French Film Theory and

VOLUME I: 1907-1929

FRENCH FILM THEORY AND CRITICISM

A HISTORY/ANTHOLOGY

1907-1939 ❧ Richard Abel

Volume I: 1907-1929

PRINCETON UNIVERSITY PRESS / PRINCETON, NEW JERSEY

Published by Princeton University Press, 41 William Street,
Princeton, New Jersey 08540
In the United Kingdom: Princeton University Press, Chichester, West
Sussex

Library of Congress Cataloging-in-Publication Data will be found on
the last printed page of this book

ISBN 0–691–05517–3 (v. 1: alk. paper)
ISBN 0–691–00062–X (v. 1: pbk.)

Publication of this book has been aided by the Paul Mellon Fund
of Princeton University Press

This book has been composed in Linotron Garamond type

Princeton University Press books are printed on acid-free paper and meet
the guidelines for permanence and durability of the Committee on Production Guidelines for Book Longevity of the Council on Library Resources

First Princeton Paperback printing, 1993

10 9 8 7 6 5 4 3 2

Printed in the United States of America

What was a Heffalump like?

Was it Fierce?

Did it come when you whistled? And *how* did it come?

Was it Fond of Pigs at all?

If it was Fond of Pigs, did it make any difference *what sort of Pig*?

Supposing it was Fierce with Pigs, would it make any difference *if the Pig had a grandfather called* TRESPASSERS WILLIAM?

Piglet didn't know the answer to any of these questions . . . and he was going to see his first Heffalump in about an hour from now!

Of course Pooh would be with him, and it was much more Friendly with two. But suppose Heffalumps were Very Fierce with Pigs *and* Bears?

A. A. Milne, *Winnie-the-Pooh*, 1926

Contents

CONTENTS

Note on Notes

NOTES to the preface and the critical essays introducing each of the four parts of this book appear immediately following the preface and each essay. Notes to the anthology selections immediately follow each selection. The anthology notes are mine unless otherwise indicated: those written by the author of the selection are marked AU; those by the translator, if other than myself, are marked TRANS.

Explanations, analyses, interpretations, are no more than frames or lenses to help the spectator focus his attention more sharply on the work. The only justification for criticism is that it allows us to see more clearly.

John Berger, *About Looking* (1980)

[History] has taken as its primary task, not the interpretation of the document, not the attempt to decide whether it is telling the truth or what is its expressive value, but to work on it from within and to develop it: history now organizes the document, divides it up, distributes it, orders it, arranges it in levels, establishes series, distinguishes between what is relevant and what is not, discovers elements, defines unities, describes relations. The document, then, is no longer for history an inert material through which it tries to reconstitute what men have done or said, the event of which only the trace remains; history is now trying to define within the documentary material itself unities, totalities, series, relations. . . . history is one way in which a society recognizes and develops a mass of documentation with which it is inextricably linked.

Michel Foucault, *The Archaeology of Knowledge* (1969)

As for me, I wanted to see the film *as close up as possible*. I had learned in the equalitarian discomfort of the neighborhood [cinemas] that this new art was mine, just as it was everyone else's. We had the same mental age: I was seven and knew how to read; it was twelve and did not know how to talk. People said that it was in its early stages, that it had progress to make; I thought that we would grow up together. I have not forgotten our common childhood: whenever I am offered a hard candy, whenever a woman varnishes her nails near me, whenever I inhale a certain smell of disinfectant in the toilet of a provincial hotel, whenever I see the violet bulb on the ceiling of a night train, my eyes, nostrils, and tongue recapture the lights and odors of those bygone halls; four years ago, in rough weather off the coast of Fingal's Cave, I heard a piano in the wind.

Jean-Paul Sartre, *The Words* (1964)

Preface

SOME YEARS AGO, in a whimsical mood, Bertrand Tavernier warned that anyone displaying the least interest in the French cinema, especially prior to the forties, would be seen as "an amnesic dinosaur, a collector of irrelevant relics," and would be in grave danger of "imminent departure for a mental institution."[1] So why, one has to ask, devote a whole book to French film theory and criticism written during the early decades of this century, especially when there may be even more serious objections to such a project? According to the standard textbook, after all, French film theory and criticism does not really begin until just after World War II, with the famous essays of André Bazin. Nothing written prior to Bazin, Dudley Andrew claims, has either the "solid logic and consistency" or the "diversity and complexity" of Bazin's influential ideas: hence the earlier writings can be dismissed in a couple of paragraphs as a repetitious series of enthusiastic, yet rigorless pronouncements.[2] Furthermore, according to the most comprehensive reader on avant-garde film theory and criticism, "perhaps the most fecund constellations of theoretical work" come not from France but from "the Soviet classical period and the avant-garde cinema that emerged after the Second World War" in the United States and Great Britain.[3] Such authoritative assertions, although once accepted as valid, are now open to question, particularly in the light of recent historical scholarship.

A growing number of essays and books have drawn attention to the wide range and rich perspicacity of early French writing on the cinema as well as to its supposed faults and lacks. Stuart Liebman, for instance, has suggested that "the film theories developed in France between 1910 and 1921 may . . . be regarded as seminal contributions to the discipline of film theory."[4] Similarly, Ian Christie has chided current historians and theorists for neglecting French film theory and practice in the decade between 1919 and 1929 and its "crucial importance to any understanding of the tradition of 'film as film'."[5] More specifically, David Bordwell has argued that one particular concept—the "musical analogy"—"functioned to brake a tendency to think of the cinema as an art of the real" (as representation and narration) and thus "helped theorists think of a film as an interplay of formal systems."[6] I myself have concluded that Impressionism, for instance, both as a theory in the 1920s and as a continuing critical concept, cannot begin to encompass the diversity and complexity of either early French writing on the cinema or actual film practice.[7] Yet much of this discussion has remained confined within the context of special interests geared to privileged *auteurs* or narrowly defined avant-garde movements.[8] What is needed now is a historical study that, building on this scholarship, can take as its subject the sheer plenitude of early French writing on the cinema—with all of its contradictions—as well as the unusually sustained continuity of its development as a discourse over several decades.

Such a study—and the further debate it should produce—is circumscribed, however, by the limited availability of primary texts. In scattered books and journals, to be sure, recent translations of some major figures have appeared—for example, Abel Gance, Jean Epstein, Germaine Dulac, René Clair, Antonin Artaud, Ricciotto Canudo, André Antoine, Georges Méliès.[9] And the French themselves have collected and published a good number of texts, although marketed almost exclusively under the rubric of individual authors—for example, Gance, Epstein, Clair, Colette, Louis Delluc, Léon Moussinac, Philippe Soupault, Marcel L'Herbier.[10] Yet these early French writings are nowhere as accessible (in English) as are the early Soviet writings on the cinema, which they certainly rival in importance (if not in influence) and on which they seem to have had some, as yet unexamined, impact.[11] Finally, no one book has collected them into a portable archive for wider dissemination.[12] Demonstrating the value and usefulness of early French writing on the cinema, therefore, must coincide with an effort to recover as much of that writing as possible.

This book—and its companion volume, *French Film Theory and Criticism, 1929–1939*—to appropriate the language of Michel Foucault, is conceived, then, as an archaeological project.[13] In this volume, I mean to excavate the period from 1907 to 1929 in France and resurrect the significant texts that intersected with—seeking either to determine or to respond to—the historical development of the silent cinema. To open up a space or "horizon of utterance" for the performance of voices, both recognized and unrecognized, banded together or separate, competing for dominance. To foreground especially those that have long been forgotten or suppressed. I also mean to engage in a dialogue with those voices, creating what Linda Gordon has called "a tension between historical empathy and rootedness in one's own present.[14] To trace some of the intertextual linkages, for instance, within the structured network of discursive and nondiscursive practices in French society (economic, social, political, ideological), out of which film theory and criticism emerged and within which it has remained partially enmeshed. To question the underlying assumptions or "given conditions" of what eventually became, during this period, a relatively autonomous cultural discourse—namely, French film theory and criticism— a discourse with its own subject, loosely defined set of methodologies, and often fascinatingly contradictory manner of articulation. Through such a double operation of re-presentation, this book thus offers both a critical map or historical framework for early French film theory and criticism as well as a site or "archive" for others subsequently to engage with, reimagine, and rewrite.

SETTING the boundaries of a space or the endpoints of a period, of course, has something of the arbitrary about it. Beginnings are always questionable, if only in raising the specter of the "myth of origins."[15] Why 1907? The choice is determined by a number of factors. Prior to that date, the cinema still often was considered as an extension or derivative form of photography, just as it had been at the 1900 Universal Exposition in Paris.[16] By then, however, the transformation of the French film industry into a major new institution of spectacle entertainment, dependent upon the continuous production and exhibition of fiction films, had begun in earnest and was well established by 1908–1909.[17] The first specialized film journals appeared between 1903 and 1909, and the first regular newspaper column devoted to the cinema in 1908. Furthermore, beginning specifically in 1907, "the year of the cinema," according to one writer,[18] also sets two crucial texts in juxtaposition—the first by a major filmmaker, Georges Méliès, summing up French film practice to that point; the other by an influential literary critic and acutely observant spectator, Rémy de Gourmont, surveying current films and cinema audiences and looking toward the future. Endings are no less suspect. Why 1929? Here the sound film "revolution" imposed a different kind of transformation on the French film industry, one that altered the material bases of film production and exhibition and, in turn, threatened to reorder the very terms of discourse on the cinema. As a consequence, certain prominent voices and discourse positions suddenly either waned in influence or else fell silent, and critics such as Moussinac even proclaimed "the death of the avant-garde." Closing off at 1929, of course, has the advantage of restricting all the texts selected to those concerned exclusively with the silent cinema. But it also allows this first volume to culminate in the series of polemical debates—over the nature and function of both film in general and the avant-garde in particular—which so animated the ciné-clubs and specialized journals in the late 1920s.

Within the boundary of these two decades, however, it is possible to demarcate smaller, perhaps even more arbitrary boundaries. Two early periods, before and during the Great War, constitute crucial stages in the development of French film theory and criticism; and the way they are marked off from one another suggests a principle of division for the others. From 1907 to 1914, we encounter something akin to what Foucault has called the initial *threshold* of a discursive practice.[19] Two assumptions are relevant here. First, out of a network or weave of accepted discursive practices and established institutions, as he might put it, a series of conflicts or struggles erupts—to clear a space for something distinct but not yet autonomous. Here that network includes, without being exhaustive, several sciences and technologies, the socioeconomic institutions of an emergent monopolistic capitalism, the journalistic practices of disseminating information and advertising, the cultural institutions of popular spectacles, the practice and criticism of the established arts, as well as then-current philosophies of aesthetics and related theories of perception and cognition. Second, just as no one text on the cinema in this period can be said adequately to mark a point of origin for French film theory and criticism, so too are nearly all texts constituted as *combinatoire*, by more or less synthesized bits and pieces of other discourses. In other words, these early writers tend to act as *flâneurs*, strolling here and there and cobbling together a variety of idioms and social practices.[20] By focusing on such transitional texts in a still unintegrated discursive practice, as Richard Terdiman argues, one can detect all that more easily the rough "fit" of its operation as well as the movements of resistance to it.[21]

From 1915 to 1919, after the onset of the war had interrupted all discourse on the cinema (as well as film production), we confront a second threshold in the development of French film theory and criticism as a discursive practice. The sets of terms articulated or half-articulated before the war, particularly those defining the cinema as a mass entertainment and a new art form, begin to settle in place, through various transformations and "hardenings"—with Emile Vuillermoz and Louis Delluc in the forefront of a further series of struggles. Out of the *combinatoire* of previous texts, a spectrum of aesthetic positions emerges. According to how they take up and answer a number of crucial questions—concerning the raw material of cinema, the possible forms of films and their methods of realization, and the value or function of cinema[22]—these half-dozen positions establish a range of both actual and potential, narrative and non-narrative film practices. From then on, French film theory and criticism is largely occupied with working out the ramifications of those positions and their interrelation or dialogue with other discourses and cultural practices.

The subsequent decade of French writing on the cinema might seem to constitute a single period that would coincide with the historical "flowering" of the silent film. Yet the major shifts and breaks that mark the contours of that discourse suggest a pattern of demarcation similar to that of the previous decade. The end of the Great War, for instance, permitted a sudden expansion of the public forum devoted to discourse on the cinema—in newspapers, film journals, books, and ciné-clubs—and an explosion of voices and texts throughout the next several years. The middle of the decade brought several significant changes as well: the influential critic and *cinéaste* Louis Delluc died in 1924; certain difficulties in financing (partly in response to the election of a quasi-leftist government) occurred in the film industry and compromised many filmmakers; several prominent ciné-clubs and specialized cinemas now formed the nucleus of a viable alternate cinema network; and arguments for a non-narrative avant-garde developed from then on in earnest. Consequently, it seems reasonable, as well as convenient, to break the period of the 1920s into two roughly equal five-year units—from 1920 to 1924, and from 1925 to 1929.

In one sense, this four-part periodization schema imposes a "natural" grid of order onto the discursive flow of French writing on the cinema. In another, more important sense, however, it merely provides an arbitrary set of neatly symmetrical, manageable units with which to "bite into" or disrupt that discursive flow and the conceptual clusters that circulate throughout. "A history, like a society, is a continuum that historians and sociologists compulsively violate and tear up into *periods* and *categories*," Regis Debray writes, "[after all] if it were not broken up, the continuum would in effect be unintelligible."[23] Early on, for instance, key terms such as realism, *photogénie*, and *cinégraphie* repeatedly crop up in everything from polemical statements to simple reviews and seem anything but fixed securely in meaning. Moreover, certain "binary oppositions" provide a locus of intelligibility at particular moments of debate and contestation. Is the cinema, for example, principally a commercial enterprise or an artistic endeavor? Is its primary function aesthetic or socioecomonic? Is it a unique new art form or a synthesis of all previous arts? Specifically, is it more closely allied with theater and prose fiction or else with music or painting? Is it narrative or descriptive, expressive or revelatory? Is it a popular or an elite form, national or international in appeal, and individual or collective in its production? Is the filmmaker a *metteur-en-scène* or an *auteur*?

By the end of the Great War, different sets of these terms coalesce into a half-dozen conceptual clusters or loosely defined "theories," both narrative and non-narrative, that recur in various formulations throughout the next decade. Initially caught up in a "classical" French tradition of Romantic Idealism, they undergo rewriting within the context of such diverse intellectual currents as Modernism, Surrealism, Freudian psychoanalysis, and Marxism. Nearly all of these conceptual clusters or "theories" are formulated in opposition—whether explicit or implicit, offensive or defensive— to what the French perceived, but rarely described, as the "classical Hollywood cinema," whose continuity systems almost exclusively served the story and character action.[24] Their writings can be seen, then, as a sustained effort to define uniquely French "theories" of the cinema. Finally, no one writer can be said to have attempted, let alone achieved, a rigorously systematic, coherent theory of film—although certain texts by Epstein,

Dulac, Canudo, and Moussinac may come close. Such a notion of theory, however, seems premature for the period, as well as highly dubious as an aesthetic absolute. Instead, individual texts tend to produce an "ephemeral" form of writing "in sync" with an ephemeral and rapidly changing art. As "speculative" essays generating insights and ideas in order to provoke action and further debate, these French texts thus constitute a polemically engaged discourse that resists our conventional efforts at canonization.

THE FOUR SECTIONS that comprise this book all include introductions that act as chapters in an ongoing "critical history" followed by complementary anthologies of texts in translation. Each introduction follows a similar format, with "local" variations to meet the demands of a particular period of reference. First, I offer a sketch of the public forum or sphere in which French film theory and criticism was articulated—a survey of the important film journals, literary and art journals, newspapers, and books that devoted attention to the cinema. Next, I single out some of the discursive and nondiscursive practices and institutions that at the time significantly intersected with this particular discourse—or, in the case of the first section, the discourses and institutions out of which French film theory and criticism emerged. Then I take up what seem to be the central concepts, problems or questions, and aesthetic positions of the period's writing on the cinema, analyzing their articulation and interpenetration across key texts as well as suggesting ways to question the distinctions and dichotomies that underlie them. Lastly, I make connections between features of these positions or "theories" and certain prior and contemporaneous aesthetic principles and concepts in the other arts. And I draw some parallels or points of resemblance to later French film theory and criticism—specifically, to the writings of André Bazin, Jean Mitry, and some of the more recent work of the 1970s.

The choice of texts for each section follows certain principles. Generally, I have sought to select texts that best represent or put in play the significant voices, positions, and issues of a particular period. This means that not all texts are equally articulate, coherent, and easily comprehensible; and some may seem maddeningly incoherent or contradictory, but such incoherence can be significant. Given the restrictions of length or space, I have tended to amass a large number of shorter documents rather than to privilege a few longer texts that might be taken as a "canon" or set of monuments and thus skew one's sense of the range and variety of writing. On the one hand, a good deal has had to be excluded in choosing excerpts from the few important books on the cinema;[25] moreover, material that I considered repetitious or irrelevent has been cut from some of the individual essays (and these cuts are clearly marked by ellipses). Also excluded have been some texts that are sufficiently well known and readily available in English, as well as those that, though polished and comprehensive, merely reiterate what was said aptly and clearly enough long before. On the other hand, I have included clusters of reviews devoted to influential or controversial films—for example, *La Dixième Symphonie* (1918), *Caligari* (1919), *El Dorado* (1921), *La Roue* (1922–1923), and *Napoléon* (1927)—not only because they particularize some of the major debates of a period but also because much of the best French writing was done in response to specific films. Finally, the texts are arranged chronologically rather than thematically or according to author.[26] This allows the reader literally to follow the historical progression of this discourse through more than two decades; but, more importantly, it allows for some thinking different from my own. The reader can draw his or her own connections and relations among these texts and, therefore, formulate a reading or interpretation that may deviate from that which I lay out in the introductions.

In the end, of course, my own writing and selecting are guided by a set of interests and aims. Despite an insistence on the multiplicity of this discourse, I tend to focus on the development of French film theory and criticism within the framework of discourse modes that position the cinema as (1) an instrument of scientific research and technological innovation, (2) a medium of information and education or social persuasion, (3) a form of popular spectacle or mass entertainment, and (4) a new form and language of art. Admittedly, the latter two discourse modes receive far greater attention, especially as the book goes on. Concentrating on them, however, does allow me to relate the cinema to broader cultural concerns in France and especially to analyze the emerging patterns of an autonomous film aesthetics. Yet if my thinking remains bound to a tradition that privileges the aesthetic, I trust that I also conceive and analyze the subject of the aesthetic as a cultural and ideological practice within the context of a larger cultural history. And I hope that I have succeeded at least halfway in picking up and untangling, as Walter Benjamin would say, some of the lost "threads that represent the weft of the past as it feeds into the warp of the present."[27] In the end, may the method and format of this book offer a model for others doing research on related bodies of film theory and criticism. For here the writing of history is accompanied by the unearthing of something close to an archive, which—through further sifting, interrogation, and analysis— may well contain the seeds of that history's rewriting.

1. Bertrand Tavernier, "Le Cinéma français des années 30, essai d'anthropologie sociale," *Positif*, 117 (June 1970), 16.

2. Dudley Andrew, *The Major Film Theories* (New York: Oxford University Press, 1976), 12–13, 134–35.

3. P. Adams Sitney, "Introduction," *The Avant-Garde Film: A Reader of Theory and Criticism* (New York: New York University Press, 1978), viii.

4. Stuart Liebman, "French Film Theory, 1910–1921," *Quarterly Review of Film Studies* 8 (Winter 1983), 2.

5. Ian Christie, "French Avant-Garde Film in the Twenties: From 'Specificity' to Surrealism," *Film as Form: Formal Experiment in Film, 1910–1970* (London: Arts Council of Britain, 1979), 37.

6. David Bordwell, "The Musical Analogy," *Yale French Studies*, 60 (1980), 142.

7. Richard Abel, *French Cinema: The First Wave, 1915–1929* (Princeton: Princeton University Press, 1984), 279–81, 286–89.

8. See, for instance, Richard Abel, "The Contribution of the French Literary Avant-Garde to Film Theory and Criticism (1907–1923)," *Cinema Journal* 14 (Spring 1975), 18–40; Eugene McCreary, "Louis Delluc, Film Theorist, Critic, and Prophet," *Cinema Journal* 16 (Fall 1976), 14–35; Paul Hammond, "Off at a Tangent," *The Shadow and Its Shadow: Surrealist Writings on the Cinema* (London: British Film Institute, 1978), 1–22; David Bordwell, *French Impressionist Cinema: Film Culture, Film Theory, and Film Style* (New York: Arno Press, 1980); Norman King, *Abel Gance: The Politics of Spectacle* (London: British Film Institute, 1984).

9. See, for instance, René Clair, *Cinema Yesterday and Today*, ed. R. C. Dale and trans. Stanley Appelbaum (New York: Dover, 1972); Jean Epstein, "Magnification," trans. Stuart Liebman, in *October*, 3 (Spring 1977), 9–15; Jean Epstein, "For a New Avant-Garde," trans. Stuart Liebman, in Sitney, *The Avant-Garde Film*, 26–30; Germaine Dulac, "The Essence of Cinema: The Visual Idea," trans. Robert Lamberton, in *The Avant-Garde Film*, 36–42; Antonin Artaud, "Sorcery and the Cinema (1927)," trans. P. Adams Sitney, in *The Avant-Garde Film*, 49–50; Ricciotto Canudo, "The Birth of the Sixth Art (1911)," trans. Ben Gibson, Don Ranvaud, Sergio Sokota, and Deborah Young, in *Framework*, 13 (Autumn 1980), 3–7; Jean Epstein, "*Bonjour Cinéma* and other Writings," trans. Tom Milne, in *Afterimage*, 10 (Autumn 1981), 9–38; Abel Gance, "The Era of the Image Has Arrived," trans. Anne Head, in *Rediscovering French Film*, ed. Mary Lea Bandy (New York: Museum of Modern Art, 1983), 53–54; André Antoine, "The Future of Cinema," trans. Stuart Liebman, in *Framework*, 24 (Spring 1984), 6–9; Georges Méliès, "Cinematographic Views," trans. Stuart Liebman, in *October*, 29 (Summer 1984), 23–31.

10. Recent French collections include Robert Desnos, *Cinéma* (Paris: Gallimard, 1966); Léon Moussinac, *L'Age ingrat du cinéma* (Paris: Editeurs français réunis, 1967); René Clair, *Cinéma d'hier, cinéma d'aujourd'hui* (Paris: Gallimard, 1970); Philippe Esnault, "Antoine et le réalisme," *La Revue du cinéma: Image et son*, 271 (April 1973), 3–64; Noël Burch, *Marcel L'Herbier* (Paris: Seghers, 1973); Jean Epstein, *Ecrits sur le cinéma*, vols. 1–2 (Paris: Seghers, 1974); Alain et Odette Virmaux, ed., *Colette au cinéma* (Paris: Flammarion, 1975); Philippe Soupault, *Ecrits de cinéma, 1918–1931* (Paris: Plon, 1979); Roger Icart, ed., *Abel Gance ou Le Prométhée foudroyé* (Lausanne: L'Age d'homme, 1983); Louis Delluc, *Le Cinéma et les cinéastes: Ecrits cinématographiques*, vol. 1 (Paris: La Cinémathèque française, 1985); Louis Delluc, *Cinéma et cie: Ecrits cinématographiques*, vol. 2 (Paris: La Cinémathèque française, 1986).

The only French anthologies of early film theory and criticism have been long out of print: Marcel L'Herbier, *Intelligence du cinématographe* (Paris: Corréa, 1946); and Marcel Lapierre, *Anthologie du cinéma* (Paris: La Nouvelle Edition, 1946).

11. See, for instance, the many references to French film theorists and critics in B. M. Eikenbaum, ed., *The Poetics of Cinema* (1927), trans. Richard Taylor, as *Russian Poetics in Translation*, vol. 9 (Oxford: RPT Publications, 1982).

12. Compare, for instance, Ian Christie and Richard Taylor's extensive anthology of Rus-

sian and Soviet film theory and criticism (1911–1939), soon to be published by the British Film Institute.

13. Michel Foucault, *The Archaeology of Knowledge*, trans. A. M. Sheridan Smith (New York: Harper & Row, 1972); Michel Foucault, "Nietzsche, Geneology, History," *Language, Counter-Memory, Practice* (Ithaca: Cornell University Press, 1977), 139–64; Hubert L. Dreyfus and Paul Rabinow, *Michel Foucault: Beyond Structuralism and Hermeneutics*, 2d ed. (Chicago: University of Chicago Press, 1983); and Guiliana Bruno, "Towards a Theorization of Film History," *Iris* 2.2 (1984), 41–55. I also borrow several terms later in this paragraph from Louis Althusser, "Ideology and Ideological State Apparatuses (Notes Towards an Investigation)," *Lenin and Philosophy and Other Essays*, trans. Ben Brewster (New York: Monthly Review Press, 1971), 127–86, as well as from several essays on Althusser—Michael Gordy, "Reading Althusser: Time and the Social Whole," *History and Theory* 22.1 (1983), 1–21; and Stuart Hall, "Signification, Representation, Ideology: Althusser and the Post-Structuralist Debate," *Critical Studies in Mass Communication* 2 (June 1985), 91–114.

14. Carol Lasser, "Interview: Linda Gordon," in *Visions of History*, ed. MARHO (New York: Pantheon, 1984), 77. See, also, Rob Harding and Judy Coffin, "Interview: Natalie Zemon Davis," in *Visions of History*, 113–14.

15. The best critique of the "myth of origins" with respect to the cinema appears in Jean-Louis Comolli, "Technique and Ideology: Camera, Perspective, Depth of Field, Parts 3 and 4," trans. Diana Matia, in *Narrative, Apparatus, Ideology: A Film Theory Reader*, ed. Philip Rosen (New York: Columbia University Press, 1986), 425–30.

16. In the organizational framework of the 1900 Paris Exposition, the cinema was classified under Photography; and the committee responsible for the Photography exhibits included only two men associated with the cinema—Jules-Etienne Marey and Louis Lumière. See Emmanuelle Toulet, "Le Cinéma à l'Exposition Universelle de 1900," *Revue d'histoire moderne et contemporaine*, 33 (April–June 1986), 179–209.

17. Observers throughout the French press in 1907–1908 commented on the upsurge in film production and exhibition. Permanent cinemas in Paris, for instance, increased from only 10 in 1906 to 87 by the end of 1908—Emmanuelle Toulet, "Le Spectacle cinématographique à Paris de 1895 à 1914," Thèse de l'Ecole des Chartes (Sorbonne, 1982), 344. For a description of the places where films were screened in the Boulevard area of Paris, between 1895 and 1908, see Jacques Deslandes, *Le Boulevard du cinéma à l'époque de Georges Méliès* (Paris: Cerf. 1963), 73–87.

18. J. B., "Le Cinématographe,' *L'Orchestre* (12 July 1907).

19. Foucault, *The Archaeology of Knowledge*, 186.

20. The critical use of the term *flâneur* originally comes from Walter Benjamin, *Charles Baudelaire: A Lyric Poet in the Era of High Capitalism*, trans. Harry Zohn (London: New Left Books, 1973), 35–66.

21. Richard Terdiman, *Discourse/Counter-Discourse: The Theory and Practice of Symbolic Resistance in Nineteenth-Century France* (Ithaca: Cornell University Press, 1985), 120–21.

22. Andrew, *The Major Film Theories*, 6–8.

23. Regis Debray, *Teachers, Writers, Celebrities: The Intellectuals of Modern France*, trans. David Macey (London: New Left Books, 1981), 39.

24. A comprehensive definition and exposition of the "classical continuity system" can now be found in David Bordwell, Janet Staiger, and Kristin Thompson, *The Classical Hollywood Cinema: Film Style and Mode of Production to 1960* (New York: Columbia University Press, 1985).

25. See, especially, Henri Diamant-Berger, *Le Cinéma* (Paris: Renaissance du livre, 1919); Léon Moussinac, *Naissance du cinéma* (Paris: Povolovsky, 1925); Henri Fescourt and Jean-Louis Bouquet, *L'Idée et l'écran: Opinions sur le cinéma*, vols. 1–3 (Paris: Haberschill et

Sergent, 1925–1926); and Léon Moussinac, *Panoramique du cinéma* (Paris: Le Sans Pareil, 1929).

26. There are, however, four exceptions to this chronological order of selected texts. Although Marcel L'Herbier's "Hermes and Silence" (April 1918) appeared after Emile Vuillermoz's critique of the essay (February 1918)—because of publication difficulties—I have placed the L'Herbier text before the Vuillermoz text so that readers will better understand what Vuillermoz is criticizing. Also, because Marcel Gromaire's six-part essay, "A Painter's Ideas about the Cinema," was published over a three-month period (beginning on 1 April 1919), I have placed it after Jean Cocteau's "Carte Blanche" column (28 April 1919), the latter of which is related closely to earlier articles by Louis Delluc and Louis Aragon. Perhaps the most unusual choice has been to move Ricciotto Canudo's "Reflections on the Seventh Art," from its posthumous publication date, in 1926, to a point coinciding with its probable composition, so that its summation of Canudo's position on the cinema follows and complements Delluc's last major statement in "Prologue," *Drames du cinéma* (1923). Finally, I have placed all the writings on Gance's *Napoléon* (1927) together in a group, even though Vuillermoz's second review of the film appeared shortly after several other essays by Jean Prévost, Antonin Artaud, and Jean Epstein, in November 1927.

27. Walter Benjamin, *One Way Street and Other Writings*, trans. Edmund Jephcott and Kingsley Shorter (London: New Left Books, 1979), 362, quoted in Terry Eagleton, *Walter Benjamin or Towards a Revolutionary Criticism* (London: Verso, 1981), 57.

Note: Were it possible to revise this volume extensively, I would add one or two articles from Edmond Benoît-Lévy's *Phono-Ciné-Gazette* (1905–1909), include the full text of Victorin Jasset's historical sketch of the early cinema in *Ciné-Journal* (1911), and reword some of my translations for greater accuracy and felicity. For this paperback version, however, only minor corrections have been made.

Richard Abel
January 1993

Acknowledgments

THIS BOOK—and its companion volume, *French Film Theory and Criticism, 1929–1939*—originally was to have been written jointly by myself and Stuart Liebman. In fact, it was Stuart who initially conceived the project some six years ago and who had just as strong a commitment to its realization as I did. Unfortunately, by the end of the first year of research and writing, a number of unforeseen problems forced him to abandon his work on the project, and I determined to carry on with it alone. For having been able to see this book through to completion, however, I owe an enormous debt to Stuart. He has acted as a steadfast, enthusiastic supporter of the project throughout these past several years. He has closely read and critiqued each of the introductory historical essays more than once, generously contributed elegant translations of selected texts, and corrected some of my own translation efforts. The finished book, of course, is quite different from what it would have been, had Stuart done much of the writing himself. But I trust that a good deal of its initial purpose and design remain and that, as it now exists, the book will prove just as valuable as the one we planned together, in part because it has often been addressed to him.

I am also indebted to a number of other colleagues for reading the manuscript at various stages. Dudley Andrew and Kristin Thompson provided thorough, knowledgeable assessments of the entire manuscript, and I have incorporated their specific emendations as well as many of their helpful ideas. Donald Crafton, Paul Willemen, and Richard Allen each read initial drafts of the first introductory essay and made useful suggestions. Early on, Crafton generously offered to share the research he had done some years before on the earliest French writing on the cinema; and, toward the end, Emmanuelle Toulet graciously provided more invaluable information on these early writings, through her own extensive research in Paris archives. Others who offered assistance at one time or another include Marie Epstein, Jean Dréville, Bernard Eisenschitz, Gérard Troussier, Jacques Aumont, Glenn Myrent, Lenny Borger, Philippe d'Hugue, Linda Williams, Claudia Gorbman, Janet Altman, and Marie-Claire Lorrain of the Bureau d'accueil des professeurs d'universités étrangères in Paris.

A great number of archives have been essential to this project—several different departments of the Bibliothèque Nationale in Paris, especially the Département des Arts du Spectacle (Arsenal), the Département des Périodiques, the Département des Imprimés, and the Annex at Versailles; the Bibliothèque d'IDHEC/Cinémathèque Française (thanks to Noëlle Giret) and the personal library of Gérard Troussier in Paris; the libraries of the Museum of Modern Art and the Lincoln Center in New York; the libraries of the University of Iowa, the University of Wisconsin–Madison, and the University of Southern California; the library of the Royal Film Archive of Belgium in Brussels; and the Inter-Library Loan Services of Cowles Library at Drake University.

Stuart Liebman and Claudia Gorbman have contributed excellent original translations of selected texts for the anthology sections of the book. Their contributions are credited as they appear. About twenty other translations have been published before: their original sources are acknowledged below, and the name of the translator accompanies each of these reprintings in the body of the book. The remaining translations are my own and render the original texts, I trust, with sufficient accuracy and clarity—for which I am indebted to *Harrap's New Standard French and English Dictionary* (1972).

At Princeton University Press, I am once again extremely grateful for Joanna Hitchcock's gracious encouragement and enthusiastic support for the manuscript, even as it grew inexorably into "another big book." And Charles Ault's meticulous copyediting corrected a good number of minor and not-so-minor mistakes in the manuscript as well as made the relationship between introductions and selected texts much more consistent.

This project was initiated with a summer grant from the Drake University Research Council (1981). During much of the research and writing, I was fortunate to have the support of a National Endowment for the Humanities Fellowship (1983–1984). A much-appreciated American Council of Learned Societies Fellowship (1986) and a sabbatical leave from Drake University then enabled me to complete the book while I was working on the research and initial writing stage of a further project on early French cinema.

Finally, my deepest appreciation once more goes to the woman who has consistently inspired me throughout the period of this project, who has read and commented on every version of the manuscript—a superb writer and scholar of Shakespeare in her own right—my best reader and collaborator, Barbara Hodgdon.

PERMISSION has been granted to reprint portions of this book, which originally appeared in slightly different formats in *Cinema Journal* 25.1 (1985) and *Framework*, 32–33 (1986). Translations that previously have appeared elsewhere include:

Louis Aragon, "On Decor," in *The Shadow and Its Shadow: Surrealist Writings on the Cinema*, ed. Paul Hammond (London: British Film Institute, 1978), 28–31.

Antonin Artaud, "Cinema and Reality." *Selected Writings*, ed. Susan Sontag (New York: Farrar, Straus, and Giroux, 1976), 150–52.

Ricciotto Canudo, "The Birth of a Sixth Art," *Framework* 13 (Autumn 1980), 3–7.

Henri Chomette, "Second Stage," in René Clair, *Cinema Yesterday and Today*, ed. R. C. Dale (New York: Dover, 1972), 97–98.

René Clair, *"Coeur fidèle," Cinema Yesterday and Today*, 70–73.

René Clair, "Pure Cinema and Commercial Cinema," *Cinema Yesterday and Today*, 99–100.

René Clair, *"La Roue," Cinema Yesterday and Today*, 54–55.

Colette, *"The Cheat," Colette at the Movies: Criticism and Screenplays*, ed. Alain and Odette Virmaux (New York: Frederick Ungar, 1980), 19–20.

Colette, *"Mater Dolorosa," Colette at the Movies*, 24–25.

Robert Desnos, "Avant-Garde Cinema," in *The Shadow and Its Shadow*, 36–38.

Germaine Dulac, "Aesthetics, Obstacles, Integral *Cinégraphie*," *Framework* 19 (1982), 6–9.

Jean Epstein, "Approaches to Truth," *Afterimage* 10 (Autumn 1981), 35–36.

Jean Epstein, "Art of Incidence," *Afterimage* 10 (Autumn 1981), 30–32.

Jean Epstein, "For a New Avant-Garde," *The Avant-Garde Film: A Reader of Theory and Criticism*, ed. P. Adams Sitney (New York: New York University Press, 1978), 26–30.

Jean Epstein, "Magnification," *October* 3 (Spring 1977), 9–15.

Jean Epstein, "On Certain Characteristics of *Photogénie*," *Afterimage* 10 (Autumn 1981), 20–23.

Jean Epstein, "The Senses 1 (b)," *Afterimage* 10 (Autumn 1981), 9–16.

Elie Faure, "The Art of Cineplastics," *Film: An Anthology*, ed. Daniel Talbot (Berkeley: University of California Press, 1959), 3–14.

Abel Gance, "My Napoleon," *Napoleon, Directed by Abel Gance* (London: Thames Television, 1980), v.

Jean Goudal, "Surrealism and Cinema," in *The Shadow and Its Shadow*, 49–56.

Marcel Gromaire, "A Painter's Ideas about the Cinema," *Motion Picture* 1.2 (Fall 1986), 4–5.

Fernand Léger, "A Critical Essay on the Plastic Quality of Abel Gance's Film, *The Wheel*," *Functions of Painting*, ed. Edward F. Fry (New York: Viking, 1973), 20–23.

Georges Méliès, "Cinematographic Views," *October* 29 (Summer 1984), 23–31.

Emile Vuillermoz, "Abel Gance and *Napoléon*," in Norman King, *Abel Gance: A Politics of Spectacle* (London: British Film Institute, 1984), 43–48.

Emile Vuillermoz, *"Napoléon,"* in King, *Abel Gance*, 42–43.

French Film Theory and Criticism

PART ONE

1907-1914

The cinema is the schoolhouse, newspaper, and theater of tomorrow.
    Pathé-Frères catalogue, 1901

We say this is the century of steam, the century of electricity, much as we say the stone age, the iron age, the bronze age, but we will soon be saying it is the age of the cinema.
    Edmond Benoit-Lévy, 1907

What is a film? An ordinary form of merchandise which the buyer can use as he sees fit? . . . No, a film is a "literary and artistic property." In order to present it to the public, one has to pay a royalty fee.
    Edmond Benoit-Lévy, 1907

The genuine cinema enthusiasts are not the cosmopolitan elite, but the common people of Paris.
    J. Yvel, 1914

Before the Canon

THE "CANON" OF French film theory and criticism usually is said to begin well after the cinema's formation—at the earliest with either Louis Delluc's witty, trenchant reviews during the Great War or with the explosion of writing that followed the Armistice. If we look back to the period in France before the war, therefore, we gaze out onto unfamiliar terrain, something close to a wasteland or void. Since very few voices reach us (especially in translation), we have had to settle for a brief catalogue of received notions, a smattering of shards and largely unexamined myths and monuments. Here we encounter one of those specific instances of a forgotten or, as Foucault would say, "suppressed" knowledge in the history of cinema. These earliest French writings on the cinema, from about 1907 to 1914, then, constitute the initial subject of this "archaeological" project of excavation and re-presentation.

THE PUBLIC FORUM

The best place to begin is with the public forum within which these writings emerged in France—a rather broad spectrum of publishing, but almost exclusively Parisian. The primary arena was comprised of the earliest specialized film journals, many of them closely associated with one or another of the major French film companies. First to appear was *Phono-Ciné-Gazette* (1905–1909), edited by Pathé's close collaborator and director of the Omnia-Pathé cinema, Edmond Benoît-Lévy. Beginning in October 1905, Benoît-Lévy pledged to support the new cinematograph industry—just as fiction film production and permanent cinema construction was about to intensify—by offering information on the industry's innovations and by initiating the public into the cinema's pleasures.[1] The most important journal, however, was *Ciné-Journal,* founded in August 1908 by Georges Dureau, who announced that it would play the role of an "intermediary" among various segments of the industry.[2] It would act as a "service" for the production and distribution sectors (initially it seemed to promote Gaumont, Eclair, and Film d'Art; later it praised Pathé and Aubert as well), offering weekly bulletins of "new releases, technical advances, and profitable ideas." At the same time, it would serve as a "commission agent for buyers," or cinema owners, recommending specific film titles and program combinations. In this, *Ciné-Journal* superseded Dureau's earlier journal serving the fairground exhibitors, *Argus-Phono-Cinéma* (1906–1908), and quickly seized its advantage over *Phono-Ciné-Gazette*. Dureau's success soon spawned a number of competitors: A. Millo's *Filma* (1908–1914); Charles Le Frapper's *Le Courrier cinématographique* (1911–1914), which initially seemed to favor Pathé, Société cinématographique des auteurs et gens des lettres (SCAGL), and Film d'Art; Charles Mendel's *Cinéma-Revue* (1911–1914), allied with Gaumont; E. L. Fouquet's *Le Cinéma* (1912–1914); and producer Georges Lordier's *L'Echo du cinéma* (1912–1914).[3] By 1913, the specialized film journals had become numerous enough to form their own professional organization, the Association professionnelle de la press cinématographique, and *Cinéma-Revue* was distributing one of the earliest annuals devoted exclusively to the cinema.[4]

Standing somewhat apart from this group, at least in function, was the earliest religious magazine devoted to the cinema, the phonograph, and photography—G.-Michel Coissac's *Le Fascinateur* (1903–1914), printed as a biweekly educational guide by the major Catholic publisher, La Bonne Presse.[5] Outside the industry, *Le Fascinateur* rivaled even *Ciné-Journal* in influence, because it spearheaded the early intense Catholic interest in the cinema—as both a splendid new pedagogical tool and a general corrupter of moral life.[6] The only other film journal during this period to vary slightly, in function and format, from the model represented by *Ciné-Journal* was former filmmaker and scriptwriter André Heuzé's deluxe weekly, *Le Film*, whose direction was quickly taken over by young Henri Diamant-Berger. During its five-month existence from late February to early August 1914, *Le Film* held down the proportion of its pages given over to advertising and tried, successfully it seems, to gather a readership from outside as well as inside the film industry.

Closely related to these specialized film journals were the earliest books or manuals published on the cinema. Here again Coissac and La Bonne Presse broke new ground with *La Théorie et la pratique des projections* (1906) and *Manuel pratique du conférencier-projectionniste* (1908). Others soon followed, most of them practical guides addressed to the increasing number of workers, craftsmen, and businessmen entering the film industry—for example, Jacques Ducom's *Le Cinématographe scientifique et industriel, traité pratique de cinématographie* (1911), Léopold Lobel's *La Projection cinématographique, guide pratique à l'usage des opérateurs projectionnistes* (Dunod, 1912), E. Kress's two-volume *Conférences sur la cinématographie* (Cinéma-Revue, 1912), Ernest Coustet's two-volume *Traité pratique de cinématographe* (Hachette, 1913–1915), and R. Filmos's *Vade-Mecum de l'opérateur cinématographiste* (Paul Laymarie, 1914).[7] At least two books, however, took on the subject of the history and current nature and function of the cinema— Georges Demeny's *Les Origines du cinématographe* (Paulin, 1909) and, more important, J. Rosen's *Le Cinématographe: Son passé, son avenir et ses applica-*

tions (Société d'éditions techniques, 1911). Both of these latter books assumed an audience beyond the film industry, especially among educators.[8]

A second, larger arena encompassed the daily newspapers in Paris, whose interest in the cinema, whether as popular spectacle or new art form, quickly picked up on that of the specialized film journals. Beginning in January 1908, *Comoedia*, the unique new daily devoted exclusively to current events and aesthetic issues in the arts (especially theater and music), initiated a weekly column of information on the cinema (and it, too, initially promoted Pathé films).[9] Soon the three most urban-oriented of the "big four" mass dailies—*Le Petit Journal, Le Journal,* and *Le Matin* (all staunch supporters of the Third Republic, but slightly right of center politically)[10]—were reviewing films regularly; while others such as the popular evening paper, *L'Intransigeant* (rightist politically, avant-gardist culturally), and the prestigious centrist paper, *Le Temps,* were accepting occasional reviews—for example, drama critic Adolphe Brisson's famous review of Film d'Art's *L'Assassinat du Duc de Guise* (1908).[11] By 1912–1913, the Paris dailies with the greatest literary pretensions were taking the cinema seriously. Perhaps prompted by a survey on the upsurge of interest in the cinema published by the literary magazine, *Les Marges,* two papers—*Le Figaro* and the new illustrated daily, *Excelsior*—conducted extensive inquiries, especially among dramatists and other literary figures, on the current state and future of the cinema.[12] By the fall of 1913, more than a year after a writer by the name of Yhcam (a pseudonym) had suggested the idea in *Ciné-Journal, Comoedia*'s "Cinematograph" column was appearing daily; and *Le Journal,* each Friday, was publishing a full page of information, interviews, and brief reviews under the simple heading of "Cinemas."[13] At the same time, other literary magazines across the spectrum were forced to confront the upstart new art form with articles or columns—from the old Catholic standby, *Le Correspondant,* and the conservative establishment journal, *La Revue des deux mondes,* to the formerly Symbolist review, *Mercure de France,* the erudite religious journal, *Les Entretiens idéalistes,* and Guillaume Apollinaire's iconoclastic avant-garde monthly, *Les Soirées de Paris.* Only *Les Soirées de Paris,* however, consistently sought to include the cinema in its controversial celebration of innovative art forms, through Maurice Raynal's regular column of film reviews. Because of the generally reluctant interest of the literary magazines, then, the industry-oriented film journals and daily Paris newspapers clearly dominated the French public forum and thus determined what could be said about the cinema.

In the context of this public forum, the emergence of French film theory and criticism within a range of established discourses and institutionalized practices can be seen in the way that several different essays consciously at-

tempt to define the nature and function of the cinema, in accordance with
cultural distinctions and dichotomies already in place. They tend to probe
the "new animal," as it were, with familiar labels. In 1907, for instance,
in his summary essay, "Cinematographic Views," pioneer filmmaker
Georges Méliès enumerated the historical development of four kinds of
films—"so-called *natural* views, *scientific* views, *composed subjects*, and the
so-called *transformation* views"—yet still considered the cinema a cornuco-
pia of popular spectacle, capable of encompassing an infinite variety of
subjects.[14] By contrast, that same year, in his famous "Epilogues" column in *Mercure de France*, Rémy de Gourmont observed a typical cinema
program—which included newsreels, travelogues, documentary studies,
comic sketches and chases, fantasies, melodramas—and derived a loose catalogue of functions that were far from mutually exclusive: the cinema was
a scientific apparatus, an instrument of educational or moral persuasion, a
mode of mass entertainment, and possibly a new form of art.[15] Five years
later, in *Ciné-Journal*, using a more sociological approach, Yhcam came up
with a similar classification of films according to their social function as
well as the age group of the audience: (1) artistic or theatrical (from low art
to high art), (2) educational (from preschool classes to postdoctoral work),
(3) propagandistic (moral, religious, patriotic), and (4) informational.[16]

These essays, as well as others,[17] suggest that a number of discourse
modes, each associated with a set of established institutions and practices,
were competing for dominance within the early French writings on the cinema and that the cinema-as-art discourse was only marginally significant,
at least at this point. The 1900 Paris Exposition, it is worth recalling, had
privileged the documentary and educational functions of the cinema; and
as late as 1911, Rosen focused his book almost exclusively on the educational function of the cinema and its popularization of prior artistic and scientific work.[18] Consequently, although certain discourse modes—notably,
cinema as art and cinema as mass entertainment—will receive much more
attention in the later sections of this book, here I am primarily concerned
with excavating the full field of discourses in a relatively non-linear and
non-hierarchical manner. In so doing, I mean to analyze the articulation
and interpenetration of these discourses across key texts as well as to suggest ways to break open or question the distinctions and dichotomies that
underlie them.

SCIENCE AND INDUSTRY

One of these discourse modes—that of scientific and technological advance—can be traced through these writings on the cinema in at least two
ways. In rare instances, there were discussions—actually little more than

reports—of research such as that involving the behavior of microbes, carried out by Dr. Jean Comandon and Emile Labrely in Pathé's facilities at Vincennes (annexing the microscope to the film camera), research that was first presented to the French Academy of Sciences in 1909 and eventually to the public in Paris.[19] For the most part, however, this discourse focused on the technological research that companies like Gaumont and Pathé were engaged in. Such research seems to have taken three primary forms: the reproduction of depth or dimension in the image, the reproduction of natural color, and the synchronized reproduction of sound and image—all of which aimed to fulfill a late nineteenth-century obsession, the production of a "true" or "faithful" analogue to reality.[20] The cinema thus promised to supercede the astonishing array of projection devices that had developed over the past century or more and to constitute, in Jean-Louis Comolli's terms, a perfect apparatus or *cinema machine*—promoting the "social multiplication of images" (in which "just looking" had been transformed into a commodity) and satisfying the desire of "seeing for seeing's sake" in a "frenzy of the visible."[21] For the French, specifically, the desire to see cut across sociopolitical differences and fueled an unceasing fascination for the landscapes and natural motion of newsreels and documentaries, which offered "a geographical extension of the field of the visible and . . . appropriatable."[22] The early observations of Gourmont, Anatole France, and Jules Claretie, for instance, are all strongly marked by this fascination, but even a celebrated conservative academician and literary critic such as René Doumic, who otherwise scorned the cinema, later fell under its power.[23] Here, I would suggest, we have a partial answer to Thomas Elsaesser's questions, how visual pleasure operated in the cinema prior to the development of stars and genres with familiar narratives and how the spectator was bound to the cinema as a technological apparatus or, as Steve Neale puts it, following Comolli, to "an ideology of *visibility* of the world."[24] Through the cinema's reproduction of reality, the significance of representation or description as a means to knowledge and identification—see especially Colette's review of *The Scott Expedition* (1914)—begins to emerge in new ways, ways that would later become crucial for Louis Delluc, Jean Epstein, and, eventually, André Bazin.[25]

At the same time, this discourse was controlled to some extent by the film industry—by Gaumont and Pathé in particular—for its own ends as a rapidly growing commercial enterprise. Both Gaumont and Pathé saw to it that their innovations in the apparatuses of recording and projection—especially in the areas of sound-image synchronization and color reproduction—were described and commented on in articles and essays as well as in advertisements, which, by 1914, were appearing almost weekly in *Ciné-Journal* and *Le Film*.[26] Gaumont, for instance, made the results of these ex-

9

periments a regular feature of its programs at the Gaumont-Palace, the largest cinema in Paris. The film companies also determined to exploit the cinema's ability to reproduce reality as visual spectacle beyond the format of documentaries and newsreels—for example, the so-called Lumière tradition, in which most of them were already involved. Accordingly, in 1911, Louis Feuillade appealed to the desire for a "true" reproduction of reality in several polemical Gaumont advertisements for his new line of "realist" fiction films that attempted to depict "slices of life," the aptly titled *La Vie telle qu'elle est*.[27] These advertisements countered Méliès and his earlier claim for the already outmoded genre of fantasy films—that the cinema achieved the impossible, "giving the appearance of reality to the most chimerical of dreams and to the most improbable inventions of the imagination."[28] Without disguising the melodramatic base of this new film series, these texts, somewhat disingenuously, invoked the literary naturalist aesthetic of making the spectator, to quote Rachel Bowlby, "an observer of social reality . . . as a succession of separate images or scenes."[29] Feuillade's initiative and the artistic (if not commercial) success of his films led to other such series—Victorin Jasset's *Les Batailles de la vie* at Eclair and René Leprince's *Les Scènes de vie cruelle* at Pathé—all of which early on established a strong realist tradition in the French narrative cinema.[30] In sum, Gaumont and Pathé yoked the discourse of technological innovation to that of a naturalist aesthetic, which itself masked a melodramatic base, as a means of promoting and legitimizing their commercial exploitation of the cinema.[31]

EDUCATION AND MORALITY

A more prominent discourse in these early French writings has to do with the cinema's function, whether narrowly or broadly defined, as a medium of education or information. Within a dozen years of the cinema's appearance, short films were already being used as a new pedagogical tool in certain sectors of the French educational system. In *Le Fascinateur*, for instance, Coissac drew attention to the Catholic Church as the first proponent of screening films in the classroom; while, in *Phono-Ciné-Gazette*, Benoît-Lévy encouraged adoption of a similar strategy in the recently established (1882) secular primary schools and *lycées*—although exactly how films were used in either school system or how extensively remains unclear.[32] By 1911, Rosen noted that several *lycées* in Paris were projecting films in art history courses and then praised the national adult education groups—including the Ligue française de l'enseignement and perhaps even the remnants of the leftist *universités populaires*—for organizing regional lectures and discussions around film screenings.[33] Shortly thereafter, according to the Catholic *moraliste*, Louis Haugmard, researchers began to experiment with stop-motion or single-frame cinematography for studying the germination of plants, the metamorphosis of insects, and the movements of the mouth and lips in speech.[34] The press eventually began to take note of the doctors and university professors who were using short films on an experimental basis, primarily in physiology courses for medical students—for example, Dr. Doyen (a famous Paris surgeon), Dr. Comandon, of course, and a Professor Franck (a colleague of Henri Bergson's at the Collège de France).[35] By 1913, journalists such as André Chalopin, as well as Yhcam, could envision the cinema's use at all levels of French education: "In sum, [the cinema] is a new tool, admirably perfected, and destined to render the greatest service, notably in all branches of education. . . . I am thoroughly convinced that films will become the *principal equipment* of the modern schoolteacher."[36] This vision was confirmed at a special conference on the cinema and education, in 1914, organized by the Paris city officials and the Académie de Paris.[37]

During this period, the concept of the cinema as an historical document that could preserve events for future generations—as an astonishing means "of conquering . . . the ravages of time, memory, and decay"[38]—also began to circulate in the general press as well as in the industry journals. First broached as early as Boleslas Matuszewski's pamphlet, *Une Nouvelle Source de l'histoire* (Paris, 1898), it had reached the upper levels of the French government by 1913 and was providing a firm basis for those who were advocating the establishment of a national collection or archive for the cinema. Or, as Léon Bérard, then Under-Secretary of Education and the Arts, called it, "a cinema museum, . . . a *cinémathèque*, if I dare offer that neologism."[39]

Much more attention was given, however, to a more broadly defined concept of the cinema as a medium of information and moral or social persuasion. Here the cinema became the subject of cultural criticism, in line with what Terry Eagleton has called the long tradition of "general ethical humanism, indissociable from moral, cultural, and religious reflection."[40] But it assumed added significance in the historical context of the Third Republic's "need for a secular or 'lay' morality which would serve to create social solidarity,"[41] now that religion had been banished from most state institutions. The question whether the cinema acts as a significant force of moral reform or as an immoral temptation ran through much of the writing of the period, just as it did in Germany and the United States.[42] As Miriam Hansen has argued—with respect to Germany, but the same goes for France—one of the reasons why this question may have proved so troubling was that the cinema constituted a new social space that threatened to blur or even undermine the conventional boundaries between public and private, upper classes and lower classes, adults and children, even male and female.[43] The French film industry itself raised the issue, in order to contain it and reassert those boundaries, in an endeavor to elevate its status as a commercial enterprise. Evidence of this can be seen in the attempt to imitate popular illustrated family magazines such as Hachette's *Lectures pour tous*—see Gourmont's clucking remarks about Pathé's obvious attempt to produce "family-oriented" story films that never "make fun of good principles"—and in Feuillade's solemn recitations on the elevated moral nature of his *La Vie telle qu'elle est* series films (otherwise advertised as "thesis plays") and on the "virtue which emerges from and inspires them."[44] And the early cinema posters and advertisements provided supporting evidence—they often placed a partially nude female figure representing France beside a camera or projector as if to guide or direct its operation. Despite these overtly propagandistic efforts by the producers and distributors, certain authorities also began to admonish the film industry, and the exhibitors in particular, to assume more firmly a moral and even paternalistic responsibility in French society. The Paris police prefect, Louis Lepine, for instance, publicly described cinema managers essentially as "educators and moralists"; and Kress exhorted those same managers to "select their films like good family fathers."[45]

This question of the cinema's social function was aggravated by a political decision, taken in 1906 (coincident with a similar decision in Germany), to abandon the national system of control over the theater yet insist on the power of censorship that local mayors and provincial prefects could exercise over popular spectacles.[46] This decision was supported initially by an extensive moral reform campaign in France, a strong component of which was led by Catholic publications as well as secular educators—for example, *Le Fascinateur*, which consistently editorialized against violence and grotesquerie in the cinema.[47] Much of the censors' and reformers' concern rested on the fact that children and adolescents constituted almost 25 percent of the cinema audience; their presence prompted writers such as Rosen and Yhcam to suggest that separate cinemas be established for them[48] All this seems to have come to a head in 1912, when some of the popular crime series films produced by Eclair, Pathé, and Gaumont were banned locally for setting a bad example for French children.[49] Newspapers across the political spectrum joined in this moral campaign at one time or another—for example, from the rightist *Le Gaulois* to the centrist *Le Temps* and the left Republican *La Lanterne*.[50] In opposition, Georges Dureau of *Ciné-Journal* led a spirited defense of the cinema, particularly directed at the Radical politician, Edouard Herriot, then mayor of Lyon.[51] Dureau pointed to the deterrent effect of such films as the newsreels showing the arrest of the anarchist Bonnot gang—earlier Yhcam had cited the moral effect of the most notorious crime film based on the Bonnot gang, Jasset's *L'Auto grise* (1912)[52]—and then to the accepted and legally protected circulation of far more dubious material in books and magazines. Dureau's campaign seems to have been halfway successful, partly because the industry redoubled its own "reformist" tendencies but also because so many writers consistently extolled the salutory effect of newsreels, travelogues, and documentaries, in spite of the problematic fiction films.[53] Critics as different as Gourmont and Doumic singled out these films as "educational" for both the masses and the elite. Gourmont loved the way they reproduced landscapes and satisfied his interest in traveling through (and learning about) other countries; Doumic accepted the fragmentary nature of such films with some mockery: they offered an education that was "encyclopedic and incoherent" and therefore "eminently modern."[54] Both, however, could just as well have been describing previous spectacle attractions—for example, the profusion of "Panoramas" and "Cinematic Voyages" at the 1900 Paris Exposition—which the cinema was now extending in a cheap, continuous fashion.[55]

Whatever the form of cinema, however, many writers were now beginning to realize that the invention of the cinematographic apparatus had the potential to create an "intellectual revolution . . . comparable to that produced centuries before by the invention of the printing press."[56] Some, like the management of the Lille-Cinéma just quoted, were fearful of the moral and social consequences of this new invention. Others such as Haugmard, who shared this concern, began to sense that it could also function usefully as a form of propaganda, to solidify or shape the national consciousness and even control foreign peoples.[57] French comic films in particular, wrote a Colonel Marchand, "are obviously a weapon of conquest in Africa and many other places as well."[58] This range of opinion formed part of a now largely forgotten Classical Renaissance movement, which itself constituted just one component of the conservative Nationalist Revival that came to dominate France just prior to the war.[59] Against this overtly nationalistic strain of discourse ran a counterstrain based, in part, on the euphoric belief that the cinema was developing into a form of universal language or, as Yhcam put it, a far more potent visual equivalent of Esperanto.[60] "The phonograph and the cinema," wrote the Pathé engineeer, Frantz Dussaud, as early as 1906, "will bring peace to the world."[61] As a complement to sociologist Gabriel Tarde's concept of human solidarity based on shared modern leisure activities, this line of thinking celebrated the cinema as a force for international unity and harmony.[62] As expressed most poetically by Ricciotto Canudo, in the tradition of Rousseau, the cinema represented the reemergence and "ultimate evolution of the ancient *Festival* . . . within which together all men could forge . . . their isolated individuality."[63] Here the desire to reverse the process of the alienation of art in capitalist society and reintegrate that art into a society of real community, however, foundered on nostalgia and naiveté. For it largely ignored, just as the early French ciné-clubs would do later, the socioeconomic forces controlling film production and distribution.

MASS SPECTACLE ENTERTAINMENT

This discourse mode of cultural criticism shades into another having to do with the cinema's function as a spectacle or a mass entertainment and as a continually changing commercial product, particularly in the form of fiction films. By 1914, in France, the cinema had largely supplanted the theater and café-concert as the chief public entertainment in the provinces and had become a strong rival to them both in the larger cities.[64] Many professionals and craftsmen in the older spectacles had begun to work, either occasionally or exclusively, within the new industry, under the direction of marketing and distribution entrepreneurs such as Pathé and Gaumont.[65] Throughout the period before the war, those writing on the cinema had to face a series of unexpected questions. Why had the cinema succeeded so well? To whom did the cinema, especially the new fiction films, really appeal? And what constituted a successful, that is, profitable, fiction film?

The answer to the first question became a familiar litany repeated by many different writers, even those such as Doumic and Haugmard, who deplored the phenomenon. For the spectator, the cinema was inexpensive—it cost only a fraction of what one had to pay to attend either the theater or the music hall.[66] It offered a variety of short films to view (even films produced in foreign countries were usually comprehensible), and one could come and go as one pleased at any of several break points in the program.[67] Its reproduction of movement gave the illusion of life or reality as no other spectacle did, and its mechanical reproduction and exhibition guaranteed the same performance by actors as Henry Krauss, Réjane, Mistinguett, and Max Linder over and over again. On this basis, writers naturally tended to compare the cinema to other forms of popular entertainment such as vaudeville or to illustrated magazines and newspapers—all of them anti-organicist forms constructed out of discrete, disconnected elements.[68] And implicit in their observations were patterns of mass consumption, which provided another answer to the question of what stimulated the spectator's visual pleasure. For the cinema functioned much like the modern department store (which the French had pioneered), offering a profuse variety of commodities or views to become absorbed in or browse through.[69] Here the "new bourgeois leisure activity [of] shopping" had its equivalent in the experience of "just looking" at the reified images or simulacra of reality continually renewed for repeated consumption.[70] Both cultural institutions thus tended to produce displays of "exotic" illusions or dream worlds (which the 1900 Paris Exposition accomplished on a grand scale), whose implicit purpose was to stimulate the desire to consume or, rather, to empathize with and enjoy the spectacle of commodity consumption itself.[71]

The question—who attended the cinema?—interestingly enough, reveals as much about the writers as it does about the audience. In France, as in other countries, the cinema quickly developed a mass audience and took a crucial place in the emerging mass culture industry of the late nineteenth and early twentieth centuries.[72] The film industry itself sought to foster this new audience, as Emmanuelle Toulet has shown—for example, Pathé headed its 1908 catalogue with a dozen different socially marked figures standing in line at a cinema.[73] And observers such as Maxime Leproust, Gourmont, Coissac, and Dureau early on took note of this mixture of classes, genders, and age groups at the cinema.[74] By 1911–1912, however, writers began to emphasize the diversity as well as the homogeneity of cinema spectators. Dureau, for instance, stressed how the middle bourgeoisie had become regular cinema-goers, attracted in particular by the various series of "artistic films" (adaptations of literary classics, especially historical reconstructions).[75] By contrast, F. Laurent devoted a series of articles in *Le Cinéma* to the working-class cinemas which had sprung up in and around Paris.[76] In the anarchist weekly, *La Guerre sociale*, Gustave Hervé even announced the formation of "Le Cinéma du Peuple" (its founders included the anarchist publisher Jean Grave, among others), whose purpose (though never realized) was to reorganize film production and distribution for the benefit of the working classes.[77] Others insisted, as good propagandists for the industry, that the cinema was now and ought to remain, whether bourgeois or working class, a respectable family affair.[78] Unfortunately, none of these texts, although perhaps Yhcam's sociological observations come closest, can rival Emilie Altenloh's invaluable *Sociology of the Cinema* (1914), which undertook an extensive study of German cinema audiences at the time, and especially the large percentage of women spectators.[79]

What is particularly telling in France, however, is the way the writers (most of them bourgeois intellectuals) placed themselves in relation to this mass audience. Some like Doumic and Haugmard generally took a position of social and moral superiority, with its attendant tone of condescension masking fear. Others like Gourmont and Brisson were somewhat ambivalent about finding themselves wrapped up in the experience of an "alien" milieu. Brisson, for instance, seemed actually surprised at his interest in a "childish drama" in 1914: "Around me people are having a good time; I myself am scarcely bored."[80] Even Haugmard sometimes could transcend his moralizing attitude. Notice his realization, given the continuing disintegration of family life under capitalism, that going to the cinema was one of the few ways that working-class families could gather together during the week.[81] However, Yhcam was the only one who consistently wrote as a kind of spokesman for the mass cinema audience, championing its interests against those of the industry, the arts, and the press. He pointedly recalled, for instance, that the masses had flocked to and appreciated the cinema long before the respectable bourgeoisie and intellectual elite did.[82] His position also set him apart on the question of spectator involvement or participation. Most other writers assumed the cinema demanded no intellectual effort from spectators and allowed them to sink into a state of passive reception. Yhcam alone believed that the spectator was an active collaborator at the cinema: "There is no other spectacle in which the imagination of the spectator plays a greater role." During the war, Louis Delluc would make this position a fundamental premise of his film criticism.

Discussions of which films during this period were successful and profitable tended to be descriptive. From Gourmont, in 1907, to Brisson, in 1914, all writers pointed out the primary appeal of fiction films. They checked off a loosely differentiated list of fiction film "genres": fairy tales or fantasies, comic sketches, chases, adventures, melodramas, classics, or "artistic films." The importance of the latter two "genres" was clear in several Dureau editorials—for example, one celebrated the proliferating series of "films d'art," and another surveyed the marketing strategies involved in either choosing works to adapt or coming up with catchy titles for original scenarios.[83] Moreover, the short series films (comics, westerns, criminal and detective adventures) remained consistently popular, despite the moral reformist campaigns, against which a young critic such as Maurice Raynal celebrated the "lurid stories" of Feuillade's *Fantômas* (1913–1914) in a deliberately provocative, antisocial gesture.[84] The so-called realist film, however, received little attention—perhaps, as Haugmard speculated, because the mass public preferred material other than what reminded them of their own milieu and customary preoccupations.[85]

One of the few times writers began to get prescriptive, interestingly enough, was on the question how long fiction films should be.[86] Between early 1911 and early 1912, the average length of a French fiction film went from 300 to almost 900 meters (from one to three reels); and by late 1913, it had begun to creep toward 1,500 meters (five reels).[87] Dureau was perhaps the first to note this change, in the late spring of 1911; and soon he was involved, along with Charles Le Frapper of *Le Courrier cinématographique* briefly, in a futile campaign against it in the pages of *Ciné-Journal*.[88] As early as October 1911, Dureau sided with the cinema owners who were complaining about how to fit these new three-reel films into their programs.[89] In later 1912, he still believed the long film "fad" would soon pass—he admired Pathé's *Les Misérables* (four parts, 3,400 meters), but as an exception.[90] By late 1913, his prescribed norms for comic sketches (300 meters) and dramas (300, 600, and sometimes 900 meters) were woefully anachronistic.[91] Even the cinema owners had accepted an average length of 1,000–1,200 meters for fiction films; and reviewers such as Des Angles in *Comoedia* were advocating what seemed to be an industry policy of suiting the length of the film to the subject.[92]

As this discourse mode of the cinema as popular spectacle shades into that of film as art, it seems appropriate to summarize briefly the network of analogies that the French used to describe the cinema during this period. Behind the continual equating of the film image with reality or life, of course, lay the unspoken, as yet undeveloped concept of the screen as a transparent "window on the world." Instead, the most prominent analogy was aptly gastronomical, for an industry of consumable goods—the cinema as a dinner menu in which the "feature" film was the chief course or entree and variety was essential.[93] In fact, one writer even described the rapacious appetite of the cinema audience as that of a "mass Minotaur."[94] This reached the point of parodic cliché when filmmaker André Hugon accused the industry of simply imitating the Italians and producing a lot of bad dishes over and over—by manufacturing films like macaroni.[95] Other analogies played on the cinema's creation of a new visual language and sense of community as well as on its alliance with certain traditions in the other arts. For the management of the Lille-Cinéma, for instance, the cinema served as "the book of the people," much like the stained glass windows, mural paintings, and cathedral sculptures had in the Middle Ages.[96] For Canudo, of course, it fulfilled "the rich promise of the *Festival* which has been longed for unconsciously, the ultimate evolution of the ancient *Festival* taking place in the temples, the theaters, and the fairgrounds of each generation."[97] The most tantalizing analogy, however, turned the cinema into a kind of addictive drug or a dream state, as Gourmont suggested, in which "the images pass, borne aloft by light music."[98] Here one of Jules Romains's early Unaminist sketches, which sought to intuit the collective consciousness of modern urban spaces, offered a marvelous description of the cinema as a collective dream experience.[99] By relocating value in the transformative power of the fading genres of fantasy and comic trick films—for example, Méliès, the Onésime comic series, and perhaps even Emile Cohl's animation films—Romains pointed toward the later enthusiasm of the Dada-Surrealists for such works and thus provided a crucial link between the prewar and postwar periods.

CINEMA AS ART

The final discourse mode—concerning the cinema as art, especially but not exclusively as narrative art—puts in play a good number of the questions and conceptual terms that will be taken up in later texts. As early as 1907, Edmond Benoit-Lévy had defined film as a "literary and artistic property," which Pathé then seized on to support his company's shift from selling to renting films.[100] The attempt to justify the cinema as a new art form, however, did not reach a sustained, polemical level until 1911. As a polemics, this discourse, too, seems to have originated within the film industry, principally as a strategy for expanding and consolidating its markets. The crucible or flashpoint seems to have been the first International Congress of the Cinématographe, which met in Brussels in September 1911.[101] Several of the speeches and debates at this congress were published soon after in one of the earliest industry annuals; and one report, by the Brussels lawyer Charles Havermans, used the issue of "authors' rights" (referring to the writer whose work was adapted for the cinema) to summarize the arguments pro and con on whether the cinema was an art.[102] One position, which had already been used against photography, assumed that sunlight, the mechanical operation of the camera, and the chemical processes of the laboratory were the sole agents of production in a film. The other argued that "the thought, taste, and feeling" of a number of individuals (scriptwriter, director, cameraman, and actors) controlled and directed that process of production. Film, therefore, was a construction of the mind and imagination, much like the work of the painter or musician, and was executed by means of a particular medium of material elements. The language of Haverman's report was taken up in other texts in 1911, where its large claims (for legal purposes) gave way to a less broadly defined concept of art in which writers focused on positioning the cinema in relation to the other arts, and the theater in particular.[103]

For a variety of reasons, the French cinema, perhaps more than any other national cinema of the period, was seen as closely allied with the theater. Considerable competition marked relations between the two, of course, and conservative high art advocates from Edmond Sée (1907) to Doumic (1913) consistently ridiculed the writers of "cinematographic plays" in comparison to their masters in the theater. Yet in France that competition and ridicule never reached the acrimonious level it seems, according to Hansen, to have reached in Germany.[104] Several 1908 court decisions, assuring authors' rights and royalties for film adaptations, curtailed the Société des auteurs' attacks on the film industry for illegally reproducing plays on the screen and supported the establishment of Film d'Art (allied initially with the Comédie Française), Pierre Decourcelle's Société cinématographique des auteurs et gens des lettres (SCAGL), and other similar film production companies.[105] The resulting influx of theater personnel into the industry, the proliferation of "artistic films" series, and the frequent and applauded adaptation of classic and popular dramas finally had the effect, Dureau argued, of producing a situation in which the artistry of individual films now attracted audiences to the cinema as often as the experience of cinema-going itself.[106] However, this also created an aesthetic problem for writers in clearly distinguishing the cinema from the theater. Whereas the legal differences between the two seem to have been resolved rather quickly, the aesthetic differences took a good deal of time to work out.

Early on, Méliès had located a significant difference between the cinema and the theater in the person of the filmmaker—"he must be the author [scriptwriter], director, designer, and often an actor if he wants to obtain a unified whole"—but his essentially auteurist position seems to have fallen into disrepute along with his career.[107] Instead, the most influential articulation of this difference came in Brisson's review of the first Film d'Art production, *L'Assassinat du Duc de Guise* (1908). For Brisson, the distinctive element of the cinema was the actor's performance—that is, his gestures and movements, which in the theater were subordinate to or dependent on words or speech.[108] Those gestures and movements must be refined and stylized, he argued, into a language or grammar that, unlike pantomime, which was fixed and unchanging, would be "sober," "true" (drawn directly from life), and flexible or varied to suit the dramatic situation. Complementing the actor's performance, he also suggested, was the choice and arrangement of props and their continuity through a number of scenes or tableaux. The importance of Brisson's formulations can be seen several years later when filmmaker Victorin Jasset described the acting in *L'Assassinat du Duc de Guise* as "revolutionary" in the context of 1908, when Dureau virtually repeated the critic's words in arguing that acting in the theater and the cinema were governed by different rules, and when Yhcam recommended the institution of special companies of actors exclusively devoted to the cinema.[109] Despite this difference, most writers of the period shared the view that the cinema was still a new form of theater—especially the melodrama whose highly formalized, emotional mode of representation insisted on expressing what language left unsaid.[110] And they accepted the idea that, as in the theater, the dramatist or scenario writer was the real author of the film. "The cinema actor must really collaborate with the author of the scenario," wrote Dureau, "he is the body for which the scriptwriter is the soul."[111] Even Yhcam insisted that the director too must subordinate himself as *metteur-en-scène* to the author of the scenario. This was such a "universal" position, once Méliès had become so unfashionable, that it was not until just before the war that filmmakers such as Léonce Perret and Georges Lacroix at Gaumont began to protest in letters to the press against the lack of attention accorded their work.[112]

In their efforts to distinguish the cinema further, some writers began to tease out features that it shared with arts other than the theater or that seemed unique to it. Early on, for instance, fantasy films were still popular enough for Méliès, Gourmont, and, later, Romains to suggest that the metamorphoses produced by "camera tricks" were a distinctive feature of the cinema, impossible to achieve in the theater. Méliès also stressed how the flatness of the photographic image made the blocking and pacing of the actors' performances all that more important for clarity in telling a story.[113] Somewhat later, Gaumont began to call attention to the function of lighting in its films, especially in its *Films esthétiques* series (1910), which attempted to appropriate the composition, color toning, and allegorical references of representational painting.[114] Such "artistic" films seemed modeled on the highly successful "Visons d'Art" at the 1900 Paris Exposition, whose seven programs devoted to the various regions of France (accompanied by recited texts), according to Emmanuelle Toulet, attracted "a public thirsting for aesthetic impressions."[115]

The most prominent feature the French noticed, however, was camera framing; and the impetus came from the American Vitagraph films, which captured their attention beginning in 1910. The Vitagraph films, argued Jasset, carried the calm, poised performances that characterized the early Film d'Art films one step futher.[116] They clarified and heightened the natural and understated effect of the actors' facial expressions through the use of closer shots or what came to be known as the "plan américain" (the shot of an actor cut off at the knees). Yhcam seconded this argument but had strong reservations about the technique. Although it did satisfy the desire to perceive the actors more clearly, it also apparently violated an unstated aesthetic principle of representing the human body in full—by cutting off the legs and even the heads on occasion.[117] So frequent had the close shots become in American films that he derisively labeled his era "the age of legless cripples." A similar reservation marked Yhcam's observations (perhaps alone among French writers) on the sequencing of images in a film. Films ought to begin with establishing shots (to create reference points), and enlargements or magnifications should be used with discretion (and even be signaled to the spectator!), for unexpected and unexplained changes in the size of figures and objects disturbed his sense of continuity and coherence.[118] Although none of these writings attempted to delineate the primary features or "raw material" of the cinema systematically, at the base of Yhcam's prescriptive statements, so at odds with his more sociological observations, there seemed to rest a traditional French aesthetic of representation and narrative or expository continuity, which may well derive from conventions of nineteenth-century theater as well as academic painting.[119] Futher research on these conventions in relation to the early cinema may explain, in part, what has often been seen as a certain "regressiveness" in the French cinema prior to the war, especially compared to the American cinema—or, rather, how the French cinema may actually have constituted an early form of counter-cinema.[120]

If most writers saw the cinema as either an extension of the theater or else a new medium of emerging unique elements, a very few envisioned it, in the Romantic tradition, as a medium or formal system synthesizing all the arts. Méliès, once again, had understood that the cinema drew on nearly all the arts to some degree—"dramatic techniques, drawing, painting, sculpture, architecture, mechanical skills, manual labor of all sorts."[121] The most systematic attempt to articulate an aesthetics of synthesis, however, was the remarkable manifesto by Canudo, "The Birth of a Sixth Art," (1911), in which a Wagnerian concept of the *Gesamtkunstwerk* meshes uneasily with a Futurist faith in machine dynamism.[122] For Canudo, the cinema could incorporate and synthesize the arts of both space (painting and sculpture) and time (music and dance) into a completely new form of theater, namely, "Plastic Art in Motion." The "significant elements" that governed this synthesis Canudo called the *real* and the *symbolic*, the one having to do with the mechanical reproduction of reality and the other with the speed with which the new machine changes, combines, and charges images. Here Canudo seemed readily to accept a kind of continuity that Yhcam resisted. As the ultimate representation of the action and dynamism allegedly characteristic of Western civilization, the cinema was also capable, through the "stylization of life into stillness," of a Symbolist evocativeness or expressiveness—whether that be the emotional life of a character, the "cosmic soul of the artist," or the "essence of things." This utopian, quasi-mystical vision culminated with the cinema reconciling science and art in a new festival of the sacred, producing a "new joyous unanimity." Rich, repetitious, deliberately provocative, and sometimes frustratingly incoherent in its concatenation of terms and discourses—for example, the mechanical and the spiritual, the real and the stylized, communal experience and individual expression—Canudo's essay provided the impetus for Abel Gance's first liturgical incantation on the "sixth art."[123] And it even marked Brisson's last important essay on the cinema, in which he defined it as "this amalgam of observation and invention, of reality and dream, containing the elements of an art that is expressive, powerful yet delicate, an art that has scarcely emerged and whose rapid progress is marked by an extraordinary vitality."[124]

Canudo's text laid the groundwork for two loosely related lines of thinking that would much occupy the French. Paradoxically, one of these passed through Yhcam. Despite his assumption that the cinema's forte lay in its "realistic" representation of action and space—that characters acted and did not reason in the cinema, which critics such as Haugmard and Doumic deplored—Yhcam believed in a subjective cinema. Perhaps influenced directly by Canudo (for example, the references to Wagner and the Futurists), he called attention to then-current technical methods of suggesting a character's state of mind.[125] Interestingly, these methods involved single images or shots and not connections between shots: soft-focus images, lighting contrasts, and superimposition. Such techniques, for instance, might heighten the effect of certain scenes in a film version of *Les Misérables*, an idea that Albert Capellani and his cameraman Pierre Trimbach seem to have used in the famous adaptation of Hugo's novel released by Pathé in late 1912.[126] Again, the technological was being appropriated for an aesthetic position. Similarly, although Yhcam demanded that sound effects (in the cinema) sustain the lifelike realism of film action and that the musical accompaniment remain neutral so as not to deflect attention from the screen image, he also praised the strange muteness marking film characters for the way it impelled the spectators themselves actively to imagine or produce the dialogue.[127] This led him to postulate an "ideal cinema" uninterrupted by explanatory or dialogical intertitles; but it also suggests that he may be alluding to a form of "inner speech," as in melodrama, by which spectators were bound up or identified with film characters and thus experienced a heightened visual-verbal pleasure—in a way that compensated for a supposed lack in the silent cinema's ability to produce what Noël Burch has called "the full diegetic effect."[128] The basis for further developments along this line of thinking may well have been provided by Henri Bergson, in 1914, when he enlarged briefly on an analogy that he had introduced in *L'Evolution créatrice* (1907): "As a witness to its beginnings, I realized [the cinema] could suggest new things to a philosopher. It might be able to assist in the synthesis of memory, or even of the thinking process. If the circumference [of a circle] is composed of a series of points, memory is, like the cinema, composed of a series of images. Immobile, it is in neutral state; in movement, it is life itself."[129] If the analogy were simply reversed, the implication would be that the cinema could simulate the analytical processes of perception, memory, and conceptualization, in a narrative form.

The other line of thinking extended to the cinema the then-current Modernist concern for re-defining the nature of the subject in painting and music—by directing attention to the formal patterns of the medium's own specific material.[130] Here a different analogy was developed quite systematically, and as an actual project, by the Russian-born artist, Léopold Survage, in the last issue of Apollinaire's *Les Soirées de Paris*.[131] Survage used the analogy between the rhythm of sound in music and the rhythm of form and color possible in a succession of images to envision a new kind of cinema that would be neither narrative nor documentary.[132] On the one hand, this would be an abstract or non-representational cinema in which the forms and colors of the film image functioned like musical notes or chords. On the other, put in motion, to be transformed and conjoined, these forms and colors would somehow "become capable of evoking feeling [orchestrated sensations]," specifically the changing emotional state of the artist.[133] Thus, at the end of a series of simple equations, Survage claimed, the projection of such a film would mysteriously produce in the spectator "something of an analogy to the inner dynamism of the author." Although the war kept Survage from realizing his project (he did succeed in completing nearly a hundred "color plates" or paintings between 1912 and 1914), his essay apparently was the first in France to edge the cinema away from a Symbolist aesthetic in which all the arts were seen as evolving toward music—in Canudo's words, "all our spiritual, aesthetic, and religious life *aspires to become music*"[134]—and toward a Modernist aesthetic of purely formal innovation and play.

CONCLUSION

What is clear from this exploratory analysis of discourse modes is that the earliest French writings on the cinema—with the exception perhaps of Méliès, Canudo, and Yhcam's texts and, to a lesser extent, those of Gourmont and Survage—tended to be fragmentary and unsystematic, either narrowly focused on a question of the current moment or else roughly synthesized bits and pieces of several discourses. Most of the texts address only a limited range of the questions that Dudley Andrew suggests any theory of film worth its salt must address.[135] But that is to be expected in the formative stages of a new discursive practice whose subject is constituted by a rapidly changing industry, technology, popular spectacle format, and art form. Much more attention is given in these texts, for instance, to the value and function of the cinema as well as to the forms and kinds of films being made and shown than to the raw material or determining features of the medium and even to the methods and techniques of realization. Consequently, in the process of disentangling and laying bare the multiplicity of early French writing on the cinema, this has meant that certain discourse modes (technological, political, educational, moral, cultural), which often tend to be ignored or suppressed in the establishment of a tradition or "canon" of film theory and criticism, have been privileged.[136] Yet in the jostling and blending of discourse modes—and the friction of their strains—a network of nodal points has emerged. Some texts situate the cinema as a tug-of-war between antagonistic polarities: national/international, commercial exploitation/aesthetic communion, commodity reification/epistemological exploration, cinematic specificity/artistic synthesis. Others find the cinema disrupting or questioning conventional cultural dichotomies such as high art/low art, fantasy/realism, narration/description, Symbolist/Modernist, French/American. Finally, the discourse modes having to do with the cinema as popular spectacle and art have put in play most of the formulations that, either sharpened or transformed into conceptual frameworks for a diverse range of narrative and non-narrative forms, will dominate the period of the war.

A final note. In 1912, Yhcam called on the French press to establish a forum of serious criticism to counter the common practice of exhibition that consigned films to an ephemeral life and, in so doing, to stimulate and guide the cinema's advance. His perception of such a lack in both film journals and newspapers seems accurate, for the earliest reviews of individual films during this period tended to be either purely descriptive or summarily judgmental. When *Le Courrier cinématographique*, for instance, initiated an "impartial criticism" of the week's film releases in August 1911, Le Mauvais Oeil (the reviewer's apologetic pseudonym) simply encapsulated the story of each film and labeled it "very good," "good," "acceptable," or "poor."[137] The same practice was still operating almost three years later in critic Ernest Le Jeunesse's "Ciné-critique" column in *Le Journal* and in Serge Bernstamm's column under the same heading in *Le Film*.[138] Among this weekly and biweekly deluge of brief stories and tag lines, a small number of reviews stand out, either because of the specific films they call attention to, the assumptions they make in their sketchy evaluations, or the sensibilities they bring to the film experience and the styles they employ to convey that experience. I have chosen to include several of these reviews— Brisson on *L'Assassinat du Duc de Guise* and Raynal on *Fantômas* as well as Feuillade's advertisement for *Les Vipères*—less as exemplary pieces of criticism than as exploratory ways of addressing an individual film or group of films. Moreover, they constitute the beginnings of a repertory that Yhcam was perhaps one of the first to recommend as a means by which films could remain in distribution and available for continual rescreening.

1. "Extension de notre but," *Phono-Ciné-Gazette,* 13 (1 October 1905), 197.

2. Georges Dureau, "Deux mots au lecteur," *Ciné-Journal,* 1 (15 August 1908), 1–2.

3. See, for instance, G.-Michel Coissac, *Histoire du cinématographe: De ses origines jusqu'à nos jours* (Paris: Cinéopse, 1925), 448.

4. Coissac, *Histoire du cinématographe,* 445. The Association professionnelle de la presse cinématographique was formed one year after two similar organizations were institutionalized by the French film distributors and exhibitors—see Coissac, *Histoire du cinématographe,* 439–41.

5. Coissac, *Histoire du cinématographe,* 447–48. René Jeanne and Charles Ford, *Le Cinéma et la presse, 1895–1960* (Paris: Armand Colin, 1961), 75–77. Claude Bellanger, Jacques Godechot, Pierre Guiral and Fernand Terrou, *Histoire générale de la presse française,* vol. 3, *De 1871 à 1940* (Paris: Presses universitaires de France, 1972), 334.

6. It is worth recalling that the secularization of the French primary and secondary schools had occurred just twenty years before, that Catholic secondary schools still attracted 43 percent of all secondary-level students in 1899, and that the French legislature had just excluded the Catholic religious orders from teaching in 1904. See R. D. Anderson, *France, 1870–1914: Politics and Society* (London: Routledge and Kegan Paul, 1977), 12–13, 105.

7. An extract from Ducom's manual was reprinted as "Les Sujets de cinématographe," in *Ciné-Journal*, 165 (21 October 1911), 33, 35–37. Ducom was an engineer and sometime filmmaker at Gaumont—see Jacques Deslandes and Jacques Richard, *Histoire comparée du cinéma*, vol. 2 (Paris: Casterman, 1968), 326–28. For an extensive bibliography of books and brochures then available in France (in French, English, German, and Italian), see the "Bibliothèque générale de cinématographie" supplement to *Cinéma-Revue*, 3 (April 1913).

8. Demeny's book was addressed specifically to the lectures and discussions in the provinces sponsored by the reformist Ligue française de l'enseignement.

9. Henri Desgranges, publisher of the sporting magazine, *L'Auto*, launched *Comoedia* on 1 October 1907. It provides one of the most complete sources of cultural history in France just prior to the war.

10. I thank Paul Willemen for spurring me to ascertain a clearer sense of the ideological spectrum that characterized the French press before the war and within which these writings on the cinema emerged. The primary source, of course, is Bellanger et al., *Histoire générale de la presse française*, vol. 3.

11. Adolphe Brisson, "Chronique théâtral: *L'Assassinat du Duc de Guise*," *Le Temps* (22 November 1908), 3–4. *L'Intransigeant* had been closely linked with the Boulangist movement some twenty years before. It shared this combination of right-wing politics and avant-garde cultural practice (Apollinaire was its art critic) with Charles Maurras's new radically conservative daily, *Action française*.

12. Selected responses to the inquiries launched by *Le Figaro* and *Excelsior* were reprinted in *Ciné-Journal*, respectively, in August 1912, and November–December 1913. For information on *Les Marges*, see the Exposition catalogue, *1913* (Paris: Société des Amis de la Bibliothèque Nationale, 1983), 63.

13. The emergence of daily columns or weekly half pages devoted to the cinema quickly followed the appearance, beginning in *L'Intransigeant*, of similar daily columns devoted to writing and publishing—see André Billy, *L'Epoque contemporaine, 1905–1930* (Paris: Jules Tallandier, 1956), 160–62.

14. Georges Méliès, "Les Vues cinématographiques," *Annuaire général et international de la photographie* (Paris: Plon, 1907), reprinted in Georges Sadoul, *Lumière et Méliès*, rev. ed., Bernard Eisenschitz, ed. (Paris: Lherminier, 1985), 204.

15. Rémy de Gourmont, "Epilogues: Cinématographe," *Mercure de France* (1 September 1907), 124–27. Gourmont's sense of the kinds of films included in a cinema program corresponds closely to the "genres" listed in the 1907 catalogue of Pathé-Frères films. See Georges Sadoul, *Histoire générale du cinéma*, vol. 2 (Paris: Denoël, 1948), 298–326.

16. Yhcam, "La Cinématographie," *Ciné-Journal*, 191 (20 April 1912), 36–37.

17. See, also, "Les Merveilles du cinématographe: Les diverses utilisations du cinéma," *Cinéma-Revue*, 3 (March 1913), 72–75, and Dr. Toulouse, "Psychologie du cinéma," *Cinéma-Revue*, 3 (March 1913), 81–83—the latter reprinted from *Le Figaro*. Dr. Edouard Toulouse was director of a laboratory of experimental psychology in Paris and founder of the French state organization on mental hygiene. A similar spectrum of discourse modes most likely can be found in other countries as well during this period.

18. J. Rosen, "Avant-Propos," *Le Cinématographe: Son passé, son avenir et ses applications* (Paris: Société d'éditions techniques, 1911), 2. For an excellent analysis of the position of the cinema within the 1900 Paris Exposition, see Emmanuelle Toulet, "Le Cinéma à l'Ex-

position Universelle de 1900," *Revue d'histoire moderne et contemporaine*, 33 (April–June 1986), 170–209.

19. See, for example, R. D., "Une Séance à l'Académie des Sciences," *Ciné-Journal*, 62 (24 October 1909), 6–7; Félix Poli, "Microscope et cinématographie," *Ciné-Journal*, 63 (1 November 1909), 5–8; Edmond Perrier, "Le Cinématographe au service de la science," *Ciné-Journal*, 64 (9 November 1909), 12–14; Georges Fagot, "La Cinématographie des microbes," *Ciné-Journal*, 96 (25 June 1910), 17; Coissac, *Histoire du cinématographe*, 534–40; and Pierre Trimbach, *Quand on tournait la manivelle . . . il y a 60 ans . . . ou les mémoires d'un opérateur de la Belle Epoque* (Paris: CEFAG, 1970), 125.

20. That passion for reproducing reality was already invested in landscape painting and photography, which had taken on "an explicitly scientific dignity as a means of investigating the visual aspect of Nature"—Charles Rosen and Henri Zerner. *Romanticism and Realism: The Mythology of Nineteenth-Century Art* (New York: Viking, 1984), 54. See, also, Léon Vidal's desire, summing up that of his contemporaries, for the addition of color and sound to photographic images, as expressed in the *Bulletin de la société française de photographie* (1895), 397, quoted in Toulet, "Le Cinéma à l'Exposition Universelle de 1900," 207.

21. Jean-Louis Comolli, "Machines of the Visible," in *The Cinematic Apparatus*, ed. Teresa de Lauretis and Stephen Heath (New York: St. Martin's Press, 1980), 122. See, also, Deslandes and Richard, *Histoire comparée du cinéma*, vol. 2, 33–55; Susan Sontag, *On Photography* (New York: Viking, 1977), 93; and Rachel Bowlby, *Just Looking: Consumer Culture in Dreiser, Gissing, and Zola* (London: Methuen, 1985), 6.

22. Comolli, "Machines of the Visible," 122–23. See, also, Comolli, "Technique and Ideology: Camera, Perspective, Depth of Field, Parts 3 and 4," trans. Diana Matias, in *Narrative, Apparatus, Ideology: A Film Theory Reader*, ed. Philip Rosen (New York: Columbia University Press, 1986), 432–33; and Noël Burch, "Primitivism and the Avant-Gardes: A Dialectical Approach," *Narrative, Apparatus, Ideology*, 489–90.

23. Gourmont, "Epilogues: Cinématographe," 124–27. Anatole France, "Entretien," *Le Cri de Paris* (August 1908), reprinted in *Phono-Ciné-Gazette* (1 September 1908). Jules Claretie, "La Vie à Paris," *Le Temps* (19 November 1908), reprinted in *Ciné-Journal*, 15 (26 November 1908), 5–7, and 16 (3 December 1908), 8–9. René Doumic, "Revue dramatique: L'Age du cinéma," *Revue des deux mondes* 133 (15 August 1913), 919–30. While Anatole France was one of the leading writers in the Dreyfusard camp in the early 1900s, Doumic remained a staunch defender of the anti-Dreyfusard faction.

24. Thomas Elsaesser, "Film History and Visual Pleasure: Weimer Cinema," in *Cinema Histories, Cinema Practices*, ed. Patricia Mellencamp and Philip Rosen (Washington, D.C.: American Film Institute, 1984), 53. Steve Neale, *Cinema and Technology: Image, Sound, Colour* (Bloomington: Indiana University Press, 1985), 22.

25. Colette, "L'Expédition Scott au cinématographe," *Le Matin* (4 June 1914), trans. Sarah W. R. Smith in *Colette at the Movies*, ed. Alain and Odette Virmaux (New York: Frederick Ungar, 1980), 16–17. Cf. André Bazin's articulation of the passion to reproduce reality in relation to the early cinema in "The Myth of Total Cinema," *Critique* (1946), trans. Hugh Gray in Bazin, *What Is Cinema?* (Berkeley: University of California Press, 1967), 17–22.

26. In addition, *Ciné-Journal* was beginning to sketch out a history of the cinema's technological development by reprinting Jules-Etienne Marey's 1900 essay on his research in the late 1880s—"Les Origines de la cinématographie," *Ciné-Journal*, 101 (30 July 1910), 11–12, and 102 (6 August 1910), 9–11—and by publishing Coissac's initial outline of an institutional cinema history—"Le Cinématographe," *Ciné-Journal*, 117 (19 November 1910), 10–11; 118 (26 November 1910), 5–8; and 119 (3 December 1910), 5–6.

27. [Louis Feuillade], *"Les Scènes de la vie telle qu'elle est," Ciné-Journal*, 139 (22 April 1911), 19. See, also, [Louis Feuillade], *"La Tare," Ciné-Journal*, 155 (12 August 1911), 15.

28. Méliès, "Les Vues cinématographiques," 207.

29. Bowlby, *Just Looking*, 15–16.

30. For a brief summary of the commercial failure of the *La Vie telle qu'elle est* series, see Henri Fescourt, *La Foi et les montagnes* (Paris: Paul Montel, 1959), 86–87. For a historical overview of the early realist tradition in the French cinema, see Georges Sadoul, *Histoire générale du cinéma*, vol. 3 (Paris: Denoël, 1951), 245–75; and Richard Abel, *French Cinema: The First Wave, 1915–1929* (Princeton: Princeton University Press, 1984), 94–97.

31. Christine Gledhill makes a crucial distinction, which demands further elaboration, between melodrama and realism as aesthetic and epistemological modes of perception and expression in "Dialogue," *Cinema Journal* 25 (Summer 1986), 45.

32. See the La Bonne Presse ad in *Le Fascinateur*, 36 (1 December 1905), 381; "Ciné-Nouvelles," *Phono-Ciné-Gazette*, 65 (1 December 1907), 419; Edmond Benoît-Lévy, "L'Education sociale par le cinématographe," *Phono-Ciné-Gazette*, 87 (1 November 1908), 774–75; and G.-Michel Coissac, "Le Cinématographe et l'Eglise Catholique," *Ciné-Journal*, 47 (11–17 July 1909), 1–5, reprinted from *Le Fascinateur*. For further information on the secularization of the French school system and the Catholic Church's response to that secularization, see Anderson, *France, 1870–1914*, 12–13, 105, and Roger McGraw, *France, 1815–1914: The Bourgeois Century* (Oxford: Fontana, 1983), 216–19. For a brief survey of the related battle between the French university system and the Catholic Church, see Regis Debray, *Teachers, Writers, Celebrities: The Intellectuals of Modern France*, trans. David Macey (London: New Left Books, 1981), 42–44.

33. Rosen, *Le Cinématographe*, 138. See, also, Paul Leglise, *Histoire de la politique du cinéma français: Le Cinéma et la IIIᵉ République* (Paris: Pierre Lherminier, 1970), 45–46, and Pascal Ory and Jean-François Sirinelli, *Les Intellectuels en France, de l'Affaire Dreyfus à nos jours* (Paris: Armand Colin, 1986), 24. In 1913, Jean Benoit-Lévy began a long career as a major producer of educational films in France—see Coissac, *Histoire du cinématographe*, 573–74.

34. Louis Haugmard, "L' 'Esthétique' du cinématographe," *Le Correspondant* (25 May 1913), 762–71. See, also, Coissac, *Histoire du cinématographe*, 543–44.

35. See, for instance, "Le Cinéma à l'école: L'Ecran remplacera le tableau noir," *Ciné-Journal*, 43 (11 June 1909), 4–6; "A l'Académie des sciences," *Ciné-Journal*, 71 (27 December 1909), 12; "Les Merveilles du cinématographe," 72–75; "Le Microscope et le cinématographe," *Cinéma-Revue*, 3 (May 1913), 129–32; J. Comandon, "Rôle de la cinématographie dans les études biologiques," *Cinéma-Revue*, 3 (November 1913), 341–48; Dr. Doyen, "Mes Films chirurgicaux," *Le Journal* (2 January 1914), 7; Michel Georges-Michel, "Henri Bergson nous parle au cinéma," *Le Journal* (20 February 1914), 7; J. Comandon, "Pour epargner les animaux servons-nous du cinématographe," *Le Film*, 18 (26 June 1914), 8; Coissac, *Histoire du cinématographe*, 526–29; and Fescourt, *La Foi et les montagnes*, 123–28.

36. André Chalopin, "Le Cinéma dans l'enseignement," *Le Journal* (24 October 1913), 7.

37. Coissac, *Histoire du cinématographe*, 575–76.

38. Neale, *Cinema and Technology*, 54.

39. Hector Blond, "L'Opinion de M. Léon Berard, Sous-Secrétaire d'Etat des Beaux-Arts," *Le Journal* (31 October 1913), 7. See, also, Augustin Thierry, "Le Cinématographe et l'histoire," *Le Courrier cinématographique*, 19 (18 November 1911), 6; Fernand Hauser, "Le 'Cinémathèque' s'impose," *Le Journal* (19 November 1913), 7; and Raymond Borde, *Les Cinématheques* (Lausanne: L'Age d'homme, 1983), 30–37.

40. Terry Eagleton, *The Function of Criticism* (London: Verso, 1984), 55–56.

41. Anderson, *France, 1870–1914*, 91.

42. Miriam Hansen, "Early Silent Cinema: Whose Public Sphere?" *New German Critique*,

27

29 (Spring–Summer, 1983), 167–71. Lary May, *Screening Out the Past* (Chicago: University of Chicago Press, 1980), 43–59.

43. Hansen, "Early Silent Cinema," 157–59. Cf. Jean-Paul Sartre's vivid description of his early cinema experiences in *The Words*, trans. Bernard Frechtman (New York: George Braziller, 1964), 121–22.

44. Gourmont, "Epilogues: Cinématographe," 125. Feuillade, "*Les Scènes de la vie telle qu'elle est*," 19.

45. The Paris police prefect spoke at the International Congress on the Cinema, organized by the Association of Exhibitors, in Paris, 25–27 March 1912; E. Kress wrote in "Comment on installe et administre un cinéma," *Conférences sur la cinématographie*, vol. 2 (Paris, 1912)—both cited in Emmanuelle Toulet, "Le Spectacle cinématographique à Paris de 1895 à 1914," Thèse de l'Ecole de Chartes (Sorbonne, 1982), 512. The notions of maleness and femaleness attributed to the early cinema demand further study, especially in light of Linda Williams's study of the representation of the human body in Eadweard Muybridge and Georges Méliès—"Film Body: An Implantation of Perversions," *Ciné-Tracts* 3.4 (Winter 1981), 19–35—and of Annette Michelson's fascinating analysis of Villiers de l'Isle-Adam's fantasy novel, *L'Eve future* (Paris, 1889), whose narrative turns on the fabrication of a beautiful woman as a simulacrum by the inventor Thomas Edison—"On the Eve of the Future: The Reasonable Facsimile and the Philosophical Toy," *October*, 29 (Summer 1984), 3–20.

46. Leglise, *Histoire de la politique du cinéma français*, 27–32; Hansen, "Early Silent Cinema," 168.

47. See, for instance, *Le Fascinateur* (1 May 1909)—cited in Toulet, "Le Spectacle cinématographique à Paris," 513–14—and Rosen, *Le Cinématographe*, 118.

48. Rosen, *Le Cinématographe*, 119–132; Yhcam, "La Cinématographie," *Ciné-Journal*, 191 (20 April 1912), 37, 39. Children were recognized as a significant part of the cinema audience as early as 1907—see Maxime Leproust, "Le Théâtre-Cinéma," *Phono-Ciné-Gazette* (1 January 1907), 13–14, and J. Ernest Charles, "Psychologie cinématographique," *Gil Blas* (20 March 1908), reprinted in *Argus-Phono-Cinéma* (29 March 1908), 11–12.

49. The principal offenders were Eclair's *Zigomar* (September 1911 to March 1912), *L'Auto grise* (April 1912), and *Hors la loi* (May 1912); Pathé's *Charley Colms* (March 1912) and *Le Collier de la danseuse* (May 1912); and Gaumont's *Main de fer* (August 1912).

50. Emmanuelle Toulet provides a succinct survey of the 1912–1913 discussion of the cinema's moral and social function in the French press—"Le Spectacle cinématographique à Paris," 511–35. For a summary of these charges against the cinema, see Lucien Cellerier, "Littérature criminelle: Romans d'aventure et cinématographe," *L'Année pedagogique* (1913), and E. Poursey, *La Démoralisation de la jeunesse par la littérature et l'imagerie criminelle* (1913).

51. Georges Dureau, "Le Cinéma tel que le juge la grande presse française," *Ciné-Journal*, 199 (14 June 1912), 3–4; Dureau, "La Liberté des spectacles menacés," *Ciné-Journal*, 200 (22 June 1912), 3–4; Dureau, "Lettre ouverte à M. Herriot, maire de Lyon et à ses imitateurs," *Ciné-Journal*, 201 (29 June 1912), 3–5; Dureau, "La Censure devant les syndicats," *Ciné-Journal*, 203 (13 July 1912), 5–11; Decroix, "La Liberté doit être la même pour la presse et pour la cinématographe," *Ciné-Journal*, 207 (10 August 1912), 17.

52. Yhcam, "La Cinématographie," *Ciné-Journal*, 194 (11 May 1912), 14.

53. Two surviving examples of this "reformist" tendency would be Feuillade's *L'Erreur tragique* (1913) and Perret's *Léonce cinématographiste* (1913), both of whose plots turn on the revelation that the supposed immorality of the cinema proves erroneous in the end. For an analysis of Feuillade's *L'Erreur tragique*, see Abel, "Before *Fantômas*: Louis Feuillade and the Development of Early French Cinema," *Post Script*, 7.1 (Fall 1987), 4–26.

28

54. Gourmont, "Epilogues: Cinématographe," 124, 126; Doumic, "Revue dramatique: L'Age du cinéma," 919. Cf. "Ce que nos hommes de lettres pensent du cinématographe: Edmond d'Harancourt," *Ciné-Journal*, 231 (25 January 1913), 17.

55. See Rosalind Williams, *Dream Worlds: Mass Consumption in Late Nineteenth-Century France* (Berkeley: University of California Press, 1982), 58–78; Toulet, "Le Cinéma à l'Exposition Universelle de 1900," 188–94; and Burch, "Primitivism and the Avant-Gardes," 490–91.

56. Lille-Cinéma, "La Question cinématographique," [1912], reprinted in Marcel L'Herbier, ed., *Intelligence du cinématographe* (Paris: Corréa, 1946), 51–52. Cf. Vachel Lindsay, *The Art of the Moving Picture* (New York: Macmillan, 1915), 252.

57. Haugmard, "L' 'Esthétique' du cinématographe," 767–68.

58. "Lettre du Colonel Marchand," *Le Film*, 2 (7 March 1914), reprinted in L'Herbier, *Intelligence du cinématographe*, 93. Even Georges Dureau succumbed to this thinking in "Donnons aux films une âme nationale," *Ciné-Journal*, 242 (12 April 1913), 3–4.

59. For an informative description of the Classical Renaissance movement, see Billy, *L'Epoque contemporaine*, 22–32. For further information on the Nationalist Revival phenomenon, see Eugen Weber, *The Nationalist Revival in France, 1905–1914* (Berkeley: University of California Press, 1968); Anderson, *France, 1870–1914*, 26–28, 50; and McGraw, *France 1815–1914*, 282–84. *Action française*, which served as the ideological vanguard of the Nationalist Revival, seems to have ignored the cinema during this period.

60. Yhcam, "La Cinématographie," *Ciné-Journal*, 194 (11 May 1912), 16.

61. Quoted from an article in *Phono-Ciné-Gazette* (15 June 1906), in Toulet, "Le Spectacle cinématographique à Paris," 508.

62. For an analysis of Gabriel Tarde's writings of the 1890s and early 1900s, see Williams, *Dream Worlds*, 368–79. This division between nationalist and internationalist strains of discourse can be seen, in part, as an extension of the sharply polarized camps that the Dreyfus Affair (1898–1899) produced among French intellectuals and politicians—see Albert Thibaudet, *French Literature from 1795 to Our Era*, trans. Charles Lam Markman (New York: Funk & Wagnals, 1967), 366–75; Debray, *Teachers, Writers, Celebrities*, 51–54; Madeleine Rébérioux, *La République radicale? 1898–1914*, 2d ed. (Paris: Editions du Seuil, 1985), 3–41; and Ory and Sirinelli, *Les Intellectuels en France*, 13–60.

63. Ricciotto Canudo, "Naissance d'un sixième art," *Les Entretiens idéalistes* (25 October 1911), reprinted as "L'Esthétique du septième art," in Canudo, *L'Usine aux images* (Paris: Etienne Chiron, 1926), 12–26.

64. See, for instance, Adolphe Brisson, "Le Cinéma et le théâtre en province," *Le Film*, 10 (1 May 1914), 27–28.

65. Producer-director Camille de Morlhon argued, for instance, that one of the theater's problems was that it depended far too heavily on the work of established authors and refused to stage plays by young, unknown writers, who then turned their attention to the cinema— Morlhon, "La Crise théâtrale," *Ciné-Journal*, 280 (3 January 1914), 25, 29, 32, 35.

66. The average prices for the four leading spectacles in Paris in 1912 were: theaters, 5 francs; concerts, 4 francs; music halls, 3 francs; and cinemas, 0.75 francs—Toulet, "Le Spectacle cinématographique à Paris," 540.

67. The Gaumont-Palace programs, for instance, were divided into four parts, each of which included several films and sometimes live performances.

68. For a fascinating analysis of the emergence of the daily newspaper as a discursive practice in France, see Richard Terdiman, *Discourse/Counter-Discourse: The Theory and Practice of Symbolic Resistance in Nineteenth-Century France* (Ithaca: Cornell Univeristy Press, 1985), 117–46. Jerrold Seigel makes a similar connection between the daily newspapers and the

29

famous literary cabarets in the late nineteenth century, in *Bohemian Paris: Culture, Politics, and the Boundaries of Bourgeois Life, 1830–1930* (New York: Viking, 1986), 225–26.

69. See Williams, *Dream Worlds*, 66–70, and Bowlby, *Just Looking*, 1–8, 66–82.

70. Bowlby, *Just Looking*, 4, 71.

71. Walter Benjamin, "Reply to Adorno [9 December 1938]," trans. Harry Zohn, in *Aesthetics and Politics* (London: New Left Books, 1977), 140–41.

72. For a brief survey of the development of mass culture and the culture industry, see Peter U. Hohendahl, "Introduction," *New German Critique*, 29 (Spring–Summer, 1983), 3–7.

73. Toulet, "Le Spectacle cinématographique à Paris," 558–60.

74. Leproust, "Le Théâtre-Cinéma," 12–14; Gourmont, "Epilogues: Cinématographe," 124–25; Coissac, "Le Cinématographe et l'Eglise Catholique," 1–5.

75. Georges Dureau, "L'Avènement de la cinématographie," *Ciné-Journal*, 173 (16 December 1911), 3–4. See also, Lille-Cinéma, "La Question cinématographique," 53. These writers tend to confirm Noël Burch's theory of a "Primitive" mode of representation based on the popular melodrama, vaudeville, and Grand Guignol, which was superceded by an "Institutional" mode of representation based on the "legitimate" bourgeois stage. Unfortunately, this theory does not account for the differences between French and American film practices within such an "Institutional" mode—Burch, "Primitivism and the Avant-Gardes," 495.

76. F. Laurent, "Le Cinéma à la foire," *Le Cinéma* (31 May 1912), and "Sur les Boul's Extérs," *Le Cinéma* (14 June 1912).

77. The "Le Cinéma du Peuple" program (1913) is reprinted in Sadoul, *Histoire générale du cinéma*, vol. 3, 272. For a brief analysis of the anarchist publisher, Jean Grave, see Eugenia W. Herbert, *The Artist and Social Reform: France and Belgium, 1885–1898* (New Haven: Yale University Press, 1961), 14-21.

78. "[Untitled article]," *Le Courrier cinématographique*, 20 (25 November 1911), 2–3.

79. Emilie Altenloh, *Zur Soziologie des Kino: Die Kino-Unternehmung und die sozialen Schichten ihrer Besucher*, diss. Heidelberg (Leipzig: Spamersche Buchdrukerei, 1914). For a fine introductory analysis of this text, see Hansen, "Early Silent Cinema," 176–80.

80. Brisson, "Le Cinéma et le théâtre en province," 27–28.

81. Haugmard, "L' 'Esthétique' du cinématographe," 765.

82. Yhcan, "La Cinématographie," *Ciné-Journal*, 191 (20 April 1912), 36. Cf. E. Kress, who also considered the fairgrounds as the genuine propagandists of the cinema—"Comment on installe et administre un cinéma," 36–37. See, also, J. Yvel, *Le Cinéma et l'echo du cinéma réunis* (28 April 1914), reprinted in Toulet, "Le Spectacle cinématographique à Paris," 560.

83. Georges Dureau, "Film d'Art et films d'art" *Ciné-Journal*, 94 (11 June 1910), 3–4. Georges Dureau, "Il faut savoir présenter les films," *Ciné-Journal*, 226 (21 December 1912), 3–4.

84. Maurice Raynal, "Chronique cinématographique," *Les Soirées de Paris*, 26–27 (July–August 1914), 363–64. See, also, Fernand Nozière, "L'Esprit dramatique du cinéma," *L'Intransigeant* (September 1913), reprinted in Marcel Lapierre, ed., *Anthologie du cinéma* (Paris: La Nouvelle Edition, 1946), 277–80.

85. Haugmard, "L' 'Esthétique' du cinématographe," 766.

86. At least one other question did elicit a long debate, that of musical accompaniment for films. See, for instance, Henri Leissus, "La Musique au cinéma," *Le Courrier cinématographique*, 2 (20 July 1911), 8; Georges Dureau, "Le Cinéma et la musique d'accompagnement," *Ciné-Journal*, 153 (29 July 1911), 3–4; Henri Leissus, "La Musique au cinéma," *Le Courrier cinématographique*, 4 (4 August 1911), 4; Louis Janssens, "Lettre et notice sur la

synchronization ciné-musicale," *Le Courrier cinématographique*, 9 (9 September 1911), 4–6; E. Kress, "Comment on installe et administre un cinéma," 26–27; Louis Janssens, "Le Cinéma ne peut se passer de musique mais il en veut une pour lui," *Ciné-Journal*, 214 (28 September 1912), 5, 7; Paul Gilson, "De la musique au cinématographe," *Ciné-Journal*, 215 (5 October 1912), 6–7, 10; Paul d'Acosta, "Des Lois: De la musique au cinéma," *Ciné-Journal*, 228 (4 January 1913), 9, 11, 14.

87. It should be remembered that one of the earliest long films that made a considerable impression in France, almost comparable to Film d'Art's *L'Assassinat du Duc de Guise* (1908), was Michel Carré's five-reel *L'Enfant prodigue*, which premiered at the Théâtre des Variétés, on 16 June 1907. *L'Enfant prodigue*, however, was recorded from a single camera position, with a minimum of editing. See Toulet, "Le Spectacle cinématographique à Paris," 488, 494–95.

88. Georges Dureau, "Les Longues Bandes," *Ciné-Journal*, 141 (6 May 1911), 3; Charles Le Frapper, "Les Grands Films," *Le Courrier cinématographique*, 3 (28 July 1911), 3–4. Le Frapper also criticized Feuillade's *La Tare* for being overlong at 900 meters and praised Film d'Art for keeping within the supposed limits of 300–600 meters—Le Frapper, "Casse-cou!!" *Le Courrier cinématographique*, 5 (11 August 1911), 3–4.

89. Georges Dureau, "Quelques mots sur les longs films," *Ciné-Journal*, 166 (28 October 1911), 3–4.

90. Georges Dureau, "Les Grandes Bandes," *Ciné-Journal*, 225 (14 December 1912), 3–4; Dureau, "Le Succès des *Misérables*," *Ciné-Journal*, 230 (18 January 1913), 3.

91. Georges Dureau, "Les Films de long métrage," *Ciné-Journal*, 264 (13 September 1913), 3–4.

92. Des Angles, "Les Films démesurés," *Comoedia* (6 October 1913), 3.

93. Georges Dureau, "Du Choix d'un programme," *Ciné-Journal*, 61 (18 October 1909), 1–2, 4.

94. De Mare, "L'Avenir du cinéma," *Argus-Phono-Cinéma* (30 March 1908), 1–6.

95. André Hugon, "L'Invasion," *Le Film*, 3 (13 March 1914), 3.

96. Lille-Cinéma, "La Question cinématographique," 53.

97. Canudo, "Naissance d'un sixième art," 15.

98. Gourmont, "Epilogues: Cinématographe," 126. Cf. Edmond Sée, "Cinématographe," *Phono-Ciné-Gazette* (15 March 1908), 530.

99. Jules Romains, "La Foule au cinématographe," *Les Puissances de Paris* (Paris: Eugène Figuière, 1911), 118–20. For a succinct analysis of Romains's Unanimist vision and his early writings, see Denis Boak, *Jules Romains* (New York: Twayne, 1974), 22–60. The empathetic, if sometimes sentimental, attitude expressed in Romains's sketches on "the crowd" contrast markedly with the classic French study on collective crowd psychology— Gustave Le Bon's deeply conservative, moralistic *Psychologie des foules* (Paris: Alcan, 1895), which was immediately translated into English as *The Crowd: A Study of the Popular Mind* (London: T. Fisher Unwin, 1896). For an introduction to Le Bon's work, see Robert A. Nye, *The Origins of Crowd Psychology: Gustave Le Bon and the Crisis of Mass Democracy in the Third Republic* (London: Sage, 1975).

100. As quoted from an unknown article in *Phono-Ciné-Gazette,* written under the pseudonym of Francis Mair sometime in 1907, in Coissac, *Histoire du cinématographe,* 348, and quoted again in Leglise, *La Politique du cinéma français,* 35.

101. M. Benoit-Lévy, "Rapport Général (Le Congrès de Bruxelles)," *Ciné-Journal*, 107 (10 September 1911), 5–8.

102. Charles Havermans, "Le Droit d'auteur," *Annuaire du commerce et de l'industrie photographique et cinématographique* (Paris, 1911), reprinted in L'Herbier, *Intelligence du cinématographe*, 189–92.

103. See, for instance, Georges Dureau, "La Cinématographie est une oeuvre d'art: Elle n'est au service exclusif ni de la morale ni de l'enseignement," *Ciné-Journal*, 160 (16 September 1911), 3–4, and E. Kress, "La Prise de vues cinématographiques," *Conférences sur la cinématographie*, vol. 1 (Paris: Cinéma-Revue, 1912), 103–6.

104. Hansen, "Early Silent Cinema," 164–70. For a representative sampling of this debate in Germany, see Anton Kaes, ed., *Kino-Debatte: Texte zum Verhältnis von Literatur und Film, 1909–1929* (Tübingen: Max Niemeyer, 1978). Kaes's introduction to *Kino-Debatte* is translated by David J. Levin as "The Debate about Cinema: Charting a Controversy," in *New German Critique*, 40 (Winter 1987), 7–33.

105. "[Untitled article]," *La Patrie* (8 January 1907), reprinted in *Phono-Ciné-Gazette* (15 January 1907), 6. See, also, Sée, "Cinématographie," *Phono-Ciné-Gazette* (15 March 1908), 530; D'Antin's untitled article from *La Liberté*, reprinted in *Argus-Phono-Cinéma* (17 October 1908); and E. Maugras and M. Guegans, *Le Cinématographe devant le droit* (Paris: Giard et Brière, 1912). This was also the year in which a revision of the Berne copyright law extended copyright protection to films, at least in Europe—see E. Potu, *La Protection internationale des oeuvres cinématographiques, d'après la convention de Berne, revisée en 1908* (Paris: Gauthier-Villars, 1912), and Jean Marchais, *Du Cinématographe dans ses rapports avec le droit d'auteur* (Paris: Giard et Brière, 1912). For several years, Pierre Decourcelle had been adapting his own popular novels into plays, which probably explains his interest in setting up SCAGL in 1908: the cinema provided him with one more medium of adaptation—see Yves Olivier-Martin, *Histoire du roman populaire en France, de 1840 à 1980* (Paris: Albin Michel, 1980), 208–9.

106. Georges Dureau, " 'Film d'Art' et films d'art," *Ciné-Journal*, 94 (11 June 1910), 3–4. Rosen, *Le Cinématographe*, 112–13. Georges Dureau, "La Valeur d'un programme influence-t-elle les recettes?" *Ciné-Journal*, 275 (29 November 1913), 3–4.

107. Méliès, "Les Vues cinématographiques," 209.

108. Brisson, "Chronique théâtrale: *L'Assassinat du Duc de Guise*," 3-4.

109. Victorin Jasset, "Etude sur la mise-en-scène en cinématographie," *Ciné-Journal*, 167 (4 November 1911), 31, 33, 35; Georges Dureau, "L'Art du théâtre et celui du cinématographe ne sont pas régies par les mêmes règles," *Ciné-Journal*, 169 (18 November 1911), 3–4; Yhcam, "La Cinématographie,' *Ciné-Journal*, 192 (27 April 1912), 29.

110. This language is borrowed from Gledhill, "Dialogue," 45.

111. Dureau, "L'Art du théâtre et celui du cinématographe," 3–4.

112. Léonce Perret, "Lettre," *Ciné-Journal*, 246 (10 May 1913), 17; E.-G. Lacroix, "Propos d'un metteur-en-scène," *Le Journal* (17 February 1914), 7.

113. Méliès, "Les Vues cinématographiques," 211.

114. No more than a half-dozen films were released under the *Films esthétiques* series title in 1910, but they were preceded by others such as *Les Heures: Film artistique* (February 1909) and *Les Sept Péchés capitaux* (September 1909). In terms of lighting, Gaumont was the most advanced of the French film companies—see Barry Salt, *Film Style and Technology: History and Analysis* (London: Starword, 1983), 89–98.

115. Toulet, "Le Cinéma à l'Exposition Universelle de 1900," 202.

116. Jasset, "Etude sur le mise-en-scène en cinématographie," *Ciné-Journal*, 170 (25 November 1911), 25–27.

117. Fescourt remarks, for instance, on Gaumont's aversion to the use of close shots in his company's films before the war—*La Foi et les montagnes*, 101.

118. Yhcam, "La Cinématographie," *Ciné-Journal*, 193 (4 May 1912), 16–17.

119. For an intriguing analysis of the relationship between nineteenth-century painting, drama, and fiction in England and France, which may well be extended to early cinema, see

Martin Meisel, *Realizations: Narrative, Pictorial, and Theatrical Arts in Nineteenth-Century England* (Princeton: Princeton University Press, 1983), 29–51, 91–96.

120. See, for instance, Barry Salt and Ben Brewster's hypothesis that, before the war, the French and Scandinavian cinemas seem to have developed an alternative form of staging that depended on a "deep space" interior set—Salt, *Film Style and Technology*, 113, 116; Brewster, "La Mise-en-scène en profondeur dans les films français de 1900 à 1914," *Les Premiers Ans du cinéma français*, ed. Pierre Guibbert (Perpignan: Institut Jean Vigo, 1985), 204–17; Brewster lecture delivered at the University of Iowa, 15 November 1985.

121. Méliès, "Les Vues cinématographiques," 207.

122. Canudo, "Naissance d'un sixième art," 13–26. Canudo's garbled attempt to synthesize science and art vaguely echoes the formulations of the Neo-Impressionists and the Futurists on art. See, for instance, Felix Fénéon, "Les Impressionnistes en 1886 (VIIIᵉ Exposition Impressionniste)," *Vogue* (June 1886); Felix Fénéon, "Le Néo-Impressionnisme," *L'Art moderne* (1 May 1887); Paul Signac, *D'Eugène Delacroix au néo-impressionnisme* (Paris, 1889); and Umberto Boccioni, Carlo Carra, Luigi Russolo, Giacomo Balla, and Gino Severini, "Futurist Painting: Technical Manifesto," *Poesia* (11 April 1910). See, also, Stuart Liebman, "French Film Theory, 1910–1921," *Quarterly Review of Film Studies*, 8 (Winter 1983), 9–11.

123. Abel Gance, "Un Sixième Art," *Ciné-Journal*, 185 (9 March 1912), 10.

124. Brisson, "Le Cinéma et le théâtre en province," 27–28.

125. Yhcam, "La Cinématographie," *Ciné-Journal*, 194 (11 May 1912), 14–15.

126. Albert Capellani (1870–1931) was the chief producer-director for SCAGL between 1909 and 1914, and was best known for his literary adaptations—for example, *L'Arlésienne* (1908), *L'Assomoir* (1909), *Le Courrier de Lyon* (1911), *Notre Dame de Paris* (1911), *Les Mystères de Paris* (1912), *Les Misérables* (1912), *Germinal* (1913). *Les Misérables* was one of the longest and most successful French films produced by that date, running 3,400 meters and released in four parts over a four-week period: 30 November 1912, 7 December 1912, 14 December 1912, and 21 December 1912. See Dureau, "Le Succès des *Misérables*"; Pierre Trimbach, *Quand on tournait la manivelle*, 34, 57–58; and Charles Ford, *Albert Capellani: Précurseur méconnu* (Bois d'Arcy: Centre National du Cinéma, 1984), 14–15. Several earlier films by Feuillade, it should be noted, used insert vignette images to suggest a character's state of mind—for instance, *La Mort du Mozart* (1909), *Christophe Colomb* (1910), and *Le Coeur et l'argent* (1912).

127. Georges Dureau takes an opposite position on sound effects in the cinema—"Les 'Bruits de Coulise' au cinématographe," *Ciné-Journal*, 162 (30 September 1911), 3–4. For a thorough enumeration of such effects, see Kress, "Comment on installe et administre un cinéma," 26–31. Also, cf. Sartre's analysis of how his silent film heroes "communicated by means of music; it was the sound of their inner life"—see *The Words*, 123–25.

128. Jacques de Baroncelli advocated a similar concept of an "ideal cinema" without intertitles in "Les Sous-titres sont-ils nécessaires?" *Ciné-Journal*, 358 (24 June 1916), 46, 48. Yhcam's observation suggests that dialogical intertitles were not yet standard in French films by early 1912, yet surviving prints indicate otherwise. Noël Burch defines the term, "full diegetic effect," in relation to the early cinema, in "Narrative/Diegesis—Thresholds, Limits," *Screen*, 23 (July–August 1982), 16–24. For a recent substantive critique of Burch's position, see Edward Branigan, "Diegesis and Authorship," *Iris*, 7 (1986), 37–44.

129. Georges-Michel, "Henri Bergson nous parle au cinéma," 7. Recently, Gilles Deleuze has reexamined Bergson's writings in order "to isolate certain cinematographic concepts," specifically several "theses on movement" in the cinema—Deleuze, *Cinema 1: The Movement-Image*, trans. Hugh Tomlinson and Barbara Habberjam (Minneapolis: University of Minnesota Press, 1986), 1–11, 56–66.

130. See, for instance, Ricciotto Canudo, "Notre Esthétique: A propos du *Rossignol* de Igor Stravinsky," *Montjoie!* 4–5–6 (April–May–June 1914), 7.

131. Léopold Survage, "Le Rythme coloré," *Les Soirées de Paris*, 26–27 (July–August 1914), 426–29. Survage deposited a second document, "La Couleur, le mouvement, le rhythme," with the Académie des Sciences de Paris, on 29 June 1914, reprinted in Survage, *Rythmes colorés, 1912–1923* (Saint-Etienne: Musée d'art et d'industrie, 1973), [7–8]. Cf. Abel Gance's more conventionally Symbolist project, "La Legende de l'arc-en-ciel," which he conceived after reading Lucien Chassagne's "Le Second Stade de l'art de l'avenir: Les symphonies de la lumière," *Le Journal* (22 August 1913)—see Rogert Icart, *Abel Gance ou le Prométhée foudroyé* (Lausanne: L'Age d'homme, 1983), 46–48.

132. Bruno Carra had developed a similar, even more thorough, theory of abstract cinema in "Abstract Cinema—Chromatic Music," *Il pastore, il gregge e la zampogna*, 1 (Rome: Libreria Beltrami, 1912), trans. Caroline Tisdall in *Futurist Manifestoes*, ed. Umbro Apollonio (New York: Viking, 1973), 66–70. See, also, Standish Lawder, *The Cubist Cinema* (New York: New York University Press, 1975), 21–26; Robert Russell and Cecile Starr, *Experimental Animation* (New York: Van Nostrand Reinhold, 1976), 35–40; and Liebman, "French Film Theory, 1910–1921," 6, 10.

133. The theoretical basis of Survage's project thus is rooted in late eighteenth-century and early nineteenth-century Romanticism, especially German Romanticism, as well as "French avant-garde Realism"—see Rosen and Zerner, *Romanticism and Realism*, 34, 52, 73, 155. Survage's language here is also close to that of Georges Braque's "Personal Statement" (1910): "I must therefore create a new sort of beauty, the beauty that appears to me in terms of volume, of line, of mass, of weight, and through the beauty interpret my subjective impression. Nature is a mere pretext for a decorative composition, plus sentiment"—quoted in Kenneth Eric Silver, *Esprit de Corps: The Great War and French Art, 1914–1925* (Ann Arbor: University Microfilms, Inc., 1981), 110.

134. Canudo, "Notre Esthétique," 7. Canudo is paraphrasing Walter Pater.

135. Dudley Andrew, *The Major Film Theories* (New York: Oxford University Press, 1976), 6–8. Cf. Noël Carroll, "Film History and Film Theory: An Outline for an Institutional Theory of Film," *Film Reader*, 4 (1979), 81–96.

136. I have chosen to focus on the "relative autonomy" of French discourse on the cinema as an ideological practice rather than attempt to privilege its relationship to the economic infrastructure or "generative mechanism" on which that discourse depends—see Robert C. Allen and Douglas Gomery, *Film History: Theory and Practice* (New York: Knopf, 1985), 15.

137. Le Mauvais Oeil, "Les Films tels qu'ils sont," *Le Courrier cinématographique*, 5 (11 August 1911), 11.

138. Ernest Le Jeunesse, "Ciné-critique," *Le Journal* (20 March 1914), 6; Serge Bernstamm, "Ciné-critique," *Le Film*, 15 (5 June 1914), 9–10.

Selected Texts

GEORGES MÉLIÈS, "Cinematographic Views"

Méliès's original text was written during the summer of 1906 and published near the end of the year as "Les Vues cinématographiques" in the *Annuaire général et international de la photographie* (Paris: Plon, 1907), 362–92. This translation by Stuart Liebman is a slightly cut version of that original text, and considerably longer than the short version published in *La Revue du cinéma* (15 October 1929) as advance publicity for the Méliès gala organized by Paul Gilson and Jean-George Auriol at the Salle Pleyel on 6 December 1929. A translation of the short version by Stuart Liebman appeared in *October* 29 (Summer 1984), 23–31.

IN THIS talk, I propose to explain as best I possibly can the thousand and one difficulties that professionals must surmount in order to produce the artistic, amusing, strange, or simply the natural subjects that have made the cinematograph such a craze all over the world.

Many volumes would be needed for old hands like myself to write down everything they have learned by the seat of their pants during long years of constant labor, and the space I have at my disposal is unfortunately very limited.

My intention is also primarily to consider unknown aspects of the construction of cinematographic views, most notably the difficulties audiences are unaware of but which are encountered at every turn during the execution of works that seem wholly simple and natural.

In exhibition halls I have often heard the most absurd remarks unquestionably proving that a large number of spectators are miles away from imagining how much work goes into the views they were watching. Some of them, understanding nothing of the way in which "that can be done," simply and naïvely say: *It's only a trick!* Or else: *They must have taken those in a theater!* and, satisfied by their explanation, they conclude with: *It doesn't matter, it's well made all the same.*

Obviously, one can only have reflected for a minute to express such an opinion; the absence of daylight in theaters, the impossibility of properly illuminating the stage and sets in a regular and continuous manner; the very particular kind of mimicry in cinematographic views, so different from that in the theater, as you will see later on; the very limited length of the reels—these are some of the causes that make it impossible or almost so to make films under these conditions. When filmed, even the way in which the theatrical sets are painted makes a woefully bad impression, as I will explain in the chapter about decor. Many concern themselves very little with these matters and do not even attempt to take them into account.

But there is a group of spectators who will not be annoyed, but rather will be delighted to obtain some information to satisfy their curiosity, which, moreover, is very justifiable and natural in intelligent people who always seek to know the explanations behind what they are looking at.

It is this category of spectator, certainly the most numerous, that I will try to satisfy. . . .

THE DIFFERENT GENRES OF CINEMATOGRAPHIC VIEWS

There are four broad categories of cinematographic views, or at least, all such views may be linked to one of these categories. There are so-called *natural* views, *scientific* views, *composed subjects*, and the so-called *transformation* views. I have deliberately set up this classification in the very order in which cinematographic views have successively appeared since the first screenings. In the beginning, views were exclusively of natural subjects; later, the cinematograph was employed as a scientific machine before finally becoming a device used in the theater. From the beginning, its success was enormous; at first this success depended on people's curiosity about animated photographs; but once the cinematograph was put in the service of theatrical art, its success was transformed into a triumph. Since then, this marvelous instrument's popularity has only grown with every passing day until it has assumed prodigious proportions.

NATURAL VIEWS

Those who took up cinematography all began by making natural views; whatever particular area they devoted themselves to, all have also continued to make such films from time to time. These views consist of cinematographically reproducing scenes from ordinary life: views taken in the streets, in the squares, by the sea, on riverbanks, in boats, on trains; panoramic views, ceremonies, parades, funeral processions, etc. In short, they have replaced the *documentary photographs* that used to be taken by portable photographic cameras with *animated documentary photographs*. After at first taking very simple subjects, astonishing solely because of the novelty of *movement* in photographic prints which had always been frozen and immobile, cameramen today, by travelling throughout the entire world, present extremely interesting spectacles that we can watch without putting ourselves out. They show us countries that we probably have not seen, along with their costumes, animals, streets, inhabitants, and customs—all rendered with a photographic fidelity. The landscapes of India, Canada, Algeria, China, and Russia, the waterfalls, the snow-covered countries and their sports, the misty or sun-drenched regions, everything has been filmed for the pleasure of people who do not like to put themselves out. There are many cameramen who specialize in this kind of work because it is the easiest. To have an excellent instrument, to be a good photographic cameraman, to know how to choose a vantage point, to be unafraid of travelling, and to move heaven and earth to obtain the authorizations that are often necessary are the sole qualifications required in this branch of the industry. That is unquestionably a great deal, but we will see further on that all this is only the basis of the art form. Every photographer can take views from nature, but not everyone can compose scenes.

SCIENTIFIC VIEWS

Very soon after the appearance of animated photographs, several people had the idea of using the cinematograph to record anatomical studies of human and animal movement on film. Before the invention of the cinematograph properly speaking, M. Marey had already succeeded in photographing a bird in flight and a horse galloping with truly extraordinary results by decomposing the movement with the assistance of a photographic apparatus with many lenses.[1] Today, thanks to the cinematograph, the automatic instrument par excellence, this is a mere game everyone can play. Others have attached microscopes to the cinematograph and presented us with enlargements of the workings of infinitely tiny creatures that are very curious to watch. Finally, others have availed themselves of the cinematograph to record and reproduce the surgical operations of a master for a specialized audience of students, or to provide them with practical lessons about glass blowing, steam or electric machine components in movement, pottery-making, and all sorts of diverse industries. Strictly speaking, this special branch of cinematography could be placed in the category of natural views, since the cameraman limits himself, as in the first case, to filming what is happening in front of him, except in those cases involving microscopic studies that require special instruments and know-how. But in any case, one must not silently ignore this cinematographic specialty.

COMPOSED SUBJECTS OR SCENIC GENRES

All subjects, of any sort, in which action is readied as it is in the theater and performed by the actors in front of the camera may be placed in a single category. The varieties within this category are innumerable; it includes comic skits, comic operas, burlesques and comedies, peasant stories, the so-called chase scenes, clown acts, acrobatic acts, graceful, artistic, or exotic dance turns, ballets, operas, stage plays, religious scenes, scabrous subjects, plastic tableaux, war scenes, newsreels, reproductions of news items, accident reports, catastrophes, crimes, assassinations, etc.—many more than I can list—as well as the most somber tragedies. The cinematographic realm knows no bounds; all subjects that the imagination can provide are suitable, and it seizes upon them. It is especially this category and the following one that have given immortality to the cinematograph because the subjects conceived by the imagination are infinitely varied and inexhaustible.

THE SO-CALLED TRANSFORMATION VIEWS

I now come to the category of cinematographic views exhibitors call *transformation views*. I find this trade name, however, unsuitable. Since I myself created this special area, I think I may say that the term *fantastic views* would be far more accurate. For if a certain number of these views in fact include scene changes, metamorphoses, or transformations, there are also a large number without transformations. They have instead many trick effects of theatrical machinery, mise-en-scène, optical illusions, and a wide range of processes that can only be called *trick shots*, hardly an academic term, but one that has no equivalent in refined discourse. Whatever the case may be, this category's domain is by far the most extensive, for it encompasses everything from natural views (documentary [*non-préparées*] or contrived [*truquées*] although shot outdoors) to the most imposing theatrical performances. It includes all the illusions that can be produced by prestidigitation, optics, photographic tricks, set design and theatrical machinery, the play of light, dissolves (*dissolving views*[2] as the English have called them), and the entire arsenal of fantastic, magical compositions that turn the most intrepid into madmen. With no intention of disparaging the first two categories, I am nevertheless going to speak solely about the latter two for the very simple reason that there I shall be entirely on home ground and able, consequently, to expound them with full knowledge of the facts. Since the day—and this goes back ten years—when countless producers of cinematographic views began to throw themselves into the making of outdoor views and comic scenes, whether good, bad, or excellent, I abandoned the simplest types and specialized in subjects whose interest lies in their difficulty of execution. To these I have exclusively devoted my efforts.

Cinematographic art offers such a variety of pursuits, it demands so much work of all kinds, and requires such sustained attention that I sincerely do not hesitate to proclaim it the most enticing and most interesting of the arts, for it makes use of almost all of them. Dramatic techniques, drawing, painting, sculpture, architecture, mechanical skills, manual labor of all sorts—all are employed in equal measure in this extraordinary profession. The amazement of those who have happened to watch part of our work always affords me the utmost pleasure and amusement.

The same phrase invariably comes to their lips: "Really, its extraordinary! I never imagined that so much space and material were needed, that so much work was required to obtain these views! I didn't have any idea at all of how they were made."

Alas, afterwards they know little more, for one has to put, as they say, one's nose to the grindstone, and for a long time, for a thorough knowledge of the innumerable difficulties to be surmounted in a profession in which everything, even the seemingly impossible, is realized, and the most fanciful dreams are given the semblance of reality. Finally, needless to say, one must absolutely realize the impossible, since one photographs it and renders it visible.

THE SHOOTING STUDIO

For the special kind of view that concerns us, a studio has to be contrived ad hoc. Briefly, it combines a photographic studio (in gigantic scale) with a theatrical stage. The structure is made of iron and glass. The cabin of the camera operator is located at one end, while at the other end, a stage is situated, constructed exactly like one in a theater and fitted with trapdoors, scenery slots, and uprights. Of course, on each side of the stage there are wings with storerooms for sets, and behind it there are dressing rooms for the artists and extras. The stage includes a lower section containing the workings for the trapdoors and buffers necessary for the appearances and disappearances of the diabolical gods in fairy plays (*féeries*), and slips in which flats can be collapsed during scene changes. Overhead, there is a grate with the rollers and winches needed for maneuvers requiring power (flying characters or vehicles, oblique flights of angels, fairies, or swimmers, etc., etc.). Special rollers help to move the canvas panoramas; electric projectors help to light and to intensify the ghosts. We have, in short, a quite faithful, small-scale likeness of a *théâtre de féerie*. The stage is about thirty-two feet wide with an additional nine feet of wings upstage and downstage. The length of the whole, from the forestage to the camera, is fifty-five feet. Outside, there are iron hangars for the construction of wooden props, sets, etc. . . . and a series of storerooms for the construction materials, props, and costumes.

LIGHTING WITH DAYLIGHT AND ARTIFICIAL LIGHT

The ceiling of the studio is glazed partly with frosted glass and partly with regular glass. In summer, when the sun strikes the sets through the windows, the results could be disastrous because the shadows of the roof's iron beams can be conspicuous on the backdrops below. Moving shutters operated by wires which permit them simultaneously to be opened and closed in the wink of an eye protect against this problem. The frames of these shutters are trimmed with tracing paper (of the kind architects use for drawing their plans); when closed, these provide a softly filtered light

39

similar to that of frosted glass. Even lighting is extremely difficult to obtain during the performance of a scene which sometimes lasts four consecutive hours and more for a subject that, when projected, lasts two to four minutes. When it is cloudy, and the accursed black cumulus clouds take pleasure in constantly crossing in front of the sun, the photographer's friend, exasperation is quick to manifest itself in the one who directs the cameramen, assistants, mechanics, actors, and extras. One must have patience for every sort of ordeal; sometimes, it is better to wait for daylight to return; sometimes one ought rather to close the shutters if there is too much light or to open them if there is not enough, and one must do all this without losing sight of a thousand details inhering in the work in progress. If I am not crazy by now, I probably never will be, because overly bright, cloudy, and hazy skies have tried my patience severely . . . and during my career they have caused innumerable failures along with enormous costs; every tableau that must be started over or is impossible to perform because the bad weather disconcerts the actors, doubles, triples, or quadruples its price, depending on whether you try it two, three, or four more times. I have watched scenes, the ballet *Faust* among others, which have been performed over the course of eight straight days, but last only two-and-a-half minutes and cost 3,200 francs. There's something to make you angry about.

After much groping, and even though it was often said to be impossible, I have recently succeeded in setting up artificial lighting by using special electric equipment consisting of battens, track lights, and props, similar to those in theaters. These completely create the effect of daylight and in the future will eventually protect me from the sore trials of the past. God be praised! I will not go mad . . . at least on account of the clouds. . . . Diffuse light is achieved with the help of a large number of arc lamps and mercury-vapor tubes combined. This artificial light is used at the same time as daylight, and its intensity varies according to need.

THE COMPOSITION AND PREPARATION OF SCENES

Composing a scene, a play, a drama, a fairy play, a comedy, or an artistic tableau naturally calls for the creation of a scenario drawn from the imagination and then a search for the effects that will bring it off for the audience; creating sketches and models of the sets and costumes; finding the chief attraction without which no view has a chance of success. As far as illusions or fairy plays are concerned, the invention, combination, and outlines of the tricks and the preliminary study of their construction requires special care. The mise-en-scène as well as the movements of the extras and the placement of the production crew are also arranged in advance. The work is absolutely analogous to readying a play in the theater, but with this difference: the author must know how to work out everything by himself on paper, and consequently he must be the author [scriptwriter], director, designer, and often an actor if he wants to obtain a unified whole. The person who devises the scene ought to direct, for it is absolutely impossible to make it succeed if ten different people get involved. Above all, one must know exactly what one wants and go over the roles that each will have to perform. One must not lose sight of the fact that one does not rehearse for three months as in the theater, but only for a quarter of an hour at most. If you lose time, the light goes down—and goodbye photography. Everything, especially the stumbling blocks to be avoided during the performance, must be anticipated. In the scenes requiring machines there are many.

THE SETS

The sets are produced by following a chosen model; they are constructed in wood and cloth in a workshop adjoining the shooting studio and painted in distemper like theatrical sets, except that the painting is executed exclusively in grisaille through all the intermediate gradations of gray between black and pure white.[3] This gives them the look of funerary decorations, with a strange effect on those seeing them for the first time. Colored sets come out very badly. Blue becomes white, reds, greens, and yellows become black; a complete destruction of the effects ensues. It is therefore necessary that sets be painted like photographers' backdrops. The painting, unlike that of theatrical sets, is very carefully done. The finish, the correctness of the perspective, the trompe l'oeil skillfully executed to tie the painting to real objects just as in panoramas[4]—all is needed to give an appearance of truth to the entirely artificial things that the camera will photograph with absolute precision. Anything poorly made will be faithfully reproduced by the camera and you must therefore keep your eyes peeled and produce the sets with meticulous care. I only know this: in material matters, the cinematograph must do better than the theater and it must not accept conventional practices.

THE PROPS

Props are made of wood, cardboard, flour, molded pasteboard, and dirt, or ordinary objects can simply be used. But if you want to get the best photographic results, the best thing to do, even for the sofas, chimneys, tables, furniture, candelabra, clocks, etc., is exclusively to use specially made objects that have been painted in carefully graduated shades of gray depending on the nature of the object. Important films are often colored by hand before they are projected, but if the objects are bronze, mahogany, red, yellow, or green, this would not be possible because they become deep black

41

and consequently not transparent when photographed; therefore they cannot be made sufficiently translucent for projection. That's something the public is generally unaware of, and they certainly do not suspect how much time and care it takes to make all these props which merely seem to be ordinary objects.

THE COSTUMES

For the same reason, most costumes must be specially made in tones that photograph well and that can later be colored. That is why it is necessary to have an enormous store of costumes of all sorts, from all periods and countries, and of different qualities, along with their accessories, not to mention the hats, wigs, weapons, and jewels belonging to the greatest lords or to the filthiest bums. The store of costumes, however large it may be, is always inadequate. Even with ten thousand costumes in our current repertoire, one is obliged from time to time to go to theatrical costumers to complete the set, for example, when many similar costumes are needed, primarily in parades or in processions with many performers. Naturally, costumers and workers who repair and maintain them are necessary; the same is true for the linens and the tights, the shoes and the equipment.

THE ACTORS AND EXTRAS

Contrary to general belief, it is very difficult to find good performers for the cinematograph. An actor of excellence in the theater, even a star, is worth absolutely nothing in a cinematographic scene. Often professional mimes are bad because they perform in pantomime according to conventional principles, just like mimes in a ballet who have a special, immediately recognizable performance style. Though very superior in their specialty, these artists are disconcerted as soon as they come into contact with the cinematograph. This is because cinematographic miming requires training and special qualities. No longer is there an audience for the actor to address, either verbally or with gestures. The camera alone is spectator, and nothing is worse than to look at it and to concern oneself with it while performing, which is what invariably happens at first to actors accustomed to the stage but not to the cinematograph. The actor must realize that, while remaining completely silent, he must make himself understood by the deaf spectators who watch him. His performance must be unostentatious and very expressive, with few gestures, but ones that are very distinct and clear. Perfection of facial expression and great accuracy of pose are indispensable. I have seen numerous scenes performed by well-known actors; they were not good because the principal element of their success, the word, was not available in the cinematograph. Accustomed to speaking well in the theater, they used gestures only as an accessory to speech, while

42

in the cinematograph, the word is nothing and the gesture is everything. Nevertheless, some, Galipaux among others,[5] have made some good scenes. Why? Because he is accustomed to using solo pantomime during his monologues, and he is endowed with a very expressive face. He knows how to make himself understood without speaking, and his movements, even if deliberately exaggerated—which is necessary in pantomime and especially in photographed pantomime—are always appropriate. When accompanying his speech, an actor's gesture is very telling, but it is no longer comprehensible when he mimes. If you say, "I am thirsty," in the theater, you do not close your hand and bring your thumb to your mouth to simulate a bottle. It's completely useless since everyone understood that you are thirsty; but in pantomime, you are obviously obliged to make this gesture.

That's all quite simple, isn't it? And yet, nine times out of ten, this does not work for anyone not accustomed to miming. Nothing can be improvised; everything must be learned. It is also advisable to consider how the camera will render a gesture. In a photograph, the characters overlap each other, and the greatest care must always be taken to make the principal characters stand out and to moderate the fervor of the supporting characters who are always inclined to gesticulate at the wrong time. This produces a jumble of bustling people in the photograph. The audience no longer knows whom to look at and no longer understands any of the action. The phases of action must be successive, not simultaneous. The actors must consequently pay attention and perform only in turn, at the precise moment when their participation becomes necessary. There is one more thing that I have very often had difficulty in making clear to performers who are always inclined to show off and get themselves noticed to the great detriment of the action and the whole; generally speaking, they are too spontaneous. How much tact is needed to moderate their excessive spontaneity without offending them! Strange as it may seem, each performer in the rather numerous troupe that I employ has been chosen from twenty or thirty I have tested in succession before obtaining what was needed, even though all were very fine artists in the Parisian theaters in which they worked.

Not everyone has the necessary qualities, and good will, unfortunately, does not replace those qualities. Those who have them take quickly to the task; others never do. Female performers who are good at mime are rare. Many are fine, intelligent, beautiful women, but when they must mime a somewhat difficult scene, woe is me! A thousand times woe! Those who have never witnessed the tribulations of a director have never seen anything. I hasten to add that there are, very fortunately, exceptional cases of women who perform very gracefully and intelligently. Conclusion: forming a good cinematographic troupe is a long and difficult business. Only

43

those with no concern for art satisfy themselves with first comers playing a confusing and uninteresting scene.

TRICK EFFECTS

It is impossible in this already long talk to explain in detail the execution of cinematographic tricks. That would require a special study; moreover, practice alone clarifies the details of the processes used, some involving unheard of difficulties. I can say without bragging, since all those in the profession are well aware of this, that it was I myself who successively discovered all the so-called "mysterious" processes of the cinematograph. The producers of composed scenes have all more or less followed the beaten path, and one of them, the head of the world's largest cinematographic company (considered from the viewpoint of its huge, low-cost production), told me himself: "It is thanks to you that the cinematograph has managed to sustain itself and to become an unprecedented success. By joining animated photographs with the theater, that is, with an infinite variety of subjects, you prevented its decline, which would otherwise have rapidly occurred with outdoor scenes whose inevitable uniformity would have quickly bored the audience."

Without false modesty, I confess that this glory—if glory it is—pleases me most. Do you want to know how the idea of applying trick effects in cinematography first came to me? Very simply, upon my word. One day, when I was photographing as usual at the Place de l'Opéra, the camera I used at the beginning (a primitive one in which the film tore or frequently caught and refused to advance) jammed and produced an unexpected result; a minute was needed to disengage the film and to make the camera work again. During this minute, the passersby, a horse trolley, and the vehicles had, of course, changed positions. In projecting the strip, rejoined at the point of the break, I suddenly saw a Madeleine-Bastille trolley change into a hearse and men changed into women.

The substitution trick, called the stop-motion trick, had been discovered and, two days later, I produced the first metamorphoses of men into women and the first sudden disappearances which at first had such great success. It was thanks to this very simple trick that I made the first fairy plays, *The Devil's Manor, The Devil in the Convent, Cinderella*, etc. . . . One trick led to another. Even before this new type was successful, I used my ingenuity to find new techniques and I conceived in turn of the fade (obtained by a special device in the photographic camera), appearances, disappearances, metamorphoses obtained by superimpositions on black grounds or on sections set aside in the sets; then came superimpositions on white grounds that had already been exposed (something everyone declared to be impossible before they saw it), realized with the help of a stratagem I cannot discuss because imitators have not yet entirely discovered its secret. Then came the tricks with cut-off heads, the doubling of characters, of scenes performed by a single character who through doubling ends by portraying all by himself up to ten similar characters performing a comedy with each other. Finally, using my special knowledge of illusions acquired through twenty-five years of practice at the Théâtre Robert-Houdin, I introduced mechanical, optical, and prestidigitation tricks, etc., to the cinematograph. With all these methods combined and competently used, I do not hesitate to say that in cinematography it is today possible to realize the most impossible and improbable things.

I will conclude by saying that much to my chagrin the simplest tricks are those that make the greatest impact, while those achieved through superimposition, which are much more difficult, are hardly appreciated except by those who understand the problems involved. Among others, the views performed by a single actor in which the film is successively exposed up to ten consecutive times in the camera, are so difficult that they become a veritable Chinese water torture. The actor, playing different scenes ten times, must remember precisely to the second, while the film is running, what he was doing at the same instant in earlier takes and the exact location where he was in the scene. On the one hand, this condition alone allows performances by ten actors (who are really one and the same) to be attuned with each other; and, on the other hand, if during one of the takes an actor makes an untoward gesture, if his arm moves in front of a character photographed in the preceding take, it will be transparent and *out of focus*, which *wrecks* the trick. You can see from this just how difficult it is and how angry you get when, after three or four hours of work and sustained attention, a tear rips through the film after the seventh or eighth superimposition, forcing you to abandon the film and do everything over again since it is impossible to repair a film containing a break in which the image is still latent and which cannot be developed until the tenth and last superimposition is recorded.

This is perhaps all "Greek" to the uninitiated, but I repeat that more detailed explanations would lead us too far astray.

In any case, it is the trick, used in the most intelligent manner, that allows the supernatural, the imaginary, even the impossible to be rendered visually and produces truly artistic tableaux that provide a veritable pleasure for those who understand that all branches of art contribute to their realization.

TAKING THE VIEWS: THE CAMERAMAN

Needless to say, the cameraman for this special genre of views must be highly trained and very much au courant with a host of little tricks of the trade. A difficult sort of view such as an execution cannot be taken by a beginner. He would invariably ruin the most easily achieved tricks if he forgets even the smallest thing while turning the crank. A mistake in cranking, forgetting a number while counting out loud during a take, a second's distraction can make everything go wrong. A calm, attentive, thoughtful man capable of withstanding all annoyances and tensions is what is needed because annoyances and tensions are practically inevitable while taking views with the almost continual problems and innumerable unpleasant surprises. These observations will make you understand why the taking of fantastic views is so problematic, whether caused by the director, the mechanics, the actors, or the cameraman taking the shot. It is hardly an easy thing to be in perfect agreement, to get everyone's attention, and to cooperate precisely all the while necessarily fighting against material problems of all sorts.

This will suffice to explain why after having thrown themselves into the new genre the majority of photographers have given it up. One needs someone more than a simple cameraman for all this; and, if there are innumerable cinematographers, those who have succeeded in doing something different than the others are far less numerous. No more than one per country, even less, since every country in the world is dependent on French producers for artistic views. . . .

The cinematograph has today become a colossal industry employing more than 80,000 people in different parts of the world. That's hard to believe but a fact nonetheless, and its success only grows stronger every day. Why? Because an interesting spectacle is an irresistible attraction in every country, and because the cinematograph has provided superb spectacles of this kind in all those countries lacking theaters and other distractions at an affordable price, since the *impresario*, once he has paid for the piece, doesn't have to pay the performers every day.

Oh, if it could only be like this for theater directors!!! But that's the way it is. Only the artists who have performed coolly and flawlessly in cinematographic views are as happy. Their performances cannot be uneven, good one day and bad the next; if they perform well at the *premiere*, they will be excellent in perpetuity. What an advantage!!!

GEORGES MÉLIÈS (1861–1938) was director of the Théâtre Robert-Houdin, the foremost magic theater in Paris, from 1888 to 1914. In December, 1895, he attended the first film screening of the Lumière brothers, and over the next eighteen years his company, Star Films, produced more than one thousand short films, first at his theater (where they were also screened) and then at a film studio that he built at Montreuil-sous-bois.

¹ Etienne-Jules Marey (1830–1904) was a celebrated physiologist and professor at the College de France, who experimented with such precinematographic recording devices as the photographic gun and chronophotography in his studies of human and animal movement.

² English in the original—TRANS.

³ Orthochromatic filmstock was sensitive to the purple-to-green portion of the spectrum, so that objects in these colors showed up as white or light gray on film. It was not sensitive, however, to yellow and red, and objects in these colors showed up as dark gray or even black.—TRANS.

⁴ For a description of the historical precedents for such panoramas and of the ways in which real objects were linked with large-scale projected images, see L.J.M. Daguerre, *An Historical and Descriptive Account of the Daguerreotype and the Diorama* (New York: Winter House, 1971); see, also, Helmut and Alison Gernsheim, *L.J.M. Daguerre* (New York: Dover, 1968).—TRANS.

⁵ Félix Galipaux was a popular music hall actor who, with Coquelin Cadet, created a vogue for monologue performances in the 1880s. According to Jacques Deslandes, Galipaux first performed for the camera in 1896–1897 when Emile Reynaud produced a film of *Le Premier Cigare*, one of Galipaux's well-known music hall routines—see Deslandes, *Histoire comparée du cinéma*, vol. 1 (Paris: Casterman, 1966), 297–98. Galipaux later appeared in films by Zecca and in a number of Méliès's films, including *An Adventurous Automobile Trip* (1905). According to Georges Sadoul, Galipaux also starred in some of the first sound films produced in France by Pathé, including *La Lettre* and *Au Telephone* (1905)—see Sadoul, *Histoire générale du cinéma*, vol. 2 (Paris: Denoël, 1948), 459.—TRANS.

RÉMY DE GOURMONT, "Epilogues: Cinematograph"

From "Epilogues: Cinématographe," *Mercure de France* (1 September 1907), 124–27.

DOES THE CINEMA pose a threat to the theater, at least the kind that is principally a spectacle which appeals to the eyes? Probably so. Cinematographic photography has all the splendid charm of static photography. The one has almost eliminated engraving; the other has almost taken the place of the spectacles performed directly by human figures. The cinema does not merely provide a more than adequate and inexpensive reproduction of such organized spectacles; it reproduces (that is, in the best conditions) panoramic spectacles, whether natural (such as landscapes) or contrived (such as a hippopotamus hunt—posed certainly, but posed on the very banks of the Upper Nile with the local people and animals performing in their own environment).¹ The best theater machinery would cost hundreds of thousands of francs just to produce the caricature of such a hunt. The cinema renders landscapes marvelously. Yesterday it showed me the Rocky Mountains and the Zambezi Falls: the wind bent the fir trees on the mountains; the water sprang up at the bottom of the falls. I saw life stirring. At the Zambezi, a small bush, partially caught in a whirlpool, wavered constantly on the brink of the abyss; and its trembling, come from such a distance away, inspired in me a strange emotion. I became entranced by this battle; when they give us a new view of this spectacular foaming falls, I will be looking for that bush which is courageously resisting the force of the water: perhaps it will have been vanquished, or perhaps it will have become a tree.

47

I love the cinema. It satisfies my curiosity. It allows me to tour the world and stop, to my liking, in Tokyo and Singapore. I follow the craziest itineraries. I go to New York, which is far from beautiful, by way of the Suez, which is hardly more so; and during the same hour I travel through the Canadian forests and the Scottish highlands; I ascend the Nile as far as Khartoum and, a moment later, from the bridge of a transatlantic liner I contemplate the bleak expanse of the ocean.

Is this portion of the cinema program the most enjoyable? I do not know for sure, but I do not think so. Public taste, it seems to me, runs to whimsical, comic, or dramatic sketches mimed before the camera. There are fairylands, ballets, apparitions, metamorphoses, and sudden changes done by means of camera tricks, whose secret I cannot fathom: this is a feature that belongs exclusively to the cinema. The fairy tales of live characters are the least supple of all; the transformations lack the nuances that one might expect to get through a kind of fusion of images, through a shimmering rainbow of colors. The cinema renders colors perfectly; and, since they are transparent, it gives them a brilliance which one does not often find in the ordinary theatrical spectacle.[2] There is, however, one fault which has to be corrected: flesh tones appear a uniformly pale white, which is very disagreeable. From shoulders to hands, human figures must appear in their natural colors; once that is accomplished, the cinema will have reached perfection.

The scenes of domestic life staged for the cinema, whether comic or tragic, consume the public with a passion. Their principal merit is their clarity. They are always simple with the most elementary intrigue. What saves them from utter banality is the context in which they develop as well as the rapid changes in setting. A mimed story that lasts ten minutes unfolds in twenty different settings. If a chase is enacted, as it often is, a variety of landscapes unrolls. I have seen a film from this genre which took me all over Spain. The rapidity of these changes adds to the sense of liveliness. The feeling is very intense, and one forgets the story's vulgarity and savors such details. I was curious to hear that, in Rouen, a Saturday afternoon crowd applauded the chimerical figures on the screen, lavished encouragement or disapproval, shouted at the innocent hero to follow prudent counsel and spurned the wrongdoer. A bit more, and they would have tossed sugar cubes to the faithful dogs which often play a sympathetic role in these innocent games. Such is the power of the illusion that a series of photographs projected on the screen can stimulate our passions just as reality can.

The cinema has a purpose. It is intensely moral. The Pathé company, which supplies a great many of the films, does not joke about good principles. In their films, one is certain that virtue will always be rewarded, crimes punished, lovers reunited and married, unfaithful husbands carefully beaten by outraged wives. The cinema is popular and family oriented. It has a tendency to want to educate. When that finally does happen in films, at least relative to those which are now so caught up in the current morality, we will have something a little more elevated. For instance, the stories of Mérimée and Maupassant make mimed spectacles of a fine intensity. Most of the dramas of Shakespeare offer very captivating scenes. I recommend such transpositions without compunction for they have not retouched the work; they have respected the word.

Speech is what the theater respects least. That is also one of the charms of the cinema, that it does not pretend to speak. One's ears are not offended. The characters keep their customary nonsense to themselves. It's a great relief. The silent theater is the ideal distraction, the best place to repose: the images pass borne aloft by light music. One need not even bother to dream.

But the public does not go to the cinema to dream; they go to enjoy themselves and they do, since the biggest theaters have now opened their doors. The Chatelet, the Variétés, and the Gymnase all now include cinema programs, and one can queue up at the small boulevard cinemas that specialize in them.[3] The price is still reasonable everywhere. For two francs you can have an orchestra seat, and for a franc you can still get a seat which in the theater would cost five or six times more. So the cinema has solved the problem of the cheaper theaters; it is an advantage that the public has clearly appreciated, especially that segment which only goes to a spectacle to pass the time and for whom the particular program is a matter of indifference, as long as it offers a certain picturesqueness. There is a great future for the cinema in this, and more than one theater this winter will be forced to accept the *mode* and replace actors with their shadows. A cinema spectacle is shown once to everyone, and it could well run day and night for a century. It is a huge magic lantern that needs only one screen, an electrical source, and an operator. With that, at the Variétés, a beautiful pantomime [*L'Enfant prodigue*] unreels that is little different from the actual spectacle of which it is the living image. The actors perform once only, and that once is for years; their gestures are fixed; they could all perish in a catastrophe while the cinema spectacle would continue on forever the same.

From the scientific point of view, the cinema is one of the strangest and most splendid inventions of our time. Some improvements will make it a perfect and truly magical instrument. I do not doubt that one day it will offer us landscapes with all of their colors, and their nuances of sky and forest.[4] Then we will really come to know the vast world, including its most inaccessible pockets, and the diverse customs of men will come alive before us like a troop of charming dancers. Let's take advantage of that. Only the

49

churlish and uncurious scorn these spectacles. For intelligent people, they are a singular and sometimes stunning achievement. The past year, the cinema taught me more about Morocco than did all the confused tales of travellers. I saw the army on the march and the artillery of the sultan; and I understood the stupidity of those politicians who took the power of that puppet so seriously.[5] It was a lesson for the eyes. That is all that counts.

RÉMY DE GOURMONT (1858–1915) was an initial supporter of the French Symbolist movement who wrote poetry, short stories, novels, philosophical and scientific essays, and literary criticism. It was as an essayist and critic that he gained most recognition, and his "Epilogues" column in *Mercure de France* perhaps best articulated the slightly left-of-center political opinions and advanced aesthetic standards of the Belle Epoque period.

[1] Here Gourmont clearly places certain kinds of films within the context of popular nineteenth-century panoramas, dioramas, and circus and theatrical spectacles. For a history of those spectacles, see Jacques Deslandes, *Histoire comparée du cinéma*, vol. 1, *De la cinématique au cinématographe, 1826–1896* (Paris: Casterman, 1966).

[2] Gourmont is probably referring to the hand-tinted color process characteristic of Méliès's films or the stencil-color process introduced by Pathé.

[3] For a guide to the theaters, vaudeville houses, music halls, and cinemas that offered film programs at the time when Gourmont was writing, see Jacques Deslandes, *Le Boulevard du cinéma à l'époque de Georges Méliès* (Paris: Cerf, 1963), 73–97.

[4] The first step was taken with color photographs by MM. Lumière. Projected on the screen, they were just like the natural world, with perhaps a bit too much brightness.—AU.

[5] In 1905, France had been on the verge of annexing Morocco as a colony, but was stymied, first, by German diplomatic pressure and, then, by certain factions of resistance in Morocco itself. The crisis toppled Théophile Delcassé, who had been the French foreign minister for an unprecedented seven years, and fueled the beginnings of the Nationalist Revival movement.

ADOLPHE BRISSON, "Theater Column: *L'Assassinat du Duc de Guise*"

From "Chronique théâtral: *L'Assassinat du Duc de Guise*," *Le Temps* (22 November 1908), 3–4.

FILM D'ART invited us to attend its initial spectacle performance at the Salle Charras. You know the origins of this ingenious enterprise. It can scarcely be considered ordinary because Henri Lavedan has given it, along with his name, his unstinting personal cooperation. . . . M. H. Lavedan has surrounded himself with able collaborators. He is being assisted by the great talent of the actor and director, M. Le Bargy, as well as by the practical experience of M. Pathé.[1]

Other dramatic authors will hasten to answer his call, curious to experiment with a new form of theater, and, if possible, to codify its aesthetic. What is a cinematographic play? What should it become? What are its essential features as well as the rules to which it must adapt? What are its conditions, its limits? How can these be made clear? Let's see.

First, whatever speech alone is able to express—thought, abstract ideas, intense passion—is excluded. We are in the world of the concrete. The actors must perform and they must perform clearly; their movements must be unified, coherent, according to the laws of cause and effect. In some way, their movements must be refined, freed of all superfluity, and reduced to the essential.

Now, this work of refinement is a work of art. Ever since Nature was simplified by human effort, there has been style. The actor who poses for the cinema and tries to do exactly what is expected of him *stylizes* the actions of the character he must embody by means of a sober balance of gestures and proper facial expressions.

In the theater, the details of dialogue and the varieties of intonation, to a degree, take the place of an exactness of gesture. Here, gesture is unadorned and obliged to be true. It cannot be otherwise without producing an intolerable sense of unease. In such a school, if they chose to enroll, Conservatory students would learn to be careful.

But can this form of art, from which the word has been excluded, be confused with pantomime? . . . Not at all. Pantomime has a language or grammar of immutable signs whose sense never varies. One of them means "avarice," another "pride," another "conquettishness," and so on. The cinema abstains from using this alphabet. Its province is life itself.

To observe, select, fix, and stylize living figures and momentary phenomena—that is the task it has set for itself. It aspires not only to reproduce current affairs but to animate the past, to reconstruct the great events of History, through the performance of the actor and the evocation of atmosphere and milieu.

L'ASSASSINAT DU DUC DE GUISE BY HENRI LAVEDAN

This drama, factual it turns out, can be recounted in outline in all of its tragic horror.[2] The Duke of Guise tears himself from the arms of Marguerite of Noirmoutiers to rush into an ambush where a coldly plotted death awaits him. The King arms the assassins, stations them along the route of the victim, goes from one to another—"Ferret, Mouse, Fidget"—touches their swords, asks to see them, and assures himself they are ready by testing the rapier points with his fingertips. And the Duke arrives, fearless, determined, haughty, confident of his courage.

As he steps over the threshold of the royal chamber, eight arms are raised to strike and slash him. He takes several steps, dragging this pack at his heels. We follow him through the palace corridors; we witness his agony. He falls. His body is stretched out, lacerated, soiled with blood, his clothes in tatters. On the ground are the King's cushions (emblazoned with a crowned H) which Guise by chance was able to seize in order briefly to defend himself and ward off the blows.

The task completed, the murderers whisper, "See, it is done." And Henri approaches, pleased yet apprehensive. He frisks the body. A note discovered there revives his unsatiated hatred. "Fie on the villain! Whatever it is, I don't want to see it."

And the six murderers, with great difficulty, haul the great body of the Duke down the spiral staircase which leads to the ground floor. They conceal it in sheaths of straw, throw the lot on the glowing andirons of the hearth, and fan the fire.

The "visual story" that Lavedan has reconstructed, with a passionate concern for detail, engraves itself in the memory with unforgettable strokes. It never drags. In fact, the images succeed one another a little too quickly and too feverishly sometimes; they are perhaps too dense, too compact, yet they are strangely evocative. It is a most impressive history lesson. Nothing is as good as this visual instruction.

In M. Albert Lambert as the Duke and M. Le Bargy as the King, [Lavedan] has found remarkable actors. In the future this kind of role should become a specialty for Le Bargy. No more lover's roles, but those of venomous traitors, of cunning villains. He will be an incomparable Iago or Sallust. . . .

. . . One further word. M. Camille Saint-Saëns has written a masterpiece of symphonic music to accompany *L'Assassinat du Duc de Guise*.[3] This was one of the most enjoyable parts of this slightly hesitant, imperfect, yet fascinating performance, which shows real promise.

ADOLPHE BRISSON (1860–1925) was a Parisian journalist and editor of the popular intellectual review, *Les Annales politiques et littéraires*. In 1903, he became the drama critic for *Le Temps*, and, for the next ten or fifteen years, his theater reviews were probably the most widely respected in Paris.

[1] Film d'Art was financed initially by Pierre Lafitte, the wealthy publisher of several illustrated magazines such as *La Vie au grand air, Femina, Je Sais Tout*, and *Fermes et chateaux*. Henri Lavedan was a celebrated fifty-year-old dramatist and had been a member of the Académie Française for nearly ten years. Le Bargy was a famous actor-director at the Comédie Française who persuaded his fellow actors from the theater to work in this production. Charles Pathé provided equipment and studio space, and Pathé-Frères helped distribute the film.

[2] The historical basis of this film and its ideological ramifications for 1908 should not be ignored. The Duc de Guise had been a leader of the Catholic Sainte Ligue and an instigator of the Saint-Barthélemy massacre against the French Protestants in 1572; he rose to such prominence that he threatened the crown of Henri III, who had him assassinated in 1588. The film represents the Duc de Guise as an "innocent" Catholic martyr in contrast to a devious, cowardly, "appeasing" King.

JULES ROMAINS, "The Crowd at the Cinematograph"

From "La Foule au cinématographe," *Les Puissances de Paris* (Paris: Eugène Figuière, 1911), 118–20.

THE LIGHTS go down. A cry escapes from the crowd and immediately is taken back. It begins much like the great clamour which dying throngs have wailed into the night down through the centuries. These people are creatures who love the daylight. Their kind emerged from the compressing and transforming power of light. But the night of the cinema is far from long. They scarcely have time to suspect their death and the happiness of imperishable feeling; they are like swimmers who plunge their heads underwater and then keep their eyelids and lips and teeth tightly clenched, in order to experience a discomfort, an oppression, a suffocation, and then suddenly burst back through the surface into life.

A bright circle abruptly illuminates the far wall. The whole room seems to sigh, "Ah!" And through the surprise simulated by this cry, they welcome the resurrection they were certain would come.

The group dream now begins. They sleep; their eyes no longer see. They are no longer conscious of their bodies. Instead there are only passing images, a gliding and rustling of dreams. They no longer realize they are in a large square chamber, immobile, in parallel rows as in a ploughed field. A haze of visions which resemble life hovers before them. Things have a different appearance than they do outside. They have changed color, outline, and gesture. Creatures seem gigantic and move as if in a hurry. What controls their rhythm is not ordinary time, which occupies most people when they are not dreaming. Here they are quick, capricious, drunken, constantly skipping about; sometimes they attempt enormous leaps when least expected. Their actions have no logical order. Causes produce strange effects like golden eggs.

The crowd is a being that remembers and imagines, a group that evokes other groups much like itself—audiences, processions, parades, mobs in the street, armies. They imagine that it is they who are experiencing all these adventures, all these catastrophes, all these celebrations. And while their bodies slumber and their muscles relax and slacken in the depths of their seats, they pursue burglars across the rooftops, cheer the passing of a king from the East, or march into a wide plain with bayonets or bugles.

JULES ROMAINS (1885–1972) was a major French poet, dramatist, novelist, and essayist, whose advocacy of a Unanimist theory of literature—an intuitive depiction of the new collective consciousness of modern life, set forth in *La Vie unanime* (L'Abbaye de Créteil, 1908)—established his early reputation.

[LOUIS FEUILLADE], *"Scènes de la vie telle qu'elle est"*

From *"Les Scènes de la vie telle qu'elle est," Ciné-Journal* 139 (22 April 1911), 19.

IN OFFERING for public approval a new series of films, to be called *Scènes de la vie telle qu'elle est*, the Gaumont Company expects that the release of these films will mark a noteworthy date in the history of the Cinematography of Art.

The scenes of *La Vie telle qu'elle est* are like nothing that has been achieved so far by film producers anywhere. They represent, for the first time, an attempt to project a realism onto the screen, just as was done some years ago in literature, theater, and art.

It falls to the Gaumont Company to be the first to attempt this; the public will tell us if the effort is successful.

These scenes are intended to be slices of life. If they are interesting and compelling, it is because of the quality of virtue which emerges from and inspires them. They eschew all fantasy, and represent people and things as they are and not as they should be. And by treating only subjects which can be viewed by anyone, they prove more elevated and more significant as moral expression than do those falsely tragic or stupidly sentimental, heart-rending little tales which leave no more trace in the memory than on the projection screen.

Lately public taste has favored "films" in which one can see excellently trained actors perform naturally, simply, with neither bombast nor ridiculous pantomime.[1] The public has been much infatuated with talented actors who more often than not mask the poverty of a scenario and its total lack of ideas and who offer a touch of piquancy to those eternally insipid idylls in which we see the young woman marry the young man of her dreams, despite all odds. We have a higher ambition—to serve up another entree. Much as in the *Film esthétique* series, where we tried to produce an impression of pure beauty, which encompassed the exhibitions of grand spectacle as well as the processions of mid-Lent—and which some cinema owners presented to their clientele as the last word in great art—so here, in the scenes from *La Vie telle qu'elle est*, we have tried to give an impression of previously unrecognized truth.

The innovative plan that we have conceived is intended to divert the French cinema from the influence of Rocambole[2] in order to raise it toward a higher destiny; and if this plan could not have been accomplished completely, we would have waited patiently for a more propitious moment.

Today, however, we are persuaded that the execution of these scenes from *La Vie telle qu'elle est* is worthy of their conception; and we offer them confidently to the public, to judge for itself.

The first film of the series is called *Les Vipères*. Here the vipers are "scandalmongers." This film is so realistic, so closely observed, so true to life that it has the power, clarity, and concise eloquence of a document. Besides the fact that no one has filmed this subject before, at least to our knowledge, we have never tried harder to create the right atmosphere, strike the right note, and achieve the maximum effect without abandoning the simplicity that gives the work its most unambiguous significance.

And our cameramen have toned down all the magic of their photography in *Les Vipères*.[3] To control the light according to the necessities of the hour and the space of composition is child's play to them; their reputations were made long ago. But, in this circumstance, they have surpassed themselves. So that here is a film which truly merits being called an honest and sincere work of art and which the public will not fail to welcome with open arms.

LOUIS FEUILLADE (1874–1925) was a journalist and scriptwriter who, in 1907, took over from Alice Guy (1873–1968) the position of chief producer-director at Gaumont. Feuillade directed all of the films in the *Films esthétiques* series as well as those in the *Scènes de la vie telle qu'elle est* series. This text was a written advertisement for Gaumont.

[1] Feuillade is probably referring to the Vitagraph films that, as Victorin Jasset noted some six months later, were having a great impact on French audiences.

[2] Rocambole evolved from arch criminal to fearless detective as the hero of some thirty adventure novels written by Ponson du Terrail in the middle of the nineteenth century. Here he is used to stand in for all of the adventure heroes of the French *séries* films (criminal, detective, western), which were so popular from 1907 to 1914.

[3] The cameraman for *Les Vipères* may well have been Guérin, who is known to have worked with Feuillade on *Fantômas* (1913–1914) and *Les Vampires* (1915–1916).

VICTORIN JASSET, "An Essay on Mise-en-scène in Cinematography"

From "Etude sur le mise-en-scène en cinématographie," *Ciné-Journal* 165 (21 October 1911), 51; 166 (28 October 1911), 33, 35–37; 167 (4 November 1911), 31, 33, 35; 168 (11 November 1911), 38–39; 170 (25 November 1911), 25–27.

WHEN IT WAS announced that M. Le Bargy was going to rehearse actors from the Comédie Française and make cinematographic plays, people anxiously talked about what these theater people who knew nothing of the Ciné's rules would produce; they spoke of huge amounts of film footage and appalling costs.

Production went slowly. Film d'Art ran into casting, equipment, and staging difficulties; but, finally, the films were finished. They were certainly astonishing. The mass public may have reacted coldly, uncomprehendingly. But people in the film industry understood that all the rules they had observed until then were passé. Well-known artists acted by standing still instead of running around; they achieved an increasing intensity of effect. It was amazing. Admittedly, the first film produced by Film d'Art was marvelously executed. Even if one criticized the technical flaws, which could be excused on the grounds that the actors had gone to great lengths to overcome difficulties they had never faced before, *La Mort du Duc de Guise* was still a masterpiece.[1]

Le Bargy had portrayed his character with care; he had performed with a wealth of detail that was a revolution to attentive eyes. What the most experienced filmmakers had not dared to do, fearing to break with old conventions, a novice had pulled off.

He brought in new principles and took no account of the experience of his predecessors, and his strategy was exactly right. Except for some technical rules, nothing remained of what the old school had so slowly built up. It was the end of the old ways.

What exactly was the influence of Film d'Art on the cinematographic schools? Almost nothing at first, but then enormous in its consequences. It opened the eyes of the American school, transformed it, and made that school what it is today.

The case of Film d'Art in itself was not a big deal from the commercial point of view. The hopes that it had created were not realized.

This sudden, misunderstood transformation was received coldly by the public. The chosen subjects were often boring. For every one film that was a success, another miscarried. The costs became too high. In brief, the artists grew weary. Le Bargy, who was its heart, abandoned the company, which remained Film d'Art in name only; and he joined an ordinary commercial enterprise with a familiar trademark.[2]

But the principles remained. And little by little the French school began to wise up. From every side, the artists who had seen what the Ciné could produce provided support and cooperation.

That the first period of transformation had its ridiculous side there can be no doubt. One does not break with tradition in a single blow. But the blow had been struck; the exhibitors began to understand and admit that the public could be interested in things artistic. And everywhere arose series of films that bore the labels, "art," "gold," "diamond," "first edition," "aesthetic." The Italians merely added two hundred or so extras to their films and for them that was Film d'Art.

About the same time, an organization of French writers and men of letters founded another school. Its purpose was the regeneration of the cinematographic scenario.[3] . . .

Around 1909–1910, the first Vitagraph comedies appeared in France.

Before that, their production had been awful, at best banal. Then suddenly, masterpieces emerged. A new school was born and gained recognition in the marketplace everywhere, not only among artists but also among the mass public who welcomed it with enthusiasm.

The American school differed from our own on three principal points:

1. camera framing
2. actor performance
3. scenario construction

Theirs was an absolutely new method that clearly distinguished the Americans from the European school.

The Americans had noticed the effect of physical expression and gesture in close shots, and they made use of the overall [long] shot only when they needed to include characters who remained slightly more immobile.

Rapid movement alarmed them, so the acting was absolutely calm, to the point of exaggeration. Moreover, the actual scenario called for dramatic, theatrical, even pathetic situations; they made films as simple and as naïve as possible, avoiding stage tricks and spectacular effects, trying as best they could to approximate real life, and often constructing an action in a straight line that ended in a bright, happy denouement. As it was, their method was greatly superior to anything we had done previously, and the public's infatuation was the best proof of that. Their acting company, though numerous, actually included several performers that the public noticed immediately, became familiar with, and claimed as their own. The periodic return of these same performers was awaited and cheered. The public wanted nothing but Vitagraph films. From then on, the French companies sought to imitate them.

What exactly was the strategy behind the Vitagraph films?

For the overeager public, the opinion could be summed up this way. The American films had talented actors who performed deliberately for the camera. So it was very simple and easy to do the same with French actors.

But that opinion was gravely mistaken. The American strategy represented, on the contrary, patient and methodical effort, special exercises by the actors, and lengthy observations by the filmmaker. It was not the work of a single person. Instead, it represented the subjugation of everyone to rules from which there had to be no deviation for fear of falling back into old ways.

When we saw one of their films on the screen, the [visual] harmony and the calm, poised performance of the actors gave us the real illusion of life. But for the filmmaker who watched closely, this apparent simplicity depended on [new] tricks and effects, and on a form of acting that was abso-

57

lutely false. However, all that was only necessary [behind the scenes] in order to provide the public with the complete illusion of reality.[4]

VICTORIN JASSET (1862–1913) was a prodigious stage manager (particularly at the Hippodrome), set designer, costumer, and writer who worked for Gaumont between 1905 and 1907 and then was hired as head producer-director at Eclair, where he became best known for his detective and criminal *séries* films—for example, *Nick Carter, Zigomar*, and *Protéa*.

[1] Sometime between 1908 and 1911, *L'Assassinat du Duc de Guise* became *La Mort du Duc de Guise*. When Pathé re-released the film before and then again during the war, it carried the latter title.

[2] Within a year after the release of *L'Assassinat du Duc de Guise*, Film d'Art was in trouble financially, and dramatist Paul Gavault took control of its film production. By late 1911, Film d'Art was still heavily in debt and was taken over by Charles Delac, the owner of Monofilm, a small film distribution company. See Georges Sadoul, *Histoire générale du cinéma*, vol. 3 (Paris: Denoël, 1951), 33–34.

[3] This was the Société cinématographique des auteurs et gens de lettres (SCAGL), founded by the popular novelist, Pierre Decourcelle (1856–1926), and his financial collaborator, Eugène Gugenheim. SCAGL operated as a subsidiary of Pathé-Frères, and Albert Capellani was its artistic director and chief filmmaker.

[4] Jasset was one of the first French writers to give some attention to a specifically filmic system of representation and narrative continuity. That he focused on an American system then in vogue acknowledged a dominance that would be well established by the end of the decade.

RICCIOTTO CANUDO, "The Birth of a Sixth Art"

Translated by Ben Gibson, Don Ranvaud, Sergio Sokota, and Deborah Young from "Naissance d'un sixième art," *Les Entretiens idéalistes* (25 October 1911), reprinted as "L'Esthétique du septième art," in Canudo, *L'Usine aux images* (Paris: Etienne Chiron, 1926), 13–26. The translation first appeared in *Framework* 13 (Autumn 1980), 3–7. Reprinted, with minor changes, by permission of the publisher.

I.

IT IS SURPRISING to find how everyone has, either by fate or some universal telepathy, the same aesthetic conception of the natural environment. From the most ancient people of the east to those more recently discovered by our geographical heroes, we can find in all peoples the same manifestations of the aesthetic sense; Music, with its complimentary [*sic*] art, Poetry; and Agriculture, with its own two compliments [*sic*], Sculpture and Painting. The whole aesthetic life of the world developed itself in these five expressions of Art. Assuredly, a sixth artistic manifestation seems to us now absurd and even unthinkable; for thousands of years, in fact, no people have been capable of conceiving it. But we are witnessing the birth of such a sixth art. This statement, made in a twilight hour such as this, still ill-defined and uncertain like all eras of transition, is repugnant to our scientific mentality. We are living between two twilights: the eve of one world, and the dawn of another. Twilight is vague, all outlines are confused; only eyes sharpened by a will to discover the primal and invisible signs of things and beings can find a bearing through the misty vision of the *anima mundi*. However, the sixth art imposes itself on the unquiet and scrutinous spirit. It will be a superb conciliation of the Rhythms of Space (the Plastic Arts) and the Rhythms of Time (Music and Poetry).

II.

The theater has so far best realized such a conciliation, but in an ephemeral manner because the plastic characteristics of the theater are identified with those of the actors, and consequently are always different. The new manifestation of Art should really be more precisely *a Painting and a Sculpture developing in Time*, as in music and poetry, which realise themselves by transforming air into rhythm for the duration of their execution.

The cinematograph, so vulgar in name, points the way. A man of genius, who by definition is a miracle just as beauty is an unexpected surprise, will perform this task of mediation which at present seems to us barely imaginable. He will find the ways, hitherto inconceivable, of an art which will appear for yet a long time marvelous and grotesque. He is the unknown individual who tomorrow will induce the powerful current of a new aesthetic function, whence, in a most astonishing apotheosis, the *Plastic Art in Motion* will arise.

III.

The cinematograph is composed of significant elements "representative" in the sense used by Emerson rather than the theatrical sense of the term, which are already classifiable.

There are two aspects of it: the *symbolic* and the *real*, both absolutely modern; that is to say only possible in our era, composed of certain essential elements of modern spirit and energy.

The *symbolic aspect* is that of velocity. Velocity possesses the potential for a great series of combinations, of interlocking activities, combining to create a spectacle that is a series of visions and images tied together in a vibrant agglomeration, similar to a living organism. This spectacle is produced exactly by the excess of movement to be found in film, those mysterious reels impressed by life itself. The reels of the engraved celluloid unroll in front of and within the beam of light so rapidly that the presentation lasts for the shortest possible time. No theater could offer half the changes of set and location provided by the cinematograph with such vertiginous rapidity, even if equipped with the most extraordinarily modern machinery.

Yet more than the motion of images and the speed of representation, what is truly symbolic in relation to velocity are the actions of the characters. We see the most tumultuous, the most inverisimilitudinous scenes unfolding with a speed that appears impossible in real life. This precipitation of movement is regulated with such mathematical and mechanical precision that it would satisfy the most fanatical runner. Our age has destroyed most earnestly, with a thousand extremely complex means, the love of restfulness, symbolized by the smoking of a patriarchal pipe at the domestic hearth. Who is still able to enjoy a pipe by the fire in peace these days, without listening to the jarring noise of cars, animating outside, day and night, in every way, an irresistible desire for spaces to conquer? The cinematograph can satisfy the most impatient racer. The motorist who has just finished the craziest of races and becomes a spectator at one of these shows will certainly not feel a sense of slowness; images of life will flicker in front of him with the speed of the distances covered. The cinematograph, moreover, will present to him the farthest countries, the most unknown people, the least known of human customs, moving, shaking, throbbing before the spectator transported by the extreme rapidity of the representation. Here is the second symbol of modern life constituted by the cinematograph, an "instructive" symbol found in its rudimentary state in the display of "freaks" at the old fairgrounds. It is the symbolic destruction of distances by the immediate connaissance of the most diverse countries, similar to the real destruction of distances performed for a hundred years now by monsters of steel.

The *real aspect* of the cinematograph is made up of elements which arouse the interest and wonder of the modern audience. It is increasingly evident that present day humanity actively seeks its own show, the most meaningful representation of its self. The theater of perennial adultery, the sole theme of the bourgeois stage, is at last being disdained, and there is a movement towards a theater of new, profoundly modern Poets; the rebirth of Tragedy is heralded in numerous confused open-air spectacles representing disordered, incoherent, but intensely willed effort. Suddenly, the cinematograph has become popular, summing up at once all the values of a still eminently scientific age, entrusted to Calculus rather than to the operations of Fantasy (*Fantasia*), and has imposed itself in a peculiar way as a new kind of theater, a scientific theater built with precise calculations, a mechanical mode of expression. Restless humanity has welcomed it with joy. It is precisely this theater of plastic Art in motion which seems to have brought us the rich promise of the *Festival* which has been longed for unconsciously, the ultimate evolution of the ancient *Festival* taking place in the temples, the theaters, the fairgrounds of each generation.[1] The thesis of a plastic Art in motion has recreated the *Festival*. It has created it scientifically rather than *aesthetically*, and for this reason it is succeeding in this age, although fatally and irresistibly moving towards the attainment of Aesthetics. . . .

V.

I move on now to a great aesthetic problem, which must be emphasized.

Art has always been essentially a stylization of life into stillness; the better an artist has been able to express the greater number of "typical" conditions, that is, the synthetic and immutable states of souls and forms, the greater the recognition he has attained. The cinematograph, on the contrary, achieves the greatest mobility in the representation of life. The thought that it might open the unsuspected horizon of a new art different from all pre-existing manifestations cannot fail to appeal to an emancipated mind, free from all traditions and constraints. The ancient painters and engravers of prehistoric caves who reproduced on reindeer bones the contracted movements of a galloping horse, of the artists who sculpted cavalcades on the Parthenon friezes, also developed the device of stylizing certain aspects of life in clear, incisive movements. But the cinematograph does not merely reproduce one aspect; it represents the whole of life in action, and in such action that, even when the succession of its characteristic events unravel slowly, in life, it is developed with as much speed as possible.

In this way cinematography heightens the basic psychic condition of western life which manifests itself in action, just as eastern life manifests itself in contemplation. The whole history of western life reaches to people in the dynamism characteristic of our age, while the whole of humanity rejoices, having found again its childhood in this new *Festival*. We could not imagine a more complex or more precise movement. Scientific thought with all its energy, synthesizing a thousand discoveries and inventions, has created out of and for itself this sublime spectacle. The cinematographic visions pass before its eyes with all the electrical vibrations of light, and in all the external manifestations if its inner life.

The cinematograph is thus the theater of a new Pantomime, consecrated *Painting in motion*. It constitutes the complete manifestation of a unique creation by modern man. As the modern Pantomime, it is the new *dance of manifestations*.

Now, it is necessary to ask of the cinematograph, is it to be accepted within the confines of the arts?

It is not yet an art, because it lacks the freedom of choice peculiar to plastic *interpretation*, conditioned as it is to being the *copy* of a subject, the condition that prevents photography from becoming an art. In executing the design of a tree on a canvas, the painter expresses without any doubt, unconsciously and in a particular and clear configuration, his global interpretation of the vegetative soul, that is of all the conceptual elements deposited deep in his creative spirit by an examination of all the trees he has seen in his life; as Poe said, with the "eyes of dream." With that particular form he synthesizes corresponding souls and his art, I repeat, will gain in intensity in proportion to the artist's skill in *immobilizing* the essence of things and their universal meanings in a particular and clear configuration. Whoever contented himself with copying the outlines, with imitating the colors of a subject, would be a poor painter; the great artist extends a fragment of his cosmic soul in the representation of a plastic form.

Arts are the greater the less they *imitate* and the more they *evoke* by means of a synthesis. A photographer, on the other hand, does not have the faculty of choice and elaboration fundamental to Aesthetics; he can only put together the forms he wishes to reproduce, which he really is not reproducing, limiting himself to cutting out images with the aid of the luminous mechanism of a lens and a chemical composition. The cinematograph, therefore, cannot today be an art. But for several reasons, the cinematographic theater is the first abode of the new art—an art which we can just barely conceive. Can this abode become a "temple" for aesthetics?

A desire for an aesthetic organization drives entrepreneurs towards certain kinds of research. In an age lacking in imagination, such as ours, when an excess of documentation is everywhere, weakening artistic creativity, and patience games are triumphing over expressions of creative talent, the cinematograph offers the paroxysm of the spectacle: objective life represented in a wholly exterior manner, on the one hand with rapid miming, on the other with documentaries. The great fables of the past are retold, mimed by ad hoc actors chosen from the most important stars. What is shown above all is the appearance rather than the essence of contemporary life, from sardine fishing in the Mediterranean to the marvel of flying steel and the indomitable human courage of the races at Dieppe or the aviation week at Rheims.

But the entertainment makers are already experimenting with other things. It is their aim that this new mimetic representation of "total life" take ever deeper root, and Gabrielle D'Annunzio has dreamed up a great Italian heroic pantomime for the cinematograph.[2] It is well known that there exist in Paris societies which organize a kind of "trust" for cinematographic spectacles among writers. Hitherto the theater has offered writers the best chance of becoming rich quickly; but the cinematograph requires less work and offers better returns. At this moment hundreds of talented people, attracted by the promise of immediate and universal success, are concentrating their energies towards the creation of the modern Pantomime. And it will come out of their strenuous efforts and from the probable genius of one of them. The day such work is given to the world will mark the birthday of a wholly new art.

VI.

The cinematograph is not only the perfect outcome of the achievements of modern science, which it summarizes wonderfully. It also represents, in a disconcerting but important way, the most recent product of contemporary theater. It is not the exaggeration of a principle, but its most logical and ultimate development. The "bourgeois" dramatics, like all of our playwrights, should spontaneously acknowledge the cinematograph as their most discreet representative, and should in consequence ready themselves for its support by making use of it, because the so-called psychological, social drama, etc., is nothing but a degeneration of the original comic theater, counterposed with the tragic theater of fantasy and spiritual ennoblement, the theater of Aristophanes and Plautus. Vitruvius, describing as an architect the many different sets used in ancient performances, talks about the solemnity of columns and temples of the tragic theater, about the wood of the satyric theater, and about sylvan adventures and the houses of the middle classes where the *commedias* took place. The latter were but the representation of daily life in its psychological and social aspects, that is, of customs and characteristics. . . .

VII.

The cinematograph, on the other hand, adds to this type of theater the element of *absolutely accurate* speed, in this way inducing a new kind of pleasure that the spectator discovers in the extreme precision of the spectacle. In fact, none of the actors moving on the illusory stage will betray his part, nor would the mathematical development of the action lag for a fraction of a second. All movement is regulated with clockwork precision. The scenic illusion is therefore less engaging, in a sense less physical, but terribly absorbing. And this life, regulated as if by clockwork, makes one think of the triumph of modern scientific principle as a new Alviman, master of the mechanics of the world in Manichean doctrine.

The rapid communion of vital energies between the two opposite poles of the *very touching* and the *very comical* produces in the spectator a sense of relaxation. Everything which in real life presents itself as an obstacle, the inevitable slowness of movements and actions in space, is as if suppressed in the cinematograph. Moreover, the *very comical* soothes the mind, lightening existence of the weight of the somber social cape, imposed by the thousand conventions of the community and representing all kinds of hierarchies. The comic can suppress hierarchies, it can join together the most different beings, give an extraordinary impression of the mixture of the most separate universes, which in real life are irreducibly distinct from one another. Since the comic is essentially irreverent, it gives a deep sense of

63

relief to individuals oppressed in every moment of their real lives by social discriminations, so emphatically present. This sense of relief is one of the factors of that nervous motion of contraction and expansion called laughter. Life is *simplified* by the grotesque which is nothing other than a deformation *per excessum* or *per defectum* of the established forms. The grotesque, at least in this sense, relieves life of its inescapable grimness and releases it into laughter.

Caricature is based on the display and masterful combination of the most miminal facets of the human soul, its weak spots, which gush forth from the irony of social life, which is itself, after all, somewhat ironical and insane. With irony, in the convulsive motion of laughter, caricature provokes in man this feeling of extreme lightness, because irony throws over its raised shoulders Zarathustra's "dancing and laughing" cape of many colors.[3]

The ancients were able to perceive in irony the roots of Tragedy. They crowned their tragic spectacles in laughter, in the farce. Conversely, we precede rather than follow the dramatic spectacle with Farce, immediately upon the raising of the curtain, because we have forgotten the significance of some of the truths discovered by our forebears. Yet the need for an *ironic spectacle* persists. And the Farce of the Orestes Tetrology of Aeschylus, the Farce which could not be found, must have been originally immensely rich in humor to have been able to lighten the spirit of the elegant Athenian women oppressed by the sacred terror of Cassandra. Now I do not know of anything more superbly grotesque than the antics of film comics. People appear in such an extravagant manner that no magician could pull anything like them out of a hat; movements and vision change so rapidly that no man of flesh and blood could present so many to his fellows, without the help of that stunning mixture of chemistry and mechanics, that extraordinary creator of emotions that is the cinematograph. A new comic type is thus created. He is the man of blunders and metamorphoses who can be squashed under a wardrobe of mirrors, or fall head-first breaking through all four floors of a four-story building, only to climb up out of the chimney to reappear on the roof in the guise of a genuine snake.

The complexity of this new kind of spectacle is surprising. The whole of human activity throughout the centuries had contributed to its composition. When artists of genius bestow rhythms of Thought and Art on this spectacle, the new Aesthetics will show the cinematographic theater some of its most significant aspects.

In fact the cinematographic theater *is the first new theater*, the first authentic and fundamental theater of our time. When it becomes truly aesthetic, complemented with a worthy musical score played by a good orchestra, even if only representing life, real life, momentarily fixed by the photographic lens, we shall be able to feel then our first *sacred* emotion, we shall have a glimpse of the spirits, moving towards a vision of the temple, where Theater and Museum will once more be restored for a new religious communion of the spectacle and Aesthetics. The cinematograph as it is to-day will evoke for the historians of the future the image of the first extremely rudimentary wooden theaters, where goats have their throats slashed and the primitive "goat song" and "tragedy" were danced, before the stone apotheosis consecrated by Lycurgus, even before Aeschylus' birth, to the Dionysian theater.

The modern public possess an admirable power of "abstraction" since it can enjoy some of the most absolute abstractions in life. In the Olympia, for instance, it was possible to see the spectators fanatically applauding a phonograph placed on the stage and adorned with flowers whose shining copper trumpet had just finished playing a love duet. . . . The machine was triumphant, the public applauded the ghostly sound of far away or even dead actors. It is with such an attitude that the public go to the cinematographic theater. Moreover, the cinematograph brings, in the midst of even the smallest human settlement, the spectacle of distant, enjoyable, moving or instructive things: it spreads culture and stimulates everywhere the eternal desire for the representation of life in its totality.

On the walls of the cinematographic theater at times one can see inscriptions commemorating the latest achievements of this prodigious invention which accelerates our knowledge of universal events and reproduces everywhere life and the experience of life since 1830 to the present day. Among the latest heroes are Renault, Edison, Lumière, the Pathé brothers. . . . But what is striking, characteristic, and significant, even more than the spectacle itself, is the uniform will of the spectators, who belong to all social classes, from the lowest and least educated to the most intellectual.

It is desire for a new *Festival*, for a new joyous *unanimity*, realized at a show, in a place where together, all men can forget in greater or lesser measure, their isolated individuality. This forgetting, soul of any religion and spirit of any aesthetic, will one day be superbly triumphant. And the Theater, which still holds the vague promise of something never dreamt of in previous ages: *the creation of a sixth art, the plastic Art in motion*, having already achieved the rudimentary form of the modern pantomime.

Present day life lends itself to such victory. . . .

RICCIOTTO CANUDO (1879–1923) was an Italian expatriate who settled in Paris in 1902 as a scholar, writer, and literary entrepreneur. A friend of Apollinaire and D'Annunzio, he established a movement called Cérébrism, edited a "French imperialist" art journal called *Montjoie!* (1913–1914), and hosted a circle of intellectuals and artists interested in the cinema who met regularly at the Café Napolitain.

¹ Canudo's concept of the *Festival* seems to come out of ancient Greek culture rather than

out of the European Medieval period or Renaissance. It is a mark of Canudo's contradictory interests or his ambition to synthesize widely divergent ways of thinking that, on the same page, he can bring together ancient Greek theater and Italian Futurism or a classical literary tradition and a potential new art form, the cinema.

² Gabriel D'Annunzio (1863–1938) never wrote any scenarios for the cinema during this period. Some of his works were adapted by others, including his son, Gabriellino D'Annunzio, before the war; and his name was attached to Pastrone's *Cabiria* (1913), but only for publicity reasons.

³ The reference to Zarathustra as well as the "birth of tragedy" suggests how fashionable Nietzsche had become in France after the first translations of his work in 1900.

ABEL GANCE, "A Sixth Art"

From "Un sixième art," *Ciné-Journal* 185 (9 March 1912), 10.

THE CINEMA? No, as my friend Canudo says, it is a sixth art that has yet to advance beyond its first stammerings.

A sixth art which, at this moment, just like French tragedy in the time of [Alexandre] Hardy [1540–1632], awaits its Corneille, its classic in a word, in order to lay down its true foundations.

A sixth art, glittering with movement, diverse objects, and peaceful landscapes. Here we can take each of the tableaux of the best theaters, make the characters descend from their frames, live as their creators imagined them, then return them to their immortal poses—now known to everyone.

A sixth art where the wings of the Victory of Samothrace actually quiver and the huntress Diana can escape through the thicket imagined by [Jean] Goujon [1514–1569]. . . .

A sixth art where we can evoke in minutes all the great disasters of history and extract from them an immediate objective lesson.

A sixth art which, with one and the same sadness, will bring tears to the eyes of the Arab and the Eskimo, simultaneously, and which, at the same time, will offer them the same lesson in courage and health.

A sixth art which, one day when some inspired artist will consider it more than a simple amusement, will spread its faith throughout the world more fully than the theater or the book.

At the cinema, the knitted brow, the tears, the laughter are so close to the spectator that it is impossible not to be moved; on the face of Juliet dying can we not read there several of great Will's lines, and in Dante's dream several stanzas from *The Divine Comedy*?

Let the cinema be naturally grandiose and human instead of what the popular novels of the past fifty years have been to literature. Let it be innovative instead of following either a maudlin sentimentality or the mechanical comic film which seems in fashion, because the true way has yet to be mapped out. Let it not be theatrical especially, but allegorical, symbolic. To plumb the depths of each civilization and construct the glorious scenario that sums it up, embracing all the cycles of all the epochs, finally to have, I repeat, the cinematographic classic that will guide us into a new era—that is one of my highest dreams.

Does it help to say now that to reach this briefly glimpsed prodigious end, I will be obliged to be commercial as have others before me (did not Wagner and Molière enrich their producers during their lifetimes?)? Yet the day will soon come, I trust, when my ravings become tangible, and they will demonstrate what can be hoped for from this wonderful synthesis of the movement of space and time.

ABEL GANCE (1889–1981) was a young dramatist and actor (and friend of Ricciotto Canudo) who wrote scenarios for Gaumont and Pathé from 1908 to 1911 and then formed his own small film company, Le Film Français, to direct several short films between 1911 and 1914. Gance only began to make a name for himself during the war when he joined Film d'Art and became the company's second major filmmaker after Henri Pouctal.

YHCAM, "Cinematography"

From "La Cinématographie," *Ciné-Journal* 191 (20 April 1912), 36–37, 39, 41; 192 (27 April 1912), 25, 27, 29, 31, 33; 193 (4 May 1912), 16–17; 194 (11 May 1912), 9, 11, 14–15, 16; 195 (18 May 1912), 19, 21, 23–24.

IN THE BEGINNING, cinematography constituted no more than a scientific curiosity, a sort of photographic "Praxinoscope"; but it rapidly set out on a double path of evolution.

On the one hand, men of science had a presentiment of its importance for kinetic studies and scientific documentation; on the other, the *showmen for children* foresaw the possibility of widespread commercial exploitation and remuneration.

We have to remember that it was the fair vendors who launched the cinema as an amusement speciality; it's on the fairgrounds that the mass public began to take a fancy to this delight for the eyes, which suddenly took off on such an extraordinary development.

The masses flocked to and appreciated the cinema-theater well before society people and the artistic and intellectual elite; still, it's fair to say that, because of technical imperfections, the first films were rather disheartening.

It was only later, after the strenuous labor of inventors and design engineers, that we could catch a glimpse of the artistic future of cinematography.

Leaving aside the technical aspect of cinematography as much as possible, we are going to pursue the study of films from several different points of view.

67

At the outset, we will establish a general classification system, set up as a base from which to derive the desiderata we need.

First class—the cinema considered from the theatrical point of view.
A. For children
B. For adolescents and their parents
C. For adults only
D. For artistic and intellectual study

Second class—the cinema considered as an instrument of intellectual development.
A. Preschool
B. Primary school studies
C. Secondary school studies
D. University studies
E. Scientific documentation

Third class—the cinema as employed for the propagation of feelings and ideas.
A. Moral sentiments
B. Religious sentiments
C. Political ideas
D. Patriotic sentiments

Fourth class—the cinema considered as a mode of information and publicity.
A. The newsreel
B. Advertising film . . .

First principle: the cinema program must correlate with the public to which it is addressed.

. . . The cinema spectacle can achieve an extraordinary artistic development, but it seems that only its adversaries have really understood this.

The recent commission report of the third Congress on Cinematography [12 May 1911] would restrict the cinema's role and future by counseling authors to write scenarios for children to the exclusion of all others.

The cinema-theater is perfectly capable of interesting and captivating adults as well as children; we must disabuse the public of the idea that the cinema is only a spectacle for children, a sort of perfected puppet show.

The cinema-theaters should be divided into two perfectly distinct kinds: on the one hand, spectacles for children, written especially for them and offering all the guarantees of requisite morality; on the other, spectacles for adults, spectacles in which the author retains his freedom completely and takes on the theater itself as a rival.

Actually, a good number of scenarios are neither fish nor fowl; they almost always go beyond the intelligence of children but without reaching a point which would interest adults.

To summarize, films should be categorized into three series:

First series—for children and adolescents

Second series—a "mixed" series capable of interesting adults while containing nothing which might tarnish the purity of children

Third series—for adults, where children and adolescents cannot be admitted

The first months of 1912 have seen the apogee of the cinema-theater, I believe; now we are going to witness a period of decline, because scenarios have not advanced and merely repeat themselves with all their faults. The mass public is growing bored, and the halls little by little will become empty. To maintain its position and augment its public, the cinema-theater has to evolve; and the managers of theaters and café-concerts are making their performers go all out in an effort to curb that evolution.

The cinema spectacle is not a pale imitation of the theater; it is a separate spectacle which corresponds to a new and very real Art, a special art which should be left to its own devices, with its own special authors and actors.

Something as astonishing as this new art could appear, for the cinema spectacle can create impressions infinitely more vivid than the theater can, even though the characters are no more than mute shadows; and this is because the system of conventional gestures disappears to be replaced by an improbable realism.

The dimness of the hall constitutes an important factor which, through the state of contemplation it produces, contributes much more than one might think to the impression created; the spectator's attention is caught and concentrated on the luminous projection, without any possible distraction.

The effect produced by the characters' silence is one of the most fascinating aspects of the cinema-theater. The spectator *does not perceive that the character is mute* for, through a particular form of psychism, through an auditory allusion, he senses the sentence that *he himself* puts in the mouth of the character. The spectator in some way hears himself speak, and the impression is all the stronger because he himself imagines the sentences of silent dialogue.

There is no popular spectacle in which the imagination of the spectator plays a greater role than in the cinema-theater.

Art in the cinema-theater is an art of suggesting dreams; so nothing must startle the spectator or else the dream disappears.

69

However, the *noises of life* are necessary, for the spectator cannot supply them through imagination, as he can for the dialogue.

When a gunshot goes off without a propman reproducing the noise, the dream ceases abruptly, for the spectator is awakened by the improbability of a silent gunshot; it's the same with a plate which falls and breaks in a deep silence.

Each of us has paid attention to the suggestive influence of murmuring waves in films of the seashore; in sum, the "noises of life" are necessary to the perfection of the spectacle.

As for musical accompaniment, while we await specialized scores, its only possible condition is to be *neutral*. That is extremely valuable—one could even say indispensable—for it prevents us from realizing that the characters are mute. When, by contrast, instead of being neutral, it asserts itself blatantly in a way opposite the subject of the film, it's abominable.

I have seen a young girl lull her dying mother to sleep by playing a harp (silently, of course), while the orchestra played "Sword of My Father" from the *Grande Duchesse* [Offenbach] with a diabolical brio.

The orchestra should drop the potpourri of operettas and operas, quadrilles, boisterous marches, and café-concert refrains in order to take up the neutral symphonic genre, which is to the advantage of the manager, besides, since nearly all of this music long ago fell into the public domain.

"Come to Me, Darling!" doesn't suit the death of Isolde any more than a funeral march suits the amusing fantasies of Prince Rigadin.

II. ON THE SCENARIO AND CINEMA ARTISTS

Here is the current method of concocting cinema scenarios.

The production company receives ideas for scenarios from any number of people.

A reading committee (?) examines these ideas and selects a certain number of them; the selected ideas are turned over to the directors.

The director constructs a scenario from the selected idea, and has full discretion to modify the selected idea to his liking, even changing it completely.

The director then explains the scenario to his actors and proceeds immediately to the shooting.

The author of the selected idea receives several francs in payment for it.

In short, there is only one author, properly speaking, and that author is the director.

In such conditions, it is hardly astonishing that the scenario is usually so feeble.

From the beginning, the film production companies have been terrified of authors or, more precisely, of authors' rights.

The situation in which salaried authors handle their own mise-en-scène is something the companies have found comfortable and advantageous. On the one hand, it's only fair to point out that, given a poor set of ideas, certain directors have done wonders and produced remarkable results. Yet the average film has remained quite trifling, and the crisis undermining the cinema-theater has no other cause than the company executive's misconceptions regarding exactly how to organize the composition of scenarios.

On the other hand, the authors of plays, novels, and short stories have come forward to claim authors' rights for the films in which the scenario idea was taken from their works. Concluding that the companies did not want to bargain with them, they have taken to composing adaptations of their works themselves.

The results have not been promising, nor can they be.

First of all, the best theatrical plays never make anything but bad films; one shouldn't ask for something other than what the cinema can provide.

For instance, as a result of its connections, SCAGL found itself appealing to stars, famous actors and actresses, which seduced it into paying enormous fees for unremarkable results—for the conventional performance of actors come off badly in the cinema. With the exception of actors such as Prince, Polaire, or Mistinguett, it's far better to appeal to artists who are making a career for themselves from cinema performances.

The cinema and the theater are two different things. On the one hand, the libretti for the cinema must be specially composed all of a piece and in a fashion very different from those destined for the theater. On the other— and I know I am repeating myself—the conventional performance of theater actors becomes perfectly ridiculous when reproduced by the cinema.

The cinema-theater ought to have special authors, special directors, and special troupes of cinema actors.

The cinema-theater has to assert itself as a new Art, with its own original methods, and it should be furious at being considered as a simple reproducer of what is properly called the theater.

Author's rights should be based on the number of meters of positive prints produced because, under the current conditions of cinema-theaters, an advance against receipts would be unthinkable. Under this recommended system, the author's rightful shares would comprise a proportion of the price of the positive print; he would be paid by the distribution company after the sale of the film. . . .

III. THE CLOSE SHOT

Pantomime and ciné-theater have the muteness of actors in common; but in pantomime the actors' performance is conventional and exaggerated, while in the ciné-theater it has to be natural and understated.

To fulfill its destiny, the ciné-theater should represent life as it is lived, while pantomime has never sought to represent more than an artificial, imitative life.

The troupe of actors at Vitagraph was the first to recognize and apply this principle, and the undeniable and undisputed success of this famous company owes largely to that.

In order to produce the maximum effect, while practicing a restraint which thwarts broad gestures, the Vitagraph actors have had to work especially on the play of facial features; and in order that their facial expressions could be seen clearly by the spectators (in all corners of the hall), the director has had to project the actors in close shots as often as possible.

This method, which gives good results, has quickly degenerated into an excessive practice, as the enthusiasts who have followed the Vitagraph films for the past two years will easily recognize.

Naturally, little by little, this misuse has been pursued conscientiously by the directors of other companies.

Now we have reached what could be called *the age of the legless cripple*. For three-quarters of the time, the actors in a scene are projected in close shot, cut off at the knees; from the artistic point of view, the effect produced is highly disagreeable and shocking.

In the theater, the play of facial features can be seen only through opera glasses; in the cinema, the use of opera glasses has the flaw of emphasizing the cinematic imperfections of the image. Therefore, we must find a way to replace the magnification produced by a projection in close shot.

Here the directors find themselves faced with an almost insurmountable dilemma—on the one hand, the play of the actors' facial features is not perceived satisfactorily; on the other, as a result of magnification, the legs of the actor vanish from the screen.

These past few days, I have seen a film where an actor and a horse, placed side by side, were both partially cut off at the knees; then when the man mounted the horse, he found himself suddenly decapitated. To pass instantaneously from being legless to being headless is really pushing things a bit far.

The second inconvenience resulting from the misuse of the close shot is, in the eye of the spectator, to produce the impression of characters of an unnatural grandeur. And when the aggrandizement diminishes and they return to normal, the same characters seem too small; the eye takes a certain time to get used to this.

Turning to another matter, certainly from an economic point of view there is an interest in renting films principally to the large cinemas which can hold a great number of spectators because, except for rental costs, the general expenses remain appreciably the same for a small or large cinema, so the receipts can be doubled.

In the final analysis, given the continual increase in cinema enthusiasts, the screen has become much too small; it no longer corresponds to the grandeur of the new cinemas. Screen size no longer correlates with the actual needs of the ciné-theater industry. Fortunately, an increase in the dimensions of the film negative does not offer insurmountable difficulties. I believe that the future of the ciné-theater is in no way compromised, on the contrary. When the screen reaches huge dimensions, for example, 24 x 18 meters, the spectacle offered will become so beautiful and produce such powerful effects that there will be a new upsurge in attendance. And the big cinemas of the future will again become too small for the increased number of enthusiasts. . . .

In documentary films, the director should always begin by projecting the subject with a clear reference point, for example, a dog with a man.

If, later, he wants to increase the size of one or the other, in order to better capture details, he should announce to the audience that the subject is being projected in an enlargement of two, three, or four times.

It is the same for flowers, plants, small animals, and, ultimately, all the subjects of natural history and anatomy.

On big screens, the characters should be projected with an average magnification so that the play of facial features is clearly perceived by those farthest back in the hall—for we should take into account the fact that, in the cinema, the seats farthest back are the most expensive.

Exaggerated magnifications should be used only in special cases and with the greatest discretion.

In order for the ciné-theater to assume the place which is its due within Art, the director should attach great importance to the composition of the tableaux. It is more than likely that sooner or later the collaboration of a painter will become indispensable, especially when the three-color film process will have achieved the requisite improvements, which cannot be delayed much longer.

From the point of view of composition, what is most striking is the lack of air or space which results from the accumulation of a mass of overly large characters on an overly small screen.

The actors cannot circulate; they obscure one another. When the scene represents a room, we never see more than a part of it. When it is a question of representing a person in a bed, the bed often occupies a grotesque position and takes up all of the room.

When it is a question of a salon or reception rooms, the director is obliged to project in depth; and the spectator sees no more than a corridor whose width in close shot corresponds at most to the space necessary for three or four characters.

Given the actual dimensions of the screen and the requirements for magnification, directors find themselves, I repeat, faced with insurmountable difficulties; and the results they do achieve, in such poor conditions, deserve all our praise. . . .

IV. SCRIPTS AND SCENARIOS, GENERAL CONDITIONS

At the present time, a film is exhibited in the same cinema for seven days at the most, and often only for three. Then it is shelved, and we don't see it any more—its life is finished; it is permanently buried and forgotten.

This ephemeral life of film is discouraging for authors. Why seek to achieve a work of art, why endeavor to create what might be considered a masterpiece in this form if, after seven days of exhibition, the work has to disappear?

It is safe to say that the scenarios which inundate us, with a few exceptions, are not worth even seven days of exhibition. But doesn't the low value of the films result precisely from the fact that they are not made to last and that they have, I repeat, only an ephemeral life?

Why could not the very best films, those which possess a genuine, intrinsic value, come to form a *repertory*, a repertory which would stay [in distribution] and could be rerun?

Why could not those scripts which are in a class by themselves be published with their mise-en-scène, exactly like theater playscripts, and come to constitute a *library of cinema-theater*?

Until now, the press has disdained to publish criticism of exhibited films, yet in Brussels, for example, there are many more people who go to the cinema than go to the theater.

On Sundays, a hundred thousand people pass into the cinemas while ten thousand go to the theater.

Why this disdain on the part of the press?

Almost everywhere the press works against the cinemas. It agrees to accept some advertising on a quarter page because that is a commercial enterprise; but in the body of the paper there is either scornful silence or virulent and undeserving attack. . . .

The ciné-theater is in fashion as a topic of conversation. This being indisputable, it follows that the first newspaper which establishes a "Cinema" column, in order to give its readers all kinds of information on their favorite subject, won't fail to see its printing run jump dramatically.

It is a little ridiculous to see the newspapers, which often carry stories and serials that would make a policeman blush, pretending to be "prudish," taxing the cinema-theaters for immorality and preaching abstention.

But despite the vain efforts of a press which is far too self-satisfied for its friends, the "cinématophobes," the cinema has become one of our customs, the habit has caught on, and the press campaigns are devoted to a lost cause.

IN THE composition of scripts for the cinema, first of all, the author finds himself faced with a very tough problem for, if his characters can *act*, they cannot *reason*; and it is only through their manner of acting that they can convey what is going on in their minds.

The author does have the resource of projecting explanations [expository intertitles], but these explanations break up the spectacle and produce a bad effect—they are anti-artistic. The best thing would be to reach the point of being able to compose a completely intelligible film without any need for expository texts.

We could envision a method which would constitute a theatrical art that is both original and interesting; this would involve projecting the characters and, simultaneously, their states of mind.

This method would be strongly analogous to the ultramodern painting of the *Futurists* who sought to paint not only a character but also what is happening in his mind. If the initiative attempted by the Futurists only ended in ridicule, an effort of this kind initiated in the cinema, on the contrary, would give results altogether more interesting.

In the ciné-theater, this method is currently practiced when there is a dream or hallucination. In order to achieve a moral effect as "the final word" in his film, *L'Auto Grise* [1912], [Victorin Jasset] projects the hallucination of one of the bandits who sees his own head fall under the blade of the guillotine. This method could be generalized by applying it to the waking state.

The Wagnerian opera employs the same tendency when the orchestra endeavors to reproduce musically the feelings which are stirring the character on stage.

In sum, theatrical art has always sought to dissect the psychic states of its characters and, in some fashion, make them manifest for the spectators.

For example, "La Tempête sous un crâne," that marvelous chapter in the famous Victor Hugo novel, [*Les Misérables*], is perfectly possible to render cinematically, by the following method.

Jean Valjean, in the guise of M. Madeleine, would appear alone on the screen, in the foreground or middle ground, while all the thoughts succeeding one another in his mind would be projected in the background—that is, *made material by means of the cinematic image*. Naturally, the gestures and facial expressions of the actors would remain in perfect synchronization with the projected image.

The author could vary the intensity of the thinking through the focus—the clarity of the image corresponding to the clarity of the thought, and vague thoughts corresponding to soft images produced by a lack of focus. He could vary the intensity of the light and leave the images of dark thoughts in shadow.

This example may raise the possibility of a new theatrical art in the future which can only be achieved through the cinema. . . .

The major dramatic authors, accustomed to and spoiled by the great success of their plays, have been stunned at how little effect the same plays produce in the cinema, so they have taken the cinema as a holy terror.

It is precisely because they know their craft so marvelously well that dramatic authors achieve such miserable results in the cinema.

First of all, the dramatic author is subject to a limited number of acts and scenes in the theater, while the cinema triumphs through the boundless multiplicity of different images.

Furthermore, in the theater the first act always serves to establish the play and uncover the basis of the plot; in the cinema this exposition is utterly impossible.

In the theater, the character can tell us that he has just completed a voyage during which a series of incidents happened to him of capital importance to the plot.

In the cinema, this kind of storytelling is impossible. The character must complete the voyage *before the eyes* of the spectator, and all the events which occur have to be *seen* by the spectator.

In the theater, the monologue is the current rage; in the cinema, a silent monologue would be the height of ridicule.

The cinema spectators must *see* a sequence of actions which constitute the drama, nothing should remain unclear. Also, the methods of construction in the cinema are completely different from those appropriate to the theater.

Before tackling the cinema script, the dramatic author ought to undergo a new apprenticeship; but having reached the age of celebrity, that is something he rejects out of hand.

In the cinema, there are no "[verbal] effects for the public." These effects are replaced by tableaux; and to execute them in good form, one has to know the rules of composition, which are precisely those of good painting.

A good author of cinema scripts is far from being a "somebody." If it is true that it's useless for him to speak beautifully, he nevertheless has to conquer enormous difficulties to put on a purely cinematic drama.

But, and herein lies his power, the scriptwriter of the cinema solves the problem of the diversity of languages. For him there is no need of either *Volapuc* or *Esperanto*. His drama is understood everywhere and by everyone, by the Chinese as well as the Parisians, by the Spanish as well as the English, by the Russians as well as the Arabs. His field of action has no boundaries; he writes for the universality of peoples. And we must be audacious enough to say that the dramatic art of the cinema is the greatest of the arts and that it has a great future as long as it gradually escapes the languages in which it is still enmeshed.

IN ITS 27 April issue, *Ciné-Journal* offered an extract from the fascinating inquiry run by *Les Marges* on the increasing aesthetic interest in the cinema. Yet, as a result of a natural prejudice, the editor addressed himself only to authors in order to resolve a question which is purely sociological. Consequently, all the responses were beside the point.

A sociologist would have begun by answering that it was not aesthetic interest in the theater but the average level of wealth which had increased.

In our era, people go to spectacles more often because they have more money to spend on their leisure. This is not an evolution of taste but an evolution of wealth.

Statistics show us that, in all periods and countries, the taste for spectacles varies solely according to the level of wealth and the price of tickets. If the cinema-theater has suddenly achieved such a considerable development, it is solely due to the lowering of ticket prices.

The cinema has allowed a huge number of people to satisfy their taste for the theater, a taste which they already had, but which the meagerness of their means did not allow them to satisfy.

Specifically, a person who could only go to the theater once on five francs can frequent the cinema five times, for the price of tickets is about five times less expensive. Such is the reason, perhaps the sole reason, why the theaters are being abandoned in favor of the cinema.

Before going to a spectacle, a man looks in his wallet; the size or weight of its contents then determines the choice of spectacles.

Offer anyone the choice of a free ticket to the Opéra, the Comédie Française, the café-concert, or the cinema, and that person will choose the Opéra or the Comédie Française every time, because then taste alone determines the choice. If the same person has to pay for his ticket, the question of how much money he has becomes uppermost.

EXACTLY who wrote these articles under the pseudonym of Yhcam is still unknown.

LOUIS HAUGMARD, "The 'Aesthetic' of the Cinematograph"

From "L' 'Esthétique' du cinématographe," *Le Correspondant* (25 May 1913), 762–71.

THE CINEMA has become not only a national institution in every country but a "worldwide" phenomenon. It attracts the Parisian masses as well as the natives of the least civilized countries on earth. In several years, its development has been prodigious; six years ago there were only two cinemas in Paris, and today there are 160. Day and night, the screenings follow fast on one another, and the cinemas are anything but empty.

In every quarter of the big cities, we see a "cinema-theatre," a "cinema-concert," or a "cinema-brasserie"—which at least are better than the "magic-cinemas" and "folies-cinemas." The "publishing houses" [production firms] have acquired a good deal of fame, and different enterprises associated with this new kind of entertainment are taking in the most remarkable profits. Fortunes are growing, and an unexpected source of revenue is now available to dramatic authors, whether experienced or inexperienced, as well as actors, whether unemployed or illustrious. It's a new branch of business, important and very modern, which requires an enormous amount of publicity. Color posters catch the passerby's eye, like those for soup or a dry goods shop, a serial novel or a music hall program. This development, which is so extraordinary in its rapidity and extent, this profusion or "invasion" of the cinema is a phenomenon which deserves the attention of the casual observer who loves to contemplate things. While omitting all that is commercial and financial in this business, allow me to meditate a little on the value of the movies, on their role, on their consequences; and allow me to discuss, since it would be useless to resist it, the good that could be derived from this phenomenon, which is as immense as it is disquieting.

THE PREPARATION of the cinematographic mechanism, if I can call it that, demands a series of indispensable elements: a natural or artificial decor, a limitless set of tools for trick effects and trompe-l'oeil, the activities of the producer, creator or director, companies of actors, armies of extras, as well as voyagers, explorers, and globe-trotters. Each of these elements requires a staff and a distinct yet cohesive and harmonious organization. Think what has to be set in motion—individuals and props, ingenuity and time—in order to come up with these two films: *Onésime se réfugie dans le tube aux enveloppes pheumatiques* and *Un Episode de Waterloo*,[1] the last of which requires a diplomatic ball, a nicely orchestrated simulacrum of combat, the multiple comings and goings of the protagonists, and even "the field covered with dead over which night falls."

The companies of actors, of which the best known are French, American, and Italian, function as in the theater. All of these people rehearse and perform conscientiously before the camera, which reproduces their silhouettes and physiognomies in boundless multiplicity, with an ubiquity which is no more than a chimera. Some actors have become specialized in the craft and have created "types." I will cite only Max Linder . . . , André Deed . . . , and especially M. Prince of the Variétés and his Rigadin. . . .[2]

They even say that—for performing in the films of childhood which are named after him—the boy who plays "Bébé" receives a salary equal to that of the assistant manager of an office.[3]

And they work on every sort of subject, whatever the place or time. History, legend, fantasy, anything from current events and daily life, from the seas to the different continents; there is nothing that cannot be used, with honesty or artifice, in the confection of a film, whether wildly improvised or documented with relish.

FOR FILM, whether hybrid or homogeneous, assumes all sorts of forms: the fantastic film, the sentimental film, the comic or dramatic film, buffoonery and acrobatics, the "artistic" film and the serial, the scientific film, the police film, the "historical" film, the moralizing film, everything from the real to the imaginary, and sometimes "enhanced by natural colors.". . .

And when it is "the biggest hit of the Hippodrome"[4] and the poster adds "1,000 meters long, an hour of intense emotion," can the casual observer resist the appeal? 1,000 meters long! An hour of intense emotion! Here indeed is the repast which awaits the modern man who is curious about life's violence and pungency.

Moreover, it's a question of gauging the ingredients to the different quarters and their publics, in order to compose a program capable of interesting every category of spectator and their different tastes: to combine, for example, a Western, a "drawing room comedy in colors," a "social document" in two or three or even four parts, a comic chase, and "The Fall of Troy" [Giovanni Pastrone, 1910]—a picturesque promenade with views of the celebrated monuments and some inevitable buffoonery. . . .

INDEED, the movie public is not uniform. Many different "milieux" can be found there, and all kinds of minds. I know an artist who sits before the screen to study the movements of animals in their elusive spontaneity, which is difficult if not impossible to observe in reality. Nevertheless, it is the people especially—in the broadest sense of the term—who frequent the cinema halls. For them, such halls are a substitute for theaters and solve the problem of a "costly theater seat." Here the ticket prices suit the most modern budgets; and, better yet, you don't have to dress up to enter a fully lighted hall and sit before a simulacrum of the stage and sometimes even a curtain, which draws back to reveal the mysterious white rectangle on which marvels unfold. Just as the newspaper killed off books for many people, so the cinema is replacing the theater. It's not only less expensive, but it demands only a minimal intellectual effort. The mental strain required is minor; if there is any fatigue at the end of the cinema program, it will be purely nervous and wholly passive. The program explains in advance the details of the "plays" when there is no "barker" who comments concurrently on the action—much like the old "moving spirit" or plaintive singer in the provincial fairs long ago, who, with a long wand in his hand, marked each stage of the story on a huge canvas where episodes were juxtaposed in shocking or pathetic colors.[5]

Thus any mental work is already prepared in advance in order to minimize the active effort of the spectator.

A SHORT TIME ago it still happened that on autumn and winter evenings one read at home; today in the general disintegration of natural communities, and particularly the family, the cinema constitutes a means of family restitution, when it is not serving only to facilitate all sorts of rendezvous. Yes, indeed, the cinema provides its mass public with something more and better than the theater. A theater generally offers no more than one kind of play and one quality of emotion. Here, every genre is represented, and every category of emotion; and the "stories" which unfold, ceaselessly active and infinitely rapid, are well crafted to please a very modern crowd. To the worker who regularly visits the cinema in his quarter, they constitute a well-stocked weekly gazette containing a little information, a melodramatic serial or cloak-and-dagger novel considerably pruned, sickly sweet or laughable "variety acts," sometimes a bit of literature much adulterated, and that's not counting the interludes—a "unique demonstration of muscular tension" or "Olympic" acrobats, the performances of two dogs (Rita and Dora, "the best trained tricksters of the century"), or a M. Bergeret who isn't whom you think, but the "celebrated imitator of La Scala."[6]

The "masses" are like grown-up children who demand a picture album to leaf through in order to forget their miseries; and here vivid images are given to them in profusion: conjured up historical facts, elegant and worldly dramas which initiate them into milieux they otherwise could not enter (just as many unfortunate creatures cannot know the "world" of the theater), exotic landscapes reproduced in all their luminous and trembling photographic truth. Everything has been achieved except for the most perfect illusion, when the ear itself will perceive a great number of sounds cunningly imitated—a speeding automobile and a galloping horse, the breaking sea waves and the torrential river, falls and blows. In sum, we really have an "armchair spectacle."

What good is voyaging or travelling no matter where, when we have before us this cinematographic "newspaper" which is a "vivid universal newspaper" and "beats the record for information"? At the movies, people get away from their miserable and monotonous lives, from which they love to escape; they have their favorites among the film actors, who they recognize at each new screening and who they welcome into the intimacy of their hearts. For here everything passes in the domain of silence, and it's useless for the spectator—though he does anyway—to manifest his admiration or sympathy for the performer, except to communicate his feeling to his neighbor, which perhaps explains this coming together in a "vast enclosure." Much like the bourgeois whose taste for a play in the theater depends on its distance from his own milieu and his customary preoccupations, I have observed that the mass public accords only mild favor to plays which refer to the material of its own life, for example, the representation of diverse crafts. Although the cinema is no more than a "circus" for adults, to the popular imagination and sensibility, which is so deprived and weary, it offers a "pleasant journey."

LET THEM display for my gaze several seconds of a fire "taken on the run," of a moment in a duel at the carnival in Nice, or Bielovuccie's crossing of the Alps, a downhill race of skiers, or a shipwreck pounded by the waves of a storm, I'm delighted but also educated. It even happens when they show me scenes of a private nature, when they let me penetrate behind the scenes of political or social life: I can then note how an official act is fabricated, how a "reality" is elaborated, all of which no longer appear veiled and hazy but are directly "seen." Through this perhaps I can lose some biases and get rid of certain mistaken notions.

The movies would have all that much more utility if they assumed an educational or didactic manner. We no longer ignore the fact that science has used and will continue to use cinematography to its advantage, as an instrument of control and experimentation. Instantaneous photography has allowed scientists to verify the accuracy of certain equestrian poses on the frieze of the Parthenon. The chronophotographs of M. Marey concerning the flight of birds have revealed precious pieces of information for the warping of airplane wings. M. Marage has filmed the movements of the lips and mouth in speech pronunciation and, from that, reproduced artificially the utterance of vowels and consonants. The study of the development of a plant or the blossoming of a flower, of phagocytosis or Brownian movement have been aided by cinematography, as have operations such as those of Dr. Doyen; and recently Amundsen has allowed us sedentary and flabby spectators to participate in his heroic adventures.

In the movies, an artist could use the properties of perspective, draw on all the material of nature, snare the elusive moment, for the cinema transposes both time and space. I am thinking of the animals observed freely in their wild state—with difficulty, but the cinema should have its heroes and even martyrs.

In such domains, the cinema succeeds perfectly for the spectator who accepts the results: instructing by entertaining. Yet if the field of scientific application is boundless, that of its social applications is no less so. The cinema allows us to determine emotions and feelings at will. It's likely that views of military maneuvers and stately reviews can function to keep up the patriotic will of a nation. Through film, the political biography will become commonplace. Every country will soon know how to use the cinema as an incomparable means of preaching for the general edification of its people. In Romania, didn't they revise the history of their independence by means of films? The army was mobilized, half of the soldiers dressed like Turks (who were sent into battle unwillingly)—they demolished some things and reconstructed others, in order to simulate the great battles of the past. The actors who played the major roles were decorated; and that provided a stirring lesson in history for school children.

In the United States, in honor of the four-hundred-year anniversary of the landing of Columbus, they resorted to caravels reconstructed in 1892. Finally, we know that the city of Paris possesses a library of films commemorating the principal Parisian public ceremonies, and not long ago we were able to see a rough sketch of the septennial of [former prime minister] M. Falliéres and several moments of the life of the new president, just as in an album of "true" images. All that, of course, is excellent; but. . . .

JUST AS photography, in the eyes of many artists, would have been fatal for art if it had not restricted itself to fixing a brief image or establishing a record, so, too, the cinema will be an agent of artifice and falsification if it doesn't limit itself to the reproduction of natural reality. If, instead, it remains the realm of fraud, counterfeiting, and trickery, how will a naïve public be able to sort out differences and make crucial distinctions, without risking inevitable misunderstanding and multiple errors? It would seem, however, that the cinema willingly puts up with chastisements about "make up": "staged" scenes are inferior to "natural" scenes in the completeness of their reproduction. The jerky brusqueness of human gestures, the overall exaggeration in physiological expression—prescribed, it seems, to make up for the absence of speech—exaggeration which quickly degenerates into grimace, is unsatisfactory and displeasing as long as natural movement, "continuous" movement—that of water, animals, trees—is so harmonious and perfectly satisfying. Here, as ever, nature remains the best and most beautiful model. Yet, will the taste for movement perhaps reach the point of preventing the masses from being interested in fixed, immobile scenes, such as in painting and sculpture? That would be a terrible consequence of "cinema."

There's no need to discourse at length on the infinitely dangerous power it possesses and which touches everything: the novel, the theater, the noblest poetry, in order to popularize them, that is, distort them; history, in order to "fictionalize" or falsify it, so as to provide a biased and incomplete education; current events, in order to feed all sorts of vanities and trigger imitations, for the image is enticing to naïve minds.

Moreover, if the reporting of immoral, licentious, or sensual spectacles, of the deeds of criminals, as well as of capital offense executions has been forbidden, *imagined* scenes relating to such police matters positively abound; and those which are *real* have reached the point of subtle ingenuity in quantity. Thus they show us the automobile in which the deliveryman was assaulted, even down to the mark of the bullet on the wheel, then the judge interrogating the policemen.[7] Imagine the influence on the minds of children, for instance, of such burglary scenes and the ingenious methods used to throw pursuers off the track. In Berlin, the chief of police thought it appropriate to forbid children under the age of fifteen from entering cinema halls.

WHY DOES an evening at the movies, however crammed with all sorts of films, despite everything, leave one with an impression of emptiness, of nothingness? Why is the pleasure one experiences there no more than a "ghostly pleasure," without any lasting effects in the memory? Scarcely is the spectacle over and it is forgotten.

It is because only facts are photographed. All the rest is sacrificed, all that which is intellectual and interior life; and in the human order, only intelligence and soul really count! This exclusive capacity to reproduce only the factual entails its consequences. Action, only action, which is rapid and brutal. From this comes the almost total suppression of any psychology. Cinematography is a form of notation by image, as arithmetic and algebra are notations by figures and letters; here, it is convenient, in the statement [intertitle] or the exposition, to limit as much as possible everything which has nothing to do with the sign itself. It is the triumph of simplification.

At the movies, lots of letters, usually in good basic English (whatever the milieu or period), fill up gaps in the inner life of the characters; and they occur as frequently as possible.[8] So it's necessary to translate, to transpose. Consequently, every theatrical play adapted for the cinema, despite the added multiplicity of scenes, runs the risk of becoming obscure; the prescribed exaggeration of gestures, separated from language, is transformed into pantomime: and pantomime, when it is not an amusement of the refined and blasé, is no more than an art for primitives.

Cinema action only allows us to ascertain the conventional value of certain gestures, something not found in the theater, because there the accompanying words keep us from giving them our full attention or even dispense with gesture altogether, since it, too, is a translation.

Because of all this, it's obvious that Racine would be a poor author for "cinema." *Britannicus* has been rudely transformed [Camille de Morlhon, 1912] into a romantic drama. The result is painful. Narcissus passed a writing implement—a fountain pen, no doubt—to Nero; and since the banquet guests were seated on chairs, one had to pity the divine poet, despite the most modern infusions of capital to dress up the drama.

For such historical evocations to succeed in avoiding vulgar errors and the most laughable anachronisms, or at least make us pardon them, what's needed is nothing short of a vast erudition, a superior sense of tact and, ultimately, culture, none of which is to be found in the usual tradesman or tutor.

I imagine that a man of taste, with a skepticism that's sometimes morose and sometimes indulgent, would say something like this:

"Since the cinema uses every available real or imaginary resource and takes a thousand forms, like Proteus, I would guess that some of its forms are tolerable and even endowed with a certain charm. I myself take delight in films that spread 'selected landscapes' before me, mountains or plains, and the vast sea over which a powerful steamer glides or a delicate sailing ship dances, and films that transport me to unknown lands which I could never visit. I would remember the delicious legends which intelligent films could illustrate using authentic landscapes of grace and truth; I would remember fairy tales suggested by brief tableaux, since the cinema can actualize any dream. What good are Hoffmann, Andersen, and the creators of fantasy? What good are poets who invent, when the cinema is there to record scientifically, for the incredulous masses, the wildest phantasmagorias of ancestral myths? . . ."

Yet there still is the crude vaudeville, which is execrable, and the dark melodrama, and the farce—all, alas, irresistible. . . .

Despite these frightful forms, one gleans a few lovely moments.

The cinema resurrects reality, prolongs it, and gives to the ephemeral an unlimited posthumous life.

No more written archives, only films. Memorable events, diligently catalogued and classified, will be deposited in stores of human motion. There we will find the "pressings" of public life, the "preserves" of the past, though scarcely exempt from falsification.

You know that recently one of the most important film production companies [Pathé] received the Czar's authorization to commemorate the three-hundred-year anniversary of the rise of the Romanoffs, with the assistance of historical costumes and four thousand extras. Should we deplore that or rejoice?

Alas, in the future, notorious personalities will instinctively "pose" for cinema popularity, and historical events will tend to be concocted for the film company cameraman.

Then getting excited over ephemeral events, after the fact, will become an ethnic custom. But aren't we already engaged in something like it when we read a history book or even the current events of a newspaper? Our emotions, coming long after the event which prompts them, are artificial and vain. . . .

Unfortunately, many deconsecrated chapels are becoming cinema halls; and that is symbolic, if one realizes that, for an important segment of the working class, the cinema is already a "religion of the people" or, rather, "the irreligion of the future"! At the movies, bewitched crowds will learn not to think anymore, to resist all desire to reason and construe, faculties which will atrophy little by little; they will know only how to open their large and empty eyes, just to look, look, look. . . . And this will be an indubitable sign of decadence, a remarkable symbol of the end of the race. The cinema will be the "amphitheater" of enfeebled civilizations, "*circenses*" for peaceful peoples, the sole means of action for neurasthenics. Will it then perhaps comprise the elegant solution to the social question, as the modern cry would have it: "Bread and 'cinemas'?"

And we shall progressively draw near to those menacing days when universal illusion will reign in universal mummery. . . .

LOUIS HAUGMARD was a *moraliste* writer and journalist who contributed this and other articles on cultural phenomena—for example, the 1900 Paris International Exposition—to the Catholic weekly newspaper, *Le Correspondant*. In 1910, he published a small book on Edmond Rostand.

[1] The *Onésime* film was part of a comedy series directed by Jean Durand (1882–1946) and starring Ernest Bourbon, between 1912 and 1914.

[2] Max Linder, André Deed, and Prince Rigadin were the three most popular French film comics of the prewar period.

[3] Louis Feuillade's *Bébé* comic series (1910–1913) at Gaumont preceded his more famous *Bout-de-Zan* series (1912–1916), starring René Poyen.

[4] The Hippodrome or Gaumont-Palace was remodeled into a cinema in 1911, and it quickly became the most profitable Paris cinema of the prewar period.

[5] The reference to a "barker" or commentator who explained the scenes in a film as it unreeled suggests that this exhibition practice may have persisted in some cinemas in France, as it did in Germany, up to the war.

[6] The reference is probably to Emile Bergeret (1845–1925), a dramatist and polemical critic who wrote for *Eclair* just before the war.

[7] The reference may well be to the *Bandits en automobile* series (Eclair, 1912), which Jasset had based on the Bonnot gang's exploits.

[8] Haugmard's remark indicates that American films were becoming increasingly prominent, and perhaps even dominant, in Paris by early 1913.

RENÉ DOUMIC, "Drama Review: The Cinema Age"

From "Revue dramatique: L'Age du cinéma," *Revue des deux mondes* 133 (15 August 1913), 919–30.

THE CINEMA program is very ingeniously composed so that there is something for everyone. First comes the serious part, instructive or, as they say, "documentary." It is an object lesson. Don't forget that we are in primary school. They give lectures; they write tracts on this subject: the education of the people by means of the cinema. . . . All this is fragmentary, with few linking transitions, even close to incoherent. But it must be said, once and for all, that incoherence is essential to cinema programs. Education by means of the cinema is encyclopedic and incoherent, and that makes it eminently modern.

Another part includes the "actualités" or newsreels. We already have a press illustrated with photographs; but how preferable to the immobile photographs of these magazines and newspapers are the photographs that move! Everything that merits the public's attention each week unreels on the screen. First place is given rightly to sports. . . . Then come the leaders and personalities, both foreign and Parisian. . . .

The cinema is also a theatrical enterprise, and, from my point of view, that is its most important characteristic. They write plays specially for the cinema. Some writers do that exclusively. Actors have made their reputations in them. A number of dramatic authors who have been acclaimed for their stage plays also have not disdained this new manner of "writing" for the theater. And some of our actors, both men and women, who are celebrated in the theater for their speech, willingly perform in this theater where silence rules. . . .

In all these cinema-dramas, however different they may be, you can easily note one common trait. They make much of going places and travelling through many countries. They move about here, there, and everywhere. The craft of the cinema-drama consists in placing the characters in circumstances where, whether they are running away or meeting, they make the greatest number of exits and entrances. The perfect cinema-drama, if they give us one someday, will achieve perpetual motion.

A genre or art form has value according to its limitations. Its end is determined by its means. If the cinema kept to those limitations, I would have little to say. But it ought to restrict its ambitions to what is its proper domain; with success has come all manner of pretensions. Before an enthusiastic crowd, for instance, they recently showed *Quo Vadis?* [Enrico Guazzoni, 1912], a mammoth cinematic reconstruction adapted from the famous novel by Sienkiwicz. Everything trooped through it: Nero, Petronius (that master of style), the imperial box, Christians and wild beasts, vestal virgins, etc. Between every two cinematic tableaux on the luminous screen, you know, there appeared an explanatory inscription, usually copiously written. This interminable succession of tableaux and placards, in which the complete novel was cut up into wordless images—images which, moreover, seemed to me more than mediocre in their grouping of actors, their decors, and costumes—was the most stupefying film that I have ever seen. . . .

Let's enumerate, if you will allow me, some of the advantages which arm the cinema in the battle in which, by force of circumstance, it is engaged with the theater. First of all, it is cheaper. You know how the ticket prices are rising, steadily and stupidly, in all of our theaters, whether for music or oratory, for classical plays or melodramas. The latest invention of the managers is to make the public pay, above and beyond the ticket price, a poor tax which was already included in that price. It's a brilliant invention, I realize, but disaster for our pocketbooks. The pleasure of going to the theater in Paris has become a costly pleasure, reserved more and more for foreigners who need not worry about costs; whereas, the shopkeepers and very many of the Paris bourgeoisie hesitate, if only because they have a family and are trying desperately to advance themselves through work. The cinema offers them pleasure for a modest sum. In the popular cinemas, a couple of sous for a ticket even buys a drink and a barley sugar for the children. In the theater, we have to suffer through interminable entr'actes, with the result that the show is more often than not composed of entr'actes with a few short acts between them. In the cinema, you have just one or two entr'actes among the different parts of the program. They give you all that for your money, and it costs almost nothing at all. You can arrive when you want to, for you are always on time: the show is broken up into pieces, and you don't need to see what has gone before. You can leave when you want, when you begin to get bored; you don't have to know how everything ends. And nothing tires your intelligence. What an attraction! One understands immediately. And when one doesn't, one can console oneself, knowing that one hasn't missed a thing. For we are becoming less capable of the slightest effort everyday. To make an effort to do something, how terrible!

Let's continue to review what makes the cinema "superior," because we have not yet come to the end. No matter how much the theater would, if it could, follow the latest fashion and style, it will remain the same "old hat." It is contemporary with the old civilizations: it is ancient, medieval, and even ecclesiastical. The Greeks celebrated the exploits of Bacchus, and the French commemorated the Passion of Christ. The cinema is scientific. I say that with respect. It's scientific in and of itself, being the result of scientific discoveries. It's scientific in its present and future, considering that it will successively take up new processes and will be steadily improving, as have motoring and aeronautics. Just as it is scientific through the means it employs, it is likewise so through a good portion of the programs to which it invites us, which are fragments of reality rather than fictions invented by artists and poets. It is scientific to see Alphonse XIII and the Queen of Spain stopping in Paris: it is not, to listen to the dialogue of Rodrigue and Chimène.[1] It is scientific to see the friends of M. Cochon besieged in the stronghold of the Boulevard Lannes: it is not, to follow the cadets of Gascoigne to the siege of Arras.[2] The theater is national and even regional, as in all the different countries there are languages that have not been supplanted by Esperanto. A French or English or German play, in order to be understood outside its country of origin, must be translated and lose something in the process. The cinematic film can be understood in all languages. The cinema is international.

And that is not all. . . . Nevertheless, we are not in a hurry to conclude that the game is lost. Competition can have its good effects, as long as one knows how to defend oneself: and that's my hope for the theater. Let it defend itself, for it is threatened. The threat is greater than one might think. I know of twelve philosophers who are deserting the theater for the cinema because they adore its curious lack of consciousness. There they see new proof of the vanity of all things. And it amuses their dilettantism. All of contemporary life—like so many stakes in the game, so many aroused passions—all the pain that we induce in ourselves, all that ends up in flickering shadows on a cinema screen! Let the theater defend itself energetically and without delay if it does not want to fulfill that terrible prophecy: the one will destroy the other. First of all, dramatic authors who are concerned about their art must be scrupulous in collaborating with the rival industry. Some time ago, an established firm asked the most famous writers of the theater to construct some films.[3] I do not know what happened with this project, but it is easy to see that it was disagreeable, even offensive. I would say the same of actors who are not above playing simple clowns. That the same actor can appear at the Comédie Française and the Cinéma-Montparnasse or the Sebasto-Cinéma should not be tolerated. At this point, especially, the theater must indulge in some serious reflection and try to reform itself. It is annoying and devoid of imagination and fantasy: while the cinema entertains. It is often absurd and devoid of psychological observation: while the cinema gives the illusion of reality. It is monotonous, usually turning on the fatal triangle of adultery. It is scandalous and risqué: the cinema—since the exhibition of crime is forbidden—is relatively moral. Today the theater's worst error is that it is losing its uniquely literary qualities. That is what is leading to its ruin. It is now coming up against an unusually powerful rival: on the other's terms, it will never do as well as the opposition. If it wants to survive, there is only one way: that is to distinguish itself, in its essential features, from the cinema, which is a theater for illiterates.

RENÉ DOUMIC (1860–1937) was a noted scholar of rhetoric, literary historian, and drama critic. He served as editor-in-chief of the prestigious and conservative *La Revue des deux mondes* (after Brunetière) and was elected to the Académie Française in 1910.

[1] Rodrigue and Chimène are the famous hero and heroine of Corneille's *Cid* (1636).

[2] The reference is probably to Louis XIII's victory over the Spanish at Arras in 1640.

[3] Doumic is probably referring to Henri Lavedan and Le Bargy's early efforts at Film d'Art.

MAURICE RAYNAL, "Cinema Column: *Fantômas*"

From "Chronique cinématographique," *Les Soirées de Paris* 26–27 (July–August 1914), 363–64.

AND NOW, dare I or don't I? Well, take courage and trust in the grace of God! Now . . . *Fantômas*![1]

What nobility! What beauty! It's one of those things that stuns you; its serene majesty, like inimitable brilliance, leaves you breathless, dazed, and mute. If only I had in my hand the pen of Brunetière![2] But I must launch a similar enterprise with nothing but feeble rhetoric, and my enthusiasm and youth. Fantômas, forgive me! But you, Armand Silvestre and Marcel Olin, lucky authors, what have you accomplished here? Others, M. Romain Rolland perhaps,[3] will no doubt later ransack the life of your hero; but you will always have the inestimable glory of having discovered, recognized, understood, and (should I say?) loved him, and thus provided us with so many excellent pretexts to shore up faltering conversations.

There is nothing in this involved, compact, and concentrated film but explosive genius. Take the gas fire scene, for example. An indisposed marquis goes to sleep after having lit his gas fire. What does Fantômas do? He runs to the gas meter, turns it off, and the flame dies out. That's not all. Very deliberately, he turns on the meter again: the gas seeps out to fill the room, and the aristocrat is asphyxiated. How simple, how great! And that young man who is hiding stolen jewels in the huge bell of a church tower, nonchalantly, without expecting the slightest difficulty. Fantômas sends him back to fetch them, hoists him up inside the bell, and, for a mischievous prank, amuses himself by withdrawing the ladder to leave him high up, suspended from the clapper, over the abyss! So when they ring the bell and the unfortunate young man, now a human clapper, is smashed against the bronze casing, both him and the jewels, there is this sublime spectacle of a rain of blood, pearls, and gold down on the church faithful. Further on, notice with what delicacy the hero "borrows" 500,000 francs from the marquis. As you say, M. Fantômas—for I dare not write Fantômas for short—as you say, monsieur, in order to excuse yourself: "Fantômas is sometimes hungry!" It is like the best of Hugo, and more beautiful in fact! Myself, I think Fantômas is a roman à clef; but who is going to provide us with the key? Who will live long enough to see that. Several well informed people, however, tell me that Fantômas will be recognized as the brother of Juve, the police inspector. My God, is that possible? I myself would swear that they were one and the same person!

MAURICE RAYNAL (1884–1954) was a young writer who became attached to Apollinaire's circle before the war. Later he would become a noted, if more conventional, art critic and art historian.

¹ The occasion for Raynal's review was the fifth and final film of Feuillade's *Fantômas* series, *Le Faux Magistrat*, which was released by Gaumont in April 1914.

² Fernand Brunetière (1849–1906) was a celebrated essayist and editor of the prestigious *La Revue des deux mondes* in the last decade of the nineteenth century. Raynal's reference is typically tongue-in-cheek, for Brunetière's rightist, Catholic principles would have been much offended by *Fantômas*.

³ Romain Rolland (1866–1944) was a prominent novelist and passionate essayist whose idealistic principles made him the spiritual leader of many Europeans who refused to fight in World War I.

LÉOPOLD SURVAGE, "Colored Rhythm"

From "Le Rythme coloré," *Les Soirées de Paris* 26–27 (July–August 1914), 426–27.

COLORED RHYTHM is in no way an illustration or an interpretation of a musical work. It is an art unto itself, even if it is based on the same psychological phenomena as music.

ON ITS ANALOGY WITH MUSIC

It is the mode of succession in time which establishes the analogy between sound rhythm in music and colored rhythm—the fulfillment of which I advocate by cinematographic means. Sound is the element of prime importance in music. . . . Music is always a mode of *succession* in time. A musical work is a sort of subtle language by means of which an author expresses his state of mind, his inner dynamic being. The performance of a musical work evokes in us something of an analogy to this inner state of the author. The more sensitive the listener—just as with an instrument of amplification—the greater the intimacy established between listener and author.

The fundamental element of my dynamic art is *colored visual form*, which plays a part analogous to that of sound in music.

This element is determined by three factors:

1. Visual form—which is abstract, to give its proper label
2. Rhythm—that is, movement and the changes which visual form undergoes
3. Color

FORM, RHYTHM

By abstract visual form I mean the complete abstraction or geometrization of a shape, an object, within our surroundings. Ultimately, the form of such objects, however simple or familiar—say, a tree, a chair, a man—is complicated. To the degree that we study the details of these objects, they become more and more resistant to a simple representation. To represent the irregular shape of a real body abstractly means to reduce it to a geometric form, whether simple or complex, and these transformed representations or forms will be to the actual world as musical sounds are to noises. But that alone does not suffice to represent a state of mind or to channel an emotion. Immobile, an abstract form still does not express very much. Round or pointed, oblong or square, simple or complex, it only produces an extremely confused *sensation*; it is no more than a simple graphic notation. Only by putting it in motion, transforming it and combining it with other forms, does it become capable of evoking a *feeling*. . . . Such a transformation in time erases space; one form converges with others in the midst of change; and they merge together, now advancing in parallel, now sparring with one another or dancing to the measure of the cadence which propels them; and that is the author's mood, his sense of gaiety, his sadness, or the deepest depths of his reflection. At this point there may come an equilibrium. But no! It is unstable, and the transformations begin anew; and through this the visual rhythm becomes analogous to the rhythm of music. In both domains, rhythm plays a similar role. Consequently, in the graphic realm, the visual form of any body is of value only as a means to express or evoke our inner state, and not at all as the representation of the significance or importance which such a body actually has in our daily life. From the point of view of such a dynamic art, visual form becomes both the expression and the effect of a manifestation of form-energy, within our environment. In this, form and rhythm are bound up together inseparably.

COLOR

Whether produced by dyes, by rays, or by projection, color is, at one and the same time, the cosmos, the material world, and the energy-field of our light-sensitive apparatus—the eye. And since what influences us psychologically is not sound or color, in isolation, but the alternating series of sounds and colors, so the art of colored rhythm, thanks to its principle of mobility, augments the alternating layers already present in ordinary painting. But there a group of colors is fixed simultaneously on an immobile surface and exists unchanging in its interrelations. Only through movement does the character of color acquire a power superior to that of the static harmony [of painting].

Through this, color in turn is bound up with rhythm. Once it ceases to be an accessory to objects, it becomes the content, or even the spirit, of abstract form.

Technical difficulties still exist, however, in the realization of cinematographic films for the projection of colored rhythm.

In order to produce a work lasting just three minutes, one has to unreel 1,000 to 2,000 images through a projector.

That's a lot! But I won't pretend to execute them all myself. I need only provide the crucial stages. Animators, with a little common sense, would know how to deduce the intermediate images from indicated numbers or figures.

Once the sheets of images were finished, they would be placed in succession in front of a three-colored camera lens.

LÉOPOLD SURVAGE (1879–1968) was a Russian-born painter who came to Paris in 1908. His first important exhibition was with the Cubists at the Salon des Indépendents in 1913 and 1914, which included some of the canvases from the Colored Rhythm series.

PART TWO

1915-1919

We are witnessing the birth of an extraordinary art. The only truly modern art perhaps, assured already of its place and one day soon of astonishing glory, because it is simultaneously and uniquely the offspring of both technology and human ideals.

Louis Delluc, 1917

To concentrate all the force of feeling or thought on an inanimate object, to crystallize around an inert accessory scattered feelings, fleeting memories, passing dreams, is that the work of an artisan or an artist? . . . Is it to produce the work of an artisan or an artist that all these magical forces are intelligently arranged in the cinema, so as to recreate a world as seen "through a temperament"?

Emile Vuillermoz, 1918

On the screen, objects that were a few moments ago sticks of furniture or books of cloakroom tickets are transformed to the point where they take on menacing or enigmatic meanings. . . . To endow with a poetic value that which does not yet possess it, to willfully restrict the field of vision so as to intensify expression: these are the two properties that help make cinematic *decor* the adequate setting of modern beauty.

Louis Aragon, 1918

Photogénie and Company

A S RICH, insightful, and combative as it was during the long grim years
of the Great War, French writing on the cinema flourished within a
range of formats somewhat narrower than it had prior to 1914. The reason,
of course, lay in the cutbacks in printing materials of all kinds, mandated
by the mobilization of men into the army, the rationing of paper supplies,
and increased censorship.[1] For more than a year, once it resumed publication in March 1915, *Ciné-Journal* provided almost the only forum of discussion for people both inside and outside the film industry.[2] Its only formidable rival emerged when Henri Diamant-Berger launched *Le Film* once
again as a deluxe weekly, in March 1916. Then when Diamant-Berger
made Louis Delluc, a young drama critic and novelist, editor-in-chief of
the magazine in June 1917, *Le Film* quickly became the principal forum
for a whole series of debates, polemics, and exploratory essays on the condition of the French cinema. And it maintained its singular position well
into 1919, until both Delluc and Diamant-Berger left the magazine to take
up filmmaking and until several new film magazines began to appear in
competition, either addressed to the film industry—for instance, Paul de
la Borie's *La Cinématographie française* and G.-Michel Coissac's *Cinéopse*—or
to the general public—for example, Pierre Henry's *Ciné-pour-tous*. In the
meantime, Georges Dureau sought to consolidate *Ciné-Journal*'s position
by publishing one of the earliest surviving annuals devoted to the full spectrum of companies and organizations within the French film industry, the
Annuaire général de la cinématographie française et étrangère (1918), for which
Coissac wrote a long sketch on the cinema's historical development.[3] By
contrast, following the direction of their work at *Le Film*, Diamant-Berger
and Delluc published, almost simultaneously, the earliest French books on
the cinema for a general audience: Diamant-Berger's *Le Cinéma* (Renaissance du livre, 1919) and Delluc's *Cinéma et cie* (Grasset, 1919).[4]

The Paris newspapers initially curtailed their coverage of the cinema as
well. *Comoedia*, for instance, ceased publication for the duration of the war;
and only *Le Journal*, of the mass dailies, continued its weekly information
section on the cinema, but on a much reduced scale. This began to change
with what seemed to be an invasion of American films into the French cinemas in late 1915 and early 1916.[5] The rightist *Le Gaulois*, for instance,
announced a weekly column, "A travers les cinémas" (3 March 1916),

which sparked the attention of larger circulation papers such as *Excelsior*; and then an important new platform suddenly emerged in the centrist *Le Temps*.[6] This came about through the efforts of the foremost prewar music critic, Emile Vuillermoz, who took over Adolphe Brisson's pioneering interest in the cinema.[7] In November 1916, Vuillermoz launched a biweekly column, "Devant l'écran," which soon attracted a wide readership (especially among artists and intellectuals) and which may well have influenced Diamant-Berger and Delluc's transformation of *Le Film*, in the late spring of 1917.[8] Eventually, Delluc took up Vuillermoz's challenge by opening his own weekly column, "Cinéma et cie," in *Paris-Midi*, in May 1918. The extent of his following, despite the paper's relatively small circulation, is reflected in the fact that, by January 1919, Delluc could turn his column, then simply called "Cinéma," into a daily event.[9] In effect, Vuillermoz and Delluc easily dominated the Paris newspaper discourse on the cinema by the end of the war.

In the literary and intellectual reviews, interest in the cinema also increased as the war drew to a close and American films consolidated their dominance on French screens. Most of the magazines gave the cinema only occasional attention—from the radically conservative *L'Action française* and the now well established *Mercure de France* to popular illustrated weeklies such as Hachette's *Lectures pour tous*.[10] Several of the smaller avant-garde journals, however, shared the enthusiasm that Apollinaire's *Les Soirées de Paris* had shown for the cinema before the war. These included Pierre Albert-Birot's *SIC*, Pierre Reverdy's *Nord-Sud*, Jean Galtier-Boissière's nonconformist *Le Crapouillot* (first addressed to infantrymen at the front), *La Rose rouge*, and *Littérature*, the latter edited by the Young Turks, Philippe Soupault, Louis Aragon, and André Breton. And their enthusiasm coincided with the development and proliferation of an original French publishing format, the *film raconté* or ciné-roman, which constituted a new form of the popular *roman-feuilleton* (serial novel).[11] Launched by the mass daily, *Le Matin*, and then bound in book form by La Renaissance du livre, Pierre Decourcelle's serialization of the famous Pearl White serial, *Les Mystères de New York* (1915–1916), proved so immensely popular that *Le Petit Parisien* and *Le Journal* soon were printing weekly installments of other French and American serials—for example, Louis Feuillade's *Judex* (1917) and Henri Pouctal's *Chantecoq* (1917)—and publishers such as Jules Tallandier and Arthème Fayard were rushing out series of ciné-romans for what seemed to be an insatiable market.[12]

The discourse modes that effectively made up the prewar writings on the cinema underwent a radical change in this period. That change came in response to the conditions imposed by the war itself (which altered production, distribution, and exhibition practices)[13] as well as to the polemical attempt to establish the cinema as an art. There was less consideration now of the cinema as a scientific or technological instrument, except when this provided a material or epistemological base for an essentially aesthetic discussion. Interest in the cinema as a medium of information and education remained high, but the subject tended to provoke less debate than before, partly because of the ideological demands of the war. Consequently, the discourse modes that treated the cinema as a spectacle entertainment and as a new art form—whether narrative, descriptive, or non-narrative in construction—now dominated the writings. As Vuillermoz, Delluc, and others reconsidered some of the concepts put in play prior to the war, rethought the relationship between the cinema and the other arts, and, consciously or not, explored the implications of several different competing aesthetic theories with regard to the cinema, they began to focus attention more and more on the raw material or determining features of the new medium as well as on the methods and techniques that might allow it to become an art. In the excitement of discovery and exploration, their ideas often jostled and contradicted one another, but neither they nor their colleagues were all that intent on producing a systematic, coherent theory of the cinema as art. Instead, they used the theoretical or critical essay as a speculative instrument—which soon became a model—to generate or provoke insight, new ideas, and action.

THE INDUSTRY, CENSORSHIP, AND IDEOLOGY

Aesthetic concerns may have been primary to French writers during this period, but they did acknowledge and sometimes critically reflect on the film industry's material conditions and the cinema's social function, given the socio-political context of the war. Repeatedly, the press called attention to and sought ways to overcome various weaknesses in the production, distribution, and exhibition practices of the industry. In *Le Film*, for instance, Diamant-Berger carried out a persistent crusade to address what he and others perceived as a grave crisis threatening the very existence of the French cinema. In March 1917, he launched an extensive survey on the crisis among prominent figures in the industry.[14] In June 1918, he published Charles Pathé's self-serving speech admonishing his colleagues to imitate the American film industry, and he followed that, in September, with a set of similar recommendations of his own.[15] Early in 1919, after a trip to the United States, he published an eight-part series, "Pour sauver le film français."[16] Even Vuillermoz, in *Le Temps*, criticized the poor technical resources of the French film studios, the general poverty of French films (both in quality and quantity), and the failure of the French government to protect its own industry from the flood of American film imports.[17] However,

97

there was no thought of criticizing the basic competitive, capitalistic structure of the French film industry. The writers all seemed to agree on that structure's survival, no matter how vulnerable the industry seemed to the threat of the American cinema's expansion or how much they disagreed on particular production practices, exhibition strategies, and so on. Furthermore, from Pathé to Delluc, his frequent antagonist, no one advocated any kind of governmental assistance for the industry—with the exception of wanting to control film imports. Delluc, in fact, was perfectly willing to let those French companies go under that could not stand up to the competition.

Much less attention was given to the matter of increased government censorship during the war. In June 1916, the Minister of the Interior organized a temporary national Commission du Contrôle des Films, whose principal function was to review the weekly newsreel, *Annales de la guerre*, produced by the army's special film unit.[18] While this new agency was widely accepted, the continued censorship of fiction films—for example, Feuillade's *Les Vampires* (1915-1916) and *Judex* (1917)—by local mayors and police prefects was not.[19] Consequently, when the Minister of the Interior extended the commission's mandate to include fiction films, in May 1917, and then appointed a committee to recommend a national system of regulation for film distribution and exhibition, most writers accepted this as a practical means of protecting the film industry from the vicissitudes of local censorship.[20] In practice, however, the mandate led to cuts and changes in all sorts of films—from Thomas Ince's *Civilization* (1916) to Gance's *Mater Dolorosa* (1917)—and the rejection of visas for Griffith's *Birth of a Nation* (1915) and *Intolerance* (1916).[21] By July 1919, when the government finally established a permanent commission (which included prominent figures from the industry), complaints were beginning to surface again in the press; and Diamant-Berger devoted a whole chapter to attacking the very principle of censorship in his book, *Le Cinéma*.[22]

Politically or ideologically, writers were less divided than one might suppose during the period of the war, and sometimes apparent divisions proved illusory. For convenience, it would be tempting to set up a paradigm of more or less clearcut oppositions—nationalist/internationalist, authoritarian/democratic, rightist/leftist, even classical/modernist—that could distinguish writers and texts. Such a simple paradigm has its usefulness. Many writers, for instance, tend toward the internationalist-democratic-leftist-modernist end of the spectrum, with Delluc certainly the most consistent and vehement spokesman for that position.[23] Yet, under scrutiny, such a paradigm also breaks down or cracks open. For one thing, a writer such as Guillaume Apollinaire, who probably would have fallen into the internationalist camp before the war, now was chauvinistically proclaiming a "new spirit" of lyrical classicism specific to France and encouraging poets to find a way to express that spirit in the new medium of the cinema.[24] Even Delluc himself, despite his international claims—for instance, "Beauty has no fatherland"—and his constant celebration of American films, proselytized as much as anyone for a uniquely French cinema, particularly one that could be distinguished from the American cinema.[25] For another, the one figure who might be said to occupy the polar position opposite Delluc, the contentious Léon Daudet of *Action française*, actually defended the cinema (even the crime serials) against censorship and stressed its international base as an art form.[26] Then again, as shown above, a major tenet of the so-called international position—the prewar dream of an international community predicated on the "universal language" of cinema—blindly ran counter to the wholesale acceptance of a competitive, capitalistic industry, in which the American cinema was fast establishing its hegemony. Ultimately, enough writers and texts slip back and forth across the dividing lines of such a paradigm so as to blur distinctions and raise the question of which distinctions really matter—see, for instance, Marcel Gromaire's synthesis of much of the wartime French thinking on the cinema, in *Le Crapouillot* (1919), in which he returns to a position advocating a classical film art after he has argued cogently and comprehensively for a variety of modernist film forms.[27]

THE HIGH AND LOW ROADS TO FILM ART

While such ideological oppositions turn into a welter of cracks and contradictions in these texts, some of which will resurface later, the "fault lines" separating attacks on and defenses of the cinema per se clearly run along two intersecting tracks. Attacks on the cinema came principally from those—as before, most of them were literary critics—who argued that it lacked certain essential features of the established arts and therefore could never pretend to be art. Paul Souday, who was just beginning to build his reputation as the foremost literary critic of the period, epitomized this position in a front-page article in *Le Temps*, in September 1916. Upholding the attitude of such prewar critics as Doumic and Haugmard and assuming the stance of the conservatives and moderates who wanted to restore the classical traditions of French art as a patriotic strategy during the war, Souday claimed that the rise of the abominable silent dramas of the cinema, especially at the expense of the theater (where the sublime poetry of the word reigned supreme), was "disastrous for the public spirit and taste."[28] Later he even resorted to the prewar argument that the cinema was merely a mechanical copy of reality.[29] Strangely, the young poet and scriptwriter, Marcel L'Herbier, took a similar position in his first important essay on the cinema—the long, convoluted, and contradictory "Hermès et le silence," *Le Film* (April 1918).[30] Neatly separating the arts from the cinema—the one associated with strict rules, the personal expression of genius, the "beautiful lie," the ideal, the absolute; the other linked to reality, chance, mere transcription, the mechanical, the popular or democratic—L'Herbier concluded that the cinema, at least for the moment, was no better than a craft. This kind of elitist, autocratic position, which assumed that the word or verbal language was the supreme medium of human expression, kept a great majority of French writers from taking the cinema seriously well into the 1920s.

Defenses of the cinema ran on two sides of a tangential fault line. Vuillermoz is representative of those who took the high road, perhaps most persuasively in his column lambasting the pseudophilosophical pretensions of L'Herbier, in *Le Temps* (February 1918).[31] There he repeated most of the points first raised by Charles Havermans in 1911 and then catalogued some of the ways that film could become a high art form, by producing "beautiful lies" and "plastic harmonies" as well as expressing thought and feeling. In this defense, he saw himself as a serious critic who was refocusing his considerable skills as a reputable music critic on a new medium and a new art form. From the beginning, Vuillermoz conceived of his task as that of an educator, trying to wean the cinema away from its fairground origins and popular film formats, while offering guidance to individual filmmakers, the general industry, and a rather elite audience. ". . . I plan to examine the lessons offered us by American and Italian filmmakers, whose qualities and faults are so highly distinctive. I will note what our own French films often lack and point out the oddly antiquated ideas about mise-en-scène that hamper the progress of an art which has no past and which is already burdened down with questionable 'traditions.' . . . We must defend the cinema against itself."[32] Vuillermoz did not care to speak to or educate the masses, for, like the actor Armand Bour and others, he distrusted their ability to comprehend film art.[33] In fact, he seems to have shared L'Herbier's initial distaste for the popularizing, democratizing, leveling (Americanizing?) effects of the cinema. If by the end of the war, it had become a "genuine 'night school' for the workers," he noted, the "education" it provided, for the most part, was intellectually tyrannical, emotionally intoxicating, and ultimately enslaving.[34] What the sociologist Gabriel Tarde might have seen as a prime example of his concept of modern commodities generating positive models of imitation (imitative behavior taking place in a semiconscious state), Vuillermoz saw clearly as exploitation.[35] But his answer was to turn away and recommend the institution of a special subscribers-only cinema, modelled on the elite theaters, whose carefully selected program would appeal to a cultured clientele of connoisseurs.[36]

Somewhat like Yhcam before the war and despite his own literary background, Delluc took the low road in his defense of the cinema, reversing the poles of the high art/low art hierarchy, just as he rejected the chauvinism of his countrymen's wartime patriotism. Throughout the war, of course, he maintained that the cinema was an international art and became the leading French advocate of the artistry of American films.[37] And that advocacy was shared by many young writers—see especially Philippe Soupault's marvelous description of how he and his friends discovered the American cinema during the war.[38] In contrast to Vuillermoz and in terms that may have linked him to the radical wing of the French Naturalist movement—and the anarchist writer, Octave Mirbeau—Delluc celebrated the cinema as a popular art: it offered an unusually direct medium of expression and communication among peoples.[39] Indeed, he refused even to consider himself a critic, at least in the traditional sense. "I learned long ago not to want to do the work of a critic; I am neither heedless nor shrewd enough to assert the faults and failures of a spectacle. Let me limit myself to noting when I am satisfied or bored. . . . It is from the crowd actually that I gather the best impressions and the clearest judgments."[40] Besides the mock modesty of personal taste, the source of Delluc's authority lay not so much in an aesthetic or moral standard but in the audience, the crowd. And what he meant by the crowd can be gathered from one of his early columns in *Paris-Midi*, in August 1918, where Delluc confessed that his favorite cinemas were not the elegant bourgeois cinemas of west Paris and the boulevards but those in the working-class quarters and especially a little one near the Gare de l'Est, thronged by "mechanics, pimps, laborers, and women warehouse packers."[41] The spectators there delighted him "not only because of their silence and attention but because of their acuteness, taste, and insight," particularly with regard to American films. "What the crowd thinks of a dramatic film, a piece of clowning, or a newsreel," he concluded, echoing Mirbeau, "is an education. And what is more pressing to recognize, a source of information."[42] Instead of educating the masses, as someone like Gromaire expected of the cinema, Delluc was receiving an education from them. His weekly and then daily film reviews in *Paris-Midi*, therefore, can be seen as an attempt to speak *for* and *to* a mass public (including the working class), to offer a forum (mediated, of course) for the circulation of public opinion. Yet Delluc displayed a rather naive faith in the unorganized power of the spectator as consumer (whether working class or not), seemingly unaware of such organized institutions as the consumer cooperatives (founded by Charles Gide), which by then had become a real force in French society.[43]

Whatever their position on the high art/low art hierarchy, and some like Jacques de Baroncelli hesitated humorously between the two, writer after writer echoed the call first articulated before the war for the cinema to become a new form of art.[44] Diamant-Berger, for instance, conceived of the cinema initially as "a new formula . . . dependent on neither books nor the theater," a formula that was still not fully recognized.[45] Colette, his first regular film reviewer for *Le Film*, considered her critical work a witness to "the crude *ciné*'s groping toward perfection"; and her review of De Mille's *The Cheat* (1915) turned the Omnia-Pathé cinema, where it was playing in July and August 1916, into a veritable "art school" to which writers, painters, and dramatists flocked like students.[46] Vuillermoz saw that "the art of the cinema had reached that stage in its technical development where all of its potential seemed in reach of being realized," and he determined to discover, and explain, how "the luminous screen . . . was a magnificent window opening out onto life and dream! . . ."[47] And several writers now were taking up the call to create a repertory of the best films, which could be available for continual rescreening.[48] Perhaps Delluc summed up this advocacy position best in one of his several professions of faith: "We are witnessing the birth of an extraordinary art. The only truly modern art perhaps, assured already of its place and one day soon of astonishing glory, because it is simultaneously and uniquely the offspring of both technology and human ideals."[49] Furthermore, "everything having to do with method, material, and technique in the cinema," Delluc admitted, was still in the process of being discovered.[50] Instead of developing the concept of film as a synthesis of the other arts, which had been prominent prior to the war and which some writers such as Apollinaire and Guillaume Danvers still were trying to promulgate,[51] most now sought further to delineate its uniqueness, particularly but not exclusively as a narrative art.

A SPECTRUM OF NARRATIVE FILM THEORIES

By this time, all agreed with Adolphe Brisson's prewar contention that the cinema differed radically from the theater; and they repeatedly condemned the French film industry for continuing to rely on theatrical conventions, especially for their actors whose artificial poses looked ridiculous compared to the natural spontaneity of American actors. This condemnation assumed a form of French narrative film that dominated the war period, largely through the production and distribution output of Pathé, and yet, like the serial, had no apologists among the writers.[52] Its contours can be gathered negatively from the writings of Vuillermoz, Delluc, Bour, André Antoine, and others. The subject of these films tended to be recent melodramas and "thesis plays" written for the theater, sometimes adapted by their authors and performed by noted stage actors and actresses.[53] Intertitles served to generate and develop the narrative (the word still carried authority), while the images functioned as "illustrations" and performance "turns," seeking to express the melodramatic excess beyond language. And scenes tended to be shot in studios, using flimsy theatrical decors, with the camera positioned at a ninety-degree angle to the actors in a "stage" space. Such films, critics agreed, were simply cheap, short-lived, usually cut-down versions of current literary works in circulation. Underlying their critique, however, were crucial questions—which Gromaire set out most clearly—the answers to which the writers did not agree on at all.[54] If it was not merely an adjunct to the theater (or novel), exactly what form and function should this new art take? What were its characteristic features, and how could they be shaped and controlled to create art? The spectrum of answers provided by French writing on the cinema coalesced into four or five major conceptions of narrative film art.

What can be considered the "progressive" mainstream industry position during this period developed in response to these film adaptations as well as to the impact of the American cinema. This position is expressed most tellingly in the few, but influential, pronouncements of Charles Pathé and the extensive writings of Henri Diamant-Berger, particularly as summed up in Le Cinéma (1919).[55] The first principle was that a film told a story and hence the author—that is, the person most responsible for the film as a work of art—was the scenarist or scriptwriter.[56] "The scenario," said Diamant-Berger categorically, "is the film itself as it will be recorded on the filmstock."[57] The primary text, therefore, as in the theater, strangely enough, was the script or scenario; yet instead of adaptations, Diamant-Berger seemed to prefer original scenarios stressing action. The director's task, again as in the theater, was to execute the scenario in such a way as to respect the author's intentions. To this task, Pathé added the demands of overseeing the production budget and setting the shooting schedule; the director's only allowance for change occurred in the editing process, and that was minimal—to detail or emphasize a gesture or an emotional effect. Interestingly, Vuillermoz, among others, also tended to accept the scenario as the primary text—see, for instance, his review of Gance's La Dixième Symphonie (1918).[58] There was a counter-claim, however, to which Delluc, for one, sometimes became attached: the filmmaker—particularly if he were an Ince, a Griffith, a De Mille, or even a L'Herbier—was the real author of the film.[59] And this, in embryo, became the first French conception of a politique des auteurs. That the French hesitated in deciding between these two claims can be measured by the fact that the Société des auteurs des films, which was organized officially in late 1917, included both script-writers and directors in its membership.[60]

Much like their counterparts in the American film industry, Pathé and Diamant-Berger focused their attention, respectively, on the subject of the scenario and on the construction of the decoupage or shooting script. For Pathé, of course, the French cinema's woes stemmed from a "crisis of the scenario."[61] His solution called for choosing subjects that would appeal to "Anglo-Saxon" spectators (to regain an American audience), which meant abandoning situations and feelings specific to the French. In effect, as Vuillermoz, Delluc, and others complained, this would turn the French cinema into a poor country cousin of the American cinema.[62] For Diamant-Berger, who seemed a bit more independent, the answer lay in a careful, meticulous crafting of the decoupage, using a central idea, a dramatic framework, and a detailed psychology of characters to produce a classical narrative construction of exposition, development, and denouement.[63] In this decoupage (for which he offered an exemplary model), the *shot* formed the basic unit of narrative action, emotion, and meaning. Although he understood that the sense of any one shot or scene depended on its context among other shots or scenes, that context was narrowly defined in exclusively narrative terms. To control the flow of action and feeling, as well as the spectator's pace of comprehension (so that *everything* was intelligible), he advocated a general rule of conveying "only one impression per shot" and ending the shot "as soon as the impression is perceived."[64] Among several suggestions for handling these shots and their interrelation, Diamant-Berger cautioned—much as Yhcam had before the war—against the overuse of closeups, except where they were justified by the narrative. This caution seems to have been shared by others and suggests there was a generally held classical French attitude of moderation and balance in opposition to a perceived sense of American exuberance and disorder. See Colette, for instance, when she singled out for criticism the emerging shot/reverse shot convention in American films: "the technique that separates two speakers of a dialogue, that projects them each in turn in huge close-ups, just when it is important to compare their faces together."[65] Or see Armand Bour, who was disturbed by the overly hectic pace of American crosscutting or parallel editing.[66] What is significant in Diamant-Berger's position, however, is the value he attached to editing, to the shot-by-shot or moment-by-moment construction of a story, which is completely clear in the measured, relentless advance of its action. Almost alone among French writers of the period, he focused exclusively, rigorously, on narrative and offered a clearcut mainstream French position against which others could define themselves.

Parallel with Pathé and Diamant-Berger's advocacy of a narrative cinema only slightly different from the American, there developed a second position (superceding that of Feuillade and Jasset before the war) out of the Realist tradition in French art and literature. Its chief proponent was the famous theater director turned filmmaker, André Antoine, seconded, but not uncritically, by Louis Delluc. For Antoine, too, the cinema was a narrative art, but its overriding aim—as with his earlier theatrical productions—was to convince the spectator of the verisimilitude of the spaces and actions represented on the screen.[67] Accordingly, perhaps in imitation of Pathé's pronouncement to his company employees, he set out a number of principles to accomplish this. First, like Yhcam, he called for the formation of a special troupe of actors, unattached to the theater, who would learn "to act solely by means of their intrinsic nature and external appearance." Next he advocated the use of real locations for decors to counter the French film industry's reliance on ill-suited theatrical sets and costumes in the old glass studios. Technological advances such as the mobile electrical generator now made this more practical than ever before.[68] And, perhaps most importantly, he stressed the need for multiple camera set-ups: the actors would perform as if they were living in their location decors, and the camera (which they would ignore) would "follow them step by step and catch all their aspects unawares, from whichever side they presented."[69] On the one hand, this implied a mobile camera and a documentary-like style of filmmaking; on the other, it assumed that the realism of a specific scene was a rhetorical construction of multiple shots and constantly changing perspectives in the editing. Accepting Diamant-Berger's concept of narrative construction, which depended on a clear flow of action, Antoine went on to emphasize the accretion of details and multiple perspectives for atmosphere and sustained verisimilitude. It was as if he were announcing the founding of a *plein air* school of filmmaking, in memory of the celebrated *plein air* school of painting depicted in Emile Zola's novel, *L'Oeuvre* (1896).

Out of Delluc's reviews of Antoine's and others' films emerged a variation on this realist narrative cinema. Interestingly, Delluc criticized Antoine's own film practice—in *Les Frères corses* (1917) and *Le Coupable* (1917)—precisely according to the first two of these principles.[70] His actors, for instance, "had not yet forgotten their Conservatory training," especially in the exterior scenes. Furthermore, Delluc considered the stories Antoine chose for his films too convoluted and literary for his purposes and contrary to his own nature. Although he thought *Les Frères corses* one of the best French films of the war, he found its scenario "unwieldy in structure." Delluc himself advocated simple, original narratives—for instance, the bitter, brutal tales of Thomas Ince films or the simple, bleak stories of Scandinavian films such as Victor's Sjöstrom's *The Outlaw and His Wife* (1918).[71] Ultimately, for him, the story was just one of several ordinary events or incidents, but one given a privileged status, within a specific natural or social milieu. Such narratives, he argued—along with Baroncelli,

Bour, and Gromaire—would eliminate the need for intertitles and rely, perhaps exclusively, on the images to develop the story.[72] And Delluc went Antoine one better by recommending that real people—"peasants, soldiers, charwomen, milkmaids, railway workers"—should be used, not just as extras, but as important actors in the cinema.

> Ah, how I wish [Antoine] had a story of his own, a vivid, original modern scenario. . . .
>
> Perhaps a story of workers or, better yet, peasants. He would go to the country, into the real countryside, where he could capture life as it really exists, in the very act of shooting. Perhaps the heroes of his story would play themselves. I would like a peasant to be played by a peasant.[73]

For an example of what he meant, see his praise for Henry Roussel's use of local people in the first half of *L'Ame du bronze* (1918).[74] In Delluc's notes and suggestions, then, there emerged a notion of film narrative grounded in the pro-filmic realism of a particular milieu and perfectly "legible" in its actions alone.[75]

A fourth conception of narrative cinema developed in tandem with the progressive mainstream and the two realist positions. In line with Yhcam's prewar speculations, here the cinema served as a medium for the expression of the subjective, the interior life of a character, as an integral part of the narrative—a possibility which Diamant-Berger and Antoine explicitly denied. Although the rightist literary critic, Léon Daudet, touched on this notion in 1916, in an article in *Action française*,[76] it was Vuillermoz, with his training in Symbolist aesthetics, who acted as its chief proponent throughout the war period. Paradoxically, he found evidence of the subjective in the editing patterns of Antoine's first film, *Les Frères corses*. What especially impressed him were the smooth, almost magical transitions in the fiction (through dissolves and fades) between one time period and another, between a present reality and a past memory or fantasy. More generally, he was mesmerized by Antoine's skill in being able "to enliven his drama with quick glimpses, allusions, echoes, inferences, forebodings, memories, hallucinations, and dreams; to illuminate it with fugitive suggestions analogous to the flashes of mental associations which traverse our imagination and multiply its creative power tenfold."[77] This same miraculous power of evocation was confirmed for him later in Baroncelli's *Le Roi de la mer* (1917) and Gance's *La Dixième Symphonie* (1918).[78] The latter's "ingenious visual and emotional transposition of the andante and scherzo of the [hero's new] symphony" Vuillermoz even envisioned as "an exploration of the subconscious."[79] Here the technological means of the cinema apparatus served to represent an interior as well as an exterior reality, in a fiction in which memory, dream, or fantasy could interpenetrate and even determine the narrative action. So impassioned was Vuillermoz's defense of *cinégraphie* as a new Symbolist mode of subjective expression that his attack on L'Herbier even persuaded the young poet of its validity. In the conclusion to a short dialogue that he offered as a preface to his first film, *Rose-France* (1919), L'Herbier defended "the cinegraphic representation of a succession of actions and reactions, that is, of dramatic gestures and images representing the dreams or reflections which those gestures have provoked in the hero of the *drama* . . . so far as it expresses . . . the active and passive visage of life. . . ."[80] He had become one of the cinema's first acolytes of an expressive, subjective aesthetics.

THE EMERGENCE OF PHOTOGÉNIE

The realist and subjectivist "blueprints" for a narrative film art intersect with and are determined, in part, by a rather different conception of the cinema that seems to have been of unusual interest in France and that laid the groundwork for the later theoretical work of André Bazin.[81] In this conception, the object of attention shifted from action and narration to description or representation.[82] In other words, the focus turned from temporal progression to spatial composition or mise-en-scène. Why was description or representation in the cinema so important to the French? Certainly there was a fascination for visual spectacle per se, to which both Delluc and Bour, for instance, attest in their critiques of repeated tour-de-force lighting effects. But there seems to have been a more important reason, at least for the writers. This came from the power of representation as a means to knowledge, a power that had generated a good deal of scientific as well as artistic experimentation in Europe since at least the later Renaissance.[83] For French writings on the cinema, this cognitive power was located in the new apparatus of the camera and, by extension, the projector and screen. Some evidence of this can be seen in the continuing French fascination during the war for short scientific films and newsreels. Even in the fiction films, however, it was nature or reality—as a subject of meditation, in the Romantic tradition—and not the story or the author's intentions or emotions that served as the basic raw material in this conception of the cinema. Here, then, the camera functioned as a mediator between the spectator and a certain reality or "world" and as an instrument of revelation.[84] Furthermore, it positioned the spectator before that mediated reality—to use Michael Fried's terms analyzing eighteenth-century French painting—as both there and not there, in a state of rapt attention or absorption.[85] For description, as Roland Barthes notes, "has its spiritual equivalent in contemplation."[86] This essentially pre-narrative or a-narrative conception of the cinema assumed several different forms in French texts, some of which meshed harmoniously with a framework of film narrative and others of which were more or less disruptive of that framework.

On the matter of mise-en-scène and the camera/spectator's relation to actors and natural decors in particular, Vuillermoz and Delluc's reflections again were representative of two different lines of thinking, the latter of which gradually assumed more and more significance. Vuillermoz's attachment to a Symbolist aesthetic again governed his thinking here. The camera, for instance, turned certain actors into "astral bodies" whose essence was delivered up to the spectator in a direct, intimate, and profound encounter—"as absolute gift."[87] This intimacy was comfortable for the masses, Vuillermoz believed, because these stars became "friends" to follow through different adventures. And the pleasure elicited by this new star/spectator bond was one of the chief reasons for the cinema's "mysterious attraction." Vuillermoz himself was more interested, however, in the cinema's mission of discovering and revealing "the spirit of things." Initially, this seemed to him to depend on the camera itself, as if it were a magical instrument of revelation almost free of human agency. "The thirst for the real," he wrote, "must extend to believing in the religion of things, to the discovery of their soul, to seeing a sort of secret pantheism which animates the greatest painters and sculptors."[88] The philosophical basis for this mission Vuillermoz found in Henri Bergson, whose theory of art seemed "a perfect apologia for *cinégraphie*." If "Art has no other aim than to brush aside . . . everything that masks reality from us in order to position us face to face with reality itself," he quoted Bergson as saying, then the cinema indeed was the Fifth Art because its "eye . . . cuts out of space and fixes in time inimitable images; [it] seizes in flight and immortalizes the fleeting moment when nature possesses genius. . . ."[89] On the screen, he concluded, in a phrase that would often be repeated in French texts, "a landscape is a state of mind." Eventually, Vuillermoz settled for a more expressive position, congruent with his concept of a subjective narrative cinema: this was effected not by the camera alone but also by the filmmaker, who had to become a poet. For it was he who "transforms, recreates, and transfigures nature, according to his emotional state . . . , concentrates all the force of feeling or thought onto an inanimate object, . . . imposes his personal vision of beings and things on thousands of spectators. . . ."[90] "The image," L'Herbier would add pithily, "is no more than the epiphany of an imagination."[91]

Delluc sometimes shared Vuillermoz's thinking, especially when he was caught up—as were most of his colleagues—in an idealist language when dealing with representation in the cinema. In his early essays, for instance, Delluc tended to define the destiny of the cinema as providing the spectator

"with impressions of evanescent beauty" and as training him "to see [anew]
into nature and the human heart."[92] But his observations on actors and natural landscapes, perhaps following Baroncelli, soon broke away to open up
another perspective. He too tried to account for the new phenomenon of
the film star, particularly the American film star. His marvelous descrip-
tions of Sessue Hayakawa, Charlie Chaplin, William S. Hart, and others
"mythologized" them as masks or personae transcending any one specific
film or story—". . . of Hayakawa one can say nothing: he is a phenomenon. . . . The beauty of Sessue Hayakawa is painful. Few things in the cinema can reveal to us, as the light and silence of this mask do, that there
really are *alone* beings."[93] In contrast to Vuillermoz, then, Delluc perceived
these extraordinary creatures, not as characters within the context of a continuity system dependent on the shot/reverse shot convention and on point-
of-view shots, but rather as seemingly detached mirror images for the spectator that disturbed as much as they delighted. For in them, particularly
the images of male actors, he discovered an essentially modern human condition, of suffering and unspoken alienation. The cinema's power of representation turned on a male-oriented, quasi-psychoanalytical system of
looking—to be developed further by Jean Epstein—which led Delluc to a
poignantly pessimistic form of self-knowledge.[94]

In a different mood, Delluc also began to single out and celebrate the
revelatory description of natural landscapes or milieux for having a significance of their own as well as providing the generative matrix out of which
an original story could evolve.[95] In Baroncelli's *Le Retour aux champs* (1918),
for instance, he perceived "a profound sense of atmosphere" in certain
scenes, whose images evoked "all the poetry of a rustic evening" and where
"silent things" in isolation became radiantly alive.[96] By early 1919, he was
advocating that Baroncelli's *Ramuntcho* (1919) be taken as a study or sketch
for that "animated impressionism which [he hoped would] become characteristic of the French cinema."[97] And by the end of the year, several Scandinavian films seemed to confirm his thinking—witness how Delluc called
attention to "the barren mountain landscapes" and "desert-like snow" of
Sjöstrom's *The Outlaw and His Wife*.[98] Drawing implicitly on French
Impressionist painting and French Realist and Naturalist fiction, Delluc
saw that the cinema, too, could represent nature simply and honestly—
"screened" not through a temperament but through the apparatus of the
camera—and thus become the site of an exercise in perception and reflection.[99] Through Delluc, then, and to a lesser extent Antoine, the term
impressionism came to refer to an almost painterly way of emphasizing the
revelatory representation of natural landscapes (and their Frenchness) on
film, above and beyond the demands of the narrative.

Delluc's interest in the uniqueness of the film image and the mediating power of the camera/screen led to one of the most widely circulated concepts in French texts throughout the silent period—*photogénie*. For all its later diffuseness and polyvalence, and its seminal importance for the later theories of André Bazin and Jean Mitry,[100] several things seem clear about Delluc's initial use of the term. It assumed that the "real" (the factual, the natural) was the basis of film representation and signification. But it also assumed that the "real" was transformed by the camera/screen, which, without eliminating that "realness," changed it into something radically new. "The miracle of the cinema," Delluc wrote, "is that it stylizes without altering the plain truth."[101] And that transformation or stylization was facilitated by several features of the camera and its associated technical components—especially framing, lighting, and mise-en-scène relations within the frame. Delluc came to this concept through the observations of his colleagues as well as his own perceptions—for example, Colette's appreciation of the "still life" images (shots empty of actors) and certain close-ups of Emmy Lynn in Gance's *Mater Dolorosa* (1917), Soupault's celebration of the cinema as a totally new means of perception, and his own discoveries about film star presences.[102] But the effect of *photogénie* was singular: to make us *see ordinary things* as they had never been seen before. "We believe," said Jean Cocteau, "we are seeing them for the first time."[103] To borrow a term from the Russian Formalists, *photogénie* defamiliarized the familiar. Interestingly, Delluc and others linked this notion of the cinema's power, not to photography, as one might have expected, but to painting and poetry.[104] In this conventionally disparaging view of photography, a contradictory note of elitism crept into the French writings. The photograph might share the "real" or "authentic" as a basis of representation with the cinema, but it lacked movement and life and, supposedly, the power of transformation, which the cinema instead shared with modern painting and poetry. The images of the factory in Roussel's *L'Ame du bronze* (1918), for instance, reminded Delluc of the poetry of Charles Baudelaire and the Belgian anarchist poet, Emile Verhaeren.[105] A Fairbanks film had ". . . the new force of modern poetry, the real thing, what you glimpse on the street in a face, in a sign, in a color, everywhere and incessantly, and what a film-maker can isolate expressively. Landscapes, horses, dogs, furniture, glasses, a staircase, a lamp, a hand, a jewel—everything assumes a fantastic nature. And true!"[106] Aesthetic creation in the cinema, consequently, depended not on subjective invention but on the impassive camera eye's discovery of the new within the already given.

In his first published essay, "Du Décor," which Delluc solicited for *Le Film* (September 1918), Louis Aragon pushed the perceptions behind the notion of *photogénie* even further. First of all, selected objects or parts of the decor could become "remotivated" and meaningful in relation to a figure such as Chaplin, simply within the mise-en-scène of a shot or scene. "The set is Charlot's vision of the world, and the discovery of its mechanics and laws haunts the hero to the point where, by an inversion of values, any inanimate object for him becomes a living thing and any person a mannequin whose starting crank he must seek out."[107] A similar process of transformation occurred, Delluc noted, in the films of William S. Hart.[108] More importantly, Aragon focused on the way film could isolate and magnify objects through framing, especially in close-ups, and then re-position them through editing. Such close-ups were thus stripped of the exclusively narrative function that Diamant-Berger assigned to them. Much like the prewar collage art of Picasso, Braque, and Gris, Aragon argued provocatively, American films—Pearl White serials as well as Chaplin comedies—isolated and recontextualized scraps or fragments of daily life.[109] These image-objects were "transformed to the point where they took on menacing or enigmatic meanings."[110] And the pleasure of these transformations and re-positionings, the poet Pierre Reverdy added, depended on the intensity and duration of the surprise they elicited.[111] In one sense then, for Delluc, Aragon, Reverdy, and later Gromaire, the power of *photogénie* seemed able to create access to a completely new world of mystery, quite different from Vuillermoz's fantastic pantheistic world. In another sense, it countered the classical aesthetic of coherence and unity in an artistic work, which dominated the majority of French writings on the cinema, by privileging the play of discontinuity at all levels of the text. Disruptive of space and time, story and spectacle, *photogénie* contained the potential for a modernist aesthetic.

THE SPECTRUM OF NON-NARRATIVE FILM THEORIES

The French writers' tendency to focus on unusually expressive, revelatory, or disruptive moments in the cinema complemented and fueled their speculations on the possibility of organizing or patterning an entire film according to principles that were other than narrative. In one of the most influential of these speculations, Vuillermoz—the former music student of Gabriel Fauré—perceived the cinema as a form of musical composition. Where others such as Baroncelli, Colette, and Danvers anticipated the eventual collaboration or integration of film and musical accompaniment,[112] Vuillermoz excitedly pursued the implications of the analogy he had discovered between cinematic and musical composition. ". . . it is exactly like a symphony! The cinema orchestrates images, scores our visions and memories according to a strictly musical process: it must choose its visual themes, render them expressive, meticulously regulate their exposition, their opportune return, their measure and rhythm, develop them, break them down into parts, reintroduce them in fragments, as the treatises on composition put it, through 'augmentation' and 'diminution' . . ."[113] Vuillermoz especially praised Antoine's films for their "subtleties and ingenuities of editing." *Le Coupable* (1917), for instance, he described as a symphony (not wholly successful) in which the images "of the great, grim maternal city" of Paris created an accompaniment of "deep and moving bass chords" to the "brave, noble melody" of the drama.[114] Here Vuillermoz seemed to assume that the sense or impression of a shot or sequence of shots was sustained through a scene just as a note or chord once struck could last through several bars of music. Similarly, Griffith's *Intolerance* overcame its many narrative and philosophical defects as a cinegraphic composition of visual rhythm. Griffith knew instinctively, he wrote, how "to harmonize his plastic phrases, to calculate their melodic curve, their echoes, and their breaks"; thus "his luminous phrases possessed a deliberate trajectory, and their cadence was timed to the exact second."[115] It was this visual rhythm and its emotional effect, Vuillermoz argued, as Survage had just before the war, that worked on the spectator as much as, if not more than, the logical and emotional development of a particular film narrative. And he took to designating the filmmaker, in terms later appropriated by Abel Gance and others, as a composer or conductor of "symphonies of light."[116]

Several others modes of organization emerged that could also work in tandem with narrative. Contradicting some of his previous advocacy positions, Delluc, for instance, demanded a "lyrical" form of film, "stylized in its material form and symbolic in its subject."[117] A central idea should govern the shape of such a film, of course, but it would be articulated symbolically or connotatively through the *photogenic* becoming *cinematic*—that is, being deployed systematically over the course of a film. Although only sketchily developed, some sense of what Delluc meant can be gathered from his reviews of Baroncelli, Gance, and L'Herbier films. Baroncelli's *Le Roi de la mer* he criticized for failing "to stress the symbolic note"—there were not enough exterior images of Far East and Far West harbors regularly inserted to set off and emphasize the intimate scenes in the single interior space.[118] What Vuillermoz considered as musical counterpoint in Antoine, Delluc conceived as symbolic or poetic counterpoint in Baroncelli. The two critics clashed interestingly—almost as classical versus modern—on the specifics of the symbolic process in Gance's *La Dixième Symphonie*. Whereas Vuillermoz praised the symbolic "correspondance" between the film's "dream landscapes" and the music of the hero's symphony (making visible "the music of the soul"), Delluc criticized this as a retrograde rhetorical strategy in which Gance overlaid conventional symbolic figures (drawn from literature and art) onto images from which emanated a "natural" *pho-*

togénie.[119] By contrast, despite the slightness of its story and the weakness of its actors, Delluc praised L'Herbier's *Rose-France* for the fluid poetic harmony of its framing and editing patterns.[120] This praise reciprocated L'Herbier's own conversion, at the end of "Hermès et le silence," to a similar conception of "lyrical" or "symbolic" cinema grounded in the factual, which he shored up with the help of the democratic spirit of Walt Whitman and the pragmatism of William James, filtered through his characteristic erudite palimpsest of discourses.[121]

This "synthetic" film form—with its indexical and symbolic "language," its parallel or counterpointed narrative and symbolic trajectories—constituted one solution, as Delluc and others saw it (redefining Canudo), to the problem of creating a cinema that would appeal to both a mass and elite audience. Apollinaire's famous speech at the Théâtre de Vieux-Colombier, on 26 November 1917, in which he encouraged his fellow poets to work in the cinema, may well have kicked off a concerted effort by a loosely related group of writers to produce just such a film form.[122] In collaboration with André Billy, Apollinaire himself was then finishing up an original scenario, *La Bréhatine*, whose melodramatic storyline catered to a recent fad for "Breton" films.[123] Philippe Soupault soon began to experiment in writing short scenarios and a hybrid form of cinematic poetry, one of which, "Indifference," was published in *SIC*, January 1918.[124] In response to what seemed to be French film industry resistance—the Apollinaire-Billy and Soupault scripts remained unfilmed; L'Herbier's poetic script for Mercanton and Hervil's *Le Torrent* (1917) was much changed in production—Delluc suggested that scenarios evidencing an unusual degree of "lyricism" ought to be published as a new kind of literary text.[125] And he himself inaugurated the practice, in the spring of 1918, by having *Le Film* publish L'Herbier's original scenario for Mercanton and Hervil's *Bouclette* (1918) and Gance's initial draft of a scenario for *J'Accuse* (1919).[126] Shortly thereafter, when they, too, ran into problems with film industry rejections, Blaise Cendrars, Pierre Albert-Birot, and Jules Romains all published original film scripts as a new form of prose narrative.[127] In contrast to the popular *films racontés* or ciné-romans, which tended to subdue and stabilize a film's sequence of images and close off its meaning, these scenarios constituted a new textual form of play in which the writers sought to recover and redeploy, in verbal language, what they most admired in the cinema—the transformation of the ordinary and the everyday through surprising juxtapositions and marvelous metamorphoses.[128]

Inklings of an exclusively poetic composition in the cinema were evident in Aragon and Reverdy, who mused briefly on the implications of juxtaposing disparate images.[129] But it was Vuillermoz, strangely enough, who first articulated the idea of a radical collage/montage construction most clearly. Again, in one of his initial columns, he singled out, explicitly for poets, one of the most marvelous features of the cinema. "This ability to juxtapose, within several seconds, on the same luminous screen, images which generally are isolated in time or space, this power (hitherto reserved to the human imagination) to leap from one end of the universe to the other, to draw together antipodes, to mesh thoughts far removed from one another, to compose, as one fancies, a ceaselessly changing mosaic out of millions of scattered facets of the tangible world . . . all this could permit a poet to realize his most ambitious dreams. . . ."[130] And in his review of Antoine's *Les Frères corses*, Vuillermoz even suggested that the rapid, multiple, shifting combinations and juxtapositions of images on film might function as a visual form of Apollinaire's *simultanéism* in poetry.[131] As an exclusive means of organization for film, the collage aesthetic of prewar French poetry could synthesize the isolated, disparate, transformed fragments of everyday life and give pattern to their disruptive power through the montage of a "simultaneous present." Vuillermoz himself unexpectedly dropped this idea to exploit his musical analogy and actually regressed to a rather conventional sense of the symbolic. But *simultanéism* reappeared just after the war in texts by Cocteau and Cendrars. Both advocated the exploitation of certain unique features of film—for instance, varied perspectives, variable speed recording, and rapid cutting—as essential rhythmic components of the creation of a "simultaneist poetry" in the cinema.[132] And Cendrars's visionary meditation on the new art read like an attempt to fuse film and poetry into a single collage form of discourse. From there it was only a short step to the earliest writings of Jean Epstein.

Finally, the aesthetic of a formal or "plastic" composition, which Survage had pioneered before the war, reemerged in the postwar writings of Gromaire and Albert-Birot.[133] Here the raw material of the cinema lay in the graphic elements of the image or shot—as a "plastic sign"—and in the rhythmic ordering of those elements.[134] A painter who saw himself as the locus of Impressionist, Futurist, and Cubist influences, Gromaire developed this position with unusual thoroughness, to the point of celebrating the cinema as an autonomous art. Each shot or image would function as an abstraction synthesizing the elements of color (light), line and form, and movement. Through the sequential combination, superimposition, and juxtaposition of shots in the editing, however, the whole film would operate as an analytical structure of unexpected "plastic" discoveries or surprises. To produce this kind of cinema, Albert-Birot recommended a strategy that owed a good deal to Gustave Flaubert and would gain wide currency in the 1920s. The filmmaker would choose the most banal subject possible in order to foreground and explore such features as superimposition, slow motion, fast motion, and rapid cutting. While Gromaire never advocated a film form that was completely abstract—like his colleagues, he always tied it to the representation of reality, to narrative, and to human emotion—he did suggest a number of unique strategies to exploit the "plastic" elements of the cinema. These ranged from a rather conventional symbolic condensation of *King Lear* to special animated cartoons as well as projects that combined photographs and drawings or paintings—a different way of relating the real and the stylized. In the end, his exuberant playfulness and freewheeling speculation led Gromaire, like Delluc (in substance if not in tone), to imagine this as a means of creating a rich and beautiful as well as useful art for the masses.

CONCLUSION

Several things should be clear from this synoptic analysis of French writings on the cinema during the war years. Certainly, Vuillermoz, Delluc, and, to a lesser extent, Diamant-Berger established and directed the basic parameters of discussion. And they did so in response to a whole series of American films as well as to selected works by Antoine, Gance, Baroncelli, Roussel, and L'Herbier. Despite, or perhaps because of, his high-art stance, Vuillermoz advanced and defended a number of key concepts: the cinema was an *expressive* medium for the *subjective* (whether the inner life of a fictional character or that of the filmmaker himself); and it was a construction that could be organized or orchestrated (in parallel with its narrative development) as a poetic mosaic, or, more importantly for him, as a *musical composition*. While he shared some of Vuillermoz's positions, Delluc played the advocate for several different ideas. The cinema was a *photogenic* or *revelatory* medium of absorption and defamiliarization, whether it focused on inanimate objects, faces, or landscapes—and the latter representation he came to celebrate as *impressionism*. At the same time, it was a construction in which the *photogénie* of the image (symbolic as well as indexical, connotative as well as denotative) could be deployed *poetically* in parallel with the narrative. A number of others writers—especially Aragon, Cendrars, and Gromaire—then extended those parameters to include modernist conceptions of the cinema as an exclusively *poetic* or *plastic composition*. Against Diamant-Berger's conception of a French variant on the American narrative cinema, consequently, there emerged a broad spectrum of possible French forms of both a narrative and a non-narrative cinema. Although the writers generally eschewed questioning the basic economic structure of the film industry as well as advocating any explicit social commitment, this spectrum of theoretical speculation did stand more or less in opposition to the Classical Renaissance tendency, which, by then, was dominating French culture, and certainly evidenced a valiant struggle to include the cinema within the most "advanced" thinking going on in the arts. French writing on the cinema during and after the war, therefore, seems to have put in place much of the conceptual basis for the production and exhibition practices of the French avant-garde during the 1920s.

1. Claude Bellanger, Jacques Godechot, Pierre Guiral, and Fernand Terrou, *Histoire générale de la presse française*, vol. 3, *De 1871 à 1940* (Paris: Presses universitaires de France, 1972), 408–23.

2. *Ciné-Journal* resumed publication on a biweekly basis and then returned to a weekly format in October 1915.

3. G.-Michel Coissac, "Le Cinématographe: Son passé, son présent, son avenir," *Annuaire général de la cinématographie française et étrangère* (Paris: Ciné-Journal, 1918), 457–507.

4. La Renaissance du livre was one of the more prominent publishing houses in Paris at the time. Established in 1893, it had recently become a "mass market" firm with its Modern Bibliothèque and Livre Populaire series. Bernard Grasset had entered publishing just ten years before Delluc's book appeared, and his novels were already winning Prix Goncourt awards by 1911 and 1912. See André Billy, *L'Epoque contemporaine, 1905–1930* (Paris: Jules Tallandier, 1956), 129–30; and Regis Debray, *Teachers, Writers, Celebrities: The Intellectuals of Modern France*, trans. David Macey (London: New Left Books, 1981), 61, 64–66.

5. For information on the importation of American films into France during the war, see Richard Abel, *French Cinema: The First Wave, 1915–1929* (Princeton: Princeton University Press, 1984), 10–12, and Kristin Thompson, *Exporting Entertainment: America in the World Film Market, 1907–1934* (London: British Film Institute, 1985), 71–74, 85–90.

6. The circulation figures for these three dailies, in November 1917, were as follows: *Le Gaulois*, 22,000; *Excelsior*, 132,000; *Le Temps*, 58,500—Bellanger et al., *Histoire générale de la presse française*, vol. 3, 428.

7. Emile Vuillermoz had been a student, along with Maurice Ravel, of the composer, Gabriel Fauré, whose biography he would later write. In 1910, he helped found the Société musicale indépendente and edited the society's journal of music criticism.

8. The change in *Le Film* also occurred in the context of several major cultural events in Paris in the spring and summer of 1917—for example, the opening of the Cocteau-Picasso-Satie-Diaghilev ballet, *Parade*, and Apollinaire's play, *Les Mamelles de Tirésias*—as well as in the context of Allied military failures on the Somne and in Champagne in the spring and of heightened *Action française* campaigns against suspected German collaborators—for example, the pacifist *Bonnet rouge* and Miguel Vigo-Almereyda (who was arrested and died mysteriously in August 1917).

9. In November 1917, *Paris-Midi* had a circulation of just 19,000—Bellanger et al., *Histoire générale de la presse française*, vol. 3, 428. Jean Cocteau's "Carte blanche" column in *Paris-Midi* also occasionally focused on the cinema.

10. *Action française* reached a peak circulation of 156,000 in November 1917, largely through Léon Daudet's virulent attacks on German spies and collaborators within France. Those who admired the paper at the time, and especially the work of Charles Maurras, included Marcel Proust, André Gide, and Guillaume Apollinaire. See Bellanger et al., *Histoire générale de la presse française*, vol. 3, 428; Eugen Weber. *Action Française: Royalism and Reaction in Twentieth-Century France* (Stanford: Stanford University Press, 1962), 111; and Pascal Ory and Jean-François Sirinelli, *Les Intellectuels en France, de l'Affaire Dreyfus à nos jours* (Paris: Armand Colin, 1986), 70.

11. For further information on the French ciné-roman, see Christian Bosséno, "Le Cinéma et la presse (II)," *La Revue du cinéma: Image et son*, 342 (September 1979), 94–97; Alain and Odette Virmaux, *Le Ciné-roman: Un genre nouveau* (Paris: Edilig, 1983), 13–42; and

Richard Abel, "Exploring the Discursive Field of the Surrealist Film Scenario Text," *Dada/ Surrealism*, 15 (1986), 58–71.

12. *Les Mystères de New York* was serialized by Pierre Decourcelle (1856–1926) and published in *Le Matin*, beginning on 27 November 1915, each chapter coming one week in advance of the film's twenty-two weekly episodes. Georges Dureau was quite concerned about the confusion that might be caused by this mixture of forms, in "Genre nouveau," *Ciné-Journal*, 323 (22 October 1915), 3–4. By contrast, Guillaume Danvers saw *Les Mystères de New York* as a turning point for the serial format, in "Nouveau Spectacle," *Ciné-Journal*, 330 (11 December 1915), 15, 18. Both *Judex* and *Chantecoq* were written by Arthur Bernède. The ciné-roman series included Romans-Cinémas (La Renaissance du livre), Cinéma-Bibliothèque (Jules Tallandier), and Les Grands Films (Arthème Fayard).

13. See Abel, *French Cinema*, 9–14.

14. Henri Diamant-Berger, "Une Enquête: La crise du film français," *Le Film*, 51 (5 March 1917), 3–7; Diamant-Berger, "Une Enquête," *Le Film*, 52 (12 March 1917), 6–8, 10; Diamant-Berger, "Une Enquête," *Le Film*, 53 (19 March 1917), 6, 8; Diamant-Berger, "Une Enquête," *Le Film*, 55 (2 April 1917), 3–6, 9–10. Diamant-Berger first took note of problems in the French film industry in "La Routine," *Le Film*, 7 (13 May 1916), 5, and in "L'Inertie," *Le Film*, 8 (20 May 1916), 5. See, also, the results of a survey by Henri Lapauze's journal, *La Renaissance*, reprinted by Henri Coutant as "Une Enquête," *Ciné-Journal*, 375 (21 October 1916), 3–4.

According to Georges Sadoul, the percentage of French films was much smaller than that of American films for all those released in France between 1917 and 1919—Sadoul, *Histoire générale du cinéma*, vol. 4, (Paris: Denoël, 1974), 51. According to Kristin Thompson, French films still maintained a slight edge over the American films, if one looks only at the monthly figures for December 1916 and January 1917—Thompson, *Exporting Entertainment*, 88. However, if one looks at the figures for films released in March 1917, French films totaled 20,712 meters while American films totaled 25,672 meters—reported in *Le Film*, 56 (9 April 1917), 16.

15. Charles Pathé, "Etude sur l'évolution de l'industrie cinématographique française," *Le Film*, 119 (24 June 1918), 6, 8, and 120 (1 July 1918), 8, 10, 12, 14. Henri Diamant-Berger, "Pour sauver le film français," *Le Film*, 130 (9 September 1918), 5–8.

16. Henri Diamant-Berger, "Pour sauver le film français," *Le Film*, 150 (29 January 1919), 5–8; 151 (4 February 1919), 5–7; 152 (9 February 1919), 5–8; 153 (16 February 1919), 5–9; 154 (23 February 1919), 5–6, 8, 10; 156 (9 March 1919), 5–8; 157 (16 March 1919), 5–6, 8; 158 (23 March 1919), 5–8, 10.

17. Emile Vuillermoz, "Devant l'écran," *Le Temps* (16 April 1917), 3; Vuillermoz, "Devant l'écran," *Le Temps* (15 August 1917), 3; Vuillermoz, "Devant l'écran: Espoirs," *Le Temps* (2 December 1917), 3; Vuillermoz, "Devant l'écran: Désertion," *Le Temps* (20 April 1918), 3; Vuillermoz, "Devant l'écran: La crise," *Le Temps* (15 May 1918), 3.

18. Henri Diamant-Berger, "La Censure," *Le Film*, 15 (8 July 1916), 5; René Jeanne and Charles Ford, *Le Cinéma et la presse, 1896–1960* (Paris: Armand Colin, 1961), 201–4. Paul Leglise, *Histoire de la politique du cinéma français: Le cinéma et la IIIᵉ République* (Paris: Pierre Lherminier, 1970), 27–28, 30–33.

19. See, for instance, the exchange of letters between Diamant-Berger and Léon Brézillon, president of the Exhibitors Association, in *Le Film*, 33 (28 October 1916). For a summary of the attacks on the cinema that supported the censorship practices, see Betrand de Laflotte, *Les Films démoralisateurs de l'enfance: Rapport présenté au comité de défense des enfants traduits en justice* (Paris, 1917), and Edouard Pouplain, *Contre le cinéma, école du vice et du crime. Pour le cinéma, école d'éducation, moralization et vulgarisation* (Besançon, 1917).

20. G.-Michel Coissac, *Histoire du cinématographe: De ses origines jusqu'à nos jours* (Paris: Cinéopse, 1925), 435–36. Leglise, *Histoire de la politique du cinéma français*, 10, 61–67.

21. Diamant-Berger, *Le Cinéma* (Paris: La Renaissance du livre, 1919) 247–48. See, also, Marcel Lapierre, *Les Cent Visages du cinéma* (Paris: Grasset, 1948), 139–40. *Birth of a Nation* apparently was scheduled to be screened at the Casino de Paris sometime in the fall of 1916—"Echos," *Ciné-Journal*, 370 (16 September 1916), 7. *Intolerance* was actually previewed within the industry in October 1917—"Un Grand Film," *Ciné-Journal*, 84 (22 October 1917), 5.

22. Diamant-Berger, *Le Cinéma*, 241–49.

23. See, also, Abel Gance's unpublished note, from 1918, on an international, socialist cinema—Roger Icart, *Abel Gance ou Le Prométhée foudroyé* (Lausanne: L'Age d'homme, 1983), 105.

24. Guillaume Apollinaire, "L'Esprit nouveau et les poètes," *Mercure de France*, 491 (1 December 1918), trans. Roger Shattuck, in *Selected Writings of Guillaume Apollinaire*, ed. Shattuck (New York: New Directions, 1971), 228–30.

25. Louis Delluc, "La Beauté au cinéma," *Le Film*, 73 (6 August 1917), 4–5; Louis Delluc, "Antoine travaille," *Le Film*, 75 (20 August 1917), 7.

26. Léon Daudet, "Le Cinéma," *Action française* (2 May 1916), reprinted in Jacques Dyssord, "En Marge du cinéma," *Mercure de France* (16 August 1916), 665, 672. This reprinting suggests how ideologically close *Mercure de France* came to *Action française* during the war period—Weber, *Action Française*, 111.

27. Marcel Gromaire, "Idées d'un peintre sur le cinéma," *Le Crapouillot* (1 April–26 June 1919), reprinted in Marcel L'Herbier, ed., *Intelligence du cinématographe* (Paris: Corréa, 1946), 239–49.

28. Paul Souday, "Au Cinéma," *Le Temps* (6 September 1916), 1. For a thorough analysis of this Classical Renaissance in French art, see Kenneth Eric Silver, *Esprit de Corps: The Great War and French Art, 1914–1925* (Ann Arbor: University Microfilms, Inc., 1981), 109–71. For a description of its beginnings prior to the war, see Billy, *L'Epoque contemporaine*, 22–32; and Ory and Sirinelli, *Les Intellectuels en France*, 51–60.

29. Paul Souday, "Bergsonisme et le cinéma," *Le Film*, 84 (15 October 1917), 9–10.

30. Marcel L'Herbier, "Hermès et le silence," *Le Film*, 110–111 (29 April 1918), 7–12. L'Herbier published a preliminary sketch of this essay as "La France et l'art muet," *Le Film*, 100 (11 February 1918), 7–8.

31. Emile Vuillermoz, "Devant l'écran: Hermès et le silence," *Le Temps* (23 February 1918), 3.

32. Emile Vuillermoz, "Devant l'écran," *Le Temps* (29 November 1916), 3.

33. Armand Bour, "L'Art du cinéma," *Le Film*, 132 (23 September 1918), 12–14.

34. Emile Vuillermoz, "Devant l'écran: Intolerance," *Le Temps* (4 June 1919), 3. Despite his condescension, Vuillermoz was one of the few critics to notice the significance of the new eight-hour workday, which was instituted just after the war.

35. For an analysis of Gabriel Tarde's social theories, see Rosalind H. Williams, *Dream Worlds: Mass Consumption in Late Nineteenth-Century France* (Berkeley: University of California Press, 1982), 342–84.

36. Emile Vuillermoz, "Devant l'écran," *Le Temps* (25 April 1917), 3. Emile Vuillermoz, "Devant l'écran," *Le Temps* (27 January 1918), 3.

37. Louis Delluc, "*Illusion* et illusions," *Le Film*, 68 (25 June 1917), 5–6. Louis Delluc, "Les Mauvais Français," *Le Film*, 84 (15 October 1917), 10–12.

38. Philippe Soupault, "The USA Cinema," *Broom*, 5 (September 1923), 65–69. The French version of this essay appeared as "Le Cinéma USA" in *Théâtre et Comoedia illustré*, 26 (15 January 1924).

39. Louis Delluc, "Le Cinquième Art," *Le Film*, 113 (13 May 1918), 7–8. The reference to Octave Mirbeau in Delluc's "La Foule," *Paris-Midi* (24 August 1918), suggests that the young critic was approaching the mass audience of the cinema much as Mirbeau might have done. For an analysis of Mirbeau's anarchism in relation to his writing and of his polemical work during the Dreyfus Affair, see Eugenia W. Herbert, *The Artist and Social Reform: France and Belgium, 1885–1898* (New Haven: Yale University Press, 1961), 146–56, 202–6.

40. Louis Delluc, "Abel Gance après *La Zone de la mort*," *Le Film*, 85 (22 October 1917), 7.

41. Louis Delluc, "La Foule," *Paris-Midi* (24 August 1918), 2. Delluc's attitude toward the working-class cinema audiences of Paris contrasts sharply with the crudely behavioristic attitude of Lev Kuleshov in Moscow—see *Kuleshov on Film*, ed. Ronald Levaco (Berkeley: University of California Press, 1974), 44–45. To be sure, Delluc did not hold consistently to this point—for instance, he roundly condemned the Feuillade and Pathé-Exchange serials, which nearly always attracted a mass audience in France.

42. Louis Delluc, "La Foule devant l'écran," *Photogénie* (Paris: de Brunoff, 1920), 120.

43. For an analysis of Charles Gide's consumer cooperative movement, see Rosalind Williams, *Dream Worlds*, 287–310. Consumer cooperatives were also important to E. Bernstein, an influential theorist of the German Socialist Democratic Party at the turn of the century—see Lucio Colletti, "Bernstein and the Marxism of the Second International," *From Rousseau to Lenin: Studies in Ideology and Society* (New York: Monthly Review Press, 1972), 92–93.

44. Jacques de Baroncelli, "Pantomime, musique, cinéma," *Ciné-Journal*, 329 (4 December 1915), 41–43.

45. Diamant-Berger, "La Routine," 5. Cf. Henri Diamant-Berger, "La Vérité en marche," *Le Film*, 93 (17–24 December 1917), 7–10.

46. Colette, "Cinéma: *Forfaiture*," *Excelsior* (7 August 1916), reprinted in Alain and Odette Virmaux, ed., *Colette au cinéma* (Paris: Flammarion, 1975), 35–38. Cf. "Echos: *Forfaiture*," *Ciné-Journal*, 364 (5 August 1916), 19.

47. Emile Vuillermoz, "Devant l'écran," *Le Temps* (23 November 1916), 3.

48. See, for instance, Guillaume Danvers, "Rétrospectives," *Ciné-Journal*, 324 (30 October 1915), 23, 27, and Henri Diamant-Berger, "La Hausse des locations," *Le Film*, 82 (8 October 1917), 3–4.

49. Delluc, "Le Cinquième Art," 8.

50. Delluc, "Les Mauvais Français," 11.

51. Guillaume Danvers, "Une Opinion: Problème de la nationalité d'un film, comment la définir," *Le Film*, 9 (22 May 1916), 6–7. Apollinaire, "L'Esprit nouveau et les poètes," 228.

52. The titles and credits of Pathé's wartime production can be found in the weekly issues of *Pathé-Journal, Ciné-Journal*, and *Le Film*. There is at least one exception that surveys the critics and supporters of the police serial—H. C., "La Question dominante: Le bon et mauvais cinéma," *Ciné-Journal*, 351 (6 May 1916), 3–4, 9.

53. See, for instance, Emile Vuillermoz, "Devant l'écran," *Le Temps* (21 February 1917), 3.

54. Gromaire, "Idées d'un peintre sur le cinéma," 239–40.

55. See, especially, Diamant-Berger, "Le Scénario," *Le Cinéma*, 35–53, and Charles Pathé, "Etude sur l'évolution de l'industrie cinématographique française," (24 June 1918), 6–8, and (1 July 1918), 8, 10, 12, 14. Cf. Abel Gance's unpublished report on "The Producer," presumably written in 1917—Norman King, *Abel Gance: A Politics of Spectacle* (London: British Film Institute, 1984), 58–61.

56. Throughout the war period, the brief reviews of the weekly film previews in *Le Film* always called attention to the author of the scenario but rarely to the director.

57. Diamant-Berger, "Le Scénario," 37.

58. Emile Vuillermoz, "Devant l'écran: *La Dixième Symphonie*," *Le Temps* (6 November 1918), 3. Cf. Armand Bour, "Pour la suprématie du scénario," *Le Film*, 98 (28 January 1918), 7–8, 12–13.

59. Louis Delluc, "Cinéma," *Paris-Midi* (2 February 1919), 2, and (12 May 1919), 2. Yet Delluc could contradict himself, as in his emphasis on the scriptwriter in "Notes pour moi," *Le Film*, 91 (3 December 1917), 12. And Vuillermoz could occasionally take an auteurist position, as when he explained how ten different filmmakers—having the same script, actors, and decors—could produce ten very different films, in "Devant l'écran: Hermès et le silence," 3.

60. Henri Diamant-Berger, "Echos," *Le Film*, 90 (3 December 1917), 15. Coissac, *Histoire du cinématographe*, 443.

61. Pathé first articulated his concern about a "crisis of the scenario" in response to an inquiry by Diamant-Berger in *Le Film*, 52 (5 March 1917), 4–6. One sign of these two men's close ties is that Diamant-Berger became an independent director-producer in 1919, with the encouragement and financial support of Pathé.

62. Vuillermoz revealed his own elitist stance when he objected strenuously to Pathé's recommendations to eliminate poets and artists as major characters in French films—"Devant l'écran," *Le Temps* (30 June 1918), 3.

63. Diamant-Berger, "Le Filmage," *Le Cinéma*, 145–68. The best analysis of the development of the classical narrative continuity system in the American cinema can be found in Kristin Thompson, "The Formulation of the Classical Style, 1909–1928," *The Classical Hollywood Cinema: Film Style and Mode of Production to 1960* (New York: Columbia University Press, 1985), 157–240.

64. Diamant-Berger's mainstream "theory" of French narrative cinema bears some similarity to that of the *juste milieu* painters of the nineteenth-century, whose primary goal was "the instant readability of the image"—see Charles Rosen and Henri Zerner, *Romanticism and Realism: The Mythology of Nineteenth-Century Art* (New York: Vintage, 1984), 116–17, 209.

65. Colette, "La Critique des films," *Le Film*, 64 (28 May 1917), 6.

66. Armand Bour, "L'Art du cinéma," 14.

67. André Antoine, "Propos sur le cinématographe," *Le Film*, 166 (December 1919). Cf. André Antoine, "L'Avenir du cinéma," *Lectures pour tous* (December 1919), trans. Stuart Liebman, in *Framework*, 24 (Spring 1984), 45–52. For a slightly different, but more extensive analysis of Antoine, from which I have borrowed several ideas, see Stuart Liebman, "André Antoine's Film Theory," *Framework*, 24 (Spring 1984), 33–43. See, also, Abel, *French Cinema*, 95–97.

68. For information on the mobile electrical generator, see "Le Monde du cinéma," *Ciné-pour-tous*, 7 (1 October 1919), 2; "Le Studio ambulant de Mercanton," *Le Journal du Ciné-Club*, 23 (18 June 1920), 3; and "La Réalisation—Le décor," *Ciné-pour-tous*, 52 (5 November 1920), 3.

69. Vuillermoz uses almost exactly the same language in one of his first columns, "Devant l'écran," *Le Temps* (27 December 1916), 3. As evidenced in his films, *La Terre* (1919) and *La Hirondelle et la mésange* (1920/1984), Antoine tended to use at least two cameras set at ninety-degree angles to one another in order to cover a scene.

70. Delluc, "Antoine travaille," 5, 7; Louis Delluc, "Notes pour moi," *Le Film*, 102 (25 February 1918), 12–13.

71. See, for instance, Louis Delluc, "Lettre française à Thomas Ince, compositeur des

films," *Le Film*, 119 (24 June 1918), 11–15. Like most French writers, Delluc assumed mistakenly that Ince directed the films associated with his name; yet on most of them he was actually the producer. See, also, Louis Delluc, "Cinéma: *The Outlaw and His Wife*," *Paris-Midi* (10 November 1919), 2.

72. Jacques de Baroncelli was one of the first to posit an ideal film form that avoided intertitles—"Les Sous-titres sont-ils nécessaires?" *Ciné-Journal*, 358 (24 June 1916), 46, 48.

73. Louis Delluc, "Notes pour moi," *Le Film*, 102 (23 February 1918), 12.

74. Louis Delluc, "Notes pour moi," *Le Film*, 98 (28 January 1918), 16.

75. Behind Delluc's position probably lay the early Romantic artists' ambition of achieving "immediacy" in a form of expression "directly understandable without convention and without previous knowledge of a tradition"—Rosen and Zerner, *Romanticism and Realism*, 39–40. This conception of film narrative provided the basis for several of Delluc's own films: *La Fête espagnole* (1920), *Fièvre* (1921), and *Le Chemin d'Ernoa* (1921).

76. Daudet, "Le Cinéma," 672.

77. Emile Vuillermoz, "Devant l'écran: *Les Frères corses*," *Le Temps* (7 February 1917), 3.

78. Emile Vuillermoz, "Devant l'écran," *Le Temps* (6 June 1917), 3.

79. Vuillermoz, "Devant l'écran: *La Dixième Symphonie*," 3.

80. Marcel L'Herbier, "*Rose-France*," *Comoedia illustré* (5 December 1919), reprinted in Noël Burch, *Marcel L'Herbier* (Paris: Seghers, 1973), 60–61.

81. See, especially, André Bazin, "The Ontology of the Photographic Image," *Problèmes de la peinture* (1945), trans. Hugh Gray, in Bazin, *What Is Cinema?* (Berkeley: University of California Press, 1967), 9–16, and Bazin, "The Evolution of the Language of Cinema," *Age nouveau*, 92 (July 1955), trans. Hugh Gray, in Bazin, *What Is Cinema?* 35–37.

82. Recent influential studies on the distinction between narration and description include Gérard Genette, "Frontiers of Narrative" [1966], *Figures of Literary Discourse*, trans. Ann Sheridan (New York: Columbia University Press, 1982), 127–44; Roland Barthes, *S/Z* [1970], trans. Richard Miller (New York: Hill and Wang, 1974); and Svetlana Alpers, "Describe or Narrate? A Problem in Realistic Representation," *New Literary History*, 8 (Autumn 1976), 15–41.

83. For an important study of the cognitive power of representation, see Svetlana Alpers, *The Art of Describing: Dutch Art in the Seventeenth Century* (Chicago: University of Chicago Press, 1983). Rosen and Zerner take up this idea as well and provide an important link between seventeenth-century Dutch painting and nineteenth-century French Realism in the work of the art critic, "Théophile Thoré—*Romanticism and Realism*, 192–202.

84. As Edward Branigan argues, this double conception of the camera provides a key construct for André Bazin's film theory—"What Is a Camera?" *Cinema Histories, Cinema Practices*, ed. Patricia Mellencamp and Philip Rosen (Washington, D.C.: American Film Institute, 1984), 91–93.

85. Michael Fried, *Absorption and Theatricality: Painting and the Beholder in the Age of Diderot* (Berkeley: University of California Press, 1980), 71–160, but especially 78, 103–5, 130–34.

86. Roland Barthes, *Empire of Signs*, trans. Richard Howard (New York: Hill and Wang, 1982), 78.

87. Emile Vuillermoz, "Devant l'écran: Les initiés," *Le Temps* (15 December 1917), 3.

88. Emile Vuillermoz, "Devant l'écran," *Le Temps* (23 May 1917), 3.

89. Emile Vuillermoz, "Devant l'écran," *Le Temps* (10 October 1917), 3. Vuillermoz is quoting from Bergson's *Matière et mémoire* (1905).

90. Vuillermoz, "Devant l'écran: Hermès et le silence," 3.

91. Marcel L'Herbier, "Suggestions pour illustrer et défendre une conception française

du cinématographe," *Rose-France* pamphlet (February 1919), reprinted in Burch, *Marcel L'Herbier*, 62.

92. Delluc, "La Beauté au cinéma," 4.

93. Delluc, "La Beauté au cinéma," 5. See, also, Louis Delluc, "L'Expression et Charlie Chaplin," *Le Film*, 106–107 (2 April 1918), 48, 50–54; Delluc, "Cinéma: *Grand Frère*," *Paris-Midi* (14 February 1919), 2; and Delluc, "Cinéma: *Grand Frère*," *Paris-Midi* (17 February 1919), 2. In "The Face of Garbo," Roland Barthes rewrites Delluc with startlingly little change—*Mythologies*, trans. Annette Lavers (New York: Hill and Wang, 1972), 56–57.

94. Recently, Thomas Elsaesser hypothesized that a deeply ambiguous male gaze or, rather, image of the male gaze (as opposed to point-of-view shots), constituted a characteristic feature of 1920s German cinema—Elsaesser, "Weimar Cinema as a Specific Form of (Inter-)Textuality: Sexual Ambiguity and the Attenuation of the Hermeneutic and Proaretic Codes of Action," paper presented at the Society for Cinema Studies Conference, New York University, 14 June 1985. See, also, Miriam Hansen, "Pleasure, Ambivalence, Identification: Valentino and Female Spectatorship," *Cinema Journal*, 25 (Summer 1986), 6–32. The subject of the male look in French and German silent cinema would seem to be well worth further examination.

95. Here again Delluc's thinking is rooted in the early nineteenth-century Romantic artists' desire to let nature itself "speak," to make "pure landscape" carry the weight and full symbolic meaning traditionally given to historical (narrative) painting—Rosen and Zerner, *Romanticism and Realism*, 51–58.

96. Louis Delluc, "Notes pour moi," *Le Film*, 116 (3 June 1918), 14, 16.

97. Louis Delluc, "Cinéma," *Paris-Midi* (1 February 1919), 2. Louis Delluc, "Cinéma," *Paris-Midi* (2 February 1919), 2. The Impressionists, it might be recalled, were the first to attach as much importance to the "study" or "sketch" as to the "finished work." In a related vein, someone might profitably examine how the use of oval masks for landscape shots in French silent films can be related to the "Romantic vignette" in nineteenth-century landscape lithographs—Rosen and Zerner, *Romanticism and Realism*, 79–81, 93–96.

98. Delluc, "Cinéma: *The Outlaw and His Wife*," 2.

99. For the standard study of the principles of French Realism that lie behind Delluc's formulation, see Linda Nochlin, *Realism* (New York: Penguin, 1971). For Delluc's probable sources in French Realism and Flaubert, see Rosen and Zerner, *Romanticism and Realism*, 143–50. For a possible connection between Delluc and Diderot, see Fried's analysis of Diderot's art criticism in *Absorption and Theatricality*, 71–160.

100. Besides the two Bazin essays previously noted, see Jean Mitry, *Esthétique et psychologie du cinéma*, vol. 1 (Paris: Editions universitaires, 1963). For a summary analysis of the "raw material" of Mitry's theory, see Dudley Andrew, *The Major Film Theories: An Introduction* (New York: Oxford University Press, 1976), 188–92. As Ian Christie suggests, the concept of *photogénie* also had an impact on early Russian film theory—Ian Christie, "French Avant-Garde Film in the Twenties: From 'Specificity' to Surrealism," *Film as Film: Formal Experiment in Film, 1910–1975* (London: Arts Council of Great Britain, 1979), 38. See, especially, Boris Eikhenbaum, "Problems of Cine-Stylistics" [1927], trans. Richard Sherwood in *The Poetics of Cinema* (Oxford: RPT Publications, 1982), 5–18.

101. Louis Delluc, "Cinéma," *Paris-Midi* (5 March 1919), 2. Here, as elsewhere, Delluc essentially redefines Canudo's earlier conception of the "real" and the "symbolic."

102. Colette, "La Critique des films," *Le Film*, 66 (4 June 1917), 4; Philippe Soupault, "Note 1 sur le cinéma," *SIC*, 25 (January 1918), 3. Colette's language here echoes an unpublished note of Abel Gance's from November 1915—Icart, *Abel Gance*, 58. This attribution of value, power, and newness to the real and the everyday in particular had a preced-

ent in Camille Mauclair and the prewar Decorative Arts Reform Movement—see Rosalind Williams, *Dream Worlds*, 203–6.

103. Jean Cocteau, "Carte blanche," *Paris-Midi* (28 April 1919), reprinted in Cocteau, *Poésie Critique* (Paris: Editions des quatre vents, 1945), 19.

104. This line of thinking coincides with (or perhaps follows) that articulated in "The Futurist Cinema," first published in *L'Italia Futurista* (15 November 1916), trans. R. W. Flint, in Umbro Apollonio's *Futurist Manifestoes* (New York: Viking, 1973), 208. Paradoxically, the surprise and "mythologizing" effect of *photogénie* reappears much later in Roland Barthes' concept of the *punctum* in photography—see *Camera Lucida*, trans. Richard Howard (New York: Hill and Wang, 1981), 32–38.

105. Louis Delluc, "Notes pour moi," *Le Film*, 98 (28 January 1918), 16.

106. Louis Delluc, "Cinéma et cie: Douglas Fairbanks," *Paris-Midi* (1 June 1918), 2. Again, Delluc's concept of modern beauty may have had a precedent in Camille Mauclair— see Rosalind Williams, *Dream Worlds*, 185–93.

107. Louis Aragon, "Du Décor," *Le Film*, 131 (16 September 1918), 9. Max Jacob expresses this idea in embryo form in "Théâtre et cinéma," *Nord-Sud*, 12 (February 1918), 10.

108. Delluc, "Cinéma: *Grand Frère*," 2.

109. Aragon, "Du Décor," 10.

110. Aragon's novel, *Le Paysan de Paris* (1926), would rely heavily on such transformations of everyday image-objects, especially those found in the shopping arcade of the Passage de l'Opéra, its principal setting.

111. Pierre Reverdy, "Cinématographe," *Nord-Sud*, 16 (October 1918), 7.

112. See, for instance, Baroncelli, "Pantomime, musique, cinéma," 42; Guillaume Danvers, "Une Idée: Essai de synchronisme cinématographique musical," *Le Film*, 12 (17 June 1916), 6; and Colette, "Cinéma: *Forfaiture*," 2.

113. Vuillermoz, "Devant l'écran, *Le Temps* (29 November 1916), 3.

114. Vuillermoz, "Devant l'écran," *Le Temps* (10 October 1917), 3.

115. Vuillermoz, "Devant l'écran: *Intolerance*," 3.

116. Emile Vuillermoz, "Devant l'écran," *Le Temps* (25 April 1917), 3. Cf. Vuillermoz, "Devant l'écran: *La Dixième Symphonie*," 3.

117. Louis Delluc, "Notes pour moi," *Le Film*, 94 (31 December 1917), 12.

118. Louis Delluc, "Accessoires," *Le Film*, 69 (9 July 1917), 9–10.

119. Delluc, "Notes pour moi," *Le Film*, 99 (4 February 1918), 13; Vuillermoz, "Devant l'écran: *La Dixième Symphonie*," 3.

120. Louis Delluc, "Cinéma," *Paris-Midi* (23 February 1919), 2, and (9 July 1919), 2.

121. L'Herbier, "Hermès et le silence," 10–12.

122. Apollinaire's speech was published a year later, shortly after his death, in *Mercure de France*, 491 (1 December 1918), 385–96.

123. Guillaume Apollinaire and André Billy, "La Bréhatine," *Archives des lettres modernes*, 126 (1971), 75–96. For an analysis of this scenario, see Alain Virmaux, "*La Bréhatine* et le cinéma: Apollinaire en quête d'un langage neuf," *Archives des lettres modernes*, 126 (1971), 97–117.

124. Soupault, "Note 1 sur le cinéma," 4. Louis Delluc reprinted Soupault's short scenario poem in *Le Film*, 101 (18 February 1918), 18–19. Delluc's connection with the circle of young Dada-Surrealists who looked to Apollinaire for inspiration was such that he published Louis Aragon's first poem, "Charlot sentimental," *Le Film*, 105 (18 March 1918), 11, as well as Apollinaire's short poem, "Avant le cinéma," *Le Film*, 135–36 (21 October 1918), 17. See, also, Soupault, "*Une Vie de chien*," *Littérature*, 4 (June 1919), 24, and "*Charlot voyage*," *Littérature*, 6 (August 1919), 22.

125. Louis Delluc, "Notes pour moi," *Le Film*, 94 (31 December 1917), 14. Delluc's

efforts were far more successful than anything that Edmond Benoit-Lévy's short-lived "Ligue française du cinématographe" (which included older writers such as Edmond Rostand) ever did—see Henri Diamant-Berger, "Les Poètes et le cinéma," *Le Film*, 112 (6 May 1918), 5–6; and Coissac, *Histoire du cinématographe*, 443.

126. Marcel L'Herbier, "Bouclette," *Le Film*, 106–107 (2 April 1918), 75–94; Abel Gance, "J'Accuse," *Le Film*, 108–109 (15 April 1918), 10–23.

127. Blaise Cendrars, *La Fin du monde filmée par l'ange N.-D.*, composition en couleurs par Fernand Léger (Paris: Editions de la sirène, 1919). Pierre Albert-Birot, "2 x 2 = 1," *SIC*, 49–50 (15–30 October 1919), 389–92. Jules Romains, "Donogoo-Tonka ou les miracles de la science," *Nouvelle Revue française*, 74 (November 1919), 821–69, and 75 (December 1919), 1016–63. Fragments of Cendrars's scenario had appeared earlier in *La Caravane* (October 1916) and in *Mercure de France*, 491 (1 December 1918), 419–30. Romains's scenario was also published in book form by the *Nouvelle Revue française* in 1920.

128. For further information on these ciné-romans and scenarios, see Alain and Odette Virmaux, *Le Ciné-roman: Un genre nouveau* (Paris: Edilig, 1983), 13–42, and Abel, "Exploring the Discursive Field of the Surrealist Film Scenario Text," 62–64.

129. Aragon, "Du Décor," 8–10. Reverdy, "Cinématographe," 7.

130. Vuillermoz, "Devant l'écran," *Le Temps* (29 November 1916), 3.

131. Vuillermoz, "Devant l'écran," *Le Temps* (7 February 1917), 3.

132. Cocteau, "Carte blanche," 19–20; Blaise Cendrars, "Modernités—Un nouveau art: Le cinéma," *La Rose rouge*, 78 (12 June 1919), 108. For a brief analysis of how such a "simultaneist poetry" operates in Gance's *J'Accuse* (1919), on which Cendrars worked as assistant director, see Abel, *French Cinema*, 299–300.

133. Gromaire, "Idées d'un peintre sur le cinéma," 239–49; Pierre Albert-Birot, "Du Cinéma," *SIC*, 49–50 (15–30 October 1919), 388–89. See also Blaise Cendrars, who summarized Survage's prewar project (and misspelled his name) in "Modernités—De la parturition des couleurs," *La Rose rouge*, 12 (17 July 1919), 188.

134. Here again the theoretical basis for this conception of film art can be traced to what Rosen and Zerner call "French avant-garde Realism"—*Romanticism and Realism*, 155.

Selected Texts

JACQUES DE BARONCELLI, "Pantomime, Music, Cinema"

From "Pantomime, musique, cinéma," *Ciné-Journal* 329 (4 December 1915), 41–43.

A T FIRST the cinema was nothing more than a sort of divertissement scarcely superior to the shadow play and the magic lantern. This unremarkable period was a time of . . . flickerings. There were cloudy, wet images, sometimes marked with forgotten fingerprints in the film glycerine alongside the sprocket holes, and uncertain "lunar" images, peopled with jerky, graceless figures who were often flattened out between a couple of unskillfully mounted lights. I exaggerate only a little. When they had perfected the filmstock, regulated the acting according to [the rules of] art, optics, and chemistry, and finally integrated the action with the lighting, a degree of harmony appeared on the screen. Life was projected in the semblance of movement. They had translated beings and objects into black, gray, and white (still a bit too abstract), but these marvels nonetheless enchanted us. So the public saluted cinematography as a power—I was going to write: an aesthetic dynamism—a craft that was coming into its own. We fell for it and were smitten. We watched passionately as groups of actors and scenes arranged themselves, as the action began. The seat was welcome, the price civil and modest, so we returned to the cinema spectacle.

In those days, however, an embarrassment spoiled our pleasure. The people who moved about in their revelings on the screen, despite their everyday concrete existence, seemed to drift in a dream or fantasy. They seemed a bit like fish in a clear stream (that is, on the best days). Sometimes we saw them stop, make a gesture or hold an expression, and look at the audience. A wordless romance. We guessed they had felt something, an emotion, and could not speak of it. A mouth opened. Would it emit that unfurling "balloon" which, in the psalm-books and stained-glass windows, exhaled from the lips of a golden legend with a mysterious scent of sanctity and radiant clarity? Nay. We saw an air bubble escape, the kind that sometimes rises from the mouth of a carp, and which passes for mere opinion. Nothing more. It was painful. In front of statues that looked too perfect, people once cried out: "But now speak!" And it was this cry that the cinema audience was tempted to take up once more. The explanatory intertitles posted between the tableaux did little to ease our impatience. Rising up in one unanimous effort, all the spectators begged for some verbal spark.

Then they gave us genuine cinema actors. Common sense is difficult to acquire. They understood—for the cinema did not lack for intelligent and well-cultured men—that a film role had to be studied, analyzed, fathomed, and rehearsed, just like any ordinary theater role. Even more closely. An actor did not just have to enter into the skin of a character, but into his thoughts and feelings. So they discovered wonderful actors. Only a few at first, but more and more are being converted, and inclination no longer is enough. The new actors have put their whole selves into their roles. They have sat down in front of a mirror, like the spectator before the screen, observed their image as something strange and possessed (lacking a definite script of responses and tirades), as a kind of psychological map, as a series of "moods" and "moments"; they have spoken in turn to their reflected body, face, mouth, gaze: "You are going to mean." They have done mime. A feeling, the deepest of their being, has come to lodge in a fold of the lip, to realize itself in a contraction of the eyebrow, to take shape in a gesture, a pose. They have rediscovered a primitive source of "language," rich, poignant, universal, and they have seen whole cinema audiences, as they say, eating out of their hands. It is pantomime (and its reflection), but how much more deliberate and severe. Pantomime is immediate; the cinema mediates. Before appearing on the screen, an expression must undergo a dosage of lights and shadows, the interplay of screen and mirror, like a sort of luminous distillation. In order to appear before the public, the actor's mood or moment has to percolate through physics and chemistry; nevertheless, the operation robs it of none of its emotional value. . . .

If [theater] pantomime has attained such a high degree of representation and reality, however, why go further?

Why the cinema?

Why? Because the cinema is more truthful or, and this comes to the same thing in art, because it better provides the illusion of truth, which alone is beautiful, as they say, as well as pleasing. To our spectators' eyes, the cinema is much more than the shadow of reality; it is the incandescent photograph of a reality that lives again. Before our eyes, a wave stirs matter into an image. Just as the rhythmic sequence of projection, which separates and combines the phases of the shadow images, gives a sense of continuity, so do the number of tableaux and scenes give a sensation of life. The actors are pure mimes. They have submitted to gravity and, rather awkwardly, to time and space—without mentioning any other form of bondage. They move, in a word, less quickly than the mind. They offer us less, according to Pascal (pardon me!), than the imagination can conceive. Finally—to exhaust our shafts—we see them *play* before us much as we accidentally notice the stage scenery quiver. Behind our perception, admittedly, our critical sense concedes ground. Sometimes there is even total abandonment, a voluntary blanking out. For, caught by the sensitive filmstock and projected on the screen, the same play performed by silent actors and arranged beforehand by all the devices of the filmmaker and the cameraman (who fixes, develops, and transforms the negative image to positive, and then lights the projector lamp), the same play with its tricks and effects, its make up and its "make believe," assumes the character of a direct document, of life taken . . . from life.

Is this representation perfect, however? Does it envelope us as in a net all the way through to the very end of its cast? No. Despite its progress—which is remarkable—the cinema, like pure pantomime, has its limits.

The moment occurs that I spoke of earlier, when the actor comes into a close shot, lifts his eyes, makes a gesture, opens his mouth, and says nothing. Again, the shock; one cannot escape the discomfort. We have before us an incomplete creation. A feeling, whose formation and release we have followed like the chords of an ascending scale, suddenly stops, wanders, loses its way, and fails to reach its note of resolution. Here, we are asking not for a word to dislodge the emotion but for music to complete it. And we believe, as some seem to understand today, that the cinema will be fully realized only through music.

Some may think that we mean nothing by that but to confirm the error—the horror—of the poor orchestra which during the love scene warbles a popular love song or at a moment of pathos unlooses a street singer's *lamento*. These choices are wrong and inappropriate. We insist on good performers and genuine music. Just as it is important to select authors who write directly for the cinema, so is it necessary to have musicians. The best should be brought in. Those of us who suffer on account of third-rate acting and the stifling of famous voices wish to instill the mime-drama, the librettos, and the *written* (not just sketched) cinematographic play with the resonant state of being and its physical complement that words are not going to provide. [Good musicians] would quickly realize that our art is superior to that of concert music. The best and the brightest of them have a thousand times felt the painful futility of the descriptive phrase. Such a phrase may have awakened ideas, emotions, feelings, surely; the pastoral oboe and the bucolic flute have recalled the alternate couplets of Virgil, perhaps the Arcadia of Poussin. But neither flute nor oboe has made a shepherd visible.[1] And if you believe that music can only settle on things like sunlight on marble statues, without penetrating them, you will see its limits; if you assume that it has a greater hold on ideas or feelings, you will sense its powerlessness since it can only proceed through approximation, evocation, or suggestion. The moment it tries to be precise, to get close to its subject, it goes wrong and evaporates. There is nothing but confusion and chaos. Follow certain concerts with the text in hand, and you will see what dischord there is between the written word and the sound.

That which presently is lacking in the image, the music will provide. The cinema possesses the secret of movement and color. The eclogue will rediscover, before our eyes, the Arcadian vales, the shepherd's hut; the reed pipe will make the spring water sing; the flute will echo the laughter of nymphs who glide through the willows along with the moonlight. In the {film} drama we will see the melody delineate a gesture, follow the contour and rhythm of a feeling, clarify and define it, and in its turns and motifs harmoniously enclose a human soul. With that, the cinema will create moments that are unique, pure, thrilling, ideal.

And that is the supreme reality.

JACQUES DE BARONCELLI (1881–1951) was a Paris jounalist who edited Eclair's newsreel from 1912 to 1914 and then began to make his own fiction films in 1915, shortly before writing this essay. He later became a reputable director of literary adaptations, especially those set in the provinces—for instance, *Ramuntcho* (1919), *Nêne* (1924), *Pêcheur d'Islande* (1924).

¹ Baroncelli's classical ideal (Greek and French) links him more closely to Paul Souday or the Classical Renaissance movement in art before and during the war than to his critical admirer, Louis Delluc.

COLETTE, "Cinema: *The Cheat*"

From *Colette at the Movies: Criticism and Screenplays*. Edited and introduced by Alain and Odette Virmaux. Translated by Sarah W. R. Smith. English translation © 1980 by the Frederick Ungar Publishing Company. Reprinted by permission. The original French text first appeared as "Cinéma: *Forfaiture*," in *Excelsior* (7 August 1916).

IN PARIS this week, a movie theater has become an art school. A film and two of its principal actors are showing us what surprising innovations, what emotion, what natural and well-designed lighting can add to cinematic fiction. Every evening, writers, painters, composers, and dramatists come and come again to sit, contemplate, and comment, in low voices, like pupils.

To the genius of an oriental actor is added that of a director probably without equal; the heroine of the piece—vital, luminous, intelligent—almost completely escapes any sins of theatrical brusqueness or excess.¹ There is a beautiful luxuriating in lace, silk, furs—not to mention the expanses of skin and the tangle of limbs in the final melee, in which the principals hurl themselves unrestrainedly against each other. We cry "Miracle!"; not only do we have millionaires who don't look as if they've rented their tuxedos by the week, but we also have characters on screen who are followed by their own shadows, their actual shadows, tragic or grotesque, of which until now the useless multiplicity of arc lamps has robbed us. A monochrome drapery, a sparkling bibelot, are enough to give us the impression of established and solid luxury. In an elegant interior there is no sign (is it possible?) of either a silk-quilted bed in the middle of the room or of a carved sideboard.

Since our French studios don't hesitate to lay on special trains, hire crowds, dam rivers and interrupt railroad service, buy villas and dynamite ships, I wish their magnificence would extend to furniture, women's dresses, men's clothing, to accessories that are stylish, complete, and irreproachable, to everything that the assiduity of the public has given it the right to demand.

Is it only a combination of felicitous effects that brings us to this film and keeps us there? Or is it the more profound and less clear pleasure of seeing the crude *ciné* groping toward perfection, the pleasure of divining what the future of the cinema must be when its makers will want that future, when its music will finally become its inevitable, irresistible collaborator, its interpreter; when the same slow waltz or the same comic-opera overture will no longer accompany, and impartially betray, a tragedy, a love duet, and an attempted murder?

COLETTE (1873–1954) was a novelist and essayist who had already gained some notoriety as the author of the *Claudine* novels and *La Vagabonde* (1910). She wrote film reviews for several months in *Le Film* (May–July 1917), and then her interest in the cinema shifted to composing scenarios—*La Vagabonde* (1918) and *La Flamme cachée* (1920)—for her close friend, Musidora, the star of Feuillade's *Les Vampires* (1915–1916).

¹ Cecil B. De Mille directed *The Cheat* (1915), which starred Sessue Hayakawa and Fanny Ward.

PAUL SOUDAY, "On the Cinema"

From "Au Cinéma," *Le Temps* (6 September 1916), 1.

NO DOUBT about it, the cinema doesn't spare a thing. All the entrepreneurs have to do is ask, and society people of both sexes pose for cinematographic scenes; and these fashionable films are displayed before the public, one and all. For a couple of sous, anybody can be invited to ultra-aristocratic receptions, and the most restricted salons are open, at least to the eyes. M. Prudhomme took his son *to watch* their betters eat ice cream at Tortoni's,¹ and now cinema enthusiasts can watch others chat, flirt, and play bridge at the home of an engaging marquis or an opulent baron. This new fad has come to us from Italy, but people probably aren't just dropping in out of the blue. In wartime, programs are usually a bit threadbare; but once peace arrives, society events undoubtedly will be back in full swing, and the Bovarys who dream of carriage horses and spring fashions can either rouse or stifle their desires before the screen.[2] . . .

Actually, there are serious objections to the cinema. The short films of vaudeville clowning which make up the bottom of the program are painfully silly. When they borrow a subject from literature, the result is even worse. Several months ago in Paris, someone exhibited a film called *Salammbô*.[3] It was as an abomination to end abominations. . . .

. . . the cinema's experiences with drama are anything but happy. It doesn't even have the advantage of avoiding the worst calamities by doing without words. If the characters are mute, during short entr'actes explanatory notices are posted, whose style and orthography make one long for the dialogue of the worst dramatists. Certainly the intellectual level of much of the theater is not very high, but the cinema is lower than even the café-concert. And since it beats the competition on ticket prices, it is going to kill off an art form that is already trying to navigate with just a single wing; only the subsidized theaters and an insignificant number of others in Paris and in several large cities in the provinces are still putting up a fight. This will be disastrous for both the public spirit and taste since what will have disappeared will have been replaced by something totally worthless.

The real interest of the cinema should be confined to accurate documentary views: the cataracts of Niagara, the sources of the Nile, tropical seas, Far Eastern ports, polar bear hunts near the North Pole or lion hunts in the center of Africa, etc. Moreover, there's no need to exaggerate the value of this vast album of moving, flickering images. The cinema only has to have average visual acumen, and it can describe objects as well as voyagers do in their tales—and even better if the voyager is named Chateaubriand, Théophile Gautier, or Pierre Loti.[4] What's exciting is not so much the external and banal aspect of reality—whatever automatically strikes any retina or lens—but its atmosphere, its life, its soul, what is perceptible only through the direct and mediating presence of a somewhat refined sensibility. See what's to be seen, if one can, and read good authors. As for me, the cinema and the photograph are the last resort, ultimately, of those who lack imagination or whose imagination only gets rolling with great effort. Rémy de Gourmont, who did not lack imagination, enjoyed the cinema as a means of avoiding fatigue: "One need not even bother to dream," he said. In any case, this province used to be the cinema's raison d'être, but now it is straying farther and farther afield and having "successes" which would have roused a Flaubert to furious indignation, even before the cruelty inflicted on *Salammbô*.

PAUL SOUDAY (1869–1929) directed the currents of literary opinion in Paris, circa 1915–1925, from his position as literary critic at *Le Temps* and *La Revue de Paris*.

¹ Joseph Prudhomme, the fictional creation of Henri Monnier (1799–1877), was an inept, self-satisfied caricature of the French petite bourgeoisie.

² Books led Emma Bovary of Flaubert's *Madame Bovary* (1863) to think that she could escape her provincial bourgeois existence through romantic dreams and fantasies; here Souday condemns the cinema for doing the same thing to her modern descendents. There is an untranslatable pun in *bais* that alludes to Emma's romantic tryst with Rochefort in a traveling horse carriage.

³ *Salammbô* (1915) was an Italian spectacle film released by Gaumont in Paris, in April 1916.

⁴ Chateaubriand (1768–1848), Gautier (1811–1872), and Loti (1850–1923) were all major French writers celebrated for their travel books about "exotic" lands.

EMILE VUILLERMOZ, "Before the Screen"

From "Devant l'écran," *Le Temps* (29 November 1916), 3.

HERE I TOUCH on one of the most marvelous technical possibilities of cinema art. This ability to juxtapose, within several seconds, on the same luminous screen, images which generally are isolated in time or space, this power (hitherto reserved to the human imagination) to leap from one end of the universe to the other, to draw together antipodes, to interweave thoughts far removed from one another, to compose, as one fancies, a ceaselessly changing mosaic out of millions of scattered facets of the tangible world . . . all this could permit a poet to realize his most ambitious dreams—if poets would become interested in the cinema, and the cinema would interest itself in poets!

This form of development of thought, with its thematic echoes, its conducive motifs, its allusions, its rapid insinuations or slow solicitations, it is exactly like a symphony! The cinema orchestrates images, scores our visions and memories according to a strictly musical process: it must choose its visual themes, render them expressive, meticulously regulate their exposition, their opportune return, their measure and rhythm, develop them, break them down into parts, reintroduce them in fragments, as the treatises on composition put it, through "augmentation" or "diminution." More fortunate than painting and sculpture, the cinema, like music, possesses all the riches, all the inflections, and all the nuances of beauty in movement: cinema produces counterpoint and harmony . . . but it still awaits its Debussy!

Among the interesting accomplishments in *Invasion des Etats-Unis*¹ should be noted certain details of the naval battle: the startling appearance of the artillery batteries, rising up from their hiding places with the supple movement of a living creature to stretch out their throbbing necks, fire, and return to the depths of their shelter; the charming lighting of certain interiors. Through the exactness of its rhythm, the precision of its movement, and the fluidity of its expression, the simple tableau of the family dinner after the meeting should be an example to directors who so annoyingly bungle and excessively banalize images of this kind. Here is first-rate advice to hold on to. In the midst of this involved "score," it is an *andante* of simplicity and exquisite charm.

The acting avoids the easy excesses which we have too often had to suffer in those "expressive" grimaces which the camera lens seems to favor. The cinema could renew the powerful and nuanced art of pantomime: most of the time, it gives that little thought. Our actors, hard pressed by their tyrannical master—they never have a minute to lose as the camera turns—simplify their physical performance, displaying only the essential character traits, connecting two opposed expressions without bothering with the necessary transitions. American actors take more time, perform more simply and "reduce," as suits them, their eyebrow wrinklings and smiles. Thus they achieve remarkable effects of reality.

One needs a volume to describe the microcosm that constitutes a film of two kilometers! The form of an article does not suffice. But no matter: the most modest notes have their usefulness in such a tangled domain, for an art which has never deigned to take pride in analysis! Besides, it will soon demonstrate that it has been perfectly worthy of respect, and we alone are guilty: people always get the spectacle they deserve! . . . The screen is there to prove it to us once again.

EMILE VUILLERMOZ (1878–1960) was a student of Gabriel Fauré and, as the foremost French music critic of the 1910s and 1920s, championed the works of Fauré, Debussy, Ravel, Honegger, Stravinsky, Florent Schmitt (one of his classmates), and others. Later he would write biographies of Fauré, Debussy, and Ravel, as well as several histories of music.

¹ *Invasion des Etats-Unis* was the French title for Vitagraph's *The Battle Cry of Peace* (1915), directed by J. Stuart Blackton and Wilford North, which advocated the United States' entry into World War I.

EMILE VUILLERMOZ, "Before the Screen: *Les Frères corses*"

From "Devant l'écran: *Les Frères corses*," *Le Temps* (7 February 1917), 3.

SCAGL has persuaded Antoine to tackle the mise-en-scène of the screen: this week saw the premiere of his first film.

The event deserves to be emphasized. It's both a confession and a promise. The cinema is committing itself officially to enter on the path of artistic experiment and serious work. It is accepting a rigorous discipline, giving itself over to an energetic, tenacious master who is quite capable of upsetting established rules and routines, getting rid of favorite performance tricks, and imposing on the cinema a sense of ambition and an undreamt-of aesthetic. The experiment is at least courageous, and the cinema should be grateful to him.

Will it be fruitful and crucial for the evolution of style? . . . Only the future will tell. [Yet] Antoine's choice of a title for his first film is particularly reassuring and opportune.

Still there's no need to hide the fact that he will have to foment a second coup d'état in order to really succeed. It's not enough to transpose the decrees of his previous dictatorship into this new domain: a new art form requires a new set of techniques. The great shortcoming of current cinematographic techniques is that they are theatrically retarded. . . . And that's why the glorious stage exploits of Antoine could very well handicap him rather than give him an advantage in the battle which he is undertaking on this new terrain.

His first film is more a parade of arms than a real combat. He's holding back, testing the metal of his adversary, studying his moves before plunging in.

He has taken for his theme Alexandre Dumas's picturesque tale, *Les Frères corses*.[1] The subject is excellently chosen. Only film could give a suitable plastic life to this dramatic story, in which the imagination must continually confront distant visions, distinct landscapes, two characters who are more Siamese than Corsican, mysteriously endowed with a unique sensibility and separated from one another by three hundred leagues. . . . The cinema's miraculous gift of ubiquity, its power of immediate evocation, its wealth of interchangeable images are all needed to execute this tour de force. The thousands of tiny frames in a moving filmstrip act like the cells of the human brain: the same overwhelming rapidity of perception, the same multiplicity of many-faceted mirrors which effortlessly juxtapose the farthest horizons, suppress distances, abolish the bondage of time and space, embrace all the cardinal points [of the compass] simultaneously, and transport us in a fraction of a second from one extreme point of the universe to another! . . .

Antoine, of course, has done remarkable things with this visual proteanism; he has been able to intensify his drama with quick glimpses, allusions, echoes, inferences, forebodings, memories, hallucinations, and dreams; to illuminate it with fugitive suggestions analogous to the flashes of mental associations which traverse our imagination and multiply its creative power tenfold. As soon as a situation gives birth to some remote thought, a mental impulse toward the past, or a flight of memory across space, the screen picks up its quick spark and offers us its image.

Moreover, the director of *Frères corses* has been able to indulge in a very curious "framing" superimposed on his action. He has first "inscribed" all the arabesque details of the author's writing chamber, shown us Alexandre

Dumas biting on his cigar, pursuing his dream in spirals of blue smoke, resolutely seizing a quill pen in his heavy, bejeweled hand, and rapidly covering a new notebook with his large handwriting: "Toward the beginning of March, in 1841, I was traveling in Corsica. . . ."

And the resurrection occurs before our very eyes: the words become images, things flock together at the call of their names, swirling visions rise to the surface of the screen, coming from distant ages and far horizons to beat their wings at the window pane of this mysterious prison of dreams! The story thus materializes naturally until the moment when, the last fantasy extinguished, we rediscover the writer rounding off his final phrase: "I bent over him; he remained quiet and immobile . . . ," blotting his fresh page, folding up his finished manuscript, and stretching with a sigh of relief.

Within this frame, a second framework of action develops. Dumas becomes an actor in the drama, watches himself perform, finds himself in the residence of Lucien de Franchi, enjoys the fine story of a vendetta which in turn becomes incarnate before his eyes, sees himself in the chamber of Louis de Franchi, at the Opéra, in the Café Anglais, at a duel, in the woods of Vincennes. . . . Here there are subtleties and ingenuities of editing that confirm the infinite suppleness of cinematographic technique and its astonishing attribute—which one could call "symphonic"—of combining chords of impressions and writing a kind of visual counterpoint for several instruments. It's the plastic formula of *simultanéism* which torments Guillaume Apollinaire.[2]

Here is a virtual storehouse to mine. The composition of *Frères corses* is full of "stage" directions of this kind. When Lucien de Franchi enchants his host by telling him of the alternating revenges of his grandmother Savilia and the savage Giudice-Jacops—softening them a bit, for the cinema, which assassinates and steals so willingly, is incredibly modest—the images of the story are not projected on the same plane of consciousness as are the images of the interlocutors: from time to time the evoked scene pales and evaporates so that the lamp can slowly brighten again to light the eloquent storyteller and attentive novelist. Thus do we glide from dream to reality with unusual fluidity.

Here we see the spirit in which the new "composer" of films is working. Admittedly, he will probably not be compensated for his discerning research by an immediate outburst of enthusiasm from the cinema regulars. Who will be grateful for his scrupulous lighting effects, his care in not giving the lighting of a salon (where a single veiled lamp keeps vigil) the same hue as that of the Opéra foyer, the interior of a curtained stage box, a restaurant, or house hallway? In the cinema, where they light hospital rooms exactly like costume balls, with formidable batteries of arc lamps, halflight always seems to be taken as a fault.

Will they equally appreciate at face value the successful researches into the atmosphere of 1840, so fascinating and refined, the costumes worn with such ease by the intelligent actors—Krauss[3] has produced an unforgettable character there!—the Opéra ball, seen from the high angle of a box, with its quadrille of longshoremen, carnival revelers, and tramps who are virtual Gavarni creations?[4] Will they sense the charm of tender intimacy in the room where the handsome, high-collared platonic lover admires his romantic "angel," his "sensitive one," seated by the fireside in the starched folds of her taffeta dress, chastely lowcut, her pure, ringlet-framed profile inclining over her embroidery while under the flickering lamp the hours slip away gently, rhythmically timed to the balance wheel of a little *colonnette* pendulum—affecting as a romance by Louïsa Puget? . . .

Wish it well without expecting too much. A public that likes police serials [for instance, *Judex*] is rather badly prepared for interpretations of this kind and perhaps will not immediately perceive their nuances and limited ends. Antoine need not defend himself if the public does not divine this meticulous attention to detail; he need not be discouraged if they are incapable of distinguishing straight away this authentic collector's item from the cheap imitations around it. Once more, this is only a trial run, and one that's a bit confidential and deceptive in its modesty, but it justifies the most ambitious hopes.

The cinema means to spruce up its weapons and coats of arms; this *nouveau riche* has decided to take lessons in deportment: let's congratulate it on having chosen a good professor. Monsieur Jourdain was astonished to be speaking prose without knowing it; soon the cinema will see that it can be making poetry as well.[5]

[1] Alexandre Dumas père (1802–1870), one of the most popular French novelists and dramatists of the nineteenth century, was best known for such novels as *Les Trois Mousquetaires, Vingt Ans Après*, and *Le Comte de Monte-Cristo*.

[2] Guillaume Apollinaire (1880–1918) was an influential poet, critic, and editor before the war. *Simultanéism* or *simultaneity* was one of several concepts Apollinaire adopted to proselytize the new art of the Cubists and others, particularly Robert Delaunay, around 1911–1913. Briefly, *simultanéism* was an aesthetic in which the subject was all but eliminated and attention was focused on the composition of purely formal elements—producing a form of abstract art or "pure painting."

[3] Henry Krauss (1866–1935) was an actor trained in the Théâtre Antoine who, like Antoine, turned to the cinema in the early 1910s. Best known as an actor—for example, *Notre Dame de Paris* (1911), *Les Misérables* (1912), *Germinal* (1913)—he also directed several important films during the war—for instance, *Papa Hulin* (1916). *Le Chemineau* (1917), and *Marion de Lormé* (1918).

[4] Paul Gavarni (1804–1866) was a noted painter and illustrator who, along with Honoré

Daumier, caricatured the customs of the bourgeoisie in the pages of Charles Philipon's notorious satirical daily, *Le Charivari*.

⁵ Monseiur Jourdain is the famous character from Molière's *Bourgeois Gentilhomme*, who becomes more and more ridiculous as he attempts to turn himself into a man of culture.

COLETTE, "Film Criticism: *Mater Dolorosa*"

From *Colette at the Movies: Criticism and Screenplays*. Edited and introduced by Alain and Odette Virmaux. Translated by Sarah W. R. Smith. English translation © 1980 by the Frederick Ungar Publishing Company. Reprinted by permission. The original French text first appeared as "La Critique des films," in *Le Film* 66 (4 June 1917), 4–5.

LET US SEND beyond the sea and the mountains films like *Mater Dolorosa*. Here, the coordinated result of two efforts, the interpreters' and the director's, appears in its full beauty. It is thanks to that effort that we forget that Gémier,¹ with his narrow mouth and his light, narrow eyes, is utterly unphotogenic. The screen, cruel to fading beauty, is also capable of betraying the best talents. Some hand has given Gémier help here, turning his face toward the most favorable light, using close-ups not as one would play with binoculars but to underline a paternal smile, a wrinkle of masculine sorrow. It is the same hand that groups, brings closer, disentangles the three actors of the intimate drama: the husband, the suspected wife (Emmy Lynn),² and the child. Gémier—I should say the husband—has been reproached for the inflexible rigor with which he separates, in order to make her confess, a young mother from her child. The film gains, all the same, from Emmy Lynn's lovely tears and from the child's scenes, which one can hardly resist. And I applaud a new use of the "still life," the touching use of props, as in the fall of the veil on the floor. We will eventually succeed in creating significant decor, sets full of undertones, an agreeable anxiety suggested, at the right moment, by a shot of a scene without actors. An empty chair at the bottom of the garden, a rose abandoned on a deserted table—did the great painter Le Sidaner need any more to hold us, dreaming, in front of a little table? I know very well that's Le Sidaner. But have patience. The miracle of cinematography is in young hands, astonished hands, hands often inept, erring, paralyzed with routine. Patience!

While we're waiting, let us praise *Mater Dolorosa*. Let us praise Emmy Lynn, exhausted young mother, who surpasses everything she promised us in the theater. Agree with me, since I take so much pleasure in it, that the action progresses in scenes lit with a rare richness—gilded whites, sooty and profound blacks.³ And my memory also retains certain somber close ups in which the speaking, suppliant head of Emmy Lynn floats like a decapitated flower.

¹ Firmin Gémier (1865–1933) was a famous actor and director who collaborated with Antoine at the Théâtre Antoine and the Théâtre de l'Odéon, and occasionally worked in the cinema. His most celebrated stage role came in Sophocles' *Oedipus Rex*, which he staged in the early 1920s.

² Emmy Lynn briefly enjoyed some success as an actress in the films of Abel Gance and her husband, Henry Roussel, during the late 1910s and early 1920s.

³ Léonce-H. Burel (1892–1977), who was responsible for the "rare richness" in lighting, was one of the top cinematographers of the French silent period. He worked first with Abel Gance on such films as *Mater Dolorosa* (1917), *La Dixième Symphonie* (1918), *J'Accuse* (1919), and *La Roue* (1922), and then with Jacques Feyder on *Crainquebille* (1923), *Visages d'enfants* (1925), and *L'Image* (1926). In the 1950s, he worked often with Robert Bresson.

LOUIS DELLUC, "Beauty in the Cinema"

From "La Beauté au cinéma," *Le Film* 73 (6 August 1917), 4–5.

A CHANCE evening at a cinema on the Boulevards gave me such extraordinary artistic pleasure that it seemed to have nothing at all to do with art. For a long time, I have realized that the cinema was destined to provide us with impressions of evanescent eternal beauty, since it alone offers us the spectacle of nature and sometimes even the spectacle of real human activity. You know, those impressions of grandeur, simplicity, and clarity which suddenly cause you to consider art useless. Obviously, art would be utterly useless if each of us was capable of appreciating consciously the profound beauty of the passing moment. But the education of a responsive mass of people is going too slowly for us to deprive ourselves yet of the many centuries of artworks which ensure the exalted confidence of others' spirits. The cinema is rightly moving toward the suppression of art, which reveals something beyond art, that is, life itself. Otherwise, it would merely be a median term between stylization and transient reality. And it has so much progress to make up for in order to reach perfection that we cannot say exactly when the screen will have trained us sufficiently— and this will be wonderful—to see into nature and the human heart.

Already much more than a reflection of this vibrant natural beauty has been revealed to us here and there. I would say much more about travelogues except that they are far too short. If the companies which lease them still do not comprehend that, it serves them right. Why do these views— I have seen some whose lighting and photography prove the cameraman's skill—last no more than a hundred meters? The poster announces Japan, Peru, or the Himalayas, and it barely lifts the curtain. The success of certain documentary films, significant in subject matter and intelligently exhibited, however, has provided evidence of the public taste for these armchair voyages. And the public is ready to go farther than the North Pole.

Advice to the cinema owner who would be the first to let us pass an entire evening in Italy, Spain, or Poland. Tourists would hasten there in droves.

This week everyone in Paris is praising a film which is, in fact, astonishing. Who has not yet seen the passage of that military convoy of ships in stormy weather. It is beautiful. I have had occasion to see this film three times, in three different cinemas, with three kinds of audiences. The enthusiasm has been the same in all three. As well as the heavy sigh at the end, which came all too soon. There, that's beauty, real beauty—I would say the beauty of chance, but the cameraman must be given his due. He has learned how *to see* with such skill that we have exactly the same experience of the sea, sky, and wind as he himself had. It is not just a film. It is natural truth, and the thought that such views will be offered us in abundance for the next several years is a great consolation. After this, how can one indulge in the blunders of a totally new art which the French have shackled with all manner of embellishments? No matter, it will unshackle itself.

The same program included two masterpieces. . . . Yes, *Ames d'étrangers* [*Alien Souls*, 1916] and *Charlot cambrioleur* [*Police*, 1916], are they not masterpieces? Quickly, tell me why, even if you believe I am paid to admire them. Ha, if I were to make money, then I would admire them even more! But, no, I am not even speaking of the films; that would be criticism, and today I am not trying to pass for a critic, let alone a contented critic. I am satisfied, that's all, for I have seen beautiful things.

So, now that I am off and running, let me assure you that *Ames d'étrangers* seems superior to most superior films. The mise-en-scène, the photography, the acting, even the scenario with its lovely, though unequal developments, but all at great cost. That said—for personal pleasure—let's move on. . . . Of the Charlot film, there is no point in speaking of photography, mise-en-scène, or any other detail that is inevitably ready to be used by the theatrical genius of Charlie Chaplin. That said, too, let's pass on to pure beauty. Pure beauty, which I now demand and always find in natural landscapes, is sometimes synthesized in a gesture, a face, a talent.

Sessue Hayakawa and Charlie Chaplin are, whatever film they appear in, two expressions of beauty. They are the two masterpieces I am talking about.

These two mimes do not act in the same way. Yet the rigorous renunciation of the word is as powerful in one as in the other. On that point we can compare them, if one wants comparisons; but, to tell the truth, a less visible and more poignant bond unites them—the absence of intellectuality. Hayakawa, through his race and virile style, and Chaplin, through his honest and mathematical naiveté, achieve equally genuine performances, although equally exaggerated in the eyes of the crowd. Of Chaplin alone can one say he has talent; of Hayakawa, one can say nothing: he is a phenome-

non. Explanations here are out of place. No explanations, then, but veri-
fications—rather than the false differences and similarities which one accepts unconsciously—for there are other striking things, with unusual
causes and effects, to discover.

Hayakawa dominates the crowd through his melancholy. Once more I
am not speaking of talent. I consider a certain kind of actor, especially him,
as a natural force and his face as a poetic work whose reason for being does
not concern me when my avidity for beauty finds there the expected chord
or reflection. So then, his melancholy, yes, of course. It is not his cat-like,
implacable cruelty, his mysterious brutality, his hatred of anyone who resists, or his contempt for anyone who submits; that is not what impresses
us, and yet that is all we can talk about. And his melancholy? His eyes are
so cold in the face of suffering that, when open, they seem as if they had
been closed forever. And especially his strangely drawn smile of childlike
ferocity, not really the ferocity of a puma or jaguar, for then it would no
longer be ferocity. The beauty of Sessue Hayakawa is painful. Few things
in the cinema reveal to us, as the light and silence of this mask do, that
there really are *alone* beings. I well believe that all lonely people, and they
are numerous, will discover their own recourseless despair in the intimate
melancholy of this savage Hayakawa.

And Charlot? Ah yes, he is something else. Something else? Not so fast!
Yes, something else. I have said it because a phenomenal actor is not the
same thing as a phenomenon. Yet, there also, charm triumphs. He goes
beyond the actor's art. Not for him the art of traditions, disguises, tricks,
acrobatics, eccentricities, and clownings, but a prodigious truth, at bottom, the truth of what he does for himself rather than for the spectator.
Charlie Chaplin enjoys himself at least as much as we do in his films, and
that is not far from the most that is possible. He enjoys himself too much.
Like all sad people. And don't tell me any more that one cannot speak of
Charlot's melancholy. It is to melancholy that he clings so delicately when
his baroque madnesses are not enough to save him: and that is his charm.
Latin people submit to Charlot just as to Sessue Hayakawa. I have never
seen a cinema audience resist the enterprises of these two men. Understand
me, the spectacle of true beauty reveals us to ourselves. And to recognize,
behind the tragic will of Hayakawa and the comic frenzy of Chaplin, an
echo of suffering or dreaming, such is the secret of an infatuation.

The cinema will make us all comprehend the things of this world as well
as force us to recognize ourselves.

LOUIS DELLUC (1890–1924) was best known as a drama critic for *Comoedia Illustré* when
he took over the editorship of *Le Film* in June 1917. Through his reviews and essays in *Le
Film, Paris-Midi*, and later his own film journals, *Le Journal du Ciné-Club* and *Cinéa*, Delluc
became the most influential film critic of the war and postwar period.

LOUIS DELLUC, "Antoine at Work"

From "Antoine travaille," *Le Film* 75 (20 August 1917), 5–7.

THE STRUGGLE goes on. Here's Antoine in the cinema. I don't know if he had been thinking about it for a long time, but we had. What would he do if he tried the cinema one day? Now we are going to find out.

His first attempt, *Les Frères corses*, can count as one of the best French films, and there aren't very many. In it, Antoine has conveyed a sense of life, taste, color, and charm of great value. His error was to launch his first effort with a scenario that's unwieldy in structure. That, I think, has been harmful—or could be harmful—to the film's success. And then the nature of the story favored a romantic verve which encouraged him to indulge in all the material charms of the theater of which he is such a virtuoso master.

It's not the least worry of this new struggle that Antoine has tougher obstacles to overcome than do the small fry of our film directors (and you know how small some are!). His theatrical genius—in mise-en-scène, performance, literary knowledge—has become his worst enemy.

The abyss that separates the theater from the cinema now seems unusually immense. Antoine doesn't seem to realize that. He realizes it less than most, in fact. And he has undertaken his first cinematographic efforts using the same methods he applied to *Julius Caesar, Ramuntcho*, or *La Faute de l'Abbé Mouret*.[1] He considers decors in the theatrical sense of the term: to begin with, he chooses historical settings that are too obviously theatrical in character. He also chooses actors from among the most gifted; you can see they are gifted for they still remember their Conservatory training. In the tableaux which are totally reconstructed—the admirable Opéra ball, for instance—this method produces marvels and perfectly harmonizes the lighting, sets, and costumes. But as soon as we find ourselves outside in scenes of exterior life, we are embarrassed by the musty smell of the theater which is so out of place in the cinema. Only it's not really Antoine's fault.

It's the fault of his habits, first of all. But that doesn't much matter. In practice, he will quickly forget his former knowledge. A first attempt is only an attempt; the first films of Thomas Ince were mediocre, and I'm sure De Mille only realized *The Cheat* after the dullest endeavors, which are already forgotten. And if our Antoine had the curiosity (as he should) to see his *Frères corses* when they released it to the public, he would certainly have noticed what was excessive as well as lacking. An Antoine who has discovered wonders, in writers as well as in his throng of actors, is a man who will continue to discover things. He will not search long for historical chateaux which are hardly indispensable. He will see, he is already seeing, the need to work straight from nature: just wait, I bet, unlike some, he won't make fun of the breezes which stir all the curtains in American interiors. And he won't associate himself any more—you will see that one day—with actors who are too good as actors.

Peasants, soldiers, charwomen, milkmaids, and railway workers should, if and when they wish to, become cinema actors, not extras but actors. We should search among them for those with the least possible acting skill. A provincial girl from Alcazar is more interesting in front of the cameraman than the most well-known of our official, subsidized ingenues. The more reason to use those who know nothing and who till the earth or work with their faces pressed up against their sewing machines. And from among our actors and actresses, keep the two dozen or so who have "reduced" their talent to the most vivid sobriety, indeed to impassivity. And if Antoine hasn't done this all at once, so what? He's only asked to begin. Now he's begun. And he will transform his copious theatrical skills without difficulty into surprising initiatives in the cinema.

If you have found him slow to do so, that's not his fault. It's the fault of capital. That's a paltry catchword to whimper about the miserable conditions of the cinema. I shouldn't insist on it, they tell me so obligingly, when I claim our directors should have the same conditions that are provided abroad. And they've laughed self-importantly; the film directors and their collaborators here believe they're invincible. They aren't even trying to find remedies. Two or three companies alone go on stubbornly trying to produce a maximum of art and intelligence with a minimum of capital. As for the others, they have no desire to be saved. Well, let them perish; no one will be sorry.

The case of Antoine is most alarming. Here's a great man who can do great things. How come millions aren't flowing out of all those pockets? Art is a business, dammit, and one makes money in the cinema, especially if the film happens to be signed by Antoine. I'd like them to decide to put their money into something other than tinned crabmeat or houses of prostitution.

Imagine Antoine with some capital. It's never going to happen, I know full well; just look at the theater. In order to mount a production of Tolstoy, Ibsen, d'Annunzio, or some other madman, you can find enough money to pay for the decors but not a sou more (and even that's not certain), so you have to produce vaudeville revues! But in the cinema, there's gold. Are you deaf and dumb or idiots, gentlemen? There's a mine to exploit, a formidable mine which you scarcely dare cut into and which may well be inexhaustible.

Antoine has vast projects. He would already have realized them if the French cinema were not subject to our disastrous traditions of economy and prudence. Abroad, it's said, volleys of laughter greet our interiors—those cheap drawing rooms and bedrooms, gaudy tapestries, scraggly and unseasonable green plants—but here they don't realize it. They economize more and more, and they earn even less. Don't you think that, if Antoine had gone to America, for instance, Triangle[2] would already have put at his disposal all the marvelous materials that he needed? And what credit would they have extended to him? Okay, over there, they can do that; we can't. But why can't we?

You know what Antoine has in preparation. I intend to speak a lot, and in detail, about the *Roche aux mouettes*, *Quatre-Vingt Treize*, and *Travailleurs de la mer*.[3] This could be extraordinary. But, here's the rub, what a struggle! Antoine always wants unheard-of things, and so many ambitions and strong wills have run aground in the cinema, until now at least.

Here's hoping Antoine is victorious. If he succeeds completely, I am going to say so; if he doesn't limit himself to making good films and persists in trying to achieve the splendors he so desires, that will be a sacred victory. And not only for Antoine, but for all of us. For if an artist as brave and all-embracing as he is can attain his aim, that means anything is possible. We will finally reach the threshold of a national art, an art which is more national than international and which has not yet—or scarcely—recognized how to be really French.

[1] Delluc is referring to several of the more lavish productions that Antoine mounted at the Théâtre de l'Odéon just before the war, whose huge debts forced him to resign as the Odéon's chief producer-director.

[2] In order to compete with the newly formed Paramount Corporation, in July 1915, three film production companies merged into the Triangle Corporation—Triangle Fine Arts (Griffith). Triangle Kay Bee (Ince), and Triangle Keystone (Sennett). Between 1915 and 1918, Triangle released more than 200 films, including some of the best of William S. Hart and Charles Ray.

[3] Antoine acted as an assistant to Albert Capellani (1870–1931) on *Quatre-Vingt Treize*, most of which was shot in 1914, and then finally was completed and released in 1921. Antoine filmed *Les Travailleurs de la mer* on the coast of Brittany in the summer of 1917; it was released in February 1918. *Roche aux mouchettes* was never made.

PHILIPPE SOUPAULT, "Note 1 on the Cinema"

From "Note 1 sur le cinéma," *SIC* 25 (January 1918), reprinted in *Ecrits de cinéma, 1918–1931* (Plon, 1979), 23–24.

ONE DAY on an empty lot in Vincennes, before an assembled crowd of idlers, an individual named Pathé presented a cinématograph invented by the Lumière brothers: man was endowed with a new eye.

After that, those who worked busily with this extraordinary invention deceived themselves terribly; they made the cinema the colorless mirror and mute echo of the theater. No one yet has stopped making this mistake.

However, since the means that the cinema makes available to the artist are quite different from those of the theater, it's important to establish a difference between the screen and the stage, to *separate cinematographic art from theatrical art*. That's the significant point of this first note.

Already, the richness of this new art is apparent to those who know how to see. Its power is tremendous since it reverses all natural laws: it ignores space and time; it upsets gravity, ballistics, biology, etc. . . . . Its eye is more patient, more penetrating, more precise. Thus the future belongs to the creator, the poet, who makes use of this hitherto neglected power and richness; for a new servant is available to his imagination.

Now, however, without wishing to exceed the limits of this note, I propose to those who have the material means that they realize this first scenario effort.

INDIFFERENCE

I am climbing a vertical road. At the top extends a plain where a violent wind is blowing. In front of me rocks puff out and become enormous. I bow my head and I pass between them. I arrive at a garden with monstrously high flowers and weeds. I sit down on a bench. There suddenly appears beside me a man who changes into a woman, and then into an old man. At this moment another old man appears who changes into a child and then a woman. Then soon, and little by little, a mixed crowd of men and women, etc., gesticulate, while I remain immobile. I get up and all disappear, I take a seat on the terrace of a café, but all the objects, the chairs, the tables, the spindle trees in the barrels, gather around and worry me, while a waiter circles around the group with ever-increasing speed; the trees lower their branches, the tramway and the cars pass at top speed, I take off and leap over the houses. I am on the roof facing a clock which grows and grows while its hands revolve faster and faster. I throw myself down from the roof and onto the sidewalk where I light a cigarette.

PHILIPPE SOUPAULT (1897–) was the first of the young Dada-Surrealists to become interested in the cinema. Besides writing several scenarios and cinematic poems, he contributed film reviews to *Littérature* and *L'Europe nouvelle*, both of which he also helped to edit.

LOUIS DELLUC, "Notes to Myself: *La Dixième Symphonie*"

From "Notes pour moi," *Le Film* 99 (4 February 1918), 3–4.

LA DIXIÈME SYMPHONIE by Abel Gance. Circumstances are giving Gance a special significance and position which will double his artistic importance as well as his personal authority. We know that, over the past ten years, the French cinema has not advanced one step. Let them boo me if they wish, but let them prove me wrong. I swear that the films produced during this lapse of time are in no way superior to the first attempts—naive and intelligent—which were called *Les Misérables, Le Bossu*, and *Les Trois Mousquetaires*.[1]

They asked us to indulge in wishful thinking by baldly adopting first Italian and then American ways, which naturally were only secondary to the original authors' intentions. Hence for six months now we have been drowning in chiaroscuro and "modern passion." Yet they aren't making any more of the *ciné* than before; they are only indulging in lighting effects. And the scenarios are as silly as they are poorly devised, or—worse—they are adopted from rickety plays, melodramtic novels, and childishly acrobatic sketches. And, worst of all, the acting is still behind the times in its "theatrical" manner. Their heavy masks come manufactured in bulk by the French Theater.

Yet . . . A quietly assured labor is gnawing away at the old shanty sheltering this childish play. Is it all going to collapse? That will be easy. One crack will be enough. For the general level of incomprehension, which has hampered any progress and forced everyone to carry on with insignificant things, has all been due to the company managers. Outside of two or three of them, they have persisted in mediocrity under the pretext that the public wants this or that—and the public really wants nothing but something new. These servile figures of power have imposed on us miserable stars (the rejects of stage crowd scenes or understudies of a dangerous notoriety), pitiful authors overwhelmed by the weight of their non-existence, and directors who perpetuate their weaknesses as stage managers on the screen and who would like to mount masterpieces like one mounts a cattle drive.

Do you really think they are going to realize and acknowledge that after reading this? Not if they can help it. Or not if all's said and done! Their conviction has only made them blind! Like Panurge's sheep,[2] they have produced, by imitation, historical films, then *grand guignolisms*, then a kind of modern romanticism *à l'italienne*, then photo-reliefs in the manner of *The Cheat*. Well, now, it will be enough to press on them three or four true films, which repudiate all their imitations, and they will madly imitate those, in spite of themselves. . . .

La Dixième Symphonie magnifies and synthesizes all the revolutionary developments which we have noticed these past months, but in such detail that no one has taken any interest. A small number of films recently have failed to achieve what this film has. You can enumerate them better than I. Each has had the misfortune to carry within it a flaw—or defect—which was too heavy not to drag it down: a role badly miscast, a director in disagreement with the author, an author ignorant of the technical means necessary for his ideas, a disorganized scenario. All this has occurred, singly or en masse, in the latest good films.

La Dixième Symphonie happily avoids these shortcomings. Undoubtedly, this is owing partially to chance. And it may also possess a flaw.

I recognize this flaw, but I know that it will diminish or rather that it could become a fine attribute, perhaps even the primordial attribute of Gance. This man is far from simple. In fact, he is too close to bombast, not in words, but in thinking: he wraps the plainest ideas in the richest clothing. The enthralling talent of d'Annunzio predates the cinema. And however radiant it may be, it's out of date. It's unnecessary for Gance to conceive of an idea as he would a character in *Feu* or *Forse che si*.[3] The cinematic craft pushes one toward an excess of externalization which renders such a style dangerous.

I'm being brash on purpose. What am I risking? That Gance will become the complete master of himself and rebel against the temptations of his nature? That's not impossible. He just might be able to discipline his personality, without repudiating it. That would take the greatest will power.

He tends to repeat himself in the same scene. I'd like to talk about the third part of the film. It's the climactic scene of a melancholy musician's performance of his new symphony: this provokes a series of simultaneous inner dramas, as the story explains itself to us. There is Séverin-Mars[4] at the piano, the piano itself, the hands of the composer, the score, the guests who are listening, the women dreaming and the men reflecting—all this is wonderful. If I'm not crazy, the public is going to respond to this with a surge of intense feeling.

Yet, at the same time, Emmy Lynn is also listening. She is even listening intently. During the first part of the scene, her *inner* immobility is affecting. Then the daemon of plasticity breathes over her, or rather over Gance, and she opens her wings: in the movement of arms and veils, Gance has had a great vision—a great white bird, a peplos in the wind, or something else. But I saw nothing of all that. Because the appearance of this poetic apparition, so slightly artificial or at least transposed from literature, embarrassed me in a moment that is otherwise true to life.

Perhaps this will please spectators. Indeed it's quite pretty to look at. But it's no good; it overlays something fine with something pretty but unnecessary. It's simply a mistake. Don't tell me, Gance, that the execution hasn't measured up to the intention. No, you were thinking of the Victory at Samothrace. I wasn't. The Victory at Samothrace suffices unto itself. Leave it where it is, unless you are devoting an essay, a poem, or a play to it. In a film, visibly present like that, it's extraneous. For three-quarters of an hour, you alone kept us interested. Would you have us believe that you aren't sufficient unto yourself? It's too late. We have only come for *La Dixième Symphonie*.

Consider also, Gance, that we suffer terribly from the quotations of Heine, Charles Guérin, or Rostand which you toss in our path.[5]

La Dixième Symphonie is a finished work. It has character, a central idea, a sense of life. This is a film by someone which could not have been executed by someone else because its author is manifest here everywhere, in every way.

It would take a closely written catalogue to enumerate all the alluring, vivid details that Gance has lavished on this film. Each has its place and thrives. The birds, the flowers, the dog, the musical instruments, the fabrics—how meticulous they all are and how graceful. We have the sense of living intimately with all of these people.

And the people are not so bad either.

Séverin-Mars dresses like Paul Mounet and acts like Guitry.[6] Yet he is completely himself. And he is "Gance" above all in the bargain. Jean Toulout is destined naturally for the *ciné*, yet he has been badly used in general, which could do a great disservice to his reputation.[7] Let him continue to work with artists, and he will realize characters as subtle as Fred Ryce. He's very good.

It's the same with Mlle. Emmy Lynn. A special form of tact is needed to put her in the best light. And there are dream roles for her in Gance's films, where she is both docile and audacious, just as Gance is both delicate and despotic.

The imagination of M. Lefaur, the gracefulness of Mlle. Nizan, a dozen anonymous actors enlisted in a cast who have done wonders—these are some of the elements which Gance has fashioned into something successful and artistic.

We will speak further of *La Dixième Symphonie*. Soon they will be releasing new films just as satisfying. *La Dixième Symphonie*, however, has the honor of being the most complete and accomplished work in this period of cinematographic renewal.

---

[1] These were all major French feature-length films produced prior to the war—André Heuzé's *Le Bossu* (1912), Albert Capellani, *Les Misérables* (SCAGL, 1912), and Henri Pouctal's *Les Trois Mousquetaires* (Film d'Art, 1913).

[2] The reference is to the popular tale in Rabelais's *Pantagruel*, in which Panurge (Pantagruel's faithful companion) buys a whole flock of sheep from a merchant and dispatches them, one by one, into the sea.

[3] These are the titles of two of D'Annunzio's more famous works.

[4] Séverin-Mars (1873–1921) was a major film actor and playwright who starred in three of Gance's films: *La Dixième Symphonie*, *J'Accuse*, and *La Roue*.

[5] Heinrich Heine (1797–1856) was a major German poet who also wrote in French. Charles Guérin (1873–1907) was much admired as a classical poet of solitude, duty, and

faith, before and during the war. Edmond Rostand (1868–1918) was the author of the French verse dramas, *Cyrano de Bergerac* (1897), *L'Aiglon* (1900), and *Chantecler* (1910).

[6] Paul Mounet (1847–1922) was the actor brother of Mounet-Sully (1841–1916), the famous prewar Comédie-Française tragedian. Lucien Guitry (1860–1925) was another celebrated actor in Paris and father of Sacha Guitry.

[7] Jean Toulout (1882–1962) went on to play major roles in Dulac's *La Fête espagnole* (1920) and *La Mort du soleil* (1922). Fescourt's *Mathias Sandorf* (1921) and *Les Misérables* (1925–1926), and Gastyne's *La Merveilleuse Vie de Jeanne d'Arc* (1929).

MARCEL L'HERBIER, "Hermes and Silence"

From "Hermès et le silence," *Le Film* 110–11 (29 April 1918), 7–12.

Hermes, god of Speech and the felicitous lie.—O.W.[1]
. . . the harmonious Silence of Truth.—St. A.[2]

EVER SINCE an invention of a miraculous kind, whose importance seems commensurate only with that of printing, undertook the task of seeming to destroy speech (as the book once did), to the point, some believe, of destroying the very structure of society—ever since [that invention] incorporated movement and aimed at a silent, popular, faithful translation of the daily drama of life or of natural landscapes—[ever since] the cinema, that subtle machine-which-transmits-life, appeared as a pragmatic source of power promising the most fantastic future, foreign nations have employed it with a methodicalness, an ingenuity, and a perseverance with which the French mind has not always been able to keep pace.

And while, for example, according to the statistics of American productivity, film will soon figure as the fifth most important source of wealth, here instead we are content to produce the "fifth art," which is either probably not enough or else too much. In any case, however, this argues, with an indubitable urgency, that the French mind, whose heritage it has been to innovate and perfect, must now assume, on clear directives and without delay, the obligation that it prove once more that nothing of its original inspiration has been lost and that, moreover—tomorrow as yesterday—in the league of world opinion, it can claim a victory that is definitive rather than merely an accepted cliché.

Nevertheless, some would have us swoon immediately in amazement.

Following speech, the arts of drawing, music, and dance, all of which apparently commenced to exist when man began to suffer and fashioned his first God out of his first tears and, dissatisfied with the latter's inertia, then prayed, sang, danced, or constructed holy places for the propitiation of the promised joy.

. . . Following these eternal works which were raised up out of the ephemeral nature of things, all of them forged with a fecund nostalgia, and

147

which together functioned through the course of centuries, as God's judgment through the genius of man; following what we will name in admiration by chance of memory: the Temple of Angkor, the Venus of Cnidus, the extraordinary pantomimes which made Herodotus tremble on the sacred lake of Sais, the dark Rembrandts in which shadows encroach like a storm of intelligence, or Beethoven's "silver key that opens the fountain of tears," or finally Speech, whose divinity when it is manifest makes of each "paradise lost" a paradise regained—following these memorable miracles, testimony to the immemorial arts, I say, to then establish the cinema straight off as the "fifth art" and as an Art equal to the other Arts, even though it is without origin, being the only one that cannot trace its stock back to the same source of human sadness, shouldn't that indeed be enough to disconcert us?[3]

However, as soon as we enter the debate and evoke the line of argument accepted up till now—I don't mean by certain hack writers whose mission, here below, seems to be to speak loudly about what the really ignorant think is little known, but by a good number of people who certainly are capable of understanding aesthetic theorems—we find ourselves assailed again by fresh surprises.

For, truth to tell, if we thought—in retort to a summary sentence by which our dear Laurent Tailhade,[4] a short time ago, condemned the cinema in toto because of some abject films—that M. Vuillermoz, sitting on the tribunal of *Le Temps*, would appeal the said sentence and take the floor in the name of the "silent art" (which we have condemned, he would whisper, without meaning to), at least we would not expect him to defend the concreteness of the image with the same fire of apodictic conviction as he has devoted to the subtle divisions of musical abstraction.

How astonished we are that, instead of limiting himself to defining the authority of *cinégraphie* as the "fifth art," he would go to the extent of judging it worthy of becoming "the most powerful of the plastic arts"—and, then again, after having glanced through Bergson in the hope of grafting his new faith onto some old metaphysical plantstock, that he would end by discovering in all this speculative orchard only the fruit of a text that was fruitless for all his gloss.

But our slackening surprise suddenly swells into full sail with the kind of analysis which, in another paper, M. Paul Souday exhales in a blast that would extinguish the glowing beliefs of his colleagues.[5]

Indeed, this eminent critic, hoping to prove the contrary of M. Vuillermoz's allegations that "Bergsonism does not accord with the cinema," constructs a line of argument exactly in the same manner as his (the just appreciation of which, I think, we can leave to someone else): namely, that if, for the convenience of propaedeutics, some psychologist amuses himself by comparing, for example, the impression of facts in the memory to the mechanical impression of printing, and if, later on, the same psychologist comes to examine his own memory and condemns it in the name, I suppose, of a more evolutionary power, we could logically conclude that the psychologist condemns printing, even more, that he condemns books! . . .

As reckless as such a line of argument seems, however, it is exactly what M. Paul Souday is pleased to accept as directing the critical faculty of the French mind, wandering in the cinegraphic wasteland.

As a double result that, since Bergson indeed compares conceptual thought to the mechanism of the cinema and, then again, pronounces himself against "the philosophy of ideas," [Souday] hastens unperturbed to the induction that "Bergson doesn't like the cinema."

Amusing logic, don't you agree? . . .

Let's look ahead further and speak clearly. If it's true that in its fundamental aspiration, Bergsonism can be summarized as a desire to merge with the "flux," as a desire to elevate the soul over the mind, as a desire to satisfy the soul "in its deepest, most genuine, and purely emotional region" (a region that's anti-verbal and anti-fictive), and finally as a tendency to descend toward the zone of deep-seated instinct, is not Bergsonism, I say, in all its propensity if not its essence, precisely analogous to current *cinégraphie*?

In this way, on the whole, at least in his conclusion that *cinégraphie* is by and large Bergsonian, M. Vuillermoz sees admirably well.

But doesn't such "correctness" still involve a begging of questions; for can we assert, as he does, without contradiction, that *cinégraphie* is similar to Bergsonism, which implies the substitution of the vital truth of movement for the falsehood of artistic crystallization, and at the same time that is is similar to the ancient arts, whose aim is always just the opposite?

Briefly, can we insist on a "fifth art" when the cinema's goal is clearly contrary to the goal of the other arts?

YET, IF we question the aestheticians on the abstract end of the four major arts, despite the differences in their discussion, it should be evident that those arts all share the same character in common, which is produced by *revolutionary* idealism. For there what leaps distinctly into the artist's mind directs him toward those concrete expressions which are works of art.

As for us, let's emphasize that in these teleological currents our opinion is firm. It accords with those famous sentences which are scarcely paralogical digressions but rather, like all paradoxes, vertiginous approaches to the brink of truth—those famous sentences which Wilde had to improvise for *Intentions* in front of the great bronze Hermes enthroned at the center of his dwelling, as the *signifiant* obedient to the artificial kingdom of speech, to the kingdom of that *logos* which, following Saint John, is God and, following Spinoza, is Untruth:

Namely, that "art is essentially a form of exaggeration, of emphasis"—a transcendent game "whose object is the Lie, that is, the expression of beautiful falsehoods"—thus "Art begins with abstract ornamentation, with a task that is purely fictive and applies only to the unreal, to the nonexistent," and, consequently, "art destroys what ceases to be strictly imaginative."

. . . isn't the contrast sufficiently marked between the end of those immemorial Arts and the end of what, from its infancy, has been called the fifth [art]?

For does it not seem clear to everyone that the end of *cinégraphie*, the art of the real, is completely opposite: to transcribe as faithfully and truthfully as possible, with neither transposition nor stylization, and by methods of accuracy which are uniquely its own, a certain phenomenal truth?

And, in fact, separated from the music which inevitably accompanies its images, and from the words which inevitably are provided by the intertitles *to be read* (music and literature, from which it has no right to profit if it insists that we accept it as an art unto itself, because they are borrowings from the other arts and are external to it)—in other words, reduced to its essence, [*cinégraphie*] strives to present, even obsequiously, as we see it, exactly the opposite of what the consoling arts of unreality attempt to make manifest in their desire for the absolute.

Thus, for example, at the antipodes of pure poetry, for which the only reality is the artificial flower of a word in the branches of language—for which dawns, landscapes, lovers, and life itself are no more than words and inflections of the soul—[*cinégraphie*] represents a life, by contrast, naturally in accord with universal matter, a life of bare fact in which drama is confined to gestures—where the landscape is as little stylized as in photography—where love lacks the absolute as much as it does tears—a life that can seem a mere printing press of images.

So then, let them try to keep us from detailing other differences between artistic and cinegraphic practice.

It is enough for us to single out the one as esoteric—that is, it is executed with means and results that are aristocratic, Aryan, hermetic, and virile; the other, exoteric—obeying a different sort of superiority, which has to do with its need to satisfy all the crowds, at the same time in every country, it is democratized, popularized, and leveled down to be nearer the mass of men.

The one, with its traditional laws, its strict conventions of unity, its artificial and chivalrous rules, reflecting a society strongly hierarchical and highly cultured; the other, without order, constraint, or control, reflecting a worldwide condition of culturelessness and helter-skelter irresponsibility.

The one, ultimately, personal, as in religious Salvation, and opposed to all collaboration (for to collaborate is to recognize an equivalence in the world and, therefore, to condemn in the eyes of art anything that makes an exception for genius); the other, by contrast, can only be practiced through the meanderings of an incessant, close, and multiple collaboration which involves scriptwriter, director, actors, and cameraman, as well as the capricious light of the sun and even that singular mechanism (which means to create all by itself and according to its own rules), that is, the film camera.

In short, after acceding to these arguments, all of which seem considerable and the first decisive, henceforth, if we really want to give some provincial magazines the satisfaction of maintaining that *cinégraphie* is the fifth art, at least at the top of their columns, we must still reach a consensus on the quality and quantity of artistic potential which *cinégraphie* allows.

It's a simple question, it seems, ever since it was posed, on condition that we really want to distinguish the *arts* from Art.

For if the Arts, the major Arts about which we have written, constitute a world uniquely promised to genius—art, on the other hand (that is, this kind of personal or professional ingenuity that we call art or craft), can occur anywhere, with anyone, with the weaver as with the lace-maker or fashion designer, with the doctor or lawyer, with specialists, and sometimes even with the serial writer . . . all the more so with the artisans of *cinégraphie*.

In the final analysis, to anyone who refuses to relent before these arguments (and who wishes to hold on to the visible effects streaming by on the screen), who, in this dispute, proposes that beauty can be projected in certain figures or certain gardens or certain reflections of moonlight on the sea, which he qualifies as purely artistic, to him, I say, his satisfaction is quickly discredited once we compare such beauty forthwith to that other sort of beauty which he must surely admire: that of chromo color–prints or even prettily illustrated postcards. . . .

The opposite of an art—and scarcely susceptible of art—for it only glows, when it glows at all, with a beauty borrowed from the other arts— that is how, in our opinion, one must judge the current cinema, according to the way one examines it in the context of the wellsprings of the past and considers it according to a view steeped in the weighty hypotheses of centuries of untruth—as we have seen some do who, retrospectively, summon it to raise itself up into an ode or some tenth symphony, patronized by the tenth muse.[6]

But let us, by contrast, judge *cinégraphie* from a pragmatic point of view, let us consider it from the horizon of the future, and things suddenly change. *Cinégraphie* is reestablished, as if miraculously, to the point of seeming, on the one hand, a force that's more efficacious, powerful, dynamic, and protean than the daily press or the telegraph, and, on the other hand, a force for the "masses" who are rid of a noble but empty superterrestrial nostalgia and who have repudiated the deceptive infinity of art, in which their sovereignty is unsatisfied, through the habitual lack of spiritual play, and who have finally become conscious of this full pleasure in living that Walt Whitman sings of[7]—for the "masses," where everything tends toward this contemplation of the factual, which Guyau holds up as the irreligion of the future.[8] In the organization of worldwide exchanges, above all, the cinema must be this medium of a visual press that, after the completion of his compulsive daily task, his sociability become universal, man may willingly read, for a small sum in a democratic community, yielding to his propensity for such established trifles of entertainment for which William James has sketched out the earthly gospel.

However, the cinema also must, sometimes in its fiction films, but especially in its documentaries, be something completely different from the theater of discourse, the novel of analysis, or the scholarly report expressed in writing. And the newsreel's views of the war already go further than the realist drama since it alone, to our minds, is capable of showing things with such sharpness, such precision, and especially such peculiar sublimation, all of which it carries out mechanically.

Furthermore, we have to point out the kind of film, and its miraculous means, which is produced by our own originality: that is, by French talent.

For let's admit something: since, in the future, the cinema is going to become an incessant weapon which "will pursue a ferocious bombardment of images and ideas across the fields of battle and peace," and since, even now, its aesthetic consists of popularizing, repeating with a scientific ubiquity, and profiting commercially from the unique works of the earlier museums of art, are we not all drafted, down to the least artist, in strict modesty, to attempt to achieve this task, imposed by the epoch, of fragmenting indefinitely, by means of evocations, suggestions, recollections, or precise images, through the fugitive miscellanies of film, the stock of these famous testimonies in which man was crystallized beneath the presence of a god?

. . .

So, in order to gain the right advantage, henceforth, let it be understood that the silent art draws itself up as an ineluctable threat to the Latin art of speech, to the traditional law of this superior god, respectively Hermes in Greece, Mercury in Rome, and Ogmios in Gaul, who once held the greatest peoples as well as the grandest centuries of our ascendance under his dominion which, in its effigies, is symbolized in the chains that fall from his mouth to envelope his proselytes in golden threads.

Indeed, compared to Hermes, who wishes to embalm generations with the elixir of bountiful untruth, Silence here looms up in our eyes and encloses in cinegraphic precision another untruth . . . a new untruth . . . the simple fact.

A secular oscillation that the French mind cannot hope to hold back. Just as it cannot hope, through its irrepressible *élan*, to rediscover, face to face, in this adverse era, all the love that fate now tosses away as fodder in time and space, to these eternal gawkers of the hereafter.

But at least let us remain steadfast at the center of French continuity; and strengthened by our clearsightedness and fortified by our example, let's demonstrate that, in this grand destiny which is concluding because another grand destiny is commencing, and for the survival of its glory, we are going to learn how to assert ourselves as the eager accessories of fate, that we are going to aid nature in spreading the mysterious waters of its innovation, and that, with a firm heart, we will wink at the new politics of human expression.

Thus, without renouncing the tottering secrets of old, which our blood has placed in us as our essential conscience, let us not turn away from the prodigious potential that *cinégraphie* encompasses; rather, let us soon take charge of its faltering existence with our intelligence and trust.

"That which is natural in things comprises the greater part of one's eternal soul."

Ah! Let's follow Baruch's universal and thus become, as sons of Sophocles and Racine, attuned to this new kind of symphony which is constructed out of leitmotifs of landscapes, counterpoints of gestures, fugues of shadows. . . .

So that our seal will be stamped on its destiny, let us lead it out of the thick naturalism in which it still wallows and toward an initially elementary symbolism which will, through more and more suggestive means, yet achieve the inherited grace of art and, what is especially significant, the tragic intention of things.

. . . And won't this be a way of putting our own preference to use more skillfully by serving with all our effort this nascent art of the image? For as we hasten its blossoming and sanction its vogue, as a consequence, the superior art of Speech and the male spirit of speculation, thus abandoned, will become, as we foresaw with Renan,[9] more and more the exclusive prerogative of a smaller and smaller elite.

Thus, even before the art of photography blossomed, the art of painting cleverly took refuge in subjective expressions and abstractions.

So Glory be to the art of the image, the universal language of the common people! Let's help this new source of power extend the boundaries of its empire to the limits of the earth so that its victory proves that this world is not dead—its virility seeming dead, who knows, it may still be fulfilled with the nourishment of this feminine form of play—and, from its surfeit, the intransigent lovers of speech will regain the freedom to employ, according to their own pleasure and not the demands of worldly appetite, the spirituality of that language which they say is what God employs "when he wants to explain himself to the Angels."

For it would be unworthy of our past if we wept indefinitely over the extinction of that age in which we would be recognized as the incomparable successors of Philo, Menander, Cerinthe, and those who in Alexandrian times would proclaim, with the Trismegistus, the divine Hermes, the son of a Pléiade, and descendent of the stars, lucid words which, with a dialectic of diamonds, would overlay the infinite palimpsest of the sky.[10]

Let's bend away from Hermes toward the protean figure of Silence.

. . . Above all, let's not for a moment be discouraged by the fact that in this basically communal and scientific enterprise, improvisation counts for little compared to patience, discipline, and the minutiae which, all told, are nothing here but qualities.

And if two nations actually still outdistance us in the nascent cinegraphic art, let that not be cause for dissuading us from our efforts.[11]

But let's recall now that once before, invaded by the auto-sacramental as well as the *Comedia dell'Arte*, if we at first retreated, we soon organized out of our sense of spirituality a systematic resistance and double offensive which was rewarded with a double victory, the one named Corneille, the other Molière.

Invaded anew by the activity of two friendly nations, and being at first, admittedly, retrograde, let's organize a similar resistance which likewise will be crowned soon with a victory.

Thus a cinematic means of expression will be born, worthy of us who no longer believe, and worthy of Silence, this new god, in whom we are coming to believe.

MARCEL L'HERBIER (1890–1980) was a minor poet and aesthete who discovered the cinema first through seeing *The Cheat*, in 1916, and then through service in the French Army Film Unit. He wrote several scenarios for Eclipse—for instance, Mercanton and Hervil's *Le Torrent* (1917) and *Bouclette* (1918)—before gaining financial support for his first film, *Rose-France* (1919).

¹ Oscar Wilde (1854–1900). As the Greek god of eloquence, commerce, and thieves, Hermes makes an apt figure for containing the several contradictions in L'Herbier's essay.

² Saint-André (1505–1562) was one of the important Catholic leaders at the beginning of the wars of religion in the sixteenth century.

³ L'Herbier's presumptuous erudition (a clutter of references and allusions), his overwrought syntax, and his studied mock-ironic tone are well exemplified here.

⁴ Laurent Tailhade (1854–1919) was a minor French poet and critic who had once been an outspoken literary anarchist in the 1890s. After an anarchist bombing in 1894, he penned this famous phrase: "What do vague humanitarian sentiments matter, so long as the action is beautiful."

⁵ See Emile Vuillermoz, "Devant l'écran," Le Temps (10 October 1917), 3, and Paul Souday's response to Vuillermoz—"Bergsonnisme et le cinéma," Paris-Midi (12 October 1917)—which Louis Delluc reprinted in Le Film 83 (15 October 1917), 9–10. These two essays did most to raise the question of the possible relationship between the cinema and the philosophy of Henri Bergson (1859–1941).

⁶ While Vuillermoz speaks of the Fifth Art ("something like a fifth carriage wheel," Delluc writes ironically), Canudo of the Seventh Art, it is Jean Cocteau who puts forward this notion of the Tenth Muse—AU.

⁷ L'Herbier's reference to Walt Whitman suggests the impact the recent translations of the American poet's work were having on French writers during the war.

⁸ Marie Jean Guyau (1854–1888) was a minor philosopher who tried to establish a secular morality free of any religious basis, to coincide with the Third Republic's legislative measures of the 1880s.

⁹ Ernest Renan (1832–1892) was an influential historian of religion and scholar of philology.

¹⁰ Here as elsewhere, L'Herbier associates himself with the Classical Renaissance then coming into dominance in French art, by seeing French culture as a privileged continuation of ancient Greek culture. And, in his use of sexual and political language, he approaches the extreme right-wing views espoused by Léon Daudet in Action française, which in turn would be promulgated by François Vinneuil (the pseudonym of Lucien Rebatet) and others in the 1930s.

¹¹ L'Herbier's reference is to the American and Italian cinemas, the latter of which, somewhat mistakenly, the French still considered equal to or better than their own cinema.

EMILE VUILLERMOZ, "Before the Screen: Hermes and Silence"

From "Devant l'écran: Hermès et le silence," Le Temps (9 March 1918), 3.

UNDER THIS TITLE, M. Marcel L'Herbier has drawn up an indictment against the cinema, of which we offered a detailed resumé two weeks ago and the complete text of which Mercure de France will publish soon.[1] You will recall the singular case of this young poet who composes symbolic dramas for the screen, helps shoot and edit them, signs them, and exhibits them for the masses, all the while nonchalantly declaring that "the cinema, even in its very design and purpose, is the opposite of art."

The attitude is cavalier. It will overjoy all the enemies of the ciné who have been waiting for just this sort of fugue from an unusually refined bookish type who has come into the land of light, into the coarse company of camera operators! Ultimately, from this condemnation, we conclude that the subtle aesthete has been captivated by a sport from which, in passing, we might well agree to free him, just to kill time, yet we refuse to take him seriously and treat his attitude with disdain once we find ourselves in good company.

This ingratitude will grieve the cinema enthusiasts who had greeted this chosen neophyte with the most open sympathy and entrusted him with a good deal of credit while waiting for him to plumb the mysteries of this new religion.

The impatient novitiate has not engaged in such sage caution. With no more than a glance, he has passed judgment on the situation and produced a definitive opinion on the future of a gospel of which he has read only the first page. Allow us to be astonished at the fickleness of his renunciation.

M. Marcel L'Herbier wishes to grant every quality and virtue to *cinégraphie* on the sole condition that it renounce forever its ambition to become an art. When he composes a film, he does not produce an artistic work, he says, but the work of a craftsman. He brings to his task merely a kind of dexterity, a professional ingenuity which is nothing more than the intelligence, imagination, or sensibility of a good typist or a skillful mechanic. Shall we defend his first works against himself? . . . No . . . Let his own cruelty declare him to be correct, for the moment.

But by what right does he take on the future? None of his subtle arguments should discourage honest seekers who divine in the *cinégraphie* a new, unexploited mode of expression, whose marvelous possibilities at this point it is highhanded to deny.

His objections, moreover, are not all that peremptory. It is difficult, for instance, to refuse the cinema the right to be accepted among the arts, under the silly pretext that it is not old enough and that it has nothing in common with the venerable arts which man discovered on his arrival on the planet.

In principle, we see no theoretical impossibility in the idea that a new art, completely unforeseen, may emerge tomorrow out of a discovery in physics or chemistry which will modify our perceptions and yield pleasures absolutely undreamt of today. But even while maintaining a prejudice against this "birth," which seems to impress our poet, it is not impossible to have some regard for the commoners' sport which he excludes from the temple of the Muses. *Cinégraphie* has an undeniable ancestry; it is a plastic art whose modes of execution have been transformed by science. The distance which separates it from sculpture and mime and drawing is no greater than that which separates a canvas by Claude Monet from the carved stones of the Ice Age or an orchestral score by Ravel from a melodic outpouring of Pithecanthropus.

Has science not completely recreated, over several centuries, what we designate under the immutable name of painting or music? Can one deny that such a prosaic intervention as placing in the hands of our Impressionists tubes of color which were lacking to the reindeer painters in the caves of the Madeleine[2] or that placing beneath the fingers of our virtuosos a good grand piano instead of dried gourds has had an influence on our artistic sensibility? The application of light-sensitive celluloid and animated projection as well as the realization of "plastic harmonies" is but a stage in visual orchestration. *Cinégraphie* comes from an excellent family, and a poet can frequent it without losing face.

The following anathema seems, at first, more thoughtful and formidable. It's developed with a charm and lyricism which render it especially dangerous. Art is, by definition, "beautiful lies": with its absurd honesty, the screen is the negation of this for it is content to trace, photograph, and thus copy reality.

After such a statement, we would be quite disturbed about M. L'Herbier's technical education if we didn't give ideology its due in an indictment of this kind; and we couldn't make much of a case for his future as a director. Well, what about it, does he actually think that the cinematographist is a copier? Does he really believe in the faithfulness of the camera? That would be a very unusual artlessness! But the screen thrives on "beautiful lies"; it creates nostalgic moonlit scenes out of bright, sunny Marseillean scenes skillfully tinted and toned by unscrupulous cameramen! The most sublime deceptions dominate this supple and wily art which, more than any other, excels in trickery and mystification. Everything is permitted, and reality poses no obstacle at all.

When the author of *Le Torrent*[3] baptizes the cinema as "the machine that imprints life," he did not provide himself with a worthy ideal. The formula is nice and catchy, but it is limiting to the point of perfidy. If M. Marcel L'Herbier adopts it for his works, we would have nothing more to expect from him. The film documentary, the faithful witness of our daily existence, can render us appreciable services by mechanically printing life; but *cinégraphie* is unworthy of our interest if it doesn't become, by contrast, "the machine with which to imprint dreams."

It has done so already. Intentionally or not, the cinematographist interprets his vision and incorporates into it a little of his feeling and thought. A landscape allows him to recognize himself. He transforms, recreates, and transfigures nature, according to his emotional state. Just as spontaneously as other artists, he knows how "to revisualize a sunset with the light and shadow of his soul."

Place ten directors before the same landscape and give them the task of treating the same film scenario, with the same cast of actors, and you will obtain ten absolutely different results. Each of them will experience the character of the landscape in his own personal fashion and will choose an hour, a kind of lighting, a pattern of movement, according to his temperament. "Corot," said Rodin, "saw goodness scattered over the crowns of trees, over the fields of grass, and over the surface of lakes; Millet saw suffering and resignation there." *Cinégraphie* has its Corots and Millets!⁴

In order to impose his personal vision of beings and things on thousands of spectators, as he does each day, does not the painter of the screen remain faithful to the cult of Hermes and fill humanity with a generous outpouring of "beautiful lies"?

To concentrate all the force of feeling or thought on an inanimate object, to crystallize around an inert accessory scattered feelings, fleeting memories, passing dreams, is that the work of a craftsman or an artist? With a brioche and a flagon of wine, Chardin draws us far away from the subject of his canvas: these two talismans open up a world, invite us into a distinctive atmosphere, and reveal to us "the soul of a bourgeois, peaceful, honest, modest, and comfortable."⁵

Cinégraphie can, in its own way, make inanimate objects speak and give laughter and tears to things. It knows, equally, how to draw an affecting harmony from a human face, effects of an extremely subtle power and charm. It lays out the whole gamut of expressions of trees, clouds, mountains, and seas. No element of beauty or passion is shielded from its penetrating glance. It can suggest, evoke, cast a spell; it can effect audacious associations of ideas through the rapprochement of images. It can mix up visual counterpoints with an irresistible force, impose harsh dissonances, or hold major chords. It can develop a feeling broadly or let it be read with a discreteness or lightness of touch that is almost imperceptible. It knows how to let a scherzo or andante soar with incredible suppleness, how to plunder the juice of every flower, like a bee, and distill it in the cells honeycombing a film. It recognizes no impossibilities of any kind, in neither space nor time.

Is it to create the work of an artist or an artisan that [*cinégraphie*] intelligently arranges all these magical forces so as to recreate a world as if seen "through a temperament"? Is it to create the work of an artisan that it adroitly cuts up and welds together the thousand tiny fragments of reality which are snatched from the forces of nature to constitute a deceptive "superreality," more intense than the truth? Is it to create the work of an artisan that it brings together a hundred disparate "moments" of a woman's suffering or love, fixed in motion, at the fleeting instant of their expressive paroxysm, and "adds them up" on the screen in order to achieve a movement, a gradual build up, a crescendo whose power the theater cannot encompass? . . .

But why multiply the examples? Does M. Marcel L'Herbier really need to be convinced of this blasphemy by a voice other than his own, since he isn't afraid to exclaim: "Let us not turn away from the prodigious potential that *cinégraphie* encompasses, rather let us soon take charge of its faltering existence with our intelligence and trust. . . . Let us [direct it] toward an initially elementary symbolism which will, through more and more suggestive means, yet achieve the inherited grace of art and, what is especially significant, the tragic intention of things . . . ?"

For a simple artisan, this is an awfully noble task! If M. Marcel L'Herbier has decided to undertake it, we will no longer think of haggling over the title he attributes to himself. And we will not rank ourselves among the aestheticians who naively apply to cinegraphic interpretations the stupefying judgment of Pascal: "How vain is the painter who for his likenesses of things gains the respect of others, when he himself fails to respect the originals! . . ."

¹ L'Herbier's "Hermès et le silence" was commissioned for *Mercure de France*, which, however, demanded many cuts in the manuscript for publication. Louis Delluc accepted it as is for *Le Film*, and it was then reprinted two years later in *Les Feuilles libres*. Vuillermoz's summary of the text—in "Devant l'écran. Hermès et le silence." *Le Temps* (23 February 1918)—suggests that he had access, perhaps with L'Herbier's permission, to the manuscript that *Mercure de France* was considering for publication.

² The reference is to the famous prehistoric caves in the region of Dordogne.

³ L'Herbier wrote the scenario of *Le Torrent* for Louis Mercanton and René Hervil; the film was released by Eclipse in late 1917.

⁴ Camille Corot (1796–1875), one of the great French painters of the nineteenth century, was especially noted for the "simple, pure" style of his landscapes. Jean-François Millet (1814–1875) became famous for his "romantic-heroic" vision of human labor in French rural areas.

⁵ Jean-Baptiste Chardin (1699–1779) was a painter of "lesser" genres—still lifes, portraits, games and amusements—whose ability to depict "the little details of ordinary life" was much admired. As Michael Fried argues, Chardin seemed especially concerned with representing and extending moments of absorption—Fried, *Absorption and Theatricality*, 44–53.

LOUIS DELLUC, "The Crowd"

From "La Foule," *Paris-Midi* (24 August 1918), 2. Delluc's essay was included (and expanded) in his second book on the cinema as "La Foule devant l'écran," *Photogénie* (Paris: de Brunoff, 1920), 104–18.

AND THE CINEMA? Why can't the "faithful and elegant clientele" of the most typical cinemas of west Paris get by without watching [the most wretched] popular films? Likeable idlers, artists, prostitutes, industrialists, and a vast majority of the high bourgeoisie—all this satisfied and comfortable public, pared down by years of dazzling Parisian living—would seem compelled to suffer nothing less than what is beautiful or at least novel. The remarkable American films are celebrated there, and everything modern is truly a la mode in these select sanctuaries where the chairs, the usherettes, the bar, the orchestra, and the lighting testify to the most desirable breeding.

However, the worst serials are regularly posted on the marquees and, of course, provoke a great deal of laughter. From *Pardaillan* or *Le Courrier de Lyon* up to the recent *Judexes*,[1] few weeks have gone by without a distinguished audience having spent an hour in joking, chuckling, and engaging in other ferocious convulsions. An admirable comic film, a Charlie Chaplin perhaps, disappoints their need for devastating mockery. And that is why we will see so-called popular films in such pleasant cinemas a long time from now, for they permit refined creatures to parade their superiority in public.

When [the French comic] Mascamor and his tragic cello note, whose effect was so amusing, were in vogue, the wealthy spectators were ruthlessly critical to their heart's content. Have you noticed how this ruthlessness is irrelevant? Obviously prejudiced, this sort of public gets angry irritably, just as in farce, when it ought to do so spontaneously.

ANOTHER audience. Barkeepers, charcoal sellers, cinema proprietors from Paris and its suburbs flocked together for the preview of Pathé's *La Dixième Symphonie*.

La Dixième Symphonie was the most publicized and awaited film by the young director, Abel Gance, whose first efforts—*Mater Dolorosa* and *La Zone de la mort*—combined a dazzling audacity of technique and performance into an interesting, imaginative exaltation. *Mater Dolorosa*, which was no more than a rough sketch, has a genuine significance in the artistic history of our cinema.

Here and there, with flashes of power, *La Dixième Symphonie* asserts the same qualities of visual conception. Perhaps it would have been better if its obvious literary flavor were the result of passing glances rather than being the essential motor [of the film], yet nothing prevents us from thinking that some day Gance will be able to reestablish a proper equilibrium of relations. Even the force of the film's qualities assures us of their future collusion.

That same authorial willfulness also insists on those errors which already appeared grave [in the earlier films]: a calculated disorder, a tendency to substitute for the basic detail, an overabundance of deflecting sensibility which sometimes stands in for sincere human or lyrical intensity.

Need I add that the cinema managers present at the Pathé preview the other day preferred these errors. One of them spoke to me enthusiastically about the chorus of maids that sobbed at the symphony's audition. And another exclaimed about the symbolic dance inserted into the drama. He had understood nothing and would just as easily admire a gaudily colored calendar with the traditional figures of Spring, Summer, Autumn, and Winter. The epigraphs which served as intertitles and were signed—Chopin, Rostand, Charles Guérin, etc.—equally caused much weeping. I am not talking about the ray of sunlight on the Buddha, the white statue under the lamp, nor particularly about the sentimental or cynical complications of the characters who undoubtedly wasted away their personalities by frequenting [Oscar] Wilde or [Claude] Lorrain or a retrospective Baudelaire who never existed.[2]

Myself, I prefer Séverin-Mars's hands on the piano and Séverin-Mars himself and his pensive and passionate sobriety; and the shudderings of Emmy Lynn, in all those moments when she is not thinking of the Victory at Samothrace or Sarah Bernhardt; yes, Emmy Lynn and her dazzling photogenic *substance*; and the old man who listens in a corner of the room, and the animals and flowers and "all that is passing away," and . . . and . . . many other things.

But what I like is not what they like. And the mass public perhaps will agree with the cinema managers and applaud all that is willful and overwritten in the generous ensemble. Have not the best plays of Henry Bataille triumphed because of the morbid trickery and tortuous psychology of those fragments which, in fact, have tarnished their overall vivid, pathetic beauty?[3]

The important thing is that the author of *La Dixième Symphonie* not think exactly like this public. And that *La Dixième Symphonie* have a healthy following—and that they follow it.

ANOTHER audience. At the Saturday evening screening of the only cinema palace of the town, the Tout-Aurillac,[4] a first-run and second-run house. Convalescents, billeted soldiers, respectable families, respectable young girls, the smoke from pipes, the ritornellos of an untuned piano, all in a deep, dark, cold cinema with *Le Courrier de Washington*[5] on the marquee.

They also screened *La Lumière qui s'éteint*,[6] an English film previewed in Paris last winter. Despite its almost unanimous lack of culture, the audience was deeply moved by the *inner* adventure of Masie, Dick, and Torp. And you know what became of the great Kipling's work on film. An ordinary anecdote, badly decorated and photographed, with a sad, heavy actor playing Dick—when will we see Douglas Fairbanks in the part?—a fop as Torp, a fool as Masie, and unbelievable Arab battles in, let's be blunt, a cardboard Sudanese Khartoum. There is a film to do over again.

Why was this rough peasant audience affected in front of this artless and unauthorized gaucherie? Will it understand even more when the same drama becomes a quite beautiful film?

IN A FRIGHTFULLY little cinema in Clermont-Fernand,[7] I have seen what is called the popular sensibility. The screen's charm has expanded the taste of the masses who have been so resistant to letting themselves be cultivated by any of the other arts. Several hundred workers and simple women were wrapped up in the delicacy of a little Japanese film, without action, comprised of gestures, flowers, and decorated papers. After which there was an episode from *Coeur d'heroine* with Irene Vernon Castle.[8] You might think this audience was affected particularly by the drama or by the serial-like changes in fortune. They scarcely took any notice of that. For any hour of happiness, they lived only for the clothes of Irene Castle, the harmony of the settings, and the remarkable grace of the furniture.

Moreover, in another town and in another cinema, but in front of a very similar audience, Sessue Hayakawa, the Japanese actor from *The Cheat* who was appearing in *Ames d'étrangers*, was followed, understood, and appreciated completely. The same film which I had seen in an elegant cinema in Paris had caused people to smile. And it is the elegant cinema that got it wrong.

Here is one of the most miraculous things about the fifth art. It touches the unanimity of the masses without demanding the cerebral preparation of a book or music. And that is why the French intellectual elite is protecting itself from admiring the cinema and especially from admitting its love for the cinema. What a revelation, right? To suddenly declare to the most cultured Latin types that they can admire something which has nothing to do with classical studies. The war has upset everything and perhaps will facilitate their quick and delighted accommodation, yet more than one cultured writer has whimpered to himself that it is rape or sacrilege or treason. Why not dream of entering the Polytechnique without examination?[9] Why not do away with nine-tenths of the bureaucrats of our government?

Added to that is the anxiety of social tradition, so rigid and so blithely blind when it is a question of progress. Mirbeau[10] fulminated against the misoneism of the gentlemen of his age. What would he say if he had spent his spare time away from pamphleteering at the cinema? At least he would have discovered with an exquisite astonishment the striking acuteness of the people, from the moment the screen comes alive.

This acuteness gains enormously from the fact that the people are timid. As long as he is not at a café-concert, the worker is reserved. Thus a performance at the Comédie-Française especially is only tolerable on Sunday evening, on condition that one is seated in the top gallery. Not being well brought up, the masses do not readily allow themselves to behave badly. There is no doubt, for instance, that if Mme Ida Rubenstein[11] had reserved 3,000 seats for Parisian factory workers at the Châtelet during its performances of Verhaeren and D'Annuzio, she would have received interesting impressions and a proper homage. But those Parisians of the boulevards, *invited* yet unprepared according to the usual rules, simply gave vent to their freedom of mind by howling like animals. Such an attitude has the principal disadvantage of preventing them from hearing.

The popular public hears because it listens. It listens because it is silent. Silence genuinely helps in looking and seeing. To chatter away in front of a film is as imprudent for its comprehension as to chatter during *Pélléas* or *Parsifal*.[12] The Opéra subscribers who dash to the Colisée[13] every Friday evening should be prevented from telling you whether a film is anything but a film. Their evening is spent in animated conversations, broken by sharp laughter, distinguished coughs, and sometimes ferocious yelpings when one or two loges have deigned to signal that the spectacle was especially ingenious. I would be desolate if they changed what is now a Friday ritual at the Colisée.

But I prefer quieter spectators. The best, to my amusement, I have found in the *faubourgs*. I say this without malice for they please me not only because of their silence and attention but also because of their acuteness, taste, and insight. Perhaps if others regarded the screen with attention and silence, they too would see this mysterious beauty which until now has exhibited such partiality in choosing its devotees. But I am not certain of that. Ah, how awkward it is to have to read so many books, especially when those who have stuffed their lives with literature embarrass themselves before the screen!

For a long time I have been going each week to the rue de la Fidelité, near the Gare de l'Est,[14] into a little cinema frequented pell-mell by mechanics, pimps, laborers, and women warehouse packers. The appearance of the first Triangle films provoked a strange enthusiasm there. Yet these films are full of elegant subtleties. Those who remember *Molly, La Lys et la rose, Peggy, Illusion, L'Autel de l'honneur*[16] know that their luxury was conceived so audaciously that it could have no relation to the people. Yet the people were delighted. At the most, they made fun of religious questions: *The Christian*, an English film drawn from the fine novel by Hall Caine, provoked much laughter; and *Le Redemption de Panamint* was only pardoned its orthodoxy thanks to the smile of Dustin Farnum.[16]

In the distant Olympic-Palace, at the bottom of the rue de Vanves, Ince's complex, inspired film, *La Mauvais Etoile*, was received with such respect that I imagined the audience to be an apostolate which would salute it with a grand ovation.[17] In the audience were men "in peaked caps" and women "without hats."

On densely crowded Saturdays, in the Barbes-Palace,[18] Douglas Fairbanks and his ingenious, sportive poetry have awakened a childlike happiness in spectators, as if those normally indifferent to art were discovering a new spark. Truly it is far from discouraging to be a spectator of such spectators.

Wild surges of passion? At the Lecourbe cinema, at the Grenelle, near the Mirabeau bridge, even at La Chapelle.[19] And if we had the time—at the Place d'Italie, Levallois, Menilmontant, the avenue de Saint-Ouen . . .

---

[1] *Les Pardaillan* (1913) starred Suzanne Grandais; *Le Courrier de Lyon* (1911) was an early three-reel film directed by Albert Capellani. Louis Feuillade's *Judex* (1917) and *La Nouvelle Mission de Judex* (1918) were the most popular French serials of the war.

[2] Delluc is caricaturing the Belle Epoque dandy and his artistic tastes.

[3] Henry Bataille (1872–1922) was a popular dramatist of sexual intrigue, before and during the war. A good number of his plays were made into films after his death—Léonce Perret's *La Femme Nue* (1926), Julien Duvivier's *Maman Colibri* (1929), Luitz-Morat's *La Vierge folle* (1929), and André Hugon's *La Marche nuptiale* (1929).

[4] Aurillac is an agricultural center in the Auvergne region, midway between Lyon and Bordeaux.

[5] *Le Courrier de Washington* was the French title for the Pearl White serial, *Pearl of the Army* (1916).

[6] I have been unable to trace the original British title of *La Lumière qui s'éteint*.

[7] Clermont-Fernand is the industrial center in the Auvergne region, just west of Lyon.

[8] *Coeur d'heroine* was the French title for *Patria* (1917), an American serial directed by Theodore Wharton and Jacques Jaccard for Wharton-International Film Service.

[9] The Polytechnique is the principal advanced school for applied sciences and engineering in France.

[10] Octave Mirbeau (1848-1917) was a novelist and dramatist of the Naturalist school, outspoken in his revolutionary anarchist ideals, and deeply committed to an emerging working-class movement.

[11] Mme Ida Rubenstein (1880–1960) was a Russian-born dancer and famous benefactor of the arts in France.

[12] *Pélléas et Mélisande* (1902) was a celebrated lyrical drama written by Maurice Maeterlinck (1862–1949), with music by Claude Debussy (1862–1918). *Parsifal* (1882) was the last operatic work of Richard Wagner (1813–1883).

[13] The Colisée cinema was the first major cinema on the Champs-Elysées. Despite Delluc's protestations, it became one of his favorite cinemas after the war.

[14] This cinema was in the tenth arrondisement, two or three blocks down from the Gare de l'Est and just west of the Canal Saint-Martin and the Hôpital Saint-Louis.

[15] These titles, in order, include Famous Players' *Molly* (1915), starring Mary Pickford; Paul Powell's *The Lily and the Rose* (1915), starring Lilian Gish; and three films starring Charles Ray—Charles Miller's *Peggy* (1916), *Home* (1916), and *Honor's Altar* (1916).

[16] *Le Redemption de Panamint* was the French title for the Famous Players–Lasky film, *The Parson on Panamint* (1916).

[17] This cinema was in the fourteenth arrondisement, just south of the Montparnasse cemetery. *La Mauvaise Etoile* was the French title for Triangle's *Civilization's Child* (1916), starring Ana Lehr and William H. Thompson.

[18] The Barbes-Palace was probably in the eighteenth arrondisement, just east of Montmarte, near the Barbes-Rochechouart metro station.

[19] These cinemas were in the fifteenth arrondisement, in southwest Paris, except for La Chapelle, which was up above the Gare du Nord and the Gare de l'Est.

LOUIS ARAGON, "On Decor"

Translated by Paul Hammond in *The Shadow and Its Shadow: Surrealist Writings on the Cinema*, ed., Paul Hammond (London: British Film Institute, 1978), 28–31. Reprinted by permission. The original French text first appeared as "Du Décor," in *Le Film* 131 (16 September 1918), 8–10.

O N T H E S C R E E N the great demon with white teeth, bare arms, speaks an extraordinary language, the language of love. Men of all nations hear it and are more moved by the drama enacted before a wall decorated poetically with posters than by the tragedy we bid the subtlest actor perform before the showiest set. Here *trompe l'oeil* fails: naked sentiment triumphs, and the setting must equal it in poetic power to touch our heart.

The door of a bar that swings and on the window the capital letters of unreadable and marvelous words, or the vertiginous, thousand-eyed façade of the thirty-story house, or this rapturous display of tinned goods (what great painter has composed this?), or this counter with the row of bottles that makes you drunk just to look at it: resources so new that despite being repeated a hundred times they create a novel poetry for minds able to respond to it, and for which the ten or twelve stories told man since the discovery of fire and love will henceforth unfold without ever tiring the sensibilities of this time which twilights, gothic castles, and tales of peasant life have worn out.

For a long time we have followed our elder brothers on the corpses of other civilizations. Here is the time of life to come. No more do we go to Bayreuth or Ravenna with Barrès[1] to be moved. The names of Toronto and Minneapolis seem more beautiful to us. Someone mentioned modern magic. How better to explain this superhuman, despotic power such elements exercise even on those who recognized them, elements till now decried by people of taste, and which are the most powerful on souls least sensitive to the enchantment of film-going?

Before the appearance of the cinematograph hardly any artist dared use the false harmony of machines and the obsessive beauty of commercial inscriptions, posters, evocative lettering, really common objects, everything that celebrates life, not some artificial convention that excludes corned beef and tins of polish. Today these courageous precursors, painters or poets, witness their own triumph, they who knew how to be moved by a newspaper or a packet of cigarettes, when the public thrills and communes with them before the kind of decor whose beauty they had predicted. They knew the fascination of hieroglyphs on walls which an angel scribbled at the end of the feast, or that ironic obsession imposed by destiny on the unfortunate hero's travels. Those letters advertising a make of soap are the equivalent of characters on an obelisk or the inscription in a book of spells: they describe the fate of an era. We had already seen them as elements in the art of Picasso, Georges Braque, and Juan Gris.[2] Before them, Baudelaire knew the import you could draw from a sign. Alfred Jarry, the immortal author of *Ubu roi*, had used scraps of this modern poetry. But only the cinema which directly addresses the people could impose these new sources of human splendor on a rebellious humanity searching for its soul.

We must open our eyes in front of the screen, we must analyze the feeling that transports us, reason it out to discover the cause of that sublimation of ourselves. What new attraction do we, surfeited with theater, find in this black and white symphony, the poorest of means deprived of verbal giddiness and the stage's perspective? It isn't the sight of eternally similar passions, nor—as one would have liked to believe—the faithful reproduction of a nature the Thomas Cook Agency[3] puts within our reach, but the magnification of the kinds of objects that, without artifice, our feeble mind can raise up to the superior life of poetry. The proof of this lies in the pitiful boredom of films that draw the elements of their lyricism from the shabby arsenal of old poetic ideas, already known and patented: historical films, films in which lovers die of moonlight, mountain, and ocean, exotic films, films born of all the old conventions. All our emotion exists for those dear old American adventure films that speak of daily life and manage to raise to a dramatic level a banknote on which our attention is riveted, a table with a revolver on it, a bottle that on occasion becomes a weapon, a handkerchief that reveals a crime, a typewriter that's the horizon of a desk, the terrible unfolding telegraphic tape with magic ciphers that enrich or ruin bankers. Oh! that grid of a wall in *The Wolves*[4] which the shirt-sleeved stockbroker wrote the latest prices on! And that contraption Charlie Chaplin struggled with in *The Fireman*!

Poets without being artists, children sometimes fix their attention on an object to the point where their concentration makes it grow larger, grow so much it completely occupies their visual field, assumes a mysterious aspect and loses all relation to its purpose. Or they repeat a word endlessly, so often it divests itself of meaning and becomes a poignant and pointless sound that makes them cry. Likewise on the screen objects that were a few moments ago sticks of furniture or books of cloakroom tickets are transformed to the point where they take on menacing or enigmatic meanings. The theater is powerless where such emotive concentration is concerned.

To endow with a poetic value that which does not yet possess it, to willfully restrict the field of vision so as to intensify expression: these are two properties that help make cinematic decor the adequate setting of modern beauty.

If today the cinema does not always show itself to be the powerful evocator it might be, even in the best of those American films that enable a screen poetry to be redeemed from the farrago of theatrical adaptations, it is because the *metteurs en scène*, though sometimes possessed of a keen sense of its beauty, do not recognise its philosophic qualities. I would hope a filmmaker were a poet and a philosopher, and a spectator who judges his own work as well. Fully to appreciate, say, Chaplin's *The Vagabond*, I think it is indispensable to know and love Pablo Picasso's "Blue Period" paintings, in which slim-hipped Harlequins watch too-upright women comb their hair, to have read Kant and Nietzsche, and to believe one's soul is loftier than other men's. You're wasting your time watching *Mon gentil-homme batailleur* if you haven't first read Edgar Allen Poe's "The Philosophy of Furniture," and if you don't know *The Adventures of Arthur Gordon Pym* what pleasure can you take in the *Naufrage de l'Alden-Bess?*[5] Watch a thousand imperfect films with this aesthetic in mind, then, and only then, seek to extract beauty from them, these synthetic elements for a better mise en scène. Films are the only film school, remember that. It's there you'll find useful material, providing that you can pick it out. This innovation isn't so presumptuous: Charlie Chaplin fulfills the conditions I'd like to see insisted on. If you need a model, look to him. He alone has sought the intimate sense of cinema and, endlessly persevering in his endeavours, he has drawn comedy towards the absurd and the tragic with equal inspiration. The elements of the decor which surround Charlie's persona participate intimately in the action: nothing is useless there and nothing indispensable. The decor is Charlie's very vision of the world which, together with the discovery of the mechanical and its laws, haunts the hero to such an extent that by an inversion of values each inanimate object becomes a living thing for him, each human person a dummy whose starting-handle must be found. Drama or comedy, depending on the spectator, the action is restricted to the struggle between the external world and man. The latter seeks to go beyond appearances, or let himself be duped by them in turn, and by this fact unleashes a thousand social cataclysms, the outcomes of some changes or other of decor. I insist you study the composition of the decor in a Chaplin film.

Let the cinema take care: it is fine to be deprived of everything verbal, but art must take the place of speech and that entails something more than the exact representation of life. It is its transposition following a superior sensibility. Cinema, master of all its distortions, has already timidly tried this method, which seduced all our great painters after Ingres. An independent spirit has become its defender in audacious projects, as yet unrealizable. But the cinema tends to remain a succession of photographs. The essential "cinegraphic" is not the beautiful shot: hence I would violently condemn those Italian films which have had their day and whose poetic nonvalue and exultant nullity is obvious to us now. To seek out filmmakers possessed of an aesthetic and a sense of beauty is not enough: this would get us nowhere, we would soon be left out in the cold. We need a new, audacious aesthetic, a sense of modern beauty. On this understanding the cinema will rid itself of all the old, impure, poisonous alloy that links it to a theater whose indomitable enemy it is.

It is vital that cinema has a place in the artistic avant garde's preoccupations. They have designers, painters, sculptors. Appeal must be made to them if one wants to bring some purity to the art of movement and light. One wants to leave it to academicians, to johnny-come-lately actors, and that's madness, anachronistic. This art is too deeply of *this* time to leave its future to the men of yesterday. Look ahead for support. And don't be afraid to offend the public who have indulged you up to now. I know those to whom this task falls must expect incomprehension, scorn, hatred. But that should not put them off. What a beautiful thing a film barracked by the crowd is! I have only ever heard the public *laugh* at the cinema. It is time someone slapped the public's face to see if it has blood under its skin. The consecration of catcalls that will gain cinema the respect of people of feeling is still missing. Get it, and the purity that attracts spittle emerges at last! When, before the naked screen lit by the projector's solitary beam, will we have that sense of formidable virginity,

The white awareness of our canvas?[26]

O purity, purity!

LOUIS ARAGON (1897–1982) was a young writer whose first published essay and poem appeared in *Le Film*. After the war, he gained some notoriety as a novelist, poet, and editor, first as a leader of the Surrealist movement and then as a member of the French Communist Party.

[1] Maurice Barrès (1862–1923) was the right-wing novelist, essayist, and politician whose cult of "la terre et les morts," perhaps best expressed in *Les Déracinés* (1897), provided a crucial emotional basis of support for the Nationalist Revival movement. The Surrealists organized a mock funeral of condemnation after his death in 1923.

[2] Picasso, Braque, and Gris were three of the leading Cubist painters prior to the war.

[3] The Thomas Cook Agency was the dominant travel agency operating in England and on the continent in the early years of this century.

[4] *Les Loups* (*The Wolves*) was the French title for Reginald Barker's *Between Men* (1915), starring William S. Hart.

[5] What films these two titles refer to is still unknown.

[6] Aragon quotes the final line from the poem "Salut" by Stéphane Mallarmé.

EMILE VUILLERMOZ, "Before the Screen: *La Dixième Symphonie*"

From "Devant l'écran: *La Dixième Symphonie*," *Le Temps* (6 November 1918), 3.

THIS FILM CRITIC has been invited to give his opinion of a new French film which represents, so we are told, the best artistic effort of the season: *La Dixième Symphonie* directed by Abel Gance and enacted by Emmy Lynn, Séverin-Mars, Toulout, Lefaur, and other actors and actresses of genuine talent. Because of its fine qualities as well as its numerous faults, this film is essentially representative enough to allow me to confirm, with the aid of specific examples, certain objections against the current direction of the silent art which have been growing in number.

Abel Gance is both the "baby in the family " and the "ace in the hole" of French filmmaking. He's a young actor who once briefly crossed the stage and then found his way into the cinema studios. He's an aesthete, a seeker, a man of discerning mind, full of fine visions, with a keen eye for ingenious details and rich lighting effects. He loves his art with a passion; he dreams of ennobling it with his discoveries—in collaboration with a young virtuoso, the cameraman Burel, his valued companion in combat; and he has already made films which mark a distinctive advance in our current production.

Yet for reasons which are hardly mysterious, the producers among us are not accustomed to supplying their embroiderers with the costly materials on which to design their arabesques. Instead, the embroiderer must manufacture the material himself. Abel Gance, who is a subtle embroidery craftsman, has not yet found on his loom enough sumptuous brocade worthy of being accentuated with filigrees of gold, glass beads, satin, and twisted silver thread. Thus he himself has been forced to weave his own canvas, in order to be able to execute his work.

Could he dispense with doing that? I don't know. But it is obvious—and I believe he is intelligent enough to agree with this graciously—that this never has been his forte. Here I touch on the fundamental problem in the current conditions of our cinema. The film producers have never understood that an illuminator of manuscripts is never a dramatic author, that a delicately skillful typesetter can never be taken for a poet, that a prestigious pianist is hardly ever a composer of genius. In the cinema, the pianist must compose his own score, the typesetter must write his own verse, the decorator must construct his own novels and dramas. We are in the land of "imitation"!

Abel Gance's dramaturgy is moving in its candor and contrivance. Once again, I don't doubt that he would be the first to smile. Impatient to display his virtuosity as a performer, he has improvised, as he went along, a theme which allowed him to execute his variations and round off his arpeggios. But I cannot call this "musical." And I believe it is my duty to say so very clearly, not only because it is distressing to see a young artist of merit go astray, but because the confusion which is emerging between the music of the pianist and the music of the composer tends to be detrimental to the latter. Our producers are satisfied too easily with the former. Just look at how, after *Mater Dolorosa*, *La Zone de la mort*, and *La Dixième Symphonie*, they have been determined to make Abel Gance the champion of the *French scenario* by staking a critical amount [of money and prestige] on his "J'Accuse!" and on his "serial social drama" [Ecco Homo], and you will realize the peril is serious enough to be denounced.

I have to say this, and even insist on it, at the moment when *La Dixième Symphonie* is about to appear on our screens, and as I invite artists, novelists, dramatists, painters, sculptors, and musicians to carefully study this distinctive work. The film is of genuine interest and may attract some very valuable collaborators to *cinégraphie* if it is understood in advance that there is no need to dwell on its scenario, which is an ordinary melodrama of the kind most current, with its drawing room brigand, a bully and blackmailer, its revolver shots, its letters of exposure, its summary and incoherent psychology, and its improbable conventions.

The scenario of *La Dixième Symphonie* cannot withstand the test of narrative analysis. . . . It is hardly an acceptable formula for the *French scenario*. However, the film is a magesterial lesson in *cinégraphie*. It provides us with an extremely rich and subtle French formula of expression and "photo-mimic" language. To the screen's detractors it will clearly demonstrate how supple, flexible, and profound the keyboard of this great organ of vision can be under the fingers of a fine organist of light.

Abel Gance has asserted himself as a consummate virtuoso in the execution of this work. His technical skill is excellent and allows for the subtlest interpretations. It will reconcile more than one of its adversaries to animated photography. It will prove to the writers and poets who most disdain the screen that *cinégraphie* can express almost anything, and with eloquence and lyricism. It would be good to be able to underline each expressive discovery, each experiment in nuance, each luminous harmonization. To show that this young translator, who is still being held up at the crossroads of aestheticism, is en route toward beauty. This stopping point is decisive. Go see the ingenious visual and emotional transpositions of the andante and scherzo of the symphony revealed in the composer's study; go see those tiny dream landscapes, those glades where the fairies dance in robes of moonlight, airy and immaterial as will-o-the-wisps. Here even now is an exploration of the subconscious; here is an attempt at a "correspondence" which opens onto fruitful paths. One senses that some day one might photograph the music of the soul and fix its changing visage on the screen in rhythmic images. The frontiers of the silent art are being extended, the glimmers of light are growing, the windows are opening.

Despite the flaws in its scenario, this film addresses and answers most of the objections made by the enemies of the French cinema. It demonstrates that we have a technical skill as supple as that of the Americans, but more subtle and psychological in its suggestions. It attests to the fact that we also have actors worthy of the greatest missions. . . .

We have in hand now all the weapons that will permit us to defend the French cinema against its foreign competition. . . .

LOUIS DELLUC, "Cinema: *The Cold Deck*"

From "Cinéma: *Grand Frère*," *Paris-Midi* (14 and 17 February 1919), 2.

*T*he *Cold Deck*, an American film with Rio Jim (Pathé).[1]
William Hart, the popular Rio Jim, is the tragedian of the cinema. He mounts a horse much like Mounet-Sully descends a staircase. . . .

In his domain, William Hart has the same godlike serenity and the same violent ways. He is no ordinary cowboy of the circus or of a thousand and one dashed-off films. He is the synthesis of that plastic beauty which marks the schematic and almost stylized Far West. Transcending the specific details of his characters, William Hart reveals a profoundness of spirit. They used to call him "the man from nowhere."[2] What a lovely title! We never know where Rio Jim comes from. He just passes through. He crosses the West—and the West is so huge. He arrives on horseback. He leaps down onto the ground where other men live. Generally, the time that he remains there is devoted to suffering, that is, to loving. When his forehead has been ravaged enough, his fingers tortured, and all his cigarettes crushed out, he refuses to continue to suffer on earth or in an enclosed room—he mounts his horse again and, that done, disappears. His departure can last through an entire film. And so his equestrian prowess lives on. The paradox of his mad rides, his responsibilities as a bandit or apostle, his constant clearing out, all give us a tremendous lift. It seems we breathe better when Rio Jim makes off on his horse across the valley.

Go see *The Cold Deck*, this beautiful American film—dazzling, vivid, strange—where there are amusing costumes, reconstructed buildings done with a sense of taste and feeling, endless vistas with better horses than can be found anywhere else (my compliments)—and William Hart.

NEVER HAS William Hart been so nobly tragic and so simply grandiose. He emerges in the milieu of the usual crowds and decors of this stylized Far West of the cinema, where the splendid fatalism of Sophocles comes alive for us—but it is still too early to say whether the cinema will have as intense a presence as the great Greek spectacles which whole peoples attended. The gold miners, the improvised town, the ranch and mountain, the saloon, the dancing couples, the card tables, the alcohol, the horses—the mystery of Hart looms over all this and makes everything as mysterious as he is.

The stagecoach runs like a great insect over partially drifted roads. Trees serve for bridges. Ravines gobble up horses. People dance back to back and drink eyeball to eyeball. The sheriff, a thin, nervous bird of prey turned civil servant, is encamped there where his silhouette can be impressive. The little sister, clothed in old-fashioned flowery dresses, alights from a distant bourgeois country. The croupiers—tall dandies in damask waistcoats, huge cuffs, embroidered shirtfronts, and ironic bow ties—coldly watch the gold change pockets and cheat when necessary. Brutes fling glasses across the room, which spill in rainbow showers over the bystanders.

The dancing girl, the enigmatic lover of the hero, wraps her handsome brown body in a beautiful black shawl. But it's a blonde that he will fall in love with. Jealousy ravages the camp. Sickness takes the little sister. Hart passes through indifference, love, pity, arrogance, and ruin. He invokes a God in whom he doesn't believe, with the face of a martyr and the arms of Christ—and he races off to attack the stagecoach. He kills and plunders, the little sister is dead, the father of the blonde is assassinated, the assassin will be hung, the beautiful dancing girl will leave the country, and Hart will remain on the mountain with his memories and his future—since the little blonde will marry him. But his horse is dead.

I believe that the cinema exists.

[1] The French title for Hart's *The Cold Deck* (1917) was *Grand Frère*.

[2] *Rio Jim, L'Homme de nulle part* (Rio Jim, the Man from Nowhere) was the French title for Hart's *The Silent Stranger* (1915).

JEAN COCTEAU, "Carte Blanche"

From "Carte blanche," *Paris-Midi* (28 April and 12 May 1919), 2.

FROM THE TIME of its discovery, the cinema was made to serve old ideas and was put in the hands of merchants who held it back. They photographed theater. But America made films in which theater and photography slowly gave way to a new form because they were better equipped than we were and they acted like engineeers who instead of stripping the airplane completely of its wings simply reduced them slightly.

Events occur in succession—interlocked, superimposed—and overrun the text. Simultaneous action transports us from one end of the earth to the other; restores a detail, as in a magnifying glass, to its proper place in the scenario; makes a hand or foot intervene like a character; takes us under the table where they are playing tricks on a giant figure whose mind can be read in its eyes like a schoolbook alphabet.

For, if the theater is the art of memorable lines, where gesture and voice take the place of anything the public would have to ascertain in the actor's eyes, the cinema, by contrast, is the art of nuances where the actor is released from the text and finds a freedom and responsibility previously unknown.

Certain photographs foreshadowed the seductive modeling of actual films. Gaugin's soft, pale paintings, photographed by M. Druet, took on the impact of bas-reliefs. Thanks to skillful lighting, the actors of the cinema are veritable statues in motion. At the end of a cinema program, figures in the crowd outside seem small and lackluster. We remember an alabaster race of beings as if glowing from within. On the screen, enormous objects become superb. A sort of moonlight sculpts a telephone, a revolver, a hand of cards, an automobile. We believe we are seeing them for the first time.

I want disinterested artists to exploit perspective, slow motion, fast motion, reverse motion, an unknown world onto which chance often opens the door. As a new means of expression, the cinema will serve a new art and impose new conventions, for art is a play of conventions which are transformed to the point where the players grow tired. We will see the architecture of forms, volumes, shadows, and planes come alive, evoking life far better than any essentially inexact performance of reality can.

While awaiting this spectacle, be content with what is offered and seek out the best. The best, uncontestably, is Charlie Chaplin. His films have no rivals—neither the theater film where the spectator has the impression of being deaf, nor the Far West film where the landscape blends in with the drama, nor the serial where mysterious men, sons of Eugène Sue, Dumas, and Edison, do good and evil under the cape of Rodolphe and with the fortune of Monte-Cristo.[1]

Chaplin is the modern Punch. He addresses all of us, everywhere. Esperanto laughter. Each of us gets his kicks for different reasons. With Chaplin's help, I'm sure, we could raise the tower of Babel. While he never underlines any of the effects, such as those quick-witted feats which he ceaselessly comes up with, the others have to be satisfied with pratfalls.

His most recent film, *Sous les armes* [1918], would be a masterpiece if they had not diminished his comic performance by enclosing it within a dream.[2]

There's no way to describe this film which moves along like a drum roll, where the decors and extras fit in with nary a false note. But I salute, in passing, this one fable of the war: Charlot does reconnaissance, camouflaged as a tree. They discover him. He escapes with a formidable enemy close on his heels. The canter of a little tree that hops about in the forest and plays hide and seek with a huge Wotan, it's a hoot!

"The light spirit," we see, vanquishes "the gross one."

HAVE YOU seen the American film, *Carmen du Klondyke*, directed by M. Ince?³ I offer it not as an example of plotting, but because it contains a masterly scene: the struggle between two men at night, in a torrential rain, in the light of arc lamps.

In the middle of a drenched, blinded, terrified crowd, the two men roll about in the deep mud and water. To follow them, the camera recoils, approaches, and slides away. We watch as if through the very eyes of the tug of war. Two madmen splash down and rise up again, as if coated in nickel, and reach out grasping to kill one another. Are they kingfishers, seals, lunar men, or Jacob and the Angel?

Is this a Buddha, this great naked body that staggers to its knees and dies like a whole school of fish in a slurry of mercury?

M. Ince can be proud, for such a spectacle is as memorable as the most beautiful books in the world.

JEAN COCTEAU (1889–1963) was a rising young poet, lyricist, playwright, and literary entrepreneur who retreated after the "scandal" of the Diaghiliev-Cocteau-Picasso-Satie *Parade* (1917) to the more conventional and patriotic *Le Coq et l'Arlequin* (1918). His interest in the cinema, evidenced here and in several earlier poems, remained dormant throughout the 1920s, as he concentrated on his work in the theater.

¹ The reference is to Feuillade's *Judex* (1917) and *La Nouvelle Mission de Judex* (1918) and to Pouctal's *Monte-Cristo* (1917–1918). Eugène Sue (1804–1857), along with Alexandre Dumas, was one of the popular writers of the early serial novels of adventure—for example, *Le Mystères de Paris, Le Juif errant*. Thomas Edison, rather than the Lumière brothers or Georges Méliès, seems to stand in here as the inventor of the cinema.

² *Sous les armes* was the French title for Chaplin's *Shoulder Arms* (1918).

³ *Carmen du Klondyke* was the French title for Reginald Barker's *Carmen of the Klondike* (1917).

MARCEL GROMAIRE, "A Painter's Ideas about the Cinema"

Translated by Stuart Liebman in *Motion Picture* 1.2 (Fall 1986), 4–5. Reprinted by permission. The original French text first appeared as "Idées d'un peinture sur le cinéma," *Le Crapouillot* 1–6 (1 April–26 June 1919), reprinted in Marcel L'Herbier, ed., *Intelligence du cinématographe* (Paris: Corréa, 1946), 239–49.

I. TRANSPOSITION

WHILE OBSERVING any scene, a painter's emotions will be different than a sculptor's and sometimes contrary to those of a poet. Each will transpose his perceptions of this ordinary scene either into smooth plastic forms, into modeled spatial forms, or into lyrical verse. The cinematic composer, of course, should respond to the changing plastic forms of this same spectacle; whereas the painter synthesizes the continuous movement into stable form, the cinema enables one to organize this movement until the desired expressive effect is achieved, and all this in front of the spectator's very eyes. Because the cinema is primarily *visual*. What will be the lyric plastic form of cinema, in short, its own proper language? In what way does it share characteristics of painting, of the theater, of dance, and in what way will it be absolutely new? That is our question.

What method should be chosen to transpose commonplace sights into cinema? Up till now, the tendency has been to proceed by way of a scenario to the film. What I mean is that the author of the scenario is in general unfamiliar with the director and the actors, or even misunderstands their purpose. Now, the three essential factors of a film, its "living material," are the director, the actors, and the landscape. One must proceed by using them as the basis of the imagined form; the film must be conceived expressly for them! One does not merely *adapt* a literary work for the cinema. If one wishes to make a film of *Don Quixote*, then in order not to betray Cervantes' intentions, one must disregard the letter and compose according to the spirit of the book, recasting it entirely, just as Molière did with the classics. The only thing that matters is what is created; what excites us is the creation. Here's another object lesson: Charlie Chaplin, who up till now has been the only one with genius enough to really come alive on screen, often performs in a desert; he has not been well served by his surroundings because the landscape is not selected expressly for him.

The landscape must be transposed. One must choose! On screen, a detail suffices to suggest the whole or to be the leitmotif of a film. Light is a first-class actor, but our film profiteers only imagine colored picture–postcards for tourists. Look at a Rembrandt, or just throw the windows wide open!

One must transpose the characters, strip what is merely adventitious from them, and create types (this has been done in burlesque comedy). Greek actors carried a mask and their physical appearance confirmed their moral identity; we must study the art of the English clown who performs without speaking; let's study the so-called deformations of modern painters that are really powerful affirmations; on screen we must organize the characters' entrances, time them, and place them correctly within the set and the surroundings. The cinema was a skeleton; let's put some muscle on it!

Before us, an unexplored artistic province is opening up, a strange province inhabited by machines, where life moves continually and hurries toward unbounded horizons. It [the cinema] is an essentially modern art because it is mobile and restless and as multifaceted as a democracy. A film is a poem developing in provisional phrases, in measured waves; it ends and starts anew without suffering any loss of unity. Thanks to the cinema, I saw a rose blossom. It was an extremely beautiful sight that our film producers ought to think deeply about.

II. COLOR

Here, even more than in painting, color means light. Color in cinema is closely related to color in engraving; before putting a film together, it would be a good idea to leaf through the etchings of Rembrandt or Claude Lorrain. No one would dispute how manifold—from gay to tragic—the expressions of light are. In addition, one must emphasize that these expressions can be intensified to such a degree that the other means would be little more than a muted accompaniment: light explodes like a powerful song; it constitutes the whole film; all of the drama depends on it. I remember a mediocre film, *Le Coupable*, adapted from Coppée.[1] The scene of the assassination, even though it was extremely brief, derived all its tragic overtones from the fall of a lamp (looming dark shots crossed by vibrating lights) followed by diffuse light. This very successful scene overwhelmed the others.

Impressionism, highly questionable in painting, is here logical since cinema proceeds by a process of decomposition. We can follow the sun's course across the "Haystacks" of Claude Monet, and the sunlight will be the whole show. Outdoors, light is brutal and shimmering. The chiaroscuro in which we spend three quarters of our lives is infinitely rich. Woefully inadequate photographers instinctively attempt to imitate chiaroscuro by shooting out of focus. They uncomprehendingly intuit how alive the atmosphere is. There are dense atmospheres, as milky or as metallic as an evening sky. We must conjure up the very air in which the characters move; we must really bathe them in it; let them appear to emerge from narrow, luminous curtains or from rich draperies of shadow. Let the interiors be intentionally furnished with blacks and shades of gray; reflected light can eliminate long speeches; different materials can make tones into closely related, equivalent, or contrasting luminous forms.

And light reflected off water and underwater visions, these so to speak subconscious dramas, what has been done with them up till now? What "Extraordinary Tales" Edgar Poe would have conceived! And artificial light, and the sudden luminous explosions with fantastic shadows, where light seems to escape from the darkness and do battle with it!

On screen, a boundless depth is at our disposal. In successive shots, light surges toward the horizon. The moving shots surmount each other and fancifully change colors; one could say it is like the successive panels of an imaginary silken umbrella speaking a luminous language.

More than any sentimental libretto, color is the soul of cinema. Imagine a film: some exceptional characters, a few actions, a unity of place. The drama of light would be everything. How classical!

III. FORM, MOVEMENT

If color is the soul of film, moving form is its essential logic, the implacable intellectual basis constitutive of its nature as a work of art. Here everything is new. With the exception of the dance, no other art form affects us through moving plastic forms. Here, the entire spectacle moves; the forms must be orchestrated. The most ingenious librettos are of little value if they are not conceived as moving structures. Let us replace the poor written explanations and the outmoded romanticism of current performance styles with the drama of these unknown forces and the search for new relationships.

The aesthetic emotion is constituted above all by surprise; here, the spectacle unfolds in fleeting phrases; they must continually be "nourished" with unexpected discoveries. Now, to modify the structures, one must continually find new ones. What an unlimited wealth of combinations there are! The shots combine, are superimposed, or are contrasted with each other in ways varying in meter and color, and each meter follows a special path, be it of length or depth through foreshortening. In the primitive cinema of today, confusion reigns; the eye loses itself in a mad jumble uncontrolled by any idea. One must simplify and select. On screen, everything matters just as much as it does on a painted surface. A gesture that is sketched and then broken off or one that is too hurried ruins the rest. Stressing the way a gesture develops, or highlighting the expressive motif of a landscape shows it in a clear and convincing way. Slow motion will become a standard strategy. Because of this, an author must adopt a different manner than he does for the theater, and he must also create a new sign language in conformity with the plasticity proper to cinema. One may start with a slow movement as a theme for an entire section or arrive at it as a conclusion. A single movement will become reason enough for a scene. And let's not forget the role of color! I do not want in any way to diminish the importance of the story for a moment, but it must be translated into vibrant plastic form. I recognize very clearly the danger of a deadly conventionality if the performers and the director are people of meager talents. But academicism is only a danger for those who accede to it. Our investigations are too many and too varied to become bogged down in a system. Who, therefore, will try to interpret our ordinary gestures? They are as complex as words and as rich in nuances. Marvelous animated plastic forms surround us. And the modern world so abounds in sets possessing such simple grandeur that it will be enough to have them appear, ready for all kinds of syntheses.

Just as the dispositions of gestures, shots and their meters are inexhaustible, we must imagine how much a subject's scale can lend a great variety of expressiveness to the forms. When magnified or reduced in scale, the same object offers tremendous contrasts, and imagining an unusual film in the spirit of Rabelais, one conceived in terms large- and small-scale images, gives me great pleasure.

IV. DRAMA

Moving plastic forms, the language of cinema, require the symbolism of a libretto to reenforce the eloquence of the images. I do not use "imagistic language" in a metaphorical sense. New relationships between the story and the image must be found. These relationships will constitute expressive *symbols*. In the cinema, one will not succeed in expressing abstract ideas such as Love or Will by means of scenes modeled after those in the theater; they must be translated into clear symbols specially conceived for moving plastic forms.

The cinema, like music, is an autonomous art. To imagine a film based on a literary work is truly to compose an opera for the eyes, as different in nature from the work originally inspiring it as a musical opera drawn from the same work. Since visual music, composed of colors and forms, has an infinite number of combinations at its disposal, the feelings to be translated must be presented in terms of qualitatively very varied symbols. Ibsen calls for symbols translatable into color. Racine insists upon majestic symbols translatable into noble forms.

If one wishes to conjure up the powerful figure of King Lear in the cinema and, in order not to be unfaithful to Shakespeare, to lose as little of his expressive intensity as possible, one must choose the symbols best conveying the essence of his character. If necessary, they must be created. A secondary character who cannot be translated into cinematic terms, but who represents a feeling, will be profitably replaced by an equivalent symbol. For example, the character of Gloucester, who to some degree parallels the character of Lear and reenforces his actions, may be evoked by some symbolic episodes that simplify the story and thereby translate Shakespeare's conception more faithfully. King Lear would be the dominant character, moving and multifaceted, while his three daughters, distant and synthetic characters, would appear as the causes of the actions, symbolic motives of the king's deeds. Lear's companions, Kent and the Fool, the first honesty and courage, the other irony and madness, would afford a perpetual commentary on him. At the end of the play, Cordelia's death is an image of tragic despair, a perfect evocation of the phrase: "The weight of this sad time . . ." Lear's curses, the Fool's rejoinders, are immediately translatable into images, and numerous symbols of this sort will permit written captions to be reduced to a minimum. *The image must be self-explanatory.* "Every inch-inch [*sic*] a king. . ."—it is pointless to write this phrase on screen. The forms alone must convey the meaning. And what is more, don't forget the effects that can be achieved by using slow motion.

Remember that in the cinema, the sets are more important than in the theater, and that elevated to the role of an actor, they may replace secondary human characters. The savage heath and the relentless storm are integral parts of Lear's madness. In the same way, the costumes are first and foremost bits of black and white color that ought to reflect his tragic madness or the serenity of destiny. Finally, objects have a definite role to play. In the first act, the map of the kingdom is the symbol of the partition. And the crown is broken in two.

VI. COMEDY

Here the clarity of symbols must permit the total elimination of written captions. They break up the action and add nothing to it. In cinematic comedy or farce, the "words" must be translated into images full of wit. In this regard, Charlie Chaplin is the inspired precursor of the new cinema. Psychologically, he seems very human, but the performance of this malicious and adroit little fellow who triumphs over brute force is very skillful. Charlot performs for the cinema. Conceived for the screen, his movements fluctuate humorously according to the rhythm of successive images, and they are broken down into simple elements. Charlot performs with his whole body. His impassive face intermittently assumes a more pronounced expression; a grimace may underscore [the feeling], but his body expresses the nuances. One must regret that an actor of such power is not better supported; each of his co-actors ought to devise characters as simple and as stylized as possible.

In a film lacking a dominant actor, it is even more necessary to compose in this manner so that each character, by being subordinated to the ensemble, will reenforce the unity of the whole and will not destroy the desired effect.

Up till now, have any comic landscapes or interiors ever been chosen? The mediocre Rigadin performs amid furnishings lacking any character or in impersonal landscapes; and yet, there are certain gardens in the Parisian suburbs that Bouvard and Pecuchet would be proud of.[2] We must create sets for every play! In today's cinema, lyricism and humor are non-existent.

On screen, the costumes are a judicious assemblage of whites and blacks, and must lend themselves to every possible plastic arrangement. Costumes will be specially conceived for a specific film and *will play a role*. Depending on the role to be performed, some will use costumes made of painted paper decorated with comic camouflage that will integrate the actor with the landscape; fantastic armor made of heavy or extremely flowing materials will be used. Depending on the film, masks, which have recently reappeared in the theater, will be similar to those used in Aunt Sally games, to those in Guignol, or to those on the comic sculptures of our ancient stonecutters. There will be hieratic characters—objects in the role of characters—and whirling characters, all used to emphasize some major types drawn from contemporary life and then stylized.

This alliance between reality and fantasy, the anxiety-less breaking of the state of equilibrium that provokes laughter, can also be found in objects. In contemporary cinema, objects don't count. Now, isn't it obvious that secondary scenes can be performed by "still-life" images? Props must be specially created for them by transforming objects from everyday life. Couldn't delicious grotesque effects be developed from a Henry the Second style buffet in the Saint Antoine quarter whose inadequacies could be magnified?[3] If they were made conspicuous, the trashy ornaments and furnishings would be jarring to the extent that they highlight a contemporary vice. Certain beautiful objects, also transformed and appearing in separate scenes, would be terrific witnesses for the prosecution.

VI. IMAGES

I said before that a certain sort of impressionism was legitimate in cinema; needless to say, this applies only to the analytic procedures by which the mind organizes successive images. But each image, taken by itself, must be a powerful synthesis. Aside from the work of several masters, Impressionism is merely a hoarding of bric-a-brac. Now, on screen as on canvas, a lofty idea needs a grand and restrained expression. One must eliminate everything that adds nothing, and move away from drab realism. Progress will require a great deal of method and logic.

If they are well conceived, films lacking a comic or tragic story will delight spectators. The pure image, the *beautiful* image, will originate in contemporary documentary films, but it will be enriched by imaginative and formal elements. There can be no art without transposition. Once transposed, any scene from life possesses an extraordinary richness, and in this respect cinema has no limits; it can examine everything, organize the whole and evoke everything from microscopic visions to intimate or colossal landscapes in color and plastic form. One can discover original relationships between the multifarious manifestations of life. What contemporary cinema lacks most is the masterful intelligence of a creator of images.

Even though the value of cartoons depends on the cartoonist, from now on we can, thanks to them, discern a new aesthetic. Cartoons will no longer necessarily be caricatures; henceforth, cartoonists will contrive moving arabesques, either purely ornamental or syntheses of human or animal movements. Only here will color be possible because coloring photographic images only leads to incorrect tonalities without any meaning. In my opinion, color cartoons can become as remarkable and impressive as stained glass, as quaint as colored magic lantern slides or "Images d'Epinal." But it is important not to confuse photographic color, black and white, with colors that express something else; it is pointless once more to repeat the pitiful attempt at coloring etchings in another domain.

It might be amusing to combine photography and drawing in the same film, and if necessary in the same image, in order to highlight the organization of imaginative and documentary elements. Moreover, this would be an exceptional way to avoid conventionality. Curiosity will also lead us to color images in a single tint with harmonies, dissonances, and nuanced shades accompanying the images for the entire length of the film.

Finally, were it not for the puritanical hypocrisy of our times, disconcerting enough because of the various forms it assumes, it may be desirable to extract many different harmonious effects from the nude. The slow-motion camera has already produced images of athletic exercises that present the gracefulness of antiquity vainly sought in M. Duncan's pastiches.[4]

VII. CONCLUSION

Impressionism in the form of Neo-Cubism continues to exist and hinders the realization of any great pictorial achievements. Will the cinema liberate painting by attracting all those formal innovators for whom painting is not right? Many investigations, that inevitably remain mere investigations in painting, can be brought to fruition in cinema. The art of animated plastic forms ought to tempt the more or less avowed adepts of Futurism, provided, however, that their Futurism remains a means, and that they really want to wake up and contemplate the present, to become aware of the real beauty of forms, and to recognize the legitimacy of the idea of perfection.

From the simple fact of a new form of plastic expression, new values will be created. The new cinema will satisfy our need for an art more strictly allied with modern dynamism, an art possessing the elegantly cerebral character of a mathematical proof. The Futurists will no longer be able to rest content with childishly indicating the givens of a problem on canvas: they will have to express their ideas with help of mechanical movement. And maybe then they will take into account that, if an art is to be born, animated sculpture, like static sculpture, requires *beautiful* forms, that is, forms profoundly satisfying the rational mind as well as forms that are *expressive*, that is, forms that logically satisfy one's feelings. The taste for the bizarre is already falling out of fashion. The world needs to be reassured; it has known too much anguish not to desire peace, and the serenity of Titian is far more contemporary in spirit than the pedantry of some aesthete who likes facile advertisements. Whether some want it or not, we are proceeding towards a classical art (though one far, far from the Institute [de Beaux Arts]). The new cinema will be classical or will not be.

The cinema can transport ideas from one end of the world to the other. It has the gift of ubiquity and the power to speak directly to the masses. In this respect, its discovery can be compared to that of printing; with this difference, however, and it is important, that printing came along at a time when literary works already existed while the cinema still awaits its poet.

May art no longer be a privilege. The common folk are marvelously responsive. For everyone's health, art must be experienced by everyone. That beauty is not a dream, that the richness of life is a common experience, must be shown to the masses. Art is useful.

Will the new cimena be the spokesman for a new faith?

MARCEL GROMAIRE (1892–1971) was a young painter without formal training who came under the influence of Fernand Léger after the war and whose first exhibition came at the Salon d'Automne in 1921.

¹ The film Gromaire is referring to, of course, is Antoine's *Le Coupable* (1917), adapted from the novel by François Coppée (1842–1908)

² These are the names of the infamous collectors and cataloguers in Flaubert's satirical novel, *Bouvard et Pecuchet* (1881).

³ The Henry II buffet was a standard decorative feature of high and middle bourgeois French homes in the early part of this century. The working class Saint Antoine quarter lay around the Saint Antoine Hospital between the Place de la Bastille and the Place de la Nation, in the eleventh and twelfth arrondisements.

⁴ This may be a reference to Raymond Duncan, the brother of Isadore Duncan.

BLAISE CENDRARS, "The Modern: A New Art, the Cinema"

From "Modernités—Un nouveau art: le cinéma," *La Rose rouge* 7 (12 June 1919), 108.

VORTEXES of movement in space. Everything is falling. The sun is falling. We are falling in pursuit. Like a chameleon, the human mind disguises itself by camouflaging the globe. The cardinal hypotheses of science taper to a point, and the four gods of the winds are moonlighting. Fusion. Everything bursts open, collapses, makes a promise today, grows hollow, stands erect, blossoms. Honor and money. Everything changes. Customs and political economy. New civilization. New Humanity. Figures have created an abstract, mathematical organism, of useful devices, of machine parts. And it's the machine that recreates and shifts our bearings. There is a new direction. From this point of view, arbitrarily, the cinema has given man an eye more marvelous than the multifaceted eye of the fly. A hundred worlds, a thousand movements, a million dramas occur simultaneously within the field of this eye. Emotion: they don't know where it is anymore. The tragic unities are out of place.

We understand that the real has no other meaning. Since everything is rhythm, word, life. Focus the lens on a hand, an eye, an ear, and the drama is outlined, expands on a ground of unexpected mystery. We already have no further need of conversation: soon character will be judged useless. In fast motion, the life of the flowers is Shakespearean; in slow motion, everything classical is there in the flexing of a biceps. On the screen, the least effort becomes painful, musical, enlarged a thousand times. We attribute to it a significance that it has never before known. All theatrical drama, its situations and stage tricks, become useless. Attention is fixed on the sinister scowl. On the hand covered with criminal callouses. On the piece of fabric that continually drips blood. On the watch chain that tightens and expands, like the vein on a man's temple. What is going to happen? And why is the material so tragically impregnated with humanity? Chemistries become untangled and come undone. Hindu poem. The least throb germinates and bears fruit. Crystallizations come to life. Ecstasy. Animals, plants, minerals represent ideas, sensations, ciphers, numbers. As in the Middle Ages, the rhinoceros is Christ; the bear, the devil; jasper, vivaciousness; chrysoprase, pure humility, six and nine. We see the wind our brother, and the sea is an abyss of men. All this is no more than an abstract symbolism, obscure and complicated, but part of a living organism that we surprise, dislodge, and track, and which has never been seen before. Evidence. Depths sensitized in a drama of Dumas, in a police novel, or in a banal film made in Los Angeles.

Above the spectators' heads, the bright cone of light wriggles like a dolphin. Characters stretch out from the screen to the lantern lens. They plunge, turn, pursue one another, crisscross, with a luminous, mathematical precision. Clustered beams. Rays. Prodigious spirals into which everything is falling. Projection of the sky falling. Life from the deep.

BLAISE CENDRARS (1887–1961) was a devoted traveler, writer, and editor (Editions de la sirène), whose poetry was second only to Apollinaire's in importance during the 1910s. In 1918–1919, Cendrars assisted Abel Gance in scripting, directing, and editing *J'Accuse* (1919), and then went on to do the same on *La Roue* (1922–1923).

HENRI DIAMANT-BERGER, "The Scenario"

From "Le Scènario," *Le Cinéma* (Paris: Renaissance du livre, 1919), 35–53.

THE SCENARIO is the film itself. As written, it is the film as it will be recorded on the filmstock. It's wrong to believe that the film is a development of the scenario, that the scenario contains only the rough substance of the film and that it is left to the director to release that substance and refine it, according to his own personality. The author of the scenario must bear responsibility for the film. There are directors who act as collaborators with the author. That is legitimate, of course; but in that case their collaboration must occur prior to the shooting and must be discussed with the author. The author should be obeyed; accordingly, he should follow the execution of his scenario in order to make sure its production respects his intentions. . . .

As for writing a scenario, it requires a subject that is complete and encompasses a central idea, that has characters and scenes, and that includes an exposition, a development, and a denouement. That takes a dramatic framework, situations, and a detailed psychology. A film must, however, meet the demand for expressing some new feeling or narrating an original action. One has to consider each scenario as a separate product, as a specific edifice, each of which requires special study and preparation proportionate to its significance. . . .

It is useful to preface the detailed work of the scenario with a commentary which sums up the progress of ideas, indicating the predominant ones, and acts as a psychological guide across the decoupage of shots. It is also useful, after that, to provide the list of roles with a quite complete physical and moral description of the principal characters. Such outlines should be developed only at the moment of the character's first appearance. Anything which can help in the selection of actors and in their acting should be explained in the most meticulous fashion. To provide this help, one could write out an initial sketch in a form that is close to that of a novel, and then go back over it to cut it up exactly into timed scenes. The action should be broken down precisely into tableaux. By *tableau* I mean each shot which unfolds without interruption in a single place, without any modification of the camera's field of vision.

Each set decor should be carefully described, down to the smallest details, for the interiors as well as those in the open air. The trapezoid of the playing area should be indicated with all its perspectives. . . .[1]

A film is not succession of shots and photographs. It is a mode of expression of thought. A film overloaded with photographic effects gives the same impression as a sentence overloaded with images, allegorical references, redundancies, hypallages, and epithets—all means which taken separately can converge into a genuine impression but whose pretentious accumulation fatigues and repulses. . . .

For each shot, the scenario should anticipate as much as possible the mode of its cutting—fade, oval iris, circular iris—and the length of its running time. It is appropriate to indicate the approximate length of each shot, knowing that the film unreels at the speed of about twenty meters per minute.

184

Of course, the scenario should include all the intertitles written out in full, as well as letters and printed material of any sort. . . .

HENRI DIAMANT-BERGER (1895–1972) was the young publisher of *Le Film* from 1914 to 1919. In 1916, he became involved in producing several documentaries on the war, and by 1919, he had set himself up as a semi-independent film producer for Raymond Bernard's *Le Petit Café* (1919) and *Le Secret de Rosette Lambert* (1920) as well as his own *Les Trois Mousquetaires* (1921–1922).

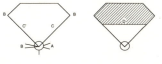

1 Pierre Trimbach, who worked as a cameraman for SCAGL prior to the war and then briefly with Antoine afterwards, provides a diagram of what Diamant-Berger means by this trapezoid playing area.

Pierre Trimbach, *Quand on tournait la manivelle . . . il y a 60 ans . . .* (Paris: CEFAG, 1970), 32–33.

HENRI DIAMANT-BERGER, "The Decoupage"

From "Le Filmage," *Le Cinéma* (Paris: Renaissance du livre, 1919), 145–68.

THE DECOUPAGE, which is the definitive form of the scenario, should indicate in advance, of course, all the shots in their actual order; and it should anticipate their exact length. The film should be written exactly as it will be shot. Changes at the last moment are an exception and often flawed. Currently, we do our shooting of close shots and unplanned landscape shots at random; later they are brought into line [with the other shots] when everything else is finished. Such a lack of order is nonsense. . . .

The Americans have an extremely rapid, nervous, tumultuous decoupage which is usually quite successful yet sometimes enervating. Their essential trick or knack is to conduct several actions at once and to cut them off one by one at the moment of climax.[1] Another of their methods is to show us enormous heads, with or without expression, or animate objects, suddenly inanimate, in order to arouse an unexpected feeling. Either can provide exquisite dramatic results, on condition they are used in moderation.

Most films give an impression of dragging on gratuitously because they are badly cut. A bad decoupage can be recognized by the exaggerated length of its shots, which exhaust each of a series of feelings without ever leaving us in doubt about anything.

These drawn out shots have the same effect as does a theater play which is nothing more than a succession of long monologues or a book which never begins a new paragraph. These two comparisons, which it would be amusing to detail, demonstrate, however, that it is not a question of making a film which is all chopped up into shots of two meters or even less, but that certainly the cinema should give us only one impression per shot and that the shot should end as soon as that impression is perceived. . . .

The cinema should show only what is of interest to us at the opportune moment. The close-up is the simplest and most aggressive method to use for this end. But it has a drawback: that's the enormous magnification of heads and objects. This magnification is useful much of the time, but can be wearying, especially when it does not meet the requirements of expressing something. It would be well to gauge this magnification more precisely than has been done up to now. For it gives the objector or enlarged facial expression an unusual importance. Everything which is presented to us in a detached manner need not be put on the same plane and emphasized in the same way. . . .

Let's not forget that one principle determines all these methods and any others yet to be created: for every idea there should be a single shot and, conversely, there should be no shot without an idea. . . . Let's take a simple example: one evening a woman enters her room; she turns on the light and, while removing her jewelry, catches sight of a burglar in the mirror. She calls for help, and before it arrives the burglar escapes. This is a scene which has a beginning, a critical moment, and an end. It, of course, joins past action to subsequent action and even allows for the interpolation of different decors. . . .

Here, without an over-indulgence in details, is the scene that I am taking as an example, cut up as it should be in order to be filmed.

1. The iris opens on an empty room (this set would already have been shown before so we know who lives in it). The burglar comes in cautiously, holding a flashlight.	5 meters
2. A closer shot of his entrance.	2 meters
3. A full shot of the room. He crosses the room slowly and walks toward a desk.	2 meters
4. An auto stops before the front door, Mme A. gets out and enters the house.	4 meters
5. The burglar is about to break into the desk (lighting effect).	2 meters
6. The vestibule. Mme A. takes off her coat, dismisses her maid with a gesture, and walks toward her room.	5 meters
5A. The burglar hears a noise and extinguishes his flashlight,	2 meters

7. then hides behind a curtain.	2 meters
1A. Mme A. enters and crosses the room, after she has	5 meters
2A. flipped on the light switch and	
3A. made her way to her dressing table.	
7A. The burglar parts the curtain and looks out.	1.5 meters
8. Mme A., seen from behind, sits before her dressing table and takes off her string of pearls.	2 meters
7B. The burglar comes out from behind the curtain and moves forward.	1.5 meters
9. Shot of the mirror. She lifts her eyes and sees the burglar advancing from behind her.	2 meters
10. She turns quickly and faces him.	1.5 meters
11. He stops, menacingly.	1 meter
12. She stretches out her arm.	1 meter
13. Close-up. She presses on a button.	1 meter
14. Close-up. A bell is struck.	.5 meters
11A. He has heard and is about to leap at her.	1 meter
15. Two servants run past in the hallway.	1.5 meters
12A. She defies him with a look.	1 meter
11B. He makes up his mind to flee.	1.5 meters
16. Longer shot. He opens the window.	2 meters
1B. Full shot of the room. He leaps through the window just as the servants push open the door.	3 meters

This scene, as cut up into twenty-six pieces in the scenario, calls for fifteen camera setups and measures fifty meters in length. You will notice, of course, that a scene thus exhibited out of context carries a completely arbitrary significance and that, according to its placement in a film, it should be treated in a manner that is either more or less synthesized or balanced.

I have not indicated this manner precisely in order to give an idea of a logical decoupage, one which, in projection, will provide a completed scene.

You will note that naturally the length of the pieces is inversely proportionate to the rapidity of the shots; moreover, it is useful to offer a lengthier view whenever one comes to a new setup. One must consider that a shot of at least 1.2 meters is required to convey the simplest impression. A piece of information less than that is too slight [to register]. Pieces of several centimeters in length are usable only in extremely special decoupages.[2] The median length of shots is from two to five meters. . . .

The decoupage is as indispensable to the cinema as dialogue is to the theater or punctuation is to writing. Obviously, the length of neither shots nor scenes has been codified. That remains a question of synthesis or balance as well as of individual personality, which doesn't have to be dissected here further. . . .

¹ Diamant-Berger is probably referring to the crosscutting technique that was most associated with D.W. Griffith.

² Contemporary examples of "special decoupages" would have been Gance's *J'Accuse* (1919) and Griffith's *Intolerance* (1916), which was first released in Paris in May 1919.

LOUIS DELLUC, "Cinema: *The Outlaw and His Wife*"

From "Cinéma: *Les Proscrits*," *Paris-Midi* (10 November 1919), 2.

I HAVEN'T SEEN this title yet on any of this week's posters. I trust the film is going into distribution and that next week we will see it everywhere. It's a marvelous work. It would be scandalous—but aren't the ways of our cinema scandalous enough already—for a film of this quality not to be seen. . . .

We know what the factory of American beauty has produced. Charlie Chaplin sums up six years of creative activity with his genius. But are the Americans alone? Soon you will get to see how carefully and attentively the Russians, Norwegians, and Germans have been working. Here is one instance of this worldwide effort, in which France still comes in last: *The Outlaw and His Wife* [1918].

The powerfully convincing actor [Victor] Sjöstrom and his remarkable partner, who plays the role of Halla, create an astonishing couple.¹ This is the story of the entire life of an island people. The visual beauty of the images is doubled by their psychological harmony. The sober, discreet development of the narrative reminds me of the impressive measured pace we associate—O Prometheus!—with the best Greek theater. And the public is swept away with emotion. For the public is awestruck by the barren landscapes, the mountains, the rustic costumes, both the austere ugliness and the acute lyricism of such closely observed feelings, the truthfulness of the long scenes which focus exclusively on the couple, the violent struggles, the high tragic end of the two aged lovers who escape life through a final embrace in a desert-like snowscape—all things which ought to horrify them (as any cinematographist will tell you). I have seen French spectators applaud at the end of a Scandinavian film.

¹ Victor Sjöstrom (1879–1960) was a Swedish actor and theater director who turned to the cinema in 1912. His best Swedish films include *Ingeborg Holm* (1913), *The Pastor* (1914), *Terje Vigen* (1917), *The Outlaw and His Wife* (1918), *The Girl from Stormycroft* (1919), *Masterman* (1920), and *The Phantom Carriage* (1921). In 1924, Sjöstrom came to the United States to work for MGM, where he directed *He Who Gets Slapped* (1924), *The Scarlet Letter*

(1926), and *The Wind* (1928). Edith Erastoff, the actress who played Halla, was Sjöström's third wife.

ANDRÉ ANTOINE, "A Proposal on the Cinema"

From "Propos sur le cinématographe," *Le Film* 166 (December 1919).

IT IS CUSTOMARY to repeat that the cinema differs totally from the theater, without taking the trouble to examine, in the slightest detail, why and how. I have attempted to tease this out with as much clarity and conciseness as possible.

According to an amusing definition by the good Febvre, who like most actors initially professed some disdain toward the screen, the Theater of the Deaf obviously has the same goal as the cinema: simply to gain the attention of the assembled listeners. But just as on stage the principal means of expression is *the spoken word*, here, by contrast, another absolute convention imposes itself: the suppression of the *word*. This is the first crucial difference which entails the need for a particular technique to convey the feelings of the characters and the vicissitudes of the action. And immediately from this follow particular rules regulating the construction of the film scenario, which are contrary to those which determine that of a theatrical play.

Therefore, if the dramatic work remains inexorably subject to the limitation, arrangement, and synthesis of scenes, by contrast, suggestions in the cinema depend on a multiplicity of images and a profusion of details, which are unrestricted by any material obstacle of execution. Let's not conclude too quickly, however, that the cinema's means of expression are superior to those of the theater just because the one permits the realization of what the other can only suggest through verbal stories. Since the screen is still deprived of depth and color, but will inevitably grow richer with photographic improvements which are barely glimpsed now, it is only in the future that we may be able to determine with complete certainty whether its production can rise unreservedly to the level of works of art.

While awaiting these developments, its seems that the work of a film author, who must be above all an inventor of images, remains purely plastic and exactly opposite that of the dramatic author, who is turned toward the physiological or psychological study of human beings. Thus, the more an author asserts himself as a great dramatist, the more his art, if truly great, will be refractory to the screen. That is why, at this moment, despite their justifiable notoriety, the authors who have ventured into the cinema have produced nothing of significance, while similarly no scenario writer has yet successfully resolved the quest for the formulas of a new art, at least with any formulas really free of our stage baggage. From this, we conclude that the kingdom of tomorrow will be reserved for plastic artists rather than literary ones.

It is simply wrongheaded, from the start, to adopt theatrical instructions and methods for an art which is not at all like what has been proposed to us up to now and to lay claim to means of expression which are quite unsuited for it.

The problems posed by the confection of a scenario increase when you examine the requirements of shooting and acting. There, too, with rare exceptions, on the screen we have only seen those actors who depend on the ancient formulas of the theater, for it is always those actors we have had recourse to—a practice which has been based, from the beginning, on the lack of any special troupe in a profession which is as new as it is uncharted. Our best actors arrive on the screen with the experience and talent which has established their reputation, and so they are not at all willing to adapt themselves to a new art, to suppress their customary and principal instrument: *the spoken word.* We go on hoping, a little ingenuously, that a great actor will remain inspired after falling silent on the screen, since it is usual to cut the hooves of a champion race horse, even when banking on his victory. This grave inconsistency at first passed almost unnoticed because our actors initially performed only in works already saturated with the current theater; but it will become more evident from now on, to the degree that our scenarios, finally enlightened by experience, produce genuine cinematic works. To our surprise, we have finally discovered that respected actors become much inferior on the screen, and the distinction between the cinema actor and the stage artist is becoming explicit. This calls, henceforth, for the formation of an acting troupe which is in no way bound to the stage. These new subjects will be exclusively plastic; their selection will be very special for they will be required to act solely by means of their intrinsic nature and external appearance. Their education will focus on their "envelope" of expression, which will let them translate a drama as easily as the spoken intonations and artifices of diction do now, which constitute the keyboard of the speaking actor. The usual conventions regulating the performance of an actor gone astray in the cinema, that is, his powers of expression through gesture, possess an intolerable falseness and inflexibility. Just as the dramatic author remains limited, so does his usual actor merely display gestures created to complement the expression of speech. Deprived of this supporting language, he becomes worthless and unsuited for silent acting.

You see the immense transformation that is required in the cinema actor's education. Yet no one has even begun to undertake this; instead, we are satisfied in this land of silence to use artists whose gestures, if I dare say so, simply *make noise.*

As for the mise-en-scène—that is, the choice of sets, the movements of the characters, the arrangement of groups—it seems that the experience of a perfect director in the theater, who is used to handling actors and extras and is skillful in the placement of furniture and props, has been altogether sufficient. Until now, the drawbacks have not been too evident because the conception of the work remained identical (that is, purely theatrical) to that of the scenarists and actors. And it would seem, indeed, that the conditions of arranging and presenting objects and people do seem similar to the theater, until one considers that the stage image remains fixed while in the cinema it is perpetually in motion. Our photographic technicians or cameramen, once they discovered themselves to be stand-ins for the spectators, have never failed to set the camera in this or that accustomed place during the creation of a film. All the elements of the spectacle have been reduced, as on stage, to a fixed point; the entire set has been composed to be seen straight on, that is, from the prompter's box. Thus, along with the unconscious complicity of actors who, through this contrivance, have regained the use of all the routines of their customary craft, the presentation of a film hardly differs from a theatrical spectacle. For a duet or a crucial dialogue, the protagonists group themselves instinctively at the [front] edge of the screen. By contrast, one of the inestimable contributions of the cinema is to multiply the aspects of a character a hundredfold, to break up his movement, expressions, and poses ad infinitum, according to distances and scales which endlessly change, through the multiplication of settings and the incessant shifting of the spectator. Our methods of shooting, therefore, must become supple and ceaselessly renewed. Already, the camera is being handled with more independence and freedom; it is ceasing to be the fixed and immutable point around which everything is organized. Just as in the theater it was necessary to get all the actors to consent to accept the fourth wall as real and to live in the ensemble of decors instead of constantly turning toward the listener, so it ought to become necessary for the actors in the cinema *to make a strict rule of ignoring the cameraman.* Instead, it is he who should follow them step by step and catch all their aspects unawares, from whichever side they are presented.

As for the sets, the furniture, and the props, we always work in ways that are badly outdated. Before the camera lens, which agrees to work only in certain conditions of lighting and perspective, we display objects perfectly refractory to photography. We continue to fabricate *theater sets*, to rent *theater costumes* and furniture, objects whose line, cut, and dimensions are hardly designed for a maximum effect in front of the camera. This or that set and furniture which look satisfactory under stage lighting become unacceptable in the cinema studio—another profound difference which necessitates a completely new technical skill.

191

I will go beyond the endpoint I set for myself here by dealing with another question crucial to the improvement which is becoming imperative—the necessary suppression, *especially for interior scenes*, of all work in our studios, which then would be used exclusively for trick shots, experiments, etc. In order to budge as little as possible, they now construct and paint, at great cost and with an enormous waste of time, interior sets which are inherently defective. It would be more logical to go *find them where they already exist*. The eternal objection of insufficient light and room or space for shooting, so often repeated, is becoming invalid since our improved electrical equipment now permits all sorts of innovations. Here, we can finally conclude, is the essential difference between the cinema, which is a *creation enacted in the open air*, and the theater, whose principal aim, by contrast, is *the imitation of nature*.

MANY perceptive minds have already said or thought such things, and some of them are well on their way to realization. America, to whom we presented the cinema once having invented it, has largely repaid us through an exemplary development and initiative that is beginning to free the new art from the inarticulate barbarism which has gripped it for far too long. The absence of cumbersome and pernicious theatrical traditions has allowed our rivals to outdistance us. Nothing is lost, however, if we determine to work with more boldness, for we can discern in the production of our competition, after a period of superb flowering, a sort of regression. Already their films no longer astonish us, and they are starting to weary the once enthusiastic listeners.

Can it be that the Americans, who once had the advantage of being born free of the routines and traditions which suffocated us, are beginning to return to the old formulas? After the naive and spontaneous scenarios of their debut, now they are buying up our plays, cutting up our novels, and importing their own theatrical actors and stars.

I like to think that our formidable competitors seem to be contracting these formulas—as if, after instinctively catching sight of the goal, they have stopped to look back—so that some among us can make an effort to forge ahead.

ANDRÉ ANTOINE (1858–1943) was an influential theater director—Théâtre Libre (1887–1896), Théâtre Antoine (1896–1906), and Théâtre de l'Odéon (1906–1914)—whose conceptions of theatrical production derived from nineteenth-century Realism and Naturalism in fiction and particularly from the famous eighteenth-century French theorist and critic, Denis Diderot. Antoine directed a series of important realist films during and just after the war, including *Les Frères corses* (1917), *Le Coupable* (1917), *Les Travailleurs de la mer* (1918) and *La Terre* (1919/1921).

PART THREE

1920-1924

Certainly what the cinema will become within the next few years will rudely obliterate these hours which we now proclaim to be of such a high order. Yet the future of cinema drama still lies in themes of simple humanity.

  Louis Delluc, 1921

The cinema is no more literature than it is painting, sculpture, architecture, or music; it is a profoundly original art which can borrow from the other arts certain elements of its definitive form but whose [governing] laws remain to be precisely discovered.

  Léon Moussinac, 1921

We recognize Cinema as the synthesis of all the arts and of the profound impulse underlying them. . . . It will be a lucid and vast expression of our internal life, infinitely more vibrant than all previous forms of expression.

  Ricciotto Canudo, 1923

The cinema is poetry's most powerful medium, the truest medium for the untrue, the unreal, the "surreal" as Apollinaire would have said. This is why some of us have entrusted to it our highest hopes.

  Jean Epstein, 1924

Cinégraphie and the Search
for Specificity

BETWEEN 1920 and 1924, the French public forum open to writing on the cinema expanded dramatically. In the previous five years, under the constrictions of the war, a broad spectrum of "theories" of narrative and non-narrative films had been articulated within a limited range of discursive formats. Now those rough notions were extended, "systematized," or even reformulated—by veterans such as Louis Delluc, Emile Vuillermoz, and Ricciotto Canudo as well as by newcomers, Léon Moussinac, Jean Epstein, Germaine Dulac, and René Clair. And they were disseminated widely, and debated enthusiastically, through a newly formed network of newspapers, journals, ciné-clubs, and *conférences* or exhibitions.[1]

THE PUBLIC FORUM

Within two or three years of the war's end, across the political spectrum, nearly every one of the major Paris newspapers had either a weekly page or daily column devoted to the cinema.[2] The "big four" mass dailies, all supporters of the conservative Bloc National government, almost simultaneously launched daily film reviews in the fall of 1921—*Le Petit Journal* (René Jeanne), *Le Journal* (Jean Chataigner, André Antoine), *Le Matin* (Jean Gallois), *Le Petit Parisien* (J.-L. Croze). Daily or weekly columns also appeared in older papers associated with the Right—for example, *L'Intransigeant* (Boisyvon), *Le Figaro* (Robert Spa)[3]—as well as newer ones linked to the Left—for example, *L'Oeuvre* (Lucian Wahl, Auguste Nardy), *Le Quotidien* (Wahl), *L'Humanité* (Léon Moussinac), and *Paris-Soir* (Chataigner, Jeanne).[4] At least four Paris papers, however, were particularly influential during the period. *Le Temps* retained some prominence through the biweekly film review column of Emile Vuillermoz. *Le Petit Journal* presented a model cinema page, which was widely imitated, because young René Jeanne offered space in the paper to major French filmmakers and other film reporters and critics.[5] *Bonsoir*, the leftist evening paper affiliated with Gustave Téry's *L'Oeuvre*, but similar in tone to *Le Canard enchaîné*, provided probably the liveliest discussions of the cinema through the reviews of Auguste Nardy, Pierre Scize [Joseph-Michel Piot], Marcel Achard, and Louis Delluc.[6] And *Comoedia*, once revived, dominated them all (under the direction of J.-L. Croze), particularly by 1922, when it invited Vuillermoz to write a weekly column and then devoted a series of reviews and articles to Abel Gance's *La Roue* (1922–1923)—pieces written by Vuillermoz, Moussinac, Jean Epstein, Fernand Léger, and Gance himself. The cinema's cultural significance finally had reached the point where journalists such as Jeanne, Wahl, and Croze could now maintain a quasi-independent status outside the film industry, by reviewing films and editing newspaper sections devoted to the cinema.

As a sign of the cinema's acceptance as a legitimate art form, the literary and intellectual journals also began, on a consistent basis, to open their pages to essays on the cinema as well as to film reviews.[7] Beginning in 1920, for instance, the prestigious *Mercure de France* took a turn to the left and invited Léon Moussinac to contribute a lengthy trimonthly film column, which soon developed into a model review form.[8] The conservative *Revue hebdomadaire* established a regular column for André Lang to do a series of film interviews and reviews, which he reprised in the even more staid *Annales politiques et littéraires*. Jean Galtier-Boissière's maverick *Le Crapouillot* published several special issues devoted to the cinema (in 1920 and 1923) as well as a third film review column by Moussinac. Another key avant-garde journal, Le Corbusier and Ozenfant's monthly *L'Esprit nouveau* (1920–1925) promoted pieces on the cinema by Delluc, Epstein, B. Tokine, and the art historian, Elie Faure.[9] And Ricciotto Canudo's short-lived *Gazette des sept arts* (1922–1923) turned over much of its space to proselytizing for film art. In 1922, a new weekly review journal, Larousse's *Les Nouvelles littéraires*, sought to rival *Comoedia* as the principal journal dedicated to cultural events in Paris; and it soon included an important cinema column by Canudo.[10] A year later, another new weekly competitor, *Paris-Journal*, opened film review columns to Georges Charensol and the young Surrealist poet, Robert Desnos. Finally, the deluxe *Théâtre et Comoedia illustré*, now published by Rolf de Maré, manager of the Théâtre des Champs Elysées, included a monthly film supplement (1922–1925) in which, after a brief stint by Claude Autant-Lara, René Clair wrote trenchant film reviews while young Jean Mitry transcribed some half dozen interviews with prominent French filmmakers.

The specialized press devoted to the cinema witnessed a similar explosive expansion. At least five weekly journals now were addressing the various sectors of the film industry—*La Cinématographie française, Cinéopse, Filma, Ciné-Journal,* and *Le Courrier cinématographique*—and *Filma* took over from *Ciné-Journal* the strategy of publishing an important annual on the industry, *Tout-Cinéma*. The mass dailies and publishing houses were busy creating a market for popular weekly film fan magazines—for example, Jean Vignaud's *Ciné-Miroir {Le Petit Parisien}*, Pierre Desclaux's *Mon-Ciné* and

Le Film complet—as well as weekly or biweekly ciné-roman series—for instance, Tallandier's Cinéma-Bibliothèque, Fayard's Les Grands Films, and J. Ferenczi's Le Roman complet.[11] The most interesting development, however, came in the journals which were more or less independent of both the film industry and the mass press. When Diamant-Berger and Delluc left *Le Film* in 1919, and its influence waned, a number of new film journals vied to take its place. Pierre Henry's biweekly *Ciné-pour-tous* (1919–1923) and Delluc's own weekly *Le Journal du Ciné-Club* (1920–1921) offered inexpensive alternatives to *Le Film*, but tended to stress up-to-date information on current film production and exhibition. Jean Pascal and Adrien Maître's *Cinémagazine* (first published in January 1921), however, provided all this in addition to space for lengthy reviews and essays from important writers across the spectrum—from those closely associated with the industry like Guillaume Danvers and Juan Arroy to independents like Vuillermoz, or from those linked to the Right like Jeanne and Boisyvon to those on the left like Moussinac. The degree of its success soon allowed *Cinémagazine* to have its own reporter, Robert Florey, in Hollywood as well as publish an annual, *Almanach du cinéma*, which competed on a par with *Tout-Cinéma*. Probably the most influential of these new film journals, however, was Delluc's deluxe weekly, *Cinéa*, whose purpose was to offer a platform for the cinema much as did the prestigious *Comoedia illustré* (for which he briefly wrote film reviews) for the theater. For at least a year and a half after its inception (6 May 1921), through the essays and reviews of Lionel Landry, Wahl, Epstein, Jean Cocteau, Delluc himself, and others, *Cinéa* did indeed function as the primary forum of discussion and debate on film art, especially an *independent French* film art. And its position was resecured in late 1923, when Jean Tedesco took over ownership and editorship from Delluc, bought out Henry's rival magazine, and merged the two into the deluxe weekly, *Cinéa-Ciné-pour-tous*.

Even though much of his time was taken up now with writing and directing a series of fiction films, Delluc also continued to turn out a small set of published books on the cinema. These included another collection of reviews and essays in *Photogénie* (de Brunoff, 1920), an affectionate tribute to Chaplin in *Charlot* (de Brunoff, 1921), and probably the first collection of original film scripts in *Drames du cinéma* (Le Monde nouveau, 1923).[12] Perhaps inspired by Delluc's seemingly tireless example, and encouraged by Blaise Cendrars, Jean Epstein devoted a final chapter to the cinema in his first book, *La Poésie d'aujourd'hui: Un novel état d'intelligence* (Editions de la sirène, 1921), and then focused exclusively on the new medium in *Bonjour Cinéma* (Editions de la sirène, 1921).[13] In this, the most significant book on the cinema of the period, Epstein not only collected his first important essays on the cinema (from his own short-lived Lyon film journal,

Promenoir, as well as from *Cinéa*) but also produced a witty parody of a film program—with poster photos of film stars, adulatory "fan" poems, a "serial episode," and several "features" (the central essays). Together, Delluc and Epstein's books offered a sharp contrast to Ernest Coustet's industry-oriented survey of early film history and current methods of production in *Le Cinéma* (Hachette, 1921), the second edition of Léopold Lobel's *La Technique cinématographique* (Dunod, 1922), and André Lang's collection of interviews with filmmakers, *Déplacements et villegiatures littéraires et suivi de la promenade au royaume des images ou entretiens cinématographiques* (La Renaissance du livre, 1924), which highlighted a controversy sparked off by André Antoine's diatribe against much of the French film industry.

Alongside the public forum of newspapers, magazines, and books, in the early 1920s, there also developed a special forum initially unique to France—the ciné-club movement. It was Delluc again who established in Paris the precedent of a public *conférence* on film—a combination of lecture, film screening, and discussion—first at the Pepinière cinema in 1920 and later at the Colisée cinema in 1921 and 1922. In addition to the critical discourse of his film journals, these *conférences* were the means by which he sought (unsuccessfully, it turned out) to create a mass ciné-club movement based on his faith in film as a popular art, a movement that would either change the policies and practices of the French film industry or else offer an alternative structure to that industry.[14] One of these—the first Paris screening of *Caligari* (1919), in November 1921—even challenged the postwar antipathy to anything German in order to promote the cinema as an international art, much as Fernand Léger had fought for the inclusion of German art in the reopened Salon des Indépendents one year earlier.[15] In 1921, Ricciotto Canudo then systematized Delluc's *conférence* format within the context of a select group of cinéphiles—artists, writers, and professional filmmakers—who met regularly as the Club des amis du septième art or CASA. In contrast to Delluc, however, Canudo used his group to promote an elitist notion of high-art cinema, principally through the special expositions on film art which CASA sponsored at the prestigious Salon d'Automne, perhaps the most important annual exhibition of painting in Paris, beginning in November 1921.[16] Other less elitist ciné-clubs soon emerged in imitation of CASA—notably the Amis du cinéma established by *Cinémagazine* (with branch organizations in several provincial cities) and the Club français du cinéma founded by Moussinac, the latter of which seems to have taken a position midway between Delluc and Canudo by explicitly attacking the commercial restrictions of the film industry as well as defending filmmakers as artists (with all the rights that entailed). In 1924, this emergent alternative cinema network culminated in a six-month-long exposition devoted to French film art, organized by Moussinac—as if in fulfillment of one of Canudo's dreams—at the major Paris art gallery–museum, the Musée Galliera.[17] And the high point of the exposition was a series of lectures and film screenings—including those of critics Landry and Moussinac, filmmakers L'Herbier and Dulac, and architect–set designer Robert Mallet-Stevens—a veritable public seminar on the cinema as an art form.[18] With the Musée Galliera exposition, the French ciné-club movement seemed to have confirmed its dedication to the cinema as an elite art form.

THE SPECTRUM OF MAJOR FILM THEORIES

In 1921, Lucien Wahl conducted an extensive survey on "The Future of the French Cinema" in the conservative weekly, *La Renaissance*.[19] This survey can stand as representative of the spectrum of thinking on the much-lamented "crisis" that continued to persist after the war in the French film industry, especially vis-à-vis the American and German industries. Opinion ranged from Charles Pathé, who repeated his position of three years earlier, Jacques de Baroncelli, who argued oddly against overproduction, and Henri Etiévant, who demanded that French banks simply provide more capital investment, to René Jeanne's call for an end to government censorship and the institution of import quotas, Ricciotto Canudo's contention that only French artists and intellectuals could rescue the cinema from ruin, and Léon Poirier's suggestion of an international consortium of film production and distribution.[20] The crisis also quickly surfaced in the controversy, mediated by André Lang, over André Antoine's scathing appraisal of French filmmakers and the industry in *La Revue hebdomadaire*, in 1923.[21] During that controversy, Louis Delluc attacked the concept of mass production—recycling the same films week after week under slightly different labels—with characteristic irony; and Léon Moussinac cautiously called for a "revolution" against those who controlled the film industry.[22] The actual changes in the industry during this period, however, either lagged behind the writers' wishes or else were deflected in a different direction. The ciné-club movement, for instance, became associated with high-art institutions such as the Salon d'Automne and the Musée Galliera. Film production devolved into a cottage industry where a small number of producers such as Louis Nalpas, Diamant-Berger, Abel Gance, and Marcel L'Herbier briefly attempted to set up "schools" or ministudios of filmmaking. Yet most—for example, Baroncelli, Poirier, Delluc, Dulac, Jacques Feyder—were forced to operate on an individual basis, project by project, to maintain some semblance of independence.[23]

Aesthetic concerns, rather than those having to do with politics and the film industry, however, most preoccupied French writing on the cinema in the early 1920s, even more than they had during the war period. Historians of film theory and criticism have long seen this period as dominated by a single more or less coherent aesthetic of "French Impressionism." Elsewhere I have argued against the limitations of this critical tendency to impose a unified aesthetic grid on the rather diverse and exploratory postwar film practice in France.[24] Here I would like to reassert and extend that argument, in accordance with the previous introductory sections, by amplifying and analyzing the heterogeneity of French discourse on the cinema. Instead of privileging "French Impressionism," I mean to reinsert it, "demystified" as much as possible, within the historical complex of voices that emerged from the war period. This complex of voices pulsated with as much polemical fervor as before, but now there was a certain degree of systematizing evident, especially in the writings of Canudo, Moussinac, Vuillermoz, Dulac, and, perhaps most singularly, Epstein. Although their work resists a consistent, mutually exclusive classification system, on the question of the cinema's function and form these writers generally fall into at least four major, well-established "camps" or centers of gravity—mainstream narrative, Impressionism, Realism, plastic non-narrative—which competed for dominance in the early 1920s.

Due to the efforts of Diamant-Berger, Pathé, and others during the war, the once "progressive" mainstream concept of a narrative cinema now largely defined French film production and hence turned into an unarticulated assumption in most French writing. An exception appeared in Louis Feuillade's brief introductions to his serials, *Barrabas* (1920) and *Les Deux Gamines* (1921).[25] Ten years before, Feuillade had sought, rather prematurely, to make film an adjunct of painting as well as Realist fiction. Now, after six years of highly successful serial filmmaking, he defended the cinema's value as a popular mass spectacle, in terms of a concise ideological formula. As *the* popular art of the time, the cinema functioned chiefly as entertainment, as a means of escape from the constrictions of ordinary life in an industrialized society and into an imaginary world "where our faculties find freer exercise."[26] What counted, therefore, was the *story*, anything else of interest was subordinated to and determined by the story. Feuillade's position dovetailed with what René Clair and others eventually came to define (in current terms) as the classical Hollywood cinema: technique at the service of the progress of the story. Except that Feuillade insisted that a particular kind of story worked best, at least for the French—romantic adventure fiction, which soon actually came to dominate French film genres such as the serial and historical reconstruction film.[27] And Louis Nalpas, even more than Feuillade, whether he was working as an independent producer or as the executive producer of Jean Sapène's Cinéromans, proved especially adept at resurrecting such popular nineteenth-century French fiction in a string of successful serials—for example, Henri Fescourt's *Mathias Sandorf* (1921), *Rouletabille chez les bohemiens* (1922), and *Mandrin* (1924).[28]

A further exception can be seen in the writings of André Antoine. In apparent opposition to the industry's excessive predilection for adventure story entertainment, Antoine continued to advocate a counter position in a series of acrimonious articles written after Pathé forced him to abandon filmmaking in 1921. For Antoine, the cinema was still in a period of transition. On the one hand, he condemned Feuillade, Pathé, and Diamant-Berger for their "bad taste" in choosing stories to film and for their reliance on "conventional" methods of filmmaking.[29] On the other, he criticized Gance, L'Herbier, and Delluc for an "artistic pretension" that, he thought, only upset most audiences who were unprepared to follow their work.[30] Instead, the cinema ought to confine itself to adaptations of "famous novels and plays"—exemplified in the work of Baroncelli, Poirier, and himself—adaptations that would guarantee commercial success and at the same time, Antoine argued, allow filmmakers gradually to discover the artistic potential of film.[31] Thus, the literary source text retained its privileged position in his "theory," guaranteeing the cinema's status as art. And the cinema's function remained—as it had in his early theater work—simply to represent the external human behavior of the source story in a three-dimensional space with as much verisimilitude as possible. Antoine reiterated the principles of filmmaking he had laid out just after the war, with one addition. He now insisted on shooting a scene, especially on location, with five or six cameras running simultaneously, in order to be able to choose the shots that best conveyed the actors' facial expressions and gestures at any one moment.[32] What was becoming the norm for shooting scenes of spectacle in the French historical reconstruction films Antoine wanted to apply to smaller scenes involving just a few people. Consequently, despite the vehemence of his attacks, by now Antoine's "theory" had become little more than a variation on the mainstream concept of a narrative cinema.

Whether perceived as American or French, this mainstream position provided a form of status quo against which, as a matter of course, most other French writers of the period rebelled along one of two divergent lines first developed by Vuillermoz and Delluc during the war. The elitist argument that the film medium was capable of producing "high art" or a form of art comparable to the established arts gained wider and wider credence. At one point or another, almost all French writers—including Delluc, Moussinac, and Epstein—paid lip service to this position, which, through a transformation of Delluc's initial use of the term, became synonymous with "French Impressionism."[33] Clearly, its leading exponents, however, were Canudo, Vuillermoz, and Dulac, who consistently engaged in a Romantic- and especially Symbolist-inflected discourse. Replete with terms drawn from as well as references to the other arts, that discourse assumed that *culture* constituted "the deepest record, the deepest impulse, and the deepest resource of the human spirit," the province of a secular and "natural" priesthood of artists.[34] For these writers as well as many others, in an industrialized society that marginalized individual perception and devalued the "data" of the senses, the narrative cinema, then, ultimately ought to function as a pretext for personal vision and lyrical expression. In the hands of a true (read "alienated") artist, Canudo hoped, this "new string on the eternal lyre" could "still the currents of inner life or feeling and crystallize them, . . . fix life's elusiveness and synthesize its harmonies," and eventually produce the individualized style of a master.[35] The artist could speak to the spectator directly, "enter into communion with him," reveal the "very soul of things," or share his "intense inner life."[36] For the cinema's uniqueness, according to Canudo, lay in its "extraordinary and striking faculty of *representing immateriality*."[37]

Audiences for such film art would be limited, Vuillermoz assumed, because not many spectators could understand the "cinégraphic language . . . stammered out by a few extraordinary artists."[38] The forms such film art took would be restricted as well. Within the commercial narrative cinema, Vuillermoz and Dulac tended to prefer "psychological films" for the latitude they offered in the expression of inner emotions or feeling.[39] Meanwhile, Canudo continued to dream of the "synthetic" film that would "reproduce the emotion of life in its entirety" in a kind of "synthesis-temple" of all the arts—a notion that L'Herbier seems to have attempted to realize in *L'Inhumaine* (1924).[40] Moreover, Canudo pushed for another, "purer," conception of form—a conception that he actually put in practice through the CASA exhibitions at the Salon d'Automne.[41] Here, as in Symbolist poetry, film art approached the condition of an "intransitive art"—as an end unto itself, a self-fulfilling passion. If it took a group of apostles or audacious snobs to proselytize for such an elite concept of film art, Lionel Landry proclaimed, then so be it. "Perhaps a milieu of snobbery is necessary," Landry wrote, "for the blossoming of a new art form."[42] That label would later stick.

In contrast to this elitist position as well as the industry's almost exclusive interest in story entertainment and adaptations, Delluc and his friend Moussinac persisted in their vision of the cinema as a "democratic art"— that is, a Realist narrative art of, by, and for the people.[43] Only through this conception might the cinema resolve the sharp separation or alienation of culture from material social life, a separation that Canudo and Vuillermoz seemed to encourage. For Delluc and Moussinac, what continued to be crucial, principally through the example of American and Swedish films, was the story and particularly the natural landscape or urban milieu out of which it evolved.[44] At its best, as Canudo summarized Delluc's thinking (without reference), the cinema transformed *nature* itself or the ambiance of a natural landscape into a *character*.[45] The subjects Delluc and Moussinac preferred, therefore, were original scenarios of simple, banal stories drawn from real life, especially working-class or provincial life.[46] News items or *faits-divers* transformed into tragedy, as Moussinac put it, in praising Griffith's *Broken Blossoms* (1919) and Delluc's own *Fièvre* (1921).[47] Here, in light of Gance's *La Roue*, Canudo contributed a variation on this conception (looking back to Zola) with his celebration of the cinema's representation of the "collective spirit" or "crowd psychology" of a particular social milieu.[48] In fact, this Realist conception of the cinema generally echoed the French Naturalists' valorization of the relative truth of simply representing the "local color" and factual data of a specific milieu. And it was complemented by the continuing French fascination for documentary films—for instance, *The Shackleton Expedition* (1920) and *Nanook* (1922)—as evidenced by both writers and audiences.[49]

Contrary to what was typical in the French film industry, Delluc and Moussinac also argued that the conception of the original scenario and its realization ought to be the work of a single individual.[50] In order to be a film artist rather than a simple *metteur-en-scène* of adaptations, one had to become an *auteur* or *cinéaste*, to use Delluc's favorite term.[51] The two critics were just as insistent that the filmmaker must become an artisan or craftsman as well.[52] Poet and scriptwriter Marcel L'Herbier, for instance, had become a kind of model filmmaker because he had learned through apprenticeship to be a fine film craftsman, just as Delluc himself had become a model critic by learning how to be part of "the crowd" or mass audience. In *Photogénie* (1920), Delluc reaffirmed his faith in the ability of most French audiences (especially working-class audiences) to understand and appreciate film art, whatever its national origin.[53] And a similar faith asserted itself early on in Moussinac and later even in Robert Desnos.[54] Now, however, Delluc and Moussinac were as ready to help educate those audiences as they were to learn from them. And they continued to be vague, despite Moussinac's growing attachment to the French Communist Party, about the broad new social community—whether class-determined, national, or international—that they hoped the cinema was in the process of building.[55] The possibility for such a community seemed to be fast disappearing in the context of a conservative political and socioeconomic swing that was then reaching a peak in France, the power of the growing multinational capitalist constituency of the film industry (especially as dominated by the Americans), and the success of Canudo and others in appropriating film into the framework of established art institutions.

In addition to these opposing Impressionist and Realist theories of cinema, the non-narrative, "plastic" conception of the cinema began to circulate ever more widely, especially in the writings of Elie Faure, Fernand Léger, and Jean-Francis Laglenn. Through them—perhaps because the first two worked in close association with the group of artists who published *L'Esprit nouveau*—the Modernist ideas previously articulated by Survage and Gromaire were reformulated, in part, within the context of a "Purist" theory of art.[56] For Faure and Léger, especially, the fundamental nature of the cinema was not dramatic or psychological, descriptive or documentary; it was plastic—which meant it had to do principally with *cineplastics*, the representation of forms either in repose or in movement. Like Gromaire before them, neither advocated a film form that was completely abstract; but Léger, particularly after seeing *La Roue*, recognized the potential of films "where the *mechanical element* plays a major role, where the machine becomes *the leading character, the leading actor*."[57] This insight led Léger to believe in the cinema as a means to celebrate the precision, order, and harmony of the machine or the mechanical in modern life; and it brought film as a medium within the scope of his own artistic practice—for example, *Ballet mécanique* (1924).[58] The ideological implications of Léger's "new spectacle" might be said loosely to parallel Delluc and Moussinac's advocacy of the cinema as a "democratic art," but a rather different ideology became explicit in Faure's theory of cineplastics. On the one hand, much like Epstein, Faure dreamed of a kind of epistemological cinema that exclusively explored the interpenetration of the spatial and the temporal—for instance, bringing together decades or centuries of visual images within the spatiotemporal boundaries of a single film.[59] On the other, he saw the current cinema serving an essential function in a modern industrial society ever more centered on machines of travel and the architectural hubs of transportation systems. "Cinéplastics will doubtless be the spiritual ornament sought for in this period [of rest and relay in travel]—the play that this new society will find most useful in developing in the masses the sense of confidence, of harmony, of cohesion."[60] Here the ideological trappings of the "new spirit" of Purism—synthesis, construction, harmony—and its confirmation of the new industrial social order find concise articulation. Faure's text, in fact, could be taken as a credo for the famous 1925 Paris Exposition of the Modern Decorative Arts.

A singular exception to these more or less familiar positions erupted in the early writings of Jean Epstein. Using an idiosyncratic amalgam of languages drawn from philosophy, physiology, psychology, and poetics or literary aesthetics, Epstein began with a number of ideas shared by Delluc and Moussinac (as well as others by Faure and Léger) and transformed them into a theory that came close to being as elitist as Vuillermoz and Canudo's.[61] For Epstein, "situations" rather than stories constituted the real subject of the cinema. What fascinated him, according to Stuart Liebman, were situations endemic to the working conditions of a highly industrial society, especially those involving mental fatigue brought about by machine labor.[62] Through its focus on such conditions, Epstein believed (translating the negative into the positive), the cinema could reveal and explore the non-linguistic, non-rational operations of the "unconscious" in human existence.[63] Here the work of Freud first entered French discourse on the cinema, although Epstein took pains to try to distance himself from the Viennese psychoanalyst.[64] For he was convinced that the unconscious had its own "grammar" or "logic" of knowing—he called it *lyrosophy*—that provided an epistemological or ontological basis for film art, as well as modern poetry.[65] Sometimes, almost in anticipation of Antonin Artaud or Dziga Vertov, Epstein wrote as if the camera itself functioned like an analogous metal brain, independent of human agency, that broke through the conventional bounds of human perception, to reveal *being* itself or, in Bergsonian terms, the change in duration of the universe as a whole.[66] At other times, he seemed to insist on the filmmaker's intervention—through his "experimental mentality" or "analytic propensity"—to make certain that what appeared on the screen exploded the prison of real space-time and opened literally onto another intuited world that would astonish and excite strong emotions in the audience.[67] In either case, the cinema seemed to create a new system of "lyrosophical" knowing, by bringing the unconscious to consciousness, through the hyperextension of a single sense—that of seeing. Epstein, too, seemed to assume that most audiences could understand and appreciate this new form of consciousness, for he described what occurred between screen image and spectator as a mysterious relay of energy, as in breathing or taking the sacrament.[68] Yet the esoteric, highly metaphorical nature of his own language—his texts actually can be read as an attempt to put that lyrosophy in play—tended to contradict that assumption.

One last conception of cinema finally began to coalesce during this period—that of the Surrealists. Early traces can be found in the essays and reviews written by Louis Aragon and Philippe Soupault in the late 1910s; but it was Robert Desnos who, in his *Paris-Journal* review column, in 1923, began to articulate an explicitly Surrealist "theory" of cinema. What attracted the Surrealists to the cinema—particularly the popular serials and American comedies and westerns—was its power to overturn the laws of logic and social convention. "Its singular power of disorientation," to use André Breton's famous phrase, "cast us outside ourselves and at the same time awakened in us forces of which we were unaware."[69] For Desnos, the cinema acted as an enchanting substitute for the dream state or drugs, which gave access to the unconscious and to unexpected conjunctions.[70] It constituted an everchanging "storehouse" of images, where the Surrealist spectator could freely associate among selected images and reorganize them at will. Specifically, the film image functioned as a double discourse of the manifest and the repressed—for Desnos, the sexual or erotic—that stimulated the poet's transformation of the banal and the conventional into the marvelous.[71] Therefore, as Paul Hammond argues, bringing a film's secret life, its latent repressed content, to the surface had priority in the early "synthetic criticism" and cinematic poems of Soupault and his colleagues.[72] In other words, Soupault's "reviews" of Chaplin's *Sunnyside* (1919) and William S. Hart's *Blue Blazes Rawden* (1918) used a method somewhat similar to psychoanalysis: they attempted to distill the latent dream content from the manifest content of popular cinema.[73] In contrast to Epstein's early epistemological interest in the unconscious, the Surrealists considered the unconscious—in film and elsewhere—as essential to a project that was both aesthetic and sociopolitical. Desnos's film reviews, Soupault's "synthetic texts," and even a few scenarios such as Benjamin Peret's "Pulchérie veut un auto" (1923) were all part of an emerging Surrealist project radically to change perception and the experience of reality as the first step toward the actual, physical transformation of the world.[74]

THE CINÉGRAPHIE *OF FILM LANGUAGE*

On the question of the nature and function of film as an art form in French society, then, the spectrum of theories laid down during the war hardened in place, with the addition of at least two significant "bands." What was strikingly different about the early 1920s, however, was the intense interest, sometimes to the point of exclusivity, in delineating the raw material of the film medium and the methods or techniques that most contributed to its transformation into art. "The cinema is no more literature than it is painting, sculpture, architecture, or music," wrote Moussinac, "it is a profoundly original art which can borrow from the other arts certain elements of its definitive form but whose [governing] laws remain to be precisely discovered."[75] That the cinema was emerging as a new "language" was now commonly assumed by most French writers, from Vuillermoz to Moussinac or Epstein. Whether or not a film such as L'Herbier's *El Dorado* (1921) would later be recognized for its original contribution to that emergence, as Lionel Landry believed, the French were unusually preoccupied with defining the parameters of that language.[76] And whether or not the cinema constituted "a form of ideographic writing," as Vuillermoz put it early in 1920, film discourse was acquiring more and more autonomy and specificity.[77] The aim of French critics and filmmakers, Epstein concluded, was "to establish the premises for a cinematic grammar or rhetoric . . . a grammar peculiar to itself."[78] Although the assumption never became explicit, this effort often seemed intent on establishing a uniquely French system of "film writing" in contrast to the then-dominant American system of spatio-temporal continuity editing. Here the similarities and differences among texts produced alignments that sometimes cut across or redistributed the expected divisions between theoretical camps.

In one sense, this search for cinematic specificity was undertaken from two complementary positions or perspectives, that of the filmmaker and that of the film spectator. In his 1920 statement on an aesthetic of the cinema, for instance, Vuillermoz summarized the first position quite clearly.[79] There were two separate "creative acts" during the process of filmmaking. One involved choices made in writing the scenario or script and then in recording images on film—through framing, lighting, and arranging the actors and decors. The other involved choices made in assembling those images or shots into sequences that would constitute a complete film. Of the two, Vuillermoz argued, the "real construction" took place in the assemblage or editing. Both provided evidence that the cinema was an art, but the latter made it unique among the arts. Delluc and Moussinac perhaps best articulated the concept of cinematic specificity from the perspective of the film spectator. For them, too, editing seemed to take precedence as they focused attention on *rhythm* in film. Here Moussinac even tried, without much success, to provide scientific and philosophical arguments to support the idea that "rhythm is a spiritual need" and hence a crucial characteristic of film as art.[80] Nevertheless, Delluc and Moussinac asserted (and Clair seconded them), two kinds of rhythm worked in conjunction within a film: an internal rhythm involving movement within the mise-en-scène of the shot and an external rhythm involving the length or duration of the shot as well as the kinds of transitions between shots.[81] As a sign of their interest in the way external rhythm was controlled in a film, they redefined the concept of *cinégraphie*—which both Vuilliermoz and L'Herbier had first articulated during the war—to distinguish the rhythmical or structural ordering of *photogénie* throughout a film. As such, *cinégraphie* now came to occupy a crucial place both in Delluc's and in Moussinac's writing.

This simple division ultimately rested, however, on a more complex analysis of cinematic specificity. Here the French seemed to have reached a consensus on the parameters of film "language," parameters that persist in one way or another down to this day. The basic unit of film was the shot, or to quote Dulac, "the image in its most isolated expressive form."[82] More specifically, that basic unit encompassed, to use Epstein's phrase, those "photogenic elements" that operated within and between shots, namely, the specific features of mise-en-scène and especially framing in conjunction with editing.[83] Writers remained uncertain whether these elements constituted a strictly regulated grammar with a complementary fixed lexicon or a loosely defined rhetoric with a flexible set of discursive strategies—and the terms, grammar and rhetoric, circulated almost synonymously. But they seemed to agree more or less on the multidimensional nature of the shot and its constituent elements. For Dulac, "the shot simultaneously defined place, action, and thought."[84] For Epstein, the rhythm of film images—their "photogenic mobility"—functioned formally, dramatically, and psychologically.[85] For Moussinac, similarly, the *cinégraphie* of film images generated a plastic, representational, emotional, and intellectual significance.[86] The assumption here was that the cinema operated as a large-scale form constituted of several codes or "notational systems": formal, representational, narrative, and connotative or symbolic.[87] And the interrelations among these existed at the level of the shot and its constituent elements. Potentially, any one system or combination of systems might override the others and act as the principle of continuity controlling the overall structure of a particular film.

Consistent with their interest in *photogénie* and *cinégraphie*, the French tended to focus debate on how the shot and its constituent elements could produce patterns of continuity other than those of the classical Hollywood cinema, which almost exclusively served the purpose of storytelling. Delluc and Moussinac, interestingly enough, sometimes resisted this tendency. Delluc, for instance, praised Fairbanks's *Three Musketeers* (1921) as far superior to Diamant-Berger's *Trois Mousquetaires* (1921–1922) precisely because its rhythmic patterns were so neatly geared to the action of the Alexandre Dumas narrative.[88] In effect, he was chiding his former publisher for failing to learn from his very own words in *Le Cinéma* (1919). Generally, both Delluc and Moussinac agreed, the French gave far too little attention to the "continuity" or decoupage, to the development of the scenario idea (both narrative and thematic) in the form of a shot-by-shot script.[89] "Few have understood," wrote Moussinac, "that the decoupage and montage, otherwise called the idea and its visualization, are as essential as the mise-en-scène."[90] The publication of four of Delluc's scripts, in *Drames du cinéma* (1923), was offered modestly as a model. Here, in the "Prologue," Delluc briefly singled out several sequences from *Fièvre* (1921) in order to explain how specific choices in the mise-en-scène, framing, and editing controlled the process of conveying atmosphere, action, and thinking or feeling.[91] And he also suggested that one particular feature of film language dictated the development of a certain kind of story. "The possibility of rapidly alternating images . . . creates an extraordinary field for antithesis" in the cinema; and this, in turn, implies that "the confrontation between past and present, between reality and memory, ... is one of the most seductive plots of this art of *photogénie*."[92] Delluc's own film practice was indeed a testament to that.

At the opposite end of this debate on principles of continuity clustered a number of conceptions that sought to "purify" the cinema, to imagine it as an art of pure pattern and process. One particular conception especially tempted Moussinac. Here the lure of rhythmic specificity led to a fascination with technique for its own sake. "The technique [of the cinema]," claimed Moussinac, "is becoming richer with a speed and power that no other art has ever known. Everyone of us is in bondage to it."[93] By technique, he meant variable speed recording (especially slow motion), various optical devices (superimposition, vignette masks, distorting filters and lenses), "punctuation" devices (the fade, iris, and dissolve), and accelerating montage. These constituted a panoply of technological innovations (and more were expected) discovered during the process of shooting and editing "research" over the previous half-dozen years or so and now disseminated widely throughout the French cinema. Such technical features were unique to the cinema and, therefore, might define its material condition as separate from the other arts and perhaps as even more advanced (and open to further change). The French writers' focus on such techniques, of course, continued the interest in technological research that had marked prewar writing on the cinema; but it also intensified, in part, because of their confrontation with a series of major films in the early 1920s. The conjunction of L'Herbier's *El Dorado* and Wiene's *Caligari* in the fall of 1921, for instance, led the French to valorize their own interest in "special effects" produced by the camera alone in opposition to the perceived German interest in a highly stylized mise-en-scène.[94] The startling premiere of Gance's *La Roue*, in the winter of 1922–1923, then extended their interest to the rhythmic effects of editing.[95] This unusual attention to technique, it should be noted, could equally serve the purposes of Moussinac's "Realism," Vuillermoz and Canudo's "Impressionism," Faure's "cineplastics," or Epstein's "lyrosophy." But it reached the point, momentarily with Moussinac, where technological innovation in the cinema came close to becoming a privileged end in itself.[96] Indeed, this valorization of technique provided support for Canudo's effort, through CASA's screenings of film excerpts at the Salon d'Automne, to define the cinema in terms of either individual or national styles. And Canudo's notion of a "cinematic anthology was extremely valuable," Epstein argued, "because, through these fragments of film, it drew attention to cinematic style: it isolated style from narrative."[97] The exclusive fascination with technique, then, provided a crucial basis for the later concept of a "pure cinema."

The dominant principle of continuity, the one that supposedly most distinguished the French from the Americans, however, depended on the then widely accepted analogy between film and painting or, more especially, music. A few writers such as Faure and Léger privileged the "plastic" or formal relations within and between shots—for example, line, form, texture, color—as the principal basis for film art.[98] Film existed solely as "a projected image," Léger asserted, or as an orderly succession of "judiciously composed" images.[99] The shot was like a painting or sculpture in motion, its graphic elements continually recombining in rhythmic, almost mathematical patterns. After the premiere of Gance's La Roue, writers such as Moussinac and Clair even speculated on the possibility of an exclusively mathematical basis for cinematic rhythm, whether the subject be the movement of human bodies or machine parts or a union of the two.[100] Nearly every writer, at one time or another, however, accepted Vuillermoz's "musical analogy" as perhaps the crucial principle of editing continuity. "What was the cinema, after all," in Gance's famous formulation, "but the music of light."[101] Here the shot was analogous to a musical chord, in which the notes corresponded to specific features of the mise-en-scène and framing; thus a sequence of shots or a scene was analogous to several bars of music or even a stanza or a movement. Some writers such as Canudo and the composer, Arthur Honegger, suggested that this correspondence derived from an actual synchronization of film and orchestral accompaniment, whether that synchronization was defined rhythmically or emotionally. In La Roue, for instance, Honegger said he had sought to achieve an "absolute correspondence between the animating spirit of a fragment of film and its rhythmic musical corroboration."[102] Resurrecting Richard Wagner's dream of a grand synthesis of drama and music, which he had first articulated before the war, Canudo also envisioned a new form of musical drama whose narrative rhythm would be generated by already existing compositions of music.[103] Others such as Vuillermoz, Delluc, Moussinac, and Clair, however, acted as if filmic rhythm functioned like music automatically, that is, independent of any accompanying score. As Moussinac put it, the "veritable orchestration of image and rhythm . . . finally tempts us to close our ears in order to submit more completely to the [cinema's] visual suggestions and transfigurations of feeling."[104] Cinégraphie itself thus played the role of orchestral accompaniment, with the potential to transcend any narrative pretext. As Clair confessed, however, precisely how that happened remained unanswered.[105] Nevertheless, although both the "plastic" and "musical" conceptions of film language still assumed that a film image was representational in nature, if not necessarily narrative, together they, too, would foster the development of a "pure" abstract cinema.

At the time, the most sustained synthesis of this focus on technique and plastic or musical patterns in the cinema came from Dulac in her lecture at the Musée Galliera, in June 1924. That lecture served to confirm, by then, the dominance of Impressionism. Dulac's task was to catalogue "the expressive techniques of the cinema . . . in short, the whole syntax of film"—illustrating them with excerpts drawn from her own films as well as others.[106] Her catalogue overlapped to some extent with Moussinac's panoply of techniques and clearly emphasized those having to do with framing and editing.[107] Particularly significant for Dulac were the effects of camera placement (distance and angle) on the shot and the effects of the rhythmic alternation or juxtaposition of shots. "The psychological shot, the large close up as we call it"—for instance, "the large close up of Mme Lebas' ear" in *La Souriante Madame Beudet* (1923)—"is the very thought of the character projected onto the screen."[108] "Superimposition is thinking, the inner life"—for instance, in Volkoff's *Kean* (1924), when "the big, laughing mouth of the valet . . . seems to engulf Kean with contempt."[109] Finally, in *Beudet* again, the rhythmic alternation of "two characters . . . opposed ideals . . . different dreams" through a series of opening shots— for instance, close-ups of objects and actions (playing the piano/weighing money, reading a book/measuring cloth)—ends in a long shot that unites the two. "Suddenly, all the jarring incongruities of a marriage appear. It is a *coup de théâtre*."[110] As each of Dulac's analyses of film excerpts demonstrated, proper technique served "to augment a fact by grafting onto it a feeling"—or, as Clair put it, "to combine harmoniously the sentimental rhythm of the action and the mathematical rhythm of the number of images."[111] In other words, technique served to express the psychology or inner life of a character, to expand and intensify the feelings latent in a story or situation. In Dulac's theory, then, narrative ended up governing the overall shape of the film; the formal and connotative only seemed to override the narrative so that the filmmaker could "create a bit of inner life in the midst of the action."[112]

Dulac's lecture, like most of her colleagues' writing on the cinema during this period, still depended on a general concept of language long prevalent in the broader culture. This was an idealist theory of language (whether Romantic or Symbolist) that assumed that "the transcendent human subject . . . was to be seen as the source and origin of all meaning."[113] Consequently, language functioned as a means of expression for the consciousness of one individual (supposedly separate from social reality) to communicate with another. Film language, whatever its system of grammar or rhetoric, then operated simply as a specialized version of expressive theory. Another concept of language, however, circulated half-submerged in a number of writings. This might be called a protostructuralist or protosemiotic theory of language since it assumed that meaning was produced or constructed as a material practice through the interplay of a textual system of signs. The meaning of a sign or a nexus of signs was not fixed, say, in denotation or connotation—consistently signifying a character's thought or feeling. Rather, it could fluctuate, depending on the sign's context among a sequence of other signs or images. This theory perhaps first finds partial articulation in Landry's analysis of specific images—for instance, Sibilla in soft focus—in L'Herbier's *El Dorado*.[114] It lurks in Delluc's celebration of William S. Hart's westerns: "*nature morte* . . . plants or objects, exteriors or interiors, physical details, everything material . . . is animated according to where and how the composer of the film uses it."[115] It surfaces in Moussinac's analysis of cinematic rhythm: "the beauty and value [of the film image] changes, is singularly diminished or increased, according to where those images are placed in time, that is, the order in which they succeed one another."[116] It even appears briefly in Dulac: "the work affects you through a purely cinematic technique, of contrasts and parallelisms [of images]."[117] Here, then, the cinema produced texts composed of or deploying the multidimensional signs of several notational systems, texts whose own rules of "reading" were still developing or in flux.

Epstein's early writings on the cinema represent a fascinating amalgam of these different theories of language. For he was very uneasy about yielding "to facile or misleading analogies" between film and verbal language.[118] Sometimes, much like Delluc and Moussinac, he echoed the expressive theory of Dulac, Canudo, and others. More often than not, however, Epstein hesitated between privileging certain features of film language per se—for instance, the close-up and moving-camera shot, which, by intensifying and transforming perception, created a new form of consciousness—and exploring, much like Landry, how those kinds of shots, as a form of polysemous "hieroglyphic language," could be arranged in the structure of a detailed decoupage.[119] On the one hand, for Epstein, film language was animistic: it attributed "personality" to or made "the spirit visible" in both things and people. On the other, and simultaneously, its "photogenic mobility" could be shaped into a spatiotemporal system that simulated and then extended or challenged the conventions of perception and representation.[120] In other words, it provided the basis for another kind of "counter cinema"—to use Thomas Elsaesser's terminology for the Weimar cinema—in which the spectator as a constructed subject is rather openly or ambiguously inscribed within the process of narration.[121]

Much like his colleagues, Epstein gave little attention to specific instances of this structuring or inscription. But he offered at least two different, tantalizing glimpses of possible film forms. One would take a merry-go-round or dance as a crucial "poetic" situation for a narrative film. "An intelligent decoupage [would] reconstitute the double life of the dance," Epstein wrote, "by linking together the viewpoints of the spectator and the dancer, objective and subjective, if I can put it that way."[122] This reconstitution would be constructed out of a (vaguely suggested) combination of close-ups, moving-camera shots, and accelerating montage. In actual practice, in what Clair called the "visual intoxication" of the carnival sequence in Epstein's *Coeur fidèle* (1923), the relatively simple Romantic synthesis of the objective and subjective articulated here turned into a far more complex textual operation.[123] Another possible form, however, appeared in Epstein's very first book on modern poetry: that of the film poem, a form that apparently first attracted the young poet to the cinema.[124] Here, representational images would be linked together, not through *sequentiality*, but through *simultaneity*, so that their suggestive, connotative, or metaphorical significance would be foregrounded. By implication, just as in the poetry of Apollinaire and Cendrars, the precise meaning of these images would accumulate through patterns of similarity and difference, repetition and variation. Here was the germ—or quantum theory, if you will—of a cinema of simultaneity or discontinuity and dislocation. Within five years, Epstein believed, the French would be writing film poems: "150 meters and 100 images like beads on a thread that would approximate the thinking process."[125] His own films as well as others would prove him right, and this quasi-semiotic conception of film language would become even more evident in his writings of the late 1920s.[126]

CRITICAL PRACTICE

French film reviewing deserves a final note here for it had reached the point where several critics could be taken as models in writing film criticism. Reviews in the daily newspapers and industry journals still tended to depend on plot summary, amplified by comments on the felicity of the film adaptation to its source in drama or fiction and evaluations of the separate contributions of each phase or component of its production. In the reviews of Vuillermoz, Moussinac, and Clair, however, traditional aesthetic standards were now beginning to assert their power. These critics tended to focus on the unity and coherence of the work as a whole, the controlling vision of the filmmaker as *auteur*, and the specific (often technical) contributions of the film to the development of film as an art form. Moussinac's long review of *Broken Blossoms*, for instance, situated Griffith's film in the context of previous "advanced" films, including Griffith's own; singled out the technical originality and harmony of its visual composition, rhythm, and atmosphere; and objected to the philosophical pretension of his choice of subject as well as his lack of "lyricism."[127] Other subsequent reviews generally followed this format—for instance, the clusters of important texts that marked the premiere of *El Dorado* or grappled with the impact of *La*

Roue or appraised Epstein's first films. Here, Moussinac's concise analysis of *L'Auberge rouge* (1923) was exemplary:

> I note, for example: the wonderfully quick manner of the panoramic shots (especially before and after the execution: the background of trees and sky), the powerful nuances of the close shots, the calculated cutting in the scene where the hero leaves the tragic chamber in obedience to the violently opposed forces of his emotion, the mathematics of the montage at certain moments of pathos, the character types anchored with a loose faithfulness to life (the masks of the drinkers, the accordian player, the old woman, the gypsy, the judges), the details of atmosphere (produced by a combination of lighting and soft focus), the freedom with which the actors perform as an ensemble and particularly the astonishing photogenic performances of [Léon] Mathot and Gina Manès. All this puts *L'Auberge rouge* far in advance of the kilometers of filmstock bungled by our "old hands." . . . In Jean Epstein, we have one more *cinégraphist*. We have so few![128]

Moreover, several writers were beginning to engage in a "close analysis" of particular sequences or excerpts from a film. In her 1924 lecture, for instance, Dulac offered a series of specific "readings" of the process by which the composition and arrangement of shots in, say, the opening of *La Souriante Beudet* led the spectator to adopt a certain interpretation.[129]

At least one form of criticism, however, ran counter to these aesthetic standards of unity and coherence, technical competence, and even technological innovation. As might be expected, it was most evident in the writings of Epstein and Desnos. In order to promote discontinuities and the rupturing of conventional logic and "classical construction," their own texts sought to produce *frissons* that would jar the reader/spectator into seeing anew—awakening to find the cinema opening onto "a new domain of poetry and dream."[130] And poetry, as Epstein wrote, in reviewing *La Roue*, is not only "harmony, balance, and good taste"; it "erupts like a storm" and is not without excess and horror.[131]

CONCLUSION

In the early 1920s, French writing on the cinema went through a paradoxical process conceptually—hardening in some ways and expanding in others, narrowing in focus yet also diversifying. Concern over the "crisis" situation of the French film industry failed to produce a consensus on what action ought to be taken to remedy it, which tended to hamstring the uncoordinated efforts of individual companies or producer-distributors. But economic and political issues generally were subordinated to aesthetic questions, for the latter still generated a good deal of excitement and probably a greater sense of potential resolution. The former balance between high-art and low-art positions shifted slightly as Vuillermoz, Canudo, and Dulac's "Impressionism" gradually overshadowed Delluc and Moussinac's "Realism"; but both were set off to some extent from the various "Modernist" conceptions of Epstein, Faure, Léger, and Desnos. Each position included writers—for instance, Vuillermoz, Canudo, Dulac, Moussinac, Epstein—who sought to systematize their thinking about the nature, function, raw material, and technique of the cinema. Yet, as before, their texts were often marked by contradictory assumptions. For instance, several different conceptions of language—expressive, revelatory, structuralist or semiotic—underscored their attempts to define film language, producing especially fascinating effects in the writing of Epstein, Moussinac, and Canudo. Whatever position they took, however, the French were engaged conscientiously in a search for *cinematic specificity*, even to the point of isolating uniquely cinematic techniques. Generally, now, the earlier concern for *photogénie* or the singularly transformative nature of the film image gave way to a concern for *cinégraphie* or the unique rhythmic principles that governed the placement, duration, and interrelation of film images. While some writers urged that these rhythmic principles—narrative, emotional, plastic, musical, poetic—ought to be synthesized in a film, others argued that one principle in particular could exclusively shape the formal system of a film, which implicitly set out the conditions for a kind of "pure cinema." In this search for specificity, the French continued to draw occasionally on American films for models; but, more often than not, they now defined their positions in response to particular French or German films—for example, *El Dorado, Caligari, La Roue, Coeur fidèle*. An unspoken opposition to the American cinema thus fueled something close to a collective effort to establish distinctly *French* theories of cinema.

1. The next five paragraphs constitute a condensed and revised version of the initial sections of "The Alternate Cinema Network," in my *French Cinema: The First Wave, 1915–1929* (Princeton: Princeton University Press, 1984), 241–55.

2. This information is drawn from an examination of most of these newspapers, plus "La Presse cinématographique," *Almanach du cinéma*, ed. Jean Pascal and Adrien Maître (Paris: Cinémagazine, 1922), 85–86; "Journaux Parisiens," *Annuaire général de la cinématographie*, ed. Jean Pascal (Paris: Cinémagazine, 1925), 559; René Jeanne and Charles Ford, *Le Cinéma et la presse, 1895–1960* (Paris: Armand Colin, 1961), 54–62; and Claude Bellanger, Jacques Godechot, Pierre Guiral, and Fernand Terrou, *Histoire générale de la presse française*, vol. 3, *De 1871 à 1940* (Paris: Presses universitaires de France, 1972), 510–84.

3. Politically, *Le Figaro* took a turn to the right in 1922, when it was bought up by the perfume manufacturer, François Coty. Strangely, *Action française* (which was then probably enjoying its greatest influence on French intellectuals) as well as its complementary weekly, *Candide*, continued to show little interest in the cinema. For further information on *Action française* during this period, see Eugen Weber, *Action Française: Royalism and Reaction in*

Twentieth-Century France (Stanford: Stanford University Press, 1962), 172–201; J. Plumyène and R. Lasierra, *Les Facismes français, 1921–1939* (Paris: Editions du Seuil, 1963), 15–28; and Pascal Ory and Jean-François Sirinelli, *Les Intellectuels en France, de l'Affaire Dreyfus à nos jours* (Paris: Armand Colin, 1986), 77–84.

4. In 1922, Henri Dumay began publishing *Le Quotidien*, which, along with *L'Oeuvre*, became the principal advocate for the left in the 1924 elections and then the "official" paper of the Cartel des Gauches government. Eugène Merle's *Paris-Soir*, which grew out of the satirical weekly, *Le Merl blanc*, in 1923, also supported the left in the 1924 elections. For further information on the leftist press during this period, see Jean Touchard, *La Gauche en France depuis 1900* (Paris: Editions du Seuil, 1977), 111–12, 145–46.

5. René Jeanne (1887–1969) was an influential film reviewer and industry reporter who, together with Charles Ford, would later write a five-volume *Histoire encyclopédique du cinéma* (Robert Laffont, 1947) as well as *Le Cinéma et la presse* (1961).

6. For a lively account of what it was like to work for *L'Oeuvre* and *Bonsoir* in the early 1920s, see Henri Jeanson, *70 Ans d'adolescence* (Paris: Stock, 1971), 116–38. In January 1923, when the *Camelot du roi* "shock troops" of the Action française group sought to revenge the murder (by anarchist Germaine Berton) of one of their leaders, Marius Plateau, they took to street violence that ended in their wrecking the offices and presses of *L'Oeuvre* and *Bonsoir*—Weber, *Action française*, 139.

7. A good survey of the French literary and intellectual journals of the period, and their political affiliation can be found in Gérard de Lacaze-Duthiers, "Notes sur les revues françaises, pendant six ans (1914–1920)," *L'Esprit nouveau*, 1 (October 1920), 99–102.

8. Interestingly, the *Mercure de France*'s principal rival, the *Nouvelle Revue française*, did not give much attention to the cinema; nor did Henri Barbusses *Clarté*, which was allied with the French Communist Party and for which, since he was reviewing films for *L'Humanité*, Moussinac might have been expected to write.

9. B. Tokine, "L'Esthétique du cinéma," *L'Esprit nouveau*, 1 (October 1920), 84–89. Louis Delluc, "Cinéma," *L'Esprit nouveau*, 3 (December 1920), 349–51. Elie Faure, "Charlot," *L'Esprit nouveau*, 6 (March 1921), 657–66. Louis Delluc, "Pro Cinéma," *L'Esprit nouveau*, 14 (January 1922), 1666–68. Jean Epstein, "Cinéma," *L'Esprit nouveau*, 14 (January 1922), 1669–70. Here again, the heightened interest in the cinema shown by the formalist, even "classical" monthly, *L'Esprit nouveau*, contrasts with the diminished interest (or perhaps frustration) of the Dada-Surrealist journal, *Littérature*.

10. It was in an interview in *Les Nouvelles littéraires* (24 March 1923) that Jean Cocteau tried to explain why he chose to work in the theater rather than in the cinema throughout the 1920s.

11. Jeanne and Ford, *Le Cinéma et la presse*, 170. Christian Bosséno, "Le Cinéma et la presse (II)," *La Revue du cinéma: Image et son*, 342 (September 1979), 94–97.

12. At the time of his death in March 1924, Delluc also left a nearly completed manuscript entitled "Les Cinéastes," which he probably hoped to publish through Le Monde nouveau, an international journal and publishing house. See, for instance, his "Les Cinéastes à Paris," *Choses de théâtre*, 1 (October 1921), 13–18; "Les Cinéastes," *Le Monde nouveau*, 5 (15 August–1 September 1922), 34–44; and several articles on American filmmakers (Griffith, De Mille, Tourneur) in *Cinéa*. This manuscript was published for the first time in Louis Delluc, *Le Cinéma et les cinéastes: Ecrits cinématographiques*, vol. 1 (Paris: La Cinémathèque française, 1985), 123–194. Delluc also published the complete scenario for *Fièvre* in *Le Crapouillot* (16 March 1923), 22–27, and an excerpt from the scenario for *La Femme de nulle part* in *Cinémagazine*, 3 (6 July 1923), 17–19.

13. Through Blaise Cendrars, then editor of Editions de la sirène, Epstein got a job as an assistant editor at the celebrated avant-garde publishing house, when he came to Paris from

Lyon in the summer of 1921. Epstein's *Bonjour Cinéma* received a good deal of attention in reviews—for example, Lionel Landry, "A propos du livre de M. Jean Epstein," *Cinéa*, 33 (23 December 1921), 9–10; Léon Moussinac, "Cinématographie," *Mercure de France* (1 January 1922), 219–21; and Maurice Raynal, "Les Livres," *L'Esprit nouveau*, 15 (February 1922), 1745–46.

14. Delluc's conception was more broadly based than, although perhaps not unrelated to, the prewar anarchist attempt to create a "Cinéma du peuple."

15. See Theda Shapiro, *Painters and Politics: The European Avant-Garde and Society, 1900–1925* (New York: Elsevier, 1976), 175.

16. See, for instance, Frantz Jourdain, "Le Cinéma, manifestation artistique très noble et très élévée accueilli en triomphateur," *Comoedia* (28 October 1921), 4; Ricciotto Canudo, "Le Cinéma au Salon d'Automne," *Le Petit Journal* (4 November 1921), 4; Ricciotto Canudo, "Le Cinéma," *Les Nouvelles littéraires* (18 November 1922), 4; Léon Moussinac, "Cinématographie," *Mercure de France* (1 December 1922), 521; "Le Salon annuel du cinéma au Salon d'Automne," *Gazette des sept arts*, 1 (15 December 1922); advertisement for "Salon annuel du film au Salon d'Automne," *Cinéa-Ciné-pour-tous*, 1 (15 November 1923), 3.

17. Léon Moussinac, "Cinématographie," *Mercure de France* (1 April 1924), 230–31.

18. Musée Galliera, *Exposition de l'art dans le cinéma français* (Paris: Prieur, Dubois et cie, 1924), 66–67.

19. Lucien Wahl, "L'Avenir du cinéma français," *La Renaissance*, 35 (27 August 1921), 1–5; 36 (3 September 1921), 4–9; 37 (10 September 1921), 17–20; 38 (17 September 1921), 4–9. In an introductory note, Wahl suggests that his survey was sparked by a meeting with French legislators concerning the cinema, organized by the Confédération des travailleurs intellectuels. See, also, Léon Moussinac, "Cinématographie," *Mercure de France* (1 May 1921), 812–16; and René Jeanne, "Les Leçons d'une enquête," *Cinémagazine*, 1 (21 October 1921), 14.

20. Pathé's "Etude sur l'évolution de l'industrie cinématographique française" [1918], also was reprinted in *Ciné-pour-tous*, 31 (3 April 1920), 2–3.

21. Antoine's diatribe and the responses to it were first published in *La Revue hebdomadaire* in the summer of 1923—see Léon Moussinac, "Cinématographie," *Mercure de France* (15 October 1923), 515–21. Both were reprinted in André Lang, *Déplacements et villegiatures littéraires et suivi de la Promenade au royaume des images ou entretiens cinématographiques* (Paris: La Renaissance du livre, 1924), 184–234.

22. Delluc's responses were reprinted from *Bonsoir* (24 July and 1 August 1923), and Moussinac's was reprinted from *L'Humanité* (29 July 1923).

23. For an analysis of the production sector of the French film industry in the early 1920s, see Abel, *French Cinema*, 17–27. For an analysis of the transition of capitalism to its monopoly phase and of the relation of small firms to big capital in that transition, which might help explain developments in the French film industry in the 1920s, see Lucio Coletti, "Bernstein and the Marxism of the Second International," *From Rousseau to Lenin: Studies in Ideology and Society* (New York: Monthly Review Press, 1972), 97–100.

24. See Abel, *French Cinema*, 279–94.

25. Louis Feuillade, "Préface," *Barrabas* (Paris: J. Ferenczi, 1920), reprinted in Francis Lacassin, *Louis Feuillade* (Paris: Seghers, 1964), 113–14. Louis Feuillade, "Préface," *Les Deux Gamines* (Paris: J. Ferenczi, 1921), reprinted in Lacassin, *Louis Feuillade*, 116–17.

26. René Clair, "Les Films du mois: *Coeur fidèle*," *Théâtre et Comoedia illustré* (1 February 1924). Vuillermoz and Delluc had begun to perceive a certain stabilization in the American cinema even earlier—see, for instance, Emile Vuillermoz, "Esthétique," *Le Temps* (27 March 1920), 3.

27. See Abel, *French Cinema*, 71–85, 151–205. The following series of articles provides

a good sense of the development of the serial in the early 1920s—Pierre Henry, "Les Idées: Le film en épisodes," *Ciné-pour-tous*, 29 (20 March 1920), 2; Ricciotto Canudo, "Le Ciné-Roman en *n* épisodes," *Le Film*, 183 (November 1921); Louis Jalabert, "La Littérature commerciale: Le ciné-roman," *Etudes*, 171 (5 June 1922), 513–31, and 172 (20 June 1922), 675–89; Léon Moussinac, "Les Films à épisodes," *Le Crapouillot* (1 March 1923), 27–29; and Albert Bonneau, "Le Film à épisodes," *Cinémagazine*, 3 (17 July 1923), 125–28.

28. *Mathias Sandorf* was adapted from a Jules Verne novel; *Rouletabille* was based on Gaston Leroux's famous detective hero; and *Mandrin* was drawn from Arthur Bernède's novel about an eighteenth-century French Robin Hood figure. Bernède had created two of the most popular film detectives during the war—in Feuillade's *Judex* (1917) and Pouctal's *Chantecoq* (1917)—and for Louis Nalpas he would create a series of historical adventurer "outlaws"—in Jean Kemm's *Vidocq* (1923) and Luitz-Morat's *Surcoeuf* (1925) and *Jean Chouan* (1926).

29. André Antoine, "Le Cinématographe," *L'Information* (30 July 1923), reprinted in Lang, *Déplacements et villegiatures littéraires*, 197–200. Antoine's article basically reiterates what he had written in *Le Film* and *Lectures pour tous*, in December 1919.

30. Antoine, "Le Cinématographe," 195–96.

31. Antoine, "Le Cinématographe," 196–97.

32. Lang, "M. André Antoine," *Déplacements et villegiatures littéraires*, 121.

33. For instance, the idea that the story served principally as a means to produce a certain "emotion" or "style" circulated as a given assumption in most writers. See Moussinac, Epstein, and Clair in the following section of "Selected Texts." See, also, Léon Moussinac, "Cinématographie," *Mercure de France* (1 January 1922), 216–21; and Louis Delluc, "De Rose-France à *El Dorado*," *Cinéa*, 1 (6 May 1921), 13–14.

34. This definition of *culture*, which was fundamental to nineteenth-century Europe, is taken from Raymond Williams, *Marxism and Literature* (Oxford: Oxford University Press, 1977), 15.

35. Ricciotto Canudo, "Réflexions sur le septième art" [1923], *L'Usine aux images* (Paris: Etienne Chiron, 1926), 29–47. See, also, Léon Moussinac, "Cinématographie," *Mercure de France* (1 February 1921), 802–3.

36. Lionel Landry, "Films français et américains," *Le Journal du Ciné-Club*, 12 (2 April 1920), 2; Jacques Baroncelli, "La Domaine du cinéma," *Le Petit Journal* (18 November 1921), 4; Emile Vuillermoz, "*La Roue*," *Comoedia* (21 December 1922), 3.

37. Canudo, "Réflexions sur le septième art," 41–42. See, also, Marianne Alby, "Le Merveilleux à l'écran," *Théâtre et Comoedia illustré*, 30 (15 March 1924).

38. Vuillermoz, "Devant l'écran: Esthétique," 3.

39. See, for instance, "Germaine Dulac parle au CASA," *Comoedia* (9 May 1921), 4, and Emile Vuillermoz, "*La Souriante Madame Beudet*," *Comoedia* (19 January 1923), 3. Dulac's own early efforts to achieve such "psychological films" included *La Cigarette* (1919) and *La Mort du soleil* (1922).

40. Ricciotto Canudo, "Cinéma et musique," *Comoedia* (4 November 1921), 4. For an analysis of L'Herbier's *L'Inhumaine*, see Abel, *French Cinema*, 383–95.

41. Canudo, "Réflexions sur le septième art," 45–47.

42. Lionel Landry, "Le Snobisme prouvera que le cinéma est un art," *Le Journal du Ciné-Club*, 1 (14 January 1920), 13. For an attack on such snobism, see Léon Poirier. "Les Enemis du septième art," *Le Petit Journal* (23 December 1921), 4. Cf. Pierre Porte, "Le Cinéma n'est pas un art populaire," *Cinéa-Ciné-pour-tous*, 12 (1 May 1924), 26–28.

43. See, again, Delluc's heated response to Antoine, in *Bonsoir* (1 August 1923), and Moussinac's even more caustic response, in *L'Humanité* (23 July 1923), reprinted in Lang, *Déplacements et villegiatures littéraires*, 209–10 and 219, respectively.

44. See, for instance, "Les Meilleurs Films de l'Année," *Ciné-pour-tous*, 51 (22 October 1920), 4–5, and Louis Delluc, "[Les Films suèdois]," *Cinéa*, 2 (13 May 1921), reprinted in Marcel Tariol, *Louis Delluc* (Paris: Seghers, 1965), 98–99.

45. Canudo, "Réflexions sur le septième art," 29–30.

46. Louis Delluc, "D'Oreste à Rio Jim," *Cinéa*, 31 (9 December 1921), 14–15.

47. Léon Moussinac, "Cinématographie: *Le Lys brisé*," *Mercure de France* (1 February 1921), 797–804; Léon Moussinac, "Cinématographie," *Mercure de France* (1 November 1921), 787–88. Cf. Jean Epstein, "Présentation de *Coeur fidèle*" [January 1924], reprinted in Jean Epstein, *Ecrits sur le cinéma*, vol. 1 (Paris: Seghers, 1974), 124. Antoine's film project of *L'Hirondelle et la mésange* (shot in 1920–1921 and finally edited by Henri Colpi for the Cinémathèque française in 1983) may well have exemplified Delluc and Moussinac's conception of the scenario.

48. Ricciotto Canudo, "Préface," *La Roue, après le film d'Abel Gance* (Paris: J. Ferenczi, 1923), 3–4.

49. See, for instance, Léon Moussinac, "Cinématographie," *Mercure de France* (15 July 1920), 529–32; "Le Réprésentation de la vie du film," *Ciné-pour-tous*, 53 (19 November 1920), 2; Léon Moussinac, "Le Cinéma à l'école et le film d'enseignement," *Cinémagazine*, 1 (9 September 1921), 8–9, 1 (16 September 1921), 24–25, 1 (30 September 1921), 22–23; "Les Grands Films: *Nanouk, l'esquimau*," *Cinémagazine*, 2 (3 November 1922), 156-58; Léon Moussinac, "Le Cinéma: *Nanouk*," *Le Crapouillot* (16 December 1922), 28; Lionel Landry, "Documentaires," *Cinémagazine*, 3 (26 January 1923), 154; Robert Desnos, "Les Documentaires," *Paris-Journal* (6 May 1923), reprinted in Robert Desnos, *Cinéma* (Paris: Gallimard, 1966), 106–8; and Lionel Landry, "Documentaires? La plus grande sincérité s'impose dans ce genre de production," *Cinémagazine*, 4 (2 May 1924), 211–12.

50. Léon Moussinac, "Cinématographie," *Mercure de France* (1 November 1921), 784–86; Louis Delluc, "Prologue," *Drames du cinéma* (Paris: Editions du monde nouveau, 1923), ii–iii.

51. See, for instance, Delluc's series of essays on *cinéastes*—"De Griffith," *Cinéa*, 47 (31 March 1922), 7–8; "Cecil B. De Mille," *Cinéa*, 63–64 (21 July 1922), 11; and "Maurice Tourneur," *Cinéa*, 69–70 (8 September 1922), 15. Canudo, of course, offered his own term for the film artist, *écranist*—see Canudo, "Réflexions sur le septième art," 36. A good sense of the French film production process, vis à vis the American, can be found in "Les Scénaristes ou auteurs des films," *Ciné-pour-tous*, 54 (3 December 1920), 2.

52. Delluc, "De *Rose-France* à *El Dorado*," 13–14.

53. Louis Delluc, "La Foule," *Photogénie* (Paris: de Brunoff, 1920), 120.

54. Robert Desnos, "Le Rêve et le cinéma," *Paris-Journal* (27 April 1923), reprinted in Desnos, *Cinéma*, 104–5.

55. Moussinac became a member of the French Communist Party in 1924, the same year he organized the exhibition on French film art at the Musée Galliera—David Caute, *Communism and the French Intellectuals, 1914–1960* (New York: Macmillan, 1964), 75.

56. See, for instance, Christopher Green, "Léger and L'Esprit nouveau," *Léger and Purist Paris* (London: The Tate Gallery, 1970), 49–72; Green, *Léger and the Avant-Garde* (New Haven: Yale University Press, 1976); *Fernand Léger et l'esprit moderne: Une alternative d'avant-garde à l'art non-objectif, 1918–1931* (Paris: Musée d'art moderne de la ville de Paris, 1982); and Kenneth Eric Silver, *Esprit du corps: The Great War and French Art, 1914–1925* (Ann Arbor: University Microfilms, Inc., 1983), 385–405. See, also, Jean-Francis Laglenn, "Le Peintre au cinéma," *Cinéa*, 9 (1 July 1921), 14, and 42 (24 February 1922), 12.

57. Fernand Léger, "*La Roue*: Sa valeur plastique," *Comoedia* (16 December 1922), 5.

58. Standish Lawder argues that *La Roue* and this essay provided the conceptual germ for Léger's only completed film project, *Ballet mécanique* (1924)—Lawder, *The Cubist Cinema*

(New York: New York University Press, 1975), 89–95. For a more recent and more thorough analysis of Léger's project, see Judi Freeman, "Léger's *Ballet mécanique*," *Dada/Surrealism*, 15 (1986), 28–45. See, also, Abel, *French Cinema*, 394–95.

59. Elie Faure, "De la cinéplastique," *L'Arbre d'Eden* (Paris: Editions G. Crès, 1922), 277–304.

60. Faure, "De la cinéplastique," 303–4.

61. Epstein's interest in Léger's work, for instance, is evident in his essay, "Fernand Léger," *Feuilles libres*, 31 (March–April 1923), 26–31.

62. Stuart Liebman, *Jean Epstein's Early Film Theory, 1920–1922* (Ann Arbor: University Microfilms Inc., 1980), 111–18. See, for instance, Jean Epstein, "Ciné-Mystique," *Cinéa*, 6 (10 June 1921), 12.

63. Liebman, *Jean Epstein's Early Film Theory*, 119. For a fascinating attempt to read Epstein's concept of *photogénie* exclusively in psychoanalytical terms, see Paul Willemen, "On Reading Epstein on *Photogénie*," *Afterimage*, 10 (Autumn 1981), 43–47. Canudo also used the term, "unconscious," but as a synonym for the conventional idealist notion of the immaterial soul.

64. See, for instance, Jean Epstein, "Freud ou le Nick-Carterianisme en psychologie," *L'Esprit nouveau*, 16 (March 1922), 1857–64.

65. Jean Epstein, *La Lyrosophie* (Paris: Editions de la sirène, 1922). Liebman, *Jean Epstein's Early Film Theory, 1920–1922*, 124–38.

66. Jean Epstein, "Le Sens 1 bis," *Bonjour Cinéma* (Paris: Editions de la sirène, 1921), reprinted in Epstein, *Ecrits sur le cinéma*, vol. 1, 85–87, 91–93. For a possible connection between Henri Bergson and Epstein, see Gilles Deleuze, *Cinema 1: The Movement-Image*, trans. Hugh Tomlinson and Barbara Habberjam (Minneapolis: University of Minnesota Press, 1986), 8–11.

67. Jean Epstein, "De quelques conditions de la photogénie," *Cinéa-Ciné-pour-tous*, 19 (15 August 1924), 7. The early writings of Béla Baláz on the cinema seem to incorporate or at least parallel much of Epstein's language here—Gertrud Koch, "Béla Baláz: The Physiognomy of Things," *New German Critique*, 40 (Winter 1987), 167–177. Here Epstein seems to share Bergson and phenomenologist Edmund Husserl's faith in intuition as an unconscious cognitive means beyond perception and ratiocination, yet for Epstein such cognition occurred through the camera and was mediated by human "analytic propensity"— cf. Martin Jay on Max Horkheimer's critique of Bergson and Husserl in Jay, *The Dialectical Imagination: A History of the Frankfurt School and the Institute of Social Research, 1923–1950* (Boston: Little, Brown, 1973), 50–51.

68. Jean Epstein, "Grossissement," *Bonjour Cinéma* (Paris: Editions de la sirène, 1921), 104. Cf. Jean Epstein, "Le Cinéma et les lettres modernes," *La Poésie d'aujourd'hui: Un nouvel état d'intelligence* (Paris: Editions de la sirène, 1921), 171.

69. André Breton, "Comme dans un bois," *L'Age du cinéma*, 4–5 (August–November 1951), 27. See, also, Desnos's first untitled film review in *Paris-Journal* (6 April 1923), reprinted in Desnos, *Cinéma*, 95–97.

70. Desnos, "Le Rêve et le cinéma," 104–5. Epstein also sometimes spoke of the cinema effect as similar to that of a drug.

71. Robert Desnos, "L'Eroticisme," *Paris-Journal* (20 April 1923), reprinted in Desnos, *Cinéma*, 101–2.

72. Paul Hammond, "Off on a Tangent," *The Shadow and Its Shadow: Surrealist Writings on Cinema*, ed. Paul Hammond (London: British Film Institute, 1978), 5–6.

73. Philippe Soupault, "L'Homme aux yeux clairs—William S. Hart," *Littérature*, 9 (November 1919), 29; Philippe Soupault, "Une Idylle aux champs," *Littérature*, 12 (February 1920), 29.

74. Benjamin Peret, "Pulchérie veut un auto," *Littérature*, 10 (May 1923), 17–23. See Hammond, "Off on a Tangent," 6. Here the cinema began to play a significant part in the radical critique of the function of art instigated by what Peter Bürger has called the "historical avant-garde"—see Bürger, *Theory of the Avant-Garde*, trans. Michael Shaw (Minneapolis: University of Minnesota Press, 1984), 3–54.

75. Moussinac, "Cinématographie," *Mercure de France* (1 November 1921), 786.

76. Lionel Landry, *"El Dorado," Cinéa*, 12–13 (22 July 1921), 7–8.

77. Vuillermoz, "Devant l'écran: Esthétique," 3.

78. Jean Epstein, "L'Elément photogénique," *Cinéa-Ciné-pour-tous*, 12 (1 May 1924), 7.

79. Vuillermoz, "Devant l'écran: Esthétique," 3.

80. Léon Moussinac, "Du rythme cinégraphique," *Le Crapouillot* (March 1923), 9–11.

81. Louis Delluc, "La Cadence," *Photogénie* (Paris: Brunoff, 1920), 71–72; Moussinac, "Du rythme cinégraphique," 9–11; Louis Delluc, "Cinégraphie," *Le Crapouillot* (March 1923), 11–14; René Clair, "Les Films du mois: *Coeur fidèle*."

82. Germaine Dulac, "Le Procédés expressifs du cinématographe," *Cinémagazine*, 4 (11 July 1924), 67.

83. Jean Epstein, "Réalisation des détails," *Cinéa*, 45 (17 March 1922), 12.

84. Dulac, "Le Procédés expressifs du cinématographe," 67.

85. Jean Epstein, "Rythme et montage" [1923], in Epstein, *Ecrits sur le cinéma*, vol. 1, 121. See, also, Epstein, "De quelques conditions de la photogénie," 6–8.

86. Moussinac, "Du rythme cinégraphique," 9.

87. I borrow several terms here from Williams, *Marxism and Literature*, 170–71, and from David Bordwell, "The Musical Analogy," *Yale French Studies*, 60 (1980), 142–43.

88. Delluc, "Prologue," ix–x.

89. See, for instance, Louis Delluc, "Scénarii," *Comoedia* (6 April 1923), 4.

90. Moussinac, "Du rythme cinégraphique," 9.

91. Delluc, "Prologue," iv–vi.

92. Delluc, "Prologue," xiii.

93. Léon Moussinac, "Technique commande," *Gazette des sept arts*, 3 (10 February 1923), 11.

94. See, for instance, Lionel Landry, *"El Dorado," Cinéa*, 12–13 (22 July 1921), 7–8; Léon Moussinac, "Cinématographie," *Mercure de France* (1 November 1921), 789–91; J. L. Croze, "Les Grands Films: *El Dorado*," *Comoedia* (1 November 1921), 1; Jean Galtier-Boissière, "L'Art cinégraphique," *Le Crapouillot* (16 November 1921), 4; Léon Moussinac, "Cinématographie," *Mercure de France* (1 January 1922), 216–19; Jean Epstein, "Cinéma," *L'Esprit nouveau*, 14 (January 1922), 1669–70; Jacques Pietrini, "Le Cabinet du Dr. Caligari," *Cinémagazine*, 2 (3 March 1922), 264–66; Emile Vuillermoz, "Le Cabinet du Docteur Caligari," *Cinémagazine*, 2 (24 March 1922), 353–54; Lionel Landry, "Caligarisme ou la revanche du théâtre," *Cinéa*, 51 (28 April 1922), 12; Blaise Cendrars, "Sur *Le Cabinet du Docteur Caligari*," *Cinéa*, 56 (2 June 1922), 11; Ivan Goll, "Un nouveau film expressionniste: *Le Cabinet du Dr. Caligari*," *Cinéa*, 12–13 (22 July 1921), 10–11; Robert Mallet-Stevens, "Le Cubisme au cinéma," *Comoedia* (8 January 1923), 4; Jean Epstein, "Le Décor au cinéma," *La Revue mondiale*, 153 (1 March 1923), 90–91; Ricciotto Canudo, "Réflexions sur le septième art," 32–33.

95. See, for instance, Jean Epstein, *"La Roue," Comoedia* (12 December 1922), 3; Fernand Léger, *"La Roue,"* 5; Emile Vuillermoz, *"La Roue," Comoedia* (21 December 1922), 3, (31 December 1922), 4, and (12 January 1923), 3; Léon Moussinac, *"La Roue," Le Crapouillot* (16 January 1923), 13; Léon Moussinac, *"La Roue," Comoedia* (19 January 1923), 5; Emile Vuillermoz, *"La Roue," Cinémagazine*, 3 (23 February 1923), 329–31, and (2 March 1923), 363–65; René Clair, "Les Films du mois," *Théâtre et Comoedia illustré* (March 1923); "Le Merle

blanc siffle et persifle *La Roue*: Encore une catastrophe de chemin de fer," *Le Courrier ciné-matographique* (17 March 1923), reprinted in Roger Icart, *Abel Gance ou Le Prométhée foudroyé* (Lausanne: L'Age d'homme, 1983), 160.

96. In the production of *La Roue* (1922) and *Napoléon* (1927), Abel Gance came close to turning technological innovation into an end in itself, in actual practice.

97. Epstein, "L'Elément photogénique," 6.

98. See, also, Mallet-Stevens, "Le Cubisme au cinéma," 4.

99. Léger, "*La Roue*," 5.

100. Gilles Deleuze privileges this form of cinematic rhythm in order to define the "French school" (by which he means filmmakers Gance, Epstein, L'Herbier, Dulac, Clair, and Grémillon) as being primarily interested in "the mechanical composition of movement-images"—Deleuze, *Cinema 1: The Movement-Image*, 40–48.

101. Abel Gance, "Le Cinématographe, c'est la musique de la lumière," *Comoedia* (16 March 1923), 4. David Bordwell offers a cogent critique of the musical analogy in "The Musical Analogy," 141–46, and Ian Christie includes a shorter but no less substantive critique in "French Avant-Garde Film in the Twenties: From 'Specificity' to Surrealism," *Film as Form: Formal Experiment in Film, 1910–1975* (London: Arts Council of Great Britain, 1979), 39, 41.

102. Arthur Honegger, "Adaptations musicales," *Gazette des sept arts*, 2 (25 January 1923), 4. Cf. Lionel Landry, "Le Musique et le cinéma," *Cinémagazine*, 4 (30 March 1924), 363–64.

103. Canudo, "Réflexions sur le septième art," 31–33. See, also, Canudo, "Cinéma et musique," 4.

104. Moussinac, "Technique commande," 11.

105. René Clair, "Rythme," *Cahiers du mois*, 16/17 (1925), 13–16.

106. Dulac, "Les Procédés expressifs du cinématographe," *Cinémagazine*, 4 (4 July 1924), 15.

107. David Bordwell's analysis of what he calls "French Impressionist Cinema" rests, to some extent, on just such a catalogue of "techniques" that Dulac, Moussinac, and others drew up in the early 1920s—Bordwell, *French Impressionist Cinema: Film Culture, Film Theory, and Film Style* (New York: Arno Press, 1980).

108. Dulac, "Les Procédés expressifs du cinématographe," *Cinémagazine*, 4 (11 July 1924), 68.

109. Dulac, "Les Procédés expressifs du cinématographe," 66.

110. Dulac, "Les Procédés expressifs du cinématographe," 67–68.

111. Clair, "Les Films du mois: *Coeur fidèle*."

112. For a fine introduction to Dulac's work as a filmmaker and theorist, see Sandy Flitterman, *Women, Representation and Cinematic Discourse: The Example of French Cinema* (Ann Arbor: University Microfilms Inc., 1982), 19–55. For a concise contextualizing of Dulac's theory, see Stuart Liebman, "Introduction to Germaine Dulac's 'Integral Cinégraphie'," *Framework*, 19 (1982), 4–5.

113. Terry Eagleton, *Literary Theory: An Introduction* (Minneapolis: University of Minnesota Press, 1983), 58.

114. Landry, "*El Dorado*," 12.

115. Delluc, "D'Oreste à Rio Jim," 14.

116. Moussinac, "Du rythme cinégraphique," 9.

117. Dulac, "Les Procédés expressifs du cinématographe," *Cinémagazine*, 4 (4 July 1924), 15–16.

118. Epstein, "L'Elément photogénique," 7.

119. Landry, "*El Dorado*," 12. It is worth recalling that Vachel Lindsay had a chapter on

"Hieroglyphics" in his *The Art of the Moving Picture* (New York: Macmillan, 1915), 199–216.

120. Epstein, "De quelques conditions de la photogénie," 7–8.

121. Thomas Elsaesser, "Weimar Cinema as a Specific Form of (Inter-)Textuality: Sexual Ambiguity and the Attenuation of the Hermeneutic and Proaretic Codes of Action," paper presented at the Society for Cinema Studies Conference, New York University, 14 June 1985. Perhaps the clearest explanation of subject construction in film discourse can be found in Kaja Silverman, *The Subject of Semiotics* (New York: Oxford University Press, 1983), 194–236.

122. Epstein, "Grossissement," 95. Again, for a different analysis of these concepts in Epstein, see Deleuze, *Cinema 1: The Movement-Image*, 40–48.

123. Clair, "Les Films du mois: *Coeur fidèle.*" For an analysis of the textual operation of this sequence in *Coeur fidèle*, see Abel, *French Cinema*, 364–65.

124. Epstein, "Le Cinéma et les lettres modernes," 169–70.

125. Epstein, "Le Cinéma et les lettres modernes," 177. Cf. Lionel Landry's much more conventional thinking in "Simultanéisme," *Le Journal du Ciné-Club*, 6 (20 February 1920), 11–12, and Francis Picabia's repetition of Epstein's ideas in "Instantanéisme," *Comoedia* (21 November 1924), 4.

126. For examples, see my analyses of selected sequences from Epstein's *L'Auberge rouge* (1923) and *Coeur fidèle* (1923), in *French Cinema*, 355–56, 361–63.

127. Léon Moussinac, "Cinématographie: *Le Lys brisé*," *Mercure de France* (1 February 1921), 797–804.

128. Léon Moussinac, "*L'Auberge rouge*," *Le Crapouillot* (1 August 1923), 16–17.

129. Dulac, "Les Procédés expressifs du cinématographe," *Cinémagazine*, 4 (11 July 1924), 67–68.

130. Desnos, "Le Rêve et le cinéma," 104.

131. Epstein, "*La Roue*," 3.

Selected Texts

LOUIS FEUILLADE, "Introduction"

These two texts are excerpted from the introductions that Feuillade wrote for the publicity brochures that preceded the release of *Barrabas* (1920) and *Les Deux Gamines* (1921). They are reprinted in Francis Lacassin, *Louis Feuillade* (Paris: Seghers, 1964), 108, 113–14, 116–17.

BARRABAS

A FILM IS NOT a sermon, nor even a lecture, much less a puzzle, but a *divertissement* for the eyes and mind. The quality of this *divertissement* is measured according to the interest of the public for which it was made. To think otherwise would mean that the cinema is not what it is: the popular art of our time. . . .

The current trend in film production is obvious: the desire to astonish the public seems to outweigh the desire to attract and hold its attention. The result is that people are no longer astonished by anything. Innumerable processions, ostentatious sets, spectacular catastrophes, athletic performances, everyday places disguised as symbols—all that is becoming banal. We have seen so much of it! But there is one thing that the public has not grown tired of, nor will it ever—whether in the theater, in books, or in the cinema—and that is romantic adventure fiction. The taste for such fiction comes from a natural disposition of the human spirit. "Through some kind of independence, which Bacon took as evidence of the strength and dignity of our existence, we love to escape the ordinary course of life, to create an imaginary world of more diverse and exciting events, where chance has less sway and where our faculties find freer exercise. This is the involuntary inclination of all intelligent people. . . ."

These lines by a writer of the last century clearly locate the source of the [universal] charm which is produced by romantic adventure fiction. . . . It is this charm which, each morning, saved Scheherazade's life, suspended as it was by the thread of her story. It is this charm that made La Fontaine write

If I were told the Tale of the Ass Skin,
I would be absolutely delighted.

It is this charm which has made so many works of the imagination famous, in so many different genres, ever since there have been men to dream them.

Barrabas is a romantic adventure fiction. The author makes no pretense

224

of reforming morals, revealing some age-old truths from the summit of a smoking Sinai, or revolutionizing the world as it is. He has made every effort to create a number of character types and, by putting them in conflict, generate an intrigue that can captivate the spectator's attention for twelve weeks through the sheer variety of its situations and the keen anticipation of its denouement.

LES DEUX GAMINES

. . . The only thing that counts [when the public judges a film] is to know if, in its twenty-six inert reels, there lies a sleeping princess whom a magician eventually will awaken with the beam of his marvelous lamp—I mean a good story. That is the sole point: the story, the tale, the fiction, the dream; and the rest is only matter. Thus the oldest thing in the world, the fable, subjugates the most modern inventions with its immortal whims; instead of replacing the story, the most prodigious discoveries merely serve to rejuvenate it in the mind of man.

EMILE VUILLERMOZ, "Before the Screen: Aesthetic"

From "Devant l'écran: Esthétique," *Le Temps* (27 March 1920), 3.

THE FRENCH CINEMA is about to perish. Its demise is no more than a matter of months. . . . French filmmakers then either will have to become Americanized under the guidance of the American film companies [harbingers of a regularized aesthetic] or else disappear.

That is distressing. All hope of raising the intellectual level of the cinema seems more and more chimerical. American technique has reached an unmistakable state where its commercial quality enjoys a level of competence we can only envy. But the artistic value of their production is no longer improving. In fact, story interest, psychological truthfulness, ingenuity, and inventiveness are diminishing markedly instead of increasing. With us, however, in the midst of clearly embarrassing productions, glimmers of light have appeared. We have sighted a new horizon, sensed the portent of a dawn. A cinegraphic language has been created slowly, confusedly, stammered out by a few extraordinary artists, and understood by spectators even fewer in number. All this is still indistinct and incomplete, but in the general state of regression it is at least a distant promise. Must we see this miniscule star extinguished?

. . . So let's plead our case. Superficial observers deny the intervention of a creative element, whether that be an idea or artistic intention, in the unreeling of a light-sensitive filmstrip that automatically photographs anything which passes in front of the camera lens. For them, it is merely a copying machine, a passive mechanical instrument of light, analogous to the phonograph disk in the autolithography of its production. For many of our contemporaries, the *ciné* and the *phono* are lumped in the category of hand-crank instruments, mechanical pianos, music boxes, barrel organs, street corner instruments, anything which gobbles up perforated music rolls and spits out waltzes and polkas. Here, the projector devours a roll of celluloid and discharges flickering images, but, at bottom, it works on the same principle; and there is no more art in this hand-crank contraption than in the others.

The painter and the musician can select and compose, they tell us, while the cinematographist is content to copy. How wrong! The cinematographist selects and composes twice. There are two creative acts, two distinct artistic enterprises in the process of making a film. The first real creation comes in the conception of the scenario, in its decoupage, in its mise-en-scène, in the choice of lighting and atmosphere, in the choice of this or that expressive detail in the landscape or face, etc. Unless one denies the existence of dramatic art, one can hardly refuse artistic quality to these preliminary labors, which exceed the fullest and most audacious theatrical construction in subtlety, variety, and power. The great artist of the stage and screen, [André] Antoine, will not contradict me on that.

But there is a second, even subtler and more decisive artistic intervention, which owes nothing to other techniques and which is the very life of *cinégraphie*. The film has been written and "shot." Hundreds of little fragments of exposed film are there in front of the author. There are scenes recorded in the open air, dialogues, "close-ups," glades and glens, bright or crepuscular skies, moonlit landscapes, lakes, clouds, snowscapes, flowers. . . . And it is now that the real "construction" begins. This is the moment of inspiration, of personal interpretation, of life "perceived through a temperament." This is the moment of "style."

Given the same elements, a hack and an artist will come up with two absolutely dissimilar films. The first will splice all these fragments end to end, passively following the action; and we will have one of those insipid and interminable stories which our merchants of printed ribbons and bows unreel day and night. The second will take on a task of a completely different nature. He will work patiently at juxtaposing, interposing, overlapping, paralleling, and opposing all these living cells; he will calculate the rhythm of these images, their intercutting and their superimposition; he will ration out the visual impressions and psychological emotions, creating a powerful dramatic "progression," a decrescendo, a surge, a diversion, an escape into dream or a harsh reawakening to reality. He will make eloquent contrasts emerge, develop the inverse of a vision, free the spirit of things; he will cut a scene at the exact moment when its trajectory ought to prolong itself and reach completion in our unconscious, interpolate the lesson of a landscape, give voice to nature, make the "dialogue of the wind and sea" or "murmur of the forest" audible, then retrieve the interrupted scene at the exact moment when its "harmonics" are about to expire in our consciousness, inspire it with a new élan, and continue to interweave the themes of his plastic symphony until the final synthesis. If that does not produce the work of an artist, if that does not add something to the model, one must exclude painting, music, sculpture, and literature from the realm of art, for their techniques are exactly the same.

At the base of every art there is a stereotypical element, inert material to bring to life, dead cells to resurrect. The muse of the cinema is no less handicapped by this charge than are her elder sisters. There is "something of the machine" in music. An organ is an assemblage of "inexpressive" pipes which automatically produce their cry at the command of a keyboard. The virtuoso achieves a note no more pure than the untutored. However, in connecting these obedient sounds, an inspired musician can give them a divine eloquence! In harmonizing moving images, in running through his keyboard of visions, is it not possible for the cinegraphic organist to compose a masterpiece?

The more easily to condemn the cinema, they have sometimes opposed it to the omnipotence of speech, which is superior to all the other arts because words are signs which address both the ear and the eye to reach the mind. And is it otherwise with cinegraphic art? Doesn't it use plastic "signs" to speak to the mind as well as to suggest feelings through the representation of the real? Aren't its dissolve-linked images a supple and extensive language?

Besides, let's not exaggerate the limitless power of speech. Aren't certain arts committed to "coming to the rescue of powerless words"? Music and the plastic arts inhabit a domain of the personal which sometimes begins on the frontiers of language. The cinema equally. It ought to be a form of ideographic writing. Its characters, its words, are drawn from nature and life. Out of the thousand tiny details of daily observation, the thousand facets of the universe which it fragments, it creates a lexicon for itself. A film is a sentence that one writes with living words.

Does the literary writer do something other than put words end to end, words that he draws out of a box called a dictionary? He hasn't even the right to alter them, mould them, cut them up according to his fancy. He must "copy" them faithfully, "record" them passively with all their grammatical conventions, their etymological oddities, and their orthographical deformities. This is the mechanical part of the literary composition. But a writer of talent knows how to juxtapose words with such dexterity that they often find themselves rejuvenated and renewed in the process, they are illuminated by their mutual reflection, and their jingling yields an unexpected and delicious sound. And this little game is worth a Gaboriau or a Verlaine, a Mallarmé or a Dubout de Laforest![1]

The same goes for the screen where one can compose inept serials or visual poems rich in subjective evocations and infinite resonances. Let me hasten to add that, in this domain, serial writers far outnumber the poets, but the future perhaps will alter the distribution of these numbers. In any case, one has no right to bring an unjust suit against this mode of expression on the grounds of a trend. The cinema possesses the specific virtues of art and writing. It only needs to learn how to make this new string on the eternal lyre sing.

Several of our virtuosos are beginning to produce rather delectable sonorous performances. But their resonances are lost in the general tumult. Have you noticed, for instance, that the last film of Marcel L'Herbier, which Léon Gaumont is about to release, carries the stamp of a personal style in a remarkable manner. Certainly, the scenario of *Le Carnaval des vérités* is an unpleasantly common melodrama, full of psychological flaws and constructed out of very poor dramatic material. But what lovely cinegraphic *writing*! What a delicious repast for the eye, what suppleness in the lap dissolves, what taste in the selection and development of plastic themes! Disagreeable music, but delightful orchestration. This is already worthy of note. All this mastery of elocution is necessary so that we do not notice the poverty of the drama and its unjustified length. Alas, why spoil such resources on such miserable materials?

Despite everything, this effort has to be praised highly. . . .

[1] Vuillermoz is comparing Paul Verlaine (1844–1896) and Stéphane Mallarmé (1842–1898), major poets of the French Symbolist movement, with two popular adventure novelists, one of whom, Emile Gaboriau (1835–1873), created one of the first French detective heroes in Inspector Lecoq.

LOUIS DELLUC, "Cadence"

From "La Cadence," *Photogénie* (Paris: Brunoff, 1920), 71–72.

I HAVE ALSO seen an admirable technical phenomenon in C. B. De Mille's *Joan the Woman* (1917).[1]

In the scene where Joan evokes the English army trampling the courtesans of the French king—through the poignant effect of a photographic superimposition—and in the scene where the royal cortege enters the cathedral at Rheims, cadence seems tangible. Everything lives, and breathes according to a deliberate rhythm. As in a symphony where the measured élan of each note is consecrated to the overall flow of music, all the figures

march off, fade away, and are reconstituted according to a powerful orchestration. This is the most perfect example there is of an equilibrium of
photogenic elements.

It is still unusually rare for the external rhythm of a film to be fully realized. How many scenarios have been scored with all the precision that
they could have achieved? We often find excellent details in the mise-en-
scène, but almost never find the impulse, the movement, the visual cadence originally envisaged and established by the figures and words. What
can the cameraman and director do without them?

And after the film is shot, who knows how *to edit* the scenes? Only a
small number have the requisite skill for cutting the kilometers of film correctly and recognizing the algebraic music which governs the proportion-
ing of the recorded vignettes. A film company should give as much importance to the *editor* as to the director and assess their respective work equally.
Then we would more often have genuine films.

However, there still remains the question of speaking to the artisans
charged with projecting the film on the screen. Each film has a different
cadence. Paderewski[2] does not give the same performance as a Pianola.
While awaiting Paderewskis to accompany film screenings, let's at least
have mechanical pianos that won't *betray* the cadence of the created work
simply because their cadence is out of sync with the film.

[1] In De Mille's *Joan the Woman* (1917), opera star Geraldine Farrar gave one of her best
performances in silent films.
[2] Ignace Paderewski (1860–1941) was a famous Polish pianist and composer who frequently toured Europe and the United States.

LÉON MOUSSINAC, "Cinema: *Broken Blossoms*"

From "Cinématographie: *Le Lys brisé*," *Mercure de France* (1 February 1921), 797–804.

AFTER HAVING provoked unanimous acclaim in America and England
and then roused one sector of the Parisian public to stunned admiration from the moment of its premier, D. W. Griffith's *Broken Blossoms*
[1919], it seems, has been booed in several of our cinemas and, from all the
evidence so far, has even disappointed many of our sympathizers. That is
due, undoubtedly, to the public's lack of experience in general but also to
the tactless strategy of our idiotic merchants who have emphasized the brutality of a bitterly despairing and lengthily developed subject by cutting it
to ribbons. The work is singularly emaciated, and D. W. Griffith's rich,
profuse style comes off rather impoverished. No matter, I believe enough
still remains of the film to justify admiration. In the history of the silent
art, the premiere of *Broken Blossoms* will be a date as important as that of

The Cheat, whose revelation actually initiated the greater French public's education about the cinema. Without claiming to be definitive, of course, *Broken Blossoms* offers a breakthrough in technical originality, thanks to the new elements with which it abounds, and reveals a new stage in the advance of cinematic art toward its ultimate perfection, something already strongly marked in the past by films such as *Pour sauver sa race, La Conquête de l'or, Intolerance, Une Aventure à New York, Mater Dolorosa, Les Proscrits, La Fête espagnole, Le Tresor d'Arne, L'Homme du large.*[1] In the future, we should not listen to someone talk about the screen if he doesn't know such films. Knowing them is as essential as knowing certain ancient, imperfect works, such as the uneven and profuse poetry of the thirteenth- and fourteenth-century troubadours, is to poetic education. No intellectual who is encouraging the cinema to become an art form capable of completely inverting the order of knowledge as well as renewing poetry and drama should be allowed to shirk off the obligation of studying them.

Without a doubt, D. W. Griffith's *Broken Blossoms* is the masterpiece of dramatic cinema. Yet, when you have been closed up in a dark room for a long time, even the feeblest light is more dazzling than the sun at high noon. So I understand the enthusiasm here. I understand that those who have been attracted to the screen and who know something of its present difficulties can be stunned by so much skill, and be stupified by the expression of a genius as self-willed as Griffith's. However, the public doesn't know how to share the same responses, and I believe that it falls to the critic to try to evaluate works and situate them in time. It is less important for the common people, for example, to know that a certain ceramic work represents a marvelous technical advance (by reason of the material, the glaze, the color, the methods employed) than to discover a new pleasure in gazing at it. The crowd craves enjoyment first of all. That's logical enough. Craft should fade away before feeling. The value of a film such as *Broken Blossoms* thus remains a completely relative one.

It has always been so in the great periods of a new art's formation. What do we admire in the naive paintings of Duccio [1260–1319] and Cimabue [1240–1302] other than all the latent art of Giotto [1266–1337], and in Giotto all the latent art of Raphael [1483–1520]?

The cinema, which also has its catacombs in the cellar of the Grand Café,[2] will achieve the plenitude of great works. But nothing is more poignant than to see it gradually being formed, and our excitement is justified when one of its manifestations gives us the occasion to admire its progress.

Intolerance [1916] and then *Hearts of the World* [1918] revealed D. W. Griffith to us. His is the first great name in the cinema.

Since, in the present state of film art's development, nothing can be intended as complete or definitive (without being presumptuous and dangerous), it is a delight to recognize in Griffith a master who has limited his ambition to a consistently deliberate effort, to a tenaciously creative quest. This artist creates. Each of his achievements, planned and thought out patiently at length, reveals some noble truth. Thus does his genius assert his concern for genuine emotion. Too many problems are posed at once, of course, for his endeavors not to betray a certain disorder; but it is enough that someone gives us a work which already carries in itself—through the quality of its quest, the technical skill, the richness of ideas—all the great works of the future.

Previously I cited Duccio and Cimabue. The art of D. W. Griffith readily offers analogies to the art of all the primitives. The same qualities and faults are found there: discipline is the dominant characteristic; the quest for precision often produces coldness; the concern for exactness sometimes becomes overly meticulous; the passion for truth becomes brutal; finally, lyricism—that élan, that breath by which every great work lives and reigns—is conspicuously absent. In his films, Griffith rarely rises to his potential (except at the end of *Intolerance*), and his choice of expressive means often evidences a certain tiresome puerility. The subject he chooses also displays the same characteristics, but then he is an American. If the primitives only painted naive madonnas by heart, it is because they had everything to discover about the renewal of their art and because they thus prepared for the coming of the great masters in whom the Renaissance became a certainty.

D. W. Griffith's art draws its power from his sobriety. Griffith concentrates all the spectator's attention on the subject he has chosen, on the emotion he is depicting. Consequently, in *Broken Blossoms*, the poignant martyrdom of the heroine is communicated with the maximum of intensity. A news item is elevated to the level of tragedy. Griffith seizes hold of his characters, scrutinizes them, enters into them—and illuminates them. If to us, nevertheless, their psychology seems somewhat summary, that is because, in reality, it is. Griffith isn't afraid of certain excesses. He clearly means for no possible equivocation. He remembers the public he is addressing, and that public is his own countrymen above all. Therefore, the mimicry of the boxer sometimes results in grimaces, yet such a magnification seems to occur only when the character is too violently set off against the Chinese idealist, whose passionate and mystical meekness is violated only at the moment when the drama reaches its point of culmination. Poor Lucy, alternately tossed between two extremes, is the victim of this terrible game, of motivated violence against the beautiful dream of peace. Here in this battle we discover the simple and eternal opposition between the beautiful and the ugly, the good and the evil, which every art at its beginnings uses to inspire the crowd.

Broken Blossoms also reveals a consciously thought out and wonderfully expressive sense of composition. No one in our cinema, except Abel Gance sometimes in *J'Accuse* [1919], has ever approached the virtuosity of D. W. Griffith in the handling of lighting.[3] He works in black and white with extraordinary skill. In the scene of the brothel in White Chapel, where so many races are intermingled and bathed in smoke, this reaches the point of giving us a powerful impression of three-dimensional space. The "transitions" from shadow to light are remarkably realized. Such modeling reminds one of a sculptor as much as a painter.

The different tableaux give evidence of an acute sense of observation and great care in composition. If D. W. Griffith sometimes demonstrates poor taste, nevertheless, we admire his concern for detail, which comes close to perfection—sometimes, as I have already said, to the point of being overly meticulous—but which never disrupts the unity of the whole. That is because the means employed are carefully selected and efficacious. Through this, Griffith achieves style, and this style has never been more personal than in *Broken Blossoms*.

The atmosphere of the scenes is always just right. A small number of simple sets suffice, yet how conscientiously are they constructed! There is no ostentation, no pompous showing off of useless learning: the artist simply transposes life. With an incomparably quiet faith in himself and his desires, he encloses his vision of things within an ideal set decor, which for us is all that much truer than reality itself.

The sets in which the action of *Broken Blossoms* unfolds are all remarkable. The street in White Chapel, where the yellow man has opened a shop speaks to us at every hour of its sad and mysterious charm, its nostalgia; there life begins again incessantly, especially in the pallid dawn when one feels maddened by the breeze which sways the paper lantern above Evil Eye's shop; the fog rising like a shifting and pervasive smoke which makes the old building framework quiver in the quarter where Battling Burrows, the boxer, has his den; even this den, with its squalor, its bleak hearth, its bare walls, its pallet, its narrow, rickety table, and the single master's chair; and the Chinaman's room where all the Orient seems to coalesce, with its tiny window which encloses in its square of light all the infinite purity of the sky. It is incomparable in its artistry. So self-evident is this penetrating and almost obstinate sense of observation that it allows Griffith to achieve scenes as realistic and beautiful as the boxing match, the martyrdom of Lucy, and the death of the boxer.

The discipline which D. W. Griffith imposes on himself is imposed equally on the performers. From which comes his concern for composition, his stylization of the characters, the studied poses which convey the necessary feeling with a maximum of intensity. In that way, Griffith often compels an emotion that artists such as Lillian Gish, Donald Crisp, and [Richard] Barthelmass, left to themselves, even with all their talent, could scarcely achieve with as much veracity and power.[4] And as proof of this discipline and art, I offer only the ease with which Griffith makes us forget that his Chinaman is an American. The wonderful expressive power of his poses, better than the most clever grimaces, and sometimes a certain lighting effect on the forehead or the eyes are all that is needed for this miracle. Everything is genuine in such an art, and no one with impunity could introduce a trick effect into this cold silence without the risk of making it seem crude and intolerable.

What is missing in *Broken Blossoms* was already missing in the previous films of D. W. Griffith—lyricism. The overly acute sense of observation absorbs and suppresses its élan. The penetrating poetry of certain parts of *Pour sauver sa race* or *La Conquête de l'or* by [Thomas] Ince, his student, appears not at all in his works.[5] I say this with keen regret, for I am convinced that, contrary to general opinion, poetry will find one of its most prodigious means of expression precisely in the cinema. The infinite world of ideal images someday will be revealed on the screen with an unequaled intensity and a marvelous power of radiance. Griffith transposes life in its essentials, adding to it (to the point of overindulgence) the feeling and personal vision through which a work impresses itself on us. That is enough for now. Others, inspired by his thinking and by his sweeping manner, will transpose the dazzling and magnificent dreams of their imagination, and thus will a still incomplete form of art reach its perfection.

Poor taste is scarcely absent from D. W. Griffith's works. In *Broken Blossoms*, for example, at the beginning and at the end, I dislike those images of the harbor and temple bells, which are worthy of the worst collection of "artistic" postcards. I dislike—no matter what you may think—Lucy's gesture which forces her sad face into a smile. I dislike the character of Evil Eye who is burdened with so much that is conventional and arbitrary. I dislike certain childish things, just as I dislike anything childish in poetry and American art. Yet, the story, undoubtedly, is what makes the public so uneasy. And we ought to criticize that melodramatic scenario because the only thing that saves it from ridicule is the great feeling of humanity which it seems to inspire in us.

Rodin [the sculptor] said that we should not attribute too much importance to the themes that the artist interprets. That is certainly true of an art which has already attained its summits and achieved definitive works, but not for the cinema where everything, so to speak, remains to be discovered. Sometimes we have a tendency to concern ourselves solely with the means of expression. We are wrong in that. Since all the problems in cinematic art are being posed at once, authors ought to have quite a lot to say. We should encourage them to "speak about" many things.

All the films of D. W. Griffith, however, exhibit philosophical pretensions. Mme Germaine Dulac, the director of *La Cigarette* [1919], *La Fête espagnole* [1920], *Malencontre* [1920], etc., recalled recently the occasion of a conversation she had with Griffith and which she reported to us: "A single philosophical idea seems to obsess him—that of the progress of human evolution, forever retarded by the brutal forces of production. It is a theme of *Intolerance* as well as, in a variant form, of *Broken Blossoms*. The Chinaman and the poor little girl of London's lower depths are brethren, although from different races, through the equality of their spiritual evolution. But all the forces of obscurantism, roughly represented by the traditional rights of the boxer, rise up to oppose their union and annihilate it, just as Cyrus the Barbarian destroyed Babylon the Civilized in *Intolerance*."[6]

If the philosophical ideas of D. W. Griffith are debatable, the technique with which he glorifies them is clearly the most perfect we have seen on the screen. Such skill has yet to be equaled. Mme Germaine Dulac recalls in particular what we owe to this magnificent craftsman of the cinema's first hours: the discovery of close shots to isolate expression (this interior performance which visualizes the innermost soul through pose and counterpose [or shot/reverse shot]; the study of soft-focus images which blur and shade certain features; the study of the irised or masked images, sometimes tinted to match, which frame the screen; the attempts at color tonings of the black areas of the image . . .[7]

If the example of such a creative *oeuvre* provokes a fruitful emulation, that is enough to justify our admiration. The results demonstrate the power of the means employed and suggest the potential of the future. And so *Broken Blossoms* has cracked open the door of initiation even more and revealed the ever-broadening range of expression of a unique art—an incomparable teacher of the masses—the art of the next worldwide renaissance. I am awaiting the day when a poet finally seizes hold of the simple grandeur and radiant power which can be achieved on the screen, and impels the truth of our new times to emerge out of the marvelous world of images, in a breath of irresistible lyricism. There is no other means remotely capable of impressing beauty on the hearts of all men, at one blow, and thus inspiring the human race to a shared and fertile idealism.

LÉON MOUSSINAC (1890–1964) was the managing editor of *Comoedia illustré*, a senior editor for the publishing firms of Editions Albert-Lévy and then La Lampe merveilleuse, and a minor playwright and poet. He and Delluc had been boyhood friends at the *lycée* Charlemagne in Paris, and Delluc had his first articles on the cinema published in *Le Film*, in late 1919.

¹ These French titles refer, respectively, to the following films: Barker's *The Aryan* (1916), *A Sister of Six* (1917), Griffith's *Intolerance* (1916), Dwan's *Manhattan Madness* (1916), Gance's *Mater Dolorosa* (1917), Sjöstrom's *The Outlaw and his Wife* (1918), Dulac's *La Fête espagnole* (1920), Stiller's *Arne's Treasure* (1919), and L'Herbier's *L'Homme du large* (1920).

² The one-hundred-seat basement hall of the Grand Café on the boulevard des Capucines was the site of the Lumière brothers first public cinema screening, on 28 December 1895.

³ G. W. (Billy) Bitzer was Griffith's principal cameraman on *Broken Blossoms*, as he had been for the previous ten years or more; but Hendrik Sartov contributed most of the soft-focus close-ups in the film. L.-H. Burel, of course, was Gance's principal cameraman on *J'Accuse*.

⁴ Lillian Gish (1896–) was best known for her roles in previous Griffith films, including *The Battle of Elderbush Gulch* (1913), *Home, Sweet Home* (1914), *Birth of a Nation* (1915), *Intolerance* (1916), *Hearts of the World* (1918), and *True Heart Susie* (1919). Donald Crisp (1880–1974) was also best known as an actor in such films as *Home, Sweet Home* and *Birth of a Nation* as well as a director of films such as *His Sweetheart* (1916). Richard Barthelmess (1895–1963) became an important silent film star with his performance in *Broken Blossoms*.

⁵ During this period, the French generally thought of Ince and Griffith as the two master filmmakers of the American cinema, the one (mistakenly) being considered the student of the other. However, Ince was the producer and not the director of many of the films the French associated with his name. Strangely, too, while most of Ince's films were shown in France during the war, the films Griffith made between 1914 and 1918 were not shown publicly there until after the war.

⁶ The source of this quote is uncertain. Cf. Germaine Dulac, "Chez D. W. Griffith," *Cinéa* 7 (17 June 1921), 11–12.

⁷ That the French were accepting Griffith's own self-aggrandizing testimony about how he discovered and perfected most of the techniques crucial to the cinema can also be seen in "La Réalisation—les moyens d'expression," *Ciné-pour-tous* 55 (17 December 1920), 16.

JEAN EPSTEIN, "Magnification"

Reprinted, with changes, from a translation by Stuart Liebman in *October* 3 (Spring 1977), 9–15, from "Grossissement," *Bonjour Cinema* (Paris: Editions de la sirène, 1921), 93–108.

I WILL NEVER find the way to say how much I love American close-ups. Point blank. A head suddenly appears on screen and drama, now face to face, seems to address me personally and swells with an extraordinary intensity. I am hypnotized. Now the tragedy is anatomical. The decor of the fifth act is this corner of a cheek torn by a smile. Waiting for the moment when 1,000 meters of intrigue converge in a muscular denouement satisfies me more than the rest of the film. Muscular preambles ripple beneath the skin. Shadows shift, tremble, hesitate. Something is being decided. A breeze of emotion underlines the mouth with clouds. The orography of the face vacillates. Seismic shocks begin. Capillary wrinkles try to split the fault. A wave carries them away. Crescendo. A muscle bridles. The lip is laced with tics like a theater curtain. Everything is movement, imbalance, crisis. Crack. The mouth gives way, like a ripe fruit splitting open. As if slit by a scalpel, a keyboard-like smile cuts laterally into the corner of the lips.

The close-up is the soul of the cinema. It can be brief because the value of the photogenic is measured in seconds. If it is too long, I don't find continuous pleasure in it. Intermittent paroxysms affect me the way needles do. Until now, I have never seen an entire minute of pure *photogénie*. Therefore, one must admit that the photogenic is like a spark that appears in fits and starts. It imposes a decoupage a thousand times more detailed than that of most films, even American ones. Mincemeat. Even more beautiful than a laugh is the face preparing for it. I must interrupt. I love the mouth which is about to speak and holds back, the gesture which hesitates between right and left, the recoil before the leap, and the moment before landing, the becoming, the hesitation, the taut spring, the prelude, and even more than all these, the piano being tuned before the overture. The photogenic is conjugated in the future and in the imperative. It does not allow for stasis.

I have never understood motionless close-ups. They sacrifice their essence, which is movement. Like the hands of a watch, one of which is on the hour and the other on the half hour, the legs of St. John the Baptist create a temporal dissonance. Rodin or someone else explained it: in order to create the impression of movement. A divine illusion? No, the gimmick for a toy presented at the *concours Lépine*,[1] and patented so that it can't be used to make lead soldiers. It seemed to Rodin that Watteau's *Cythera* could be animated by the movement of the eye from left to right over it. The motorbike posters race uphill by means of symbols; hatching, hyphens, blank spaces. Right or wrong, they thereby endeavor to conceal their ankylosis. The painter and the sculptor maul life, but this bitch has beautiful, real legs and escapes from under the nose of the artist crippled by intertia. Sculpture and painting, paralyzed in marble or tied to canvas, are reduced to pretence in order to capture the indispensable movement. The ruses of reading. You must not maintain that art is created out of obstacles and limits. You, who are lame, have made a cult of your crutch. The cinema demonstrates your error. Cinema is all movement without any need for stability or equilibrium. Of all the sensory logarithms of reality, the photogenic is based on movement. Derived from time, it is acceleration. It opposes the event to stasis, relationship to dimension. Gearing up and gearing down. This new beauty is as sinuous as the curve of the stock market index. It is no longer the function of a variable but a variable itself.

The close-up, the keystone of the cinema, is the maximum expression of this *photogénie* of movement. When static, it verges on contradiction. The face alone doesn't unravel its expressions but the head and lens moving together or apart, to the left and right of each other. Sharp focus is avoided.

The landscape may represent a state of mind. It is above all a state. A state of rest. Even those landscapes most often shown in documentaries of picturesque Brittany or of a trip to Japan are seriously flawed. But "the landscape's dance" is photogenic. Through the window of a train or a ship's porthole, the world acquires a new, specifically cinematic vivacity. A road is a road but the ground which flees under the four beating hearts of an automobile's belly transports me. The Oberland and Semmering tunnels swallow me up, and my head, bursting through the roof, hits against their vaults. Seasickness is decidedly pleasant. I'm on board the plummeting airplane. My knees bend. This area remains to be exploited. I yearn for a drama aboard a merry-go-round, or more modern still, on airplanes. The fair below and its surroundings would be progressively confounded. Centrifuged in this way, and adding vertigo and rotation to it, the tragedy would increase its photogenic quality ten-fold. I would like to see a dance shot successively from the four cardinal directions. Then, with strokes of a pan shot or of a turning foot, the room as it is seen by the dancing couple. An intelligent decoupage will reconstitute the double life of the dance by linking together the viewpoints of the spectator and the dancer, objective and subjective, if I may say so. When a character is going to meet another, I want to go along with him, not behind or in front of him or by his side, but in him. I would like to look through his eyes and see his hand reach out from under me as if it were my own; interruptions of opaque film would imitate the blinking of our eyelids.

One need not exclude the landscape but adapt it. Such is the case with a film I've seen, *Souvenir d'été à Stockholm*. Stockholm didn't appear at all. Rather, male and female swimmers who had probably not even been asked for their permission to be filmed. People diving. There were kids and old people, men and women. No one gave a damn about the camera and had a great time. And so did I! A boat loaded with strollers and animation. Elsewhere people fished. A crowd watched. I don't remember what show the crowd was waiting for; it was difficult to move through these groups. There were café terraces. Swings. Races on the grass and through the reeds. Everywhere, men, life, swarms, truth.

That's what must replace the Pathécolor newsreel where I always look for the words "Bonne Fête" written in golden letters at the corner of the screen.[2]

But the closeup must be introduced, or else one deliberately handicaps the style. Just as a stroller leans down to get a better look at a plant, an insect, or a pebble, in a sequence describing a field the lens must include close-ups of a flower, a fruit, or an animal: living nature. I never travel as solemnly as these cameramen. I look, I sniff at things, I touch. Close-up, close-up, close-up. Not the recommended points of view, the horizons of the Touring Club, but natural, indigenous, and photogenic details. Shop windows, cafés, quite wretched urchins, a cashier, ordinary gestures made with their full capacity for realization, a fair, the dust of automobiles, an atmosphere.

The landscape film is, for the moment, a big zero. People look for the picturesque in them. The picturesque in cinema is zero, nothing, negation. About the same as speaking of colors to a blind man. The film is susceptible only to *photogénie*. Picturesque and photogenic coincide only by chance. All the worthless films shot near the Promenade des Anglais [in Nice] proceed from this confusion. Their sunsets are further proof of this.

Possibilities are already appearing for the drama of the microscope, a hystophysiology of the passions, a classification of the amorous sentiments into those which do and those which do not need Gram's solution.[3] Young girls will consult them instead of the fortune teller. While we are waiting, we have an initial sketch in the close-up. It is nearly overlooked, not because it errs, but because it presents a ready-made style, a minute dramaturgy, flayed and vulnerable. The amplifying close-up demands underplaying. It's opposed to the theater where everything is loudly declaimed. A hurricane of murmurs. An interior conviction lifts the mask. It's not about interpreting a role; what's important is the actor's belief in his character, right up to the point where a character's absent-mindedness becomes that of the actor himself. The director suggests, then persuades, then hypnotizes. The film is nothing but a relay between the source of nervous energy and the auditorium which breathes its radiance. That is why the gestures which work best on screen are nervous gestures.

It is paradoxical, or rather extraordinary, that the nervousness which often exaggerates reactions should be photogenic when the screen deals mercilessly with the least forced gestures. Chaplin has created the overwrought hero. His entire performance consists of the reflex actions of a nervous, tired person. A bell or an automobile horn makes him jump, forces him to stand anxiously, his hand on his chest, because of the nervous palpitations of his heart. This isn't so much an example, but rather a synopsis of his photogenic neurasthenia. The first time that I saw Nazimova agitated and exothermic, living through an intense childhood, I guessed that she was Russian, that she came from one of the most nervous peoples on earth. And the little, short, rapid, spare, one might say involuntary, gestures of Lillian Gish who runs like the hand of a chronometer! The hands of Louise Glaum unceasingly drum a tune of anxiety. Mae Murray, Buster Keaton. Etc.[4]

The close-up is drama in high gear. A man says, "I love the faraway princess." Here the verbal gearing down is suppressed. I can see love. It half lowers its eyelids, raises the arc of the eyebrows laterally, inscribes itself on the taut forehead, swells the masseters, hardens the tuft of the chin, flickers on the mouth and at the edge of the nostrils. Good lighting; how distant the faraway princess is. We're not so delicate that we must be presented with the sacrifice of Iphigenia recounted in alexandrines. We are different. We have replaced the fan by the ventilator and everything else accordingly. We demand to see because of our experimental mentality, because of our desire for a more exact poetry, because of our analytic propensity, because we need to make new mistakes.

The close-up is an intensifying agent because of its size alone. If the tenderness expressed by a face ten times as large is doubtlessly not ten times more moving, it is because in this case, ten, a thousand, or a hundred thousand would—erroneously—have a similar meaning. Merely being able to establish twice as much emotion would still have enormous consequences. But whatever its numerical value, this magnification acts on one's feelings more to transform than to confirm them, and personally, it makes me uneasy. Increasing or decreasing successions of events in the right proportions would obtain effects of an exceptional and fortunate elegance. The close-up modifies the drama by the impact of proximity. Pain is within reach. If I stretch out my arm I touch you, and that is intimacy. I can count the eyelashes of this suffering. I would be able to taste the tears. Never before has a face turned to mine in that way. Ever closer it presses against me, and I follow it face to face. It's not even true that there is air between us; I consume it. It is in me like a sacrament. Maximum visual acuity.

The close-up limits and directs the attention. As an emotional indicator, it overwhelms me. I have neither the right nor the ability to be distracted. It speaks the present imperative of the verb to understand. Just as petroleum potentially exists in the landscape that the engineer gropingly probes, the photogenic and a whole new rhetoric are similarly concealed in the close-up. I haven't the right to think of anything but this telephone. It is a monster, a tower, and a character. The power and scope of its whispering. Destinies wheel about, enter, and leave from this pylon as if from an acoustical pigeon house. Through this nexus flows the illusion of my will, a laugh that I like or a number, an expectation or a silence. It is a sensory limit, a solid nucleus, a relay, a mysterious transformer from which everything good or bad may issue. It has the air of an idea.

One can't evade an iris. Round about, blackness; nothing to attract one's attention.

This is cyclopean art, a unisensual art, an iconoscopic retina. All life and attention are in the eye. The eye sees nothing but a face like a great sun. Hayakawa aims his incandescent mask like a revolver. Wrapped in darkness, ranged in the cell-like seats, directed toward the source of emotion by their softer side, the sensibilities of the entire auditorium converge, as if in a funnel, toward the film. Everything else is barred, excluded, no longer valid. Even the music to which one is accustomed is nothing but additional anesthesia for whatever is not visual. It takes away our ears the way a Valda lozenge takes away our sense of taste. A cinema orchestra need not simulate sound effects. Let it supply a rhythm, preferably a monotonous one. One cannot listen and look at the same time. If there is a dispute, sight, as the most developed, the most specialized, and the most generally popular sense, always wins. Music which attracts attention or the imitation of noises is simply disturbing.

Although sight is already recognized by everyone as the most developed sense, and even though the viewpoint of our intellect and our mores is visual, there has nevertheless never been an emotive process so homogeneously, so exclusively optical as the cinema. Truly, the cinema creates *a particular system of consciousness limited to a single sense*. And after one has grown accustomed to using this new and extremely pleasant intellectual state, it becomes a sort of need, like tobacco or coffee. I have my dose or I don't. Hunger for a hypnosis far more intense than reading offers, because reading modifies the functioning of the nervous system much less.

The cinematic feeling is therefore particularly intense. More than anything else, the close-up releases it. Although we are not dandies, all of us are or are becoming blasé. Art takes to the warpath. To attract customers, the circus showman must improve his acts and speed up his carousel from fair to fair. Being an artist means to astonish and excite. The habit of strong sensations, which the cinema is above all capable of producing, blunts theatrical sensations which are, moreover, of a lesser order. Theater, watch out!

If the cinema magnifies feeling, it magnifies it in every way. Its pleasure is more pleasurable, but its defects are more glaring.

JEAN EPSTEIN (1897–1953) came to France from Poland in 1908 and became a student of medicine and philosophy in Lyon, where he worked initially as a laboratory assistant to the Lumière brothers. Through Blaise Cendrars, he went to Paris to become an editor at Editions de la sirène and begin writing on the cinema. He worked briefly as an assistant for Louis Delluc and Marcel L'Herbier and then directed his first film for Jean Benoît-Lévy, a feature-length fictionalized documentary, *Pasteur* (1922).

¹ The *concours Lépine*: an exhibition fair for inventors held annually in Paris—TRANS.

² Georges Sadoul has suggested that Epstein is here referring to film images stylized in the manner of picture postcards—Sadoul, *Histoire générale du cinéma*, vol. 5 (Paris: Denoël, 1975), 135. Epstein may also be referring to the practice of early film companies who inscribed their trademark emblem on the theatrical sets or inserted placards bearing such emblems into shots taken outdoors to prevent pirating of their prints.—TRANS.

³ Gram's solution: a solution used in the differential staining of bacteria.—TRANS.

⁴ Louise Glaum (1894–?) was best known for starring in the William S. Hart westerns, *The Aryan* (1916) and *Hell's Hinges* (1916), both directed by Reginald Barker. In the late 1910s and early 1920s, she starred in a popular series of "vamp" films. Mae Murray (1889–

1966) starred in such films as James Young's *Sweet Kitty Bellairs* (1917), Robert Leonard's *Dolly* (1917) and *Her Body in Bond* (1918). Epstein was one of the first French writers to take notice of Buster Keaton.

JEAN EPSTEIN, "The Senses 1 (b)"

Translated by Tom Milne in *Afterimage* 10 (Autumn 1981), 9–16. Reprinted by permission. The original French text first appeared as "Le Sens 1 bis," *Bonjour Cinema* (Paris: Editions de la sirène, 1921), 27–44.

I DO NOT WANT to do it the disservice of overestimating it. But what can I say that would be adequate? The passion exists, independently, like that of the painter or sculptor. People are only barely beginning to realise that an unforeseen art has come into being. One that is absolutely new. We must understand what this means. Drawing was on hand to see the mammoths die. Olympus heard the Muses numbered. Since then man has added to their official tally, which is actually a fraud in that it could be reduced to half a dozen, only styles, interpretations, and subdivisions. Small minds sank without trace after running into pyroengraving. Books, railways, and automobiles were all amazing, of course, but they had precursors. They were varieties, but now a new species has mysteriously been born.

Once the cinema ceased to be a hermaphrodite, with art rather than science proving to be its sex, we were baffled. Hitherto it had mainly been a matter of reinterpreting the prescribed rules to weary ends. This needed to be understood. It was something else again. For a long time we understood nothing, not a thing, nothing at all.

A time when the cinema was a holiday diversion for schoolboys, a darkish place of assignation, or a somewhat somnambulistic scientific trick. There's a dreadful danger in not knowing chalk from cheese. And duped the sages were in not realizing sooner that those popular, foolish (that goes without saying), novelettish, blood-and-thunderish, serialized *Exploits of Elaine*[1] characterize a period, a style, a civilization. No longer, thank goodness, in vogue. Good yarns that go on endlessly and then start all over again. *Les Trois Mousquetaires, Fantômas, Du côté de chez Swann*, and this one with the extra-dry American flavor. The most assassinated woman in the world, as Armand Rio says.

Serious gentlemen, rather too lacking in culture, applauded the lives of the ants, the metamorphoses of larvae. Exclusively. As educational for younger minds.

Then the schism of filmed theater.

Filmed theater is just what it was not. In fact it was the reverse. Even today this art, then so new that it existed only as a presentiment, lacks words because they were overexposed in images that remain, alas, unforgotten. A new poetry and philosophy. We need an eraser to efface styles, and then start constructing afresh. But are we capable of so much amputation? Neither wit, nor plot, nor theater. *The Exploits of Elaine*—it is easier today to admit that one did see a few episodes—is not simply a farrago of cliff-hanging semidenouements, or Monsieur Decourcelle would happily have buried it. Generally speaking, the cinema does not render stories well. And "dramatic action" is a mistake here. Drama that acts is already half resolved and on the healing slope to crisis. True tragedy remains in abeyance. It threatens all the faces. It is in the curtain at the window and the handle of the door. Each drop of ink can make it bloom on the tip of the fountain pen. In the glass of water it dissolves. The whole room is saturated with every kind of drama. The cigar smoke is poised menacingly over the ashtray's throat. The dust is treacherous. The carpet emits venomous arabesques and the arms of the chair tremble. Now the suspense is at freezing point. Waiting. One sees nothing as yet, but the tragic crystal which will create the nucleus of the drama has begun to form somewhere. Its ripples spread. Concentric circles. It advances stage by stage. Seconds.

The telephone rings. All is lost.

Well now,

do you really want so much to know if they get married in the end? Because NO FILMS end unhappily, and bliss descends at the appointed hour in the program.

The cinema is true; a story is false. One could argue this with a semblance of conviction. But I prefer to say that their truths are different. On the screen, conventions are despicable. Stage effects are absurd, and if Chaplin puts so much tragic expression into them, it is a risible tragedy. Eloquence expires. Presentation of the characters is pointless; life is extraordinary. I like uneasiness in encounters. Exposition is illogical. What happens snares us like a wolftrap. The denouement, the unraveling of the plot, can be nothing more than a transition from knot to knot. So that there are no great changes in emotional heights. The drama is as continuous as life. It is reflected, but neither advanced nor retarded, by the gestures and movements. So why tell stories, narratives which always assume a chronology, sequential events, a gradation in facts and feelings? Perspectives are merely optical illusions. Life is not systematized like those nests of Chinese tea tables each begetting the next. There are no stories. There have never been stories. There are only situations, having neither head nor tail; without beginning, middle, or end, no right side or wrong side; they can be looked at from all directions; right becomes left; without limits in past or future, they are the present.

The cinema is ill-suited to the rational framework of the novelette and indifferent to it; barely sustained by the air of circumstance, it offers moments of a wholly distinctive flavor. *The Honor of His House* [1918] is an improbable yarn: adultery and surgery. Hayakawa, the tranced tragedian, sweeps the scenario aside. A few instants offer the magnificent sight of his harmony in movement. He crosses a room quite naturally, his torso held at a slight angle. He hands his gloves to a servant. Opens a door. Then, having gone out, closes it. *Photogénie*, pure *photogénie*, cadenced movement.

I want films in which not so much nothing as nothing very much happens. Have no fear, misunderstandings will not arise. The humblest detail sounds the note of drama that is latent. This chronometer is Destiny. This bronze statue, dusted off with more tenderness than the Parthenon will ever earn from him, is the whole of a poor man's mind. Emotion is timorous. The thunder of an express train jumping the rails on a viaduct does not always leave it undisturbed in its familiar habitat. A casual handshake is more likely to persuade it to show its lovely tear-fringed face. What sadness can be found in rain! How this farmyard echoes the innocence when the lovers in their room look back amazed on the sweetness. Doors close like the lock-gates of destiny. The keyhole eyes are impassive. Twenty years of life fetch up against a wall, a real wall of stone, and everything must begin again if the courage can be summoned. Hayakawa's back is as tense as an obdurate face. His shoulders refuse, reject, renounce. The crossroads is a nucleus from which roads radiate elsewhere. Charlie the Tramp stirs up the dust with his huge boots. He has turned his back. On his shoulder is a bundle which probably contains nothing but a brick as a defense against unwelcome encounters. He sets off. Departure.

Do not say: Symbols and Naturalism. The words have not been discovered yet, and these ones jar. I hope there may be none. Images without metaphor. The screen generalizes and defines. We are not dealing with *an* evening but evening, yours included. The face a phantom made of memories in which I see all those I have known. Life fragments itself into new individualities. Instead of a mouth, the mouth, larva of kisses, essence of touch. Everything quivers with bewitchment. I am uneasy. In a new nature, another world. The close-up transfigures man. For ten seconds, my whole mind gravitates round a smile. In silent and stealthy majesty, it also thinks and lives. Expectancy and threat. Maturity in this tenuous reptile. The words are lacking. The words have not been found. What would Paracelsus[2] have said?

The philosophy of cinema remains to be formulated. Art remains unaware of the eruption which threatens its foundations. *Photogénie* is not simply a fashionably devalued word. A new leavening; dividend, divisor, and quotient. One runs into a brick wall trying to define it. The face of beauty, it is the taste of things. I recognize it as I would a musical phrase from the very specific intimations of emotion that accompany it. Elusive, it is often trampled underfoot like the promise of riches with which an undiscovered coal seam emblazons the earth. The human eye cannot discover it directly, unless after long practice. A lens zeroes in on it, drains it, distilling *photogénie* between its focal planes. Like the human eye, this one has its own perspective.

The senses, of course, present us only with symbols of reality: uniform, proportionate, elective metaphors. And symbols not of matter, which therefore does not exist, but of energy; that is, of something which in itself seems not to be, except in its effects as they affect us. We say "red," "soprano," "sweet," "cypress," when there are only velocities, movements, vibrations. But we also say "nothing" when the tuning fork, diaphragm, and reagent all record evidence of existence.

Here the machine aesthetic—which modified music by introducing freedom of modulation, painting by introducing descriptive geometry, and all the art forms, as well as all of life, by introducing velocity, another light, other intellects—has created its masterpiece. The click of a shutter produces a *photogénie* which was previously unknown. People talked of nature seen through a temperament, or of temperament seen through nature. But now there is a lens, a diaphragm, a dark room, an optical system. The artist is reduced to pressing a button. And his intentions come to grief on the hazards. The harmony of interlocking mechanisms: that is the temperament. And nature is different too. This eye, remember, sees waves invisible to us, and the screen's creative passion contains what no other has ever had before: its proper share of ultraviolet.

To see is to idealize, abstract and extract, read and select, transform. On the screen we are seeing what the cinema has already seen once: a double transformation, or rather raised to the power of two, since it is multiplied in this way. A choice within a choice, reflection of a reflection. Beauty is polarized here like light, a second generation beauty, the daughter—though prematurely delivered and slightly monstrous—of a mother whom we loved with our naked eyes.

This is why the cinema is psychic. It offers us a quintessence, a product twice distilled. My eye presents me with an idea of a form; the film stock also contains an idea of a form, an idea established independently of my awareness, an idea without awareness, a latent, secret but marvelous idea; and from the screen I get an idea of an idea, my eye's idea extracted from the camera's; in other words, so flexible is this algebra, an idea that is the square root of an idea.

The Bell and Howell is a metal brain, standardized, manufactured, marketed in thousands of copies, which transforms the world outside it into art. The Bell and Howell is an artist, and only behind it are there other artists: director and cameraman. A sensibility can at last be bought, available commercially and subject to import duties like coffee or Oriental carpets. From this point of view the gramophone is a failure, or yet to be explored. One would have to find out what it distorts, where it selects. Has anyone made recordings of street noises, engines, railway concourses? One might well discover that the gramophone is just as much made for music as the cinema is for theater—not at all, in other words—and that it has its own road. Because this unexpected discovery of a subject that is an object without conscience—without hesitation or scruples, that is, devoid of venality, indulgence, or possible error, an entirely honest artist, exclusively an artist, the model artist—must be put to use.

Another example, Mr. Walter Moore Coleman's detailed observations[3] demonstrate that at certain times, without being in any way synchronous, all movements (locomotor, respiratory, masticatory, etc.) in a motley group of individuals, even including both men and animals, yield a certain rhythm, a certain frequency that may either be uniform or bear a simple musical relationship. One day, for instance, while the lions, tigers, bears, and antelopes at Regent's Park Zoo were walking or eating their food at 88 movements a minute, soldiers were walking on the lawns at 88 paces a minute, the leopards and pumas were walking at 132, in ½ rhythm, *do-so*, in other words, and children were running at 116, in ¾ rhythm, *do-fa*. What we have here is therefore a sort of euphony, an orchestration, a consonance whose causes are obscure to say the least. It is known that crowd scenes in the cinema produce a rhythmic, poetic, photogenic effect when there is a real, actively thinking crowd involved. The reason is that the cinema can pick this cadence up better than the human eye and by other means; it can record this fundamental rhythm and its harmonics. Think of how Griffith kept his characters constantly on the move for many scenes in *True Heart Susie* [1919], even having them shift virtually from one foot to the other in strict time. Here is where the cinema will one day find its own prosody.

The true poet—despite what Apollinaire says—is not assassinated by this. I do not understand. Some turn aside when offered this new splendor. They complain of impurities. But is the cutting of diamonds so new a thing? I redouble my love. A sense of expectancy grows. Sources of vitality spring up in corners one had thought exhausted and sterile. The epidermis reveals a tender luminosity. The cadence of crowd scenes is a ballad. Just take a look. A man walking, any man, a passerby: today's reality preserved for eternity by art. Embalmed in motion.

Yes, there are impurities: literature, plot and wit, incompatible accessories. Wit, in particular, is the meaner aspect of the matter. The cinema aims high. Compare what the cinema makes of Adventure, Adventure with a capital A, and what a witty man like M. Pierre Mac Orlan[4] does with it.

On the one hand, a complex, ruthless, simple, true tragedy. Episodes of atrocity as pitiful as a suffering animal. The foundering of lost paradises. On the other, a slyly genial little book—published by the Editions de la sirène—which smooths away the asperities that make for a masterpiece. True passion always entails bad taste because it is intent, urgent, violent, devoid of breeding and decorum. M. Mac Orlan dolls it up, painting its face with wit; instead of a beautiful sorceress, there remains only an old lady who doesn't mind being made fun of.

No painting. The danger of *tableaux vivants* in contrasting black and white. Images for a magic lantern. Impressionistic corpses.

No texts. The true film does without. *Broken Blossoms* could have.

But the supernatural, yes. The cinema is essentially supernatural. Everything is transformed through the four *photogénies*. Raymond Lulle never knew a finer powder for projection and emotion. All volumes are displaced and reach flashpoint. Life recruits atoms, molecular movement is as sensual as the hips of a woman or young man. The hills harden like muscles. The universe is on edge. The philosopher's light. The atmosphere is heavy with love.

I am looking.

[1] The reference is to the 22-reel serial, *Les Mystères de New York* (starring Pearl White), which Pathé compiled from the three serials of *Exploits of Elaine* (1915), *The New Exploits of Elaine* (1915), and *The Romance of Elaine* (1915) and then released in Paris between December 1915 and April 1916. Pierre Decourcelle wrote a ciné-roman based on *Les Mystères de New York*, which was serialized in *Le Matin* one week in advance of each episode and thus acted as publicity for the film.

[2] The reference is to Paracelsus (1493–1541), the famous medieval Swiss alchemist and doctor.

[3] Walter Moore Coleman, *Mental Biology* (London: Woodbridge and Co., [n.d.]).

[4] Pierre Mac Orlan (1882–1970) was one of the few "serious" French writers interested in working in the film industry in the early 1920s. He wrote the scenario, for instance, for L'Herbier's *L'Inhumaine* (1924). Epstein is probably referring to Mac Orlan's *A bord de l'étoile matutine* (1921).

LIONEL LANDRY, *"El Dorado"*

From *"El Dorado," Cinéa* 12–13 (22 July 1921), 7–8.

ONCE THE LANGUAGE of the Cinema has stabilized and people are searching retrospectively for those who most contributed to that stabilization, no one will be able to deny the illustrious part played by M. Marcel L'Herbier in the formulation of its vocabulary.

The task of an inventor of a language is double. First of all, he has to experiment with signs, create them if need be, give them shading, and distinguish them one from another; then he has to assign each of them to the precise and exclusive representation of an idea, a feeling, a situation.

For the first part of this task, M. L'Herbier—in *El Dorado* even more than in his earlier works—has proved to be unequaled. He knows how to see and how to make us look on man and nature from the most varied, the most unexpected, the most appropriate perspectives that are possible to imagine. When he wants to indicate that Hedwick is a painter, he shows us an Alhambra that distorts under his gaze, columns twist in spirals, terraces buckle, porticos flatten out—when the dance hall regulars, drunk with wine and lust, appear disfigured and bestial—when the blazing landscape of white light reels around Sibilla as she staggers toward her moment of vengeance—the significance of each image is direct and immediately perceptible.

The second stage of the task calls for some degree of sacrifice. In attaching an exclusive meaning to a sign, one enriches it with all the associations of ideas which that meaning encompasses; but, at the same time, one is excluded from using it in another sense. For example, suppose that the *cinéaste* positions his characters all in the same plane and shows several of them in soft focus and the others in sharp focus. M. Marcel L'Herbier uses this effect, at a given moment, to indicate that Sibilla's thoughts are far away; her image becomes clear when she is recalled to reality. But some other *cinéaste*, even M. L'Herbier, could give to this symbol another significance: for example, an actor in the drama might not notice the character in soft focus and then suddenly perceive her. If there is any doubt, if the image has to be explained by text [an intertitle], its effect is destroyed; but if the significance excludes all other uses, that meaning is imposed and sustained everywhere and, consequently, becomes something banal. The first person who thought of naming a swollen muscle "a little mouse," through an analogy with an animal hidden under the skin, created an original image; then *musculus* became common language and today no one thinks of the earlier sense of the word. That is the price paid for any artistic invention which involves the *means of expression*: music would provide me with innumerable examples. The fact that grade-school Debussy artists have become commonplace should not make us forget the profound and charming impression they made on us at first.

Besides, who knows what will happen in five or ten or twenty years? Let's enjoy this sensation of novelty and originality, which is so refreshing in the midst of the cinema's weekly banality, without an afterthought. Let's gaze at the lovely landscapes.

Garden of Alhambra and Generalife, marble basins in the Lion's Court, fountains of russet-brown porphyry, rustling foliage; let's become intoxicated with the wild dances of *El Dorado*; let's blend in with the teeming crowd of a procession; let's admire a prestigious photography of unequaled virtuosity which honors the cameraman, M. Lucas,[1] as much as the *cinéaste*. I cited several effects a while ago; there are others, by the dozens or hundreds: the course Iliana [Sibilla] follows in the avenue which leads to the Alhambra—the silhouettes of the young couple in the floral garden—the huge door which closes on the vengeful hands of Sibilla—finally, the shadow of the clown dancing and grimacing ironically on the backdrop as the dancer is dying . . .

Now, if one admits that a film has to follow the same exigencies of logic and probability as a play does, one can raise some timorous objections. Actually, by acting as if threatened, by a woman he knows is in desparate straits, and sending her an unnecessarily brutal letter, Estira does everything he can to provoke the scandal which he dreads so much. Unnecessarily brutal also is the sentence from Hedwick which leads to the denouement: "Besides, my mother is going away." If that is so, it's a poorly timed moment to conduct Iliana to her house. Who would he have believe that a woman generous enough to take in the sick son of the dancer would not allow the mother to come see him? And, finally, if this dutiful son is ashamed to bring Sibilla into his mother's house, he could not escape noticing that it is much more improper to bring her there in her absence!

These words of a gratuitous and shocking cruelty serve to bring about a denouement which perhaps does not conform to the truth of life. Indeed, Sibilla would not die; she would mount the stage again; she would begin *to sell her wares* once more—or return to the grind—without feeling the frightful anguish that her child may be dying for lack of care, without having to provide the moral support that her presence would give him. And thus the circle would close, the drama would culminate in the eternal return to the beginning. But if M. Marcel L'Herbier had adopted this course, we would not have had the excruciating and agonizing pleasure of seeing Sibilla kill herself. This then is the occasion to apply the old adage—"the best of two solutions is the one that succeeds"—and to certify that this one has succeeded. . . .

So, at the end of this season, the French cinema asserts its authority in three works of some notoriety. We will be speaking next of *L'Atlantide*, which is valuable because of its subject matter rather than its interpretation; if one considers the two other works together, *Fièvre* and *El Dorado*, it is surprising to find that two works conceived within the same artistic milieu, set in similar locations, and performed by some of the same actors reveal such divergent tendencies. And that is excellent, for the god of the cinema has to be pleased to know that there are many rooms in his mansion.

248

LIONEL LANDRY (1875–1935) was part of Charles Péguy's literary circle and a contributor to his *Cahiers de la quinzième* before the war. Like Vuillermoz, Landry had some advanced training in music.

¹ George Lucas was L'Herbier's principal cameraman during the early 1920s—for example, *L'Homme du large* (1920) and *Don Juan et Faust* (1922)—but he also helped shoot Delluc's *Fièvre* (1921) and *La Femme de nulle part* (1922) as well as Gance's *Napoléon* (1927) and Epstein's *La Chute de la Maison Usher* (1928).

LÉON MOUSSINAC, "Cinema: *Fièvre, L'Atlantide, El Dorado*"

From "Cinématographie," *Mercure de France* (1 November 1921), 784–91.

ORDINARILY we criticize the scenarios of most French films rather sharply and are astonished that, in a country where novelists, poets, and dramatists are conspicuously brilliant, we have not yet discovered a scenarist. I want to examine the different aspects of this question, on which even those who have already long reflected on the screen's possibilities hardly have been in agreement. Perhaps we too easily perpetrate confusion. We do not distinguish the cinegraphic argument from the scenario proper. They are, however, two different things: the argument is the exposition of the generative visual idea of the film; the scenario or script is the practically realized development of this idea, and as such it is virtually the realized film.¹

If we believe—as we must—that all kinds of films will be made in the future, from the ciné-roman through the ciné-lyrical drama to the cinegraphic poem, we have to note that, in the context of current productions which lack any particular artistic value—and I was tempted to say serials—the scenario can be written by anyone who, with no training as a *metteur-en-scène*, has just enough knowledge of technique to be able to foresee the utilization of its resources and expressive possibilities.

In this case, the scenario is developed—through details and in successive, satisfactorily rhythmic images—around a subject in which the common people will find reason to be moved and rejoice. The task of the *metteur-en-scène* then is roughly parallel to that of the scenario writer. This is what happens in most ordinary American films. The *metteur-en-scène*, an excellent technician and no more, directs the original vision by using all the expected resources and practical innovations of his craft. In no case is it his task to dominate the film; he is to the film what a perfect craftsman is to a piece of furniture conceived and designed by the decorative artist.

For films which more precisely claim the title of works of art, on the other hand, there is no question of separating the realization from the conception—here the exceptional case, possible in any creative domain, cannot but confirm the rule. The *metteur-en-scène* becomes his own scenarist. He

249

is truly the original creator, for out of his imagination and his practical skills there arises an absolute insight. And it is in the necessary unity of the work of art that his originality, his creative individuality, emerges. This is not to say that he must always discover in himself the original vision which his particular genius will transfigure. It is possible for him to borrow the *argument* of his film from another's work or for a collaborator to provide him with an argument, but this is only a pretext for which he *alone* will discover the multiple forms of cinegraphic development, a general or particular image that he can recreate completely and from which he will make a purely personal work, the same way a painter or sculptor finds in a poem the pretext for a painting or sculpture. This is the reason—if we aim for such artistic research, and in this instance only—the current scenario competitions are useless.[2] They are of no use to any real creator. They will compel so many changes in order to be adapted perfectly to the thinking of the *metteur-en-scène* that they will only produce bastard works.

Each individual creates for himself a world of perfectly defined images, and the more perfectly and sharply defined are those of the person whose particular bent or intelligence extends to the expressive arrangement of images—the *metteur-en-scène*, or more precisely, since we expect better, the *écranist* according to Canudo or the *cinéaste* according to Delluc. A true scenario is incomprehensible to almost anyone; its author alone can understand it. This is not a new literary formula, as some have said.[3] Nothing could be further from literature. Rather it is a series of personal notations and technical directions, where words are sometimes saddled with veritable hieroglyphs, signs which, much like those in music, gradually are becoming stable and, once universalized but only then, will render the scenario completely legible to the initiated. The sole reproach we might actually address to the scenarios of our most original cinegraphists is that they are still too encumbered with literature. The cinema is no more literature than it is painting, sculpture, architecture, or music; it is a profoundly original art which can borrow from the other arts certain elements of its definitive form but whose [governing] laws remain to be precisely discovered.

We dream then of some marvelous creator who will be the *metteur-en-scène* of the great works of tomorrow, and of the original qualities that he will have to epitomize and combine. The synthetic power of the screen is reaching a tremendous emotional level. For this magnificent task there must be workers more resourceful than any we have yet seen in any branch of the creative activity of art. As both poet and scholar-scientist, the *metteur-en-scène* will have to demand of his intelligence, imagination, and technical skill more discoveries than we have ever seen before. And this is the reason for our excitement in the presence of a new art that is still stammering in its endeavors, whose gaucheries are all the more touching since we realize that out of them will emerge the marvelous synthesis of all the arts and the most complete expression of the mind and spirit of the twentieth century.

THESE PAST few months, three films, all quite different in conception and even opposite in their tendencies, have provided us with novelty, original-ity, and great expectations. These three films will be the honor guard of our production this season. It is especially appropriate to extol their merits rather than insist on their faults, some of which are rather serious, for it is thanks to such films that the cinema is becoming more elevated and enno-bled each day, freeing itself of the prejudices which still oppress it, and asserting its beauty.

First there is *La Boue* by Louis Delluc, which, mutilated by the censors with a stupidity that surprises no one, has become *Fièvre*.[4] This film estab-lishes, almost definitively, a formula which achieves full cinegraphic verac-ity. Delluc is one of that rare breed who are "seekers" and who conse-quently happen to make mistakes.[5] Yet even in this instance, his errors reveal an originality or define a possibility, and they will become the point of departure for new ventures. Thus Delluc creates incessantly, with an en-ergy which never slackens because of difficulties; he is one of the most in-quiring artisans of the Seventh Art. *Fièvre*, which occurs in an unusual de-cor—*the image*: a sailors' bistro in Marseille, in which several quick glimpses of the harbor accentuate its nature, like a bass pedal supporting the melody—demonstrates that in order to "make cinema" by no means is it necessary to carry a camera to the most extraordinary sites and that from the emotion of faces and gestures in a decor which encompassed them all together one can derive effects of real power through the simple play of light and shadow, of black and white. The Rare is not perforce Beauty. It can be only itself. Either nature is the living element of the drama, and it must be employed judiciously, or it justly serves as the base of the drama, and to suggest it is enough. Too often we forget this essential truth. Delluc does not. What is the landscape in *La Fête espagnole* [1920] and *Le Chemin D'Ernoa* [1921]? Everything. What is the decor in *Le Silence* [1920] and *Fièvre*? A fiction, but a fiction truer than life. A banal news item serves as the framework in *Fièvre*, and the bistro comes intensely alive, not through its walls, countertop, and tables, but rather through the darkness in which they are submerged and particularly through the characters that animate it. It is from the drama that the decor draws all of its expressive substance. The realism of the character types and the action does not exclude a kind of solemn poetry, heavy with an oriental nostalgia, an ennui of drunkenness and debauchery, and a violent disgust with sensual pleasure. We can argue with this work, whose first part is marked by an admirable unity, but it will provoke enthusiasm. As for the intelligence of certain images which possess a rare intensity and are perfectly sufficient unto themselves, that will escape no one's notice.

L'Atlantide, directed by M. J. Feyder from the Pierre Benoît[6] novel, has a certain value because of its rich photogenic subject much more than because of the manner in which this subject has been deployed. It is a beautiful film which is cluttered with many superfluous and pointless things and which could easily endure much cutting. M. J. Feyder has restricted himself too often to the plot developments of the novel. Those developments have a logic which is hardly cinegraphic. Thus the film is an illustration of the adventures of Saint-Vit, a sometimes magnificent illustration, but one which could have been consistently beautiful. As an excuse, M. J. Feyder undoubtedly knows nothing of the Swedish films. I'm certain that if he had seen *Arne's Treasure* [1919] or *The Outlaw and His Wife* [1918] before guiding his valiant caravan into the vast sands of the Sahara, his work would have been different and more complete. Each time that he makes the desert participate in the drama, the work strangely soars. While the opening is remarkable, the end, in my opinion, is the best part. The desert becomes an unforgettable actor; it assumes prior position with an incomparable authority. A power of suggestion emerges from those oppressive and deadly solitudes. We are seized by the throat, we become thirsty and hungry, our eyes burn, we suffer . . . You don't find unnecessary new plot developments at the end of the drama, for example, and you see that the vicissitudes of Tanit-Zergase's agony suffice unto themselves and that the mere outline of Saint-Vit's flight achieves a savage beauty—there is nothing more, in the simple play of black and white, than two actors face to face: man and the desert. And between them is revealed the most implacable and poignant struggle that can exist. And it emerges from a simplicity more full of genuine richness than that part of the film where we are smothered under false riches: the palace of Antinea! Apart from the death of Morhenge, soberly beautiful and very photogenic, there is nothing there to retain. The abundance and realism of the decoration leaves nothing to the imagination. That is the error of all realism. *L'Atlantide* cost a lot. It cost its artisans much deprivation and suffering as well, so it is fitting to compliment M. Feyder and his collaborators, [Jean] Angelo, [Georges] Melchior, Mme Napierkowska (so badly used), and Mlle Iribe.[7] For I imagine the shareholders will hardly do so. Still, such as it is, the film astonishes us through the richness of a subject never before deployed so grandly on the screen, and it moves us through the sober beauty of two or three remarkable scenes. That is already more than enough to merit our close attention.

Shortly after the preview of Marcel L'Herbier's *El Dorado*, I wrote:[8]

"Some will be too cowardly to speak of their complete enthusiasm or admit their excitement. They will exhaust themselves trying to uncover things to criticize. They will find some—that's all right. But I only want to tell them that they have never experienced a more passionate hour in front of the screen since the great revelations of Griffith, Ince, Gance, and Sjöstrom, that they have never been more fascinated by the intelligence of certain images since *La Fête espagnole* and especially *Fièvre* by Louis Delluc. *El Dorado* is a very lovely film and the most complete work yet by Marcel L'Herbier. It asserts itself as the logical and powerful culmination of all his efforts. After *Le Carnaval des vérités* [1920], *L'Homme du large* [1920] gave us a great expectation of beauty, and confidence in a "form" which, disencumbered of certain mannerisms of an overly willful and seemingly technical virtuosity, could quickly become a "style." Here, thanks to a greater simplicity in the development of images, that form is now realized with a soberness of expression and a force of strangely intense rhythm (in the second part especially), in which we often recognize clearly the cinegraphic veracity which had already enchanted us in certain passages of *Villa Destin* [1921].

"Thus, in the story of the dancer Sibilla, who suffers and sacrifices herself to save her child, do we not recognize precisely, thanks to Marcel L'Herbier, no more than the glorification of the eternal human truth, grievous and magnificent, which is to be enchanted by and to suffer from love. And if we think, nevertheless, that *El Dorado* does not correspond to the ideal formula of cinegraphic art, we do not have the right to distort any of its beauty through petty criticisms. We ought to speak of all the originality and audacity in a work which is equal, in technique, to the most accomplished productions of the screen. We ought to say that this film will reconcile most of those who are disgusted with the cinema and procure the sympathy of the sceptics. We ought to say that the public will be shaken by the pathetic power of the drama and be carried away by its rhythm, that artists will discover in it the subtle expression of a composition in which sensibility finally is substituted for reality and which evokes and suggests with a rare perfection. For certain images of this film, which the director has imbued with his own feeling and animated with an unusual sense of tonal values, rightly evoke, in their different ways, Goya [1747–1821], Velasquez [1599–1660], and Ribera [1588–1652]. One has to feel the extreme emotion provoked by the apparition of the hazy, oblique, high white wall of the Alhambra, for example, along which Sibilla, a somnambulent figure, walks to meet her destiny; and the great pure beauty of the scene in which the two lovers bathe their foreheads ever higher in the sunlight, so high that it seems at one moment their brows begin to absorb the light and even begin to radiate; and again the tragic death of Sibilla, which is one of the most prodigious setpieces of *photogénie* that we have ever admired.

"I am not talking about certain details of technique, or the attention that is being drawn to the deliberate plastic deformations done with such audacity by Marcel L'Herbier and which, realized for the first time on the screen, cause us to enter into the very sensibility of the images, or to the soft-focus shots already used by Griffith and which singularly accentuate the expression of the image by substituting interior for exterior emotion. And I am not speaking of the photography, which gives prodigious evidence of a remarkable virtuosity, either.

"The performances are of a perfect homogeneity. We have warmly acclaimed Eve Francis.[9] Her creation of the character of Sibilla is unforgettable. It is more complete and alive in artistry, more troubling in veracity, than her performances in *La Fête espagnole*, *Le Silence*, and *Fièvre*; she has an artistry that equals in perfection and power those of the greatest screen performers we know. We have seen nothing comparable in pathos to the scene of her death where, baring her soul and heart with a tragic simplicity, she makes us participate in her anguish, in the torment of her memories, in the surge of her tenderness, and then jolts us in the death rattle of her agony. We have advanced no further than this in cinegraphic veracity. Eve Francis creates the atmosphere, establishes the spectrum of a truly unfortunate life, poignant, intense, and radiant, with a richness of unforgettable expressions.

"At her side we find all the intelligent, sensitive, and sober expressive quality of Jaque Catelain as well as the pure, touching, simple grace of Marcelle Pradot, both already so remarkable in *L'Homme du large*; and we should not forget the right feeling for veracity with which Mme Edith Réal and Claire Prélia and M. Paulias and Philippe Hériat have created their characters."[10]

Now that I have seen *El Dorado* again, I have nothing to take back of what I wrote in the enthusiasm of that first hour. I would rather add that several alterations carried out by Marcel L'Herbier for its public premiere produce an even more powerful rhythm and that the beauty of the film's best parts has now become impassioned. I would stress only the novelty and originality of the plastic deformations realized with such mastery by Marcel L'Herbier and which are completely different from the experiments of certain German films, which we have much talked about lately and whose sole peculiarity, as in *Le Cabinet du Docteur Caligari* [1919], is to substitute for nature the fiction of a decor of Cubist extraction.

Fièvre, L'Atlantide, El Dorado. Here are three beautiful stages in the progress of French cinematography or simply cinematography; here equally are unerring reasons to make us ever more confident of a new art which is attempting gradually to discover itself—and will soon dazzle us.

---

[1] The first part of this essay was reprinted as a section of Moussinac's "Le Scénario," *Le Crapouillot* (16 March 1922), 11–12.

[2] This may well be a reference to the scenario competitions sponsored by *Cinéa* and *Bonsoir* in 1921 and 1922—see Delluc's "Prologue" later in this section.

³ Between 1919 and 1921, a number of scenarios and filmscripts were published as literary or quasi-literary works—for example, Blaise Cendrars, *La Fin du monde filmé par l'ange N.-D.* (Paris: Editions de la sirène, 1919); Pierre Albert-Birot, "2 x 2 = 1." *SIC* 49–50 (15–30 October 1919), 389–92; Jules Romains, "Donogoo-Tonka ou les miracles de la science," *Nouvelle Revue française* 74 (November 1919), 821–69, and 75 (December 1919), 1016–63; Ivan Goll, *Die Chapliniade, eine kinodichtung* (Dresden: Rudolf Kaemmerer Verlag, 1920), translated into French in *La Vie des lettres et des arts* (July 1921); Blaise Cendrars, "La Perle fièvreuse," *Signaux de France et la Belgique* 7 (1 November 1921), 345–52, 9 (1 January 1922), 481–91, 10 (1 February 1922), 530–44, 11–12 (March–June 1922), 606–66.

⁴ See Louis Delluc, "Huit jours de fièvre," *Cinéa* 20 (23 September 1921), 9–12.

⁵ In describing the milieux of French intellectuals at the beginning of this century, Ory and Sirinelli write that "the notion . . . of seeker [*checheur*] was still foreign to French society," and that, when used, it referred to artists more often than to scientists or university scholars—Pascal Ory and Jean François Sirinelli, *Les Intellectuels en France, de l'Affaire Dreyfus à nos jours* (Paris: Armand Colin, 1986), 27.

⁶ Pierre Benoît (1896–1962) was one of the most popular French adventure novelists of the 1920s. Feyder's *L'Atlantide* was extremely successful commercially, as was another adaptation of a Benoît novel, Perret's *Koenigsmark* (1923).

⁷ Jean Angelo (1888–1933) was an important French actor who debuted in *L'Assassinat du Duc de Guise* (1908). His major films in the 1920s included Tourjansky's *Le Chant de l'amour triomphant* (1923), Epstein's *Robert Macaire* (1925–1926), Renoir's *Nana* (1926), and Fescourt's *Monte-Cristo* (1929). Georges Melchior was a minor French actor whose most important role probably came in this film. Stacia de Napierkowska (1896–1939) was a famous dancer who had already starred in several films—for example, Capellani's *Notre Dame de Paris* (1911), Dulac's *Venus Victrix* (1917), and Etiévant's *La Fille de la camargue* (1921). Marie-Louise Iribe (1900–1930) acted in several films, including Fescourt's *Un Fils d'Amérique* (1925) and Renoir's *Marquitta* (1927); she also directed and starred in *Hara-Kiri* (1928).

⁸ Léon Moussinac, *"El Dorado," Le Crapouillot* (16 July 1921).

⁹ Eve Francis (1896–1981) was a celebrated stage actress and the wife of Louis Delluc. She starred in nearly all of Delluc's films as well as Dullac's *Ames de fous* (1918), *La Fête espagnole* (1920), and *Antoinette Sabrier* (1927).

¹⁰ Jaque Catelain (1897–1965) starred in most of L'Herbier's films of the 1920s as well as in Perret's *Koenigsmark* (1923), Tourjansky's *Le Prince charmant* (1925), and Fescourt's *L'Occident* (1928).

Marcelle Pradot starred in several of L'Herbier's early films and then retired from acting when she married the filmmaker in 1924.

Philippe Hériat (1898–1971) performed in several of L'Herbier's early films as well as in Delluc's *L'Inondation* (1924), Bernard's *Le Miracle des loups* (1924), Gance's *Napoléon* (1927), Cavalcanti's *En Rade* (1927), and Gastyne's *La Vie merveilleuse de Jeanne d'Arc* (1929).

LOUIS DELLUC, "From Orestes to Rio Jim"

From "D'Oreste à Rio Jim," *Cinéa* 31 (9 December 1921), 14–15.

THE TRUE dramatic film was born one day when someone realized that the translation of theater actors and their telegraphic gestures to the screen had to give way to nature. When I say nature, I mean *nature morte*.

Vegetation or everyday objects, exteriors or interiors, physical details, any-thing material, in the end, offers a new dimension to the dramatic theme. Already modeled or shaped, this lifeless or silent nature can be animated according to where and how the composer of the film chooses to use it. This prior dimension of things diminishes the character of the actor, the human element. He himself is no more than a detail, a fragment of the material that is the world. He is a note in the great composition of visual music. Things which play a large part in life and in art rediscover their true role and their prophetic eloquence. When that first step was taken toward the synthesis of cinematic orchestration, the cinema began really to exist as an art of expression. And on that day we all came away, deeply moved, in awe and joy.

It is to the Americans that we owe this miracle. In their Far West films—which they have manufactured in series ever since, for we are not the only cinema merchants—in films of which *The Aryan* certainly is the most typical, they got us interested as much in the cowboy's horse as in the cowboy himself. A dog becomes an important character. Hamming takes a hard knock, the atmosphere changes, no longer is there a star and a lot of extras. Instead, there are men and things, even footsteps, a vast symphonic mixture stirred by a rhythm which may be no more than unanimism now, but which presages the great cadence of visual symphonies in the future.

The significance of these expressive details is astonishing. So astonishing that it now seems natural—and necessary. It constitutes the harmony of true style. Are you shocked by the bucket from which Rio Jim drinks, the dice that he throws on the bar, the meaningful cards of the drunken card-players? The scale of these images overwhelms the head of the hero and con-denses the whole drama into a miniscule object enlarged a hundred times. We are familiar with these props from the adventure films; we may even dream of abandoning them or putting them to more audacious use. But let's not disown them. Let's not forget *Pour sauver sa race*, *Grand Frère*, *L'Auberge du signe du loup*, *La Conquête de l'or*, *L'Homme aux yeux clairs*, *Le Serment de Rio Jim*[1]—those marvelous hours that nourished our eyes and our love of life. The gold-laden belt, the casino table, the stone jug into which a strong brandy is poured that will inflame the mind, and those incredible pistols which suddenly spring from the belt to paralyze dozens of brutes or characters who have disturbed and threatened us. Think of those two heavy leather cuffs, studded with copper and laced with savage stylishness, which one sees on William Hart's wrists. In close-ups, they sum up his power, anger, or sadness; even the fists of Rio Jim, his bronzed fists, are often worth a fine portrait.

There is something more. I think that Rio Jim is the first character pro-duced by the cinema; he is the first film type and his life is the first genuinely cinegraphic theme. Already a classic—the tale of an adventurer who seeks his fortune in Nevada or the Rocky Mountains, who stops the stagecoach, loots the strongbox, disrupts the dancing in the saloon, burns down the pastor's house, and marries the sheriff's daughter—here is an established theme, so established you might henceforth think it banal. Yet you cannot find another as clearcut or as fascinating. All that *photogénie* is so satisfying. Gray plains devoid of obstacles, high mountains shining like white screens, horses and men full of the animal vitality and the ready intensity of a simple life that affords rhythm, dimension, beauty, and provides a burst of incomparable humanity to the simplest feelings—love, duty, vengeance—which loom there.

You won't think me ridiculous if I tell you that never before since the Greek theater have we had a medium of expression as powerful as the cinema. The Greek semicircles of stone encompassed an entire people. Spectacles performed there had to satisfy all classes of society. That did not prevent the production of masterpieces. Yet these masterpieces (uneven, yes?) made simple themes come alive, straightforward characters deprived of civilized complications. The Trojan War, the life of Oedipus, the renunciation of Dionysus, poetry and religion combined in a drama of free lines, and is it not still our best repertory? Orestes, Agamemnon, Iphigenia, Electra have crossed twenty-five centuries of different customs, literatures, horrors, and yet remain intact. They have the solidity of statues.

The semicircle in which the cinema spectators are brought together encompasses the whole world. The most separated and diverse human beings attend the same film at the same time throughout the hemispheres. Isn't that magnificent? A hero can move many millions of people who neither know nor understand one another, who may even be attacking and slaughtering one another. Rio Jim is the first figure to sustain this paradox. Where is he not known? As simple as Orestes, he moves through an eternal tragedy free of psychological snares. I spoke of *Pour sauver sa race* a moment ago. Doesn't the terrible bitch played by Louise Glaum possess the fatal splendor of Clytemnestra? Doesn't Bessie Love[2] evoke the chaste, savage energy of Electra? This film speaks to all hearts. In France, I have seen it impress the most diverse audiences—in Marseille before startled fishermen, in a small provincial village before timid and numbed peasants, enraptured. At the Belleville,[3] they cried; at the Colisée, I saw ironists cease laughing and intellectuals, once completely refractory toward the cinema, now converted enthusiasts.

Certainly, what the cinema will become within the next several years will rudely obliterate these hours which we proclaim now to be of the highest order. But the future of cinematic drama lies in themes of simple humanity. It often wastes its time on the usual clever vaudevilles, just as our

257

insipid theater does. That will not last. The irresistible pressure of creative minds is turning over the silent art to blood that is difficult to poison. Believe me, it will allow great figures to emerge out of creators yet to come, just as Aeschylus created *Prometheus*, as Shakespeare created *Macbeth* and *Hamlet*, as Wagner created *Parsifal*. It is so simple that even the cinegraphists don't believe it. Ah well, let them disbelieve. Aeschylus did not create *Prometheus* on purpose. It was forced on him. Rio Jim is the advance guard of the coming great film figures.

[1] These were the French titles, respectively, for *The Aryan* (1916), *The Cold Deck* (1917), *Her Fighting Chance* (1917), *A Sister of Six* (1917), *Blue Blazes Rawden* (1918), and *The Passing of Two-Gun Hicks* (1914).

[2] Bessie Love (1898–1986) starred in several Hart westerns—for instance, *The Aryan* (1916) and *A Sister of Six* (1917)—as well as Herbert and Alice Guy Blaché's *Her Great Adventure* (1918).

[3] A popular cinema in the center of the working-class districts of east Paris, the Belleville cinema was owned and managed by the French Communist Party, from the early 1920s on.

ELIE FAURE, "The Art of Cineplastics"

Translated by Walter Pach in *The Art of Cineplastics* (Boston: Four Seas, 1923) and reprinted in *Film: An Anthology*, ed. Daniel Talbot (Berkeley: University of California Press, 1959), 3–14, from "De la cinéplastique," *L'Arbre d'Eden* (Paris: G. Crès, 1922), 277–304.

WITH DRAMATIC STYLE lost, the present is just the moment for the theater to choose for its attempt to monopolize an art, or at least the instrument of an art, that is absolutely new; one that is so rich in resources that, after having transformed the spectacle, it can act on the aesthetic and social transformation of man himself with a power which I consider to exceed the most extravagant predictions made for it. I see such power in the art of the moving picture that I do not hesitate to regard it as the nucleus of the common spectacle which everyone demands, as being perfectly susceptible of assuming a grave, splendid, moving character, a religious character even, in the universal, majestic sense of the word. It can do so quite as well as music, which began with some sort of string stretched between two sticks, struck by the finger of some poor devil, black or yellow, blind perhaps, to an even and monotonous rhythm; it can do so quite as well as the dance, which began with some little girl skipping from one foot to the other, while around her other children clapped their hands; quite as well as the theater, which began with the mimicking recital of some adventure of war or the chase amid a circle of auditors; quite as well as architecture, which began with the arranging of a cave, in front of which, after a fire had been lighted, someone stretched the hide of an aurochs; quite as well as the frescoes, the statues and the perspectives of the temple, which began with the silhouette of a horse or a deer, dug out with a flint on a bit of bone or ivory.

The needs and desires of man, fortunately, are stronger than his habits. There will some day be an end of the cinema considered as an offshoot of the theater, an end of the sentimental monkey tricks and gesticulations of gentlemen with blue chins and rickety legs, made up as Neapolitan boatmen or Icelandic fishermen, and ladies really too mature for ingénue parts who, with their eyes turned heavenward and their hands clasped, ask the benediction of heaven and the protection of the crowd for the orphan persecuted by the wicked rich man. It is impossible that these things should not disappear along with the theater of which they are the counterpart. Otherwise, we must look to America and Asia, the new peoples or those renewed by death, to bring in—with the fresh air of the oceans and the prairies—brutality, health, youth, danger, and freedom of action.

The cinema has nothing in common with the theater save this, which is only a matter of appearances, and the most external and banal appearances at that: it is, as the theater is, but also as are the dance, the games of the stadium, and the procession, a collective spectacle having as its intermediary an actor. It is even less near to the theater than to the dance, the games, or the procession, in which I see only one kind of intermediary between the author and the public. Actually the cinema presents between the author and the public, three intermediaries: the actor—let us call him the cinemimic—the camera, and the photographer. (I do not speak of the screen, which is a material accessory, forming a part of the hall, like the setting in the theater.) This already establishes the cinema as further away from the theater than from music, in which there also exist two intermediaries between the composer and the public—i.e., the player and the instrument. Finally, and especially, there is no speaking in the cinema, which is certainly not an essential characteristic of the theater. Charlot (Charlie Chaplin), the greatest of cinemimics, never opens his mouth; and observe that the best films almost completely do without those intolerable explanations of which the screen is so prodigal.

In the cinema the whole drama unrolls in absolute silence, from which not only words, but the noise of feet, the sound of the wind and the crowds, all the murmurs, all the tones of nature are absent. The pantomime? The relationship is scarcely closer there. In the pantomime, as in the theater, the composition and the realization of the role change, more or less, every evening, which confers on both a sentimental, even impulsive, character. The composition of the film, on the other hand, is fixed once for all, and once fixed it does not change again, which gives it a character that the plastic arts are the only ones to possess. Besides, pantomime represents, by stylized gestures, the feeling and the passions brought to their essential attitudes; it is a psychological art before being a plastic art. The cinema is plastic first; it represents a sort of moving architecture which is in constant accord—in the state of equilibrium dynamically pursued—with the surroundings and the landscapes where it is erected and falls to the earth again. The feelings and the passions are hardly more than a pretext, serving to give a certain sequence, a certain probability to the action.

Let us not misunderstand the meaning of the word "plastic." Too often it evokes the motionless, colorless forms called sculptural—which lead all too quickly to the academic canon, to helmeted heroism, to allegories in sugar, zinc, papier-mâché, or lard. Plastics is the art of expressing form in repose or in movement by all the means that man commands: full-round, bas-relief, engraving on the wall or on copper, wood, or stone, drawing in any medium, painting, fresco, the dance; and it seems to me in no wise overbold to affirm that the rhythmic movements of a group of gymnasts or of a processional or military column touch the spirit of plastic art far more nearly than do the pictures of the school of David.[1] Like painting, moreover—and more completely than painting, since a living rhythm and its repetition in time are what characterize cineplastics—the later art tends and will tend more every day to approach music and the dance as well. The interpenetration, the crossing, and the association of movements and cadences already give us the impression that even the most mediocre films unroll in musical space.

I remember the unexpected emotions I received, seven or eight years before the war, from certain films the scenarios of which, as it happens, were of an incredible silliness. The revelation of what the cinema of the future can be came to me one day; I retain an exact memory of it, of the commotion that I experienced when I observed, in a flash, the magnificence there was in the relationship of a piece of black clothing to the gray wall of an inn. From that moment I paid no more attention to the martyrdom of the poor woman who was condemned, in order to save her husband from dishonor, to give herself to the lascivious banker who had previously murdered her mother and debauched her child. I discovered, with increasing astonishment, that, thanks to the tone relations that were transforming the film for me in a system of colors scaling from white to black and ceaselessly commingled, moving, changing on the surface and in the depth of the screen, I was witnessing a sudden coming to life, a descent into that host of personages whom I had already seen—motionless—on the canvases of El Greco, Frans Hals, Rembrandt, Velazquez, Vermeer, Courbet, Manet.[2] I do not set down those names at random, the last two especially. They are those the cinema suggested to me from the first.

Later, as the medium of the screen was perfected from day to day, as my eye became accustomed to these strange works, other memories associated themselves with the earlier ones, till I no longer needed to appeal to my memory and invoke familiar paintings in order to justify the new plastic impressions that I got at the cinema. Their elements, their complexity which varies and winds in a continuous movement, the constantly unexpected things imposed on the work by its mobile composition, ceaselessly renewed, ceaselessly broken and remade, fading away and reviving and breaking down, monumental for one flashing instant, impressionistic the second following—all this constitutes a phenomenon too radically new for us even to dream of classing it with painting or with sculpture or with the dance, least of all with the modern theater. It is an unknown art that is beginning, one that today is as far perhaps from what it will be a century hence as the Negro orchestra,[3] composed of tom-tom, a bugle, a string across a calabash, and a whistle, is from a symphony composed and conducted by Beethoven.

I would point out the immense resources which, independent of the acting of the cinemimics, are beginning to be drawn from their multiple and incessantly modified relationships with the surroundings, the landscape, the calm, the fury, and the caprice of the elements, from natural or artificial lighting, from the prodigiously complex and shaded play of values, from precipitate or retarded movements, such as the slow movements of those galloping horses which seem to me made of living bronze, of those running dogs whose muscular contractions recall the undulations of reptiles. I would point out, too, the profound universe of the microscopic infinite, and perhaps—tomorrow—of the telescopic infinite, the undreamed-of dance of atoms and stars, the shadows under the sea as they begin to be shot with light. I would point out the majestic unity of masses in movement that all this accentuates without insistence, as if it were playing with the grandiose problem that Masaccio,[4] Leonardo, Rembrandt were never quite able to solve. . . . I could never come to the end of it. Shakespeare was once a formless embryo in the narrow shadows of the womb of a good dame of Stratford.

THAT THE starting point of the art of the moving picture is in plastics seems to be beyond all doubt. To whatever form of expression, as yet scarcely suspected, it may lead us, it is by volumes, arabesques, gestures, attitudes, relationships, associations, contrasts, and passages of tones—the whole animated and insensibly modified from one fraction of a second to another—that it will impress our sensibility and act on our intelligence by the intermediation of our eyes. Art, I have called it, not science. It is doubly, even trebly art, for there is conception, composition, creation, and transcription to the screen on the part of three persons, the author, the producer, the photographer, and of a group of persons, the cinemimics, as the actors may properly be called. It would be desirable, and possible, for the author to make his own film pictures, and better still if one of the cinemimics, since he cannot be his own photographer, were to be the composer and producer of the work to which he gives life and which he often transfigures by his genius. This is, of course, just what certain American cinemimics are doing, notably the admirable Charlie Chaplin. It is a moot question whether the author of the cinematographic scenario—I hesitate to create the word cineplast—should be a writer or a painter, whether the cinemimic should be a mimic or an actor. Charlie Chaplin solves all these questions; a new art presupposes a new artist.

A certain literary critic has recently deplored the sacrificing of the theater to the cinema and has bracketed Charlie Chaplin and Rigadin (an actor who was formerly known in the French theater under the name of Dranem) in the same terms of reprobation. This does not mean at all that the critic in question is unequal to his task when he sticks to the field of literature; it means simply that he does not realize the artistic significance of the cinema, nor the difference of quality that necessarily exists between the cinema and the theater and between one film and another. For, with all due respect to this critic, there is a greater distance between Charlie Chaplin and Rigadin than between William Shakespeare and Edmond Rostand. I do not write the name of Shakespeare at random. It answers perfectly to the impression of divine intoxication that Charlie Chaplin gives me, for example, in his film *Sunnyside*; it befits that marvelous art of his, with its mingling of deep melancholy and fantasy, an art that races, increases, decreases and then starts off like a flame again, carrying to each sinuous mountain ridge over which it winds the very essence of the spiritual life of the world, that mysterious light through which we half perceive that our laughter is a triumph over our pitiless insight, that our joy is the feeling of a sure eternity imposed by ourselves upon nothingness, that an elf, a goblin, a gnome dancing in a landscape of Corot, into which the privilege of reverie precipitates him who suffers, bears God himself in his heart.

We must, I think, take our stand on this. Chaplin comes from America, he is the authentic genius of a school that is looming up more and more as the first in importance in cineplastics. I have heard that the Americans greatly enjoy our French films, with their representation of French customs—a fine thing, to be sure, but without the least relation to the effects of motion which are the essential foundation of cinematographic art. The French film, as we know it, is resolutely idealistic. It stands for something like the painting of Ary Scheffer at the time when Delacroix was struggling.[5] The French film is only a bastard form of a degenerate theater and seems for that reason to be destined to poverty and death if it does not take a new turn.

The American film, on the other hand, is a new art, full of immense perspectives, full of the promise of a great future. I imagine that the taste of the Americans for the "damaged goods" that we export to them is to be explained by the well-known attraction that forms of art in a state of decomposition exercise on all primitive peoples. For the Americans are primitive and at the same time barbarous, which accounts for the strength and vitality which they infuse into the cinema. It is among them that the cinema will, I believe, assume its full significance as plastic drama in action, occupying time through its own movement and carrying with it its own space, of a kind that places it, balances it, and gives it the social and psychological value it has for us. It is natural that when a new art appears in the world it should choose a new people which has had hitherto no really personal art. Especially when this new art is bound up, through the medium of human gesture, with the power, definiteness and firmness of action. Especially, too, when this new people is accustomed to introduce into every department of life an increasingly complicated mechanical system, one that more and more hastens to produce, associate, and precipitate movements; and especially when this art cannot exist without the most accurate scientific apparatus of a kind that has behind it no traditions and is organized, as it were, physiologically, with the race that employs it.

Cineplastics, in fact, presents a curious characteristic which music alone, to a far less marked degree, has exhibited hitherto. In cineplastics it is far from being true, as it is in the case of the other arts, that the feeling of the artist creates the art; in cineplastics it is the art that is creating its artists. We know that the great thing we call the symphony was engendered little by little by the number and the increasing complexity of musical instruments; but before even the instrument with one string, man already sang, clapping his hands and stamping his feet; here we had a science first, and nothing but a science. There was required the grandiose imagination of man to introduce into it, at first by a timid infiltration and later by a progressive invasion breaking down all barriers, his power of organizing facts according to his own ideas, so that the scattered objects that surround him are transformed into a coherent edifice, wherein he seeks the fecund and always renewed illusion that his destiny develops in conformity with his will.

Hence come these new plastic poems which transport us in three seconds from the wooded banks of a river that elephants cross, leaving a long track of foam, to the heart of wild mountains where distant horsemen pursue one another through the smoke of their rifle shots, and from evil taverns where powerful shadows bend over a deathbed in mysterious lights to the weird half light of submarine waters where fish wind through grottoes of coral. Indeed—and this comes at unexpected moments, and in comic films as

263

well as in the others—animals may take part in these dramas, and newborn children too, and they participate by their play, their joys, their disappointments, their obscure dramas of instinct, all of which the theater, as it seems to me, is quite incapable of showing us. Landscapes, too, beautiful or tragic or marvelous, enter the moving symphony in order to add to its human meaning, or to introduce into it, after the fashion of a stormy sky by Delacroix or a silver sea by Veronese, the sense of the supernatural.

I have already explained why the Americans have understood, as by instinct, the direction they should give to their visual imagination, letting themselves be guided by their love for space, movement, and action. As for the Italians, they might be reborn to the life of conquest and lose the memory of their classic works, were they to find in their genius for gesture and attitude and for setting (thanks in part to the aid of the wonderful sunshine, which is like the sunshine of California) the elements of another original school, less violent and also less sober, but presenting better qualities of composition than that of the Americans. In the cinema the Italians give us marvelously the crowd, and the historical drama in the motionless setting of palaces, gardens, ruins, where the ardent life that characterizes the Italian people goes on, with the quality which is theirs of never appearing out of time or out of place. A gesticulating drama it may be, but the gestures are true. The Italian gesture has been called theatrical; but it is not that, for it is sincere. Giotto's personages are not acting. If that is the impression we get from Bolognese painting, it is because the Bolognese no longer represented the real genius of Italy. Rembrandt, up to the age of forty-five, and Rubens are far more theatrical than all the Italian masters down to the painters of Bologna. Italian energy alone will render the Italian school of cineplastics capable of maintaining, in this new art in which the Americans already excel, the plastic genius of Europe—and that by creating a form that is destined to have a great future.

In any case, the chief triumph in the American conception of cineplastics—a triumph which the Italians approach most nearly and the French approach, alas, most remotely—seems to me to consist in this: that the subject is nothing but a pretext. The web of feeling should be nothing but the skeleton of the autonomous organism represented by the film. In time this web must be woven into the plastic drama. It is evident that this drama will be the more moving in proportion as the moral and psychological pattern that it covers is strongly, soberly and logically conducted. But that is all. The expression and the effects of that drama remain in the domain of plastics; and the web of feeling is there only to reveal and increase their value.

SHALL I dare to dream of a future for the art of the moving picture, a future distant no doubt, when the actor, or, as I would prefer to call him, the cine-mimic, shall disappear or at least be specialized, and when the cineplast shall dominate the drama of form that is precipitated in time? Observe, in the first place, one vital point that hitherto has not been sufficiently noted, I think, or at least the poetic consequences of which have not been made sufficiently clear. The cinema incorporates time in space. More than this, through the cinema time really becomes a dimension of space. We shall be able to see dust rising, spreading, dissipating, a thousand years after it has spurted up from the road under the hoofs of a horse; we shall be able to see for a thousand years the smoke of a cigarette condensing and then entering the ether—and this in a frame of space under our very eyes. We shall be able to understand how it may be that the inhabitants of a distant star, if they can see things on earth with powerful telescopes, are really contemporaries of Jesus, since at the moment when I write these lines they may be witnessing his crucifixion, and perhaps making a photographic or even cinematographic record of the scene, for we know that the light that illumines us takes nineteen or twenty centuries to reach them. We can even imagine, and this may modify still more our idea of the duration of time, that we may one day see this film, taken on that distant star, either through the inhabitants sending it to us in some sort of projectile or perhaps transmitting it to our screens by some system of interplanetary projection. This, which is not scientifically impossible, would actually make us the contemporaries of events which took place a hundred centuries before us, and in the very place wherein we live.

In the cinema we have indeed already made of time an instrument that plays its role in the whole spatial organism, unfurling under our eyes its successive masses which are ceaselessly brought before us in dimensions that permit us to grasp their extent in surface area and in depth. Already we find in these masses pleasures of an intensity unknown hitherto. Stop the most beautiful film you know, make of it at any moment an inert photograph, and you will not obtain even a memory of the emotion that it gave you as a moving picture.

Thus, in the cinema, time clearly becomes necessary for us. Increasingly it forms a part of the always more dynamic idea that we are receiving about the object upon which we are gazing. We play with it at our ease. We can speed it up. We can slow it down. We can suppress it. Indeed I feel it as being part of myself, as enclosed alive, with the very space which it measures and which measures it, within the walls of my brain. Homer becomes my contemporary, as my lamp upon my table before me is my contemporary, since Homer had his share in the elaboration of the image under

265

which my lamp appears to me. Since the idea of duration enters the idea of space as a constituent element, we may easily imagine an expanded cineplastic art which shall be no more than an architecture of the idea, and from which the cinemimic will, as I have said, disappear, because only a great artist will be able to build edifices that are made and broken down and remade ceaselessly—by imperceptible passages of tone and modeling that are in themselves architecture at every moment—without our being able to seize the thousandth part of a second in which the transition takes place.

I remember witnessing something analogous to this in nature itself. At Naples, in 1906, I saw the great eruption of Vesuvius. The plume of smoke, two thousand meters high, that rose above the mouth of the volcano was spherical, outlined against the sky and sharply separated from it. Inside this cloud, enormous masses of ashes assumed form and became formless unceasingly, all sharing in the modeling of the great sphere and producing an undulation on its surface, moving and varying, but sustained, as if by an attraction at the center, in the general mass, the form and dimension of which nothing appeared to alter. In a flash it seemed to me, as I looked upon the phenomenon, that I had grasped the law of the birth of planets, held by gravitation around the solar nucleus. It seemed to me that I was looking at a symbolic form of that grandiose art of which in the cinema we now perceive the germ, the development of which the future doubtless holds in store for us, namely a great moving construction ceaselessly reborn of itself under our eyes by virtue of its inner forces alone. Human, animal, vegetable, and inert forms, in all their immense variety, have their share in the building of it, whether a multitude is employed on the work or whether only one man is able to realize it in its totality.

Perhaps I may explain myself further on this last point. We all know those animated drawings, very dry and thin and stiff, which are sometimes projected on the screen and are, when compared with the forms that I have been imagining, what the outlines in chalk traced on a blackboard by a child are to the frescoes of Tintoretto and the canvases of Rembrandt. Now let us suppose three or four generations devoted to the problem of giving depth to these images, not by surfaces and lines but by thickness and volumes; three or four generations devoted to modeling, by values and halftones, a series of successive movements which after a long training would gradually enter into our habits, even into our unconscious actions, till the artist was enabled to use them at will, for drama or idyll, comedy or epic, in the light or in the shadow, in the forest, the city, or the desert. Suppose that an artist thus armed has the heart of a Delacroix, the power of realization of a Rubens, the passion of a Goya, and the strength of a Michelangelo; he will throw on the screen a cineplastic tragedy that has come out of his whole nature, a sort of visual symphony as rich and as complex as the sonorous symphonies of the great musicians and revealing, by its precipitation in time, perspectives of infinitude and of the absolute as exalting by reason of their mystery and more moving, because of their reality for the senses, than the symphonies of the greatest of the musicians.

There is the distant future in which I believe, but of which the full realization is beyond my power of imagining. While we await the coming of the cineplast, who is as yet in the shadows of the background, there are today some admirable cinemimics and at least one cinemimic of genius, who are showing us the promise of that collective spectacle which will take the place of the religious dance that is dead and of the philosophic tragedy that is dead and of the mystery play that is dead—indeed of all the great dead things around which the multitude once assembled in order to commune together in the joy that has been brought to birth in the hearts of the people by the mastery over pessimism achieved by the poets and the dancers.

I am not a prophet, I cannot tell what will have become in a hundred years of the admirable creations of the imagination of a being, a cinemimic, who, alone among living things, has the privilege of knowing that though his destiny is without hope, he is yet the only being to live and think as if he had the power to take to himself eternity. Yet it seems to me that I already see what the art of that cinemimic may presume to become if, instead of permitting itself to be dragged by theatrical processes through a desolating sentimental fiction, it is able to concentrate itself on plastic processes, around a sensuous and passionate action in which we can all recognize our own personal virtues.

In every land, mankind is attempting to escape from a form of civilization which, through an excess of individualism, has become impulsive and anarchic, and we are seeking to enter a form of plastic civilization that is, undoubtedly, destined to substitute for analytic studies of states and crises of the soul, synthetic poems of masses and great ensembles in action. I imagine that architecture will be the principal expression of this civilization, an architecture whose appearance may be difficult to define; perhaps it will be the industrial construction of our means of travel—ships, trains, automobiles, and airplanes—for which ports, docks, pontoons, and giant cupolas will be the places of rest and relay. Cineplastics will doubtless be the spiritual ornament sought for in this period—the play that this new society will find most useful in developing in the crowd the sense of confidence, of harmony, of cohesion.

ELIE FAURE (1873–1937) was trained as a medical doctor but became well known as an art historian, biographer, and critic. His celebrated *Histoire d'art* was published originally in four volumes between 1909 and 1921, and then released in a revised edition of four volumes in 1924.

[1] Louis David (1748–1825) was the leader of the French Neo-Classical school of painting under Napoleon in the early nineteenth century.

[2] May I be permitted in passing to form a wish? It is that smoking be forbidden in cinema halls, as talking is forbidden in concert halls. At the end of an hour, the atmosphere is saturated with smoke. The finest films are clouded, lose their transparency and their quality, in both tone and overtone.—AU.

[3] The reference is to the black American jazz bands and orchestras that became very popular in Paris after the war.

[4] Masaccio was an Italian painter of considerable influence in Florence in the fifteenth century.

[5] Ary Scheffer (1795–1858) became a celebrated French academic painter while Eugène Delacroix (1798–1863) struggled as a leader of the French Romantic school.

LIONEL LANDRY, "Caligarism or the Theater's Revenge"

Translated by Stuart Liebman from "Caligarisme ou la revanche du théâtre," *Cinéa* 51 (28 April 1922), 12.

EVEN AS Robert Wiene's very remarkable film was being shown to us, I already guessed that the madman through whose eyes we were supposed to see the world was only a pretext. In an article—much discussed—in *Cinémagazine*, M. Emile Vuillermoz[1] and, more recently, the director himself have let the cat out of the bag and proclaimed the sole import of the method. "The contrivance of a lunatic's tale," M. Vuillermoz declares, "is only a limited and discreet subterfuge to develop a new aesthetic while minimizing the risks."

At first, one is shocked. Because if, in the final analysis, the decisions made by Robert Wiene seem so successfully to convey an idea of the world a madman is capable of conceiving, it seems illogical that it [Wiene's approach] can be used to present a rational person's conception of the world.

I know very well that I am no longer up to date and there are no more sane people. Freud and M. Lenormand have covered all this; we are all madmen in one way or another; novels, plays, and films constitute little more than phases of someone's morbid psychology.[2] Still, one must admit that our madness assumes diverse forms. Some are intellectual, some are auditory, and others are fictive. All are not necessarily Cubist (*Caligari*, moreover, does not belong to the Cubist realm, but rather to some universe conceived according to the geometry of Riemann,[3] and characterized by the impossibility of drawing two parallel lines. In passing, it is remarkable to note the influence that the popularization of the new geometric and mechanical theories has had on the arts. Anyone who appeals to the fourth dimension is no Dadaist, and the bewildering vertiginousness of hyperspace is a new hashish that overturns all aesthetic principles).

Whatever the case may be, enthusiasm [for *Caligari*] is intense. M. Vuillermoz speaks about *Caligari* the way Théophile Gautier did about *Hernani*,[4] and the most talked-about filmmakers demonstrate their approval by imitating it—a more discreet but no less sincere kind of praise.

Everybody [does]—or nearly everybody (the exception is Louis Delluc, and considering the date, it is remarkable that his *Femme de nulle part* should be free of Caligarism when Griffith and L'Herbier have succumbed to the temptation. To include the latter is perhaps wrong, for the optical distortions he experimented with in *El Dorado* seem to me more consistent with the genius of cinema and more fruitful because they allow for *transitions* to the undistorted views). This is simply because such a method more readily provides the artist with the illusion that he can control nature.

Nature, alive and authentic, imposes itself upon man. Man tries to attach himself to it; he still needs to believe that in its vastness he counts for something. The most heart-rending scene does not benefit at all by being shot in front of Niagara Falls. A Sjöstrom, a Griffith can evoke mighty landscapes such as those in *The Outlaw and His Wife* or the breaking up of the ice in *Way Down East*; an ordinary filmmaker would do well to be more modest. (What remains of *L'Atlantide* aside from the desert?)

If, on the other hand, nature is done away with and replaced by an image that can be distorted to suit one's taste, the filmmaker will rediscover the means to reaffirm his personality. And it is so economical! Gone are the costly trips, the caravans in search of a site, the waiting for a favorable sunlight! As M. Vuillermoz indicates, ". . . canvas, cardboard, brushes, and creative imagination are all that are needed to construct an ideal world far richer than the real world, an interpreted world, transformed, intelligent and sentient, a world that thinks, dreams, and suffers like the men who inhabit it, a nature that reflects, prolongs, and magnifies the character's feelings . . ."

Unfortunately for such creations the creative imagination—that is, genius—is also as indispensable as canvas and brushes.

Unfortunately, it [genius] is much more rare. And genius needs no new recipe to manifest itself. If imagination proceeds not by using plastic distortion but by basing composition on psychology it may arrive at results every bit as striking. And with this latter approach, if genius is lacking, one is free to watch the landscapes which in themselves are inoffensive to the degree that expressionism is absent. I know very well that when, tomorrow or the day after, all products begin to be Caligarized, M. Vuillermoz will not go to screenings to see the results. But I will go, and I've already begun to suffer.

And meanwhile, while awaiting all this, the theater laughs into its white (because it is very old) beard . . .

"You are coming back to sets, to struts, and to painted canvases. What was the use of making a tour of the world to conjure the magic of Tokyo and Vancouver, the North Pole, and Cape Horn on screen to end up here! Now, you have grown wiser and you ask for my advice . . . You need only abandon all pretense and once again assume your rightful place. You, a seventh art! Sixth and a half is more like it. When it [the cinema] was based on photography, when it utilized the natural sets that I could not, when it had the whole world at its disposal, the cinema constituted an autonomous art. When all this is replaced by a set, and it is reduced to showing—without color and voices—what takes place on stage in front of an essentially realistic or symbolic painting inspired by Reinhardt, Pitoeff, Gordon Craig—or Jusseaume—what element does it possess that is its own? It is only an economical method for reproducing a pantomime . . .

"You think you are justified in denouncing the error that Antoine committed when he attempted to create realist staging in the theater. How much you have remained men of the theater! To prohibit a practice to the cinema because it is opposed to the aesthetics of the stage, is to demonstrate that you do not understand the differences between the two art forms. Precisely because the Americans were not men of the theater and lived very close to nature, they endowed the cinema with a new aesthetic. It is interesting to observe that the reaction against this aesthetic comes from Germany, ever theatrical and affected, and from France whose art, however rich or profound it may be, always seems cloistered, a salon art, and art deriving from the cabaret or the wings.

"Let those who are in truth my little children return unto me! Here are some sets to paint, some scenes to compose in the studio—just like on stage. When the audience tires of seeing the same thing on both sides of the street, someone will remember that the cinema, as opposed to the theater, can show us real trees, real waterfalls, and real flowers, and they will present a film conceived according to these new ideas, and their resounding success will create imitators . . ."

Like all old people, the theater has a tendency to speak at great length. I did not listen any further . . .

[1] Emile Vuillermoz, *"Le Cabinet du Docteur Caligari,"* *Cinèmagazine* 2 (24 March 1922), 353–54.

[2] The reference is probably to the minor French playwright, Henri René Lenormand (1882–1951).

[3] The reference is to the German mathematician, Georg Friederich Bernhard Riemann (1825–1866), some of whose geometry problems became textbook classics.

[4] The reference is to Théophile Gautier's detailed description of the opening night performance of Victor Hugo's famous drama, *Hernani* (1830), which he wrote and published just before he died in 1872. It was reprinted in Gautier's *Histoire du romanticisme* (Paris: Librairie des bibliophiles, Flammarion, 1929), 85–92.

BLAISE CENDRARS, "On *The Cabinet of Doctor Caligari*"

Translated by Stuart Liebman from "Sur *Le Cabinet du Docteur Caligari*," *Cinéa*, 56 (2 June 1922), 11. An earlier translation of Cendrars's essay appeared in *Broom*, 2 (July 1922), 351.

I DO NOT LIKE this film. Why?
Because it is a film based on a misunderstanding.
Because it is a film which does a disservice to all modern art.
Because it is a hybrid film, hysterical and pernicious.
Because it is not cinematic.
A film based on a misunderstanding because it is a sham produced in bad faith.
It heaps discredit on all modern art because the subject of modern painters (Cubism) is not the hypersensibility of a madman, but rather equilibrium, tension, and mental geometry.
Hybrid, hysterical, pernicious because it is hybrid, hysterical, and pernicious. (Long live cowboys!)
It is not cinema because:
1. The pictorial distortions are only gimmicks (a new modern convention);
2. Real characters are in an unreal set (meaningless);
3. The distortions are not optical and do not depend either on the camera angle or the lens or the diaphragm or the focus;
4. There is never any unity;
5. It is theatrical;
6. There is movement but no rhythm;
7. There is not a single refinement of the director's craft; all the effects are obtained with the help of means belonging to painting, music, literature, etc. Nowhere does one see [the contribution of] the camera;
8. It is sentimental and not visual;
9. It has nice pictures, good lighting effects, superb actors;
10. It does excellent business.

FERNAND LÉGER, "*La Roue*: Its Plastic Quality"

Translated by Alexandra Anderson as "A Critical Essay on the Plastic Quality of Abel Gance's Film, *The Wheel*," in *Functions of Painting*, ed. Edward F. Fry (New York: Viking, 1973), 20–23. Reprinted by permission. The original French text first appeared as "*La Roue*: Sa valeur plastique," in *Comoedia* (16 December 1922), 5.

ABEL GANCE'S film involves three states of interest that continually alternate: a dramatic state, an emotional state, and a plastic state. It is this entirely new plastic contribution whose real value and implications for our time I shall struggle to define precisely.

The first two states are developed throughout the whole drama with mounting interest. The third, the one that concerns me, occurs almost exclusively in the first three sections, where the mechanical element plays a major role, and where the machine becomes *the leading character, the leading actor*. It will be to Abel Gance's honor that he has successfully presented an *actor object* to the public. This is a cinematographic event of considerable importance, which I am going to examine carefully.

This new element is presented to us through an infinite variety of methods, from every aspect: close-ups, fixed or moving mechanical fragments, projected at a heightened speed that approaches the state of simultaneity and that crushes and eliminates the human object, reduces its interest, pulverizes it. *This mechanical element* that you reluctantly watch disappear, that you wait for impatiently, is unobtrusive; it appears like flashes of a spotlight throughout a vast, long heartrending tragedy whose realism admits no concessions. The plastic event is no less there because of it, it's nowhere else; it is planned, fitted in with care, appropriate, and seems to me to be laden with implications in itself and for the the future.

The advent of this film is additionally interesting in that is is going to determine a place in the plastic order for an art that has until now remained almost completely descriptive, sentimental, and documentary. The fragmentation of the object, the intrinsic plastic value of the object, its pictorial equivalence, have long been the domain of the modern arts. With *The Wheel* [*La Roue*] Abel Gance has elevated the art of film to the plane of the plastic arts.

Before *The Wheel* the cinematographic art developed almost constantly on a mistaken path: that of resemblance to the theater, the same means, the same actors, the same dramatic methods. It seems to want to turn into theater. This is the most serious error the cinematographic art could commit; it is the facile viewpoint, the art of imitation, the imitator's viewpoint.

The justification for film, its only one, is *the projected image*. This image that, colored, but unmoving, captures children and adults alike—and now it moves. The moving image was created, and the whole world is on its knees before that marvelous image that moves. But observe that this stupendous invention does not consist in imitating the movements of nature; it's a matter of something entirely different; it's a matter of *making images seen*, and the cinema must not look elsewhere for its reason for being. Project your beautiful image, choose it well, define it, put it under the microscope, do everything to make it yield up its maximum, and you will have no need for text, description, perspective, sentimentality, or actors.

Whether it be the infinite realism of the close-up, or pure inventive fantasy (Simultaneous poetry through the moving image), the new event is there with all its implications.

Until now America has been able to create a picturesque cinematographic fact: film intensity, cowboy plays, Douglas [Fairbanks], Chaplin's comic genius, but there we are still beside the point. It is still the theatrical concept, that is, the actor dominating and the whole production dependent on him. The cinema cannot fight the theater; the dramatic effect of a living person, speaking with emotion, cannot be equaled by its direct, silent projection in black and white on a screen. The film is beaten in advance; it will always be bad theater. Now let us consider only the visual point of view. Where is it in all of this?

Here it is: 80 percent of the clients and objects that help us to live are only noticed by us in our everyday lives, while 20 percent are *seen*. From this, I deduce the cinematographic revolution is *to make us see everything that has been merely noticed*. Project those brand-new elements, and you have your tragedies, your comedies, on a plane that is uniquely visual and cinematographic. The dog that goes by in the street is only noticed. Projected on the screen, it is seen, so much so that the whole audience reacts as if it discovered the dog.

The mere fact of projection of the image already defines the object, which becomes spectacle. A judiciously composed image already has value through this fact. Don't abandon this point of view. Here is the pivot, the basis of this new art. Abel Gance has sensed it perfectly. He has achieved it, he is the first to have presented it to the public. You will see moving images presented like a picture, centered on the screen with a judicious range in the balance of still and moving parts (the contrast of effects); a still figure on a machine that is moving, a modulated hand in contrast to a geometric mass, circular forms, abstract forms, the interplay of curves and straight lines (contrasts of lines), dazzling, wonderful, a moving geometry that astonishes you.

Gance goes further, since his marvelous machine is able to produce the fragment of the object. He gives it to you in place of that actor whom you have *noticed* somewhere and who moved you by his delivery and his gestures. He is going to make you *see* and move you in turn with the face of this phantom whom you have no more than *noticed* before. You will see his eye, his hand, his finger, his fingernail. Gance will make you see all this with his prodigious blazing lantern. You will see all those fragments magnified a hundred times, making up an absolute whole, tragic, comic, plastic, more moving, more captivating than the character in the theater next door. The locomotive will appear with all its parts: its wheels, its rods, its signal plates, its geometric pleasures, vertical and horizontal, and the for-

273

midable faces of the men who live on it. A nut bent out of shape next to a rose will evoke for you the tragedy of *The Wheel* (contrasts).

In rare moments scattered among various films, one has been able to have the confused feeling that there must be the truth. With *The Wheel* Gance has completely achieved *cinematographic fact*. Visual fragments collaborate closely with the actor and the drama, reinforce them, sustain them, instead of dissipating their effect, thanks to its *masterful composition*. Gance is a precursor and a fulfillment at the same time. His drama is going to mark an epoch in the history of cinema. His relationship is first of all a technical one. He absorbs objects and actors; he never submits to means that ought not to be confused with the desired end. In that above all his superiority over the American contribution resides. The latter, picturesque and theatrical in quality, in bondage to some talented stars, will fade as the actors fade. The art of *The Wheel* will remain, armed with its new technique, and it will dominate cinematographic art in the present and in the future.

FERNAND LÉGER (1881–1955) was a French painter initially aligned with the Cubists, whose work came under the influence of the "Purist" movement after the war. But Léger also became involved in attempts to produce a synthesis of the arts as a popular spectacle—for example, the ballet dramas *Parade* (1917) and *Skating Rink* (1922), L'Herbier's film *L'In-humaine* (1924), and his own *Ballet mécanique* (1924).

EMILE VUILLERMOZ, *"La Roue"*

From *"La Roue," Cinémagazine* 3 (23 February 1923), 329–31, and (2 March 1923), 363–65.

ABEL GANCE'S latest film establishes once again that even though the cinema is silent, filmmakers are not chary with words. *La Roue* has provoked numerous discussions and debates, and the hubbub shows no sign of abating. The release of this majestic work does not, however, raise complex problems, rather it highlights—and in huge close-ups even—several elementary questions on which, it seems, everyone can easily agree.

In *La Roue,* Abel Gance has spun out an incalculable number of symbols, some of which are magnificently beautiful and poetic. One can also spin out another: *La Roue* is the very image of cinema, that is, a machine that is steadily revolving and yet seems to be revolving in place. The film industry is a prisoner of this gyrating motion which forces it to follow the same circle forever, to commit the same mistakes, and to fall into the same errors. Never has this elementary truth been demonstrated so obviously as in this splendid work which I intend to examine.

La Roue proves several things. First, that the current commercial formula of cinema exhibition is absurd and dangerous, and, second, that its usual dramatic formula is no less so. Now, producers, distributors, and authors should not protest such a peremptory assertion; it constitutes a defense and not an attack. In treating the current state of affairs so harshly, I mean to serve their interests.

La Roue contains all the elements of a masterpiece, but the "iron law of supply and demand" which governs the relations between producer and consumer in the cinema is so overwhelming that it can destroy the most splendid efforts.

There is no doubt that Abel Gance possesses cinematic genius. He was born to speak the silent language of moving images. He is one of the coming generation that thinks spontaneously in lifelike visions. As a young and essentially modern art, the cinema can only find its true creators among the younger generation. Up to now, older filmmakers were content to adapt their theatrical or fictional techniques to the screen, but rarely did they stumble upon the true eloquence of images. It's the current generation alone, trained in the schools of the Tenth Muse ever since childhood, that can discover the new techniques which are essential to this new art.

Several men have an inkling of that art: Griffith in America and Gance here. Yet they are faced with a commercial and industrial set of regulations poorly suited to this new ideal. Besides, both are still entangled in the manifold traditions of print fiction and stage plays.

Let me repeat what I have said before. Gance is a genius who is lacking in talent. The scenario of *La Roue* calls for the harshest criticism. Here again, we have witnessed the triumph of the most lamentable presumptions. Abel Gance—this inspired poet and powerful visionary—has conceived a romantic adventure story of the most mediocre kind, undoubtedly in obedience to the old filmmakers' catechism of perseverance.

Evidently because they told him the mass public insisted on it, he introduced several ridiculous puppets into his story, music hall characters whose buffoonery is in such bad taste. Likewise, in order ultimately to please an American clientele, he was forced to bring his melodrama to a climax with an unlikely fist fight between the son of a mechanic and the chief engineer of the PLM company. According to the same rules of prudent international distribution, he conferred the role of a young working-class woman, French by education, to an English actress who, although charming, distorted the character by performing in a resolutely American manner.

Most of Abel Gance's errors have a commercial or industrial rationale. Separately, any one detail may be absurd, which even the company men recognize; but they argue that it was necessary at the time for one or another better reasons. An art which has so many better reasons to be absurd finds itself in a dangerous situation.

In the cinema, they screen rushes incessantly; everything is solved by arithmetic formulas. The arena of the calculator, however, could use some dancers. By cutting everything according to the supreme wisdom of numbers, they produce deplorable results.

The other arts don't operate under a regime of patronage. A publisher of music or literature, a gallery owner of painting or sculpture is no more disinterested than a producer of films; he obviously intends to make money from the works of art which have been given over to his care. In order to achieve this goal, however, he doesn't believe that authors are required to submit to such servile rules, to such rigid formulas of exhibition. He knows that a masterpiece needs a certain degree of freedom in order to establish and extend its power effectively. He also knows that the public will follow.

The film producer adopts an opposite point of view. He claims to guide the masses and to determine in advance what will please them and what will not. He believes in his infallible receipts and indisputable axioms. He is unaware that in the other arts technique is constantly being renewed and that what is right today may be wrong tomorrow. Because he lacks the courage and wisdom to escape routines like this, Abel Gance's triumph is a tattered triumph. The first-rate moments of beauty which abound in this film are too often drowned in a torrent of dramatic, theatrical, and commercial preconceptions that continue to run rampant through studios everywhere.

They say that Abel Gance's film has cost three million francs. They could only recuperate this sum, it seems, by transforming an excellent production of 2,000 meters into a vast expanse measuring 10,000 meters. For it's a fact that cinematic beauty is sold by the pound and that in the cinema the genius of an author can only be measured with the aid of a surveyor's chain. That's where we are led by the obstinacy of our film distributors who refuse to abandon their demagogic ideas.

All these reflections, which the ardent devotees of *La Roue* will perhaps read with impatience, have been dictated by the most sincere admiration for an artist whose best effort I am saddened to see go to waste, falling as it does between two stools. In the cinema, as elsewhere, one has to choose. It's childish to want to please everyone. Yet Abel Gance is becoming used to doing that. The weakness and banality of his dramaturgy is discouraging to artists and literate people. And his artistic discoveries deeply shock the ignorant, who have been raised in the school of serial novels. An excess of prudence has led to a fatal dose of doubled imprudence.

One has to choose: the wheel is revolving, and two paths are open before it. For the switchman there is a decision to make. One movement of the lever will determine the destiny of the work.

On the right is an assured, mathematical, popular success—in a prologue and six episodes—with the crass melodrama of the engine driver Sisif who loves his adopted daughter and is a rival to his son and the chief engineer, with its theatrical effects, its catastrophes, its melodramatic villains, its derailments, its fist fights, its circus interludes, and its themes of romance.

On the left is the conquest of the elite—a difficult, uncertain, heroic quest, requiring arduous battles, for the adversaries of the cinema are still numerous and stubborn. But who can resist the eloquence of those wonderful notes which capture all the secret beauty of daily life, of a trembling and vibrant life that we know not how to see and whose innumerable facets a "seer" of genius illuminates and highlights for us.

In the first case, one has to excise several hundred meters of film in which glimmers a poetry that is inaccessible for the time being to the serial customers. One has to remove from the action what is the personal contribution of Abel Gance, what an authoritative spokesman for this special public has so characteristically called "the appearance of diverse mechanical instruments," whose tactless intervention slows the exciting story. We are all agreed, it seems, that a locomotive possesses wheels, rods, and a smokestack and that it obeys signals. In order for us to understand that we are going to live in a railway environment, it is enough that a smart express train pass before our eyes and the question will be answered once and for all. Everything else is merely padding and lost time.

ON THE OTHER hand, if one wants to amaze the artists, one has to eliminate the fictional elements which take up so much space, get rid of the clowns, and preserve only the two essential themes of this symphony of black and white, which begins in the tragic gloom of charcoal dust and smoke and ends in the purity and assuaging calm of eternal snows. One has to preserve only a slim plot thread from one end to the other in order to connect the splendid tableaux in which the beauty of things is revealed. Here this beauty takes on an unfamiliar, extraordinary stirring quality.

Abel Gance knows how to see and make others see. Daily, unquestioningly, a blind humanity traverses a fairyland whose astonishing exhilaration it does not even suspect. We are too accustomed to the appearance of things. With our naive arrogance as the kings of creation, we have become habituated to imposing an anthropocentric view on the whole universe. Currently, we practice the naive finalism of Bernard de Saint-Pierre; we will end by seeing in things only the artificial and often arbitrary function that our own egotism claims to see there.

One of the first cinematic discoveries consisted of bringing this soul of things to light, something the theater could not begin to externalize. The screen showed us that things were capable of seeing, thinking, suffering.

It was a first step. It was the basis of the technique ironically called "expressive *natures mortes.*"

Naturally, they soon abused the technique: the least flower, the least trinket on a shelf, the simplest chair was used to convey something about psychology. In madly praising Abel Gance for having learned how to unveil the soul of things, one is merely paying him a rather banal compliment. His principal merit does not consist of showing us a disc plate equipped with a human face, a semaphore that makes a commanding arm gesture, or a locomotive whose whistles express articulate cries. Every film-maker now recognizes these recipes, this elementary symbolism, for whatever kind of dish is needed. The discoveries of Abel Gance are of a more subtle and profound kind. He teaches us to see not just the soul but the true face of things, he forces us to reeducate our eyes; he unmasks the scattered beauty all around us, by emphasizing and exalting it without distortion.

Certainly, the most beautiful, moving, and original parts of his film are the experimental study of a mechanical fairyland, from drive-rod traction to hissing steam, and the description of the supernatural magic of snowy landscapes. He has learned how to analyze the hallucinatory beauty of speed, the drunken frenzy of the wheels' intelligent labor, the steel rods and gear wheels, the great stirring voice of organisms made of sheet iron, copper, and steel. His "Song of the Wheel" and "Song of the Rails" are visual scores of unforgettable power and beauty. The man who has learned how to gather up such thrilling songs out of mere matter is indeed a great poet.

Like all poets, sometimes he lets himself be drawn into certain imbalances of composition.

Living in the midst of elevated symbols and magnificent allegories, he too easily lets himself be drawn into translating his characters into tones and chords. In the same exalted spirit, one can reproach his mechanic Sisif for being a superman, when he would have touched us even more had he consented simply to be a man.

The talent of Séverin-Mars, which does not always avoid a melodramatic accent or a theatrical exaggeration, only accentuates this tendency. There is a bit of overindulgence in the creator's conception and realization. Confronted with a nature and atmosphere which are so true and genuine, Abel Gance's characters appear slightly conventional.

But these reservations must not make us forget that, with *La Roue*, we find ourselves in the presence of a work of exceptional quality. This work is actually being pulled apart in four different directions, by exhibitors, publicity agents, tactless friends, and genuine artists. It is suffering the fate of Orpheus, who was torn apart by the bacchantes; but, like Orpheus, it will survive the punishment.

We must have a reshaped and tightened version of *La Roue*, relieved of the slight imperfections which have been imposed on it by circumstances.[1] All the elements of a masterpiece exist in this composition. It's perhaps the first time that a cinegraphic production has contained such pleasing and persuasive treasures. All those who love the cinema and have confidence in its future must lay claim to this "artistic model" in the work of Abel Gance.

For, if there have been more refined, more delicate, more ingenious works before this, I cannot remember ever having contemplated a production as clearsighted as it is powerful, in an exclusively cinegraphic style. *La Roue* will make those who are still unsuspecting now understand the prodigious future of this art form of moving images. Later they will come to see that *La Roue* was a prophecy. Why are we not immediately attempting to comprehend the broad range of its advance?

[1] A reedited 4,200 meter version of *La Roue* did premiere at the Colisée cinema in February 1924.

RENÉ CLAIR, *"La Roue"*

Translated by Stanley Appelbaum in *Cinema Yesterday and Today*, ed. R. C. Dale (New York: Dover, 1972), 97–98. Reprinted by permission. The original French text first appeared as "Les Films du mois: *La Roue*," *Théâtre et Comoedia illustré* (March 1923).

*L*a Roue is the archetype of the film that is Romantic in spirit. Just as in a Romantic drama, you will find in M. Abel Gance's film improbable situations, a superficial psychology, a constant attempt to achieve visual effects—and verbal effects as well—and you will find extraordinary lyrical passages and inspired moments of movement, one could even say, the sublime and the grotesque.[1]

Given a drama so obviously "thought out," so carefully stuffed with literary ideas and ambitions, it is tempting to debate these with the author. No need to bother. If a screenplay ought to be merely a pretext, here it is a cumbersome pretext, sometimes annoying, rarely necessary, but in any case not deserving of lengthy consideration. It is hardly unusual that, like most filmmakers, M. Gance has made a mistake as a screenplay writer, even if the mistake is more serious at times than we are accustomed to. If we were asked to judge M. Gance by the psychological intentions he expresses on the screen and by the titles he writes, I have to admit that my judgment would not be in his favor. But right now we are concerned with cinema.

As I see it, the real subject of the film is not its odd story, but a train, tracks, signals, puffs of steam, a mountain, snow, clouds. From these great visual themes that dominate his film, M. Gance has drawn splendid sequences. We had, of course, seen trains before moving along tracks at a velocity heightened by the obliging movie camera; but we had not been completely absorbed—orchestra, seats, auditorium, and everything around us—by the screen as if by a whirlpool. "That's only a feeling," you will tell me. Maybe. But we had not gone there to think. To see and feel is enough. Fifty years from now you can talk to me again about the cinema of ideas. This unforgettable passage is not the only one that testifies to M. Gance's talents. The catastrophe at the beginning of the film, the first accident Sisif tries to cause, the ascent of the cable car into the mountains, the death of Elie, the bringing down of his body, the circular dance of the mountaineers, and that grandoise ending amidst veils of cloud: those are sublime lyrical compositions that owe nothing to the other arts. Seeing them, we forget the quotations from Kipling, Aeschylus, and Abel Gance throughout the film, which tend to discourage us. And we start to hope.

Oh, if M. Abel Gance would only give up making locomotives say yes and no, lending a railroad engineer the thoughts of a hero of antiquity, and quoting his favorite authors! If he were willing to create a pure *documentary*, since he knows how to give life to a machine part, a hand, a branch, a wisp of smoke! If only he were willing to contribute in that way to the creation of the Film that can barely be glimpsed today!

Oh, if he were willing to give up literature and place his trust in the cinema! . . .

RENÉ CLAIR (1898–1981) was a young journalist and actor—for instance, in Feuillade's *L'Orpheline* (1921) and *Parisette* (1922). In 1922, he worked as an assistant director to Jacques de Baroncelli; a year later he was making his first film, *Paris qui dort* (1924).

[1] Victor Hugo's theory of the sublime and the grotesque, enunciated in his dramatic manifesto, *The Preface to Cromwell* (1827), became one of the French Romantics' main themes. Clair here uses the term ironically to describe Gance's ups and downs, rather than in an accurate historical way. [Note by R. C. Dale]

LÉON MOUSSINAC, "On Cinegraphic Rhythm"

From "Du rythme cinégraphique," *Le Crapouillot* (March 1923), 9–11.

IF, IN A FILM, the images have to possess a particular beauty and value in and of themselves, beyond their significance in relation to the whole, this beauty and value can be singularly diminished or increased according to the role those images are given in time, that is, the order in which they succeed one another.

For example, it's evident that if they projected, all by itself, the image in *El Dorado* where Marcel L'Herbier shows his heroine walking along the high, angled wall of the Alhambra, even if we were told of its emotional significance within the whole, we would only be struck by the quality of its "lay out" and photographic deformation; by no means would we be jolted by the realization which makes its beauty so profound when we discover *its placement* in the film.

Rhythm exists, therefore, not only within the image itself but in the succession of images. In fact, cinegraphic rhythm owes the greater part of its power to such external rhythm, and its sensation is so strong that certain cinegraphists—those who have scarcely studied it, however—search for it in ignorance. To edit a film is nothing more than to give it rhythm. For when you know in general how the montage is executed, it is hardly astonishing to realize that the images in certain films can lose 50 percent to 75 percent of their specific value.

Few have understood that giving rhythm to a film is as important as giving rhythm to the image, that the decoupage and the montage, otherwise called the idea and its visualization, are as essential as the mise-en-scène. It is no less curious that no one yet has tried to encompass this rhythm in certain mathematical relations, in a kind of measure, for practical use at the time of the scenario's construction—after all, these relations seem easy to determine since the value of the image and that of the film can be represented in time or space through figures or numbers.

If the cinema, as a plastic art of space, derives part of its beauty from the *arrangement* and *form* of the individual images, one must not forget that, as an art of time (since the parts of the whole are successive), it derives the complement of its beauty from the *expression* of the images. In that, it shares in the characteristics of all the other arts and, as the last arrival, seems called to assume first place. Yet even this expression, as we are coming to see, must depend for the greater part of its power on the placement and duration of the image within the context of the whole. Thus the cinema must be a veritable orchestration of images and rhythm.

In summary, the elements which determine the proper value of the movement of each image ought to be found in the meaning or feeling provided by the subject or theme of the scenario, which is itself expressed through representation, and in which the acting, lighting, and decors combine into what is rightly called, in one word, mise-en-scène. But the particular quality which finally determines the value of the film is rhythm.

IF WE ATTEMPT to study cinegraphic rhythm, we notice that it has a close analogy to musical rhythm; and here we can transpose many ideas expressed notably by René Dumesnil in his essay on "Musical Rhythm."[1] We should hardly be astonished at this rapprochement between cinema and music. After all, M. Vuillermoz has already noted how the cinegraphic composition obeys the secret laws of musical composition: "a film is written and scored like a symphony."[2] Luminous phrases also "have their rhythm." Similarly, that is why the cinegraphic poem—such as I conceive it and which tomorrow should represent the highest form of expression in the cinema—will be so close to the symphonic poem, the images being to the eye in the former what sounds are to the ear in the latter.

It will be richer, however, since the poet will find in the cinema a means of reshaping his thought in a plastic form which is itself expressive. The rhythmic combinations, resulting from the selection and order of images, will stimulate in the spectator an emotion complementary to the emotion determined by the subject or naked idea of the film, a complementary emotion which may not only replace the original emotion but whose ultimate expression *has* to surpass it—the subject no longer being the essential matter in the work but the pretext or, better yet, the visual theme.

Moreover, I can easily imagine that the cinema, although descriptive above all else—that is, commenting on actions and gestures—could, in the cinegraphic poem, display and comment solely on states of mind. In that especially, it will form a bond with music, whose indefinite nature allows it to produce different correspondences in different imaginations. We could say, in effect, that no one really knows what the Ninth Symphony means, but its phonic rapture so stimulates the mind, without confining it to a definite theme, to the point where the excitement thus generated inspires us to dream and recall our own memories.

Thus, in the presence of a harmonious series of images—as a corollary to the tendency we have of closing our eyes while listening to music—will we be tempted eventually to close our ears the more completely to submit to the visual suggestions and transfigurations of feeling? . . .

The importance of the rhythmic element once more comes from the following fact: contrary to the arts of space where generally the whole is perceived before the specific detail, in order to assimilate a film the mind passes from the particular to the general. From which it follows that the original visual idea has to be perceptible from the beginning, in such a way that we can follow it "through all its developments up to its final flowering." For rhythm has the power to make the memory engage in this progressive labor of assimilation, since it is memory that, reviving the principal idea each time it reappears under its different representations, leads us gradually through the perception of specific details to the synthetic impression of the whole.

This return of the general theme or of the particular expression through which the general theme extends its emotional power is so necessary that it culminates sometimes in a leitmotif. We have had some striking examples in D. W. Griffith's *Dream Street* [1921], with the images symbolizing "the

Voice of Evil" (a masterpiece) and "the Voice of Good," and with the theme of Despair (Suzanne Desprès) in Léon Poirier's *L'Ombre déchirée* [1921].[3]

Finally, if measure is the soul of musical rhythm, the effect of force and intensity is similarly the soul of cinegraphic rhythm. This effect is achieved through the expressive value of the image with respect to the images that precede and follow it. In this case, the power of suggestion in rhythm can be singularly expanded. In a dramatic moment—we know many examples of this—the rhythm can become jarring and correspond perfectly to a gasping and irregular breathing, establishing once more the firm relation which exists between the intensity of organic rhythm and that of artistic rhythm.

[1] René Dumensil (1879–1967) was a historian of music and literature, and particularly expert on Flaubert. The essay Moussinac refers to supposedly appeared in *Mercure de France*, but I have not been able to locate it.

[2] See Emile Vuillermoz, "Devant l'écran," *Le Temps* (4 June 1919), 3.

[3] Léon Poirier (1884–1968) was a Paris theater director whom Gaumont hired as the artistic director of his Séries Pax (1919–1923) and whose films included *Ames d'orient* (1919), *Narayana* (1920), *Le Penseur* (1920), *L'Ombre déchirée* (1921), *Jocelyn* (1922), *Geneviève* (1923), *La Brière* (1925), *La Croisière noire* (1926), and *Verdun, visions histoire* (1928). Suzanne Desprès also appeared in L'Herbier's *Carnaval des vérités* (1920).

ROBERT DESNOS, "Dream and Cinema"

From "Le Rêve et le cinéma," *Paris-Journal* (27 April 1923), reprinted in Desnos, *Cinéma* (Paris, Gallimard, 1966), 104–5. © Editions Gallimard 1966.

IT'S A CINEMA more marvelous than any other. Those who have a gift for dreaming know full well that no film can equal, in either unforeseen contingencies or tragedy, that indelible life to which their sleep is consecrated. From the desire to dream comes the thirst for and love of the cinema. For lack of the spontaneous adventure which our eyelids let escape on wakening, we go into the dark cinemas to find artificial dreams and perhaps the stimulus capable of peopling our empty nights. I would like a filmmaker to fall in love with this idea. On the morning after a nightmare, he notes down exactly everything that he remembers and reconstructs it in detail. It's not a question here of logic and classical construction, nor of remarks to flatter public incomprehension, but of things seen, of a superior realism, since this opens onto a new domain of poetry and dream. Who has not recognized the exclusively personal interest of the dream? The sleeper alone has experienced his wanderings, and his description will always be sufficient to make his listeners appreciate the terrible or comic interest of the dream. Poetry has expected everything from film; let's acknowledge that is hasn't always been disappointed. Often the scenario has been magnificent and the actors wonderful. We've been indebted to them for profound emotions. Yet, while poetry has freed itself from all rules and fetters, the cinema still remains bound by a rigid and strictly common logic. Despite a number of endeavors, the screen still has not given us a chance to see a scenario unfold emancipated from human laws. Dreams there especially are perverted; none operate with the incomparable magic that is their charm. None, that is, when the filmmaker is served only by his memories.

Is the public which is thirsting for such manifestations so restricted? That should not be so. Here an educational effort might prove interesting. In any case, it is discouraging to see foolish sums of money swallowed up for imbecilic popularizations like *La Roue* and not to have any money at all available to tempt the desire of those whose freedom of mind is great enough to allow full license to the filmmaker. The cinema has nothing yet equivalent in audacity to the Ballets russes, nothing naturally as free as *Couleurs du temps* and *Les Mamelles de Tirésias* in the theater.[1]

I have already said how I deplore the fact that eroticism is prohibited.[2] Imagine then the remarkable effects that we could derive from nudity and what wonderful works the Marquis de Sade could achieve in the cinema.

Couldn't we therefore establish a private cinema where films that were too bold for the ordinary public would be screened?[3] In every age, innovators have been hounded by their contemporaries. The painter and the writer are able to consecrate themselves in obscurity to superior tasks. Can the cinegraphist ever escape the prison of antiquated ideas? Will the cinema perish for lack of these eccentricities in which I continue to see only genius?

One of my friends once imagined the existence of someone who would dedicate his fortune to the maintenance of an *experimental laboratory* of this kind.[4] Will we one day encounter this millionaire, in the showy title of a bacon or steel king, who would favor such a laboratory, all the more enviable in my opinion, over "free men"?

ROBERT DESNOS (1900–1945) was a young poet who had just joined the Surrealist group organized around André Breton. His ability to produce poems while actually in or just after coming out of a dream state was legendary, and his interest in the cinema surpassed even that of Philippe Soupault and Louis Aragon. Desnos died of typhus at Buchenwald.

[1] The references are to Henri de Regnier's short story collection, *Couleurs du temps* (1909), and Guillaume Apollinaire's play, *Les Mamelles de Tirésias*, first performed in 1917.

[2] Robert Desnos, "L'Eroticisme," *Paris-Journal* (20 April 1923), reprinted in Desnos, *Cinéma* (Paris: Gallimard, 1966), 101–3.

[3] Desnos apparently is not referring to the pornographic film programs and cinemas which seem to have cropped up in Paris within a few years of the Lumière's first public film screenings. The idea of a specialized cinema was finally realized by Jean Tedesco when he opened the Vieux-Colombier, in November 1924.

[4] Desnos probably has another Thomas Edison in mind. Marcel L'Herbier's Cinégraphic company, set up in 1922, perhaps came close to fulfilling this idea of an experimental laboratory, for it both operated as a "school" in scenario writing and film production and ac-

tually financed several independent films—for example, Catelain's *Le Marchand des plaisir* (1923), Delluc's *L'Inondation* (1924), and Autant-Lara's short *Fait-Divers* (1924).

LOUIS DELLUC, "Prologue"

From "Prologue," *Drames du cinéma* (Paris: Editions du monde nouveau, 1923), i–xiv.

THEY SAY there are no cinegraphic works. Say rather that you don't see any, because film producers don't want them to be seen at any price.

I have seen some that are remarkable. The scenario competitions sponsored by *Cinéa* and *Bonsoir*, among others, have allowed me to discover several excellent ones. Yet no one has wanted to assure their realization. A dozen times have strangers done me the honor of sending me their manuscripts; they had material there for fine French films. I submitted these ready-to-shoot subjects to nearly all the film companies: they were original, vivid, lively, interesting, and reading them was a delight; they were even *commercial*, as the saying goes; but time is passing and these interesting works, inexplicably, always cause alarm. I would submit them again just to see that reaction.

ACTUALLY, the only possible way for you to see your ideas realized is to have a sizable fortune or bankers intelligent enough to cover your costs. Neither is impossible, and writers for the *movies* would be wrong to become discouraged. Let them dream of being composers whose youthful works are still being performed when they are fifty. In the cinema, old-timers don't have the authority that they do in the theater and opera. The cinema is for young minds. Anything that's not youthful is out of place there.

A work written for the cinema has no resemblance, gentlemen, to the libretto that a composer enlivens or messes up. Nor to the scenario that the ballet master or pantomimist embroiders. The cinema drama exists in and of itself. Let its image-maker cut a line or illustrate it imprecisely, he will prove himself as foolish as the tragic actors who mutilate the text of their roles.

In truth, someone who writes a drama for the cinema must direct it himself. His intended conception, intelligent and exact, means little in the hands of imbeciles: I mean the majority of filmmakers. If it comes into the hands of one of his peers, the latter will adapt himself badly to the rigorous execution of a work that's not his own: the newcomer will find himself off target, out in the cold, not measuring up. The result will be unfortunate.

Most authors of cinegraphic dramas hesitate to film their own work. A brief but bitter experience allows me to declare they are wrong. First, because there is little chance that their *translators* understand them. Next, be-

285

cause the fact of having thought through and experienced a visual composition is the best assurance that they will know how to execute it.

In all the manuscripts which have been willingly entrusted to me, I have noticed with amazement that the best of these new writers have had no other technical education about the cinema except what they have derived from their simple understanding as spectators.

READERS of the four little dramas collected in this volume will be surprised, even disappointed perhaps, to see them drafted in a jargon different from what they might expect. They will find them devoid of all technical annotation. Some believe it indispensable to *write out* the images in scenarios,[1] for example, like this:

> Antoinette remembered her happy childhood with bitterness and regret (American shot).
> The apparition of Antoinette, as a child, playing with her doll under an almond tree in flower (Distant shot, dissolve in with a shaded oval mask).
> Large close up of Antoinette dreaming (End of dissolve in, iris out).

There, that's impressive. But to what end? The director of the scenario must be capable of understanding *how* he should realize what the writer intends. When you put a letter in the mailbox, you write on the outside: M. Dupont, 18, rue Georges-Clemenceau, in Aubagne; and you don't tell the carrier what rooftop he must look for to find number 18 on the rue Georges-Clemenceau in Aubagne. He knows how to read and conduct himself.

It seems to me that after reading this

> 201. Militis explains that she is his wife.
> 202. He bought her one day in the Far East from a respectable old couple . . .
> 203. A Buddhist priest covered with jewels has blessed the marriage, in a temple of paper and bamboo, where there was a giant idol of solid gold . . .
> 204. . . . whose left eye the woman kissed . . .
> 205A. . . . before embarking on the large freighter with her husband.
> 205B. Sarah makes a gesture.

the reader will see the unfolding of shots and their equilibrium well enough. His imagination, aided by his intelligence, will evoke the images at the desired distance, in the desired length, according to the desired rhythm.

And the director, likewise, will employ the procedures of his craft almost *automatically*, just as the writer puts his thought into the form of words without recourse to a dictionary.

Even the apprentice, ignorant of any professional tricks, will learn them intuitively if he follows his reason.

Thus in the lines I have just cited, 201 will be a very clear close shot of the sailor Militis engaged in speaking to a stranger.

202 shows us what Militis is speaking about, something from the past: the change in rhythm calls for a *fade* or *dissolve*; the change in framing means a different angle of *shooting*, therefore, a shifting of the camera; the change in time and the transition to a distant country allows for *a slight soft focus* or *luminous superimposition and different tinting*; finally, since the interest of this image comes from the *decor* and the *ensemble of actors*, it should have the largest possible field of vision. The same with 203, which, still wider and more distant, means to enchant us with the charms of the temple and the idol.

204 brings us near to the Oriental woman but with a certain vagueness, aided by *soft focus*, and from the same angle.

These images of the story will achieve a *blending* of one into another so that, in 205A, the exterior long shot, the characters seem nearly insignificant beside the freighter they are going to board. The story is finished: here a *fade* or an *iris out* is indispensable.

Finally, 205B brings us back to a more proximate reality. *Sarah makes a gesture.* Yes, this woman who has listened to the storyteller suggests either her interest or her impatience with a gesture. Her face matters to us. Will this be a large close shot? No, for the indicated gesture may carry the actress outside the frame of the screen. It's best to adopt the *American shot*, that is, the view of the actress from the top of the head to the knees.

Is that complicated?

Just understand that the technique of directing a film is quite simple, even for an apprentice. He needs only two things: (1) *to know* what he is seeing or what he should see and (2) *to work* in a studio with perfectly adequate equipment. The latter is perhaps more rare than the former.

Try it.

IT'S CURIOUS that the country where cinema is really taken seriously produces so few dramas conceived cinematographically.

The initial American scenarios were rather mediocre, save those of Chaplin, but his were only monologues born of a strong and supple personality, and conceived according to the dimensions of his talent.

In Sweden, the adaptation of novels reigns almost supreme. Their productions have provided an amazing education for the French adapters. Mauritz Stiller and Sjöstrom have discovered the means to achieve something truly *cinematic* while preserving the novel, so that the *whole* work remains *whole*. Thus the entire world has been able to *read* the best works of Selma Lâgeröff on the screen in images.[2]

In France, despite the marvelous dramatic inventions of Abel Gance, Marcel L'Herbier, Léon Poirier, and several others, distributors more and more gravely mistrust anything which is not an adaptation. They are mistaken in this. Their ambition and their commerce have spread French culture throughout the world—without which this special branch of *business* would already have succumbed—thanks to works like *La Roue, El Dorado, L'Ombre déchirée* much more than to the *transfilmation* (if I dare say so) of *Roger la honte, La Dame de Monsoreau*, or *Les Mystères de Paris*.[3]

Distributors don't realize that. They believe it is enough to announce: "This is adapted from something" in order to attract the crowds. An error which they'll be sorry about and which will spare us posters of this sort:[4]

MADELEINE CINÉMA
Two of the best successes of the theater
L'ARLÉSIENNE
A triumph at the Odéon
MLL. DE LA SEIGLIÈRE
A masterpiece of the Comédie Française

It's not a question of renouncing adaptations. But it's unthinkable for this country, which blithely disowns the creation of young talents, to accept mediocre productions in which neither the flavor of the novel nor the personality of its people can be recognized. It's all well and good to adapt, but to begin to learn how is very difficult. *L'Atlantide, Jocelyn, Le Crime de Lord Arthur Saville, Mathias Sandorf, Le Père Goriot* have been adequately illustrated.[5] But how many others are as good? How many times has the life of a novel withered away through a translation which doesn't even come to life or achieve a semblance of photogenic life. Generally, our directors begin working without having a sense of the book they are to film—besides not having a sense of this subtle and imperious cinema in whose names they are working.

The Americans, who chiefly film novels, take only their essence. I have seen Frenchmen shocked by the screening of films drawn from famous works because they scarcely recognize them. They were wrong. The American *cinéaste* instinctively takes all that is cinematic in a novel. He jettisons the rest. What should he do? He is to be condemned only when he attacks a work in which there is nothing cinematic—example: *Thaïs*[6]—and wants to "photogenize" it anyway. In that, he imitates the French and Italian who would make a film out of any old book as long as it was known. This error is rather rare for, despite their faults and weaknesses of taste, the American *cinéastes* up to now have shown more flair in choosing a theme to film than have the European novelists' fellow countrymen.

Thus *Les Trois Mousquetaires* [1921–1922] filmed by Henri Diamant-Berger, despite its qualities, has not had the worldwide success of *The Three*

Musketeers [1921] filmed by Douglas Fairbanks. That is not, as some seem to believe, because of Douglas's violent charm and publicity. It's because the French version, concerned about *detail*, about historical minutiae, about the patient touching up of each and every individual and milieu, has almost completely sacrificed the rhythm of the novel. The American version is only rhythm: Fairbanks admits freely that there are few characters as devoid of interest in themselves as d'Artagnan. He lives only though his reactions to events, through his outbursts and caprices, through his rhythm finally, since Dumas—a murky storyteller, a summary psychologist, a historian of shoddy details—is a master of rhythm. The adapter is right to see only that to film in the novel.

The French public is rather badly situated, I recognize, to judge a foreign film categorically. Nine times out of ten they give one to us mutilated, deformed, and aggravated by those deadly intertitles which too often combine the useless and the inept.

The text, let's say it again, should not appear when the image can replace it. The use of intertitles is abused. They drag on the rhythm—and the spectator.

Thus in a recent film, in the middle of a scene where a young soldier says goodbye to his parents, we read this "intertitle":

> And several weeks later, one beautiful morning, Léon had to bid a fond farewell to his family just as one of those giant sea monsters in the harbor was preparing to carry him to the land of France, in the salvation of liberty.

That replaced the ships, the volunteers, and the battlefield which they could not or would not show us. And to fill a gap in the images, the *cinéaste* seemed unaware that he was forcing the spectator to imagine so many new images: the steamship, the American soldiers, the trenches, and to superimpose them over the young man's farewells—one beautiful morning!

I cite here only a sincere and serious text which goes wrong by interrupting the trajectory of our own visual emotion. It is one of the worst, the stupidest, the most scandalous. Such snares are characteristic of the powerlessness of our distributors—however excited they are by adaptation—to release a majority of *good* adaptations.

HOWEVER, I will not be surprised soon to see an important revelation of French cinegraphic dramas. The disparate eagerness of several dozen young men to compose film projects will have its recompense. The stubbornness of four or five among them to direct what they consider interesting and what they feel necessary has already achieved victories. It's not over yet. The most diverse cultured minds are more and more drawn to the animated image. They closely examine the suggestions there, on the chance of making a discovery. They know that we can, we must seek to say, in global *black and white*, in this unique medium of expression, what other languages—the book, the painting, the voice, the dance—cannot and dare not say.

We ourselves have already made an attempt. A clumsy and incomplete effort, but something promising is more precious than a brilliant and useless success.

We will continue then.

THROUGH the possibility of rapidly alternating diverse images, the cinema permits the evocation of simultaneous scenes; it allows us to witness interior scenes paralleled to exterior scenes. And it creates an extraordinary field for antithesis: the opposition of drawing room and hovel, of prison cell and sea, of war and fireside . . .

Griffith once employed this technique with the most paradoxical and prodigious mastery. *Intolerance* evoked the fall of Babylon, the death of Christ, Saint Bartholomew's [massacre] and the life of an American worker all at the same time. The rather unsporting spirit of spectators kept this experiment from achieving all the success it deserved, for to many eyes this vertiginous four-part drama quickly turned into an inexplicable chaos in which Catherine de Medici visited the poor of New York just as Jesus was baptizing the courtesans of Balthazar and Darius' armies were beginning to assualt the Chicago elevated. But the bold rhythm, the verve, the brilliance, the sumptuous ingenuity of this vast film merit our admiration and make it the most magnificent document of cinegraphic simultaneity.

This confrontation between present and past, between reality and memory, through the image, is one of the most seductive plots of photogenic art. Several *cinéastes* have employed it so far. It is delicate and sometimes disappointing work. It requires the collaboration of not only intelligent but especially intuitive actors and very special technical attention. With such carefully selected elements one can achieve the psychological precision of nuances that poetry and music guard so jealously. I know nothing more enticing than to transcribe in *moving pictures* the obsessions of memory or the profound returns of the past.[7] A woman leaves a comfortable life to see how the poor live and is revived by a violent situation and the confused atmosphere of a popular festival (relived once more). Alone one evening, a man discovers through a series of simple signs the real course of a drama in which not long ago he believed he had acted as a judge but where he had actually submitted to a criminal influence. Separation and exhaustion disjoin two lovers; they think they have forgotten one another, but then they meet again—calmly—and the drunkenness of a disorderly evening revives their former love while kindling all the appetites, dreams, and resentments of their opponents. An aged, worn-out woman makes a final pilgrimage to the house which she left out of unhappiness thirty years before; she discovers a young woman in the same situation and particularly the image of her past hours of joy, and she doesn't regret having paid so harshly for a fleeting happiness. These themes torment and haunt me. They can also enchant. These evocations should find in the spectator a deep resonance. Each of us has something inside, a story, which he believes dead and gone and that the phantoms of the screen have suddenly restored to consciousness. . . .

1 A reference perhaps to Henri Diamant-Berger's model decoupage in *Le Cinéma* (1919), or Abel Gance's decoupage of *J'Accuse* in *Filma* (May 1920), or even Blaise Cendrars's "La Perle fièvreuse," *Signaux de France et Belgique* (November 1921–June 1922).

2 See, for instance, Stiller's *Arne's Treasure* (1919) as well as Sjöstrom's *Karin Ingsmarsdotter* (1920) and *The Phantom Chariot* (1921).

3 Baroncelli's *Roger la honte* (1922) was adapted from the novel of Jules Mary. René Le Somptier's *La Dame de Monsoreau* (1923) was adapted from the Alexandre Dumas novel. Charles Burguet's *Les Mystères de Paris* (1922) was adapted from the famous Eugène Sue novel.

4 Both were André Antoine films. *L'Arlésienne* (1922) was adapted from the story by Alphonse Daudet. *Mademoiselle de la Seiglière* (1921) was adapted from the Jules Sandeau novel.

5 Feyder's *L'Atlantide* (1921), Pierre Benoît novel; Poirier's *Jocelyn* (1922), Lamartine poem; Hervil's *Le Crime de Lord Arthur Saville* (1922), Oscar Wilde novel; Fescourt's *Mathias Sandorf* (1921), Jules Verne novel; Baroncelli's *Le Père Goriot* (1921), Balzac novel.

6 *Thaïs* was an Anatole France novel which Massenet had turned into an opera.

7 The following sentences summarize the story lines of Delluc's own *La Fête espagnole* (Dulac, 1920), *Le Silence* (1920), *Fièvre* (1921), and *La Femme de nulle part* (1922).

RICCIOTTO CANUDO, "Reflections on the Seventh Art"

Translated by Claudia Gorbman from "Réflexions sur le septième art" [1923], *L'Usine aux images* (Paris: Etienne Chiron, 1926), 29–47.

I. ANOTHER CHARACTER

I HAVE SAID that the expressive domains of cinema remain basically unexplored. At least in France. A most painful qualification, given that France has unleashed all the fire of modern poetry for the last fifty years. In France the visual arts have sought new alchemies of color and form; in France music has been exploring the new harmonic magic of sounds. In France the cinema first took flight, hatched from scientific and industrial research.

There is less awareness in France than anywhere else that the cinema is an art which must not resemble any other. For it is unlike any other: totally unlike the theater in its muteness, unlike pantomime which from Augustan Rome to our era seeks merely to represent a few elementary emotional states (greed, gratification, spite), unlike the dance, since its rhythm arises from everyday life and not from life as transposed into visual harmony and musical stylization.

The Swedes brought to cinema's evocation of the human drama, with incomparable mastery, an element of ideal counterpoint, inaccessible to theater: the ambience of *nature* (a character as important as Destiny). Painting, too, had tried its hand at this but only within its limitation of immobility. The Americans, with their great westerns, have also cast nature in a major role. Though it is used to delineate the tone of the cowboy's horseback chases and gunfire more than to motivate human actions, the cowpunching characters are nevertheless true products "of the land," thanks to nature. This mathematical fatality of nature's role, that is, an indispensable cog in the clockwork mechanism that moves our emotions, is something we find rarely in Italy, where the landscape is hardly more than a beautiful natural setting. And in France.

And yet, *nature as character* is another absolute domain of the cinema. For example, the Lorraine landscape of Barrès's *La Colline inspirée* so influences the dramatis personae, that we could never mistake them for natives of the Massif Central or Chamonix.[1] Nature must not be a pretext for sightseeing, travel memoirs, or post card collections. What is perfect in Feyder's *L'Atlantide* is precisely the rendering of action in which human beings appear intimately bound to the specific milieu's own states of madness. Especially in the third part of the film: the real protagonist here is the desert, with its gaping soul and its unfathomable ferocity. Sometimes, as in Delluc's *Fièvre*, the evocation of human atmosphere—the cabaret of drunken sailors and decadent pleasure seekers—is taken to such a point that the plot seems reduced to mere incident. It is no longer nature but ambiance, milieu, that dominates and directs the acts of men.

But this is not the case in L'Herbier's *l'Homme du large* where the father, a deplorable murderer—quite contrary to Balzac's treatment—feels and acts as he would irrespective of milieu; seascapes here are merely excuses for beautiful photography. The same strategy is found in L'Herbier's other works as well, all creaking under an antiquated aestheticism. In cinema, the setting's mood, natural like the Swedes', or powerfully artificial as in some German films (*Dr. Caligari* comes to mind, of course), must determine the course of events. Action in—only in—the cinema should be nothing more than a corporeal detail, a material consequence, a visual expression of a collective psychology. The theater, on the other hand, can only focus on the *individual* and will always remain more oriented toward the specifically psychological.

Cinema will thereby prove to be the supreme artistic means of representation and expression of milieus and peoples. It will cease being "individual," copying the theater, which in turn copies life. Further, cinema must cease adapting old novels, a mockery of good taste and an insult to intelligence. It's an assassination of literary heroes: think of Baroncelli's job on the powerful Rastignac in *Le Père Goriot*—a crime more heinous than the one perpetrated against his latest heroes from Jules Mary![2]—and also Diamant-Berger's murder of those poor plumed puppets of *Les Trois Mousquetaires*, of four swaggering petty officers, in the middle of drunken binges, reveling, unruly horsecharges, and of that incredible naval battle off La Rochelle shot in the pools at the Luxembourg Gardens!

II. THE CINEMA'S DOMAINS

The cinema's domains are so numerous that at present we cannot even imagine what they might be. They will multiply like magic before artists' eyes. For generations to come, the marvels of this seventh art will bring into being all that the world's imagination glimpsed in the magical tales of our youth. Science, as well as Art, will increasingly take possession of the Screen's Enchanted Castle where—in the blink of an eye—dream is represented by a most corporeal reality. And already, scientific films, whose limits and possibilities Javorski has described, are finding admirable applications in Pathé's *Doin* series and elsewhere.

In the strictly practical and technical sense, the recent Cinema Exhibition at the Arts and Métiers school, under the aegis of the Society for Art in the Schools (headed by Gaston Vidal, Undersecretary of State, and Léon Riotor, of the City Council), has served to broaden the scope of education, particularly the crucial influence that the older generation exercises on the younger: the orientation of the child's mind, directly via images, toward particular professions or arts.[3]

But most of all, we anxiously anticipate the future of artistic works. Art's sole mission is to fix life's elusiveness and synthesize its harmonies. Its true charm—in the magical sense—is to possess the secret of the philter of oblivion, of spiritual elevation, of deepest joy.

Film will increasingly serve as Art's powerful coadjutor. When the painter and the musician truly wed the poet's dream, and when their triple expression of a single subject is achieved in living light by the *écraniste*[4]— at least while we wait for the screen's Wagner to embody all three at once— films will reach us with a supreme clarity of ideas and visual emotions. We will recognize cinema as the synthesis of all the arts and of the profound impulse underlying them. It will be our immaterial Temple, Parthenon, and Cathedral. It will be a lucid and vast expression of our internal life, infinitely more vibrant than all previous forms of expression. Cinema will be able to construct the synthesis-temple of our intense inner life, in the heavens that its new strength will illumine and "illustrate" by means of the incomparable findings of Science.

The cinema's domains can extend in all directions. The Italian assemble great numbers of people in front of the cameras and compose immense, alive, moving historical frescoes—and it "works." In Germany, for the first time, painters and *écranistes* have collaborated to attain the living atmosphere of dream. Admittedly in the admirable *Cabinet of Dr. Caligari*, "exceptional" characters sometimes appear *glued* to the decor, whose style their reality seems to contradict at times. But in the German film, *From Morning to Midnight*,[5] a pure masterpiece of human emotion and artistic synthesis, the landscapes and their moods are so unified with the characters, that all of the distortion and unreality of this vision melts into the simplest, broadest, and most poignant truth. The *écraniste* had the set designer take advantage of black and white, inscribing in its limitless range all the psychological nuances of the poor thieving cashier. (The protagonist wants a happy life, but at the end of his day of debauchery he is seized by the most intolerable loathing of life and embraces the ultimate solution of suicide.)

Abel Gance, our Walt Whitman of the screen, has ventured into another domain of emotion in *La Roue*, by means of the life of the machine. He has also created a mood of *unreality*, in accordance with his vision. Rather than rely on a set designer, he appealed to the odd world that man created to amplify his power. This world of monsters of hard and fiery matter which drones and rumbles through human life, multiplying its strength a hundredfold, is the Machine.

Between the mood of unreality synthesized by the German film's designers, and the mood of equally synthetic unreality "engineered" in Gance's French film, there is absolute reality: the artist's dream, Poetry. As Novalis says, Poetry is the absolute Real. It mobilizes the chimerical operation of artistic genius when it tears from the fabric of "real life" elements or details too numerous to count. From these details, genius composes a meaningful and moving work—not a mere photograph of beings and things in movement, but a synthesis of life.

III. ON CINEMATOGRAPHIC LANGUAGE

I do not believe that true intellectual milieus, and their epigones—the gossipy salons called art and literary circles; newspapers (those mills of daily opinion); the business organizations of artistic and literary news; the cafés where young art students, if indeed any are left, absorb the latest aesthetic trivia over imported beers—quite realize the immense toil that goes on in the world of cinema. Nor do I even know, for that matter, if the brain realizes the considerable work of the stomach in digesting a complicated meal. All humanity, after having swallowed cinema, is in the process of digesting it, and the going is not smooth.

The immense toil does not reside only in what is referred to as production. We know that the cinematograph—totally conceived in industrial terms, and the child of scientific experiment—has not yet truly embraced the world of artists, those natural organizers of aesthetic pleasures, those age-old "rhythm men" of universal sensibility; but the screen wishes to tap in on the universal sensibility, and it succeeds. Film production is growing with an intensity both wild and calculated. Reels of film, these celluloid railroad tracks, will soon wrap around the world by the thousandfold. Production is at full capacity, and is every increasing with the animal fecundity of the lower species. But the work of intellectual digestion has hardly begun—in spite of all the artistic attention which admirable *écranistes* have been devoting to such an industrialized form.

The philologist Max Muller said that thoughts are merely speech rolled around in the mouth. Indeed, the more words one knows in a language, the more thoughts one can produce with grace and flexibility. Likewise, the more a sculptor has studied painting, the more forms, designs, shapes his hands possess, and the more supple and rich his visual thinking. For this reason cinematographic language is trying to formulate (if not yet amplify) its vocabulary. The problems demanding solutions are many. The rhythm already established by the interactions of shot scale, from shot to shot, has produced an elementary graded nomenclature of close-ups, American shots, and so on. But "tone," that is, the relations of *expressive tonalities* among images of a single scene, are of growing interest to *écranistes*. Few of them really care. Many are still content to treat the camera as a moving *deus ex machina*, and they expect it to *illustrate* a text purely and simply, often in an impure and complicated way. But the best *écranistes*, those most sensitive to the aesthetic demands of our present moment, are working doggedly to transform the screen into the most marvelous and direct man-made instrument for arresting life and pinning down its meanings.

Thus, cinematographic language, even outside the story that it is to animate, is feverishly seeking its speech, articulating its syllables, striving toward an optical pronunciation. So far it generally lacks elegance, or pleasing spontaneity.

CINEMA is reinaugurating the entire experience of writing—it is renewing writing. Essentially it is a universal language, and not just by virtue of its visual and immediate expression of all human feelings. What are the letters of the alphabet? A stylization or schematization, via progressive simplification, of ordinary images which had struck the first men. From the paleo-

295

lithic era to the consolidation of the copper age, man strove also to arrest the fleeting aspects of life—external or emotional—images and thoughts, so others could know them, so as to transmit to others a felt impression. Man chose the means most certain to last, he carved images in stone. He divested them of all superfluity by retaining only their most essential cursive elements for signification.

The large linguistic families were born from this centuries-long work which determined the real, only incontestable superiority of man over the animals—his ability to arrest life, the triumph over the ephemeral and over death.

Ideographic languages like Chinese, or hieroglyphic systems like the Egyptian, still visibly manifest their origins in images. The newer alphabetical languages, although based more on sound than image, might also hark back to these origins in images.

Cinema, for its part, draws upon and multiplies the possibilities of *expression in images* which heretofore was the province of painting and sculpture. It shall build a truly universal language with characteristics entirely yet undreamed of. In order to do so, it must bring art—the representation of life—back to the sources of all emotion, seeking *life in itself* via movement. Static visual art forms, and rhythmic musical art forms, have as their sole purpose to arrest and crystallize the moving currents of internal life. The arrival of cinema heralds the renovation of all modes of artistic creation, of all means of "arresting the fleeting," conquering the ephemeral. What it can already show us—for example, in slow-motion studies of plant growth—is an affirmation of its stupendous capacity to renew the representation of life itself, fixing the instant-by-instant movement of beings and things. Cinema gives us a *visual analysis* of such precise evidence that it cannot but vastly enrich the poetic and painterly imagination. In addition, through its "horizontal" dimension—its capacity to show events occurring simultaneously—it will increase the sum total of our sensations.

In its groping infancy, the cinema seeks its voices and words. It is bringing us with all our acquired psychological complexity back to the great, true, primordial, synthetic language, visual language, prior even to the confining literalness of sound. The moving image does not replace words, but rather becomes a new and powerful entity of its own. The screen, this single-paged book as unique and infinite as life itself, permits the world—both internal and external—to be imprinted on its surface.

Thus far, confusion reigns over the definition of some concepts relating to cinema. The cinema is not only working out its various modes of production, but also the terms to describe them. Investigations are in progress: Gaston Tournier's work in *L'Echo de Paris*[6] regarding the root "kinema" (movement) has been quite instructive. Cinegraphy, cineology,

cinemania, cinephilia and cinephobia, cinepoetry and cinoedia, cinema-
turgy, cinechromism—the list goes on. Only time and chance will tell
what terminology will stay with us. For the time being, I shall stick with
"screen art," and for its practitioner, "*écraniste*."

IV. ON "CINEMATIC TRUTH"

The following remarks are inspired neither by Marcel L'Herbier's *La
Carnaval des vérités* nor by Henri Roussell's *Verité* [1922] (two beautiful
films with very different styles). All the "truths" that cinema can show us
will eventually force us to confront and define this new and complex *cinematic truth*, of which most *écranistes* are totally unaware. It alone can interest
artists in all the arts.

The undeniable and—alas—increasing inferiority of French films when
compared to other countries' production resides primarily in their ignorance of cinematic truth. Such ignorance ranges from indiscriminately
snatching actors from the theater to other choices in subject matter, sets,
landscape, even lighting. Energy is poured into industrial management
rather than aesthetic vision. Dignity and the aim of conceiving something
of human value are being sacrificed to stupidly commercial goals. The cinematograph's ruling class came from all spheres of general business, with
the traditional cupidity of merchants of the Temple. For publishers and
booksellers a book still is a work of art, but for them a film is not. Film is
measured and sold as a commodity; it's bought up by the meter or foot.
Then why all the surprise that the state treats it as nothing other than an
industrial product on the market? The cultivated man's aversion to cinema
will surely grow as the industry itself grows, because money enters into
every phase (including artistic intelligence and initiative) as a motive.

However: there is a "truth" of the cinema, which film-producing nations
perceive and practice already. If the multitudes are like dense foliage, the
flowers that bloom as the synthesis of their minds and as ideals of beauty
are artists and intellectuals. In France, the very multitude which invented
cinema has so far yielded very few flowers. We're still so astonished at the
new discovery that we try to believe at all costs that it is part of our old
heritage, that cinema is nothing more than an offshoot of theater. So we
pluck our film actors from the theater—actors who keep talking even
though cinema wants them silent. Also from theater we derive a kind of
staging, in balanced masses of figures, instead of giving free play to the
infinite intensities of light itself, to masses of black and white and their
innumerable gradations. Light must not be enslaved to the representation
of human figures. Instead, characters should appear solely as light human-
ized into dramatic symbols.

As for "dramatic truth" itself—that is, the impact of feelings and indi-

297

vidual sensations that can elicit pathos and emotion—it seems nobody could care less about exploring what would be a really *photogenic* impact. People are content with the *photogénie* of faces although any face, lit with expertise and subtlety, is photogenic. They dredge up the most belabored, simplistic, lesser literary works, as long as the work doesn't trumpet a concern for psychology, and as long as it provides plenty of the vulgar collisions of passion and greed which comprise, for everyone in the melodrama business, *action*.

Here is the big mistake of most *écranistes* and their financial bosses. They think that all a film needs (more than a play) is what they call an action. Indeed, in the theater, speech can explain things, while in cinema, the plot requires the visual portrayal of a limited range of gestures. But no one even conceives of a cinematographic truth for which screen characters—far from simply coming across as photographed actors—would represent *luminous entities*. If cinema is more than just photographed theater, or an illustrated realist novel, all the actors must be articulated in the play of light, just as painters expressed the phantoms of their dreams via the play of color. The film, the work, will then appear in its own right, independent of the other arts, not needing overexplicit intertitles or mimed speeches, free from the conventional fetters of the theater.

HERE IS one of the essential characteristics of the cinematograph. The way to transpose "truth" into art does not merely depend on what a camera can capture of reality. This truth lies fundamentally in the artist's mind, it is his *parti pris*, just like his own style. To be content with pointing the camera at some characters or landscape arranged more or less artfully is *not* doing the work of an artist, but is a vulgar and mediocre act. The cinema, far from being a stage in photography, is an altogether new art. The *écraniste*'s mission is to transform objective reality into his own personal vision. Acquiring a style means not just photographing something as an objective document, but working with the light it captures to evoke the states of the soul.

Rather than the spectacle of objective reality, art consists in evoking feelings associated with that reality. It is intolerable vulgarity, for instance, when in a film we *see* the setting and objects representing a character's thought when he is supposedly remembering something. A title tells you, "He remembered reaching the forest," and you're shown a long shot of the character approaching the forest. But that does not show his memory. In one's memories one does not see oneself. The film can only portray his memory of reaching the forest by suggesting the thoughts and feelings *accompanying* the moment. We could provide numerous examples of how the photographer's banal choices ruin the portrayal of evocative impressions.

By and large, the *écraniste* has been accepting, not creating, what he photographs. He does not create psychological atmosphere, the equivalent of description in the novel or color balance in painting. Instead of planning each shot in the way a painter conceives each detail of a composition, so that the spectator will be left with a *single image* distilled from the entire film, the *écraniste* is pleased if his shots are remembered at all, and if people say, "it's beautifully photographed." This brings to mind the inferiority of melodic opera—composed and remembered in separate melodies—to the truly symphonic musical drama.

Several authors, though, have understood that cinematographic truth has nothing to do with the truth of visible reality. They see that unless the *écraniste* has succeeded in imposing his personal emotion on his images, a single scene can produce very different emotive effects according to the spectator's mood. If a dagger piercing flesh is shown to me, my emotional reaction will depend on my feeling about the hand doing the thrusting, or the flesh being stabbed. But if the *écraniste* has succeeded in situating his action in the greater psychological context, if he has successfully prepared me for the emotion he feels, than I will respond in the manner he desires.

In the cinema, as in the pursuits of the mind, art consists in suggesting emotions, and not in recounting facts. It is very tempting to *show* everything in "true" images; this is why people think the screen shows much "truth" even when they barely feel any profound or truly aesthetic emotion. The word "truth" (which in this sense should be replaced by "gross and superficial reality") should belong to no category of art. What painter painted "truth" as writers on cinema mean it? Leonardo, with his androgynes always in the same pose? All the painters of the Nativity, with their idealized arrangements of human and animal figures around the manger? Michelangelo, with his predilection for grandeur, or Watteau, with his penchant for the graceful ornamentation so popular in his era?

Only a few *écranistes* have understood that cinematographic truth must correspond to literary truth, to pictoral truth, even to the truth of love. None of these is objective "reality." A traveling businessman once blamed Anatole France for inventing a Florence he couldn't recognize when, along the banks of the Arno, he tried to use *Le Lys rouge* as his guide instead of a Baedeker. And yet, Anatole France expressed the soul of Florence with details reflecting his visionary precision, if not documentary truth.

We see it in German expressionist films such as *Caligari, From Urick to Niscurit*, and *Torgus*;[7] in the Swedes, whose vision acquires emotional profundity embodied in their snowscapes; and in France, with Louis Delluc, especially Marcel L'Herbier, sometimes Abel Gance. The discoveries in

299

these films touch on cinematographic truth, with a stylistic fluency capable of establishing the cinematograph on equal footing with the other arts. More film artists are drawing near as well.

Still others, of whom Léonce Perret and Diamant-Berger are typical, glut themselves on their albums of picture postcards, where you can find everything *but* truth and aesthetic nobility.

V. IMMATERIALITY IN CINEMA

Camille Flammarion, having witnessed a screening of a film illustrating a soul's survival after death, has once again expressed his old faith in spiritism, adding his new enthusiasm for cinema. He was happily surprised to see the cinema confront the evocation (if no longer the representation) of immateriality. Mr. Flammarion's remarks confirm that the cinema, *when understood and conceived as an art by artists*, must develop in specific areas that are impossible in other arts.[8]

Cinema has exclusive domains. It is difficult to see or even conceive of them in the current confusion surrounding this infant art. The cinema, understood as an art—and I insist on this necessary understanding, separating us distinctly from almost all "men of cinema"—gives the impression today of something sacred, a temple for example, inadvertently open to the merchants who are most bitterly determined to deny entry to the secular and natural priesthood of artists.

This is why many intellectuals aren't aware that like all arts this one paves new avenues for the soul's expression. Understandably, they are still considering cinema as a new commodity in the mercenary global stock market, and they disdain it as something irrelevant to their concerns. In this context no one has dreamed of recognizing and defining the cinema's arenas of expression. And owing to the usual commercial haste to produce quickly, minimize risk, and make big profits, all the other genres—novel, theater—have been plundered. Producers have sunk to the lowest level in order to have the widest clientele. They have resuscitated the serial and the "chromo" to bring the melodrama's spirit and views to the screen, and they have pilfered any music they can find to envelope it all in the appropriate atmosphere.

In other words, it suffices to put any old subject onto the screen—just as musicians (talented ones included) used to put any old text to music. And finally came Wagner and Debussy . . . I have already pointed out that the "beautiful melodies" of operas correspond, for the mass audience's pleasure, to the "beautiful photography" of most of our *écranistes*.

ONE OF cinema's exclusive domains will be the immaterial, or more precisely, the *unconscious*. The image of a character's memory or thought had already tempted many an *écraniste*. It rounded out the drama, replaced speech (or the excess of dialogue and explanation) on the screen. The means were primitive, with those superimpositions reminiscent of popular icons that have saints prostrated before the madonnas in their mandalas. Now we can do better. We can already alter the visual register by means of stylistic devices such as distortions, superimpositions, and scrims and masking effects. Theater is confined to concrete speech, and when an unconscious image is desired, it can play with light: it can throw a white mantle around Hamlet's father. But it will always remain within the exact proportions of everyday reality.

Cinema permits, and must further develop, the extraordinary and striking faculty of *representing immateriality*. Both America and Sweden have just shown us: in, for example, Svenska Film's admirable *Phantom Carriage*, based on Selma Lâgerlöf's novel, and the astonishing and perfect drama *Earthbound*, by Basil King at Goldwyn.

With these films we are bordering on the perfection of a genre at its very outset. *The Phantom Carriage* is the vision of a drunkard. In *Earthbound*, we actually witness the anguishing problem of a dead man's soul. Killed in his prime by his mistress's husband, he must linger on earth until everyone he had made unhappy forgives him, and until his wife recognizes the ghost and his agony. Only love can free him from the earth where his body is already decaying. Where during his life he had created disharmony and suffering, he must regain harmony, which means repentance and love. "The dead inhabit our lives, but they are separate," an intertitle bitterly comments, as we see a shot showing the poor young murdered man take his impassive wife in his arms; she does not see or feel him, since he can no longer embrace a living being.

Certain shots in this film, combining the real and the immaterial, the living and the dead, are often powerful and very troubling. We are reminded of the promise that man might photograph the total life of the unconscious, whose unknown rhythm might rule over our own! . . .

VII. A FIRST STEP

The present artistic movement in cinema will result in affecting the commercial establishment, whose strength threatens to submerge the screen in a tidal wave of business interests. We must claim the film as a work of art, and marshal the energies and sensibilities of artists. Only by doing so will we know whether the human imagination has really enriched the world with a new mode of expressing our deepest life, or whether a new industry is merely in the process of creating—in place of cafés, which are disappearing before an onslaught of banks—modern shelters from bore-

dom, or pleasant oases where couples may conveniently grope in the darkness.

The Salon d'Automne has hastened to open its doors to modern artists
who believe in cinema as an art, who are prepared to devote their dreams
and energies to it but who find themselves discouraged by the implacable
domination of the hoi polloi and by an incompetent, insensitive, often
biased corporate press. The "Seventh Art" screenings in our newest Salon
have as their purpose to present the "state of the art" of this new force be-
stowed upon man to communicate across great distances via image and
emotion. It's a simple overview, in the form of short talks on the aesthetic
values of cinematic works, interspersed with selections from among the
best films made thus far. The program ought to demonstrate to the cultural
world that these innumerable light-engravings in the measure of man,
moving and animated by the breath of life, this triumphant "living black
and white" that can prolong man's existence beyond the limits of space,
time, and death—this is a brand-new force that can make life manifest and
comfort us in living.

But the excerpts chosen for screening at the Salon fall short of what the
modern artist can expect from contemporary genius. Although they stand
among the best and the most representative, we will no doubt one day be
able to see the primitive awkwardness through their veiled grace. The
écraniste paints, sculpts, composes with light, and never was a painter's palette at the same time so rich and so ineffable! All the same, he knows about
lines, and the play of lines one calls forms, and the play of forms one calls
movement. He knows about them via the magic of the lens and the power
which cinema's mechanical precision grants him to arrest the fleeting aspects of life. The new power is so great, and man has possessed it for so
little time, that the imperfections, the groping, and the visual mistakes
coexist right along with lightning flashes of beauty. This unevenness
might irritate us now: but tomorrow the cinema's images will appear as
moving as the simple and divine frescoes, fashioned by the bare hands of
Christian painters in the Roman catacombs, where for nine centuries they
hid their faith and kept watch over the inextinguishable aesthetic fire.

The Salon d'Automne will have had the certain glory of proclaiming to
the world of artists that the cinema is an art, synthesizing science and the
arts all at once. Artists—creative minds whose mission is to grasp the aspects and rhythms of life—will learn that rather than contemptuously
avoiding the cinema, or treating it as inconsequential entertainment, they
ought to devote their talents to it. Elie Faure has already expressed his hope
for "visual symphonies" in film. Who can create them, whom shall we ask?
Certainly not those blind businessmen currently in charge of its destiny:
they're stunned not by luminous miracles but by their impressive cash

boxes. We must go to artists themselves, to the people of taste, to the indispensable "snobs" who organize exchange, dialogue, and work. We must appeal to the writers and critics who, with the aid of courageous and clear-sighted publishers, must replace the hacks whose scribblings are not so much critical reviews as business reports.

The Seventh Art is for artists. This is the lesson that the Salon d'Automne is bringing to the cultural world. The lesson will be heeded—for nothing can long resist art, the impulse of the universal soul.

[1] Maurice Barrès (1862–1923) was a French writer who initially celebrated the rigorous, solitary individualism of *la culte du moi* and then took up the cause of a French nationalism based on close relations with the land and on race or ethnic origins. *La Colline inspirée* (1913) was a late collection of lyrical, philosophical essays.

[2] The reference is to Baroncelli's adaptation of *Roger la honte* (1922), by Jules Mary.

[3] This exhibition was part of the first Congress on Cinema and Education, which gathered together 700 educators, businessmen, and politicians in Paris, 20–24 April 1922. See G.-Michel Coissac, *Histoire du cinématographe* (Paris: Cinéopse, 1925), 578–79.

[4] Canudo's term for the film director. Literally "screenist," it implies "screen artist."—TRANS.

[5] Karl-Heinz Martin's *Von Morgen bis Mitternachts* (1920), adapted from the George Kaiser play.

[6] Gaston Tournier was the regular film critic for *L'Echo de Paris*, a rightist Paris newspaper with literary interests, which briefly challenged the "big four" dailies during the war, largely because of the patriotic articles of Barrès, and then declined in circulation and influence.

[7] Hans Kobe's *Torgus* (1920), scripted by Carl Mayer and photographed by Karl Freund. The reference to *From Urick to Niscurit* is uncertain.

[8] Camille Flammarion (1842–1925) established and directed an important publishing house in Paris.

RENÉ CLAIR, *"Coeur fidèle"*

Translated by Stanley Appelbaum in *Cinema Yesterday and Today*, ed. R. C. Dale (New York: Dover, 1972), 97–98. Reprinted by permission. The original French text first appeared as "Les Films du mois: *Coeur fidèle*" in *Théâtre et Comoedia illustré* (1 February 1924).

IT IS NOT too late to talk about *Coeur fidèle*, which was shown in a few theaters last month. This film does not date from just yesterday, but because of the ineptitude of our methods of distributions, it has not yet been seen by a wide audience. But it dates from tomorrow. We shall see it again.

Before formulating our criticism, let us say that you must see *Coeur fidèle* if you wish to be acquainted with the resources of the cinema today. Its plot is banal, a sort of *Broken Blossoms* seen through French eyes. But you know what importance should be attached to the subject of a film: the same, more or less, that is attached to the subject of a symphony. All we ask of a plot is to supply us with subjects for visual emotion, and to hold our attention.

The factor which distinguishes *Coeur fidèle* from so many other films is its having been composed for the screen, for the joy of "intelligent" eyes, so to speak. From the appearance of the very first images, the film sense is in evidence—no doubt more rational than instinctive, but undeniably there. The lens turns in every direction, moves around objects and people, seeks the expressive image, the surprising camera angle. This exploration of the perspectives of the world is thrilling: it is inconceivable that so many directors have persisted in multiplying matte shots and the tricks of still photography when they could have awakened so much curiosity with a slight tilt of their camera.

The study of the proper camera angle, the only angle right for a given image or scene, is far from having been exhausted. The Americans, who took the first steps in that direction, seem to have stopped short in fear of what still remained to be discovered. *Coeur fidèle*, among other films—and among other French films, I must add—points us once again in the direction of that study, progress in which is inseparable from progress in cinematic expression.

M. Jean Epstein, the director of *Coeur fidèle*, is obviously concerned with the question of rhythm. People talk a lot about cinematic rhythm, and the question seems to be the most important one the cinema has to answer at present. It must be said that up to now no complete answer has been proposed. It appears that rhythm sometimes crops up spontaneously in a film—especially in American films—but too often it remains sketchy and disappoints us. When it is intentional—and it is in *Coeur fidèle*—it is created by means of the reappearance of earlier images; at first this is very effective, but it soon becomes a burden to the overall movement and quite justly annoys the majority of the audience, who cannot make out what the author is driving at, and get impatient. Periodic repetition of earlier images—like assonance or rhyme in prosody—seems to be the only effective rhythmic element the film now has at its disposal. But rhyme and assonance do not bring back the same word in the sentence, whereas the repetition of images summons up more or less the same vision. Something else, which can only be guessed at now, must be found. The absolute mathematical solution has the drawback of not taking into account the sentimental value of the recalled image. No doubt it is necessary to combine harmoniously the sentimental rhythm of the action and the mathematical rhythm of the number of images. . . . But forgive me for letting myself be carried away by this question, which will perhaps seem to be of interest to only a very few readers. I advise these readers once again to go and see *Coeur fidèle* and its carnival, a beautiful scene of visual intoxication, an emotional dance in the dimension of space, in which the visage of Dionysiac poetry is reborn.

304

Coeur fidèle can be criticized for lacking unity of action. The film too often goes astray into technical experiments which the action does not demand. That is the difference between the advanced technique of our school and American technique, which is completely at the service of the progress of the story. That is also the explanation of the difference in the audience's attitude toward American films, in which the expressions are immediately accessible, and ours, which require an effort of the intelligence alone. That is the cause of many a mass dissatisfaction. . . . But let us not dwell on this. A quality director will be able to find the means to reconcile both schools for the greater good of the cinema. If a film is worthy of the cinema, that is already a most agreeable miracle! *Coeur fidèle* is worthy of it in more than one respect. Those who compare the young and still barbarous cinema with all of literature and all the arts, will not understand this. But let them subject our contemporary old drama to this comparison! The cinema will seem to them in contrast to be an inexhaustible source of poetry.

Apropos of *Coeur fidèle*, certain details in it have led some people to speak of an unpleasant return to realism. I think that the cinema need fear nothing of the sort. The suppleness of cinematic expression, which passes in a flash from objective to subjective, simultaneously evoking the abstract and the concrete, will not permit film to confine itself to an aesthetic as narrow as that of realism. No matter if the view of a gloomy cabaret or a poverty-stricken room is photographically exact. The screen gives a soul to the cabaret, the room, a bottle, a wall. It is this soul alone that counts in our eyes. We move from the object to its soul as easily as our being passed from a sight to a thought. The screen opens onto a new world, one vibrant with even more synesthetic responses than our own. There is no detail of reality which is not immediately extended here into the domain of the wondrous.

GERMAINE DULAC, "The Expressive Techniques of the Cinema"

Translated by Stuart Liebman from 'Les Procédés expressifs du cinématographe," *Ciné-magazine* 4 (4 July 1924), 15–18, (11 July 1924), 66–68, (18 July 1924), 89–92. This lecture was given at the Musée Galliera on 17 June 1924.

THE CINEMA is a silent art. Silent expression is its categorical rule and this sentence from *L'Ecriture* could be applied to those who are its servants: *Their throats will not utter a sound*. We, the authors of films, must assume the difficult task of describing *without words, without phrases*. . . .

Since I am a filmmaker, you will understand how helpless I am here in front of you.

And nevertheless, I must talk with you about a subject that is especially dear to me: the expressive techniques of cinema, about the role of different shots and shooting angles, the fade, the dissolve, superimposition, soft focus, and distortions. In short, the whole syntax of film. But just as much as this syntax must appear foreign to you, *to me* it seems easy, simple, and flexible to use in comparison with the syntax regulating writing and speech. How much I would prefer to introduce you to it by creating a live demonstration. How much more at ease I would be if, instead of all these sheets of paper, I had my cameraman and camera with me and I could, with your consent, request that you be the performers in a scene that would have as its subject a lecture at the Musée Galliera, thereby allowing me to stick to facts instead of words. In any case, I will bypass any difficulties by continually appealing to projected examples.

The Seventh Art, like most other arts, has been assigned the goal of bringing matter under control and to fix in it the *summum* of humanity. Until now, this material was called clay, colors, sounds, or words; for several years, it has also been called film stock. The Seventh Art does not stop at the stylization of an impression as sculpture and painting do. It augments a fact by grafting a feeling onto it by means of a technique that is proper to it, just like literature, the theater, and music. If the cinematic work in its evolution and its progress is related to the theater, the novel, and the musical symphony, it exists [as an art] only by virtue of its visual form. The image, faithful guardian of a gesture or a fugitive expression, attains all of its eloquence in the silence that rules over it. The composition of the image is our rhetoric; the contrasts and the sequences that it sets up are our means of silently affecting [spectators].

In order to have a common basis for our discussion, I am immediately going to project for you a fragment of an able piece of work by one of my colleagues, Marcel Silver. After seeing it, you will understand the feeling that a logical sequence of images can provoke. This film contains none of those texts that are called intertitles in the language of the profession. The image alone is king. The work therefore affects you through a purely cinematic technique, of contrasts and parallelisms [of images], and you will be able to appreciate how, despite the excellent performances in this scene, the shock of what is seen and the principal source of its emotional impact depends on the judicious choice of isolated expressions developing a theme or a thought. Thanks to the image, the sensibility of the film's author is emitted, just like an artist's is in his work. Photography, performers, landscapes obey his will. He is the only creator since he organizes according to a logic he chooses, opposes, juxtaposes, and makes rhythmical. Before going any further, let us understand each other very well. I do not consider a cinematic work to be a successor of the theater with the actor's performance as the basis of interest. When it allies itself with the theater in its techniques, the cinema demeans itself. It is no longer itself. And we ought not to consider this deplorable compromise here. We will speak about the cinematic work from the perspective of its unique resources and possibilities. . . .

(A section of [Marcel Silver's] *L'Horloge* [1924] is screened.)

Ladies and gentlemen, you have no doubt followed the two lovers' state of mind step by step. Calm . . . Long images, the young people look at each other; they are filled with boundless bliss. The spectators understand their state of mind through the juxtaposition of vast horizons which induce a reverie composed of grandeur, space, the unknown, and the mountain tops. In this majestic nature, their lips draw near. A bell tower lies in the distance.

The excitement begins once the thought of the clock suddenly shatters their happy musing. From then on, the images succeed each other in a mad rhythm. The throbbing vision of the pendulum contrasted with the two lovers rushing toward one another creates the drama. Did you notice the technique of this scene? Short images . . . the sensation of the long road the two lovers must traverse, and the obsessiveness punctuating the action. Interminable paths, a still imperceptible village. The pendulum is emphasized insofar as the author wants to give us the sense of distance in the other shots. By the choice of images, their length, and their contrasts, rhythm becomes the sole source of emotion. The distance to be covered and the pendulum's movement alone captivates our attention. And when we close in on the unredeemable, once again silence, calm.

You have been interested and moved by a technique proper to cinema, the contrast of images, their rhythm, and their duration. This is the first and a principal method of expression. . . .

I have given you two examples[1] in which contrasts of images create the action: a thrilling drama and a state of mind. I am now going to show you another and bring this first section to a close. [It concerns] the conflict of two people who love each other.

The example is drawn from *Kean* [1924], performed by Mosjoukine and directed by Volkoff.

Kean, the celebrated English actor is in love with a lady of high estate. Kean despairs about not being able to conquer this lady . . . In a bar, disguised as a sailor in order to escape the creditors who are pursuing him, he drinks and he dances. The ferocity of his wantonness increases his desire to forget his impossible love. For two minutes you watch a wild, madly rhythmical dance. You can see the wantonness in his eyes, in his gestures and his mouth. Pleasure at all costs! Once the exaltation has passed—sadness, emptiness, a long, static pose. Kean is despondent. Another image is skillfully contrasted. The location changes and we see the ambassador's wife in bed, dreaming of the handsome actor, but she is dreaming about him in his Romeo costume. She loves the artist . . . She dreams about *him*.

We have stepped into the action. Once more the rhythm and the contrasts have sufficed to move us, to present the drama.

(Screening of a section of *Kean*. A drunken party ends with the apparition of Kean as Romeo in the room of the ambassador's wife.)

I must still explain to you how the clash of images creates a sense of the atmosphere. You have just seen Kean in his drunken state plunge into a wild dance. His expressions and gestures have allowed us to understand his thoughts . . . But the more ferocious his desire, the greater, no doubt, is his inner pain. How can you show the intensity of Kean's wantonness? The actor's expression must be true and not exaggerated. In order to preserve his simplicity, another image underlines it. We are going to feel the floor move under the jumping feet of the dancers; we will see animals gripped by fear. Contrasted with the drinkers' round dance, the bottles on the bar totter on the shelves. A cat will look at them, but soon become frightened, it will seek out a corner in which to take cover. These juxtapositions of images are not hors d'oeuvres. They are placed there mathematically to create a sense of the atmosphere, the feeling of noise *in* and *through* the silence. They have a reason for being there just as a well-placed word is necessary for the brilliance of a phrase.

(Screening of a section of *Kean*.)

The examples I have commented upon have clarified the basis of our technique—the juxtaposition of images—for you.

On this basis, you will acknowledge the primordial importance that the image's quasi-mathematical compositional structure has. Every image must single out an expression or underline an intention. And that is where the work of the camera begins.

The machine is based on the effects of lenses that come closer to or move away from [an object] to frame the picture required for our dialectic. Every lens records the vision we have intellectually conceived in order to transmit it to the film.

In the sections you have just seen, the camera's placement has played a considerable role: *by situating, by underlining*, and *by isolating*. In *L'Horloge*, for example, if Marcel Silver had cropped out the mountain peaks instead of presenting them from a perspective in which sky, snow, and clouds blend together, we would not have had the sensation of the infinite. When the young people are in anguish as they rush [back to the village], we would not have sympathized with them if the small village at their feet and the very long road in front of them had not made the length of the route they had to travel evident to us.

Now, in each of these images, this combination of peaks, road, and variously proportioned shots of the village is obtained by shifts in the camera's placement.

In the same way, isn't the camera's placement isolating the wheels and crank arms perfect? If we looked over the wheels and crank arms, we would not have the impression that it was these wheels and crank arms whose din recalls for Morin the noise of the jazz band.

If the juxtaposition of images must be precise, the placement of the camera can be no less so.

The latter provokes and accentuates an impression. . . .

I move now to another technical consideration: the shot which proceeds directly from the juxtaposition of images and the camera placement. The shot is the image in its most isolated expressive form, underscored by the lens's framing . . . The shot simultaneously defines the place, an action, and a thought. Each different image that is juxtaposed is called a shot. The shot is a small piece of the drama; it is a small touch that unites in a conclusion. It is the piano on which we play. It is the only means that we have to create a bit of the inner life in the midst of the action.

I am going to project a film, *La Souriante Madame Beudet* [1923], which I directed based on a scenario by André Obey which was based on the play this author wrote in collaboration with Denys Amiel. After the screening, we will speak about shots.

(Screening of the first part of *La Souriante Madame Beudet*.)

You have undoubtedly grasped the importance of the shots in this drama. In the beginning: long shots. Indications of sadness in the empty streets, the small quaint figures. The provinces . . .

Then another unifying shot: two hands playing a piano and two hands weighing a handful of money. Two characters. Opposed ideals . . . different dreams. We already know this, and all without any actors.

Now we see the actors . . . a piano . . . behind it the head of a woman . . . a scrap of music. A vague reverie. The sun playing off the water among the reeds.

A store. Cloth is measured. An account book. A man gives orders. Up till now, everything is distant. People have only moved among things. We see them move around and position themselves . . . Movement.

One senses that poetry and reality will clash.

In a very bourgeois room, a woman reads. Very worthy, a book . . . Intellectualism. A man enters: M. Beudet . . . He is conceited. He holds a book of fabric samples . . . Materialism.

Shot: Mme Beudet doesn't even raise her head.

Shot: M. Beudet seats himself at a desk without speaking.

Shot: M. Beudet's hands count the threads of a fabric sample.

The characters are posed in shots that contrast with each other and that isolate different gestures, thereby making them stand out in relief.

All of a sudden, a long shot reunites these two people. Suddenly, all the jarring incongruities of a marriage appear. It is a *coup de théâtre*.

This is approximately the effect of the shots, their actions, and above all their psychological import. When something is shown from far away or near, the shot's value changes; when it isolates or reunites, its degree of intensity is not the same; its meaning changes.

Taken in long shots, Mme Beudet shrugging her shoulders would not have the same meaning if she shrugged her shoulders in a closer shot. When M. Beudet laughs, a laugh that sets his wife's nerves on edge, this laugh must fill the entire screen, the entire auditorium, so that the spectators feel the same antipathy as Mme Beudet does toward this vulgar husband. We need this to pardon the idea of crime that crops up later. The scale of the shots is graduated; the importance of M. Beudet's laugh is underscored in order to make an impression on the spectator and to make his flesh creep. Some people have blamed me for d'Arquillières's performance. I maintain that the character of M. Beudet would have been less three-dimensional if each of his tics had not been highlighted, or sampled, if I dare to put it this way.

Just as we work with the juxtapositions of images and with the camera placement, we also work with the shots. The psychological shot, the large close-up as we call it, is the very thought of the character projected onto the screen. It is his soul, his desire. . . . The large close-up is also an impressionistic note marking the fleeting influence of the things that surround us. Thus, in *Madame Beudet*, the large close-up of Mme Lebas's ear summarizes all that is provincial, all the gossips and narrow minds on the lookout for disputes and disagreements.

The close-up demands to be handled discretely. It is too important to be used without considering whether or not it is absolutely necessary.

As much as the long shots, the American shots—to use professional jargon—that cut the characters off at the knee, are used in shots where two or more characters are brought together. The large close-up is used above all to isolate a striking expression in a scene. It belongs to the intimate life of people or things.

The inner life made perceptible by images is, with movement, the entire art of cinema . . . Movement, inner life. These two terms, moreover, are not at all incompatible. What is more mobile than our psychological life with its reactions, its manifold impressions, its sudden movements, its dreams, its memories. The cinema is marvelously equipped to express these manifestations of our thinking, our emotions, our memories. And this leads me to speak about another technique: superimposition.

You have already seen examples of superimposition in *Kean*, when the beautiful ambassador's wife recalls her favorite actor, and in *Madame Beudet*, when the poor woman, overwhelmed by her noisy husband, dreams of a strong, powerful man who will deliver her from the one responsible [for her misery], the husband. The man summoned forth is only glimpsed in a dream. He is impalpable and unstable. It is a phantom that enters to do battle with the pusillanimous soul of M. Beudet. A transparent scene is grafted onto the more distinct one, one which portrays Mme Beudet as seen through her own imagination.

Superimposition is thinking, the inner life . . . It is achieved by combining two photographs. . . .

I still must talk about dissolves, soft focus, and distortions.

The dissolve is a means of moving from one image to the next in such a way that the end of the first is superimposed on the beginning of the next. It is also a technique with a psychological meaning. The images that are linked are related to each other so that the movement from one to the other is not jarring. The dissolve brings people and things together into a brief or lengthy whole. In one of my films, *La Mort du soleil* [1922], I wanted to depict the painful awakening of a great scientist who had been stricken with a cerebral hemorrhage. His paralyzed hand unleashes a whole realm of unhappy realities in his brain. He understands his condition . . . His eyes move towards his female colleague, then to a large painting of a corvette moving along under full sails. He looks at his hand . . . The great voyages of the mind, alas, are no longer for him. He then looks at his student who is combined in his vision with the large painting (a clear indication of his feelings) and, despairing, he turns back to the window where the leaves of the tree stand out against the shadows. Cut up in successive shots, this cinematic phrase would have lost its intellectual weight. The scientist's thought must be developed like a deduction. The dissolve assists this development. You are going to be the judges.

(Screening of *La Mort du soleil*: The sick man's room.)

Once cured, the scientist holds his student in a kind of bondage because she represents to him his power, his ideas—a complement to his brain that has been weakened by the illness. The two characters who you are going to see act independently, but nevertheless they are tied to one another . . . The dissolve highlights the ascendancy of one mind over another, an act of domination, a union that nothing can break.

(Screening of *La Mort du soleil*: The doctor dictates his book.)

Once the work is accomplished, the master becomes less harsh and domineering. These are the last pages of their collaborative work . . . A bit of tenderness comes with them. The dissolve imposes some tranquility on these two minds straining stubbornly towards a goal. We see two heads tilting symmetrically, happy in the fusion that softens the rigors of work. The scientist's head rests on that of the woman; the woman's rests once again on the scientist's, and their two profiles once more appear peaceful and studious. The dissolve doesn't play a passive role like the superimposition: it unifies.

(Screening of *La Mort du soleil*: The final dictation.)

I will give you two more examples of dissolves. One is psychological, the other is poetic.

The first, taken from *La Belle Dame sans merci* [1921], a film I directed several years ago, brings together a married woman and her husband's mistress. The legitimate spouse would like to be indignant, but the seductress's charm and her bearing sways the spirit of the deceived spouse who cannot fight against the refinements of the courtesan whose ascendancy she senses at the very moment she wants to be defiant. Strange flowers and penetrating perfumes put her spirit to sleep. These flowers and this incense are linked once again in the artist's head and enable her to understand what has happened.

(Screening of *La Belle Dame sans merci*: Perfume scene.)

The dissolve is unity in diversity. It is also a way of introducing a shot without any abruptness or to underscore a relationship between ideas.

The dissolve enables a poetic impression to be created. . . .

I will say very little to you about the fade, a process thanks to which a scene, once it is over, loses its luminosity and fades to black. It is the dot on the line, or sometimes a capital letter, depending on whether it comes at the end or at the beginning of a scene. It may also be a parenthesis when in the middle of a scene, an incident is quietly inserted. The fade is only a punctuation mark. . . .

Distortion and soft focus bring a whole visual philosophy to cinema.

In France, we have a great director, M. Jacques Feyder. In an admirable film, *Crainquebille* [1923], he has used the methods of soft focus and distortions with genius.

Soft focus . . . Crainquebille wants to persuade his lawyer of his innocence. Crainquebille is not an interesting client; he is a poor fellow without a penny. What good is it to listen to him! And in order to indicate how distracted the lawyer is, you will see all the notes that he takes on Crainquebille's case become unfocused and wavering. A visual explanation.

We are going to screen this tableau.

(*Crainquebille*: Scene with the lawyer.)

This shift from soft focus to distortion has somewhat disturbed audiences who poorly comprehend the real goal of cinema: to visualize the events or the joys of the inner life. One could make a film with a single character in conflict with his impressions.

It is almost this tour de force that Feyder has superbly realized in *Crainquebille*: Crainquebille and his feelings of fear and hope.

When considered from the standpoint of Crainquebille's mind, the soft focus, superimpositions, and distortions work magisterially. This poor Crainquebille, innocent of the offence he is accused of, no longer possesses the proper view of things . . . The policeman accusing him appears to be a giant. The defense witness seems tiny, and his testimony loses itself in a blank space next to him: the policeman's sleeve. Why is this policeman's sleeve so close to him? He didn't do anything!

A section of *Crainquebille*, one of the most powerful and most perfect French films, is going to be shown: Crainquebille at court!

(Screening of *Crainquebille*.)

This film has proved to you, I hope, the usefulness of distortions and soft focus. The ingenuous spirit of Crainquebille seemed all important to you, now that a skillful director knows how to dissect visual impressions.

What other art can achieve psychological effects such as this better than the cinema?

Isn't it remarkable that audiences corrupted by the antics in dramas rooted in exterior facts have been so uncomprehending as to necessitate an outrage, a written forward, at the beginning of *Crainquebille*? I deliberately left it there so that you could imagine the fights that we are obliged to wage to free the cinema from the routines in which even its friends sometimes imprison it.

You see, ladies and gentlemen, our palette is rich. The angle at which we shoot, pans, fades, dissolves, soft focus, distortions, superimpositions are so many touches to express ourselves without recourse to literature, without theatrical means, without excessive stage effects.

Cinema is an art that must remain itself and develop proudly next to the six others since it can, if it wishes, borrow nothing from them. What bothers us about cinema are the prejudices of the audience and the reflections of the other arts that want to help us at all costs.

The other arts can only do cinema a disservice to the extent that they express the pretension of imposing on it their rules and visions, which, moreover, they will not try to fuse with those of cinema when they are called upon to collaborate. But we who struggle, who fight in order to free our art from unfortunate intrusions and mistaken principles, have hope of victory. Just yesterday, weren't we still likened to fairground showmen? Yet today, the Musée Galliera opens its doors to us. It is now up to the general public to help us by seeking to understand our innovations and discoveries. The cinema will evolve, and will rid itself of everything that demeans it. What we have achieved up till now are merely experiments. Tomorrow we are certain that the cinema will produce pure masterpieces and will deserve even more to be called the Seventh Art, since that is how it has been baptized by those who have faith in its future.

GERMAINE DULAC (1882–1942) was a writer for the feminist magazines, *La Française* and *La Fronde*, before the war. She began directing films in 1916—for instance, *Ames de fous* (1918), *La Cigarette* (1919), *La Fête espagnole* (1920), *La Mort du soleil* (1922), *La Souriante Madame Beudet* (1923). At the time of this lecture, Dulac was becoming increasingly involved in the French ciné-club movement.

¹ The other example was an excerpt from Tourjansky's *Ce Cochon de Morin* (1924). I have deleted other sequences excerpted from Fescourt's *La Poupée du Milliardaire* (Italy, 1922) and *Les Grands* (1924).

JEAN EPSTEIN, "On Certain Characteristics of *Photogénie*"

Translated by Tom Milne in *Afterimage* 10 (Autumn 1981), 20–23. Reprinted by permission. Epstein delivered versions of this essay at the Salon d'Automne in November 1923, to the Paris-Nancy Group at Nancy on 1 December 1923, at the Pathé-Palace in Montpelier on 7 January 1924, and to the Philosophical and Scientific Studies Group at the Sorbonne on 15 June 1924. The original French text first appeared as "De quelques conditions de la photogénie" in *Cinéa-Ciné-pour-tous* 19 (15 August 1924), 6–8.

THE CINEMA seems to me like two Siamese twins joined together at the stomach, in other words by the base necessities of life, but sundered at the heart, or by the higher necessities of emotion. The first of these brothers is the art of cinema, the second is the film industry. A surgeon is called for, capable of separating these two fraternal foes without killing them, or a psychologist able to resolve the incompatibilities between these two hearts.

I shall venture to speak to you only of the art of cinema. The art of cinema has been called *"photogénie"* by Louis Delluc. The word is apt, and should be preserved. What is *photogénie*? I would describe as photogenic any aspect of things, beings, or souls whose moral character is enhanced by filmic reproduction. And any aspect not enhanced by filmic reproduction is not photogenic, plays no part in the art of cinema.

For every art builds its forbidden city, its own exclusive domain, autonomous, specific, and hostile to anything that does not belong. Astonishing to relate, literature must first and foremost be literary; the theater, theatrical; painting, pictorial; and the cinema, cinematic. Painting today is freeing itself from many of its representational and narrative concerns. Historical and anecdotal canvases, pictures which narrate rather than paint, are rarely seen nowadays outside the furnishing departments of the big stores—where, I must confess, they sell very well. But what one might call the high art of painting seeks to be no more than painting, in other words color taking on life. And any literature worthy of the name turns its back on those twists and turns of plot which lead to the detective's discovery of the lost treasure. Literature seeks only to be literary, which is seen as a justification for taking it to task by people alarmed at the idea that it might resemble neither a charade nor a game of cards and be put to better use than killing time, which there is no point in killing since it returns, hanging equally heavy, with each new dawn.

Similarly, the cinema should avoid dealings, which can only be unfortunate, with historical, educational, novelistic, moral or immoral, geographical or documentary subjects. The cinema must seek to become, gradually and in the end uniquely, cinematic; to employ, in other words, only photogenic elements. *Photogénie* is the purest expression of cinema.

What aspects of the world are photogenic, then, these aspects to which the cinema must limit itself? I fear the only response I have to offer to so important a question is a premature one. We must not forget that where the theater trails some tens of centuries of existence behind it, the cinema is a mere twenty-five years old. It is a new enigma. Is it an art? Or less than that? A pictorial language, like the hieroglyphs of ancient Egypt, whose secrets we have scarcely penetrated yet, about which we do not know all that we do not know? Or an unexpected extension to our sense of sight, a sort of telepathy of the eye? Or a challenge to the logic of the universe, since the mechanism of cinema constructs movement by multiplying successive stoppages of celluloid exposed to a ray of light, thus creating mobility through immobility, decisively demonstrating how right was the false reasoning of Zeno of Elea?

Do we know what radio will be like in ten years time? An eighth art, no doubt, as much at odds with music as cinema currently is with the theater. We are just as much in the dark as to what cinema will be like in ten years time.

At present, we have discovered the cinematic property of things, a new and exciting sort of potential: *photogénie*. We are beginning to recognize certain circumstances in which this *photogénie* appears. I suggest a preliminary specification in determining these photogenic aspects. A moment ago I described as photogenic any aspect whose moral character is enhanced by filmic reproduction. I now specify: only mobile aspects of the world, of things and souls, may see their moral value increased by filmic reproduction.

This mobility should be understood only in the widest sense, implying all directions perceptible to the mind. By general agreement it is said that the dimensions deriving from our sense of direction are three in number: the three spatial dimensions. I have never really understood why the notion of a fourth dimension has been enveloped in such mystery. It very obviously exists; it is time. The mind travels in time, just as it does in space. But whereas in space we imagine three directions at right angles to each other, in time we can conceive only one: the past-future vector. We can conceive a space-time system in which the past-future direction also passes through the point of intersection of the three acknowledged spatial directions, at the precise moment when it is between past and future: the present, a point in time, an instant without duration, as points in geometrical space are without dimension. Photogenic mobility is a mobility in this space-time system, a mobility in both space and time. We can therefore say that the photogenic aspect of an object is a consequence of its variations in space-time.

This definition, an important one, is not simply a mental intuition. A number of films have already offered concrete examples. First, certain American films, demonstrating an unconscious and highly precocious feeling for cinema, sketched the spatiotemporal cinegrams in rough outline. Later Griffith, that giant of the primitive cinema, gave classical expression to these jostling, intersecting denouements that describe arabesques virtually simultaneously in space and time. More consciously and more lucidly, Gance—today our master, one and all—then composed his astonishing vision of trains swept along on the rails of the drama. We must be clear why these racing wheels in *La Roue* comprise the most classic sentences yet written in the language of cinema. It is because in these images the most clearly defined role is played by variations, if not simultaneous at least approximately so, in the spatiotemporal dimensions.

For in the end it all comes down to a question of perspective, a question of design. Perspective in drawing is a three-dimensional perspective, and when a pupil executes a drawing which takes no account of the third dimension, the effect of depth or relief in objects, it is said that he has done a bad drawing, that he cannot draw. To the elements of perspective employed in drawing, the cinema adds a new perspective in time. In addition to relief in space the cinema offers relief in time. Astonishing abridgments in this temporal perspective are permitted by the cinema—notably in those amazing glimpses into the life of plants and crystals—but these have never yet been used to dramatic purpose. If, as I said earlier, a drawing which ignores the third spatial dimension in its perspective is a bad drawing, I must now add that cinema composed without taking the temporal perspective into account is not cinematic.

Moreover, cinema is a language, and like all languages it is animistic; it attributes, in other words, a semblance of life to the objects it defines. The more primitive a language, the more marked this animistic tendency. There is no need to stress the extent to which the language of cinema remains primitive in its terms and ideas; so it is hardly surprising that it should endow the objects it is called upon to depict with such intense life. The almost godlike importance assumed in close-ups by parts of the human body, or by the most frigid elements in nature, has often been noted.

316

Through the cinema, a revolver in a drawer, a broken bottle on the ground, an eye isolated by an iris, are elevated to the status of characters in the drama. Being dramatic, they seem alive, as though involved in the evolution of an emotion.

I would even go so far as to say that the cinema is polytheistic and theogonic. Those lives it creates, by summoning objects out of the shadows of indifference into the light of dramatic concern, have little in common with human life. These lives are like the life in charms and amulets, the ominous, tabooed objects of certain primitive religions. If we wish to understand how an animal, a plant, or a stone can inspire respect, fear, or horror, those three most sacred sentiments, I think we must watch them on the screen, living their mysterious, silent lives, alien to the human sensibility.

To things and beings in their most frigid semblance, the cinema thus grants the greatest gift unto death: life. And it confers this life in its highest guise: personality.

Personality goes beyond intelligence. Personality is the spirit visible in things and people, their heredity made evident, their past become unforgettable, their future already present. Every aspect of the world, elected to life by the cinema, is so elected only on condition that it has a personality of its own. This is the second specification which we can now add to the rules of *photogénie*. I therefore suggest that we say: only mobile and personal aspects of things, beings, and souls may be photogenic; that is, acquire a higher moral value through filmic reproduction.

An eye in close-up is no longer the eye, it is AN eye: in other words, the mimetic decor in which the look suddenly appears as a character . . . I was greatly interested by a competition recently organized by one of the film magazines. The point was to identify some forty more or less famous screen actors whose portraits reproduced in the magazine had been cropped to leave only their eyes. So what one had to do was to recognize the personality in each of forty *looks*. Here we have a curious unconscious attempt to get spectators into the habit of seeking and recognizing the distinctive personality of the eye segment.

And a close-up of a revolver is no longer a revolver, it is the revolver-character, in other words the impulse toward or remorse for crime, failure, suicide. It is as dark as the temptations of the night, bright as the gleam of gold lusted after, taciturn as passion, squat, brutal, heavy, cold, wary, menacing. It has a temperament, habits, memories, a will, a soul.

Mechanically speaking, the lens alone can sometimes succeed in revealing the inner nature of things in this way. This is how, by chance in the first instance, the *photogénie* of character was discovered. But the proper sensibility, by which I mean a personal one, can direct the lens towards increasingly valuable discoveries. This is the role of an author of film, com-

317

monly called a film director. Of course a landscape filmed by one of the forty or four hundred directors devoid of personality whom God sent to plague the cinema as He once sent the locusts into Egypt looks exactly like this same landscape filmed by any other of these locust filmmakers. But this landscape or this fragment of drama staged by someone like Gance will look nothing like what would be seen through the eyes and heart of a Griffith or a L'Herbier. And so the personality, the soul, the poetry of certain men invaded the cinema.

I remember still *La Roue*. As Sisif died, we all saw his unhappy soul leave him and slip away over the snows, a shadow borne away in angels' flight.

Now we are approaching the promised land, a place of great wonders. Here matter is molded and set into relief by personality; all nature, all things appear as a man has dreamed them; the world is created as you think it is; pleasant if you think it so, harsh if you believe it so. Time hurries on or retreats, or stops and waits for you. A new reality is revealed, a reality for a special occasion, which is untrue to everyday reality just as everyday reality is untrue to the heightened awareness of poetry. The face of the world may seem changed since we, the fifteen hundred million who inhabit it, can see through eyes equally intoxicated by alcohol, love, joy, and woe, through lenses of all tempers, hate and tenderness; since we can see the clear thread of thoughts and dreams, what might or should have been, what was, what never was or could have been, feelings in their secret guise, the startling face of love and beauty, in a word, the soul. "So poetry is thus true, and exists as truly as the eye."

Here poetry, which one might have thought but verbal artifice, a figure of style, a play of antithesis and metaphor—in short, something next to nothing—achieves a dazzling incarnation. "So poetry is thus true, and exists as truly as the eye."

The cinema is poetry's most powerful medium, the truest medium for the untrue, the unreal, the "surreal" as Apollinaire would have said.

This is why some of us have entrusted to it our highest hopes.

PART FOUR 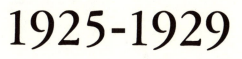 1925-1929

A subject is not a pretext, it is the very *foundation* of the work. . . . A film devoted to a narrative, performed and directed without any other aim but that narrative, handled through the objective exposition of a series of actions, has nothing to do with theater.

Henri Fescourt and Jean-Louis Bouquet, 1925

Cinegraphic images do not illustrate an action. They themselves are the action.

Germaine Dulac, 1927

Is this a new dramaturgy toward which images are now reaching? More or less stripped of all technique, they really signify only in association with each other, just as words which are simple and rich in meaning must do.

Jean Epstein, 1927

For us and us alone the Lumière brothers invented the cinema. There we were at home. Its darkness was like that of our bedrooms before we fell asleep. Perhaps the screen might be the equal of our dreams.

Robert Desnos, 1927

In order for the cinema to realize its potential, it has to be freed from the domination of capital. What will do that? The system of production of a socialist economy. And since this socialist economy is only possible through revolutionary means, we await the Revolution.

Léon Moussinac, 1927

The Great Debates

THE STARTLING expansion of French writing on the cinema, generated by the end of the Great War and sustained throughout the early
1920s, actually increased at least twofold in the second half of the decade.
Once again the increase seemed explosive rather than gradual. It was
sparked by the heady growth of magazines and books devoted to film, by
newly opened specialized cinemas, and by activist ciné-clubs which organized even more exhibitions and *conférences* on the cinema. It was fueled by a
long, often rancorous debate revolving around the question whether there
could or should be anything like a "pure cinema," a debate that then
touched off others as well. And it was fanned by a growing dissatisfaction
with the economic institutions and sociopolitical practices in which the
French cinema was enmeshed. This dissatisfaction led to a further politi-
cization of French intellectuals and the formation of several influential
groups on both the right—Les Jeunesses Patriotes and Le Faisceau—and the
left—the Surrealists and the Philosophes. Of those on the left, some now
even joined forces with the French Communist Party and came to espouse
an interest in either a populist or proletarian literature and cinema.

THE PUBLIC FORUM

During the late 1920s, the public forum for French writing on the cinema was probably more extensive than during any other period in the first
half of this century.[1] The daily newspapers and weekly magazines constituted perhaps the least important arena now, and few significant changes
occurred in their ranks.[2] Of the Paris dailies associated with the right, to
which *Le Temps* and *Paris-Soir* had now shifted, the only film critic changes
came at *Le Matin* (Jean Chataigner) and *L'Intransigeant* (Alexandre Arnoux).
An important addition on the right, however, appeared in François Coty's
L'Ami du peuple, which unexpectedly reached a circulation of one million
within two years of its launching in 1928.[3] Much like *L'Intransigeant* before
the war, despite its generally rightist political line, *L'Ami du peuple* attracted writers who supported the left on cultural affairs—its cinema page,
for example, provided a forum for reviews by Louis Chavance and Paul Gilson. J. L. Croze (now the president of the Association professionelle de la
presse cinématographique) continued to control the cinema page of the
centrist *Le Petit Parisien* as well as the arts daily, *Comoedia*. On the left, as
its influence declined somewhat with the fall of the Cartel des Gauches gov-

ernment in 1926, only one new small-circulation daily appeared—Alexis Caille's *Le Soir*, for which Robert Desnos wrote weekly reviews in 1927.

The weekly journals devoted to political and cultural affairs played an even larger role than before as they continued to provide more and more space for articles and reviews about the cinema. The *Revue hebdomadaire* added another film review column to René Jeanne's extensive list of writings; the *Nouvelles littéraires* changed film reviewers at close to one-year intervals (Jeanne, Jean Prévost, Arnoux); *Le Monde illustré* opened a film column to André Antoine; and *Le Journal littéraire* briefly included film reviews by Desnos. At least three new politically distinct journals emerged into prominence—the right-wing *Candide* (published by Arthème Fayard), for which Jeanne wrote yet another column; the international communist journal, *Monde* (edited by Henri Barbusse), to which Léon Moussinac contributed film reviews; and the much smaller, left-wing *La Lumière* (launched by Georges Boris), which published Georges Altman's earliest film writings.[4] Finally, the monthly literary magazines maintained a serious interest in the cinema. While *Mercure de France* failed to replace Moussinac after he left the magazine in early 1926, its rival, the *Nouvelle Revue française*, suddenly began to open its pages to the cinema, beginning with Prévost's film reviews and Antonin Artaud's scenario for *La Coquille et le clergyman* (1927).[5] Jean Galtier-Boissière's *Le Crapouillot* continued to devote a good deal of space to both filmmakers and film critics, and Georges Bataille's short-lived *Documents* (1929–1930) published the last of Desnos's essays on the cinema.

Most central to this public forum, of course, was a host of film magazines that seemed to grow in number annually. At the elite end of the spectrum, young Jean Dréville, for instance, edited no less than three different film journals over a two-year period: *Photo-Ciné* (1927), the deluxe, folio-format *Cinégraphie* (1927–1928), and *On Tourne* (1928), all of which especially supported the work of the French narrative avant-garde. Backed by the publishing prestige of Gallimard and the *Nouvelle Revue française*, in December 1928, Jean-George Auriol launched the deluxe monthly, *La Revue du cinéma*, which gave special attention to the Soviet and French Surrealist films and which published essays and reviews by Chavance, Gilson, Robert Aron, J.-Bernard Brunius, André Sauvage, and Lucie Derain among others.[6] At the popular end of the spectrum, two major weekly film magazines also appeared late in 1928—Gaston Thierry's *Cinémonde* (financed by *Le Petit Parisien*) and Alexandre Arnoux's *Pour Vous* (financed by *L'Intransigeant*)—but their impact would not come until the 1930s. In the meantime, *Cinémagazine* continued to circulate as the most popular semi-independent film magazine of the 1920s, and its *Annuaire général de la cinématographie* maintained a position on a par with *Filma*'s *Tout-Cinéma*.

Mon-Ciné prospered to the point of offering its own annual review of the cinema, while *Ciné-Miroir* (published by *Le Petit Parisien*) reached the extraordinary circulation of 100,000 copies per issue. Finally, Jean Tedesco's deluxe *Cinéa-Ciné-pour-tous* consolidated its position as the most important film journal encouraging discussion of a national as well as an international film art. It was here, after all, that Jean Epstein still published most of his essays and that the debate raged most fiercely over the concept of a "pure cinema."

But there was another major component of the French public forum at least equal in importance to that of the specialized film magazines. One segment was comprised of special journal issues devoted to the cinema, which *Le Crapouillot* had initiated just after the war. *Les Cahiers du mois* published the most significant of these, in 1925, in two book-length issues: one (issue 12) a collection of unfilmed scenarios,[7] the other (issue 16–17) an influential collection of lectures, essays, and notes on almost every aspect of the cinema, published in conjunction with the 1925 Paris Exposition of the Modern Decorative Arts. In the latter, Lucien Wahl cautiously described the work of a film reviewer—without establishing any clear-cut critical principles or rules—and called attention to the problems of maintaining some degree of independence from the film industry.[8] The success of this second *Cahiers du mois* issue on the cinema spurred the publication of several other similar collections: Germaine Dulac's *Schémas* (February 1927), *Le Crapouillot* (March 1927), *La Revue fédéraliste* (November 1927), and *Le Rouge et le noir* (July 1928). And it undoubtedly encouraged the Librairie Félix Alcan to publish and market a special collection of lectures and essays on the cinema in a serial format, much like the issues of a semiannual or triquarterly magazine. This celebrated *L'Art cinématographique* series collected four long pieces in each volume (almost every major French writer was represented here) and ran for eight volumes from 1926 to 1929.

Another segment of this forum was comprised of books devoted to the cinema, which numbered almost as many as were published throughout the rest of the first decades in France. Some were collections or revisions of essays and reviews written between 1919 and 1924: Moussinac's *Naissance du cinéma* (Povolovsky, 1925), Blaise Cendrars's *L'A.B.C. du cinéma* (Les Ecrivains réunis, 1926), and Ricciotto Canudo's *L'Usine aux images* (Etienne Chiron, 1926). Others were collections of more current writings: Epstein's *Le Cinématographe vu d'Etna* (Les Ecrivains réunis, 1926), René Schwob's *Une Melodie silencieuse* (1929), Moussinac's *Panoramique du cinéma* (Le Sans Pareil, 1929), Arnoux's *Cinéma* (1929), and Georges Charensol's *Panorama du cinéma* (Editions Dra, 1929).[9] At least three books dealt extensively with the film industry in one way or another: G.-Michel Coissac's *Histoire du cinématographe: Des origines jusqu'à nos jours* (Cinéopse, 1925),

André Delpeuch, *Le Cinéma* (Octave Doin, 1927), and Coissac's *Les Coulisses du cinéma* (Pittoresques, 1929). Finally, there were at least three original and influential books: Henri Fescourt and Jean-Louis Bouquet's polemical defense of a narrative cinema in *L'Idée et l'écran: Opinions sur le cinéma* (Haberschill et Sergent, 1925–1926), René Marchand and Pierre Weinstein's introductory survey of the Soviet cinema in *L'Art dans la Russie nouvelle*, vol. 1, *Le Cinéma* (Rieder, 1927), and Moussinac's more extensive survey in *Le Cinéma soviétique* (Nouvelle Revue française, 1928).

This broad public forum of writing on the cinema was heavily indebted, even more so than in the early 1920s, to the interrelated network of ciné-clubs, specialized cinemas, exhibitions, and *conférences* which—as Moussinac was one of the first to document—now constituted an alternate system of exchange more or less independent of the dominant film industry.[10] The year 1925 saw the establishment of two major ciné-clubs that would dominate the alternate cinema network for the rest of the decade—the Ciné Club de France, which Moussinac and others (Dulac, René Blum, Henri Clouzot) created out of a merger of CASA and the Club français du cinéma, and the Tribune libre, which Charles Léger formed around a nucleus of younger cinéphiles (Dréville, Auriol, Brunius, Marcel Carné, and Jean Mitry). At the same time, two major specialized cinemas opened to become the "flagship" cinemas of a loose circuit of independent cinemas in Paris— Jean Tedesco's Vieux-Colombier and Armand Tallier and Myrga's Studio des Ursulines, both of which were joined later by Jean Mauclaire's Studio 28. Together, these ciné-clubs and specialized cinemas, in imitation of the Musée Galliera exhibition of 1924, organized several series of public expositions and *conférences*—from the Tribune libre screening-discussions at the 1925 Exposition of the Modern Decorative Arts and the Ciné-Club de France *conférences* at the Vieux-Colombier, in the winter of 1925–1926, to the League of Nations' International Film Congress (organized by the Comité national français de coopération intellectuelle) in the fall of 1926 and the Ciné-Club de France lectures for the College libre des sciences sociales, early in 1927. Many of the lectures and papers delivered at these sessions were later published in *Cahiers du mois, L'Art cinématographique*, and *Cinéa-Ciné-pour-tous*.

By the end of the decade, then, just before the sound "revolution" hit France, there were over a dozen ciné-clubs flourishing in Paris (some with branches in the French provinces and in Switzerland or Belgium) and a half dozen specialized cinemas (including L'Oeil de Paris, Salle des Agriculteurs, Studio Diamant) catering to these ciné-clubs as well as to a mixed audience of intellectuals, artists, workers, and students. Perhaps the most interesting organization to emerge in this alternate cinema network— Amis de Spartacus (1928)—was founded by Moussinac and his French

Communist Party colleagues not long after his return from the first international writers conference organized by the Association of Soviet Proletarian Writers (RAPP) in Moscow, in late 1927. This one truly mass ciné-club or "Cinéma du peuple" had an overtly political orientation, which centered on the exhibition of the banned Soviet films at the Casino de Grenelle and Bellevillois cinemas. But it was also committed to the preservation of films of all sorts, in original negative as well as positive distribution prints.[11] Although Spartacus was disbanded by the Paris police prefect not long after its foundation, it laid some of the groundwork for the Popular Front film organizations as well as the Cinémathèque française, which would come into prominence in the middle 1930s.

POLARIZING THE IDEOLOGICAL GROUND OF DEBATE

Despite a good number of disagreements and internal discrepancies, French writing on the cinema in the early 1920s had operated within a kind of loose consensus. Writers generally agreed on the commitment to search for and isolate some form of cinematic specificity, more precisely to define *cinégraphie* or the rhythmic principles that governed film continuity, and to establish distinctly French conceptions of cinema. This commitment continued to motivate writers in the late 1920s, of course, as evidenced in André Levinson's "Pour une poétique du film" (1927), where he concisely summarized the principles according to which film could be defined as an art form, could be differentiated from the other arts, and could be said to be unique—primarily in its editing.[12] Generally, however, the consensus of the early 1920s seemed to break down or at least undergo some change in the late 1920s. Discourse became polarized and sometimes acrimoniously personal, drawing what seemed to be clear-cut lines between highly polemical factions. Assumptions once held in common came more and more under scrutiny. In one sense, this could be taken as a sign of health and vitality, a form of renewal or maturity. In another sense, however, this meant that the shared vision of a new art form that would transform the world—culturally, socially, even ontologically—seemed as far from realization as ever before. The French cinema once more seemed in a state of crisis, and the dimensions of that crisis informed much of French discourse on the cinema.

"The present situation is clear; we are on the brink of disaster," Jean Sapène told a stockholders meeting of Pathé-Consortium early in 1925.[13] Most writers seemed to agree with him—and as owner-director of the Société des Cinéromans (with controlling interest still in *Le Matin*), he was the leading figure in the French film industry at the time—but they did not necessarily agree with his analysis or conclusion. For Sapène, the solution lay in realignments and policy changes within the structure of the film industry: tighter controls over directors in film production and alliances with other European film companies in production and distribution. In this, he probably spoke for many in the industry who wanted to create a European cartel that could compete with the American film distributors at least in Europe, but one that also would preserve some national autonomy.[14] By contrast, Marcel L'Herbier, Abel Gance, and Cendrars, for example, spoke for those who retained some faith in the old dream of a new international community predicated on the "democratic" constituency and "universal language" of the cinema as well as, by implication, on a benevolent form of capitalism.[15] This position was representative of the idealistic, cooperative spirit of the 1926 Paris International Film Congress, whose 500 delegates sought to encourage the non-commercial—that is, intellectual and educational—functions of the cinema worldwide.[16] Implementation of the potentially progressive resolutions of the congress came to nought, however, because of the American film industry's refusal to participate and the growing weakness of its sponsor, the League of Nations. Despite this failure, Gance, for one, continued to lobby for a kind of cultural solution to what essentially was an economic and political problem, through international mediation—a League of Nations agency for worldwide film production and distribution—long after the idea could be said to be viable.[17]

More and more writers, however, were coming to see that the French cinema crisis was only part of a more fundamental crisis in the socioeconomic system that dominated Europe and the United States and that a "cultural revolution" led by the cinema could not alone effect significant social or economic change. In his analysis of modern spectacle, for instance, Fernand Léger took note of the need for an "economic revolution" that, instead of producing department store display windows to compel consumption, would create "the hoped-for new equilibrium" of human relations and make man a "beneficiary [rather than] a victim of the machine."[18] In somewhat more specific terms, René Clair advocated "a modification of the material conditions of the cinema," namely, its "whole industrial organization."[19] After attending the RAPP conference in Moscow (along with Barbusse and others) and studying the structure and facilities of the Soviet film industry, Moussinac, of course, went even further.[20] The only way that the cinema could become the "great form of collective expression" it had once promised, he argued, would be through "*a cooperative system* of production, coincident with a new economic system [which was] founded on the base of a new social organization."[21] For Moussinac, this meant a "socialist economy" modeled on that of the Soviet Union, which was "only possible through revolutionary means." As a consequence, he turned his attention to the alternate cinema network in France, which still depended heavily on the status quo of the French social economy even though it may have developed into a quasi-independent exhibition system. Moussinac's Amis de Spartacus, however, turned out to be an overly ambitious and mistimed attempt to break free of the status quo, encourage a revolutionary change, and move toward just such a new socioeconomic order.

Within this polarization of political and socioeconomic positions, more familiar oppositions either stabilized, dissolved, or else turned relatively unstable. The elite cinema advocates—for example, Dulac, Tedesco, Vuillermoz, Pierre Porte, Paul Ramain—consolidated their position within the alternate cinema network. But they came increasingly under attack from those who advocated a popular cinema, whether as a narrative form produced by a kind of industry status quo—for example, Jacques Feyder, Fescourt and Bouquet—or as a more heterogeneous form of spectacle produced by a new economic system—for instance, Léger, Moussinac, Desnos, André Sauvage. Among the latter, Léger seem to have been unique in situating the cinema as just one of several promising popular cultural forms of *modern spectacle*, each of which would be based on the dynamic rhythms and collisions of daily phenomena in the streets and organized in terms of "form, light, and color."[22] The elite cinema advocates also continued to argue strongly that the cinema ought to constitute a medium for the individual artist's expression. Those within the industry, such as Sapène, of course, assumed a hierarchical concept of collaborative production, over which they could exercise more control and possession. Here, perhaps not so unexpectedly, Moussinac, Desnos (as a representative of the Surrealists) and others often sided with the individualist position, at least in their reviews of specific films. Although Moussinac would describe the collective or group method of production in the Soviet cinema as a model for imitation, he acknowledged, given the actual conditions in France, the value of individuals whose work offered alternatives to current practice. Yet even Moussinac's survey of the Soviet cinema tended to privilege the individual genius of a Sergei Eisenstein, a Vsevolod Pudovkin, or a Dziga Vertov; and his reviews consistently assumed that certain "master" filmmakers were *auteurs* worthy of study on their own.[23] Such an assumption now marked much of French writing on the cinema.

Abel Gance, perhaps the most prominent French *auteur* of the late 1920s, represented a highly visible convergence and fusion of the elitist and popular conceptions of cinema. Gance's work during this period depended on what Norman King has called an "elitist populism"—a form of political romanticism quite widespread during the interwar years in France, notably in the writings of Elie Faure, whose book on Napoleon (G. Crès, 1921) became the primary source of Gance's *Napoléon* (1927).[24]

According to Faure, King writes, although "the people remain the source of new energy" for social change and renewal, they need "a powerful authority with high ideals and strength of purpose" to galvanize and guide them[25]—in other words, a cult of the hero based on popular intuition and spiritual regeneration. For Gance, specifically, this called for a heroic figure such as Napoleon whose "personality" would express "the visible soul of things and of a people," and whose history would offer a vision of the past and future for an entire nation. The filmmaker's own characteristically immodest contribution to this elitist populism was to turn himself into a hero: "the [film] image only exists as the representation of the power of the person who creates it."[26] Consequently, he cast himself as the prophetic artist who sought to inspire such a regeneration through his ability to fuse the visionary and the scientific (the poetic and the technological) within the then-current forms of popular culture, namely, the melodrama. Such a transformation would create a "great film" synthesizing all the arts—a synthesis such as L'Herbier had previously attempted, but as high art, in *L'Inhumaine* (1924)—and constituting a mythic "bridge of dreams from one era to another."[27] Although Gance regarded himself as nonpolitical in making *Napoléon*, critics as disparate as Vuillermoz and Moussinac found the film ideologically repellant.[28] Ultimately, as Moussinac feared, Gance's work would feed the reactionary rightist mythologizing so cherished by *Action française* and other like-minded organizations.

Despite Gance's visionary heroism, the French faith in technological innovation—whether defined generally as progress or specifically as an "avant-garde" end in itself—also came into question. Jean Goudal, for instance, broached the idea that the cinema had already reached a kind of perfection as an artificial, black and white simulacrum of reality, supported by music. The promised addition of sound, color, and three-dimensionality would only detract, Goudal argued, from its existence as a dreamlike hallucination.[29] Moussinac also prudently stepped back from his faith in technological innovation. Although he and Vuillermoz might still laud the technical inventiveness of Gance's *Napoléon*, for example, that inventiveness could not be extricated from what he perceived to be the fascist ideology of the film.[30] Yet by the end of the decade, that faith seemed to return as Moussinac accepted the supposed neutrality of technology within the social economy, despite his awareness of the current American development of television—"Other than technique, in filmmaking everything must be destroyed—and everything remains to be created."[31] As if his stance were a marker of the period, Epstein hesitated. Along with André Obey, he concluded that technological innovation for its own sake seemed to be bankrupt: by 1924–1925, "the mechanical period of the cinema [was] over."[32] Yet he also cautiously encouraged the experiments in developing a viable color filmstock, no matter how ridiculous and simplistic the initial films using it might seem.[33] Furthermore, Epstein recognized that his own films had changed significantly in their rhythm not only because of technological advances but simply because "the time it takes an ordinary spectator to read a cinematic image has decreased in five years by 30 percent."[34] A similar hesitation in attitudes would mark the French writers and filmmakers' response to the coming of sound films.

MAINSTREAM NARRATIVE CINEMA VERSUS PURE CINEMA

The spectrum of theories that had developed during the previous ten years underwent a polarization as well. This is most evident in the central debate that animated French writing on the cinema, especially between 1925 and 1927, the debate over the possible existence and value of a "pure cinema." So pervasive was the question that nearly every writer was forced to declare a position on it. The debate took shape in the public sessions at the 1925 Paris Exposition and at the Vieux-Colombier and, more importantly here, in the pages of Cahiers du mois, Cinéa-Ciné-pour-tous, Schémas, and L'Idée et l'écran: Opinions sur le cinéma. The two poles of the debate were set by Fescourt and Bouquet's provocative defense of the primacy of narrative cinema, in which they attacked the so-called avant-garde along with the very idea of a "pure cinema," and by the spirited rejoinders of various "pure cinema" advocates.

Fescourt and Bouquet's L'Idée et l'écran appeared in three booklets issued in conjunction with the release of their big-budget, four-part adaptation of Les Misérables, probably the single most important French film of the 1925–1926 season.[35] These booklets functioned, therefore, as a justification of their own film practice at Sapène's Cinéromans, which Feyder had supported implicitly in Cahiers du mois not long before. Because of poor production methods, lagging spectator education, and a dearth of original scenarios, Feyder argued, the French cinema had to rely on skillful adaptations of good French novels.[36] Furthermore, Fescourt and Bouquet wrote their tract as playlets or pseudo-Socratic dialogues in which (speaking as a single voice) they easily manipulated a rather simple-minded "pure cinema" advocate into accepting their conclusions.

Fescourt and Bouquet begin with a sketch of cinema history that describes a line of French filmmaking that deviates from American practice— through Gance, Delluc, L'Herbier, and Epstein—and ends up in an "avant-garde" compendium of techniques—an overly simplified representation, which many others have since elaborated on. Thereafter, they run through several variations on their argument. Their central point is that narrative or story provides the subject for most art, which includes painting and music as well as almost any form of literature. Too many critics, they note, have equated narrative with theater and mistakenly thrown out both in trying to distinguish the cinema from the theater. As the very *foundation* of art, then, narrative functions as the primary source of any emotional or intellectual effects. At its simplest level, this means that the film image is not only plastic, but meaningful, for "movement produces a transformation of meaning as well as a transformation of plasticity."[37] In other words, they write, "the cinema depends on two aesthetic elements: *luminous values* and *rhythm*," of course; but it also depends on *"logic* . . . the principle that coordinates shots into an ensemble."[38] Here, Fescourt and Bouquet's argument returns to that articulated in far more detail by Diamant-Berger in *Le Cinéma* (1919). In general, however, their purpose is more polemical than theoretical or practical. They do not consider, for instance, how each of the film image's constituent parts interrelate; they do not look closely at any one film text; and they end up implicitly defending the American narrative cinema as much as, if not more than, the French narrative cinema. But Fescourt and Bouquet do conclude with a question that pinpointed the crisis that a good number of "avant-garde" filmmakers and writers were going through—for instance, Epstein and Clair, whom they villify repeatedly.[39] What exactly was the French avant-garde—an end in itself or a movement in search of a new aesthetic? And, in either case, just what had it accomplished?

The "pure cinema" advocates were scarcely unanimous in their sense of avant-garde accomplishments; but, surprisingly, in light of Fescourt and Bouquet's argument, they were no more unanimous about precisely how to define "a *pure, absolute cinema*."[40] This was because the term actually covered a loose cluster of concepts of cinema—absolute cinema, abstract cinema, integral cinema, plastic music, visual symphony—over which it emerged briefly as dominant.[41] "Pure cinema" represented, in fact, the culmination of several slightly different lines of thinking—from Survage's "colored rhythm" and Vuillermoz's "musical analogy" to Gromaire and Léger's "plastic compositions" and Faure's "cineplastics," inflected by the general fascination with cinematic specificity that so marked the early 1920s. All these came together, in 1925, in what initially seemed an answer to the general French crisis of confidence and to Epstein's call "for a new avant-garde." Taken as a composite group, then, the "pure cinema" advocates seemed to act in implicit consort with Abbé Bremond who, in a famous series of articles in *Les Nouvelles littéraires* (from October 1925 to January 1926), popularized a theory of "pure poetry," which undoubtedly helped energize, though hardly originate, the "pure cinema" debate and whose internal inconsistencies the theory of a "pure cinema" shared.[42]

In *Cahiers du mois* alone, several different ideas circulated under shifting labels. Dulac, for instance, articulates a concept of cinema in which the artist's feeling or state of mind emanates through a "visual symphony made up of rhythmic [representational] images"—a visual symphony that she comes close to detaching completely from narrative cinema.[43] While seeming to agree with Dulac, Henri Chomette (Clair's older brother) instead argues for a cinema that eschews representation altogether, whether documentary or dramatic, and whose "kaleidoscopic" surface of rhythmic harmony alone could "move our sensibilities as well as our intelligence."[44] Here, Clair also singles out as essential the rhythmic relations within and between shots (echoing Moussinac), but he asserts that their value is partly determined by the "emotional quality" of actors and decors.[45] In a separate note, Clair also suggests that something like his brother's concept of cinema exists only in fragments (which recalls Canudo's privileging of film excerpts); yet Chomette himself clearly intends an autonomous form for short films and modestly refrains from mentioning his own *Le Jeux des reflets et de la vitesse* (1925) and *Cinq Minutes de cinéma pur* (1925) as models.[46] Léger and Charensol share Chomette's desire to get rid of the scenario or narrative as the subject of film, but they relocate that subject in *"the image of the object,"* in the plastic and rhythmic conjunction or juxtaposition of representational "documentary" images.[47] Strangely, while Charensol offers "the succession of . . . fixed and moving objects, machines, common utensils, and geometric forms" in Léger's *Ballet mécanique* (1924) as a model of "abstract cinema," Léger himself concludes that "very few possess the plastic culture or training" that such a cinema entails, "apart from Marcel L'Herbier and René Clair."[48] Within the specific forum of *Cahiers du mois*, at least, "pure cinema" already constituted an unstable amalgam of Romantic and Modernist, representational and non-representational, expressive and formalist assertions.

Over the course of the next year or so, this amalgam held, especially in the short pieces of Pierre Porte, who, perhaps more than any other critic, repeatedly challenged Fescourt and Bouquet's argument with a consistently limpid, modest defense of "pure cinema."[49] At times, as when he offers a brief catalogue of "schools" or individual avant-garde stylistic tendencies, Porte writes as if he were echoing Bremond's concept of "a pure appreciation of poetry": "pure cinema" seems to be little more than an abstract quality common to all "true" films.[50] At other times, Porte assumes the Symbolist expressivity of a Vuillermoz or Dulac in asserting that the cinema can have "the same ideal as the other arts, the ideal of elevating the spirit above and beyond the material world," in a kind of "transcendental poetry."[51] Then again, in the same essay, he can isolate and privilege the originality of the cinema as a material means—*"the harmony and melody of plastic movements."*[52] Here Chomette, Léger, and Charensol's concept of an

331

abstract or absolute cinema seems to become the "purest" of the "pure cinema" positions. Consequently, through his many essays in *Cinéa-Ciné-pour-tous*, Porte acted much like a point man among a broad coalition of avant-gardists.[53]

By late 1926 or early 1927, however, this amalgam had come unstuck. The good ship *avant-garde*, suggested André Obey, now seemed more like a *bateau ivre* lost at sea.[54] Louis Chavance, for instance, successfully split off the concept of "visual symphony" from that of "pure cinema," to the latter's detriment.[55] Pure cinema he identifies with a cinema comprised exclusively of geometric elements whose existence was fleeting and whose value was limited in comparison to the sustained orchestration of evocative representational images, for example, in Dulac's "visual symphony" cinema. Thereafter, only a very few writers, such as filmmakers Hans Richter and Eugène Deslaw, chose to privilege the plastic side of "pure cinema," by focusing exclusively on the rhythmic surface of the film image.[56] A greater number, including Vuillermoz, of course, continue to emphasize the "musical analogy" as a theoretical basis for film art.[57] Some, like Obey, echoing Canudo, argue for a synthetic formal composition of complementary music and film image.[58] Others, like Dulac—especially in her rewriting of Fescourt and Bouquet's historical sketch, in "Les Esthétiques, les entraves, la cinégraphie integrale" (1926)—imagine a cinema entirely autonomous from narrative, in which "lines unwinding in profusion according to a rhythm dependent on a sensation or an abstract idea affect one's emotions by themselves . . . solely through the activity of their development."[59] In several essays as well as in her own film practice, Dulac now repeatedly defends a nonrepresentational cinema that would bring to the surface from the depths an "imperceptible music."[60] This fragmentation effectively ended the brief, paradoxical reign of a theory of "pure cinema." And it led to further attacks by writers who were perhaps even less enamored of mainstream narrative cinema—for instance, Artaud, Moussinac, Epstein, and Desnos.[61] As a polemical convergence of more or less like-minded filmmakers and critics, at a particular historical juncture, however, the "pure cinema" advocates constituted a major chord of near harmony in the cacaphony of French voices debating the nature of the cinema in the late 1920s.

IMPRESSIONISM AND REALISM

Between these two antagonistic poles of mainstream narrative cinema and "pure cinema," a number of other theories either struggled to survive, underwent a dramatic resurgence, or were consolidated in iconoclastic positions. The Impressionist concept of a subjective cinema, for one, seemed to lose some of its force and to settle into a somewhat stable position, perhaps because it no longer required a polemical defense. The best sign of this probably was provided by Dulac, formerly one of its leading proponents, when she assigned "the psychological and impressionist film" a specific place of influence in cinema history (the early 1920s) and then described how "pure cinema" extended, purified, and superceded it.[62] And when it did find an explicit defense now, it came in the shape of either Vuillermoz's unoriginal "La Musique des images" (1927), Chavance's critique of its narrow focus on technique, or Paul Ramain's "theory" of an oneiric cinema or "symphonic daydream"—a half-baked synthesis of aesthetic idealism, new psychological concepts, and "pure cinema" techniques.[63] Impressionism did receive implicit support, however, from several essays that explored the relations between film and fiction. In a ground-breaking argument (for the French) that film and novel "obey the same necessities and use the same means to affect their audiences," André Levinson, for instance, pointed to, among other things, their shared concentration on a so-called "symbolic attitude," their insinuation of "a state of mind," and their similar progressive narration of action.[64] More specifically, Pierre Quesnoy found startling parallels between the handling of character, place, time, and memory in film and in the novels of Marcel Proust. These included the discontinuous "psychological evolution of characters," the recalling of forgotten memories through "some sensorial shock, some sort of triggering release in the unconscious," and the use of superimpositions to describe subjective impressions.[65] By the end of the decade, the Impressionist theory of cinema was still prominent enough, at least in practice, for Desnos to single out its "exaggerated respect for art" and its "mystique of expression" for mocking condemnation.[66]

The Realist theory of a narrative cinema, which Delluc and Moussinac had articulated in partial opposition to Impressionism in the early 1920s, at first seemed to fade in importance as well. But then it rebounded in response to the stunning impact of the banned Soviet films, the emergence of manifestos for and inquiries into a populist and proletarian fiction, and perhaps the repeated revival of Delluc's as well as other early French realist films in the ciné-clubs and specialized cinemas.[67] With his connections in the French Communist Party, Moussinac, of course, was the crucial figure here. His participation in the RAPP conference in Moscow, his firsthand experience of the Soviet film industry, his discussions with Soviet filmmakers, and his tireless efforts to exhibit Soviet films widely in France all seemed not only to restore his faith in a realist aesthetic but also to redefine it more sharply and narrowly in socioeconomic terms. In contrast to the travestied caricatures in the American and European cinemas, for instance—see the scathing review of *Metropolis* (1927) by Prévost[68]—the Soviet cinema was seeking "to portray the life of workers and peasants in particular, to translate revolutionary realities, without forgetting that this ought neither to be limited to sentimental and psychological serial episodes nor simply dissolve into a study of certain milieus and a number of personalities."[69] There the spectator "discovered in a simple, authentic story, not the sterile romantic excitement of fated events, but the omnipresent realism of his sacrifice, his labor, his desire, and his goals."[70] In contrast to the French, Moussinac also pointedly noted, the Soviet *cinéastes* were interested in "pure cinema" experiments only to the extent that they might be useful in satisfying "the moral and intellectual needs of the masses."[71] One of the things that impressed Moussinac about Eisenstein, for instance, was the way he devoted himself, especially in *Potemkin* (1925–1926), "to approximating the 'newsreel' image as much as possible, to images caught on the run and interpreted solely by the lens and the drive mechanism of the camera."[72] As conscious as he was then of the different techniques that Eisenstein, Pudovkin, and Vertov used and experimented with, Moussinac still stressed the social vision that seemed to unite them.

Soviet filmmaking practice and a Marxist aesthetic (whether Soviet or French) were not alone, however, in stimulating the resurgence of a Realist theory of narrative cinema. Encouragement also came from the relatively apolitical defenses of a populist literature, initially articulated in the late 1920s by André Thérive and Léon Lemonnier.[73] And it came most significantly from Henri Poulaille, whose influential advocacy of a proletarian literature intersected momentarily with the notions of Moussinac and his colleagues.[74] Because it arose as a "spontaneous expression of the working class," Poulaille believed that a proletarian literature was indigenous to France as well as elsewhere.[75] And generally, he also argued, it was not overtly political; instead, it merely had to be "not only humanist in tone but authentic in its depiction" of the proletarian milieu.[76] In "L'Age ingrat du cinéma" (1928), Poulaille uses this notion to call attention to an eclectic list of "true films whose scenarios are drawn from life and which are authentically human."[77] But he also pays homage to Moussinac, especially his *Le Cinéma soviétique* (1928), in roundly attacking the commercial nature of the French film industry and approaching the conclusion that the cinema could serve as a collective means of combat in some kind of social revolution.[78] It may well have been Poulaille's defense of a broadly proletarian art, then, as well as the example of Soviet films, that encouraged Moussinac to appreciate, for instance, the uncompromising realism, "the profoundly *human* meaning of the trial of death of Jeanne d'Arc," in his admirable review of Carl Dreyer's *La Passion de Jeanne d'Arc* (1928).[79] And both Poulaille and Moussinac led others, such as André Sauvage, to celebrate such films as King Vidor's *The Crowd* (1928) for its evocation of "the soul of the American city" and "the heartfelt drama of the proletariat there."[80]

JEAN EPSTEIN AND THE SURREALISTS

Among these various theories, Epstein charted a singular, rather idiosyncratic course that involved several shifts in direction and some tacking back and forth. These shifts may have been exacerbated by a personal crisis, sometime between 1924 and 1925, which seems to have coincided with his disappointing commercial filmmaking practice at Films Albatros. Evidence of this appears in several essays that turn his concept of "lyrosophical" knowing back on the filmmaker as well as the spectator, by suggesting how—as if in anticipation of Jacques Lacan's "mirror stage"—the camera/screen can function as a psychoanalytical instrument of self-revelation. At one point, Epstein recommends such a psychoanalysis of cinema as a pleasantly instructive, therapeutic experience.[81] At another point, however, he describes an analogous confrontation—the stunning vision in the multi-mirrored stairwell of a Sicilian hotel—as absolutely horrifying. "I appeared at the top of seven flights of stairs within a huge retina which had neither conciousness nor morality. There I saw myself stripped of well-kept illusions, surprised, laid bare, erased, pared down to net weight. I wanted to run far away to escape the screw-like grooves down which I seemed about to plunge toward the ghastly gravitational center of myself."[82] Here Delluc's earlier disquieting experience of self-knowledge before the cinema screen seemed perversely magnified. For what Epstein's mirror/screen permitted, as Paul Willemen puts it, was a recognition of a *photogénie* of the unspeakable, "the activities of a phantasy" by means of "the scopic relation underpinning cinematic signification"—a formulation that looks forward to Christian Metz's "Imaginary Signifier."[83] Yet despite this wavering and self-doubt over the psychoanalytical implications of the cinema, Epstein generally held firm to the lyrosophical position he had developed in the early 1920s. Only now he postulated first one and then another film form to put this lyrosophical knowing into practice.

In "Art d'événement" (1927), for instance, which served as a preamble to *La Glace à trois faces* (1927), Epstein presented an original film narrative construction analogous (in his characteristic overlapping of languages) to a chemical crystallization, to "an egg [appearing suddenly] at the fingertips of a naked magician," or to a syntactically difficult Latin sentence.[84] In one sense, this narrative construction was grounded in a quasi-semiotic conception of film language. Here film images "really signify only in association with one another, just as words that are simple but rich in meaning must do."[85] Hence the image, Epstein would later add, "is a sign, complex and

335

exact, like those of the Chinese alphabet."[86] The shot is both precise and arbitrary, single and polysemous, its signification dependent on its contextual position in relation to other shots within a constructed textual system as well as on the spectator's ability to synthesize perception and memory in a process of "reading." In another related sense, however, the particular narrative structure of *La Glace à trois faces* was shaped by and exploited the peculiar spatiotemporal nature of the cinema. Specifically, four stories are narrated, not in succession, but in parallel: "each character is introduced alone" and kept apart, but "they live together, in association with one another."[87] Moreover, their association depends on a complex interpenetration of temporal relations: "Fragments from several pasts take root in the present; the future erupts through the memories."[88] Here the narrative process of coming to knowledge within the film text is omniscient, Epstein insists, rather than subjective, as with the "Impressionists." Yet it nonetheless turns deceptive: at the end, the hero as subject "proves to be untrue" in a literal mirror image that reflects disquietingly on the spectator's own positioning as subject. What goes unsaid, interestingly enough, is the fact that, since the narrative of *La Glace à trois faces* deploys three sets of broken-off romances, all narrated by the women, this deception is strongly marked by sexual difference.

Within a year—whether influenced by the Soviet films and Dreyer's *La Passion de Jeanne d'Arc* or else by the rise of a populist and proletarian literature remains unclear—Epstein seemed to forsake such a sophisticated, highly self-conscious practice for another, far more simple and allegedly authentic. In effect, he, too, returned to some of the realist premises that he initially had shared with Delluc and Moussinac. "Les Approches de la vérité" (1928) served to introduce and justify *Finis Terrae* (1929) as a "psychological *documentary*," a drama of "events which really happened, of actual men and things," on several remote islands off the coast of Brittany.[89] There was no makeup or costumes to mask the human figure, no artificial decors to conceal the islands and sea, no technical effects (beyond the consistent use of a slightly slow motion camera), and no complicated narrative structure to deflect from what Epstein called "the mystery of men dedicated to a land that is nothing but rock, to a sea which is nothing but foam, to a hard and perilous trade [gathering sea algae], as if in obedience to some high command."[90] The narrative process of knowing for Epstein finally seemed to settle on the existential condition of a simple people not only marginal to but apparently outside modern industrial society and whose only problems were defined as diseases, which a good, compassionate doctor could cure. And a similar settling now marked spectator positioning. This shift in locations and terms—from studio artifice to natural reality, from the relations of sentimental romance to those of isolated community, from the modern industrial to the pre-industrial, from the psychoanalytic to the physical or concrete, from critical analysis to the mystical or mytho-poetic, from the uncannily destabilizing to the more or less stable—did this represent an advance or a retreat for Epstein, a stripping away of illu-sions or, what is more likely, merely another form of inescapable repres-sion?

In contrast to Epstein, the Surrealists pursued a relatively straightfor-ward course, gathering momentum as the decade wore on. Their writings neatly, if unfairly, summarized the other competing theories in circulation during the period as they lambasted, in turn, the French mainstream nar-rative cinema, L'Herbier as a practictioner of an outdated Impressionism, the "pure cinema" advocates in particular, and even Epstein, perhaps be-cause he was closest of all to the Surrealists' own position. Their principal concern remain unchanged: the exploration of the idea that the cinema op-erated as an analogous discourse to that of the dream state, thereby giving access to the unconscious, making visible "the automatic writing of the world,"[91] and constituting a new order of intellectual pleasure. Here Dr. Allendy's study, "The Psychological Value of the Image" (1926), provides an instructive contrast to the Surrealists, particularly since he was then An-tonin Artaud's physician. Allendy assumes a rather conventional hierarchi-cal model of "psychological life" with consciousness and rational thinking at the top and the "swarming subterranean realms" of the unconscious at the bottom—the latter threatening "to overflow and drown our reason at the least sign of weakness."[92] Yet within the film image—which is a unique blend of the objective and subjective—the unconscious plays a special role in the form of "symbolism . . . an unconscious, primitive, rudimentary process" that can bypass the understanding and "arouse intense feelings in us without our having the least intellectual notion of its meaning."[93] For examples, Allendy points to specific French films, notably the carnival se-quence in Epstein's *Coeur fidèle* (1923), where, among a plethora of details, three tiny mechanical figures on a barrel organ replicate the heroine's sit-uation: a woman torn between two men. Such a correspondence, Allendy argues, "impinges naturally on the unconscious of the heroine" and, through her, on that of the spectator.[94] This "domestication" of the uncon-scious within a rational process of representation and perception was carried even further in Paul Ramain's "theory" of an oneiric cinema that repressed the revolutionary potential of the unconscious within a muddled, almost Impressionist, aesthetic idealism.[95] The Surrealists instead followed Des-nos's lead in seeking to wrench the cinema free of such conventional aes-thetics.

As Linda Williams has demonstrated, two different lines of thinking ac-tually governed Surrealist writing on the cinema during the late 1920s.[96]

337

The more simple or naive was represented by Desnos, who continued to write as if film could literally reproduce the content of dreams.[97] Here film functioned as a wish-fulfillment of unconscious desire, especially in its ability to overturn the real world "through the disruptive anti-social tumult of *amour fou* [mad passion]."[98] And Desnos provided a myth of origin for such a Surrealism in the cinema that rivaled Soupault's. Theirs was a generation raised in an ideologically bankrupt prewar period, a generation tortured by a "desire for love, revolt, and the sublime;" and they found that desire fulfilled in the mysterious spaces and actions of the early crime serials. *Fantômas* (1913–1914), *Les Vampires* (1915 1916), and *Les Mystères de New York* (1915–1916).[99] Yet the scenarios Desnos wrote during this period were marked by a different conceptualization of the cinema, one that privileged formal patterns and used them whimsically to transgress established narrative conventions. In "Minuit à quatorze heures" (1925), for instance, according to Williams, various round forms are repeated to the point where they become "an ominous and inexplicable presence . . . swallowing up everything else in the scenario, including (literally) the incipient psychology of the characters."[100] Through this process of narrative interruption and diversion, similar to the way the unconscious desires interrupt ordinary thoughts and memories, Desnos's scenario offered "an analogue of the tensions between the manifest and the latent contents in a dream."[101]

This more sophisticated line of thinking, however, developed especially through the writings of Jean Goudal and Antonin Artaud. Although not a Surrealist and critical of the assumptions and methods advanced by André Breton in *The Surrealist Manifesto* (1924), especially with regard to literature, Goudal found that they suited the cinema almost perfectly. Here the film image, rather than reproducing the dream, "corresponds exactly to a *conscious hallucination*."[102] What interested Goudal, writes Williams, was "more the resemblance between the film and the dream *in language* than *in content*."[103] Specifically, this meant that film was capable of producing "the Marvelous," by combining rational and irrational elements peculiar to the cinema: the *"geometry of lines"* and the *"illogicality of detail"* (the displacing, fragmenting, and reordering of ordinary objects and movements).[104] About the same time, Clair found himself similarly fascinated by "the marvelous barbarism" of film's illogic, in the form of a "musical liberty," which pointed toward his actual film practice in the early 1930s, and in the form of an erotic pleasure that shifted Desnos's earlier repressed latent content onto film construction and the cinematic apparatus itself.[105] In both cases, the cinema functioned not as a *representation* but as a *construction*, an approximation of the *form* of unconscious desire. While director of the Bureau de Recherche Surréalistes, Artaud pushed this Surrealist concept of the cinema toward the realm of impossibility, especially in his introduction to the published scenario of Dulac's *La Coquille et le clergyman* (1928).[106] Such a film was not the recreation of a dream, Artaud insisted, but a "pure play of appearances," a "collision of objects, forms, repulsions, attractions," out of which "is born an inorganic language that moves the mind by osmosis and without any kind of transposition in words."[107] It presents, in short, "the very essence of language," a non-discursive, non-translatable language that, as Williams puts it, would *"be* the very flesh and blood of his thought."[108] Artaud's extraordinary sense of alienation, of a perpetually absent self, and his extravagant hopes for an ontological "cure" by means of the cinema almost inevitably had to end in disappointment—as they did several years later.

Besides the production of a number of publishable, filmable, and unfilmable scenarios,[109] this project of advancing a marvelous, truly revolutionary cinema led the Surrealists to champion a diverse corpus of films.[110] Desnos, for one, consistently singled out documentary films as a source of "mysterious movement"—from short studies of modern machine movement to full-length features by André Sauvage and Alberto Cavalcanti.[111] And just as consistently, he excoriated Epstein for failing to discover in his film practice that same sense of mystery that he, too, seemed to appreciate. Most writers ranged widely across the narrative cinema, finding radical or subversive elements almost everywhere, regardless of a film's national origin. Goudal, for instance, compared several magical moments in Fairbanks's *The Thief of Bagdad* (1924) with the laboratory resurrection sequence that climaxed L'Herbier's *L'Inhumaine* (1924).[112] For revolutionary candor, Desnos equated Eisenstein's *Potemkin* (1925–1926), Chaplin's *The Gold Rush* (1925), Stroheim's *The Wedding March* (1925), and Buñuel's *Un Chien andalou* (1929).[113]

The most specific analysis of Surrealist cinema, however, came in Robert Aron's fascinating comparison of Man Ray, Luis Buñuel, and Buster Keaton, in *La Revue du cinéma* (November 1929).[114] With unusual acumen, Aron traces the two French filmmakers' "delight in dislocation and desire for freedom" in the very structure of film. Both exhibit a playful use of narrative disruptions, intertitle juxtapositions, and unexpectedly satirical transformations of faces, fragments of bodies, and clothing. Yet the freedom they achieve is easy, Aron argues, because it is merely witty fantasizing, "with neither joy nor passion."[115] In *The Navigator* (1926) and *Steamboat Bill Jr.* (1927), by contrast, while seeming to accept all natural laws and social conventions, Keaton produces a comic "disorder of nightmarish or hallucinatory proportions."[116] The normal working out of the plot, in this best regulated of worlds, is lured into traps where those very laws and conventions are mocked mercilessly. In one sense, what is "revolutionary" for Aron is a film practice like Keaton's (an American practice), one that apparently follows the rules only to violate or defy them from within rather than one that irreverently dispenses with the rules altogether. In another sense, however, as if following Desnos, he simply endorses a strategy that conventionally places the spectator so that he can better identify with "the revenge of [the hero] in the very space of [his] sufferings."[117] Yet in so doing, he ignores the more radical strategy articulated by Goudal and Artaud as well as Epstein—and by the films themselves—a strategy that continually dislocates the spectator and questions the very space of desire as well as suffering. Here, as Williams argues, the Surrealists—along with Epstein, whom she does not mention—initiated "a very sophisticated attempt to expose the viewer's own misrecognition of the image" and, in cultivating "what Lacan calls the Imaginary," ultimately reveal "the ways in which the image, too, is structured by processes similar to those at work in language."[118]

CONCLUSION

By the late 1920s, French writing on the cinema clearly was functioning as an autonomous discourse. The broad spectrum of some half-dozen "theories" that had emerged during and just after the Great War now constituted a set of polarized factions, each relatively systematic in its thinking, although not necessarily consistent internally, and each having its own heritage or history on which to draw. Whereas arguments in defense of the cinema previously had been addressed to those hostile to the new medium or had comprised just one perspective in a loosely shared vision of a new art form, now they were addressed to one another, and often in the form of polemical harangues. The very concept of an "avant-garde" in the cinema came into question in a crisis of confidence compounded by a continuing crisis within the French film industry as well as another socioeconomic one developing within French society. The crisis, however, induced Fescourt and Bouquet to write the most comprehensive defense of a mainstream narrative cinema since Diamant-Berger. It provoked a series of attempts to produce a kind of aesthetic revolution in cinematic representation and visual pleasure—for instance, in Porte's "pure cinema" or Dulac's "visual symphony"; in Moussinac, Poulaille, and others' proselytizing of an authentic proletarian or populist film art; in Epstein's disquieting experiments in narrative construction and spectator positioning; and in the Surrealists' disruptive transformations of the very process of representation and "reading." Finally, it encouraged Moussinac and his colleagues to use the Soviet cinema as a model in establishing a new cultural institution—the Amis de Spartacus—and a realist aesthetic to facilitate (unsuccessfully, it turned out) the coming of a new socioeconomic order in France. French film theory and criticism, then, seemed perhaps most vital just at the moment when it was poised on the brink of another crisis, the coming of sound film, a crisis that would drastically alter the parameters of its discourse and the very ground of its debates.

1. The next six paragraphs constitute a condensed and revised version of one section from "The Alternate Cinema Network" in my *French Cinema: The First Wave*, 1915–1929 (Princeton: Princeton University Press, 1984), 260–63.

2. This information is drawn from a partial examination of these newspapers and magazines, plus "Société des Ecrivains du Cinéma," *Tout-Cinéma*, ed. E. L. Fouquet and Clément Guilhamou (Paris: Filma, 1926), 84–86; "Autres Journaux publiant régulièrement une rubrique cinématographique," *Tout-Cinéma* (Paris: Filma, 1928), 903–5; René Jeanne and Charles Ford, *Le Cinéma et la presse, 1895–1960* (Paris: Armand Colin, 1961), 63–69; and Claude Bellanger, Jacques Godechot, Pierre Guiral, and Fernand Terrou, *Histoire générale de la presse française*, vol. 3, *De 1871 à 1940* (Paris: Presses universitaires de France, 1972), 510–84.

3. François Coty wielded some financial power in the French press of the late 1920s. In 1925, he helped launch Georges Valois's *Nouveau siècle*, the official organ of Le Faisceau, the first openly fascist political party in France—see J. Plumyène and R. Lasierra, *Les Facismes français, 1923–1939* (Paris: Editions du Seuil, 1969), 34–44. In 1927, after breaking with Valois, Coty annexed *Le Gaulois* to *Le Figaro*. The stunning success of *L'Ami du peuple*, whose political line was difficult to describe (perhaps "simplistic and demagogic" or even "Boulangist" sums it up best), contributed to the breakup of the consortium of four or five major dailies that had dominated the French press financially for almost forty years. One factor contributing to that success was the sudden decline in *Action française*'s influence, partly as a result of the Vatican's decision to censure the organization that published the paper, in December 1926—see Eugen Weber, *Action Française: Royalism and Reaction in Twentieth-Century France* (Stanford: Stanford University Press, 1962), 219–39.

4. Georges Altman first wrote for the literary pages of *Monde* and *L'Humanité*, where he also contributed a number of film reviews—see Jean-Pierre A. Bernard, *Le Parti communiste français et la question littéraire, 1921–1939* (Paris: Presses universitaires de Grenoble, 1977), 307–8, 312.

5. Antonin Artaud, "La Coquille et le clergyman," *Nouvelle Revue française*, 170 (November 1927), trans. Victor Corti, in *Tulane Drama Review*, 11 (Fall 1966), 173–78.

6. Another film journal deserving mention here is Kenneth MacPherson's international *Close Up* (published in Switzerland, beginning in July 1927), which included a regular column on the French cinema by Jean Lenauer as well as articles by Robert Aron and Marc Allégret.

7. The publication of *films racontés*, unfilmed scenarios, and shooting script excerpts proliferated in the late 1920s. See such magazines as *Ciné-Miroir, Mon-Ciné, Le Film complet*, and the deluxe *La Petite Illustration*; book series from Jules Tallandier's Cinéma-Bibliothèque to Gallimard's Cinéma-romanesque; individual ciné-romans such as Henri Barbusse's *Force* (1927), Henry Poulaille's *Le Train fou* (1928), Pierre Chenal's *Drames sur celluloid* (1929); and Abel Gance's full-length découpage texts, *Napoléon vu par Abel Gance* (1927) and *La Roue, scénario arrangé par Jean Arroy* (1930).

8. Lucien Wahl, "La Critique des films," *Cahiers du mois*, 16–17 (1925), 187–94.

9. At least two publishers for these books were associated with the French Communist Party: Povolovsky, which published Moussinac's *Naissance du cinéma* (1925), and Les Ecrivains réunis, which published Epstein's *Le Cinématographe vu d'Etna* (1926) and Cendrars's

final version of *L'A.B.C. du cinéma* (1926)—David Caute, *Communism and the French Intellectuals, 1915–1960* (New York: Macmillan, 1964), 47.

10. Léon Moussinac, "Avenir et technique," *Panoramique du cinéma* (Paris: Le Sans Pareil, 1929), reprinted in Moussinac, *L'Age ingrat du cinéma* (Paris: Les Editeurs français réunis, 1967), 320–21. For a more extensive survey of the French ciné-clubs and specialized cinemas, see Abel, *French Cinema*, 256–60, 263–70.

11. See, for instance, Léon Moussinac, "Un Répertoire de films," *Panoramique du cinéma* (Paris: Au Sans Pareil, 1929), 107–9.

12. André Levinson, "Pour une poétique du film," *L'Art cinématographique*, vol. 4 (Paris: Félix Alcan, 1927), 51–88. A section of this essay was translated as "The Nature of the Cinema," in *Theatre Arts Monthly* (September 1929) and reprinted in Lewis Jacobs, ed., *Introduction to the Art of the Movies* (New York: Noonday, 1960), 145–53. Levinson, a Russian emigré, was the most distinguished French dance critic of the period and wrote regularly for *Les Nouvelles littéraires*.

13. Jean Sapéne, "La Politique du cinéma français," *Cinéa-Ciné-pour-tous*, 34 (1 April 1925), 7. There is a telling racial slur in Sapène's remarks when he complains that directors too often turn "the bouncing blond baby" of a script (which the producer has given him) into "a little nigger boy." See, also, Jean Tedesco, "Pour un cinématographe international," *Cinéa-Ciné-pour-tous*, 28 (1 January 1925), 4–5.

14. For an analysis of the international production strategies in France in the 1920s, see Abel, *French Cinema*, 27–32, 35–36.

15. See, especially, Marcel L'Herbier, "Cinématographe et démocratie," *Cinéa-Ciné-pour-tous*, 48 (1 November 1925), 7–8; Blaise Cendrars, *L'A.B.C. du cinéma* (Paris: Les Ecrivains réunis, 1926), 20–22; Marcel L'Herbier, "Le Cinématographe et l'espace," *L'Art cinématographique*, vol. 4, 1–22; Marcel L'Herbier, "Detresse du cinéma français," *Comoedia* (18 July 1927), reprinted in Marcel Lapierre, ed., *Anthologie du cinéma* (Paris: La Nouvelle Edition, 1946), 169–75; and Abel Gance, "Autour du moi et du monde: Le Cinéma de demain," *Conférencia*, 18 (5 September 1929), translated by Norman King in *Abel Gance: A Politics of Spectacle* (London: British Film Institute, 1984), 62–79.

16. For an analysis of the 1926 Paris International Film Congress, see Kristin Thompson, *Exporting Entertainment: America in the World Film Market, 1907–1934* (London: British Film Institute, 1985), 114–16. A copy of the program and list of invited filmmakers can be found at the Bibliothèque de l'Arsenal in Paris.

17. See Roger Icart, *Abel Gance ou Le Prométhée foudroyé* (Lausanne: L'Age d'homme, 1983), 203–6; and King, *Abel Gance*, 164.

18. Fernand Léger, "Le Spectacle," *Bulletin de L'Effort Moderne*, 7 (July 1924), translated by Alexandra Anderson as "The Spectacle" in Léger, *Functions of Painting* (New York: Viking, 1973), 35–47.

19. René Clair, "Cinéma pur et cinéma commercial," *Cahiers du mois*, 16–17 (1925), 89–90. See, also, René Clair, "Le Cinématographe contre l'esprit," lecture, Collège Libre des Sciences Sociales, 19 February 1927, reprinted in Lapierre, *Anthologie du cinéma*, 175–82; and Clair, "Millions," *Le Rouge et le noir* (July 1928), 46–47.

20. Bernard, *Le Parti communiste français*, 57–58. See also Hubert Révol, "La Corporation du cinéma," *Cinégraphie*, 4 (15 December 1927), 64, and Spartacus, "Le Décret des '32'," *Spartacus*, 1 (15 April 1928), 1.

21. Léon Moussinac, "Cinéma: Expression sociale," *L'Art cinématographique*, vol. 4, 35–36. See, also, Léon Moussinac, "Cinéma vivant," *Cinégraphie*, 5 (15 January 1928), 75.

22. Léger, "The Spectacle," 46–47. Nothing quite like Siegfried Kracauer's socio-psychological studies of the cinema as the central component of popular culture in Germany seems to have appeared in France—see Siegfried Kracauer, "Cult of Distraction: On Berlin's

Picture Palaces" [1926], translated by Thomas Y. Levin in *New German Critique*, 40 (Winter 1987), 91–96; Thomas Elsaesser, "Lulu and the Meter Man," *Screen*, 24 (July–October 1983), 6–8; Heide Schlüpmann, "Phenomenology of Film: On Siegfried Kracauer's Writings of the 1920s," translated by Thomas Y. Levin in *New German Critique*, 40 (Winter 1987), 97–114; and Sabine Hake, "Girls and Crisis: The Other Side of Diversion," *New German Critique*, 40 (Winter 1987), 147–164.

23. Léon Moussinac, *Le Cinéma soviétique* (Paris: La Nouvelle Revue française, 1928), reprinted in Moussinac, *L'Age ingrat du cinéma*, 200–217. See, also, Moussinac's reviews of Gance's *Napoléon* (1927), Clair's *Un Chapeau de paille d'Italie* (1928), Dreyer's *La Passion de Jeanne d'Arc* (1928), and Feyder's *Thérèse Raquin* (1928), collected in Moussinac, *Panoramique du cinéma*, and reprinted in *L'Age ingrat du cinéma*, 267–77, 284–95. Cf. Alberto Cavalcanti, "Le Metteur-en-scène," *La Revue fédéraliste*, 103 (November 1927), 11–16.

24. King, *Abel Gance*, 140–46. The concept of "elite populism," it should be noted, is not all that different from the Boulangism of Maurice Barrès in the late 1880s and early 1890s, which recognized "the people as at once a mass to be dominated and a source of instinctual energy"—see Jerrold Seigel, *Bohemian Paris: Culture, Politics, and the Boundaries of Bourgeois Life, 1830–1930* (New York: Viking, 1986), 278–79. Ann Yaeger Kaplan also sees "this bizarre combination of populism and elitism" as characteristic of fascism—Kaplan, *Reproductions of Banality: Fascism, Literature, and French Intellectual Life* (Minneapolis: University of Minnesota Press, 1986), 6.

25. King, *Abel Gance*, 142.

26. Abel Gance, "Le Temps de l'image est venu!" *L'Art cinématographique*, vol. 2, translated as "The Era of the Image Has Arrived," in *Rediscovering French Film*, ed. Mary Lea Bandy (New York: Museum of Modern Art, 1983), 53.

27. Gance, "The Era of the Image Has Arrived," 54.

28. Abel Gance, "Mon Napoléon," Théâtre de l'Opéra programme (April 1927), trans. Kevin Brownlow in "*Napoleon* directed by Abel Gance," Empire Theatre program (London: Thames Television, 1980), v; Emile Vuillermoz, "Napoléon," *Le Temps* (9 April 1927), 3; Emile Vuillermoz, "Abel Gance et *Napoléon*," *Cinémagazine*, 7 (25 November 1927), 335–40; Léon Moussinac, "Napoléon," *L'Humanité* (24 April and 1 May 1927), revised and reprinted in Moussinac, *L'Age ingrat du cinéma*, 267–77, and trans. Norman King, in *Abel Gance*, 34–41. For further reviews of *Napoléon*, see Jean Mitry, "*Napoléon* à l'écran," *Photo-Ciné*, 4 (April 1927), 55–57; Jean Tedesco, "*Napoléon* vu par Abel Gance," *Cinéa-Ciné-pour-tous*, 83 (15 April 1927), 9–10; Juan Arroy, "La Technique d'Abel Gance," *Cinéa-Ciné-pour-tous*, 86 (1 June 1927), 9–12; Jean Prévost, "Le Napoléon d'Abel Gance," *Le Crapouillot* (June 1927), 50–51; and Albert Gain, "Napoléon," *La Petite Tribune* (10 June 1927). For recent books and essays on *Napoléon*, see Bernard Eischenschitz, "From *Napoléon* to *New Babylon*," *Afterimage*, 10 (Autumn 1981), 49–55; Kevin Brownlow, "*Napoleon*": *Abel Gance's Classic Film* (London: Jonathan Cape, 1983), 14–176; Abel, *French Cinema*, 428–45; and King, *Abel Gance*, 31–33, 87–105, 145–63, 191–96, 205–11.

29. Jean Goudal, "Surréalisme et cinéma," *La Revue hebdomadaire* (February 1925), 343–57. Jean Cocteau had expressed a similar attitude two years earlier, in an interview in *Les Nouvelles littéraires* (24 March 1923).

30. Moussinac, "Napoléon," *L'Age ingrat du cinéma*, 267–77. Gance himself had no such problem with technological innovation, as evidenced in "Nos Moyens d'expression," *Cinéa-Ciné-pour-tous*, 133 (15 May 1929), 7–9.

31. Moussinac, "Avenir et technique," 327–28.

32. Jean Epstein, "Pour une avant-garde nouvelle," *Cinéa-Ciné-pour-tous*, 29 (15 January 1925), 8. Cf. André Obey, "Musique et cinéma," *Le Crapouillot* (March 1927), 9–12.

33. Jean Epstein, "Les Grands Docteurs," *Photo-Ciné*, 3 (15 March 1927), 34.

34. Jean Epstein, "Les Images de ciel," *Cinéa-Ciné-pour-tous*, 107 (15 April 1928), reprinted in Epstein, *Ecrits sur le cinéma*, vol. 1 (Paris: Seghers, 1974), 189–90.

35. Henri Fescourt and Jean-Louis Bouquet, *L'Idée et l'écran: Opinions sur le cinéma*, vols. 1–3 (Paris: Haberschill et Sergent, 1925–1926).

36. Jacques Feyder, "Transposition visuelle," *Cahiers du mois*, 16–17 (1925), 67–71.

37. Fescourt and Bouquet, *L'Idée et l'écran: Opinions sur le cinéma*, vol. 3, 9–10.

38. Fescourt and Bouquet, *L'Idée et l'écran: Opinions sur le cinéma*, vol. 1, 26.

39. Epstein, "Pour une avant-garde nouvelle," 8–10; Clair, "Cinéma pur et cinéma commercial," 89–90.

40. Pierre Porte, "Faisons le point," *Cinéa-Ciné-pour-tous*, 49 (15 November 1925), 9.

41. See, for instance, Jean Tedesco, "Pur Cinéma," *Cinéa-Ciné-pour-tous*, 80 (1 March 1927), 9.

42. D. J. Mossop, *Pure Poetry: Studies in French Poetic Theory and Practice, 1746–1945* (Oxford: Oxford University Press, 1971), 167–93.

43. Germaine Dulac, "L'Essence du cinéma: L'Idée visuelle," *Cahiers du mois*, 16–17 (1925), 64–65, translated by Robert Lamberton as "The Essence of the Cinema: The Visual Idea," in *The Avant-Garde Film: A Reader of Theory and Criticism*, ed. P. Adams Sitney (New York: New York University Press, 1978), 36–42.

44. Henri Chomette, "Seconde Etape," *Cahiers du mois*, 16–17 (1925), 86–88.

45. René Clair, "Rythme," *Cahiers du mois*, 16–17 (1925), 13–16.

46. Clair, "Cinéma pur et cinéma commercial," 90; Chomette, "Seconde Etape," 87–88.

47. Fernand Léger, "Peinture et cinéma," *Cahiers du mois*, 16–17 (1925), 107–8.

48. Georges Charensol, "Le Film abstrait," *Cahiers du mois*, 16–17 (1925), 83–84. Léger, "Peinture et cinéma," 108. Cf. Marcel Gromaire, "Le Cinéma et ses deux tendances," *Cahiers du mois*, 16–17 (1925), 205–7.

49. See, for instance, Pierre Porte, "Eclecticisme," *Cinéa-Ciné-pour-tous*, 58 (1 April 1926), 10; Porte, "Cinéma intellectuel ou affectif?" *Cinéa-Ciné-pour-tous*, 61 (15 May 1926), 9–10; Porte, "Une Sensation nouvelle," *Cinéa-Ciné-pour-tous*, 64 (1 July 1926), 27–28; Porte, "Musique plastique," *Cinéa-Ciné-pour-tous*, 68 (1 September 1926), 22–23. For Fescourt and Bouquet's response, see "Sensations ou sentiments," *Cinéa-Ciné-pour-tous*, 66 (31 July 1926), 13–14, and 69 (15 September 1926), 15–16.

50. Porte, "Faisons le point," 9. Mossop, *Pure Poetry*, 167–68, 187.

51. Pierre Porte, "Le Cinéma pur," *Cinéa-Ciné-pour-tous*, 52 (1 January 1926), 12.

52. Porte, "Le Cinéma pur," 13.

53. See, for instance, Bernard Brunius, "Musique ou cinéma?" *Cinéa-Ciné-pour-tous*, 68 (1 September 1926), 15–16; Henri Chomette, "Cinéma pur, art naissant," *Cinéa-Ciné-pour-tous*, 71 (15 October 1926), 13–14; and Tedesco, "Pur Cinéma," 9–11.

54. Obey, "Musique et cinéma," 9. The *bateau ivre* or "drunken boat" refers to the famous 1871 poem written by Arthur Rimbaud (1854–1891).

55. Louis Chavance, "Symphonie visuelle et cinéma pur," *Cinéa-Ciné-pour-tous*, 89 (15 July 1927), 13.

56. Hans Richter, "Mouvement," *Schémas*, 1 (February 1927), 21–23. Eugène Deslaw, "Comment travaille Eugène Deslaw," *Pour Vous*, 16 (7 March 1929), 4. See, also, Miklos N. Bandi, "La Symphonie diagonale de Vicking Eggeling," *Schémas*, 1 (February 1927), 9–19.

57. Vuillermoz, "Abel Gance et *Napoléon*," 340.

58. Obey, "Musique et cinéma," 11–12.

59. Germaine Dulac, "Les Esthéthiques, les entraves, la cinégraphie integrale," *L'Art cinématographique*, vol. 2, 46.

60. See Germaine Dulac, "Du Sentiment au ligne," *Schémas*, 1 (February 1927), 26–31;

Dulac, "La Musique du silence," *Cinégraphie*, 5 (15 January 1928), 77–78; Dulac, "Films visuels et anti-visuels," *Le Rouge et le noir* (July 1928), 31–41. Dulac's own short non-narrative films from this period included *Disque 927* (1928), *Thèmes et variations* (1928), and *Etude cinégraphique sur un arabesque* (1929).

61. Antonin Artaud, "Cinéma et réalité," *La Nouvelle Revue française*, 170 (1 November 1927), reprinted in Artaud, *Oeuvres complètes*, vol. 3 (Paris: Gallimard, 1956), 22–25; Léon Moussinac, "La Question du film dit d' 'avant-garde'," *Le Cinéma soviétique*, 218–20; Epstein, "Les Images de ciel," 190; Robert Desnos, "Cinéma d'avant-garde," *Documents*, 7 (December 1929), 385–87.

62. Dulac, "Les Esthétiques, les entraves, la cinégraphie integrale," 41–47.

63. Emile Vuillermoz, "La Musique des images," *L'Art cinématographique*, vol. 3 (Paris: Félix Alcan, 1927), 41–66. For an earlier, but no more original essay, see Vuillermoz, "Réalisme et expressionnisme," *Cahiers du mois*, 16–17 (1925), 72–80. Louis Chavance, "L'Impressionnisme cinématographique," *Cinégraphie*, 2 (15 October 1927), 21–22. See, for instance, Paul Ramain, "L'Influence du rêve sur le cinéma," *Cinéa-Ciné-pour-tous*, 40 (1 July 1925), 8; Ramain, "Les Chants et danses de la mort," *Cinéa-Ciné-pour-tous*, 46 (1 October 1925), 23–25; Ramain, "Sensibilité intelligente d'abord, objectif ensuite," *Cinéa-Ciné-pour-tous*, 55 (15 February 1926), 7–8; Ramain, "Pour une esthétique intellectuelle du film," *Cinéa-Ciné-pour-tous*, 58 (1 April 1926), 13–14; and Ramain, "De l'incohérence onirique à la cohérence cinématographique," *Schémas*, 1 (February 1927), 60–66.

64. Levinson, "Pour une poétique du film," 69–74.

65. Pierre-F. Quesnoy, "Littérature et cinéma," *Le Rouge et le noir* (July 1928), 91–93.

66. Desnos, "Cinéma d'avant-garde," 385–87.

67. For a survey of the revivals of French films within the circuit of ciné-clubs and specialized cinemas, see Abel, *French Cinema*, 283–84.

68. Jean Prévost, "*Metropolis*," *Le Crapouillot* (November 1927), 55.

69. Léon Moussinac, "Les Principes," *Le Cinéma soviétique* (Paris: Nouvelle Revue française, 1928), reprinted in Moussinac, *L'Age ingrat du cinéma*, 177–78. See, also, Michel Goreloff, "Le Nouveau Cinéma russe," *Cinéa-Ciné-pour-tous*, 76 (1 January 1927), 10–11; Jean Tedesco, "La Jeune Ecole russe," *Cinéa-Ciné-pour-tous*, 90 (1 August 1927), 12–15; René Marchand and Pierre Weinstein, *Le Cinéma* (Paris: Rieder, 1927); and Michel Goreloff, "Cinéma russe," *Cinéa-Ciné-pour-tous*, 100 (1 January 1928), 15–16.

70. Moussinac, "Les Principes," 182.

71. Moussinac, "La Question du film dit d' 'avant-garde'," 218. Cf. André Delons, "Cinéma pur et cinéma russe," *Cinéa-Ciné-pour-tous*, 105 (15 March 1928), 11–12. André Levinson evidenced some interest in Eisenstein's *Potemkin* as a "*film of attractions*" and briefly cited an essay on montage ("Iskousstvo Kino," Leningrad, 1926) by the Russian filmmaker, Timoshenko—"Pour une poétique du film," 87–88. Translations of Russian writings on the cinema, however, did not appear in France until 1929—for example, Vsevold Poudovkine, "Construction d'un scénario," *La Revue du cinéma*, 3 (May 1929), 2; S. M. Eisenstein, "Les Principes du noveau cinéma russe," *La Revue du cinéma*, 9 (1 April 1930), 16–27.

72. Léon Moussinac, "Eisenstein," *Le Cinéma soviétique*, 204.

73. André Thérive, "Plaidoyer pour le Naturalisme," *Comoedia* (3 May 1927); Léon Lemonnier, "Une Manifeste littéraire: Le roman populaire," *L'Oeuvre* (27 August 1929); Léon Lemonnier, *Manifeste du roman populiste* (Paris: Jacques Bernard, 1929). See Bernard, *Le Parti communiste français*, 19–21; and J. E. Flowers, *Literature and the Left in France* (London: Methuen, 1985), 80–83.

74. See, for instance, the inquiry on the question of a proletarian literature, launched by Barbusse's *Monde* (4 August–3 November 1928) and to which Poulaille was one of six principal respondents. This inquiry sparked four others as well over the next two years—*La Re-*

vue mondiale (November 1929), *Savoir et Beauté* (March–May 1930), *Les Nouvelles littéraires* (July–September 1930), and *La Grande Revue* (October 1930)—see Bernard, *Le Parti communiste français*, 29–33. See, also, Moussinac's laudatory review, "Charlie Chaplin, par Henry Poulaille," *Panoramique du cinéma*, 142–44.

75. Flowers, *Literature and the Left in France*, 79. See Henri Poulaille, "Le Littérature et le peuple," *Le Progrès* (17 December 1925); Poulaille, "Reponse," *Monde* (13 October 1928); and Poulaille, "Charles-Louis Philippe et le littérature prolétarienne," *Cahiers bleus*, 55 (29 March 1930). Poulaille and his "school" were published primarily by Georges Valois, who had returned to his earlier anarchist beliefs after his break with François Coty in 1927. For an analysis of Poulaille's theory of a proletarian literature, see Bernard, *Le Parti communiste français*, 23–28; Pierre Bardel, "Henry Poulaille et la littérature prolétarienne," *Europe*, 575–76 (March–April 1977), 168–78; and Flower, *Literature and the Left in France*, 77–80.

76. Flower, *Literature and the Left in France*, 78.

77. Henri Poulaille, "L'Age ingrat du cinéma," *Le Rouge et le noir* (July 1928), 68. Cf. his earlier defense of a Realist cinema in "L'Emotion et le cinéma," *La Revue fédéraliste*, 103 (November 1927), 78, 81–82.

78. Poulaille, "L'Age ingrat du cinéma," 69–71.

79. Léon Moussinac, *"La Passion de Jeanne d'Arc," Panoramique du cinéma*, reprinted in Moussinac, *L'Age ingrat du cinéma*, 284–88. After its preview, in April 1928, the Catholic archbishop of Paris threatened to initiate a boycott of Dreyer's film, a position that convinced the producers to cut the film severely for its premiere in October. It should be remembered that Action française and other rightist groups adopted Jeanne d'Arc as the true mythic figure of French nationalism quite early in the century, and that the date of Jeanne d'Arc's birth was proclaimed a national holiday, as a symbolic event marking the Nationalist Revival, in 1911—see Plumyène and Lasierra, *Les Facismes français* 25–26; and Eugen Weber, *The Nationalist Revival in France, 1905–1914* (Berkeley: University of California Press, 1968), 11, 69–71. Thus Dreyer's Protestant interpretation of the Jeanne d'"Arc story overtly countered this rightist mythology.

80. André Sauvage, "Panoramiques," *La Revue du cinéma*, 2 (February 1929), 1.

81. Jean Epstein, "L'Objectif lui-même," *Cinéa-Ciné-pour-tous*, 53 (15 January 1926), reprinted in Epstein, *Ecrits sur le cinéma*, vol. 1 (Paris: Seghers, 1974), 128. See, also, Epstein, "Le Regard du verre," *Les Cahiers du mois*, 16–17 (1925), 9–12.

82. Jean Epstein, "Le Cinématographe vu de l'Etna," *Cinéa-Ciné-pour-tous*, 59 (15 April 1926), 9–10, reprinted in Epstein, *Le Cinématographe vu de l'Etna* (Paris: Les Ecrivains réunis, 1926), 16, 18.

83. Paul Willemen, "On Reading Epstein on *Photogénie*," *Afterimage*, 10 (Autumn 1981), 44–45. Christian Metz, "The Imaginary Signifier," *The Imaginary Signifier: Psychoanalysis and the Cinema*, trans. Ben Brewster (Bloomington: Indiana University Press, 1982), 3–87.

84. Jean Epstein, "Art d'événement," *Comoedia* (18 November 1927), 4. See, also, Jean Epstein, "Temps et personnage du drame," *Cinégraphie*, 3 (15 November 1927), 43–45; and Epstein, "Opinion sur le cinématographe," *Le Rouge et le noir* (July 1928), 28–30. The doubled narrative and peculiar climax of Epstein's 6 1/2 x 11 (1927)—with its development of a photograph whose image is simultaneously present and absent—act as a prelude to *La Glace à trois faces*. For an analysis of these two films, see Abel, *French Cinema*, 448–62.

85. Epstein, "Art d'événement," 4.

86. Epstein, "Les Images de ciel," 90.

87. Epstein, "Art d'événement," 4.

88. Epstein, "Art d'événement," 4.

89. Jean Epstein, "Les Approches de la vérité," *Photo-Ciné* (15 November–15 December

1928), reprinted in Epstein, *Ecrits sur le cinéma*, vol. 1, 191–93. For an analysis of *Finis Terrae*, see Abel, *French Cinema*, 500–507.

90. Epstein, "Les Approches de la vérité," 193.

91. Rosalind Kraus, "The Photographic Conditions of Surrealism," *October*, 19 (Winter 1981), 31.

92. Dr. Allendy, "La Valeur psychologique de l'image," *L'Art cinématographique*, vol. 1 (Paris: Félix Alcan, 1926), reprinted in Marcel L'Herbier, *Intelligence du cinématographe* (Paris: Corréa, 1946), 305–8. Cf. Michel Goreloff, "Suggerer," *Cinéa-Ciné-pour-tous*, 91 (15 August 1927), 23–24; and Paul Ramain, "La Construction thématique des films de F. Lang: *Metropolis*," *Cinéa-Ciné-pour-tous*, 91 (15 August 1927), 21–22.

93. Allendy, "La Valeur psychologique de l'image," 304–5, 310.

94. Allendy, "La Valeur psychologique de l'image," 310–11.

95. Ramain, "L'Influence du rêve sur le cinéma," 8. See, also, Paul Ramain, "Le Film peut traduire et créer le Rêve," *Cinéa-Ciné-pour-tous*, 67 (15 August 1926), 11–14.

96. Linda Williams, *Figures of Desire: A Theory and Analysis of Surrealist Film* (Urbana: University of Illinois Press, 1981), 14–17, 26.

97. See, for instance, Robert Desnos, "René Clair et le nouveau cinéma," *Journal littéraire* (21 March 1925), and "Les Rêves de la nuit transportés sur l'écran," *Le Soir* (3 February 1927), reprinted in Desnos, *Cinéma* (Paris: Gallimard, 1966), 131–32, 150–52.

98. Williams, *Figures of Desire*, 24. See, for instance, Robert Desnos, "Amour et cinéma," *Le Soir* (19 March 1927), reprinted in Desnos, *Cinéma*, 159–60.

99. Robert Desnos, "*Fantômas, Les Vampires, Les Mystères de New York*," *Le Soir* (26 February 1927), reprinted in Desnos, *Cinéma*, 153–55.

100. Williams, *Figures of Desire*, 27. Robert Desnos, "Minuit à quatorze heures," *Cahiers du mois*, 12 (1925), reprinted in Desnos, *Cinéma*, 21–28. For further analyses of Desnos's scenarios, see Marie-Claire Dumas, "Un Scénario exemplaire de Robert Desnos," *Etudes cinématographique*, 38–39 (Spring 1965), 135–39; J. H. Matthews, *Surrealism and Film* (Ann Arbor: University of Michigan Press, 1971), 56–58; Alain and Odette Virmaux, *Les Surréalistes et le cinéma* (Paris: Seghers, 1976), 69–71; and Steven Kovács, *From Enchantment to Rage: The Story of Surrealist Cinema* (Cranbury: Associated University Presses, 1980), 59–61. For an analysis of Desnos's previously unacknowledged contribution to Man Ray's *L'Etoile de mer* (1928), see Inez Hedges, "Constellated Visions: Robert Desnos's and Man Ray's *L'Etoile de mer*," *Dada/Surrealism*, 15 (1986), 99–109. The manuscript scenario of *L'Etoile de mer* is reprinted by Rudolf Kuenzli, and translated by Inez Hedges, in *Dada/Surrealism*, 207–19.

101. Williams, *Figures of Desire*, 28.

102. Goudal, "Surréalisme et cinéma," 346.

103. Williams, *Figures of Desire*, 18. Cf. Kovács, *From Enchantment to Rage*, 251–53.

104. Goudal, "Surréalisme et cinéma," 355.

105. Clair, "Rythme," 15.

106. See, also, Antonin Artaud, "Le Cinéma et l'abstraction," *Le Monde illustré*, 3645 (October 1927), trans. Helen Weaver as "Cinema and Abstraction," in *Antonin Artaud, Selected Writings*, ed. Susan Sontag (New York: Farrar, Straus, and Giroux, 1976), 149–50; and Artaud, "Sorcery and the Cinema" [1927 or 1930], trans. P. Adams Sitney, in *The Avant-Garde Film*, 59–60. For an analysis of Artaud's scenario and Dulac's film version of *La Coquille et le clergyman*, see Matthews, *Surrealism and Film*, 64–66; Kovács, *From Enchantment to Rage*, 174–76; Inez Hedges, *Languages of Revolt: Dada and Surrealist Literature and Film* (Durham: Duke University Press, 1983), 27–33; Abel, *French Cinema*, 475–80; Naomi Greene, "Artaud and Film: A Reconsideration," *Cinema Journal* 23.4 (Summer

1984), 28–40; and Sandy Flitterman-Lewis, "The Image and the Spark: Dulac and Artaud Reviewed," *Dada/Surrealism*, 15 (1986), 110–27.

107. Artaud, "Cinéma et réalité," 24–25.

108. Williams, *Figures of Desire*, 20.

109. See, for instance, Benjamin Fondane's "paupières mûres," "barre fixe," and "mtasipoj" in his *Trois Scénarii* (Paris: Robert Baze, 1928), and Francis Picabia, *La Loi d'accommodation chez borgnes* (Paris: Th. Briant, 1928). For an analysis of Fondane's scenarios, see Peter Christensen, "Benjamin Fondane's 'Scenarii intournables'," *Dada/Surrealism*, 15 (1986), 72–85.

110. It should be remembered that André Breton, Louis Aragon, Paul Eluard, Benjamin Peret, and Pierre Unik all joined the French Communist Party in early 1927, after which the rest of the Surrealist circle followed; as a body, the Surrealists remained aligned with the French Communist Party until 1932—see Robert Short, "The Politics of Surrealism, 1920–1936," *Journal of Contemporary History*, 1.2 (1966), 10–17; and Bernard, *Le Parti communiste français*, 90–112.

111. Desnos, "Cinéma d'avant-garde," 386. See, also, Robert Desnos, "Mouvements accélérés," *Journal littéraire* (18 April 1925); [untitled], *Journal littéraire* (9 May 1925), and "*Moana*," *Le Soir* (19 May 1927), reprinted in Desnos, *Cinéma*, 137–38, 143–44, 177–79.

112. Goudal, "Surréalisme et cinéma," 356.

113. Desnos, "Cinéma d'avant-garde," 387.

114. Robert Aron, "Films de révolte," *La Revue du cinéma*, 5 (15 November 1929), 41–45. The Surrealist films that Aron discusses include Man Ray's *Emak Bakia* (1927), *L'Etoile de mer* (1928), and *Les Mystères du Chateau du Dé* (1929), and Buñuel's *Un Chien andalou* (1929). See, also, Luis Buñuel and Salvador Dali's scenario for *Un Chien andalou*, in *La Revue du cinéma*, 5 (November 1929), 3–16. For analyses of *Un Chien andalou*, see Raymond Durgnat, *Luis Buñuel* (Berkeley: University of California Press, 1968), 22–37; Matthews, *Surrealism and Film*, 84–90; Phillip Drummond, "Textual Space in *Un Chien andalou*," *Screen*, 18 (1977), 55–119; Paul Sandro, "The Space of Desire in *An Andalusian Dog*," *1978 Film Studies Annual* (1979), 57–63; Kovács, *From Enchantment to Rage*, 196–210; Williams, *Figures of Desire*, 53–105; Hedges, *Languages of Revolt*, 44–52, 69–73; Abel, *French Cinema*, 480–86; and Stuart Liebman, "*Un Chien andalou*: The Talking Cure," *Dada/Surrealism*, 15 (1986), 143–58.

115. Aron, "Films de révolte," 41–43, 45.

116. The Surrealists were much taken with the films of Buster Keaton—see, for instance, Robert Desnos, "*Paris qui dort, Sherlock Jr., Le Rail*," *Journal littéraire* (14 February 1925), and "René Clair et le nouveau cinéma," reprinted in Desnos, *Cinéma*, 127–28, and 131–32; and Luis Buñuel, "Buster Keaton's *College*," *Cahiers d'art*, 10 (1927), reprinted in Francisco Aranda, *Luis Buñuel: A Critical Biography*, trans. David Robinson (New York: De Capo, 1976), 272–73.

117. Aron, "Films de révolte," 45.

118. Williams, *Figures of Desire*, 41. As Williams suggests, "many of Lacan's most important contributions to psychoanalytic tradition . . . are all drawn from the poetic wellspring of Surrealism"—*Figures of Desire*, 44.

Selected Texts

JEAN EPSTEIN, "For a New Avant-Garde"

Translated by Stuart Liebman from "Pour une avant-garde nouvelle," *Cinéa-Ciné-pour-tous* 29 (15 January 1925), 8–10. This essay was first delivered as a lecture at the Vieux-Colombier cinema on 14 December 1924. An earlier version of this translation appeared in *The Avant-Garde Film: A Reader of Theory and Criticism*, ed. P. Adams Sitney (New York: New York University Press, 1978), 26–30.

I JUST WANT to say this: you have to love it and hate it at the same time—and love it as much as you hate it. This fact alone proves that the cinema is an art with a very well-defined personality of its own. The difficulty lies above all in the choice of what is right to hate about it. And if this choice is difficult, it is because it must be revised at extremely short intervals.

Indeed, the best friends of an art always end up becoming infatuated with their ideas. And because art as it transforms itself goes beyond its rules at every moment, these best friends of yesterday become the worst enemies of tomorrow, fanatics devoted to shopworn methods. This continual overturning of friendships is characteristic of the slow evolution of all the arts.

Thus it is that today at last—at last but a little too late—some methods of cinematic expression, still considered as strange and suspect a year ago, have become a la mode. Being fashionable has always signaled the end of a style.

Among these methods we can chiefly include the suppression of intertitles, rapid editing, the importance accorded to sets and to their expressionistic style.

The first films without intertitles were made almost simultaneously in America and in Germany. In America it was a film by Charles Ray, *La Petite Baignade* [*The Old Swimmin' Hole*, 1921], distributed and titled here, though only after considerable delay. Retreating from its novelty, the distributors were careful to add about fifteen intertitles to the film. In Germany, it was *Le Rail* [*Scherben* or *Shattered*, 1921] by Lupu Pick. I haven't come here to justify the so-called "American" title—incorrectly named for it is, alas, often French too—that beforehand explains a first time to the spectator what he is about to see in the next image, and then after it tells him a second time in case he either wouldn't see or understand. Certainly the suppression of the title has had its value as a new method, not entirely in and of itself but as a useful one among others. And Lupu Pick, who must be considered the master of the film without titles, last season presented us

349

with a kind of cinematic perfection, that is, *The Night of St. Sylvester* [1923], perhaps the most filmic film ever seen, whose shadows conveyed an extreme of human passion on film for the first time. And the theory that is the basis for the film without titles is obviously logical: the cinema is made to narrate with images and not with words. Except that one should never go to the limits of theories; their furthermost point is always their weak point where they give way. For you can't deny that watching a film absolutely free of intertitles is, for psychological reasons, depressing; the intertitle is above all a place for the eye to rest, a punctuation point for the mind. A title often avoids a long visual explanation, one that is necessary but also annoying or trite. And if you had to limit yourself to films without titles, how many otherwise beautiful scenarios would become unrealizable. Finally, there are various kinds of information that I still believe it is more discreet to provide in a text than through an image; if you must indicate that an action takes place in the evening, maybe it would be better simply to write it than to show a clock face with the hands stopped at nine o'clock.

Obviously, in a good film an intertitle is only a kind of accident. But on the other hand, advertising a film by stating that it has no intertitles, isn't that like praising the poems of Mallarmé because they don't have punctuation marks?

Rapid editing exists in an embryonic state in the gigantic work of Griffith. To Gance goes the honor of having so perfected this method that he deserves to be considered its inspired inventor. *La Roue* is still the formidable cinematic monument in whose shadow all French cinematic art lives and breathes. Here and there, attempts are being made to escape from its hold and its style; it is still difficult. And if I insist on this point, it is so that what I am going to say in a moment cannot in any way be construed as a criticism of *La Roue*. It contains, moreover, elements far more noble, more pure, and more moral than the discovery of the rapid editing technique, which seems to me nothing more than an accident in the film. But if in *La Roue* this is a very fortunate accident, how disagreeable it becomes in so many other films. Today, rapid editing is abused even in documentaries; each drama has a scene, if not two or three, made up of little fragments. Nineteen twenty-five, I predict to you, will inundate us with films that will precisely correspond to this most superficial aspect of our cinematic ideal in 1923. Nineteen twenty-four has already begun, and in a month four films using breakneck editing have already been shown. It's too late; it's no longer interesting; it's a little ridiculous. Wouldn't our contemporary novelist be ridiculous if he wrote his works in the Symbolist style of Francis Poietevin where, invariably, he uses the word "remembrance" [*resouvenance*] for "memory" [*souvenir*] and "disheartenment" [*désésperance*] for "despair" [*déséspoir*]?[1]

If you must say about a film that it has beautiful sets, I think it would be better not to speak about it at all; the film is bad. *The Cabinet of Dr. Caligari* is the best example of the misuse of sets in cinema. *Caligari* represents a serious cinematic malady: the hypertrophy of a subordinate feature, the great importance still accorded to what is an "accident" at the expense of the essential. I do not want to talk primarily about *Caligari*'s shoddy expressionism "ready-made for thirty francs," but about the principle of a film that is hardly anything more than photographs of a group of sets. Everything in *Caligari* is a set: first, the decor itself, next, the character who is as painted and tricked up as the set, finally, the light which is also painted—an unpardonable sacrilege in cinema—with shadows and halflights illusionistically laid out in advance. Thus the film is nothing more than a still life, all its living elements having been killed by strokes of the brush. Along with a thousand other things, cinema has borrowed sets from the theater. Little by little, if it is independently viable, the cinema will pay back its debts and this debt as well. No more than it revived the theater, the work of painters will not succeed in reviving the cinema. On the contrary, the work of painters cannot but succeed at impeding the normal development, sincere and pure, dramatic and poetic, of the cinema. Painting is one thing, the cinema something else entirely. If the "Théâtre d'Art" declared at its birth: "The word creates the decor as well as everything else . . . ,"[2] the "Cinéma d'Art" now being born declares: "The gesture creates the decor as well as everything else." In cinema, stylized sets ought not and cannot be. In the fragments of those few films that are almost true cinema, the sets are anatomical, and the drama played in this intimate physical arena is superlatively ideal. In close-up, the eyelid with the lashes that you count, is a set remodeled by emotion at every instant. Beneath the lid appears the gaze which is the character of the drama and which is even more than a character: it is a person. With imperceptible movements whose religious secret no emotional microscopy has yet been able to reveal, the circle of the iris transcribes a soul. Between the tuft of the chin and the arc of the eyebrows an entire tragedy is won, then lost, is won anew and lost once more. Lips still pressed together, a smile trembles toward off-screen, within those wings which is the heart. When the mouth finally opens, joy itself takes wing.

If I criticize three techniques especially misused by modern cinema, methods which now enjoy a belated vogue, it is because these methods are purely material, purely mechanical. The mechanical period of cinema is over. The cinema must henceforth be called: the photography of delusions of the heart.

I remember my first meeting with Blaise Cendrars. It was in Nice, where Cendrars was then assisting Gance in the production of *La Roue*. We

351

were speaking about cinema and Cendrars told me: "*Photogénie* is a word
. . . very pretentious, a bit silly; but it's a great mystery." Gradually,
much later, I understood what a great mystery *photogénie* is.

Each of us, I assume, may possess some object which he holds onto for
personal reasons: for some it's a book; for some, perhaps a very banal and
somewhat ugly trinket; for someone else, perhaps, a piece of furniture with
no value. We do not look at them as they really are. To tell the truth, we
are incapable of seeing them as objects. What we see in them, through
them, are the memories and emotions, the plans or regrets that we have
attached to these things for a more or less lengthy period of time, sometimes forever. Now, this is the cinematographic mystery: an object such as
this, with its personal character, that is to say, an object situated in a dramatic action that is equally photographic in character, reveals anew its
moral character, its human and living expression when reproduced cinematographically.

I imagine a banker receiving bad news at home from the stock exchange.
He is about to telephone. The call is delayed. Close-up of the telephone. If
the shot of the telephone is shown clearly, if it is well-written, you no
longer see a mere telephone. You read: ruin, failure, misery, prison, suicide. And in other circumstances, this same telephone will say: sickness,
doctor, help, death, solitude, grief. And at yet another time this same telephone will cry gaily: joy, love, liberty. All this may seem extremely simple; they may be regarded as childish symbols. I confess that it seems very
mysterious to me that one can in this way charge the simple reflection of
inert objects with an intensified sense of life, that one can animate it with
its own vital import. Moreover, I confess that it seems much more important to me to concern ourselves with this phenomenon of cinematic telepathy than to cultivate two or three almost purely mechanical methods too
exclusively.

M. Jean Choux, the film critic of the newspaper *La Suisse*,[3] has written
apropos of *Coeur fidèle* the lines that I reproduce below and that do not apply
solely to this film.

"How close-ups deify. Oh, these faces of men and women displayed so
harshly on screen, solid as enamel and more powerfully sculptural than the
Michelangelesque creatures on the ceiling of the Sistine! To see a thousand
immobile heads whose gazes are aimed at and monopolized and haunted by
a single enormous face on the screen toward which they all converge. What
an excruciating conversation. An idol and the crowd. Just like the cults in
India. But here the idol is alive and this idol is a man. An extraordinary
import is emitted from these close-ups. In them, the soul is separated in
the same way one separates radium. The horror of living, its horror and
mystery, is proclaimed. This pitiable Marie, this Jean, and this Petit-Paul,

have they no other purpose than to be this Marie, this Jean, and this Petit-Paul? It's not possible! There must be something more."

Certainly there is something more.

The cinema is its herald.

[1] Francis Poietevin (1854–1904) was a minor Symbolist poet.

[2] A reference to Jacques Copeau's famous Théâtre de Vieux-Colombier, which he founded in 1913 with the help of the writers associated with the *Nouvelle Revue française*.

[3] Jean Choux (1887–1946) was a Swiss journalist and film critic who directed a half-dozen films in Switzerland and France between 1925 and 1929, and then hit the jackpot with *Jean de la Lune* (1931).

JEAN GOUDAL, "Surrealism and Cinema"

Translated by Paul Hammond in *The Shadow and Its Shadow: Surrealist Writings on the Cinema*, ed. Paul Hammond (London: British Film Institute, 1978), 49–56. Reprinted by permission. The original French text first appeared as "Surréalisme et cinéma" in *La Revue hebdomadaire* (February 1925), 343–57.

A NEW TECHNIQUE is born: immediately the philosophers come running, armed with false problems. Is it an art?—Is it not an art?—Is it even worthy of interest?

"In short," some of them say, "the cinema is only a perfected form of photography." And they refuse to credit the new invention.

The indispensable extremists assume the other position. They tell us, "Not only is the cinema an art, it will, moreover, gradually absorb all the other arts" (Monsieur Marcel L'Herbier, in a lecture at the Collège de France, repeated in Geneva during October 1924 at the showing in that town of *L'Inhumaine* [1924], previously published in *La Revue hebdomadaire* in 1923). The proof: the cinema takes the place of architecture (30 meters devoted to the palaces in *The Thief of Bagdad* [1924]), music (a Negro jazz band goes through the motions for 20 meters), dance (25 meters on a tango by Valentino). Were they to draw the obvious conclusions from their ludicrous logic they would have us believe that in future our meals will be replaced by the image of Charlie Chaplin and the Kid tucking into a plate of pancakes.

"Given its basic technical strictures, how do we see the future of the cinema?" Now that's a more realistic question. To establish the correctness of it, to begin to answer it, we need briefly to consider the evolution of the other arts.

We see each of them in their turn follow the same general pattern.

First, they escape *literary* contamination (the renunciation of figurative painting, of thematic music); next they renounce the constraint of *logic*, considered an intellectual element restricting sensory freedom, in favor of

353

inquiring after their guiding principles in terms of their *technique* (Cubism, musical impressionism).

(You can already foresee the third stage: thirsting for total liberty, artists will thrust aside the last support of technique and claim the right to bring into play, without any modification, the very *material* forming the basis of their art.)

We do not want to conceal the excessive simplification of these views or the dangers inherent in them; but nobody can contest this conclusion: in the evolution of every art there comes a moment, which may or may not be deplored, when the artist ignores every command of intellectual or logical origin in order to question the *technical* possibilities of his art. To us this moment appears to have arrived for the cinema.

Let us open a short parenthesis here on a literary movement whose origins are not recent, but which manifests itself at present in a very noisy way.

We know the essential character of the Surrealist theses (we find an authentic expression of them in André Breton's *Manifesto of Surrealism* [1924]): that the unconscious activity of the mind, on which general attention has been focused through the work of thinkers like Freud and Babinski[1] or the novels of authors like Marcel Proust, has become the keystone of mental life. The artist's principal target is henceforth to search for a reality in the dream superior to that which the logical, therefore arbitrary, exercise of thought suggests to us. On the one hand Surrealism presents itself as a critique of existing forms of literature, on the other as a complete renewal of the field and of artistic method and even, perhaps, as the renovation of the most general rules of human activity: in short, the absolute overthrow of all values.

You might think that objections to Surrealism (about which, however, you cannot deny the relative fruitfulness) are not lacking. Monsieur André Breton, even, shows himself to be ecstatic about the obstacles which already present themselves: "To its conquest [surreality] I go, certain of not getting there, but too heedless of my death not to calculate a little the joys of such possession."

The potential difficulties seem to us capable of being subsumed under two principal headings.

First, an objection as to method. It is not easy to determine if the Surrealists situate a superior reality in the dream itself, or in a sort of union or adjustment, difficult to imagine, of the two states, dream and reality. In both cases the same objection arises. If you admit that dream constitutes a superior reality, there will be insurmountable practical problems in attaining and fixing this dream. As soon as consciousness succeeds in rummaging through the unconscious you can no longer speak of the unconscious. On the other hand if you accord a superior reality to a mystical fusion of the real and the dream, one cannot see by what means one can make two areas, by definition incommunicable, communicate with each other. (Our intention of progressing quickly here may lend too schematic an allure to our arguments. Furthermore, our real objective is not a critique of Surrealism.)

The second order of objection touches more profoundly on the antilogical ambitions of Surrealism. Men have had the habit for so long now of using a language to communicate with each other that one asks if they can ever renounce this kind of usage. In short, what we call *reason* is the part of our mind common to all men: if it is to disappear will we not lapse into an individual, incommunicable mode of expression? "I believe more and more," writes Monsieur A. Breton (*Manifesto of Surrealism*), "in the infallibility of my thought in relation to myself." Monsieur A. Breton is right; but why then have this "spiritual and mental mechanism" of Monsieur A. Breton's, once fixed in its absolute ingenuity valid only for Monsieur A. Breton himself, printed and published? Is it not so that we can make a comparison between his mind and our mind, and is this comparison even possible without some essential reference that only reason and logic can supply?

One fact seems remarkable to us. The objections we have just sketched out lose their value as soon as one applies the Surrealist theories to the domain of cinema. (That the theorists of Surrealism have wanted to apply their ideas to literature, that is to say just where they are most contestable, should not be too surprising since the same pen suits the theorist and the poet.) Applied to the technique of cinema the correctness and fecundity of the Surrealist thesis is all the more striking.

The objection to *method* (the difficulty of uniting the conscious and the unconscious on the same plane) does not hold for cinema, in which the thing seen corresponds exactly to a *conscious hallucination*.

Let's go into a cinema where the perforated celluloid is purring in the darkness. On entering, our gaze is guided by the luminous ray to the screen where for two hours it will remain fixed. Life in the street outside no longer exists. Our problems evaporate, our neighbors disappear. Our body itself submits to a sort of temporary depersonalization which takes away the feeling of its own existence. We are nothing but two eyes riveted to ten square meters of white sheet.

But we must beware of vague analogies. It is better here to go into details.

Monsieur A. Breton, wanting to establish the superiority of the dream, writes: "The mind of the man who dreams is fully satisfied by whatever happens to it. The agonizing question of possibility arises no more." And, he asks, "what reason, what reason better than another confers this natural allure on the dream, makes me welcome unreservedly a host of episodes the strangeness of which strikes me as I write"?

The answer to this question lies in what Taine[2] used to call the "reductive mechanism of images." When we are awake the images surging into our imagination have an anemic, pale color which by contrast makes the vigor and relief of real images stand out, the ones, that is to say, we get through our senses: and this difference of value is enough to make us distinguish the real from the imagined. When we sleep our senses are idle, or rather their solicitations do not cross the threshold of consciousness and, the reducing contrast no longer existing, the imaginary succession of images monopolizes the foreground; as nothing contradicts them we believe in their actual existence.

Awake, we imagine the real and the possible all at once, while in the dream we only imagine the possible. The Surrealists see an advantage in what, they say, one is used to seeing as inferior. Without going into the legitimacy of this paradox, let us return to the cinema. There we see a whole host of material conditions conspire to destroy this "reductive mechanism of images." The darkness of the auditorium destroys the rivalry of real images that would contradict the ones on the screen. It is equally important to ward off the impressions that can come to us through our other senses: who has never noticed the special nature of music in the cinema? Above all else it serves to abolish a silence that would let us perceive or imagine auditory phenomena of a realistic order, which would damage the necessary uniqueness of vision. And what spectator has not been embarrassed at times during the showing of a film at the attention he was giving, despite himself, to the music? In reality the only music that would suit the cinema would be a sort of continuous, harmonious, monotonous noise (like the humming of an electric fan), the effect of which would be to obdurate the sense of hearing in some way for the duration of the show.

Someone might object that these are conditions common to all forms of spectacle and that even in the theater the darkness is there to facilitate the audience's concentration on the stage. But let us observe that the individuals performing on a theater stage have a physical presence that strengthens the *trompe l'oeil* of their setting; they have three-dimensionality, they live amidst the noises of normal life; we accept them as our brothers, as our peers, while the camera aspires to give the illusion of reality by means of a simulacrum of a uniquely visual kind. An actual hallucination is needed here which the other conditions of cinema tend to reinforce, just as, in the dream, moving images *lacking three-dimensionality* follow each other on a single plane artificially delimited by a rectangle which is like a geometrical opening giving on to the psychic kingdom. The absence of color, too, the *black and white*, represents an arbitrary simplification analogous to those

356

one meets in dreams. Once again let us note that the actual succession of images in the cinema has something *artificial* about it that distances us from reality. The persistence of images on the retina, which is the physiological basis of cinema, claims to present movement to us with the actual continuity of the real; but in fact we know very well that it's an illusion, a sensory device which does not completely fool us. Ultimately, the rhythm of the individuals we see moving on the silent screen possesses something jerky about it that makes them the relatives of the people who haunt our dreams.

We must add one last analogy. In the cinema, as in the dream, the *fact* is complete master. Abstraction has no rights. No explanation is needed to justify the heroes' actions. One event follows another, seeking justification in itself alone. They follow each other with such rapidity that we barely have time to call to mind the logical commentary that would explain them, or at least connect them.

(Summary considerations, no doubt, but ones that allow us to make short work of certain illusions about the advisability of adding "improvements" like color, relief or some kind of sound synchronization. The cinema has found its true technique in black and white film—forget three-dimensionality and sound. To try to "perfect" it, in the sense of bringing it closer to reality, would only run counter to and slow down its genuine development.)

The cinema, then, constitutes a conscious hallucination, and utilizes this fusion of dream and consciousness which Surrealism would like to see realised in the literary domain. These moving images delude us, by leaving us with a confused awareness of our own personality and by allowing us to evoke, if necessary, the resources of our memory. (In general, however, the cinema only demands from us memory enough to link the images.)

The cinema avoids the second order of difficulty raised by Surrealism just as happily.

Though the complete repudiation of logic is forbidden language, which is born of this logic, the cinema can indulge itself in such repudiation without contravening any ineluctable internal necessity.

"The strongest image is the one that has the greatest degree of arbitrariness," declares Monsieur A. Breton, who cites, among other examples, this image from Philippe Soupault: "A church stood dazzling as a bell."

The word *church*, encompassed, by virtue of language, within a system of logical relations, just as the word *bell* is, makes the very fact of pronouncing these two words, of comparing them, evoke these two systems, makes us make them coincide. And, as they are not juxtaposable, the reader bridles at accepting the comparison.

On the other hand when the cinema shows us a dazzling church then,

357

without transition, a dazzling bell, our eye can accept this sequence; it is witnessing two facts here, two facts which justify themselves. And if the two images succeed each other with the necessary rapidity, the logical mechanism which tries to link the two objects in some way or other will not have time to be set in motion. All one will experience is the almost simultaneous sight of two objects, exactly the cerebral process, that is to say, that suggested this comparison to the author.

In language the foremost factor is always the logical thread. The image is born according to this thread, and contributes to its embellishment, its illumination. In cinema the foremost factor is the image which, on occasion, though not necessarily so, drags the tatters of reason behind it. The two processes, you see, are exactly inversed.

The above tends to demonstrate that not only does the application of Surrealist ideas to the cinema avoid the objection with which you can charge literary Surrealism, but that surreality represents a domain actually indicated to cinema by its very technique.

Just leaf through the dreamed poems Monsieur A. Breton has collected together at the end of his *Manifesto*, under the title of *Soluble Fish*, and you will see, perhaps, that the surest way of making the public accept them would be to treat them like film scenarios.

The adventures of the crate penetrated by human arms, sliding down hillsides, bashing against "trees that cast bright blue sunlight on it," then running aground on the first floor of a run-down hotel, and which is found to contain only starch, and the mysterious voyage of the barque which is the poet's tomb following the closing of the cemetery, and the tribulations of the lamppost, and the chase after the woman who has left her veil with her lover, a source of miracles and inexplicable bliss, so many marvelous tales with enough anacoluthon inevitably to shock the reader, but which, brought to the screen, would perhaps be accepted with delight by the spectator. The latter would see in its teeming lapses of logic no more than thousands of details, comic and strange, all ingenious.

It is time *cinéastes* saw clearly what profits they may gain in opening up their art to the unexplored regions of the dream. Up till now this has only been done intermittently, as if by default. They should lose no time in imbuing their productions with the three essential characteristics of the dream, the *visual*, the *illogical*, the *pervasive*.

THE VISUAL

The cinema is already so by force of circumstance.

It will remain so exclusively.

(There is nothing for it to fear, we repeat, from the paltry attempts at phonographic synchronization.)

THE ILLOGICAL

Everything that is foolish about cinema is the fault of an old-fashioned respect for logic.

Sentimentality is the respect for logic within the framework of feeling. (All elegance, all unselfconsciousness results from the severing of one or more links in the traditional chain of feelings.)

The *feuilleton* is the respect for logic within the framework of episodes. (I term *feuilleton* any sequence of events whose unfolding, using basic characters and situations, can be understood by the average concierge.)

Slowness is the respect for logic within the framework of situations and gestures.

Etc.

THE PERVASIVE

But if you are to bring to the screen only various illogical series of images, assembled according to the most capricious associations of ideas, don't you risk alienating the public?

First, we reply that we are suggesting only one possible direction for the cinema here. *Other ways remain open besides this one.* Bit by bit the education of the public will occur.

Next, we feel we must not lose our footing through complete incoherence. Man is only interested in what is close to him. I am interested in my dreams, despite their coherence, because they come from within me, because I find a particular quality in them belonging no doubt to what I can recognize in them of elements of *my* past life, though arbitrarily assembled. These memories are my own; but I have difficulty in identifying them. For want of a better word this is what I mean by the expression: the dream is *pervasive*.

This property of the dream is strictly personal, one can see that. How can a film, which must address itself to thousands of spectators, manage to be *pervasive*?

This is the place to reintroduce the human dimension.

One of Surrealism's points of departure is the observation that everything that emerges from the mind, even without logical form, inevitably reveals the singularity of that mind. Man retains his personality (all the more so perhaps) in his most spontaneous productions.

A film, then, will have a sufficiently pervasive and human character because it will have come from the brain of one of my peers.

We now come up against a serious problem. In the actual process of cinema, a film does not have one creator, it has two, three, ten, fifty. One man supplies the scenario, which usually consists of an extremely brief outline. This scenario is taken up by the director, who develops it, fills it out with

359

detail, in short brings it to the level of practical realization. It remains to note the contribution of each artist, the suggestions of the costume and prop departments, the requirements of the lighting technicians. During the course of such a many-sided collaboration doesn't the work risk losing the singular quality it owed to the individuality of the author, the singularity of its first conception?

This difficulty is, we believe, only temporary and soon tends to disappear. It is due to the exceptional conditions created by the too-rapid growth of the cinema. The cinema has met with such success since its beginnings (it is barely thirty years old, remember) that it has had to cope with demands disproportionate to its means. The public expects new films every week. To create them is the work of many. You employ whomever you can. Let us give the division of labor and the necessary specialization the time to find their way. Then, beginning with the original cell, the source idea born in his mind, the *cinéaste* will be able to supervise it, thanks to a technique he must be master of, until it is seen on the screen without the idea being bungled by a commercial organization concerned only to exploit it. On that day the cinema will have its artists, and the question whether or not "the cinema is an art" will thereby get an affirmative response difficult to contest.

The *cinéastes* are beginning to see the light.

It isn't too hard to see indications in their most recent productions that would confirm our previsions, yet with what awkwardness is this *Marvelous* in which the cinema finds its real voice still spoken of. Will results come from the comedy film side? We have memories of certain American films, almost without subtitles [intertitles], in which girls, irresponsible individuals, and animals let their whims, of the most diverting fantasy, take control of them. Do not the recent Chaplins betray the desire to construct a simplified setting which no over-precise detail can localize (Charlie Chaplin being universal, the locations he performs in could be anywhere)—and also the preoccupation with creating a dream atmosphere which is believable and makes possible the extraordinary gestures of this unfortunate with the little mustache and big feet. Remember the strange chapel with its strange congregation in *The Pilgrim* [1923], where Charlie, the bogus pastor, delivers that strange sermon; and in *Payday* [1922], Charlie, the mason in his cups, returning to a far-off lodging house that proves impossible to get to, and that nightmarish rain, and those futile, unreal attempts by the drunk to get on a tram which has no destination and will always escape, full of eternal commuters, back into the anonymous night.

Besides this burlesque Marvelous, Charlie's unique atmosphere, there is a place for that faery [*féerie*] Marvelous certain films have already brought us, the essential elements of which would be the *geometry of line* and the *illogicality of detail*.

The Marvelous in the cinema, unable to utilize the infinite resources of color, must count above all on the resources of lighting and line. Just as in the world we inhabit no line is absolutely geometrical, so a resolutely geometrical stylization creates a surprising atmosphere.

In *The Thief of Bagdad*, for instance, two details strike the spectator forcibly: the gate of the town that opens and closes through the connecting and disconnecting of identically formed panels, and Douglas Fairbanks soaring above the unreal clouds on his scleroid horse. These two images have the admirable manifest artifice of the dream.

In the same film, on the other hand, the heavy-handed Americans, wanting to show us a monster, have laboriously sought verisimilitude and concocted a sort of enormous lizard, instead of painting in, in broad strokes, a clearly fantastic creature of geometrical cardboard. The Germans made the same blunder when they sought to represent Cerberus guarding Brunhild's castle (in *The Nibelungen* [1924]). They constructed a complicated, naively realistic mechanism needing sixteen men to make the huge thing move. What effort and money expended, not necessarily in vain, but they missed the whole point!

At least we have a success in the laboratory set F. Léger designed for Monsieur L'Herbier's *L'Inhumaine*. The effect of the machines used to bring the loved woman back to life is striking, the Cubist decor coming alive and moving in a clever frenzy.

Let us quote Monsieur A. Breton again: "No matter how charming they may be, a grown man would think he were reverting to childhood by nourishing himself on fairy tales, and I am the first to admit that all such tales are not suitable for him. The fabric of adorable improbabilities must be made a trifle more subtle the older we grow, and we are still at the stage of waiting for this kind of spider." It is the fineness of this fabric we think of when calling for the *illogicality of the detail*. It is not without unparalleled sorrow that man, crushed by a thousand years of logic, will renounce the principle of identity. The American faery that we find in this same *Thief of Bagdad* (flying carpets, flames, monsters) is not much more courageous than Perrault's, whose fairies didn't go quite so far as to change a pumpkin into a horse or a rat into a coach, but prudently changed an animal into an animal, an object into an object. "There are," adds Monsieur A. Breton, "fairy tales to be written for adults, fairy tales still almost blue." Who will write these tales if not the cinema?

The preceding pages, we repeat, aim only at suggesting one possible direction for the cinema.

As for the concessions needed to suit public taste, we do not think it useful to insist on them. There will always be enough industrialists to keep up the old traditions, to go on adapting novels to be acted out by boxing champions and France's most beautiful *midinettes*.

What the cinema has produced over a quarter of a century justifies all our hopes. One does not fight the forces of the spirit.

JEAN GOUDAL (1895–?), as far as is known, composed just this one essay on the cinema.

¹ Joseph François Félix Babinski (1857–1932) was best known for his studies on hysteria—for example, *Démembrement de l'hystérie traditionnelle, pithiatisme* (Paris: Semaine médicale, 1909).

² Hippolyte Taine (1828–1893) was an influential literary historian and critic whose positivist theory of literature attempted to explain literary works in the context of race, place, and time period.

PAUL RAMAIN, "The Influence of Dream on the Cinema"

From "L'Influence du rêve sur le cinéma," *Cinéa-Ciné-pour-tous* 40 (1 July 1925), 8.

IF ONE TAKES inspiration from the ideas of Sigmund Freud on dream— which is "untranslatable in words, [and] can only be expressed by means of images"—it is quite obvious that one is correct in believing that the current cinema is based on dream *under all its guises*: both the dream that is an unconscious creation of moving images during sleep and the daydream that is a subconscious creation of the waking state—two forms which have the same cause according to certain psychologists. Moreover, inspiration is associated with dream: like dream, it is a spontaneous manifestation of the unconscious or subconscious which is translated into images.

Now, this—quasi-conscious, if one can say that—use of dream appears constantly in the majority of artistic films or real "cinema," whether it occurs as content, as means, or merely as a sporadic element.

To cite the films which are dreamlike or use dream images would be time-consuming, there are so many: from Sjöstrom's *Charette fantôme* [*The Phantom Carriage*, 1921] to René Clair's *Fantôme du Moulin Rouge* [1925] and *Midsummer Night's Dream* (in preparation),¹ by way of the same author's *Entr'acte* [1924], a film which has to be regarded as a type of dream but an incoherent one, which makes it all the more interesting. *L'Inhumaine* [1924] also is of an oneiric order. As for the German productions, from *Caligari* [1919], which is a distorted vision, the oneiric delirium of a madman, to *Waxworks* [Paul Leni, 1924], *The Hands of Orlac* [Robert Wiene, 1924], and *Warning Shadows* [Arthur Robinson, 1923], dream turns to nightmare and nightmare to hallucination.

If the cinema is dreamlike, the reciprocal is also true: dream is like the cinema. Without entering here into what I could call the physiology of the cinema, I will show briefly how dreams and cinema are merely different, yet parallel expressions of the same impulse. The images that I see unroll before my eyes in the slumber of the darkened hall are directly comparable to oneiric images, with the orchestra playing an essentially *hypnogenic* role.[2] In dreams, people are silent, food doesn't exude any odor, liquids are tasteless: it's the same on the screen.

In certain films—for example, the German *Vanina* [Arthur von Gerlach, 1922]—I have personally experienced the intolerable feeling that one has in certain dreams: running without getting anywhere in trying to escape imminent danger.

This example, chosen from among many, reveals that a cinema based on dream reaches the point of producing oneiric feelings in us. Moreover, by virtue of very complicated laws of dissociation between the representative and affective elements of a psychological state—according to P. Brunet— the representative terms of a fear can occur in a dream without being accompanied by the affective terms; so that the dreamer can see his fears materialize without experiencing any distressing emotions. What produces a certain oneiric materialization of fears here *is not* a nightmare and cannot be distinguished from the materialization of desires.

Now, *all this can be fully realized in the images on the screen*. Certain scenes, although agonizing in and of themselves, are not so for many spectators who, instinctively, unconsciously, recognize that they are seeing a fiction.

The incoherence of dream is more apparent than actual and, interposed against the logic of film, is easily repressed: the technique of film being the same as that of dream. *All the expressive and visual processes of the cinema are found in dream*, and have existed there since man first came to exist and to think. The simultaneity of actions, soft-focus images, dissolves, superimpositions, distortions, the doubling of images, slow motion, movement in silence—are these not *the soul of dream and daydream?*

Furthermore, dream is progressive, never static. So is the cinema.

Now, this affinity between the dynamic movement of the cinema and the dynamic movement of dream engenders a third connection: that of cinema and music. Music, the supreme art of dream, of audible dream, is itself dynamism and movement. This simultaneity, this soft focus, these superimpositions, these distortions, all this movement proper to cinema and dream can be found again completely, acoustically, in music: fugue, counterpoint, harmony . . . And doesn't music create, for many people, more or less rapid, clear visual images, and in constant motion? See, for example, Bach's *Caprice sur le départ d'un frère bien-aimé*, Beethoven's *Pastoral Symphony*, most of Debussy's works, Ravel's *Valse*, Rimsky-Korsakov's *Schéhérazade*, Déodat de Séverac's *Baigneuses au soleil*, Vincent d'Indy's *Poème des montagnes*, Igor Stravinsky's *Sacre du printemps*, Arthur Honegger's *Pacific 231*, and so on . . .

Therefore, dream and the fantastic are nicely externalized by music (Moussorgsky) and even better so by cinema (*Charette fantôme*). Cinema, dream, and music form, then, a kind of Trinity: three states in one. And I have to admit, inspired by all this, that the cinema, as the translator of dream, may one day become a true *optical music* that transcends the scenario and causes the subtlest emotion to blossom in the self, through *the rhythm and visual song of images alone*—without any wordplay.

That is a form of cinema, if not cinema at its best.

PAUL RAMAIN was a cinema enthusiast who founded one of the earliest ciné-clubs outside Paris, in Montpellier. He also passed himself off as a doctor of psychology, although he apparently had no formal training.

¹ *Midsummer Night's Dream* apparently was a working title for what became Clair's *Le Voyage imaginaire* (1926).

² Ramain is creating a neologism by splicing "*hypnotic*" with "*photogenic*."

JACQUES FEYDER, "Visual Transpositions"

From "Transpositions visuelles," *Cahiers du mois* 16/17 (1925), 67–71.

THE CINEMA has scarcely gotten beyond infancy. It is still in its period of formation, that of "essays," various experiments, tentative trials and errors, and also the most exciting efforts—those in which it sees opening ahead all the paths of virtual conquest and mystery, rich in possibilities. In the meantime, it can be pardoned for not always being entirely itself. Yet just as we demand that painting be above all pictorial, literature literary, and theater theatrical, so we are right to insist that the cinema above all be cinematic. The character or individuality of an art is comprised of an ensemble of means, techniques, and possibilities which constitute its own unique property.

In the current state of the art and of visual technique, film still cannot escape completely from the influence, suggestions—and snares—that the other arts in general and literature in particular impose upon it each step of the way.

Until the new order of things arrives, then, we have two kinds of scenarios: those composed directly for the screen and those drawn from theatrical dramas or novels. The future will see more and more *cinéastes* worthy of the name adopting the former to the detriment of the latter.

For two reasons, however, this first source of visual interpretation is temporarily impossible. In our age of literary overproduction, where bad books are almost as numerous as bad films, a well-launched book can easily sell its 150,000–200,000 copies. It's a publicity campaign, in effect, for a film of the same title. Producers are fond of saying that a film drawn from a celebrated book attracts many more people than does one drawn from an original scenario, whose author may die unknown—unrecognized—however inspired he may be. That's an error of judgment from which the public will recover long before the producers do.

The visual education of the spectator is proceeding slowly but surely. His revolt will be all the more sudden the less he believes in production company publicity. When that day comes, the cinema will take an enormous step forward and perhaps witness the collapse of the exhibition circuits of our cinema shopkeepers.

The second important reason why we don't create original scenarios in France is that, ever since the death of Louis Delluc [March 1924], we have not had any genuine scenario writers. Who could we compare with C. Gardner Sullivan and Jack Hawks, the authors of *The Aryan* [1916], *Civilization* [1916], *Those Who Pay* [1917], and *Blue Blazes Rawden* [1918], with Jeannie MacPherson and Francis Marion, all claimed by America, or with Hans Janowitz, Hans Kraely, Thea Von Harbou, and Carl Mayer who do Germany proud?[1]

The dramatists and novelists who could give us some powerful and original work have no sense of the cinema; they have neither seriously investigated its limitless possibilities nor studied the technical resources for those possibilities. They all ought to submit to a reeducation and serve an apprenticeship in visual composition; but, because of their age and intellectual rigidity, none would even consider that.

Now, certain modern writers—Pierre Mac Orlan, Alexandre Arnoux, Jules Romains, Georges Duhamel, Joseph Delteil, André Obey, Marc Elder[2]—have come strongly under the influence of this new art form; but that influence has not gone beyond the point of the literary development of this or that page.[3] It still has not provoked a revolution in the conception of the novel like that which the following generations will make, the generation born along with the cinema.

Given the total French production of the last few years, how many original scenarios are worthy of sustaining our attention? *Le Penseur* by Edmond Fleg; *Le Silence, La Fête espagnole*, and *La Femme de nulle part* by Louis Delluc; *L'Âtre* by Robert Boudrioz[4]—and then?

Abel Gance, the greatest director that the cinema has granted us until now, to whom we owe certain fragments in *La Roue*, which, stripped of their context, are among the most perfect in the cinema? Has Gance himself ever achieved balance and harmony in the composition of his scenarios?

DESPITE a sometimes technically deft decoupage, the film projects proposed to us currently, most of the time, possess such a banality and poverty of ideas that it is disconcerting!

Where should we turn? . . . What films should we shoot? . . . We turn to adaptations. They are but a last resort in the present state of affairs.[5]

Certain good novels, not necessarily the famous ones, provide a richness of substance, vigor, and thought, a multitude of psychological details. They penetrate more deeply into the characters, explore their dimensions, expose all of their impulses and the play of their reflexes, dismantle all of their mental machinery.

Temporarily, then, it seems preferable to film these adaptations, provided that they be perfectly visual.

Understand the importance of these words. to make *visual*. In them lies the whole art of cinegraphic transposition.

Writing is a means of expression; the film is another, essentially different. And it is agreed that the former, in light of its age, has the enormous advantage of universality.

Just as any literary translation inevitably alters the sense of the original language more or less, visual transposition more or less distorts the original work.

This distortion is matched inversely to the skill, ingenuity, and virtuosity of the *cinéaste*, who must have the desire to rethink the work on a different plane, to recreate it completely if necessary. Often then there is a displacement of the original qualities. Some passage given over to a learned vocabulary or to verbosity has to be condensed and expressed on the screen by several suggestive images. By contrast, several pages, lines, or words can become the pretext for extended visual development.

The screen, which calls for images and not words, can require a total recasting of the subject; it can demand that the scriptwriter create images which may seem quite distant from those found in the novel or play in a literary form and yet which may be closer in spirit to the author's thinking or to those he himself would have imagined.

The description of a decor, a character, the psychology of an individual, the stock phrases of an exchange, the responses of a pathetic scene—all have to become visual and be expressed by the image, that is, in light and silence. The extraordinary dynamism of the cinema, its extreme mobility in time and space, can even authorize the *cinéaste* to modify the order of development of the action.

Everything is allowed so long as the visual perfection of the work is foremost.

The *cinéaste* who visually translates a literary work has only one purpose: to make cinema, to make a film. He has to put aside all other considerations. To do otherwise is a confession of impotence on his part.

In France, we are wrong to think only of the source work, especially since the Americans always think about the work to be done. We reproach the latter for having distorted *Notre Dame de Paris*; actually they have transformed it, they have *made it visual*. If Victor Hugo were alive in our century and wrote directly for the screen, he would be obliged to submit to certain contingencies of visual expression.

Scriptwriters have imposed rules on Victor Hugo's work which he would accept cheerfully if he were alive.

There's no point, then, in crying out about sacrilege; instead, let's be astonished at the scriptwriters' ingenuity.

We often express the opinion that some works are visual and others are not. It's an easy argument which masks our helplessness. All literary, theatrical, and musical works have been or could be rendered visual. It's only the cinegraphic conception of certain directors which is not always so visual. Anything can be translated onto the screen; anything can be expressed in images.

It's possible to derive a fascinating fiction film from the tenth chapter of Montesquieu's *Esprit des lois* as well as from a page of [Balzac's] *Physiologie du mariage*, or a paragraph from Nietzsche's *Zarathustra* as well as any novel of Paul de Kock.[6]

But, to do so, it's indispensable that one possess the spirit of cinema.

JACQUES FEYDER (1885–1948) was an actor at Gaumont before the war and then directed numerous short films for Gaumont between 1915 and 1919. His first feature film, *L'Atlantide* (1921), based on Pierre Benoît's best-selling novel, was a smash hit, and he went on to direct *Crainquebille* (1923) and *Visages d'enfants* (1925).

[1] C. Gardner Sullivan (1885–1965) was head of the scenario department for Thomas Ince's productions (at Triangle, Paramount-Artcraft, and Associated Producers), and Jack G. Hawks (1875–1940) was one of his chief writers. Actually William S. Hart shared credit with Sullivan for the scripts and dialogue titles of many of his films.

Jeannie MacPherson (1887–1946) wrote scripts for Cecil B. DeMille—for example, *Forbidden Fruit* (1921), *Manslaughter* (1922), *The Ten Commandments* (1923). Francis Marion (1887–1973) was one of the best American scriptwriters from the late 1910s to the 1930s; she was particularly favored by Mary Pickford—for example, *Daddy Long Legs* (1919), *Pollyanna* (1919), *Little Lord Fauntleroy* (1921).

Hans Janowitz (1889–1954) was the scriptwriter, along with Carl Mayer, for *Caligari* (1919). Hans Kraely (1885–1950) wrote the scripts for many of Ernest Lubitsch's early films—for example, *Madame Dubarry* (1919), *Sumurun* (1920), *Anna Boleyn* (1920).

Thea Von Harbou (1888–1954) was Fritz Lang's principal scriptwriter—for example, *Destiny* (1921), *Dr. Mabuse* (1922), *Niebelungenlied* (1924)—and also his wife. She also scripted Murnau's *Phantom* (1922) and Von Gerlach's *Chronicle of Grieshaus* (1925).

Carl Mayer (1894–1944) wrote the scripts for *Backstairs* (1921), *Shattered* (1921), *Vanina* (1922), *Warning Shadows* (1923), *Sylvester* (1923), and *The Last Laugh* (1924).

[2] Pierre Mac Orlan (see note 4 to the Jean Epstein selection, "The Senses 1 (b)," in Part Three). Alexandre Arnoux (1884–1973) was a novelist and playwright who turned to writing film criticism and edited the film journal, *Pour Vous* (1928–1939). Jules Romains had just written an original scenario for Feyder at this time—*L'Image* (1926). (See, also, the biographical note following the Romains selection, "The Crowd at the Cinematograph," in Part One and note 127 to the introductory essay, "*Photogénie* and Company," in Part Two.)

Georges Duhamel (1884–1966) was a novelist and essayist—for example, *Vie des martyrs* (1917), *Les Plaisirs et les jeux* (1922), *Confessions de minuit* (1924). Joseph Delteil (1894–1978) was best known then for his lyrical study of *Jeanne d'Arc* (1925). André Obey (1892–1975) was a playwright best known for his collaboration with Denys Amiel on *La Souriante Madame Beudet* (1921), the source of Germaine Dulac's 1923 film. Marc Elder was the pseudonym of Marcel Tendron (1884–1933).

3 Pierre-F. Quesnoy argues that the influence of the cinema on literature was actually stronger than Feyder suggests, in "Littérature et cinéma," *Le Rouge et le noir* (July 1928), 85–104.

4 *Le Penseur* (1920) was directed by Léon Poirier for Gaumont; this was the only work done for the cinema by the Swiss writer, Edmond Fleg (1874–1963). *L'Atre* (1920–1923) was adapted from Alexandre Arnoux's play, *La Chavauchée nocturne*, and directed by Robert Boudrioz for Films Abel Gance.

5 Feyder could very well be talking about his own experience as a filmmaker here. After making two very successful adaptations, *L'Atlantide* (1921) and *Crainquebille* (1923), he directed two original scenarios, the first of them his own—*Visages d'enfants* (1925) and *L'Image* (1926)—both of which ran into distribution difficulties. At the time he wrote this essay, he (along with others such as Clair and L'Herbier) was forced by the economic problems of the Cartel des Gauches govenment, which tended to dry up French film production money, to sign a contract with Films Albatros to make two more adaptations, *Gribiche* (1926) and *Carmen* (1926).

6 Feyder is contrasting the classic political and philosophical texts of two writers almost no one would consider adapting for the cinema with the novels of Balzac, which were much in vogue at the time for film adaptations—for example, Poirier's *Narayana* (1920), Baroncelli's *Père Goriot* (1921), Ravel's *Ferragus* (1923), Epstein's *L'Auberge rouge* (1923), Robert's *Cousin Pons* (1924), and de Rieux's *Cousine Bette* (1924)—and with the sentimental romance novels of Paul de Kock (1793–1871), which offered a prototype for the typical French melodramatic films of the 1920s.

RENÉ CLAIR, "Rhythm"

From "Rythme," *Cahiers du mois* 16/17 (1925), 13–16.

T HE EARTH glides by under the hood of an automobile. Two outstretched fists. A mouth that cries out. Some trees snapped up, one after the other, by the muzzle of the screen.

Thought emulates speed in the flow of images. But it slows and, vanquished, gives way to surprise. It surrenders. The new gaze of the screen forces itself on our passive gaze. At that moment rhythm comes into its own.

W E SAY "rhythm" and feel satisfied with that. We find a rhythmic value in every film, with a little kindness. Yet it seems that the filmed world is notably lacking in such rhythm. Nothing is more incoherent than the "exterior movement" of most films. The formlessness of this mass of images would be disconcerting if we didn't know that it came from an era in chaos itself. Occasionally there's hope. Three quick drum beats. The spectator's

body rouses. Delight fades away. The torrent of images continues to run
slackly through the well-regulated gearing mechanism.

A GENERAL definition of rhythm. The latest, it seems, is that of Professor
Sonnenshein.[1] Rhythm is " a series of events in time, producing in the
mind that experiences it a sense of proportion among the durations of the
events or groups of events which constitute the series." So be it. But on the
screen the series of events is produced in time and space. One has to take
space into account as well. The emotional quality of each event gives to its
measurable duration a rhythmic value that's completely relative. Let's not
be too hasty to define the nature of cinematic rhythm. Instead, let's open
our eyes.

Before becoming interested in the luminous editing table where images
are assembled, I used to think that it would be easy to give orderly rhythms
to a film. I distinguished three factors in the rhythm of a film, thanks to
which one could achieve a cadence not too different from that of Latin
verses:

1. the duration of each shot
2. the alternation of scenes or "motifs" of action (interior movement)
3. the movement of objects recorded by the lens (exterior movement: the
   performance of the actor, the mobility of the decor, etc.)[2]

But the relations among these three are not easily definable. The duration and alternation of shots have a rhythmic value which is affected by the
"exterior movement" of the film, whose emotional quality is unappre-
ciated. And what metric laws can resist this balancing of spectator and
landscape, each equally mobile, on the axis formed by the screen? This
ceaseless shifting from objective to subjective, thanks to which we experience such miracles? Thus the spectator who sees some faraway automobile
race on the screen is suddenly thrown under the huge wheels of one of the
cars, scans the speedometer, takes the steering wheel in hand. He becomes
an actor and sees, in the turns of the road, rushing trees swallowed up before his eyes.

AGNOSTICISM. Does our generation know what to think about such a
question posed within each film and by film itself? I doubt it. Such an attitude has to be judged incompatible with the knowledge we pretend to
require that an artist have of his art. Let's insist in the cinema on the right
of being judged only according to its promises.

Today I myself have learned how to resign myself to readily admitting
neither rule nor logic in the domain of images. The marvelous barbarism
of this art fascinates me. Here at last are virgin lands. It doesn't distress me

369

to not know the laws of this newborn world which is free of any slavery to gravity. I feel a pleasure at the sight of these images which is, too infrequently, what I seek to awaken in myself—a sensation of musical liberty.

Gallop, canter. How the ascending horizons are inverted and the abyss finally opens its petals to welcome you into its soothing heart. Become statue, house, little dog, sack of gold, rolling river of oaks. I no longer know how to separate you from the midst of your kingdom, O huntress [Diana].

Sentences cannot long carry illogic in their arms without working themselves to death. But this series of images which is not bound up with the old tricks of thought and to which no absolute meaning is attached, why should it be burdened with a logic?

Blond, you lift your head and your curving hair reveals your face. This look, this gesture toward the imagined door—I can give them a meaning of my own. If words had given you life, it would be impossible to preserve you from their constrictive power; you would be their slave. Images, be my mistress.

You are mine, dear illusions of the lens. Mine, this refreshing universe in which I take a bearing on flattering features, according to my taste.

[1] A reference probably to Professor Edward Adolf Sonnenshein (1851–1929), a classical scholar, whose *What is Rhythm?* (1925) had just been published by Blackwell's in England.

[2] Here Clair reverses the meaning of the terms, interior and exterior movement, that Moussinac and Delluc had established several years before.

RENÉ CLAIR, "Pure Cinema and Commercial Cinema"

Translated by Stanley Appelbaum in René Clair, *Cinema Yesterday and Today*, ed. R. C. Dale (New York: Dover, 1972), 99–100. Reprinted by permission. The original French version first appeared as "Cinéma pur et cinéma commercial," in *Cahiers du mois* 16/17 (1925), 89–90.

THE CINEMA is primarily an industry. The existence of "pure cinema" comparable to "pure" music seems today too much subject to chance to merit serious examination.

The question of pure cinema is directly connected with that of "cinema: art or industry?" To answer this last question, it would first be necessary to have a precise definition of the concept of *art*. Now, our era is not favorable to such precise formulations. Next, it would be necessary for the cinema's conditions of material existence to be drastically altered. A film does not exist on paper. The most detailed screenplay will never be able to foresee every detail of the execution of the work (exact camera angle, lighting, exposure, acting, etc.). A film exists only on the screen. Now, between the brain that conceives it and the screen that reflects it, there is the entire industrial organization and its need for money.

Therefore, it seems pointless to predict the existence of a "pure cinema" so long as the cinema's conditions of material existence remain unchanged or the mind of the public has not developed.

Nevertheless, there are already signs of the pure cinema. It can be found in fragmentary fashion in a number of films; it seems in fact that a film fragment becomes pure cinema as soon as a sensation is aroused in the viewer by purely visual means. A broad definition, of course, but adequate for our era. That is why the primary duty of the present-day filmmaker is to introduce the greatest number of purely visual themes by a sort of ruse, into a screenplay made to satisfy everybody. Therefore, the literary value of a screenplay is completely unimportant. . . .

HENRI CHOMETTE, "Second Stage"

Translated by Stanley Appelbaum in René Clair, *Cinema Yesterday and Today*, ed. R. C. Dale (New York: Dover, 1972), 97–98. Reprinted by permission. The original French version first appeared as "Seconde étape," *Cahiers du mois* 16/17 (1925), 86–88.

No sooner had the cinema freed the image from its original immobility than it began to express itself in disappointing formulas. False humor, Italian melodrama, the serial, and "natural" color came along to doom our new hopes. Later, the spectator—anxious for information about the theater but depending on chance for the choice of films to see—discovered *The Cheat*, Chaplin, Mack Sennett, and *Nanook*. And his understandable discouragement gave way to a temporary reconciliation.

At present—except in the eyes of the French legislator, who still classes it along with "traveling shows"—the cinema has been able to win its least favorable judges back to its side. Yet, although it is a newborn force with numerous possibilities, it is still showing signs of only one of its potentials: the representation of known things.

In short, the only role it plays in regard to the eye is partially comparable to that of the phonograph in regard to the ear: recording and reproducing.

Of course, stop-action filming reveals to us events which our eyes did not perceive or did not perceive clearly (the opening of a rose)—but at least we had an idea about the sum of these events. Of course, trick shots give us unprecedented illusions (elimination of gravity, or of the opacity of a body through double exposure)—but only by sticking to objects familiar to our reason, concrete and well-known objects. Do you wish to escape from the real and conjure up something imagined—a soul, for example? You will have to make use of a body, which has become transparent—but is still a

371

recognizable human body. A conventional representation, but representation.

Thus, all the present uses of cinema can be reduced to films of a single world, the representative, which can be divided into two groups: documentary—mere reproduction in motion—and dramatic (comedies, dramas, fairy-pantomimes, etc.), the origin and essence of which can be found in older types of performing arts (drama, pantomime, vaudeville, etc.).

But the cinema is not limited to the representative world. It can create. It has already created a sort of rhythm (which I did not mention when speaking about current films because its value in them is extremely diluted by the meaning of the image).

Thanks to this rhythm, the cinema can draw from itself a new potentiality, which, leaving behind the logic of events and the reality of objects, engenders a series of visions that are unknown—inconceivable outside the union of the lens and the moving reel of film. Intrinsic cinema—or, if you will, pure cinema—since it is separate from all other elements, whether dramatic or documentary—that is what certain works by our most personal directors permit us to foresee. That is what offers the purely cinematic imagination its true field and will give rise to what has been called—by Mme Germaine Dulac, I believe—the "visual symphony."

Virtuosity, perhaps, but just like a harmonious concert of instruments, it will move our sensibilities as well as our intelligence. For why should the screen be denied that faculty for enchantment which is granted to the orchestra?

Universal kaleidoscope, generator of all moving visions from the least strange to the most immaterial, why should the cinema not create the kingdom of light, rhythms, and forms alongside that of sound?

HENRI CHOMETTE (1896–1941) was the older brother of René Clair. He worked as an assistant to Robert Boudrioz, Jacques Feyder, and Jacques de Baroncelli; made two short abstract films, *Jeux des reflets et de la vitesse* (1925) and *Cinq Minutes de cinéma pur* (1925); and then directed Dolly Davis and Albert Préjean in *Le Chauffeur de Mademoiselle* (1928).

FERNAND LÉGER, "Painting and Cinema"

From "Peinture et cinéma," *Cahiers du mois*, 16–17 (1925), 107–108.

THE PLASTIC ARTS all exist in a state of relativity. If you wish to consider the cinema as such, it then comes under the same law.

In my own case, I know that I have used the magnification of the frame or the individualization of a detail in certain compositions. Thanks to the screen, the prejudice against "things larger than nature" no longer exists.

The future of cinema as painting lies in the attention it will draw to objects, to fragments of those objects, or to purely fantastic or imaginative inventions.

—The error of painting is the subject.

The error of cinema is the scenario.

Freed of this negative weight, the cinema can become the gigantic microscope of things never before seen or experienced.

There's an enormous realm which by no means is restricted to documentary but which has its own dramatic and comic possibilities.

—(Similarly in painting, in the plastic composition of the easel).

I maintain that a stage door that moves slowly in close-up (object) is more emotional than the projection of a person who causes it to move in actual scale (subject).

Following this line of thinking leads to a complete renovation in cinema and painting.

—Subject, literature, and sentimentality are all negative qualities which weigh down the current cinema—in sum, qualities which bring it into competition with the theater.

True cinema involves *the image of the object* which is totally unfamiliar to our eyes and which is in itself moving, if you know how to present it.

Naturally, you have to know how to do this. It's rather difficult. It demands a plastic understanding which, apart from Marcel L'Herbier and René Clair, very few possess.

HENRI FESCOURT and JEAN-LOUIS BOUQUET, *Idea and Screen: Opinions on the Cinema*, vol. 1

From *L'Idée et l'écran: Opinions sur le cinéma*, vol. 1 (Paris: Haberschill and Sergent, 1925).

IN SUM, this famous avant-garde movement can only lead to a massive miscarriage.

—You jest!

—We do not jest. On the contrary, we think the jest has gone on far too long.

On the boulevard, at the end of a preview screening. Three characters are arguing, and from the responses below you can judge for yourself who has won the argument. Sour grapes? Lack of fairness? What do you know about those? An idea . . . We are going to make you decide. To orient you now, let's take up the conversation again from its beginning.

ENTHUSIAST: The film we just saw is worse than useless.

WE: As bad as that?

ENTHUSIAST: You saw it too: it follows the formula of a play, that is, a series of scenes presented according to the arbitrary rules of all dramatic works. There's no attempt at novelty, no technical discovery, no concern for composing the image. It's not cinematic.

WE: What do you mean by "cinematic"?

ENTHUSIAST: By "cinematic" I mean everything that fills the screen with an aura free of literary conventions. If the cinema devoted itself exclusively to drama, I would no longer consider it had a reason to exist, since drama existed before it. As something new, the cinema must provide me with new feelings.

WE: When you open the *Petit Larousse*, you find the following definition of the *cinématograph*: an apparatus intended to project animated images on a screen.

ENTHUSIAST: Doubtless!

WE: This definition is better than others. It at least has this advantage—whether presented to our elders of 1900 or those of 1910 or even our successors, it could not fail to pick up all the votes. Would it be same with yours?

ENTHUSIAST: I obviously cannot prejudge our descendants. As for our predecessors, I'm not really concerned because, before 1915, the cinema existed only in a larval stage. It did not exist intellectually.

WE: We protest! Whatever opinion you have of that period, you have no right to erase it with your memories. Imagine a philosopher who, in studying the evolution of a science, an art, or a social movement, neglected to examine its origins.

ENTHUSIAST: I repeat that from an intellectual point of view, I date the origins of the cinema around 1915–1916, with the appearance of the first good American films.

WE: However, in 1914, the cinema had a form. To make a film meant to choose an action or plot, and to present the sudden changes in that action by means of a series of concise tableaux. The acting did not differ greatly from that of the theater, but already photographic necessities had created a knowledge of lighting and decor. Léonce Perret, Louis Feuillade, Jasset, and several others used both natural and artificial lighting with virtuosity.[1] In sum, it was a question of narrating actions as clearly as possible, with the benefit of frequent and instantaneous changes of decor—something impossible in the theater.

ENTHUSIAST: All that is true, but I see nothing of interest in it.

WE: During the war, the American films you spoke about just now came into view. The most striking was *The Cheat*. Others such as *The Aryan*, the first films of Douglas Fairbanks and Mary Pickford equally caused a sensation. They created an absolute upheaval in technique through the use of "close-ups." Let's get this straight: the Americans didn't invent the "close-

374

up"; they found them in the oldest films. But no one had figured out how to use them rationally. The Americans established the "close-up" as the mark of a system, and this was an enormous step forward because the photographic lens, moving from one object to another, showed us only what was important to see instead of letting the spectator's eye wander among vast ensembles.[2]

ENTHUSIAST: That's a technique that I consider "cinegraphic."

WE: Don't cry victory! With a new technique, the Americans pursued a previously agreed-on aim: they told stories. Their films had no other purpose. Certainly, from time to time, a light touch helped construct the milieu or created an atmosphere, but only in proportion to what was required to strengthen the scenario. If they showed us some drinkers in a bar, it was because those drinkers watched the gestures and actions of the principal character. Some disreputable dancer, seated in a corner of the decor, served to describe the sad milieu which shocked the poor ingénue. There was nothing in all this except narrative.

ENTHUSIAST: Good Lord, yes! They stick to that one set of routinely marked out paths.

WE: In France, despite the war, several directors worked with ample means: Abel Gance, Louis Nalpas,[3] Jacques de Baroncelli, [Louis] Mercanton, [René] Hervil, and others. They differed from the Americans in their choice of subjects, but they adopted the same techniques. They sought to correct the performance of French actors, which had been excellent in the old days but was inappropriate for the system of "close-ups." The play of light especially held their attention. It would be unfair to say that our directors copied the Americans; they followed the same path, that's all. It was then that Louis Delluc came along.

ENTHUSIAST: I'm curious to hear what you are going to say about someone who was a pioneer of the current cinema.

WE: Delluc created a movement. Let's try to examine it.

From his first contact with American films, Delluc was dazzled, enthusiastic. Was it by the intrigue? No, it was by the "atmosphere," by the detail that cropped up, by the picturesqueness of the decor. What struck him was the drunken face of a cowboy, a pool of muddy water, a gray wall in front of which something happened. Did he concern himself with defining what entranced him? In his books and articles, you will notice penetrating comments and acerbic remarks, but the man is too subtle to trouble himself with formulas. Did he invent the word *photogénie*? In any case, he launched it. Well, search his writings for a precise, formulated definition of *photogénie*.

In the same period, people began to say: "That's cinematic. That's not

375

cinematic." At first a charming witticism, this way of passing judgment soon became doctrine.

ENTHUSIAST: Talk about Delluc's films.

WE: Let's talk rather about his scenarios, okay? We said that Delluc admired the picturesque side of American films. But if you put the purely picturesque images of *The Aryan* end to end, would you have a hundred meters of film? Delluc took the time to write scenarios, and beginning with *La Fête espagnole*, the major part of a film for him was devoted to impressionistic images. It was a revolution, which had nothing in common with American films. We see a sustained action in one, and a scenario-as-pretext in the other. The drama moves into the background: it's a question of displaying Spain, and the principal characters shift for themselves as best they can, in order to be seen. Take *Fièvre*, the tendency there is even more emphasized. Delete its intrigue, and the film remains with nearly all its characteristics intact.

ENTHUSIAST: Come on, you are less refractory than I feared. I see now that you understand the cinema.

WE: Delluc wrote in praise of Swedish films: "A subtle and profound atmosphere renders the scenario nearly useless. To live with the people and know them, what an impression! And just like that, they're suddenly stylized because we directly experience their thoughts (otherwise glimpsed only through their actions)."[4]

Delluc made several films of psychological action: *Le Silence* and *La Femme de nulle part*. There, the impressionism is "interior," but it's just the same impressionism. The thoughts and memories of characters interested Delluc; their actions not at all. He lavished attention on daydreams and subjective visions and confined the action to several meters of film.

ENTHUSIAST: Exactly!

WE: Another filmmaker was working similarly, but he lived in isolation for a long time. No one knew at first where he wanted to go. *Rose-France, Le Bercail, Le Carnaval des vérités* are slightly hermetic and hesitant sketches.

ENTHUSIAST: It's obviously with *L'Homme du large* and *El Dorado* that Marcel L'Herbier asserted his own propensities.

WE: With L'Herbier, picturesque impressions gave way to a concern for the decorative. Then again, for a long time, when speaking of "rhythm," one referred to the battle montage in *Intolerance*, certain passages in *J'Accuse*, and various other films. L'Herbier sought to combine "rhythm" and "tableaux." See the brothel scene in *L'Home du large* and the death of Sybilla in *El Dorado*.

ENTHUSIAST: It's really during this period that the cinema seemed to me to break out of its chrysalis. The soft-focus images of *Broken Blossoms* and the "distortions" of L'Herbier let me glimpse an absolutely dazzling future.

WE: With L'Herbier as with Delluc, the action moved into the background. L'Herbier called *El Dorado* a melodrama, which showed his disdain for the subject. It was an obstruction. For a number of filmmakers, technique alone counted. Before the despised public, they tossed out a scenario as if turning it out to pasture, but the initiated knew that they could do that only for certain passages.

However, there was a reaction, inspired by the Swedish films (for, in opposition to Delluc, we think the Swedish films were for the most part conceived dramatically and objectively). *The Outlaw and His Wife* and *Arne's Treasure* were much admired, but their influence remained almost nil. Technique was a la mode, and the technique of the Swedish was camouflaged, nearly invisible. Only the superimpositions of *The Phantom Carriage* held the attention of the image masticators.

ENTHUSIAST: Don't be unfair. The Swedish films were much talked about . . .

WE: . . . talked about, and that's all. The wind blew in another direction. Jean Epstein wrote: "Generally, the cinema tells a story badly and 'dramatic action' is wrong for it," and then again: "Why tell stories, stories which always assume orderly events, a chronology, a gradual process of actions and feelings. Perspectives are no more than illusions of the lens. Life isn't deduced like those China tea tables out of which come twelve more, one after another, in succession. There are no stories. There never were any stories. There are only situations, with neither head nor tail, without beginning, middle, or end."[5]

ENTHUSIAST: You aren't speaking of the Germans.

WE: We are. The Germans provided us with *Caligari* and *Destiny*, the one derived from Cubism, the other from the conceptions of Max Reinhardt. Although *Caligari* was a scenario-as-pretext, the action was tightly reined in. That of *Destiny* was even more so. But, in France, we focused only on the stylization of the film's decor.

So, the anarchy is complete: soft focus, distortions, superimpositions, Cubist decors, close-ups, rhythm, all mixed up together. Gance contributed his ingenious discovery of split-second montage. But, while he used it soberly, and to narrate something, his imitators used it without rhyme or reason. A group formed which baptized itself "avant-garde." For this avant-garde the only good film had to have some originality in its mechanical effects. They decreed that the camera was a brain, that it was the camera which interpreted man and nature.

ENTHUSIAST: Let me interrupt you here. Where you see anarchy, I see well-founded inclinations. Would you let me summarize them in a better way?

WE: We'll listen attentively. One should never decline an occasion to be educated.

ENTHUSIAST: If the camera is not a brain, at least it possesses an eye, and an eye quite different from ours. It has its own way of seeing, in space as in time; and it overturns our conceptions of the image and movement. "Luminous values" and "rhythm," these are the elements of the new aesthetic which it offers us. Filmmakers make cinematic works according to how well their films allow this harmony of value and rhythm to develop unobstructed, beyond any outside influences.

WE: Undoubtedly, it's in light of such experiments that a young director, René Clair, recently uttered the following: "Perhaps we have to reach the point of divesting the cinema of all that is cerebral and devoting ourselves to seeking the direct expression of movement."[6]

ENTHUSIAST: Exactly.

WE: Another person, Mme Germaine Deluc, for whom we have special respect, has gone even further.[7] In the course of a chat—would she hold this indiscretion against us?—she laid out an audacious theory. She longed to see only luminous forms without any material significance on the screen: lines, surfaces, tonal values shifting and combining—a visual symphony, made poignant through its own unique plastic resources.

ENTHUSIAST: An audacious conception, which distresses me not at all.

WE: Indeed, could you cite some films that you consider "cinematic"?

ENTHUSIAST: No one complete work, but interesting experiments.

WE: Many?

ENTHUSIAST: Alas, no!

WE: Ten? Twenty? Thirty?

ENTHUSIAST: A few more.

WE: A hundred?

ENTHUSIAST: That's all!

WE: A hundred films . . . and you reject the thousand others that have been produced. Because they do not square with the theory fixed in your head, you say: "That doesn't exist!"

ENTHUSIAST: Once again, the cinema has no other reason to exist except not to resemble any other form of expression.

WE: You make us think of those apostles who, in proclaiming a new faith, have only one idea: to free it of any dependence on the already existing cults, to turn it into a revealed doctrine. People are enthusiastic, then centuries pass; the enthusiasm passes as well. Then come the mythologies that demonstrate, through the evidence at hand, that the so-called religion had been inspired by all the preceding ones.

378

ENTHUSIAST: That's a pleasant digression that says my conceptions aren't original.

WE: Aren't we speaking of lines and luminous surfaces?

We think a painter would give useful advice on the arrangement of tonal values and the composition of tableaux.

ENTHUSIAST: The painter works on a fixed, clamped-down image. The cinema is composed of successive moving images.

WE: Rhythm would interest a musician. Besides, twenty articles appearing in the avant-garde journals have emphasized the resemblance that exists between cinematic rhythm and musical rhythm.

ENTHUSIAST: One addresses the ear, the other the eye. A rather big difference, it seems to me!

WE: You are quick to assert the independence of the cinema, when your theories demand it. You showed much less perspicacity several moments ago when we tried to ascertain whether certain differences existed equally between a cinematic drama and a theatrical drama.

ENTHUSIAST: It's up to you to point them out to me!

WE: We don't mean to insinuate that your conception of cinema mimics paintings and music. We note only that it has several points of contact with those two arts.

ENTHUSIAST: They are more than coincidences.

WE: So the cinema remains pure. But why wouldn't it be just as pure when it presents analogies with the theater and the novel? And, to extend the debate, what reason is there for the arts to be separated one from another by airtight partitions? What benefit do they draw from this so-called independence? Aren't sculpture and painting distinct arts, in spite of their obvious family relationship?

ENTHUSIAST: The cinema has nothing to gain from the theater, whose ways it cannot assimilate.

WE: You constantly confuse "theater" and "narrative." Is narrative the prerogative of literature alone? Take an essentially dramatic subject: the story of Prometheus. If a musician or a painter took inspiration from Prometheus to compose a work of art, would he cease making music or painting?

ENTHUSIAST: The subject would then be a pretext, the painter would study the forms of the man bound to the rock, and the musician would assemble sounds allowing only feelings of a general nature.

WE: But one driving idea, a kind of anecdote, *would animate* the two works. The subject is not a pretext, it is the very *foundation* of the work. If you want to banish narrative from the plastic arts and music, you would have to suppress the celebrated series of tableaux on the Life of Marie de Medici by Rubens, the Life of Sainte Genevieve by Puis de Chevanne and

Jean-Paul Laurens, the Gate of Hell and the Burgers of Calais by Rodin, and the third movement of the Pastoral Symphony by Beethoven. We mention these by chance: a host of names comes to mind.

ENTHUSIAST: You don't invalidate my theory. Those artists were only working at the limits of their art's independence.

WE: Yes, but one can still recount an anecdote without being a feudal vassal of literature and theater. Drama indeed is a source of emotion from which all artists have drawn. It's wrong to confuse the spirit of "drama" itself with the dramatic methods in use in the theater.

ENTHUSIAST: We are in agreement here. But it's because the filmed dramas employ these theatrical methods that I condemn them.

WE: The misunderstanding originates here. A film devoted to a narrative, performed and directed without any other aim but this narrative, handled through the objective exposition of a series of actions, has nothing to do with the theater.

ENTHUSIAST: That's right.

WE: You have remarked, quite rightly, that the cinema depends on two aesthetic elements: *luminous values* and *rhythm*. But you have forgotten a third: *logic*, that is, the peculiar quality that shots have of being coordinated.

ENTHUSIAST: Who could deny that shots form an ensemble? My theory does not contradict that at all.

WE: But you claim to draw only impressions, there where one could come to conclusions. You want to feel emotion, and seek out a rhythm; we want to think, and seek out meaning. You know the film of Dr. Comandon, *The Movement of Leucocytes*, recorded with the aid of the microscopic camera? What does the eye of the layman see on the screen? Forms which for him have no objective value, but which are nevertheless harmonious, decorative, and whose elements change position like the crystals of a kaleidoscope. That has to be sufficient for your happiness. However, does this film mean anything? Don't the learned see a drama there? Don't the images of the film, in succession, develop a logical action?

ENTHUSIAST: An action quite different, you would admit, from those of the films I call theatrical.

WE: Good! Let's take another example. Aren't you amazed by the following fact: we show you a man shooting a gun, then, in a second shot, a bottle breaking, and you deduce that the gunman broke the bottle.

ENTHUSIAST: That doesn't take much thought.

WE: It's minimal because it's only a question of two shots. But is it when it's a question of a hundred or a thousand shots? If in this way we succeeded in telling you the most involved, the most complicated story possible, why would we not have made *cinema*? Even if our story is stuffed with theatrical tricks, it will not be theater. Even if it's full of fictional situations, it will not be a novel.

ENTHUSIAST: You are playing on words.[8]

WE: Haven't you done that in saying: "That's not cinematic"? Such a state of mind leads you to repudiate narrative as a cinematic genre. For, not only does narrative merit the freedom to go where it will, one could also consider it one of the most dangerous genres to deal with. You can reach the sublime by not letting yourself be understood; it is difficult to make yourself interesting through an effort at clarity.

ENTHUSIAST: "To narrate," that's your aim?

WE: A character can be studied through an analysis of his actions just as well as through the transposition of his mental states. Judiciously arranged events produce meaning, create emotion. That's why a dramatic film, no less than a film full of plastic and rhythmic designs, can be harmonious. Its harmony is even of a higher quality because it affects not the eye but the mind directly.

ENTHUSIAST: All dramatic action is arbitrary.

WE: Yes, we understand that: "There are no stories; there never were any stories. There are only situations, with neither head nor tail, without beginning, middle, or end."

An impoverished assertion, with consequences even more impoverished! Don't kid yourself, life worldwide is prodigiously logical; "Chinese tables do engender twelve more, one after another, in succession." Ever since the world's creation, not a grain of sand has changed position spontaneously. The largest as well as the smallest events, whether accomplished by men or the elements, have causes and consequences. Only the appearances of life are incoherent. But is it a question of reproducing life in its appearances or of interpreting and analyzing it? The task of the artist rightly consists in arranging, inferring, and implying. Evolution, that's action—*drama*.

ENTHUSIAST: Apropos of logical and coordinated action, tell me about Charlie Chaplin.

WE: You are handing us the cane with which to whip you. According to his formulas, Charlot seems to you quite outside our conceptions. But that's merely an illusion. Notice, in the first place, that Charlot is *objective*. He *narrates* his life; he reveals his character by means of actions, he never confides his thought by way of evocations—with the exception of the dream in *The Kid*, which was still a narrative.

Therefore, if Charlot neglects to construct solid scenarios, it's because he makes films on the model of the old "episode play" or skit. Examine the "skits" of Charlot, and you will notice that all those actions of a minute's length call for as much logic and coordination as do more tightly constructed dramas. If the ensemble holds together, it's thanks to the virtuosity of the actor-author. Molière equally could neglect the construction of his comedies because he was Molière. Shakespeare botched the denouements of his dramas, as is well known! We don't believe that it's good for a dramatist to draw lessons from that.

ENTHUSIAST: Drama, drama . . . You can't talk about anything else.

WE: Then reread a recent essay by Jean Tedesco entitled, "Has the Art of Marcel L'Herbier Evolved?"[9] The author notices an evolution in L'Herbier: "less stylization and more humanity." Then he adds: "A solid scenario, pleasing and poignant at certain moments, will always be a necessary framework." Certainly, in writing those lines, Jean Tedesco must have been on guard not to betray L'Herbier's effort. Here's a respected man, and rightfully respected, as one of the most remarkable seekers of the French cinema, who feels obliged not to sacrifice the foundation or framework to the form.

But we have something even better to impart to you. Jean Epstein, not long ago, pronounced some memorable words. Didn't he say:

"What is an avant-garde film? And how does an intelligent public which readily accepts the cinema today recognize such a film? It stubbornly insists on several scenes of rapid montage, several distorted images, several superimpositions in the German style, and a more or less genuine absence of intertitles. These techniques, once admirable at the time of their inception, are today almost completely prohibited through the desperate relentlessness with which certain filmmakers have taken them over and abused them."[10]

"At the time of their inception" means: two years ago! If such propositions came from the lips of a philistine, you would scorn them. But Epstein certainly knows what he is talking about: and notice how, in just a few sentences, he summarizes many years of research and experimentation.

ENTHUSIAST: The artist is allowed to renew himself. That's necessary.

WE: We don't contest the principle of artistic evolution; we record certain results: "Technique once admirable at the time," says Epstein. What seems admirable to us is to see these techniques relegated to the closets of yesteryear because they are no longer "avant-garde" enough.

Is the "avant-garde" an end in itself or rather a movement destined to produce a mature aesthetic? If it is an end in itself, let's talk no more about it: it's redoing the story of Saturn devouring his own children. If it constitutes a movement whose aim is an aesthetic, admit that the results are disappointing. We have come full circle and can sum up with a brief catalogue of technical terms. Since the methods of filming are fallacious, because of their facility, your famous avant-garde movement can only lead to a massive miscarriage.

ENTHUSIAST: You jest!

WE: We do not jest! On the contrary, we think the jest has gone on far too long.

ENTHUSIAST: Our seekers are not as opinionated as you think. They are evolving and certain ones actually are finding the "avant-garde" label a little narrow.

WE: In that case, nothing distinguishes them from most other mortals. But is it the label alone that seems obsolete? Isn't the goal of their research even more so? Someone spoke, two months ago, of "divesting the cinema of all that's cerebral." At that, we cry "murder," for that is equivalent to killing intellectualism, to put it bluntly.

ENTHUSIAST: You demolish things with a good deal of passion, but without talking of reconstruction. You defend the cinematic drama but admit that at present it flounders in chaos. Do you have some formulas, some of your own methods to clarify that? Do you have a technique of narration?

WE: Let's guard against pontificating and creating inevitably arbitrary frameworks. The art of narrating is not *single*; each individual possesses his own way of doing so. But there exists, here as elsewhere, a set of biases that we have to combat.

HENRI FESCOURT (1880–1966) was a journalist and minor government official who turned to filmmaking and directed several short films for Gaumont before the war. During the 1920s, he was one of the most successful filmmakers working for Cinéromans—for example, *Rouletabille chez les bohemiens* (1922), *Mandrin* (1924), *Les Grands* (1924), *Les Misérables* (1925–1926), *La Glu* (1927).

JEAN-LOUIS BOUQUET (1900–1978) came to the cinema as an assistant to Louis Nalpas, then turned to writing scenarios—for example, Luitz-Morat's *La Cité foudroyée* (1924), Dulac's *Le Diable dans la ville* (1925)—and became Fescourt's editor on *Rouletabille chez les bohemiens* (1922), *Mandrin* (1924), and *Les Misérables* (1925–1926).

[1] Fescourt and Bouquet are perhaps the first to single out Léonce Perret (1880–1935) as a Gaumont filmmaker—for example, *L'Enfant de Paris* (1913), *Roman d'un Mousse* (1914)—who was as important as Feuillade before the war. Perret went to the United States in 1916, where he made a number of competent but undistinguished films for Brady World and Pathé-Exchange. In 1921, he returned to France to direct *L'Ecuyère* (1922) and the highly successful *Koenigsmark* (1923).

[2] Fescourt and Bouquet's brief analysis of the American systematization of the close-up during the 1910s as well as their subsequent remarks on the American subordination of atmosphere and milieu to narrative agree, in general outline, with the authoritative history of the development of the American continuity system in Kristin Thompson's "The Formulation of the Classical Style, 1909–1929," in David Bordwell, Janet Staiger, and Thompson, *The Classical Hollywood Cinema: Film Style and Mode of Production to 1960* (New York: Columbia University Press, 1985), 155–240. See, also, Barry Salt, *Film Style and Technology: History and Analysis* (London: Wordstar, 1983), 162–70.

[3] Louis Nalpas (1884–1948) was an independent producer who almost singlehandedly tried to create a major studio outside Nice between 1918 and 1921. Some of his films were hits—for example, Le Somptier's *La Sultane de l'amour* (1919) and Fescourt's *Mathias Sandorf*

(1921)—but the venture overall was not successful enough. In 1922, Nalpas became executive producer for Jean Sapène's newly reconstituted Société des Cinéromans.

⁴ Quoted from a Delluc essay on the Swedish cinema in *Cinéa* 2 (13 May 1921), reprinted in Marcel Tariol, *Louis Delluc* (Paris: Seghers, 1965), 98.

⁵ Quoted from Jean Epstein, "Le Sens 1 bis," *Cinéa* 9 (10 June 1921).

⁶ Quoted from a René Clair interview in *L'Intransigeant* (22 August 1925).

⁷ The special respect accorded Germaine Deluc may stem from the fact that she was on contract to Sapène's Cinéromans, just as Fescourt and Bouquet were.

⁸ The French words referred to are *romanesque* (fictional) and *roman* (novel).

⁹ Jean Tedesco, "L'Art de Marcel L'Herbier, avait-il évolué?," *Cinéa-Ciné-pour-tous* 44 (1 September 1925).

¹⁰ Quoted from a Jean Epstein interview in *Comoedia* (25 September 1925).

HENRI FESCOURT and JEAN-LOUIS BOUQUET, *Idea and Screen: Opinions on the Cinema*, vol. 3

From *L'Idée et l'écran: Opinions sur le cinéma*, vol. 3 (Paris: Haberschill and Sergent, 1926), 9–11, 32–33.

WE: The cinema records and reproduces external phenomena in motion. How does this reproduction operate? By means of the presentation of an image which is *transformed*. Let's hold onto the concept: *the transformation of an image*. It involves movement, and it embraces the cinema at its root as well as in all its applications. Its terms are independent of any artistic conception, which is of a necessarily secondary order.

This transformation doesn't operate solely on lines and forms. Indeed, let's not forget that it's an *image*. Look at its etymology! The image is the representation of a subject; and, with photography, the actual existence of this subject is indisputable, since there's nothing except recording.

Some would arbitrarily twist and contract the principle of photography by saying that its purest expression is to reproduce subjects—lines or forms—without any meaning. They would alter the general principle of the image even further, since the ultimate value of the image is precisely to espouse the meaning as well as the aspect of its subject.

A cinematic image is thus able to *signify*. Movement exerts a transformation of meaning as well as a plastic transformation. There is an evolution on the intellectual plane, on which we will later have occasion to speak.

Let's return to our definition: the cinema is not at all by nature an art. It becomes art only through the application of aesthetic ideas, which everyone knows are not exclusive. It expresses through the transformation of the image, which is both a movement of forms and a meaningful movement. . . .

ENTHUSIAST: Apropos of *personality*, let me share some reflections with you. The technical means of the cinema assume such expert knowledge that they demand collaborative efforts. In the current state of the cinema, who exactly is the author of a film? The scenario writer? The director? Can one work without the other, and both without a number of third parties? What would the set designer of *Caligari* say about that?

It would be a great advance for the artist to discover a medium in which he could exercise his talent in complete independence, without the meddling of other "personalities."

WE: In several arts, individualism is a necessity. In others, collective efforts are time-tested. Aside from the architect, who works with decorators, and Michelangelo, who is capable of creating Saint Peter's in Rome all by himself (in conception, of course, not in the construction), how many collaborations have there been with grandiose results?

A gothic cathedral wasn't even conceived by a single man, at least not in all its features. A number of artists of diverse talents, conforming to a conception of the ensemble, personally created a part of the work. There was agreement and harmony, above all! There was also that precious quality of the Middle Ages: humanity. The artist lived in the shadows; he worked so as to render a work immortal rather than to immortalize his own name.

Is the cinema an individualistic art? Perhaps . . . But let this individualism be dictated solely by a disinterested aesthetic! Plenty of doctrines would cause the uninitiated to think quite differently if they knew how keenly certain *cinéastes* were gnawed by the desire not to share the delights of fame with anyone.

An individual art? A collective art? Both concepts can work as long as one tries. When one creates, it's the work alone that matters; it's not a question of knowing how one can compose something that's more personal, but how one can compose something that's best. When the two qualities are combined, so much the better! But when an outside contribution can produce an improvement, the artist who refuses it is being criminal toward his work. . . .

PIERRE PORTE, "Pure Cinema"

From "Le Cinéma pur," *Cinéa-Ciné-pour-tous* 52 (1 January 1926), 12–13.

AMONG FOREIGN "intellectuals," most stubbornly persist in considering the cinema merely as an instrument to convey actions, a machine to recite stories. For, seeing it confined within the genre of adventure stories alone, they want to believe it's inept at any other function, incapable of anything resembling speculation.

Certain *cinéastes*—all of them called "avant-garde"—have protested often against such an opinion, widespread even in cinegraphic circles, an

385

opinion that seeks to reduce the cinema to being no more than the craftsman of a single genre. They have claimed that this new art is capable of
conveying something else besides adventures, of expressing as well as conveying, of revealing the expression of intellectual feats, and of bearing witness to the revelation of a transcendent poetry. Thus, in the face of the cinéphobes who persist in speaking badly of it, they attest to the power and
richness of their art.

THESE *cinéastes*—and not the least of them—profess that, far from having
to limit itself to the role of narrator, the cinema can have another ideal, the
same ideal as the other arts, the ideal of elevating the spirit above and beyond the material.

They would like to create a genre in which the cinema, once it was
uniquely and completely itself, would evoke in us the same transcendent
feelings which poetry or music evokes, but through the harmonic and melodic play of that plastic movement of which it alone is master. And I say,
"They would like to create this particular *genre*," and not "They want to
involve the whole cinema in such practices."

They want to create a cinegraphic genre whose aim will be not only to
arouse interest, amuse, or distract but whose end will be to fling us into
that aesthetic emotion, so different from distraction and amusement,
which—as everyone knows—is purely intellectual and completely disinterested.

They would like to form a genre in which the cinema seeks, not its pretext in a purely material adventure story, but rather its base, above and beyond the material, in the very inspiration of the artist.

They would like to realize a genre in which the cinema would use not
just some of its means but each and all of them and in which, once completely autonomous, it would only have recourse to its very own forces.

They share the ideal of creating a cinegraphic genre that will be to the
cinema which exists today something like what poetry is to prose in literature.

And they don't want actually to create this cinegraphic poetry so much
as to reveal its possibility to the enemies of the cinema. To those who dispute this art or speak badly of it because they consider it purely material,
because they imagine it slavishly copies the material, because, seeing it dependent on science, they want to believe it impassive, mechanical—to
those, the devoted *cinéastes* bear witness to the existence of a cinema on
which all of these petty arguments have no effect.

BUT BETWEEN the current cinegraphic genre which depends on action
alone and this genre out of which certain filmmakers tomorrow will realize

a number of poems, what is the precise difference of opinion? If, on the one side, action is everything, is there nothing on the other? A delicate and controversial question.

For myself, the cinema exists above and beyond the plot and even the action—but not everyone agrees with this. So let's engage in discussion.

The cinema exists above and beyond the action—that doesn't mean that it must always, or even sometimes, be deprived of all action. That simply means that its principle source is not in action, that its aesthetic foundation is independent of any plot.

It's this which certain of our "avant-garde" wish to establish when they say that narrative is not the aim of cinema. Their actual concern is to demonstrate that this narrative role is far from the most interesting of those which could fulfill their art. Thus, when Epstein declares: "Generally, the cinema tells stories badly" and "Dramatic action is a mistake," or when he asks, "Why tell stories, tales?" he doesn't mean to claim that the cinema has to abandon narrative entirely, but only to show that there exists for him another field of action, above and beyond any chronicle or fable, in which he can flourish uninhibitedly and offer the boldest and most personal works. Thus, when René Clair says, "Perhaps we have to reach the point of divesting the cinema of all that is cerebral and seek out the direct expression of movement," one must not—as certain people have—misunderstand that the *cinéaste* wants to eliminate all connections with action, but rather that the cinema, by rejecting the anecdote, might form a genre where it would elucidate its genius more freely and marvelously.

Similarly, if literature was confined purely to adventure tales alone, wouldn't you applaud those who revealed that it might have an ideal other than the one which compelled it always to narrate?

Action is no more than a form of veneer to the art of the cinema. It isn't necessary to its very existence. That's why we say that, when they are mixed together, the one combines with the other in an amalgam, an amalgam so coherent that it's difficult to separate the elements, an amalgam so homogeneous that to certain people it can seem a single and quite simple substance.

Such a cinema, once isolated from the matrix in which we always see it incorporated, we call *pure cinema*, not wishing to claim that action can tarnish it but rather noting that, above and beyond the action, we can better contemplate its unique specificity.

The specificity thus manifested has nothing in common with any other among the arts. Its fundamental principle—completely original in aesthetics—is *to express itself through the harmony and melody of plastic movements*.[1]

A general formula that welcomes the narrative cinema—on the condition obviously that the story be "visual." A formula that welcomes all experiments called avant-garde. A formula that welcomes a cinegraphic genre where there would be no action and even a genre where emotion would result from the play of masses and colors *in movement* alone.

On the question of a cinema perfectly separated from all contingencies other than the harmony and melody of plastic movement, and thus perfectly pure, it seems that Poiret has just mounted an experiment on his barge *Orgues*, an experiment that seems to me to realize the famous "keyboard of colors."[2] Rachilde described this effort enthusiastically in *Comoedia*:

> A visual symphony stimulated not by sound but by daubs of color and lines on the screen. What nourishment for the imagination there! Clouds, blood-red curves, incisive verticals, subtle mauves, spirals, fugitive suns, madonna blues—all this rhythm of combined colors and coupled light and shadow evoked in our minds fleeting visions: oriental skies, superhuman conflagrations, fabulous moonlight, aurora borealis, morbid twilight. No sooner did a daub take the shape of a woman's body than it disappeared. All that tortured our hearts, gnawed at our brains, and hollowed us out inside. There's no story capable of transporting us like that.[3]

Such films or rather films in which, as Epstein says, "nothing happens but so what," or rather films that would constitute pure visual poems— these are obviously only films of a certain "genre." No one ever said or could say—unless he was mad—that *all* cinema must commit itself to such a path. Certain people have said, and we say it too, that on this path the cinema has an immense future ahead of it, that here it can explore its intense specificity completely, that here it can produce works which alone can express its genius and which, free of a dependency on plotting, can achieve that same ideal which the cinéphobes deny it.

Is that why, in a recent booklet, H. Fescourt and J. L. Bouquet endeavor to prove that the cinema always has to depend on the anecdote and can only exist by means of action alone?

PIERRE PORTE contributed dozens of theoretical essays to *Cinéa-Ciné-pour-tous* from 1924 to 1927.

[1] By *movement*, I mean not only the movement of the human body—without which the basis of the cinema closely merges with that of dance and music—but *all* forms of movement, in an absolutely general sense, from the slow evolution of a shot to the brusque leap from one shot to another.—Au.

[2] Paul Poiret (1879–1944) was the most influential French fashion designer of the early decades of this century. L'Herbier invited him to design the costumes for *L'Inhumaine* (1924). The "keyboard of colors" reference probably comes from Joris-Karl Huysmans (1848–1907) and his Symbolist novel, *Au Rebours* (1884).

³ Rachilde was the pseudonym of novelist Marguerite Valette (1862–1953) who published a biography of her close friend, Alfred Jarry, *Alfred Jarry ou le surmâle de lettres*, in 1928, and whose husband was one of the founding editors of *Mercure de France*.

GERMAINE DULAC, "Aesthetics, Obstacles, Integral *Cinégraphie*"

Translated by Stuart Liebman in *Framework* 19 (1982), 6–9. Reprinted by permission. The original French version first appeared as "Les Esthétique, les entraves, la cinégraphie integrale," *L'Art cinématographique*, vol. 2 (Paris: Felix Alcan, 1926), 29–50.

To Yvon Delbos,¹ friend of cinema

IS CINEMA an art?
  Its burgeoning power that breaks through the still well-established barrier of incomprehension, of prejudice, and of laziness in order to reveal itself in the beauty of a new form, nobly substantiates its claims (to be an art).

Every art bears within itself a personality, an individuality of expression that confers upon it its value and independence. Until now, the cinema was confined to the task, simultaneously servile and splendid, of drawing its life's breath from the other arts, those ancient masters of the human sensibility and spirit. Regarded in this way, it had to abandon its creative possibilities in order to be cast, as demands required, according to traditionalist comprehensions of the past and to lose its character as the seventh art. Now (the cinema) is proceeding resolutely and gradually through adverse elements, occasionally stopping to do battle, and moving to surmount the obstacles in order to appear in the light of its own truth before the eyes of an astonished generation.

If, as we envisage it today, the cinema is merely a surrogate for, or an animated reflection, but only a reflection, of the expressive forms of literature, or of music, sculpture, painting, architecture, and the dance, it is not an art. Now, in its very essence, it is a very great art. Hence the constant and hurried transformations of its aesthetic that attempts, unceasingly and arduously, to free it from the succession of erroneous interpretations of which it is the object, in order finally to reveal its own appropriate inclinations.

The cinema is a young art. While the other arts have had long centuries to evolve and to perfect themselves, the cinema has had only thirty years in which to be born, to grow, and to move beyond its first stammerings to acquire a conscious form of speech capable of making itself understood. Through the forms that we have imposed on it, let us see what form it has, in its turn, little by little attempted to impose on us.

When it appeared, the cinema, a mechanical invention created to capture life's true continuous movement, and also the creator of synthetic movements, surprised the intellects, the imaginations, and the sensibilities of artists whom no course prepared for this new form of expression, and who believed that literature, the art of written thoughts and feelings, that sculpture, the art of plastic expression, that painting, the art of color, that music, the art of sound, that dance, the art of gestural harmonies, and that architecture, the art of proportion, were adequate forms with which to create and to unbosom themselves. If many minds appreciated the singular significance of the cinematograph, very few grasped its aesthetic truth. The intellectual elite, like the masses, obviously lacked some psychological capacity indispensable for any correct assessment that would have enabled them to consider movement from another angle: namely, that a shifting of lines can arouse one's feelings. This required a new sense, parallel to the literary, musical, sculptural, or pictorial senses in order to be understood.

A mechanical device, an originator of expressive forms and new sensations hidden in its gears, existed; but even in those of supple mind, no spontaneous release of feelings was summoned by the rhythm of a moving image and the cadence of their juxtaposition, as if by the vibrations of a long-desired and long-sought keyboard. It was the slow disclosure by the cinema of a new emotive faculty present in our unconscious that led us to the perceptual comprehension of visual rhythms and not our rational longings that made us greet it (cinema) as an art we had been waiting for.

While enfeoffed with our ancient conceptions of the aesthetic we held it back at our level of understanding, it tried, in vain, to raise us toward a hitherto unknown conception of art.

It is rather disturbing to recount the simplistic way in which we greeted its manifestations. At first, the cinema was for us nothing but a photographic means to reproduce the mechanical movement of life; the word "movement" evoked in our minds only the banal vision of animated people and things, going, coming, or shaking with no other concern than to let them develop within the borders of the screen, when it was instead necessary to consider movement in its mathematical and philosophical essence.

The sight of the indescribable Vincennes train arriving in the station was enough to satisfy us, and no one at that time dreamed that in it a new means for the sensibility and the intellect to express themselves lay hidden. No one ventured to discover these means on the other side of the realistic images of a commonly photographed scene.

No one sought to know if within the apparatus of the Lumière brothers there lay, like an unknown and precious metal, an original aesthetic; content to domesticate it by making it a tributary of past aesthetics, we disdained any careful examination of its own possibilities.

Sympathetic study of mechanical movement was scorned, but in the hope of attracting an audience, the spiritual movement of human feelings through the mediation of characters was added. The cinema thus became an outlet for bad literature. One set about arranging animated photographs around a performance. And, after having been based solely on actual experience, the cinema entered the fictional domain of narrative.

A theatrical work is (a form of) movement since it presents a development of moods and events. The novel is (a form of) movement because it recounts ideas and situations that follow each other, that collide and clash. Human existence is movement because it changes position, lives, acts, and reflects successive impressions. Rather than studying the concept of movement in its plain and mechanical visual continuity as an end in itself, unaware that the truth might lay therein, we moved from deduction to deduction, from confusion to confusion to assimilate the cinema with the theater. It was regarded as a simple means to multiply the episodes and the sets of a drama, or, thanks to alternating shots of fabricated sets and natural scenes, as a means to reinforce dramatic or novelistic situations by perpetual changes of viewpoint.

Taking the place of capturing movement from life itself was a curious preoccupation with dramatic reconstructions composed of pantomimes, exaggerated expressions, and ridiculous subjects, in which characters became the principal objects of concern when, perhaps, the evolution and transformations of a form, or of a volume, or of a line would have provided more delight.

The meaning of the word "movement" was entirely lost sight of, and in the cinema it (movement) was made subservient to succinctly recounted stories whose series of images, too obviously animated, were used to illustrate the subject.

Just recently, someone[2] had the happy idea to compare a film of long ago with contemporary films, thereby showing how this caricature of narrative cinema is still honored today in a more modern form: a photographed action far removed from the theory that, after years of mistakes, aims at pure movement as the creator of emotion.

Compared to these racy and completely puerile images, how much closer the simple sight of a suburban train entering the Vincennes station seems to the true meaning of *cinégraphie*. On one hand, an overbearing plot filmed without any visual care; on the other hand, the capturing of a raw movement, that of a machine with its connecting rods, its wheels, its speed. The first *cinéastes* who thought it was clever to confine cinegraphic action within a narrative format embellished with droll stories and those who encouraged them were the cause of an unpardonable mistake.

A train arriving in a station provides a physical and visual sensation. In composed films, nothing to equal it (was offered). A plot, an intrigue, without emotion. The first obstacle that cinema encountered in its evolution was, therefore, this preoccupation with a story to be told, this conception of a dramatic action performed by actors that was considered indispensable, this presumption of human beings as the inevitable center of attention, this total misunderstanding of the art of movement considered in and for itself. If the human spirit must embody itself in works of art, can it not do so except by means of other souls shaped by some motive?

Painting, meanwhile, can create emotion solely through the power of color, sculpture through ordinary volume, architecture through the play of proportions and lines, music through the combination of sounds. No need at all for a face. Cannot movement be considered exclusively from this perspective?

Years passed. The production methods and the skills of directors were perfected, and narrative cinema, laboring under a misapprehension, attained the fullness of its literary and dramatic form in realism.

The logic of an event, the precision of a shot, the truth of a pose constituted the armature of visual technique. The study of composition, moreover, when applied to the arrangement of images, created astonishing expressive rhythms that were likened to movement.

Pictures no longer followed independently of each other, simply linked by a subtitle [intertitle]; rather, an emotive and rhythmic psychological logic made them interdependent.

At that time the Americans were kings. Little by little, after a detour, a sense of life, if not of movement, was recovered. One still worried about a plot, but the images were decanted so that they were no longer burdened with useless gestures and superfluous details. They were balanced in harmonious juxtaposition. The more perfect cinema became by moving in this direction, the more, I think, it moved away from its own truth. Its attractive and rational form was all the more dangerous because it created an illusion (of truth).

Skillfully constructed scenarios, splendid performances and ostentatious sets propelled the cinema headlong into literary, dramatic, and decorative conceptions.

The idea of "action" was increasingly merged with the idea of "situation," and the idea of "movement" was volatized into the arbitrary linking of briefly described events.

One demanded truth. Perhaps it was forgotten that presented with the famous Vincennes train, our minds, surprised by a new spectacle, were not bound by any tradition, and the attractions we found in it were not so much the precise observation of people and their gestures but the sensation of speed (at the time small) of a train charging straight at us. Sensation, action, observation—the struggle commenced. Cinegraphic realism, the enemy of useless annotations and a friend of precision, won so many votes that with it the art of the screen seemed to have attained its zenith.

Nevertheless, after an odd detour, cinegraphic technique began to ascend toward the visual idea by dividing up the gestures that presided over the realization of acted scenes.

In order to create dramatic movement, one must successively contrast varied mimetic gestures and intensify them by using different shots corresponding to a motivating feeling . . .

By the use of interposed shots and the necessary divisions, a cadence was imposed. From the juxtaposition, rhythm was born.

Carmen of the Klondyke was one of the masterpieces in this genre.

Fièvre by Louis Delluc, which will remain one of the most perfect examples of realist film, marked it apogee. But over *Fièvre*'s realism hovered a bit of a dream that went beyond the dramatic line and rejoined "the inexpressible" above its unambiguous images. The cinema of suggestion came into view.

The human spirit began to sing. Transcending the events, an intangible movement of feelings took shape as a melody that controlled the people and things heaped up pell-mell as they are in life. Realism evolved. This film by Louis Delluc did not receive the welcome it deserved. The public, always the prisoner of habit, of tradition, and the eternal obstacle with which innovators collide, did not understand that an incident counts for nothing without the play of actions and reactions, either slow or rapid, that brings it about.

The cinema was already trying to break loose from clearly formulated events and it sought an emotional agency in suggestion. At first, *Fièvre* met with the incomprehension of the crowd. And yet Delluc hardly deviated from traditional modes. He respected the rising curve of literary action and as a result he developed a standard (narrative) line.

Fièvre is now a classic work in the repertoire of the screen. Those who hissed the film when it appeared admire it today thanks to the improvement of their cinegraphic education. Now they must seriously reflect on their conduct in order to understand that it is better to seek self-renewal in an original work than to criticize it. Yesterday's truth is always dazzling, and it impedes the blossoming of tomorrow's truth.

After the failure to appreciate the term movement, routine was the greatest obstacle that the cinema had to overcome.

Another era arrived, that of the psychological and impressionist film. It seemed childish to place a character in a given situation without penetrating the secret domain of his inner life, and the actor's performance was annotated with the play of his thoughts and his visualized feelings. By combining the description of manifold and opposing experienced impressions

393

with the unambiguous facts of a drama—actions are but the consequence of a mental condition, and vice versa—a duality of lines gradually emerged that had to be adjusted to the measure of a clearly defined rhythm in order to remain in harmony.

I remember that in 1920, in *La Mort du soleil*, before portraying the despair of a scientist who regains consciousness after having been felled by a stroke, I used, in addition to the actor's countenance, his paralyzed arm, and the objects, lights, and shadows surrounding him, and I gave these elements a visual value by calculating their intensity and rhythm to match my character's physical and mental state.

Of course this passage was cut; the spectators were not willing to endure an action slowed down by a sensitive elaboration. Nevertheless, the impressionist era began. Suggestions began to prolong the action, thereby creating an enlarged emotional domain since it was no longer confined within the limits of unambiguous facts.

Impressionism regarded nature and objects as elements equal in importance to the action. A light, a shadow, or a flower at first were meaningful as reflections of a (character's) feeling or of a situation; then, little by little, their own intrinsic value made them become necessary complements (to the action). We strained out ingenuity to make things move, and by using our knowledge of optics, we tried to change their outlines to correspond to the logic of a state of mind. Later, rhythm, mechanical movement, long suppressed by the literary and dramatic framework, disclosed its will to exist . . . But it ran up against ignorance and habit.

La Roue by Abel Gance stands out as a great step forward.

Both the psychology and the performance became clearly dependent upon a rhythm controlling the work. The characters no longer were the only important factors; rather, alongside them (the characters), the duration of the images, their contrasts and harmonies assumed a role of prime importance. Rails, a locomotive, a boiler, wheels, a manometer, smoke and tunnels: a new drama composed from a series of raw movements, and undulating lines appeared, and the idea of an art of movement, finally understood in a rational manner, recovered its rights, leading us magnificently toward a symphonic poem of images, toward a visual symphony outside all known formulas. (The word "symphony" is used here only by way of analogy.) A symphonic poem in which the image is equivalent to a sound, and as in music, feelings bursts forth not in facts and in actions, but in sensations.

A visual symphony, a rhythm of arranged movements in which the shifting of a line, or of a volume in a changing cadence creates emotion without any crystallization of ideas.

The public did not respond to Abel Gance's *La Roue* in the way it deserved and, when filmmakers used the play of varied rhythms in which the speed of a single image having the effect of a cadence sometimes flashed by like a lightning bolt—I was going to say as quickly as a triple crotchet—or when they used abstract rhythms in the synthesis of movement, protests exploded from among the spectators: useless protests that were later transformed into applause. The time it takes to become accustomed: an obstacle, time lost.

Cinegraphic movement, in which visual rhythms corresponding to musical rhythms give the overall movement its meaning and power, and which is composed of values analogous to note values, had to be completed, if I may put it thus, by the sonorities constituted by the feeling contained in the image itself. Here the architectural proportions of the set, the flickering of artificial light, the density of shadows, the balance or imbalance of lines, and the resources of perspective could play a role. Each image of *Caligari* really seemed to be a chord thrown into the moving flow of a fantastic burlesque symphony. A responsive chord, a baroque chord, a dissonant chord within the larger movement of the succession of images.

In this way, despite our ignorance, the cinema, by freeing itself from its initial mistakes and transforming its aesthetics, drew nearer in techique to music, leading to the claim that a rhythmic visual movement could provoke a feeling analogous to that aroused by sounds.

By slow degrees, narrative structure and the actor's performance assumed less importance than the study of the images and of their juxtaposition. Just as a musician works on the rhythm and the sonorities of a musical phrase, the filmmaker sets himself to work on the rhythm and the sonorities of images. Their emotional effect became so great and their interrelationships so logical that their expressiveness could be appreciated in its own right without the assistance of a text.

This was the ideal that guided me recently when, composing *La Folie des vaillants* [1925], I avoided acted scenes in order to stick to the song of the images alone, exclusively to the song of emotions within a diminished, almost nonexistent, but always dynamic action.

We are entitled to question whether cinegraphic art is a narrative art form. In my opinion, cinema seems to progress much farther by means of tangible suggestions than by means of its unquestionable accuracy. Will it not be, as I have already said, music for the eyes, and shouldn't we envision the subject serving as its pretext as comparable to the sensitive theme that inspires the musician?

The study of these different aesthetics whose developments tend toward a unique concern with expressive movement as the generator of emotion logically leads to (the idea of) a pure cinema, able to endure without the tutelage of other art forms, without any subject, without any explanations.

395

The cinema finds its principal obstacle in the slowness with which our visual sense develops and sets about seeking its fulfillment in the integral truth of movement. Can lines unwinding in profusion according to a rhythm dependent on a sensation or an abstract idea affect one's emotions by themselves, without sets, solely through the activity of their development?

In the film about the birth of sea urchins, a schematic form, generated by greater or lesser speeds of time-lapse cinematography, describes a graphic curve of varying degree that elicits a feeling at odds with the thought that it illustrates. The rhythm and the magnitude of movement in the screen space become the only affective factors. In its embryonic state, a purely visual emotion, physical and not cerebral, is the equal of the emotion stimulated by an isolated sound. If we imagine many forms in movement unified within an artful structure composed of diverse rhythms in single images that are juxtaposed in a series, then we will successfully imagine an "integral *cinégraphie.*"

Consider an example in which a bit of learning is involved, but which is composed of quite simple elements: a grain of wheat sprouting. This joyful hymn of a germinating grain stretching toward the light in a slow and then a more rapid rhythm, isn't it a synthetic and total drama, exclusively cinegraphic in its conception and expression? Of the rest, the lightly touched upon idea gives way to the shades of movement harmonized by a visual proportion. Straining lines do battle or become united, expand and disappear: the *cinégraphie* of forms.

Another expression of brute force, lava and fire, a tempest expiring in a whirlwind of elements whose speeds destroy each other and which become but a series of stripes. The contest of blacks and whites, each wishing to dominate the other: the *cinégraphie* of light.

And consider the crystallization process. (In it we witness) the birth and development of forms harmonizing in the movement of the whole by means of abstract rhythms.

Until now, only documentaries made without any philosophical ideal or aesthetic concern, with the sole aim of capturing the movements of the infinitesimal and of nature allow us to conjure up the technical and emotional particulars of integral *cinégraphie.* They nevertheless carry us toward an understanding of a pure cinema, one liberated from every property alien to it, a cinema (that is) the art of movement and of the visual rhythms of life and the imagination.

If the sensibility of an artist inspired by these modes of expression will use them to create and will coordinate them by means of a clearly defined act of will, we will draw nearer to an understanding of a new art revealed at last.

396

To divest cinema of all elements not particular to it, to seek its true essence in the consciousness of movement and of visual rhythms, that is the new aesthetic appearing in the light of the coming dawn.

Just as I wrote in *Les Cahiers du Mois*:[3] "the cinema that assumes so many varied forms can also remain what it is today. Music does not disdain to accompany dramas or poems, but music would never have been music if it had been restricted to uniting notes with words or actions. The symphony, pure music exists. Why doesn't the cinema have its own symphonic school? (The word 'symphonic' is used here only by way of analogy.) Narrative and realist films can make use of cinegraphic plasticity and continue along their chosen paths. The public, however, should not be misled: this is a mode of cinema but not the true cinema that must try to find its emotion through the artistic movement of lines and forms.

"The question for a pure cinema will be long and arduous. We have misunderstood the true import of the seventh art; we have travestied and trivialized it, and now, the public accustomed to its current forms, so charming and pleasurable, has fashioned for itself a conception of and a tradition for the art."

It would be easy for me to say: "Only the power of money impedes the evolution of *cinégraphie*." But this is only a function of that (the public's conception of the cinema), and *that* comprises the public's taste and its familiarity with an artistic mode that it likes the way it is. Cinegraphic truth will be, I believe, stronger than we are, and for better or worse, it will thrust itself upon us through its revelation of visual sense. Till now, music, comparable to cinema in technique, has not been a comparable inspiration. Two arts that arouse emotion through the agency of suggestion.

Cinema, the seventh art, is not the photographing of real or imagined life as it has been believed to be up till now. Regarded in this way, it will merely be the mirror of successive epochs and will remain incapable of engendering the immortal works that every art form must create.

To prolong (the life) of what will die is good. But the very essence of cinema is different and it brings Eternity with it since it springs from the very essence of the universe: movement.

[1] Yvon Delbos (1885–1956), newspaper editor and Radical Socialist politician, was the Minister of Public Education in the second and third Painlevé cabinets (11 October–28 November 1925). He was also Foreign Affairs Secretary in several of the Blum and Chautemps cabinets during the Popular Front period.—TRANS.

[2] A reference to M. Tallier and Mlle Myrga, directors of the Studio des Ursulines.—TRANS.

[3] Dulac, "L'Essence du cinéma: L'idée visuelle," *Cahiers du mois* 16–17 (October 1925), translated by Robert Lamberton as "The Essence of Cinema: The Visual Idea," in P. Adams Sitney, ed., *The Avant-Garde Film: A Reader of Theory and Criticism* (New York: New York University Press, 1978), 36–42.—TRANS.

397

ROBERT DESNOS, *"Fantômas, Les Vampires, Les Mystères de New York"*

From *"Fantômas, Les Vampires, Les Mystères de New York," Le Soir* (26 February 1927), reprinted in Desnos, *Cinéma* (Paris: Gallimard, 1966), 153–55. © Editions Gallimard 1966.

GENERATIONS are born under a sign: love, liberty, life, poetry, and even the parabolic curve of an era are subject to it. Some were born under the cockades of '89, to the clamor of '93 (in the bitterness of Thermidor, Brumaire, or December), or in the enthusiasm of '48.[1]

We were born under the sign of the [1900] International Exposition. The Eiffel Tower had dominated Paris for eleven years, opening an era which some called a renaissance and which was merely an eccentric spiritual endeavor and a condemnation of the triumph of matter over the spirit.

They were carefully upholding the spirit of revenge in the schools; Déroulède spoke annually in front of a bronze statue of Jeanne d'Arc, Mac-Mahon was no more than an *image d'Epinal*; Panama was a far off reef disemboweling shameful ships; our fathers were still gasping for breath after having battled over Dreyfus; on certain nights, our childhood sleep was troubled by cries of "Down with the clergy!" and resounding blows breaking down the church doors; the Fédérate wall was already welcoming the people of Paris; the empty terrain of Villeneuve-Saint-Georges was getting ready to soak up blood; they invented the automobile for tragic bandits; they raced from Paris to Peking; Europe had no more than fourteen years to forge its arms.[2]

We came to be born. We learned to read with *Les Misérables* and *Le Juif errant*. A tremendous desire for love, revolt, and the sublime tortured us. We weren't vicious; we were precocious. We hid copies of *Claudine* in our desks. We dreamed, in turn, of shipwreck in the *Vengeur*, of the Moulin Rouge, of Cléo de Mérode. For us and us alone, the Lumière brothers invented the cinema. There we were at home. Its darkness was like that of our bedrooms before going to sleep. The screen perhaps might be the equal of our dreams.[3]

Three films lived up to this mission: *Fantômas*, for revolt and liberty; *Les Vampires*, for love and sensuality; *Les Mystères de New York*, for love and poetry.

Fantômas! Such a long time ago! . . . It was before the war. But the vicissitudes of this modern epic were already fixed in our memories. At every corner of Paris, we rediscovered an episode of this terrific work; and, in the depths of our dreams, we reenvisioned the bend in the Seine where, under a red sky, a barge exploded, right next to a newspaper with headlines telling of the latest exploits of the Bonnot gang.

Musidora, how beautiful you were in *Les Vampires*! Do you know that we dreamed of you and that when evening came you entered our bedrooms without knocking, dressed in your black tights, and on awakening the next morning we searched for a trace of the disconcerting "hotel mouse" that had visited us.

Meanwhile, across the deserted streets of Paris, then in the grip of a bellicose madness, under a sky lacerated by searchlights and artillery shell explosions, as we sought the privilege of shadowy adventures of love, did you know that, in our desire for escape and evasion, we rediscovered that privilege in the wake of Pearl White, in the touring cars of *Les Mystères de New York*, and the mock battles between bogus policemen and stupendous bandits?

We have not read *Faublas*,[4] yet, despite failures and disillusionments, we will not let the image of love that we once nurtured fade away, not the cinema either, where for the first time woman appeared to us with all her wiles, her charms, and her splendor, to become, under the yoke of multiple censures, the expression of a common, lawful morality.

There are only vices for the powerless; sensuality, on the contrary, is a justification of all forms of life and expression. To the first belong literature, art, and all the manifestations of reaction: tradition, classicism, the obstacles to love, the hatred of liberty. To the sensual, instead, belong the deepest revolutionary pleasures, the legitimate perversions of love and poetry.

That's why we refuse to consider the spectacle of the screen other than as the representation of the life we desire, with the same status as our dreams; why we refuse to believe that any rule, any constraint, any realism could relegate it to the low level to which writing has fallen ever since the novelists, as good businessmen, threw public discredit on the poets; why we demand that the cinema exalt what is dear to us and only what is dear to us; why we wish that the cinema would be revolutionary.

[1] These are references to the revolutions of 1789, 1793, and 1848 in France.

[2] Paul Déroulède (1846–1914) was a polemical political writer, poet, and leader of the right-wing Ligue des patriotes. In 1899, Déroulède attempted to lead a coup against the Republic, for which he was banished for six years.

General MacMahon (1808–1893) was President of the French Republic from 1873 to 1879. His support of the Royalist forces in their struggle with the Republicans led by Léon Gambetta (1838–1882) was not enough to counteract the victory of the latter in the 1877 elections.

The Fédérate wall was where the leaders who briefly established the Paris Commune of 1871 were executed.

Villeneuve-Saint-Georges was the Paris site where, in 1908, the Confédération Générale du Travail and the Fédération du Bâtiment held a rally protesting police action against a

quarrymen's strike at Draveil; an unprovoked police cavalry charge into the rally partici-
pants left four dead and sixty-nine wounded.

Most of these references provide clear evidence of the strong leftist position of the Surrealists in 1927.

[3] The references are to Victor Hugo's *Les Misérables* (1862), Eugène Sue's *Le Juif errant*
(1830), Colette's *Claudine à l'école* (1900), and Cléo de Mérode, a famous ballet dancer from
before the war.

[4] The reference is to Louvet de Couvray's series of novels, *Les Aventures du Chevalier Faublas* (1787–1793).

ABEL GANCE, "My Napoleon"

Translated by Kevin Brownlow in *Napoleon, Directed by Abel Gance* (London: Thames
Television, 1980), v. Reprinted by permission. The original French text first appeared as
"Mon Napoléon" in a Théâtre de l'Opéra programme (April 1927).

NAPOLEON is Prometheus.

I'm not thinking here of morality or of politics, but of art. What
greater tragedy could there be than the story of a man who wrote: "All my
life I have sacrificed everything, peace, profit, happiness to my destiny."

So it wasn't in order to make a mundane "historical film" that I tried to
bring alive on the screen this epic figure who described himself as a fragment of rock thrown into space; but because Napoleon represents a microcosm of the world.

My first quest was for a cinematographic style capable of fulfilling my
vision. Since *La Roue* I had realized that it was possible at all times to separate the emotional from the narrative element of the pictures appearing on
screen. From this arose the necessity of finding new techniques of filming
to bring the required flexibility.

One of these was the use of the triple screen. In part of my film I used
the triple screen as a way of portraying simultaneously three elements: the
physical, the mental, and the emotional. It requires considerable effort to
understand and to fuse these three elements in the space of a single second;
or should I say a sixteenth of a second. And I noticed that if I missed one
image, the other two immediately became meaningless. Let's hope that
viewers' hearts, minds, and eyes will at least bear with my self-indulgence.

In general, my approach in *Napoléon* was: (1) to make the spectator become an actor; (2) to involve him at every level in the unfolding of the action; (3) to sweep him away on the flow of pictures.

I conceived Napoleon as a man who is being dragged towards war by a
strong web of circumstances and who is trying all the time and in vain to
escape. From Marengo onwards, war had become his inescapable destiny.
He tried his best to avoid it but was forced at every turn to succumb.
Therein lies the drama.

Napoleon can be seen as the everlasting and recurrent conflict between the great revolutionary who wanted to bring about a Revolution in peace, and who went to war in order to establish that peace.

He confessed this in a letter to Fiévée: "I am pitting my strength against Europe. You are putting your strength against the spirit of the Revolution. Your ambition is greater than mine, and I have greater chances of success than you."

And, later, that terrible accusation: "War is an anachronism. One day victories will be won without cannon and without bayonets."

He was a man whose arms were not long enough to encompass something that was greater than himself: the Revolution.

Napoleon was a climax in his generation, which in turn was a climax in Time.

And the cinema, for me, is the climax of life.

EMILE VUILLERMOZ, *"Napoléon"*

Translated by Norman King in his *Abel Gance: A Politics of Spectacle* (London: British Film Institute, 1984), 42–43. Reprinted by permission. The original French text first appeared as *"Napoléon"* in *Le Temps* (9 April 1927), 3.

IT IS CHARACTERISTIC of the epic, whether it is poetic, pictorial, musical, theatrical, or cinematographic, to sweep along on its stormy waves all kinds of contradictory elements and to throw together in its violent rhythm the good, the mediocre, and the worst. In making his *Napoléon*, Abel Gance has not escaped from the law of the genre. His film has splendid qualities and strident defects; it is by turns dazzling and intensely irritating. If one examines this work in strictly critical terms, one cannot possibly approve of it. But it is self-evident that where the critical faculties dominate, there can be no more epics . . .

The fundamental limitation of this gigantic composition is that it is not essentially cinematic. Without being aware of it, Abel Gance has gradually distanced himself from the seventh art and made an unexpected return to literature, to the ode, to historical drama, official painting, state sculpture, and lyrical theater. I am not speaking simply of the perfectly legitimate interventions of the chorus, of the drums, of Koubitsky present on the stage, singing the "Marseillaise" while he was miming it on the screen, or even of the actor who lent his voice to Bonaparte to harangue the Army of Italy; it is rather in the whole conception of the work that I see a tendency which represents a very unfortunate step backwards in the history of the silent art. A reproach that is all the more serious in that Abel Gance is a filmmaker who has a real cinematic genius. And it is towards the cinematic, and only towards it, that he should have directed his exceptional gifts. By seeking to imitate verbally and scenically Edmond Rostand and Georges d'Esparbès,[1] this Ingres of the screen has, alas, merely played the violin.[2]

This film is in fact made in an extremely disparate style. Sometimes, as in the first and the third parts, it nobly fulfills its technical mission; sometimes, as in the second, it is merely reduced to the rank of schoolbook illustration. Everywhere there is an abuse of visual and verbal repetitions, of effects that are overextended. Too often the image is only a camouflaged "tirade" leading artificially into a dramatic subtitle [intertitle], which from a cinematic point of view is a crime of high treason. You can too easily sense a desire to go for cheap effects and to make the actor, in the theatrical sense of the word, far too important. As in old Italian operas, there are in all this too many cavatinas, ariosos, and bravura arias sung in front of the prompter's box and not enough orchestral and harmonic atmosphere. But, by an effect of immanent justice, it is not this flattery of the masses and the concessions to the dramaturgy of the old Porte Saint-Martin[3] that will bring this formidable work the success Gance has been counting on.

He will in fact owe his success to the few moments in which he searches resolutely and wholeheartedly for the purely cinematic. That is when we find the real Gance, with all his qualities, his technical virtuosity, his insight and visionary mastery. I personally would give up the whole of the second part just for the few meters of that prodigious ride around Corsica in which a translucent horseman, literally a "journeying soul," passes through landscapes whose contours blend and intertwine with a smoothness of rhythm that is unforgettably beautiful. Every time Gance has sincerely looked for a means of expression within the resources of moving image, he has triumphed. True cinematic eloquence is indeed to be found not in printed speeches thrown to the crowds like bones to a dog, but in the beautiful visual synthesis, the striking combination, the powerful or really appropriate image conveying feeling and thought, the arrow of light that strikes us in the heart, or the reflection that almost penetrates our unconscious. Abel Gance is more expert in this sublime language than anyone else, and he proved that many times in the course of yesterday evening's performance. His triple screen, whose wealth of possibilities I was the first to describe in an earlier issue of this paper,[4] has allowed him to reach effortlessly the highest peaks of the lyricism of the image. The titanic counterpoint of the double storm of the sea and the convention shows what could be expected from so crucial a technical innovation. When the curtains are drawn back, opening out in the wall of the theater that immense breach of light, the effect produced is one of an astonishing power.

In the present state of French cinematography, Abel Gance has a liber-

ating mission to fulfill. He is capable of it. Only he is currently in a position to resist the commercial cartels that want to maintain cinema as a slave
to a profitable and demagogic Taylorism.[5] He showed us yesterday that we
were right to place our trust in him. And that is why I will always offer as
a homage to this prophet my most vehement and impassioned curses whenever he forgets to preach his noble gospel.

[1] Critics of Gance's films often compared them to the romantic verse dramas of Edmond
Rostand (1868–1918), the highly successful turn-of-the-century playwright. Georges
d'Esparbès (1865–1944) was keeper of the palace of Fountainebleau and an enthusiastic
writer about Napoleon. Gance had been invited by d'Esparbès to write his screenplays [for
the six planned films about Napoleon] at Fontainebleau in 1924, and later hoped d'Esparbès
would write a book based on his cycle of films.—TRANS.

[2] Ingres, the nineteenth-century painter, was an amateur violinist. The term "violin
d'Ingres" refers to a hobby or pastime.—TRANS.

[3] The Porte Saint-Martin district was the home of the boulevard theater in Paris.—
TRANS.

[4] Le Temps (8 January 1927).—TRANS.

[5] A reference to Frederick Winslow Taylor's "scientific management" studies, which
were used to control the labor process and promote efficiency in early twentieth-century
manufacturing industries. An indirect reference to the production practices of the American
film industry and its imitators in Europe.

EMILE VUILLERMOZ, "Abel Gance and *Napoléon*"

Translated by Norman King in his *Abel Gance: A Politics of Spectacle* (London: British Film
Institute, 1984), 43–48. Reprinted by permission. The original French text first appeared
as "Abel Gance et *Napoléon*" in *Cinémagazine* 7 (25 November 1927), 335–40.

THIS TREMENDOUS work has already been subjected to the same fate
as the map of Europe, cut up and pieced back together by the lank-
haired Corsican. We have seen it stretched and shrunk like the wild ass's
skin . . . that is, like a fragile empire set up by an overambitious soldier.
This grandiose and heterogeneous film has at last been reduced to normal
dimensions for commercial exploitation. But in this shortened form, it is
no less significant a composition. The abridged version merely underlines
the essential characteristics of its author's psychology.[1]

In this respect, we must not forget the explicit indication contained in
its rather unexpected title. We are not being offered a biography of Napoleon or a page of French history. What we are invited to look at is Napoleon
"seen by Abel Gance," that is to say the heroic encounters of the young
Bonaparte and the "Little Corporal" of French cinema. In fact there is as
much in this adventure story, and perhaps more, of Abel Gance as there is
of Napoleon.

That is not a reproach. I actually have more sympathy for the former

403

than for the latter. I have frequently had occasion to exalt the exceptional qualities of a dynamic presence who has brought to the screen the advantages of his visionary gifts, his poetic intuition, and his pictorial virtuosity. We owe to him all kinds of conquests in the untilled land of animated vision. I feel myself particularly well placed, then, to address to this conqueror—in the sense of the ancient tradition of the march to the Capitol— remarks which are intended to remind him that he is a man and that he must be mistrustful of apotheoses which lead to the paralytic state of demigod.

Abel Gance was born to make films. That is nature's express desire. Light and shade obey him and at every moment he discovers in the vocabulary of luminous vibrations turns of phrase and expressions which are strikingly new and original. He is, then, a man of 1927, perfectly capable of understanding his own times, which is, as you know, an exceptional privilege and something of a rarity in an effete society nurtured on an outdated "literary" culture.

But by a strange irony of fate, this man of today is afflicted with a handicap that he must at all costs overcome if he is to exert an effective influence on the young generation of creators who will present us with the aesthetic of our century. He is a romantic. Romantic in the most outmoded, anachronistic, and "antimodern" way. This master of the mechanical eye and of the luminous ray, this virtuoso of the electric brain conceives of lyricism in about as artificial a way as Alexandre Dumas père, Sardou, Edmond Rostand, and d'Esparbès.[2] A cruel, almost tragic anomaly: d'Artagnan as factory manager, Cyrano as director of a laboratory. This perfect filmmaker will only realize his full potential the day he has cleared his brain and his imagination of an idea of the sublime which is purely literary in essence.

It is in this sense that I have never hesitated to say to this artist, whom I esteem above all others, that his *Napoléon* is at once a fine work and a reprehensible act. On a philosophical level it is impossible to approve of such subject matter especially when Napoleon is seen by Abel Gance, that is to say systematically and tendentiously misrepresented by a man whose lyricism is sincere.

What we have to reproach him with as author of a production whose artistic quality is not at stake is in fact a rather puerile, yet dangerous desire to seek at all costs to present more or less fantasized conceptions of the poet as though they were part of history. Just as the director of *King of Kings* [Cecil B. DeMille, 1926] hides all the time behind the authority of the Gospels, giving chapter and verse for every single subtitle [intertitle] to prove that it is taken from the New Testament, Gance doesn't give a single line of dialogue or even an exclamation (even something as basic as "Death to Robespierre!") without certifying in brackets and in italics that the quotations are *authentic*. We should interpret that as meaning that they conform to the literary orthodoxy of a Frederic Masson,[3] which, it has to be admitted, is not a totally convincing argument.

There is something unpleasant in all this. Why does the author not accept responsibility for his inveterate taste for "panache," that coquettishness so typical of generals and of hearses? He ought to have the courage of his extrapolations and after showing us Bonaparte seizing an enormous tricolor from outside the Ajaccio town hall and using it as a sail during a Shakespearian tempest, he should not insert the subtitle "This Bonaparte left Corsica to go to fight at Toulon." Of course not: that is obviously not how things really happened! The departure by boat leads into a symbolic and theatrical development which is entirely Gance's own creation. He should assert his paternity here rather than trying to pass off as historical (what, after all, is history?) scenes which, however decorative they may be, should not for loyalty's sake be foisted onto the popular imagination as though they were official truths.

One has no right to let French people, or foreigners for that matter, believe that Napoleon was a kind of Douglas Fairbanks holding out singlehanded against a hundred armed opponents, leaping through the window and into the saddle of a fiery charger, galloping across the whole of Corsica like some fantastic cowboy, braving with a smile countless pistol shots at point-blank range and emerging without a scratch. One has no right either to affirm that on arriving at the encampment of the army of Italy, this young upstart had only to throw his sword vigorously on the table, and stare arrogantly at the formidable Masséna, the invicible Augereau and their fierce companions to crush their dignity completely and transform them instantaneously into cowering lackeys, slaves brought to submission by their fear of the master's whip.

All this theatrical romanticism dominates Gance's vision to an unfortunate extent, and that is certainly not the best part of his work. There is, in this overindulgent apotheosis of dictatorship, a flattery of the basest demagogic instincts of the masses who, as one knows, have never had enough of being kicked in the pants. And it's not very logical on the part of our visonary author to have tried to reconcile the irreconcilable by presenting us with a Bonaparte who is a democrat, the son of the Revolution, of Danton, Marat, and Robespierre, placing his sword at the service of an international Republic, whereas the whole of the cinematic portrait clearly denounces the tyrant, the opportunist, the unscrupulous conqueror, and the soldier who sowed throughout the whole of Europe the seeds of all the imperialisms of the future. Either Bonaparte was sincere in his love of liberty and, in that case, he should not have been portrayed as conqueror, or he was not and it would have been honest to draw attention to his duplicity.

Since Gance is so partial to historical texts, he will know that his altruistic hero had as his breviary the following dogmas: "To be a successful conqueror you have to be ferocious . . . Those who haven't learned to make use of circumstances are fools . . . I have an income of a hundred thousand men a year . . . If the aggressors are wrong up in heaven they are right down here . . . Nothing was ever founded except by the sword . . . There are moments of crisis when the public good necessitates the condemnation of an innocent person . . . You can't do anything with a philosopher. A philosopher is a bad citizen, etc."

Confronted with a social morality of this order, one has to take sides. To go all out, in such conditions, to dress up the figure of a despot in all kinds of romantic frills, to decorate the statue of a tyrant with cinematographic flowers, is to produce a work which is philosophically and historically despicable. That is what Abel Gance will realize in ten years' time, when the evolution of our poor, maimed civilization has shown him the terrible consequences of warmongering cinematography as it is being organized by the international commercial interests of today, casually throwing into a belligerent crucible the real and the sham, history and fantasy, sacred relics and the trappings of carnival, in order to preserve at all costs those convenient clichés of the masses which leaders of peoples need if they are to be able to mobilize them in the future. Making the strategy of massacre seem noble by romanticizing it, making butchery respectable or simply fresh and enjoyable is in effect, my dear Abel Gance, taking on a heavy burden of responsibility in respect of the mothers whose children will be gunned down tomorrow.

These things have to be said to relieve the consciences of many spectators whose dignity as civilized people is beginning to be deeply wounded by Parades great and small.

But, after speaking so bluntly to the author of this portrait of Napoleon, it is only fair to stress the technical values of his achievement. From the purely professional point of view, a film of this kind does the greatest honor to our national cinema. The assurance of its style and the power of its internal rhythm make an irresistible impact. Gance is the most courageous and the most secure of our orchestrators of visual symphonies. He sees everything on a grand scale. The magnificent counterpoint of images that he has created in the duet of the "double tempest," when the waves of the crowd and those of the sea rise up in synchrony, will continue to be a model of this new form of writing.

At every moment he provides glimpses of new techniques and innovations whose potential cannot yet be measured. One can never praise enough his lightness of touch when the translucent silhouette of the young Bonaparte glides through landscapes of the Enchanted Isle which blend harmo-

406

niously into each other with an unforgettable smoothness. One feels that he is the master of all the techniques of shooting images which usually signal the ethnic origins of a film: German etchings, Swedish soft-points, resplendent American chromo-lithos.

Here is a writer of the screen whose dominance of his style is magnificent.

But it is especially his invention of the triple screen which, as one of the great victories of cinematic writing, demands our attention. The use he has made of it in *Napoléon* can only give an idea of its potential, since the cameras were perfected too late to allow him to exploit the process as freely as he would have liked. But we see enough of it in this film to realize that the point has been made. There is an extremely valuable element of polyphony and a plurality of rhythms here which could completely transform our traditional conception of visual harmony. The monody of the optical melody is supplemented by the possibility of a notation of the music of images on three staves. That is truly revolutionary.

We can already see sketched out here what will eventually be the principal applications of so rich a technique. The triple repetition of the same phrase in unison is not the most promising of them. But others are quite remarkable. When the field of vision is stretched to left and right, as if the screen were opening wings of light, the impression that is produced electrifies a crowd. No superimpressions are needed to entrance it then. But, a moment later, the plurality of rhythms comes into play with its infinite resources. The central unit can sing a powerful melody to the double accompaniment of its two neighbors. Sometimes, on the other hand, it is a theme that superimpression—the muted tone of the image—makes it possible to overlay discreetly on the principal orchestration. At yet other times, the same phrase, turned round like a reversible counterpoint, will be played to the right and the left of the principal theme, a moving frieze suddenly as solid and as balanced as a purely decorative composition. Synchronism, delayed rhythms, stylization, consonance, dissonance, chords, arpeggios, and syncopation, all are now available to musicians of the screen who were until now restricted to elementary harmonization and orchestration.

We must give the warmest possible welcome to this liberation of the screen's vocabulary that we owe to a French filmmaker.

Napoléon will go all round the world. It will be acclaimed everywhere. I sincerely hope that spectators of all latitudes will not reserve their enthusiasm for the effects of literary grandiloquence imposed in this tumultuous fresco on the art of silence, and that they will pay homage not to a warrior who left France poorer and weaker than he found it and who stirred up throughout Europe a bitterness and hatred that we are still paying ransom

407

for, but to the creative spirit of a young French artist, whose pacific victories will earn our country a prestige and a glory for which we will not have to pay nearly so high a price. I also hope that Abel Gance will take more carefully into account the heavy sociological responsibilities of tribunes of the screen who have at their disposal a surreptitous but irresistible power to sway audiences. And that he never forgets that by making light of the history of yesterday he is, without realizing it, helping to write the history of tomorrow!

¹ The Opéra version of *Napoléon*, which premiered 7 April 1927, measured between 4,800 and 5,600 meters. The Apollo Cinéma version, which premiered 9–12 May 1927, measured between 10,800 and 12,000 meters. The Salle Marivaux version, released in November 1927, measured between 3,700 and 4,000 meters. For further information on the various versions of *Napoléon*, see Kevin Brownlow, *Napoléon: Abel Gance's Classic Film* (London: Jonathan Cape, 1983), 286–87, and Norman King, *Abel Gance: A Politics of Spectacle* (London: British Film Institute, 1984), 148–49.

² Victorien Sardou (1831–1908) wrote popular, tightly constructed comedies and historical melodramas—for example, *Les Pattes de mouche* (1860), *Patrie!* (1869), *La Tosca* (1887), *Madame Sans-Gêne* (1893). The latter play had just been adapted and directed by Léonce Perret for Paramount, starring Gloria Swanson—*Madame Sans-Gêne* (1925).

³ Frédéric Masson (1847–1923) was the author of a long series of books on Napoleon and his family that were enormously popular in the early part of the century.—TRANS.

JEAN PRÉVOST, "The Cinema: *Metropolis*"

From *"Metropolis," Le Crapouillot* (1 November 1927), 55–56.

*M*etropolis purposely wants to be taken as an apocalyptic vision of the machine age. Let me state at once, so I don't have to insist, that this little story is one of the silliest I have ever seen.¹

In the beginning, there are five minutes of undeniably marvelous spectacle, at a ponderous, strictly regulated pace, whose purpose is to represent men enslaved to machines. You probably remember Abel Gance's *La Roue*: the effect here is just as powerful, but the movement of the machines is infinitely more varied and the play of light as well as the superimposed diagrams of motion nicely augment the power of the machine spectacle.² The first accident is also marvelously worked out. And despite the usual problems with miniatures, I have to admit that the image of the great city and its towers is perfectly realized.³ It's something like New York as seen one day by a poet with a migraine. The movements of the crowd recall everything in *The Ten Commandments* that depicts the servitude in Egypt.⁴ And machines such as the dial-works and the huge mechanical gong have a firm, restrained Cubist design.

By contrast, the whole human part of the film is profoundly disappointing.⁵ There is an old scientist who is little more than a sentimental Caligari and a Master of the City who, once deprived of machines like the dial-works and the mechanical gong, becomes little more than commonplace. The young hero, who otherwise lacks neither charm nor intelligence, is continually compelled to make excessively quick movements. And the heroine, who stands at the center of the film, and finds herself forced to play two completely different roles, is strangely weak in the sympathetic role and unusually fascinating and even amusing in the role which ought to be hateful. Instead of once again risking the desperate experience of vainly fighting against the bad luck that overwhelms virtue in the cinema, it would be better, once and for all, to renounce any attempt to put morality in the position of being useless.

After the slow movements of the crowd at the beginning, at the end we have quite rapid crowd movements. They, too, are very successful, especially those of the children. Yet it's rather odd that the movement of the water in the deluge is consistently excellent at the first signs of its encroachment but much less so at the height of the flooding.

Finally, among the miniatures or enlarged sets, the destruction of the huge electrical machine (very likely achieved by fitting two sections of a metal model to a Windhurst machine) is stunning at first and then grows a little monotonous. One tires of everything, even catastrophes.

One scene seems designed to salvage the actors' share of the film, since otherwise they are sacrificed to the machines: that is the meeting between the old diabolical pedant and the young prophetess in the catacombs. The author has come up with an excellent idea here: the malicious projection of the lamplight into the most forbidding niches of the cavern. But the characters, who have a wonderful opportunity to display genuine emotion, fail to extricate themselves with honor. They have the look of being overwhelmed by all the machinery that surrounds them, and of being pressed, in the shortest time possible, to produce all the complicated machinations imposed on them by the scenario.

Metropolis has sprung from a biblical sensibility's reaction against the machine civilization. Unfortunately, one finds that the party on the side of ideals and hope, which can only naively be assumed in the real world, has been outshown by the spectacle of machines. The director has owned up to noticing this disparity, for he has done some cheating. The machines he offers us lose steam in the face of those who manipulate them, yet they give off an overpowering degree of heat and are extremely tiring to operate: in brief, they are very poor machines. Besides, this civilization exudes such an impression of power that one automatically thinks: just a little more effort—which could be made up by a slight increase in production—and these workers would become docile and stupid, but perfectly happy. Now that would make a dramatic situation. Finally, even in the way the problem is posed, there is a serious psychological error: it is in the nature of men and workers, even the revolutionary worker, to love the machine and detest only their fellow men. The beginning of *Metropolis* is a prodigious spectacle, but the conception of this barbarous universe comes from the mind of a false artist, who refuses to understand what he is seeing, and concludes that industry is to be damned simply because it makes too much noise.

Once again, the beginning images are quite lovely and almost cause us to forget the scenario's ineptitude, but I find it odd that Fritz Lang has put so much genius into producing the migraine fantasy of a four-year-old.

I also believe that spectators are realizing how much this work seeks to overwhelm them rather than to please them, which is curtailing their admiration. It was lovely, yes, but to what end? . . .

JEAN PRÉVOST (1901–1944) was a brilliant essayist and populist novelist who occasionally wrote articles on the cinema as well as film reviews in *Les Nouvelles littéraires, La Nouvelle Revue française,* and *Le Crapouillot,* in the later 1920s.

  ¹ The scenario for *Metropolis* was written by Thea Von Harbou and Fritz Lang.
  ² The cinematography in *Metropolis* was done by Karl Freund and Günther Rittau.
  ³ The special effects for *Metropolis* were done by Eugen Schüfftan.
  ⁴ The reference is to Cecil B. DeMille's *The Ten Commandments* (1923).
  ⁵ The cast of *Metropolis* included Rudolf Klein-Rogge (Rotwang), Alfred Abel (Fredersen), Gustav Fröhlich (Freder), and Brigitte Helm (Maria).

ANTONIN ARTAUD, "Cinema and Reality"

From *Selected Writings* by Antonin Artaud. Translation copyright © 1976 by Farrar, Straus and Giroux, Inc. Reprinted by permission of Farrar, Straus and Giroux, Inc. Translated by Helen Weaver. The original French text first appeared as "Cinéma et réalité," in *La Nouvelle Revue française* 170 (1 November 1927) and was reprinted in Artaud, *Oeuvres complètes,* vol. 3 (Paris: Gallimard, 1956), 22–25.

TWO PATHS SEEM to be open to the cinema right now, neither of which, undoubtedly, is the right one.

On the one hand there is pure or absolute cinema, and on the other there is that kind of venial hybrid art which insists on translating into more or less suitable images psychological situations that would be perfectly at home on the stage or in the pages of a book but not on the screen, since they are merely the reflection of a world that depends on another source for its raw material and its meaning.

It is clear that everything we have seen up to now that passes for abstract or pure cinema is very far from meeting what seems to be one of the essential requirements of cinema. For although the mind of man may be able to conceive and accept abstraction, no one can respond to purely geometric lines which possess no significative value in themselves and which are not related to any sensation that the eye of the screen can recognize or classify.

410

No matter how deeply we dig into the mind, we find at the bottom of every emotion, even an intellectual one, an affective sensation of a nervous order. This sensation involves the recognition, perhaps on an elementary level, but at least on a tangible one, of something substantial, of a certain vibration that always recalls states, either known or imagined, that are clothed in one of the myriad forms of real or imagined nature. Thus the meaning of pure cinema would lie in the re-creation of a certain number of forms of this kind, it would lie in a movement and follow a rhythm which is the specific contribution of this art.

Between a purely linear visual abstraction (and the play of light and shadow is similar to the play of lines) and the fundamentally psychological film which relates the development of a story that may or may not be dramatic, there is room for an attempt at true cinema, of whose substance or meaning nothing in the films that have been presented to date gives any suggestion.

In heavily plotted films, all the emotion and all the humor depend solely on the text, to the exclusion of the images; with a few rare exceptions, all the thought in a film is in the subtitles [intertitles], and even in films without subtitles the emotion is verbal, it requires the clarification or support of words, for the situations, the images, the actions all turn on a clear meaning. We have yet to achieve a film with purely visual situations whose drama would come from a shock designed for the eyes, a shock drawn, so to speak, from the very substance of our vision and not from psychological circumlocutions of a discursive nature which are merely the visual equivalent of a text. It is not a question of finding in visual language an equivalent for written language, of which the visual language would merely be a bad translation, but rather of revealing the very essence of language and of carrying the action onto a level where all translation would be unnecessary and where this action would operate almost intuitively on the brain.

In the screenplay [of *La Coquille et le clergyman*] that follows, I have tried to carry out this idea of a visual cinema in which even psychology is engulfed by actions. No doubt this screenplay does not achieve the absolute image of all that can be done in this direction; but at least it points the way. Not that the cinema must renounce all human psychology: that is not its principle—on the contrary—but it must give psychology a form that is much more vital and active, and without those connections that try to reveal the motives for our actions in an absolutely stupid light instead of spreading them before us in their original and profound barbarity.

This screenplay is not the re-creation of a dream and should not be considered as such. I shall not attempt to excuse its apparent incoherence by the facile subterfuge of dreams. Dreams have more than their logic. They have their life, in which there appears an intelligent and somber truth.

This screenplay seeks the somber truth of the mind in images which have issued solely from themselves and which do not derive their meaning from the situation in which they develop, but from a kind of powerful inner necessity that casts them in a light of inescapable clarity.

The human skin of things, the epidermis of reality: this is the primary raw material of cinema. Cinema exalts matter and reveals it to us in its profound spirituality, in its relations with the spirit from which it has emerged. Images are born, are derived from one another purely as images, impose an objective synthesis more penetrating than any abstraction, create worlds which ask nothing of anyone or anything. But out of this pure play of appearances, out of this so to speak transubstantiation of elements is born an inorganic language that moves the mind by osmosis and without any kind of transposition in words. And because it works with matter itself, cinema creates situations that arise from the mere collision of objects, forms, repulsions, attractions. It does not detach itself from life but rediscovers the original order of things. The films that are most successful in this sense are those dominated by a certain kind of humor, like the early Buster Keatons or the less human Chaplins. A cinema which is studded with dreams, and which gives you the physical sensation of pure life, finds its triumph in the most excessive sort of humor. A certain excitement of objects, forms, and expressions can only be translated into the convulsions and surprises of a reality that seems to destroy itself with an irony in which you can hear a scream from the extremities of the mind.

ANTONIN ARTAUD (1896–1948) was an actor in Charles Dullin's Atelier Théâtre as well as a poet, playwright, and dramatic theorist. He was a member of the Surrealist group from 1925 to 1927 and again briefly in 1928, around the time of the release of *La Coquille et le clergyman*. Artaud performed in a number of important late 1920s French films—for instance, Gance's *Napoléon* (1927), Dreyer's *La Passion de Jeanne D'Arc* (1928), Poiriers's *Verdun, vision d'histoire* (1928), and L'Herbier's *L'Argent* (1929).

JEAN EPSTEIN, "Art of Incidence"

Translated by Tom Milne in *Afterimage* 10 (Autumn 1981), 9–16. Reprinted by permission. The original French text first appeared as "Art d'événement," *Comoedia* (18 November 1927), 4.

IGNORING three analogous assignations made with or by three different women, a young man, happy to be on holiday as it were, alone and free, takes his sports car out of the garage and speeds away . . . until he smashes himself up on the road to Deauville. With a little stab of its beak between his eyes, a swallow flying even faster than the speeding car had killed this refugee from love.

The fifteen pages of Paul Morand's short story, *"La Glace à trois faces,"*[1] thus melt into a scenario dedicated in its simplicity and truth to the cinema. After those stories supposedly without end, here is one which sets out to have no exposition or inception, and which stops dead. The incidents do not succeed each other, yet there is an exact correspondence. Fragments from several pasts take root in a single present. The future erupts through the memories. This is the chronology of the human mind. Each character is introduced alone and the narrative keeps them definitively apart; nevertheless they live together, in association with each other.

Is this a new dramaturgy toward which images are now reaching? More or less stripped of all technique, they really signify only in association with each other, just as words that are simple but rich in meanings must do; noble thought and thought noble. And among these images two, strangers to each other, meet in the eye of the spectator across twenty meters of film, only then sounding their real note; in the same way, the notes of a chord a semi-octave apart yield their musical significance only to a musician's ear.

Among tokens of reality, banality is the least relative. This meticulous, deep-seated, dissected, intensified, itemized, applied banality will lend the cinematic drama a startling depth of humanity, an immensely enhanced power of suggestion, an unprecedented emotive force. The events in slow or accelerated motion will create their own time, the time proper to each action, to each character, our time. Our first French compositions at school are written in the present. The cinema narrates everything in the present, even in its intertitles. Learning more of grammar and rhetoric, pupils then use the past and future tenses in their narratives, alternating but agreeing. The fact is that there is no real present; today is a yesterday, perhaps already old, colliding with a possibly distant tomorrow. The present is an uneasy convention. In the flow of time it is an exception to time. It eludes the chronometer. You look at your watch; strictly speaking the present is no longer there; and strictly speaking it is there again, and always will be from one midnight to the next. I think, therefore I *was*. The future "I" is shed as "I" past; the present is merely this instantaneous and perpetual sloughing. The present is merely an encounter. The cinema is the only art capable of depicting this present as it is.

A carefree motorist seems an insignificant character; a swallow in flight even more so; their encounter; the incidence. That little mark which the bird's beak left on the man's forehead had against it the desires of three hearts, the miraculous vigilance of love, all the reflexes of living, all the probabilities in three-dimensional space, every temporal chance.

But it took—and the phrase is appropriate—place. In an instant, supersaturation produces crystallization. And so with the drama, appearing out of nowhere, appearing everywhere, like an egg at the fingertips of a naked magician. Before and after it, characters and actions suddenly fall obediently into place. In the future, a wrong road unexpectedly intersected in its turn by the ultimate. In the past, viewed enumerated, interlinked, comprehensible, comprehended. "Of course—these actors intimate—that is why we were there." As with the difficult syntax of a Latin sentence, you come back from the final verb to the subject.

And it proves to be untrue.

¹ Paul Morand (1888–1976) was a clever, refined author of novels, short stories, and travel books. "La Glace à trois faces" was published in *L'Europe galante* (1925).

LÉON MOUSSINAC, "Cinema: Social Expression"

From "Cinéma: Expression sociale," *L'Art cinématographique*, vol. 4 (Paris: Felix Alcan, 1927), 23–49.

AGREEMENTS, misgivings, and even certain attacks of conscience already are widespread [in discussions about the cinema]. Certainly we do not lack for assertions. I myself have made some . . .

However, we reach the heart of the matter with René Clair, the author of *Entr'acte* and *Le Voyage imaginaire*, for he places the cinema clearly in its social sphere, outside of which everything else is merely intellectual speculation: "A film only exists on the screen. Yet, between the mind that conceives it and the screen which reflects it, there looms a huge industrial organization and its craving for money. . . . It seems futile to anticipate the existence of a pure cinema, therefore, as long as the material conditions of the cinema remain unaltered and as long as public taste does not advance. . . ."¹ (See also Blaise Cendrars, *L'ABC du cinéma*.) Let's move on then to the conclusion of our thinking and say: in its essence and its deepest realities, the cinema corresponds to the greatest forms of collective expression: an art of space and time, universal and international, it can free itself of the foreign influences which enslave it and really live only through the independence of a new economic system formed on the base of a new social organization. This condition is a direct extension of the problem which Count de Laborde already posed in 1853: the Union of Art and Industry.² A chimera vainly pursued ever since, up to and including the 1925 International Exposition of Modern Decorative and Industrial Arts, which constituted the most glaring demonstration of the impossibility of such a union: because of the irreparable antagonisms between capital and labor.

As the consequences of ceaseless scientific discovery, mechanical inventions have stimulated the transformation of technical means; they have made it mandatory that we have constantly improving tools and an organization answerable to continually accumulating demands, on the universal as well as the national and international levels. . . . From this follow ever-

increasing outlays of working capital and ever more unreasonable demands—and logic decrees so. But because of this also the chasm widens
between an art which is dependent on the means provided by industry and
the artists themselves. Because of this heightened necessity to acquire industrial means, all those characteristics that the other arts already possessed
to some degree—in order to create—the cinema has gathered together and
elevated to their maximum power. This has led to a hastily derived conclusion which permitted the other arts to think they could separate themselves
from the cinema, by reason of their conditions of existence.

The house will burn down while the firemen play cards—upping the
ante for the pot—naturally.

Now, everyone who even glancingly considers the present situation of
the cinema, gripped as it is by commercialism, poses the same question.
The only answer—which is logical, strikingly logical—makes them uneasy or frightens them in that it shocks their habitual ways, their education, or their class biases. For myself, I have often found evidence of this
among my correspondents. They can be summarized like this:

"Monsieur, the cinema is less disinterested than the other arts. Perhaps
it's this lack of freedom which has affronted our intelligence up until now;
undoubtedly that's why we have refused to grant it our approval. Don't the
Ciné-Club de France, the *Cahiers du mois*, the Vieux-Colombier, and the
Studio des Ursulines all act in such a way as to lance a wound that cannot
be healed; don't they mean to heal it in spite of that?"

Or like this: "Besides the fine notions which I share with you, Monsieur,
I want to make you aware of the concerns that I believe constitute an essential part of the problem. Vis-à-vis the few sous needed by a writer or the
few francs which satisfy a painter or sculptor, you have stressed the considerable outlay of capital which the cinegraphic work requires and which
puts it totally at the mercy of money interests. Isn't that an irreparable defect which disfigures this new art? To hope for the independence of a better
social condition, you must concede, is to indulge in an optimism which is
far too excessive and to believe in an awfully long-range payoff! For, to return to first principles, the *cinéaste* of tomorrow—like the scriptwriter,
poet, architect, musician, photographer, painter, physician, industrial-
ist—must also find the capital with which to sustain his activity. If it
doesn't come from a huge personal fortune, how will he safeguard his independence? And, if young and unknown, how will he find the financial
means that will allow him to realize his ideas, to assert his mastery the first
time around . . . ? I'm simply afraid that, in the current state of social relations, you cannot convince me, Monsieur, of this revelation (which I too
wish for) of making an art come alive within the bounds of an industry
. . ."

Here's our answer:

"All art is made essentially through the disinterestedness of the artist; he is solely preoccupied with his creation and, to make that creation complete, lets go of it for the benefit of all—thus in the past, when the arts required of the artist rather limited material means for working, the force of genius supplied everything; it overcame obstacles, created the means itself; and, when necessary, the artist gave up a little of his own blood. But we now find that the arts—where we are discovering equivalences and facile comparisons—are, theoretically, opposed to the cinema in practice. They say that especially in the case of Music and Radio. They play freely on words (what else do you expect) and say *arts* and *Art*. They confuse ends and means. So that art proper is not only a new material such as aluminum or rubber but "the consciousness of man which has come into the world with man and which is still taking shape."

Certainly, in the current social conditions, the cinegraphic work is totally at the mercy of money interests. But this acknowledgment calls for a line of reasoning which leads to the question of all or nothing. In order for the cinema to realize its potential, it has to be freed from the domination of capital. What will do that? The system of production of a socialist economy. And since this socialist economy is only possible through revolutionary means, we await the Revolution—or prepare ourselves for it, according to the degree of our courage. We cannot go against that. It's a mathematical springboard. We will not avoid the perilous triple somersault in space between two drum rolls. It's only a question of landing on one's feet and setting out again straight ahead. . . .

Conceived well ahead of the time over which it will rule, along with other forms of expression known or yet unknown, the cinema, the firstborn of the cinematic arts, can only suffer severely, and more so than all other organisms of production, from the crisis of the social economy which has become impotent and obsolete because of recent events and which already has outlived its usefulness. It's only a question of time and more painful suffering for eyes to be opened. Everything in the present holds it up to the light and condemns it, as we have seen. But time is not wasting and knows what to do in this waiting. The heroism of true *cinéastes*—already there are several in the world—now assures the cinema of its theoretical and practical preparation. This comes thanks to improving technical means and fragmentary accomplishments that have succeeded in spite of and sometimes in opposition to business partners, stars and their hangers on, producers, distributors, and exhibitors. Here, too, exceptions prove the rule. So let's support the *cinéastes* for their cunning and their courage in holding out and fighting on, against the French film serial, the American trust, and the corrupt press consortia. They are gradually perfecting an instrument that will soon be ready for great tasks.

The cinema then isn't disfigured with an irreparable defect. It isn't marked by an excessive optimism. And if the payoff, to which the correspondent I cited earlier alluded, is more or less a long way off, is that any reason to stop working with all our effort? Then—and only then—will the *cinéaste* have no need of a personal fortune. Spiritual assets will have a value that material assets have not known. The community will guarantee the artist his independence *because that will be in the interest of the community*. To each according to his needs.[3]

[1] Quoted from René Clair, "Cinéma pur et cinéma commercial," *Les Cahiers du mois* 16–17 (1925).

[2] Marquis Léon de Laborde (1807–1869) was a French archaeologist who explored Asia Minor and the Nile Valley. Earlier in this essay, Moussinac quoted from his famous paper extolling the "applied arts," which was published in conjunction with the 1855 International Exposition in London.

[3] Part of this essay also appeared as "Le Cinéma sera!" in *Cinégraphie* 1 (15 September 1927), 3–4.

LÉON MOUSSINAC, "Eisenstein"

From "Eisenstein," *Le Cinéma soviétique* (Paris: La Nouvelle Revue française, 1928), reprinted in Moussinac, *L'Age ingrat du cinéma* (Paris: Les Editeurs français réunis, 1967), 201–6.

Of all the arts, the most important for Russia, it seems to me, is that of the cinema.—Lenin

WE KNOW that Eisenstein [1898–1948] came out of the theater; but at 23, when he was training with the greatest man of the theater today—that is, Meyerhold[1]—he barely had time to begin to define the spirit of an art and almost no time to assimilate its methods. We understand that he experienced his revelation of the cinema while attending a screening of D. W. Griffith's *Intolerance*. If the fact is questionable—and I don't think it is—it remains a distinct possibility. Indeed, the films of Eisenstein and those of the master of the American cinema share a certain number of characteristics in common. Specifically, the best qualities of the author of *Broken Blossoms* reappear in him, but with the addition of that power and lyricism which are often lacking in Griffith and which have appeared only here and there in the films of Thomas Ince, in the heroic era of the Triangle Company, and in certain images tossed up in the cinematic disorder of Abel Gance.

Personal discipline and a passion for the truth. That sometimes results in a certain brutal realism and a cruelty (which immediately recalls that of

Dostoevsky), an inspiration of rare amplitude, a poetry of collective energy, an emotion springing directly out of the mind and spirit of men, a timeless rhythm of great forms of expression, which every age creates in its own image and to the scale of its intentions. Griffith raises the commonplace to the level of tragedy by approaching it singularly through its individual, psychological aspect. Eisenstein raises the commonplace to the level of epic by envisioning it through its social and collective aspect. Two civilizations. And we already know which of the two is of more consequence.

Eisenstein, like Griffith, is not afraid of certain excesses. He doesn't hesitate to represent reality at its most horrible because he is of a younger generation that feeds on reality and digests it, something the older generations are incapable of doing, condemned as they are to remain stubborn until death in their ignorance of and their disgust for life and its rhythms—an ignorance and disgust which is their only (provisional) guarantee of security. Eisenstein, like Griffith, uses simple, timeless contrasts, as in the struggle between the beautiful and the ugly, the past and the present, truth and error, which are used in the beginnings of every art so as to exalt the masses, contrasts which naturally affect the choice of the film's cadence. Eisenstein, like Griffith, pushes his concern for detail almost to the extreme, which sometimes results in minutiae; but this is less embarrassing with him because of the rhythmic power which carries everything along. On the other hand, his concern for composition tends much less toward the perfection of the ensemble than toward a rigorous unity: hence the radiant virtue of his works, so that each marks a more complete culmination of his system, a more vigorous expression of his personality: *Strike* [1925], *Battleship Potemkin* [1925–1926], *October* [1928], *The General Line* [1929].

If one can note that he resembles Griffith in certain ways, much as Gance resembles him, Eisenstein actually far surpasses his master, through a greater breadth, a healthier and fuller constitution, a more sophisticated level of thinking, a sense of inspiration and desire that strains toward the purest destiny of the cinema and refuses to tire. Unlike the best *cinéastes* in France, Germany, and America, whose period evocations of a historical reality long dead or whose individualistic, psychological dramas have now been overtaken by the living reality of today, by the world social drama, the domain of Eisenstein is collective pathos. His personality sets him free; for he knows that the new mode of expression he is employing, and which he commands with assurance, comes with the sense of opportunity of all discoveries, so as to express the times when universality and grandeur are no longer frightening, so as to transfigure a marvelous new human phenomenon above and beyond the characters which he exalts: the communist revolution.

418

Eisenstein uses a technique at once learned and simple, according to the material means he has at his disposal: learning is forgotten in the vigor of expression. He works with some misgivings because he doesn't have an absolute confidence in his means and because he proceeds by choice or, rather, by successive eliminations in the work of composition. He doesn't go for a strikingly elaborate effect but for as many effects as possible, in order to allow for chance to operate. In other words, a romanticism rather than a scientific spirit informs certain elements of his work. Transition.

He has been strongly influenced by the theories and example of Vertov,[2] in the sense that in every part of his films he tries to make us forget the performances of the actors and the artificial mise-en-scène in black and white studios, so as to get as close as possible to the "newsreel" document, to images caught on the run and interpreted solely by the cinematographic lens and camera. From this comes the variety of shooting angles that he uses and the alternations in juxtaposed or successive shots which give so much life to certain sequences of images. Thus does he rarely show us the overall view of an ensemble [establishing shot], preferring to suggest the ensemble, as if mechanically, through the presentation of the most characteristic details—for instance, the revolt on the ship or the action of clearing the deck or the Odessa massacres in *Battleship Potemkin*.

Eisenstein never accentuates the performance of crowds to the point of making us forget the personality of certain actors, which is the heart of real cinema. In the montage, Eisenstein endeavors to spread out the oppositions of his effects and to reinforce the expression of a shot not only through the careful determination of its durational value but particularly through the maximum intensity of its expressive quality, due largely to deciding on the exact place it has to occupy in the film.

HE LOVES to work in a rich, abundant medium, which is why he rarely economizes on filmstock. And that's not because Pudovkin's way[3] is not his way of doing things but because he thinks more advantageously in practice: once the best of his effort and knowledge has been brought to bear on the composition of a shot, he takes chances—that is, he shoots the same shot several times, each time applying different methods of filming. It bears repeating that Eisenstein, as I have already alluded, trusts the lens more than his own eye, the mechanism of the camera more than his artistic system. Jean Epstein once said: the surreal of the cinema is everywhere. The *cinéaste* of *October* thinks it is there to be provoked. As long as its placement is timely and explicit enough.

We should note that Gance uses a rather similar straightforward method. With this difference—that Eisenstein constantly dominates his work, that he carefully curtails in advance the quantity of cinematographic material which he will have to eliminate, a quantity which he continually has in mind during the course of shooting; and, therefore, he does not risk, as Gance does, imprisoning himself because he has too much freedom and impoverishing himself because he has a surfeit of riches.

If, in Eisenstein's films, there still occasionally are some emphases on performances or several fragments of rhythm which clash in an ensemble of inspiration that's otherwise magnificent, it's because the *cinéaste* remains unconsciously under the influence of cinematographic compositions in which Griffith sought to achieve a certain style (in the acting: Lilian Gish's smile in *Broken Blossoms*, for example) and of otherwise remarkable German films in which either the impact of the theater survives too obviously or else the effort at "artiness" is too perceptible.

In the fragments of *October* which I have been able to see, those kinds of failings did not occur. Eisenstein has carefully eliminated them in his montage, for I think one could still find a certain number of them in the "rejected" negative. *October* thus constitutes a flow of images filmed with an astonishing mastery, a degree of plasticity carried to the maximum point of expression and richness, a precise form of dynamism, a kind of lyrical epic.

[1] V. S. Meyerhold (1874–1940) was a celebrated and controversial theater director, before as well as after the Bolshevik Revolution. In 1921–1922, Eisenstein attended the State Advanced Directorial Workshop that was supervised by Meyerhold.

[2] Dziga Vertov (1895–1954) was a major film theorist and documentary filmmaker who worked separately from Eisenstein and the other Soviet filmmakers in the 1920s. He wrote, directed, and edited a good number of short documentaries and newsreels, including the *Kino-Pravda* series (1922–1925), and then did several feature-length documentaries—*Kino-Eye* (1924), *One Sixth Part of the World* (1926), *The Eleventh Year* (1928), and *Man with a Movie Camera* (1929). On 23 July 1929, Vertov presented a lecture and screened *Kino-Eye* at Studio 28 in Paris.

[3] Vsevolod Pudovkin (1893–1953) was a student of Lev Kuleshov's workshop, an offshoot of the Moscow State Film Institute. His major silent films included *Chess Fever* (1925), *Mechanics of the Brain* (1926), *Mother* (1926), *The End of Saint Petersburg* (1927), and *Storm over Asia* (1928). His book entitled *Film Technique* (1926) seems to have become familiar to French filmmakers and critics in the early 1930s.

LÉON MOUSSINAC, "The Question of the 'Avant-Garde' Film"

From "La Question du film dit d' 'avant-garde'," *Le Cinéma soviétique* (Paris: La Nouvelle Revue française, 1928), reprinted in Moussinac, *L'Age ingrat du cinéma* (Paris: Les Editeurs français réunis, 1967), 218–20.

BECAUSE all film research in the USSR currently is directed toward increasing the social significance of the cinema, one doesn't find any of those experimental films which, according to general opinion, represent the international avant-garde cinema. A "so-called" avant-garde. For it is really an artificial, arbitrary grouping, following close on the heels of any old theory that comes along, and contradictory theories at that. "Pure cinema," as they say in Paris and Berlin, has interested the Russian *cinéastes* only in so far as it has been responsive to the needs of the human spirit or heart. The "abstract film" (Ruttman, Man Ray, Hans Richter, Chomette) is merely a laboratory experiment, useful of course, but contrary to the real destiny of the cinema, since it can only be useful to a small number of initiates and experts. That is why the Russian *cinéastes* are only enthusiastic about such works as professionals, in the laboratory, and see no point in displaying them in public to convince themselves that they are struggling against government prejudices, the ignorance of the masses, or universal commercial practices. They know full well that the cinematic poem, in which the image appeals to the eye just as sound appeals to the ear in symphonic poems, requires a level of visual education that will be reached quite naturally once the cinema has established the range and spectrum of its diffusion with more certainty.

The practical necessities just now closely correspond to the artistic necessities of this new mode of expression—and its possibilities beckon at every rung of the ladder. Life, once more, is on the ascent. Art is reaching beyond the decadent, superficial, and conventionally deluxe character of [avant-garde] cinema—or esoterism—in order to satisfy the moral and intellectual needs of the masses. In the most inspired works, it is achieving real character and power. The rest inevitably is diminutive and vulgarized. Conceived and nourished by the Revolution, Eisenstein, Pudovkin, Vertov, and several others among their comrades are not mistaken in what they are doing. . . .

JEAN EPSTEIN, "Fragments of Sky"

From "Les Images de ciel," *Cinéa-Ciné-pour-tous* 107 (15 April 1928), reprinted in Epstein, *Ecrits sur le cinéma*, vol. 1 (Paris: Seghers, 1974), 189–90.

CHANGE is vital for the artist, it's assumed, and he cannot be reproached for changing his aesthetic beliefs from time to time; but now we hear it professed that either the cinema hasn't made any progress since *L'Arroseur arrosé* [1895] or else the American western has remained the purest achievement of our art. If it is true that a paradox is capable of animating the human spirit, that paradox still has in its elegance to contain an aspect of truth. Otherwise, it's a joke.

The occasion of Jean Tedesco's screening of *La Belle Nivernaise* [1924] at the Vieux-Colombier the other day surprised me and compelled me to recognize the *actual* progress that has occurred in the cinema. This progress—to give it the relative meaning ordinarily attributed to a variable whose value is absolute—can be figured arithmetically and summed up like this: the time it takes an ordinary spectator to read a cinematic image has decreased in five years by 30 percent. Not one older film can be screened without giving an impression of slowness and attenuated rhythm. And this is not a matter of hasty generalization based on the technique they call "rapid montage"—which, parenthetically, is much abused nowadays—since such foreshortening is equally and regularly required of each and every shot, each and every intertitle.

I see here precise evidence of an evolution. Each image has a surface value and another deeper value. On the surface, we read a tableau: the frame of a decor, the fold of a costume, the allure of a gesture, the harmony of lighting. Here art is plastic. On account of this, we edit no matter what ensemble shot to a minimum of four meters in order that the spectator has the time to see everything. In the depths, if there are depths, the understanding of an image is nearly immediate. Only the distillate of the plastic ensemble acts on us, or rather the subject of the image itself, the situation of that subject in relation to other subjects contextually, in relation to the overall idea of the film. The image is a sign, complex and precise, like that of the Chinese alphabet. To allow time to admire the sign is to distract the spectator from the meaning of the text and turn his interest to its typography. Dramaturgy is one thing; calligraphy is another, and much subordinate. . . .

Cathedrals are constructed of stones and sky. The best films are constructed of photographs and sky. I call the sky of an image its moral discharge, which is why it is so desired. One has to limit the action of the sign around this discharge and interrupt it or else it distracts from the thought and feeling [of the film] and diverts attention to itself. Pleasure in plasticity is a means, never an end. Once having evoked a sequence of feelings, the images have only to channel their semispontaneous charge just as cathedral spires conduct thought into the heavens. The film itself is a melody for which only the accompaniment is written on the filmstock, but written in such a way that the melody cannot fail but be amplified within each spectator.

JEAN EPSTEIN, "Approaches to Truth"

Translated by Tom Milne in *Afterimage* 10 (Autumn 1981), 35–36. Reprinted by permission. The original French text first appeared as "Les Approches de la vérité," *Photo-Ciné* (15 November–15 December 1928), reprinted in Epstein, *Ecrits sur le cinéma*, vol. 1 (Paris: Seghers, 1974), 191–93.

ONE WINDY DAY, over the farthermost tip of the Breton islands, I saw a couple of carrier pigeons flying in from the ocean. In two great sweeps, the birds recognized the island, land! The erratic beating of their wings revealed their fatigue. They disappeared to the east. Seafarers who constantly find themselves adrift in their calculations contemplate these aerial navigators with a religious awe.

I have watched the artist Spat at work for long periods. Like the birds, the tip of his pencil is magnetized. Like their flight, its stroke is unerringly aimed at a single goal. Spat's pencil sets out and arrives; its route is the drawing. But neither Spat nor the pigeon, I think, knows during the journey precisely where he is going and how; what they know is that they have the ability to get there.

The path of a film is like the bird's flight, like a drawing by Spat. It is undoubted but unknown. The pilot is sure of it; sure of neither the objective nor the ways to reach it; sure like an insect, like the bee feeding its queen, like the ant building its hill. This certainty is the film's course. It is inexplicable and incommunicable. The pilot is alone, without hope of assistance. The best advice makes for the worst mistakes. Very late in its journey, the true nature of a film lets itself be glimpsed. This nature is so unexpected that each new film seems like a new person, spontaneously born.

Just as the wonders, big or small, presented to us by scientists are limited by the instrumentation, so dramatic conviction on the screen is limited by material or technical imperfections. Most films are an invention which the author tries to make seem real. The cinema's progress has been in lending an idea the more and more precise semblance of an external fact. Lacking sound, color, and relief, the progress was halted. Meantime, I have tried to achieve dramatic illusion in reverse, as it were, by lending an existing reality the more general characteristics of fiction. I have tried to make that marvel appear, the truth.

Drawn by what I no longer know, I went to Brittany to seek the authentic elements for this film which became *Finis terrae*. It is not that a place can equally well be the homeland of love or a battle or yet a miracle. There is always a secret bond between the traveler and the place where he apparently elects to rest. Concarneau, Audierne, Douarnenez seem Italian. La Pointe du Raz is inhabited by a clan of beggers. Sein has lost its most beautiful girls to the bars of Brest. And it looks very much as though André Savignon[1] saw Ouessant only by way of field glasses and his own eloquence. I returned home stunned, like a magician left empty-handed for the first time, wanting to tell no one.

There is, however, a mystery to this Far West. By what command do a thousand men live from birth to death on an islet less than half a kilometer square, without water unless it rains, without cultivation, at the mercy of perpetual storms in winter? What is this weighty ban that prevents them from joining the mainland civilization? Why do they prefer the risk of famine to a few hours' crossing by sea? The men are sailors or fishermen; but the women are afraid of the sea and take sick as soon as they step on board a boat. One woman, in twenty-eight years of marriage, had slept with her sailor husband only seven months in all; she kept up the house on the island and raised two children for a destiny exactly like that of their father. Another, having never been on the mainland, didn't know what kind of animals to expect there. When she saw a horse on a post card, she said, "It's a big pig." The islanders of Sein and Ouessant also look very unlike the mainland Bretons. They are of a type suggesting the Orient. They do not readily marry except among themselves. One imagines some very old colonies of seafarers, coming from whence?

So I hadn't looked properly; it was not that there was nothing to see. Warily, I took a seven-eyed camera with me on the second trip. My perseverance was rewarded by the discovery, behind the cloud of seaweed smoke, of the two islands Bannec and Balenec and their cordial colony of algae fishers, the "harvesters of the sea." In this place and people is resumed the mystery of men dedicated to land that is but rock, to a sea which is but foam, to a hard and perilous trade, thus bowing to some high command.

An irresistible persuasive power erupts from the moving picture when it has the quality of sincerity. Images of an object playing its own role in a drama always bring conviction. An object does not lie. Inevitably, on the other hand, the craft of acting is all too often a school for lies. Sincerity in expression and natural gestures had to be—and still are—avoided, distorted, drawn out, "held," stylized, because they were too fast, too illegible at normal speeds of shooting and projection; only filming at 30 or 40 frames per second can do away with this basically untruthful quality in an actor's performance.

Makeup also seriously endangers the truth of an expression. See only one film shot with the cast using no makeup, and it is impossible not to smile while observing the extraordinary distortion of a face, the paralysis of its most subtle and mobile features beneath a mask of paint.

No decor and no costume will have the look, the hang of the real thing. No pseudo-professional will have the marvelously technical gestures of the seaman or fisherman. A tender smile, an angry cry are as difficult to imitate as a sky at dawn or a stormy sea.

Finis terrae endeavors to be psychological "documentary," the *reproduction* of a brief drama comprising events which really happened, of authentic men and things. Leaving the Ouessant archipelago, I felt I was taking with me not a film but a fact. And that once this fact had been transported to Paris, something of the material and spiritual reality of the island life would henceforth be missing. An occult business.

¹ André Savignon (1878–1947) wrote picturesque essays and travel books on the seafaring peoples of France and elsewhere.

LÉON MOUSSINAC, "Technique and the Future"

Translated by Claudia Gorbman from "Avenir et technique," *Panoramique du cinéma* (Paris: Le Sans Pareil, 1929), reprinted in Moussinac, *L'Age ingrat du cinéma* (Paris: Les Editeurs français réunis, 1967), 320–28.

There will always be French films, because there will always be little old ladies in France who will want to make movies.—The director of a large Paris cinema

If we could only all agree on it, everybody from the usherette to the producer would make a profit.—Jean Sapène, director, Cinéromans–Films de France

It is highly improbable that the cinema will succeed in developing as an art, given its present economic conditions.—Jacques Feyder

JEAN TEDESCO has said that overspecialization is not the solution. Intelligent specialization, at best, will preserve what is essential in our cinema—and possibly more, particularly if a sufficient number of specialized movie house owners representing substantial material interests, not content merely with forming a living classic repertory, can organize against the powerful film producers and produce films themselves. They could make films of various lengths, original in theme and directorial style. The films could pay for themselves on in-house screens and turn a profit from foreign sales since today there are similar movie houses in all the principal cities of the world. A *cooperative system* would be the only road to this kind of production.

THE CINÉ-CLUBS laid the groundwork for the development of the avant-garde cinema, but now it appears that they have accomplished that goal. We can only surmise that the ciné-clubs will simply have to change their focus of activities. Historically, clubs like CASA (Club des Amis du Septième Art) and the Ciné-Club of France have played a role of considerable importance. We only need remember the revelations they inspired, and the struggle they led against certain forms of film conception and execution.

It was this need to respond to the public's curiosity and tastes that led to the organizing of film screenings at the "Salon d'Automne" by Canudo and myself in 1921, film presentations prepared by Louis Delluc at the Colisée (Robert Wiene's *Dr. Caligari*, Marcel L'Herbier's 1922 *Prométhée banquier*), private screenings by CASA, and then the French Cinema Club, and finally the Ciné-Club de France, at the Cinema Exhibition at the Musée Galleria with lectures and films projections (1924).

425

The distinterested propaganda published by the growing number of ciné-clubs (Film-Club, Amis du Ciéma, Club de l'Ecran, Samedis du Cinéma, Tribune Libre, etc.) is being counterattacked, however, by the commercial setup of the small specialized movie houses themselves. This is logical, of course. The viewing public today is too large for things to be otherwise. Only organizations like Les Amis de Spartacus, which have a specific critical and polemical focus, could see any significant development on the international film scene.[1]

FILM TECHNIQUE has developed admirably, contributing enormously to the style of the best films on our screens. Elsewhere I have explained how the principles of technique need to be understood.[2] Since then, still more discoveries have improved many once-rudimentary techniques of filmic expression. Recent Americana films are marvels of a technique which is effective but not affected or obvious (*Underworld, A Girl in Every Port, Solitude, The Crowd*).[3]

Several causes for concern—in addition to problems raised by the talking film and color—have arisen: namely, problems of projection and of the limits of the screen.

When Gance invented his three-screen system for *Napoléon*, I pointed out the logical direction for investigations beyond today's conventional rectangular screen (a format corresponding to the shape of the celluloid film frame). Roger Charpentier, in a study that takes as a scientific point of departure the human eye and its needs, writes in a similar vein that "the cinema has not found its niche," and that "the retina is not physiologically disposed to appreciate a white rectangle." In *Monde* (8 November 1928) he remarked: "It seems that the organ (screen) has to adapt to the function (vision). . . . It is necessary to aim toward an optical fresco (retina to be occupied totally, visual field to be decorated). . . . The screen must be established in the form of a visual field: this form can be compared to a horizontal ellipse. . . . The movie theater can be divided into two parts, the spectator side and the screen side. On the spectator side the theater is narrow so that those in the center and on the side all keep basically the same axis of vision. . . . On the screen side the theater has an elliptical section (horizontal ellipse). The general shape is a paraboloid, in which the screen would occupy the region of the focus. . . . In these conditions, the section of the spectator's visual cone, instead of being haphazard (e.g., rectangular) will approximate the physiological visual field. . . ."

THERE IS another side of the technological problem, namely decoupage and editing. I believe I was among the first to call attention to this in an article that has since become a chapter of *Naissance du cinéma*. Even its title,

"Rhythm or Death," suggests the importance I already attributed to these tasks of preparation and completion.

The USSR and USA aside, it doesn't look as if anyone—especially in France—has tried in a methodical way to address this difficult problem of film construction. Not even the essays of the most daring young *cinéastes* show the slightest concern about it. Chance and intuition seem to take precedence over principle and system. Today's filmmakers write their screenplays in haste; the most important thing for them is the filming, after which they simply grope along. As a result, most French films we see demonstrate a notable lack of movement.

The Americans have understood the pressing need to resolve the difficulty. They have devised a practical solution in creating special departments where professionals, specially trained in all the technical resources and new processes, are on hand to work out a good decoupage of the chosen subject, a decoupage reflecting these rich and varied technical resources. These specialists are called continuity writers.

The Russians, to avoid the standardizing character of this solution and to safeguard the artist's personality as much as possible, have created special collaborators who work on the decoupage much more closely in tandem with the director and screenwriter. In Moscow and Leningrad, all young filmmakers serve a long apprenticeship on decoupage and editing, and they study theory as well.

Anyone taking the time to study Pudovkin's own *Mother* can see what minute and exacting preparation went into it. Having had many opportunities to see this film, I have analyzed certain segments: it certainly contains typical examples of decoupage and editing which have been widely practiced by everyone from novices to "big names" in filmmaking. I have found the same thing in Dupont's *Variety* and Paul Fejos's *Solitude*. But one can also easily show Pudovkin's scientific rigor as opposed to those examples so typical of the "trade." Naturally, we should also keep in mind works like Carl Dreyer's *La Passion de Jeanne d'Arc* in its original version, to cite a more recent European film, and all the exemplary films of Dziga Vertov, yet unknown in France.

Abel Gance is doubtless the first who used the system of cinematic "measurements" in *La Roue*. As to the demands of "continuity"—as instinctively understood by the Americans, and which artists like Ince, Griffith, Fred Niblo, and De Mille remarkably resolved in their best films—Lev Kuleshov, who made *Dura Lex*, was writing theoretical essays on continuity before anyone else, as early as 1919 in Moscow.[4]

Some laws of decoupage are immutable, like the laws of all rhythmic compositions. One just has to discover them. Each image is closely linked to the one before and the one after, and to the whole film, by *mathematical relationships*; men of the cinema have not yet realized the importance of investigating and calculating these mathematical relationships. They are generally more concerned with enriching the figurative expression of the image than with film's *rhythmic expression*.

For a film is first of all *a construction*.

CERTAIN essential questions do not seem to cause concern to those who are responsible, nor to those who are leading the cinema toward its destiny.

Elsewhere (in *Cinema: Social Expression*) I have discussed how people too often think that film's material conditions of existence are immutable. But long-awaited, necessary, inevitable discoveries are upon us. In businesses in America there already exist television machines. Have the consequences of this discovery—which will necessarily entail, before long, the organizing of radiocinematography—been evaluated? If at present one person can participate in events with others from a distance, this means we will soon be able to receive at home—with music—any film we might want to choose from among the offerings of various broadcasting stations in the world.

Clearly these discoveries, after the inevitable crises of transition, will necessitate a reorganization of national and international economics: what will be needed is an order, a method, and an initial centralization which the current system (except in the USSR) does not have.

"Our imagination must come to the aid of our impatience. Cataclysms, painful and long-awaited deliveries should neither astonish nor frighten us because of the shocks and reverberations they announced to humanity. The cinema is being born. It arrives at the end of an era to which it does not belong, as we have seen, to herald the hidden impulses of an era which will be born along with it. It is suffering from the care of an individualism which is dying out. It is developing amid a system of hostile and indifferent forces which suffocate it even as they cradle it. . . ."

The tool, created, is perfecting itself by virtue of science serving economics—and, most often, against the Spirit.

Other than technique, in filmmaking, everything must be destroyed—and everything remains to be created.

[1] There are actually many such groups abroad. Let us mention: Berlin (Heinrich Mann Organization), Amsterdam (Film Liga), London (Film Society), Brussels (Film Club), Ostende (Cinema Club), Moscow (Friends of the Cinema and Revolutionary Cinematographic Association), New York (Film Arts Guild). Le Club français du cinéma premiered in France: Abel Gance's *La Roue*, Jean Epstein's *Coeur Fidèle*, André Obey and Germaine Dulac's *La Souriante Madame Beudet*, Louis Delluc's *La Femme de nulle part*, Lulu-Pick's *Sylvester*, *Premier Amour* with Charles Ray, Sanne's *Polikuchka*, and others. Le Ciné-Club de France then presented: J. Brunhius's *Charles XII*, Stiller's *The Legend of Gosta Berling*, Jacques Feyder's *L'Image*, Eisenstein's *The Battleship Potemkin*, André Gide and Marc Allégret's *Le Voyage au*

Congo, Marcel L'Herbier's *Résurrection*, Léon Poirier's *La Brière*, René Clair's *Le Voyage ima-ginaire*, Fernand Léger's *Le Ballet mécanique*, and so on. Les Amis du Spartacus (founded April 1928 and banned in October of the same year) premiered for the public: Pudovkin's *Mother* and *The End of Saint Petersburg*, Eisenstein's *Battleship Potemkin* and *October*. Among their revivals were Stiller's *Arne's Treasure*, Flaherty's *Moana*, and Louis Delluc's *Fièvre*.—Au.

Moussinac was the leader of each of these three ciné-clubs. That he helped Canudo organize the CASA screenings at the Salon d'Automne cannot be confirmed.

² See *Naissance du cinéma*, 36ff.—Au.

³ The references are to Joseph von Sternberg's *Underworld* (1927), Howard Hawks' *A Girl in Every Port* (1928), Paul Fejos's *Solitude* (1928), and King Vidor's *The Crowd* (1928).

⁴ Lev Kuleshov began writing on the cinema in 1917, but his principal essays appeared between 1922 and 1929. See the "Bibliography" in *Kuleshov on Film: Writings of Lev Kuleshov*, ed. and trans. Ronald Levaco (Berkeley: University of California Press, 1974), 211–15.

ROBERT DESNOS, "Avant-Garde Cinema"

Translated by Paul Hammond in *The Shadow and Its Shadow: Surrealist Writings on the Cinema*, ed. Paul Hammond (London: British Film Institute, 1978), 36–38. Reprinted by permission. The original French text first appeared as "Cinéma d'avant-garde" in *Documents* 7 (December 1929), 385–87, reprinted in Desnos, *Cinéma* (Paris: Gallimard, 1966). © Editions Gallimard 1966.

THANKS TO the persistent influence of Oscar Wilde and the aesthetes of 1890, an influence to which we owe, among others, the interventions of Monsieur Jean Cocteau, a mistaken kind of thinking has created much inauspicious confusion in the cinema.

An exaggerated respect for art and a mystique of expression has led a whole group of producers, actors, and spectators to the creation of a so-called avant-garde cinema, remarkable for the rapidity with which its productions become obsolete, for its absence of human emotion, and for the risks it obliges all cinema to run.

Don't get me wrong. When René Clair and Picabia made *Entr'acte*, Man Ray *L'Etoile de mer*,¹ and Buñuel his admirable *Un Chien andalou*, there was no thought of creating a work of art or a new aesthetic but only of obeying profound, original impulses, consequently necessitating a new form.

No, I am attacking here films like *L'Inhumaine*, *24 heures en 30 minutes*, *Warning Shadows*,² etc.

I will not harp too much on the ridiculousness of our actors. A comparison between the photographs of Bancroft and Jaque Catelain is enough to show the grotesqueness and vanity of the latter,³ who we may take to be the prototype of the avant-garde actor, just as Monsieur Marcel L'Herbier is the prototype of the director.

Technical processes not solicited by the action, conventional acting, and

429

the pretence of expressing the arbitrary and complicated movements of the soul are the principal characteristics of this kind of cinema, which I prefer to call "hair in the soup cinema."[4]

These works have had their apologists. It is enough, to be convinced of the incredible degree of error and artifice to which critics aspire, to read the article by M. Moussinac devoted to his brother-in-law's film *24 heures en 30 minutes*.[5]

Amphigory, hotchpotch, bloomer, brouhaha, and hurly-burly have a superb champion in this man who concludes by recommending to his working-class audience, who nonetheless will have too much taste to follow him, a pitiful imitation of the original films of Sauvage and Cavalcanti,[6] to the detriment of an indisputably human, sound, and poetic work: I mean, of course, *Un Chien andalou*.

And not the least droll aspect of this confusion is the joining together here in a community of ideas of the eminent critic of *L'Humanité* and that penetrating Protestant analyst, Monsieur Jean Prévost of *La Nouvelle Revue française*.

In fact the avant-garde in cinema, as in literature and theater, is a fiction. Whosoever assumes to count himself among these timorous revolutionaries is simply playing the game of "if the cap fits, wear it."

Fine disguises, but you don't fool us.

All it would take to convince you of the imposture would be to project a moth-eaten film of yours before or after the admirable *Wedding March* by Stroheim, in whom we must salute a genius as authentic as Chaplin and equally as important where influence is concerned. Here is a totally human film in all its moving and tragic beauty. Stroheim, this is a story you have lived through! I have found the characters of *Foolish Wives, Greed, Merry-Go-Round* again. What pain have you borne so long? What pain so great you cannot stop yourself reliving it, from playing over and over again a terrible role you obviously assumed long ago?

But here we must return to our avant-garde.

Even though it only "discovered" Chaplin four or five years after the man in the street, our avant-garde has taken him to its heart. There's Charlie Chaplin and no one else.

Well, no. I've liked and admired Chaplin for twelve years but I must say Stroheim moves me in a more direct way, in a way that appeals more to my temperament.

It's precisely because Stroheim has the courage to show us love exactly as it is that he is today the most revolutionary and most human of directors.

And not just for his famous apple blossoms, ridiculed by every species of artist, every enlightened soul, which are precisely the kind that move us most profoundly and legitimately, since what really amorous person has not been open to apple blossom, to postcard romance, to the sentimental refrain?

Only candor is revolutionary. Insincerity and lying are characteristic of reaction. It's this candor that enables us today to equate the real revolutionary films, *Potemkin*, *The Gold Rush*, *The Wedding March*, and *Un Chien andalou*, and to put in the shade *L'Inhumaine*, *Paname n'est pas Paris*, and *La Chute de la Maison Usher*, in which Epstein's lack, or rather paralysis, of imagination is revealed. In fact there is no more avant-garde cinema than the French cinema in its entirety, whether it be the *ciné-roman* or the Nalpas-Gance productions (poor Napoleon), Baroncelli, and all the rest. The question is, avant-garde of what?

Allow me to leave unwritten the forcible and final word that would easily answer this.

To appreciate these advanced souls to the full it would suffice to observe their attitude when sound film came along. (The talking picture is another story: we should know what it is before discussing it. Pardon me for ignoring it, not yet having seen real talking films.)

Nought but a cry of horror left those delicate lips.

They irrevocably condemned an invention just as artists at the beginning of the century had condemned the cinema lock, stock, and barrel. The same arguments were trotted out. The mediocrity of present productions was used to condemn future ones . . .

Meanwhile, outside of all artistic theorizing, in the darkness where Chaplin's walk and Stroheim's desperate kisses resonate, in the auspicious darkness of the picture palace, two young people, boy and girl, hold each other in their arms, while on the screen Betty Compson[7] signals that she has something to say. And she will say it.

---

[1] Here the author of these lines assumes a slightly modest air.—AU.

An unpublished Desnos poem provided the "scenario" or intertitles for Man Ray's *Etoile de mer* (1928).

[2] This German film is cited with due consideration, by virtue of the lamentable decadence of cinema on the other side of the Rhine.—AU.

[3] George Bancroft (1882–1956) was best known then as the star of von Sternberg's *Underworld* (1927) and *The Docks of New York* (1928). Jaque Catelain starred in the following late 1920s French films: L'Herbier's *Le Vertige* (1926), Malikoff's *Paname n'est pas Paris* (1927), L'Herbier's *Le Diable au coeur* (1927), Fescourt's *L'Occident* (1928), and L'Herbier's *Nuits de prince* (1929).

[4] *Venir comme des cheveux sur la soupe* means "to be quite uncalled for or out of place." I like the evocative power of Desnos's words so have translated them literally.—TRANS.

[5] A reference to Jean Lods (1903–1974) and one of the documentaries he made with Boris Kaufman in the late 1920s. By 1929, Desnos had been expelled from the Surrealist group and no longer felt compelled to support intellectuals who were members of the French Communist Party.

[6] André Sauvage (1891–1975) was a major French documentary filmmaker whose films

431

were often premiered at the Vieux-Colombier—for example, *La Traversé du Crepon* was included in Tedesco's first program in November 1924. The Cavalcanti reference is probably to *Rien que les heures* (1926) and perhaps even *En Rade* (1927).

[7] Betty Compson (1900–1943) starred opposite George Bancroft in *The Docks of New York* (1928).

ROBERT ARON, "Films of Revolt"

From "Films de révolte," *La Revue du cinéma* 5 (15 November 1929), 41–45.

APART FROM the films of Man Ray and Luis Buñuel,[1] you could search in vain for any other films made in France which have real merit. The anguish that emanates from these films does not come, as is usual, from a well-constructed story or from an ingenious technique. Disdaining the superficial contagion of the anecdote or the image, instead they condemn the spectator to a far deeper sense of disorder. Again and again, everything is put in question. The familiar determinism which governs the ordinary succession of actions is unsettled—in that Man Ray and Buñuel create peculiar breaks in the narrative, each of which strangely never returns to what went before. And when, at the beginning of his first film, *Emak Bakia*,[2] Man Ray sets up a camera, it is not, as a documentary author would do, to provide a preface or render homage. Rather, suspicious of the only mechanism that he cannot avoid using, to the point of undermining his requisite technical means, he forces the inflexible camera and its impassive lens to mock and betray themselves by admitting that they are the source of crazy, unreal images.

A challenge, a constant challenge to all matters of necessity, to all the rules, even the most customary rules that habitual usage seems to have deprived of all force. In their deep-seated intolerance, the authors of these films reopen the old wounds we have been saddled with, and that is hardly the extent of what they are endeavoring to get away with.

As for language, which congeals everything, and which Man Ray's intertitles divert from its usual course to become a storehouse of fantastic neologisms and puns which thumb their noses at the authorities, and which Buñuel places right next to disarming, poetic, improbable characters who exceed language's competence—these four films scarcely seek to elude chastisement. Human faces which are stamped with character and thought, looks which we can read—Man Ray erases or disturbs them: over lowered eyelids he paints expressionless eyes. He dilutes body outlines by multiplying their contours. He conceals faces under nearly opaque lattices which lay over all the characters the same smooth, expressionless, indistinct mask. Buñuel exercises the same destructive comedy on the social conventions of clothing. On a Paris street, a cyclist wears a costume embellished with surprising emblems. The fall of bodies is rendered gently, ignoring the acceleration that physical laws recognize: the bicyclist falls to the pavement with a motion that seems to slow down as he approaches the earth. Similarly, in *La Château du Dé*, a woman swimming underwater combs her hair, does some juggling, and picks up a pair of barbells, all in comtempt of the most fundamental experiences of the least of us who have taken a plunge into fresh water.

Here it is no longer fresh water, experience, or matter. All the elements are dislocated, the natural kingdoms confused. Andalusians push up like flowers in the seashore sand; forms vacillate and blur and themselves engender vague geneses. Underarm hair is transformed into a sea urchin; flowers become starfish. In order to convey this universe in which the most disparate things are joined in mongrel combinations, new words also appear in the intertitles, generated from monstrous juxtapositions: Robert Desnos expresses his anguish and mystery at night by inventing *éternèbres*, and Man Ray, following his diver, discovers a new universe which opens up through *piscinéma*.[3]

Man Ray and Buñuel have each taken a position, each exercises his delight in dislocation and his desire for freedom, using the faculties with which he is most familiar. Man Ray, who is more sensitive to forms and less sensual, watches for the miracle of object movements and found images in the world, rather than for the internal movements of his body or nerves. And in his frenzy, he plays with the objects that he distorts and dislocates—or with dream landscapes and material metaphors, which are clipped off with cruel delight by dazzling skies or documentary clichés. Attentive to the boundaries of things, to the arbitrary limits by which the body is distinguished, saboteur of precise forms—he cannot describe a chateau without dispersing it into the air or without taking the geometrical lines so loved by modern architects and charging them with mystery.

It is on the borders of our body, there where our desires pour forth and where the world assaults us, that Buñuel, squared on his haunches, relying on this inner strength, seeks to bring to bear the vertiginous. Everything on which the body rests or halts, everything which limits that strange body—distance, time—is dislocated in the course of his film. Time retreats; a character threatens his own past image with a revolver; space is obliterated for a dying man so that the slow motion agony begins within the walls of a room and ends under the trees. Bodies dress or conceal themselves, undress or dress again, covering themselves with hair or insects, according to the desire that impels them or the death that threatens. And in order to defy even desire, the body suppresses its sensuality by prescribing a slobbering, impotent mask with sorrowful upturned eyes for the lover who caresses naked breasts and buttocks.

More intellectual than Man Ray, more taken with technique so as to avoid technique, or logic so as to defy it, more sensual, in *Un Chien andalou*, Buñuel's shared desire for freedom rears up against the powers of the *cinéastes*, that is, one or another of their prisons. A freedom that seems all the more complete as it obliterates its limits, a freedom that is quickly achieved in that space of our fantasy where all laws slacken, but a freedom without vengeance, without real joy, without possession—in which a fecund exaltation appears neither in the rictus of Buñuel's character nor under the opaque lattices which protect the guests of the Château du Dé from the world and themselves.

That kind of freedom exists in American films, which seem to make every concession to the world. The prisons have jailors. Corporations exhibit the presidents of their executive committees in morning jackets and top hats. Commercial problems are posed. Armies clash in battle. And for their central hero, it's a question of success or rather, as they say in current parlance, a successful outcome. Such a hero is Buster Keaton. According to the films, his ambition is to marry the woman he loves, in spite of the business rivalry which separates their parents—or to be hired as a cameraman in the film company whose secretary he is courting . . .[4] An unpretentious conformist, Buster Keaton accepts every kind of mechanism, whether natural or man-made. Heedlessness is wrapped around him: his awkwardness takes him places steadily and triumphantly up to the very end of the film. It sweeps away all his conscientious, capable rivals, whether malicious or well-intentioned.

Awkwardness triumphant and heedlessness rewarded—these mark a comic spirit and a sense of anarchy that, expressed in the framework of current activity, are all the more aggressive and demoralizing. But Buster Keaton goes further.

In the hopeless, hierarchical society in which two of his films unfold, *Steamboat Bill Jr.* and *The Navigator*, he is the cause of a disorder of nightmarish or hallucinatory proportions. However, he accepts everything: clergyman, war, businessmen. Ships and submarines operate according to the mechanical laws of levers. Savages are cannibalistic: and hatmakers make the most of their standard models on Buster Keaton's head. Everything happens according to the rules of this best regulated of worlds. No laws are violated, nor are the laws of the universe: there is no rent in the concept of determinism. However, as one thing leads to another, without break or digression, in the normal working out of the plot, one of these films culminates in a nightmare on a deserted ocean liner, whose mooring ropes have been cut by conspirators; the other ends in a storm that carries off dwellings and separates things from the earth as well as from reason itself.

In order for hospital beds to take flight, for whole houses to lift off their foundations, and for a storm to carry off uprooted trees without ruffling the surface of the water, for the pitching of a deserted ocean liner, unmoored, lost at sea, to open and close all the cabin portal windows as one, causing a frightful panic, Buster Keaton does not need to be either revolutionary or arbitrary. The films of Man Ray and Buñuel, authoritative but in a void, claim to exercise a dictatorship of annihilation in their relations with the world. In the American films, the will to destruction seems to safeguard forms—all forms of thought, objects, and social relations—yet seeks to penetrate them in order to harrass or violate them. Efficacious as well as acerbic, it accepts the beaten paths and, secretly seeking to mock the rules, lures those forms into traps carefully camouflaged in an action or intrigue.

Action, we know what it means: intrigue, which creates no illusions. The tempests of the melodrama and the conspiracies of the theater mark those who use them with feebleness and second-rate status—and never give someone the impression that "he has arrived." Yet there the passage from the real to the unreal occurs without rupture; and in the American films adventure, love, and the supernatural are all tangled up with the material, the social, and the rational—the better to defy them and best them on the grounds which are most familiar to them. The revenge of individuals in the very space of their sufferings.

Two images combine in an elementary diptych:

In the chateau swimming pool, which Man Ray was forced to take as the subject of his latest film, a woman in a bathing suit indulges in gratuitous gestures . . . plays of light and poses that the water distorts and attenuates.[5]

In deep sea water, enclosed in a diving suit, near the anchor of a ship, Buster Keaton lifts his arms in supplication. The desperate gesture of a man obliged by social reasons to descend to the sea bottom where he is threatened with asphyxiation, and still wins.

Two images that the mind can compare with one another, but *in reality* quite distinct and producing very different sensations.

It is unfortunate that the spirit, whether acting within or outside of the world, can secrete the same images. Connected or disconnected, the mechanism is the same. Every confusion is possible, dizziness and deception. For the boundary that separates world and spirit is transparent in this world where the spirit, in its moments of power, imposes its demands and causes its desire to triumph. On one side of this boundary, revolt can be fecund: on the other, it is merely witticism and harmless onanism.

ROBERT ARON (1898–?) was a writer and cinéphile who became one of the editors of *La Revue du cinéma*. In the early 1930s, Aron, Armand Daudieu, and Alexandre Marc founded an intellectual circle and journal, *Ordre nouveau* (a forerunner of Emmanuel Mounier's

Esprit), which attempted to mediate the political differences between the right and the left in France.

[1] Man Ray: *Emak Bakia* (1927), *L'Etoile de mer* (1928), *Le Mystère du Château du Dé* (1929). Luis Buñuel: *Un Chien andalou* (1929).—AU.

[2] Man Ray's first film, *Retour à la raison* (1923) had not yet been screened publicly.

[3] *Eternèbres* is made up of *étern*al [eternal] and ten*èbres* [darkness]. *Piscinéma* is made up of *pis*cine [swimming pool] and *cinéma*.

[4] The references are to *Steamboat Bill Jr.* (1927) and *The Cameraman* (1928).

[5] *Le Mystère du Château du Dé* was financed by the Vicomte de Noailles as a birthday present for his wife.

Index

INDEX OF NAMES (individuals, organizations, places, events), titles (films, books, magazines, newspapers), and selected critical terms. Film title dates, according to year of release, are placed in parentheses. Book title dates are placed in brackets. This index includes selected references to substantive material in endnotes to the preface, introductions, and translated texts.

Library of Congress Cataloging-in-Publication Data

Abel, Richard, 1941–
French film theory and criticism.

Bibliography: p.
Includes index.
Contents: v. 1. 1907–1929—v. 2. 1929–1939.
1. Motion picture criticism—France. 2. Motion pictures—France—History. I. Title.
PN1995.A22 1988   792'.01'50944   87–25929
ISBN 0–691–05517–3 (v. 1: alk. paper)